School Counseling in the Secondary School

A Comprehensive Process and Program

Colette T. Dollarhide
University of Wisconsin–Whitewater

Kelli A. Saginak
University of Wisconsin, Oshkosh

Boston • New York • San Francisco • Mexico City • Montreal
Toronto • London • Madrid • Munich • Paris • Hong Kong
Singapore • Tokyo • Cape Town • Sydney

Colette: This book is dedicated to those people I love most: to my family, Jerry and Shiloh, who teach me about love; to my parents and siblings, who teach me about families; and to my students, who teach me about the journey.

Kelli: For my children, Andrea and Riley . . . with hope that my journey through life, including adolescence, has enabled me to be the mother I am today.

Executive Editor: *Virginia Lanigan*
Editorial Assistant: *Robert Champagne*
Editorial Production Administrator: *Joe Sweeney*
Editorial Production Service: *Walsh & Associates, Inc.*
Composition Buyer: *Linda Cox*
Manufacturing Buyer: *JoAnne Sweeney*
Cover Administrator: *Kristina Mose-Libon*

Library of Congress Cataloging-in-Publication Data

Dollarhide, Colette T.
    School counseling in the secondary school : a comprehensive process and program /
Colette T. Dollarhide, Kelli A. Saginak; contributing authors, Jim Larson . . . [et al.].
     p. cm.
    Includes bibliographical references and index.
    ISBN 0-205-32531-9
    1. Counseling in secondary education.   I. Saginak, Kelli A.   II. Title.

LB1620.4 .D65 2003
373.14—dc21

                                               2002026116

Printed in the United States of America

10 9 8 7 6 5 4 3 2 1   06 05 04 03 02

Photo Credits: pp. 27, 49, 81, 104, 133, 159, 185, 201, 223, 241, 257, 271, 299, 323, 345, 353, 361, 373, 381, 391, Jill Werner; pp. 3, 63, Colette T. Dollarhide

Contents

12 *Educating and Advocating with Parents, Colleagues in the Schools, and Colleagues in the Community (Blocks 8, 9, 10 of the DAP Model)* **241**

Colette T. Dollarhide

13 *Consulting with Parents, Colleagues in the Schools, and Colleagues in the Community (Blocks 11, 12, 13 of the DAP Model)* **257**

Colette T. Dollarhide

14 *Leadership and Coordination with Parents, Colleagues in the Schools, and Colleagues in the Community (Blocks 14, 15, 16 of the DAP Model)* **271**

Colette T. Dollarhide

SECTION V • *You As Professional School Counselor*   **297**

15 *Moral, Ethical, and Legal Issues in School Counseling*   **299**

Colette T. Dollarhide

16 *Professional Issues*   **323**

Colette T. Dollarhide

Preface

This book comes with the deeply held beliefs of the authors, because this is a work of love. It is important that you, the reader, understand these beliefs and that you understand how these beliefs shape this book and its use.

First, we believe that school counselors are counselors who work in schools. This means that while school counselors have many activities and many roles in schools, the primary professional definition of the school counselor and the comprehensive school counseling program come from the profession of counseling. Some school counselors may perform the activities of registrar, administrator, advisor, or teacher, but the professional identity of the school counselor transcends those roles, making the school counselor unique in worldview and philosophy. School counselors must understand the roles and strategies of these other school professions, but ultimately, must stand accountable to the profession of counseling for their actions.

We believe that school counseling is a deeply "soul-full" activity, meaning that we see school counseling as something that the counselor feels is important and meaningful in the world. We wrote this book to reflect that sense of intuitive meaning, in spite of the fact that much of what secondary school counselors do professionally is very intellectual in nature. At its best, counseling is a blend of intellect and intuition, of art and science. At its worst, counseling is cold intellect untempered by the warmth of feelings or unfettered intuition uninformed by any theory or developmental awareness. We wrote this book to articulate the middle ground—to ignite the fire of passion for helping young people on their journey, for helping schools to become places where all are valued for what they bring to that journey, and for the vision of a world in which entire communities do indeed raise all children. Simultaneously, we wrote this book to inform the intellect about models of school counseling, to juxtapose various theories of working with young people and schools, and to facilitate the professional school counselors' critical thinking and reflective judgment about these models and theories.

As counselors, we believe in the intrinsic value of every young person, that every person enriches the whole, and that we are diminished as individuals and as a community whenever the life-spark of any one person is extinguished. Every person lost to the abyss of addiction, self-hatred, or ignorance is a person lost to the community and is a tragedy. Yet, we are not of the belief that counselors are responsible for all choices of all students in our schools. While we as counselors must do all we can to educate young people of the dangers of their choices (and in the eyes of the law are responsible if we fail to report behavior that we know is potentially lethal and/or illegal), each person is ultimately responsible for his or her own choices. As counselors, we do all we can to help young people on their journey, but then we must let go to allow each young person to learn about responsibility and consequences. Rescuing others from the consequences of their choices is called "enabling" in the addictions literature, and counselors who are enabling are not acting ethically.

Finally, we believe that learning is an intensely personal activity. We believe that you will learn best when you have a chance to reflect on and personalize the information in this book. To that end, we have organized each chapter to facilitate your reflection and personalization. In an ideal world, we would be in conversation with you to answer your questions, stimulate your thinking, and challenge you to reach your personal best. Not being there in person, we have arranged those "conversations" to take place within the chapter.

Each chapter will begin a student quote, which we hope will help you reflect on the meaning the chapter has in the lives of students and in your life. Next, you will find the learning objectives for that chapter. After the learning objectives, you will read about a secondary school counselor who has experienced some challenge based on the topic of that chapter, and you will be asked to think about what you would do if you were in that counselor's place. Within the text, you will also find "Reflection Moments" to prompt you to pause and think about the topic, to reflect on your assumptions, biases, and perceptions to help you articulate *your* context.

At the end of the chapter, we will then revisit our secondary school counselor and the dilemma in that counselor's day. In this Integration box, you will be asked three things: 1) to reflect on how the topic of the chapter related to that dilemma, 2) to think in terms of the counselor's choices about the dilemma, and 3) to articulate what you would have done to resolve that dilemma. In the Application section, you will be prompted to apply what you have learned and to extend your learning. Finally, you will find suggested readings that will help further your understanding of the topic.

It is our hope that you will enjoy reading this book as much as we enjoyed writing it. We would not want this conversation to be one-sided and encourage you to contact either of us at our campuses to tell us about your personal triumphs and challenges as school counselors. In this age of computers, going to the web page for our respective campuses will enable you to communicate with us. Your contributions will provide us with the feedback needed to refine and improve future editions of this book.

We would like to take this moment to acknowledge those without whom this book would not have happened. Our sincerest appreciation and respect goes to Virginia Lanigan, Executive Editor; Erin Liedel, Editorial Assistant; and our outside reviewers—Thomas V. Trotter, University of Idaho; Vivian McCollum, University of Missouri, St. Louis; Susan G. Keys, Johns Hopkins; Alan Silliker, St. Bonaventure University; John S. Geisler, Western Michigan University; Doris Rhea Coy, University of North Texas—for their invaluable suggestions and assistance. We would also like to thank Jim Larson, Gary Koch, Dave Van Doren, Margaret Eichler, Carol Doyle, and M. Alan Saginak for their expert contributions.

Acknowledgments

From Colette Dollarhide:

To Brenda O'Beirne, Don Norman, Dave Van Doren, and Anene Okocha, my department colleagues at Whitewater, for their understanding and support.

To Pam Clinkenbeard, Greg Valde, and Ellen Smith for their ideas on education.

To Len Mormino in Madison School District for the student quotes.

To Jill Werner of the New Berlin School District for the student photographs.

To Elizabeth Shadel, my graduate assistant, for her help with the research and editing of this manuscript.

To Kate Schultz and Elizabeth for their help with proofreading the manuscript.

To Gary Koch, my dear friend, from North Central ACES, for accepting my need to focus on the book and decline an officer position in that august body.

To Kelli Saginak, who inspired this book in innumerable ways, and who was always willing to lend inspiration and encouragement, in spite of her own growing life roles.

And to Jerry, Shiloh, Dad, Carol, Kathy, Mike, Tricia, and my beloved nieces, for their support, love, and faith in me.

From Kelli Saginak:

This project could not have been completed without the support and dedication of some very special individuals. First, I want to thank the faculty of the Department of Counselor Education, and the College of Education and Human Services at the University of Wisconsin, Oshkosh for their continued support throughout this project.

A special thanks goes to Jody Misovec, Graduate Assistant, for the countless hours spent researching and gathering literature. The mound of paper that I have in my office proves this was no easy task.

I also want to offer my sincere thanks to all the contributors who graciously gave to this project. This textbook would not be complete had it not been for their willingness to share their expertise and their passion for youth.

An extra-special thanks goes to all the students who offered their contributions of quotes and photographs. It is through their eyes that we see the world in which they live.

I especially want to thank my co-author, Colette, for her understanding and patience, and for her fire and energy, which never once flickered or faded. She is truly a portrait of strength and perseverance. I feel especially fortunate to have been invited to go on this journey with her.

Finally, I want to thank my family, Alan, Andrea, and Riley for their love and encouragement and for standing beside me throughout this endeavor. I love you so much.

Counselors, Students, and Schools

Introduction

Collette T. Dollarhide

"As a student who wants to someday be involved in this field—thanks. I think it's great that you want to help students and also feel the importance to hear what we have to say. Thanks again."

Margaret, age 18

Learning Objectives

By the end of this chapter, you will:

1. Reflect on your own philosophy of counseling.
2. Reflect on the nature of schools.
3. Begin to articulate your own philosophy of education.
4. Understand the diversity of issues faced by today's students and professionals in education.

A Day in the Life of a Counselor: The Hurdle for Henry

Henry went from his undergraduate degree in sociology into his master's degree in counseling, specializing in school counseling. He had a troubled childhood and adolescence; his passion for helping young people was his life's calling and his only mission on this earth. He had never worked in a school, but had experience volunteering with troubled youth, and his commitment to young people was almost tangible. He accepted a job as a high school counselor.

During his first months on the job, Henry performed counseling tasks very well. He interacted well with the students, and yet was cool toward other professionals in the school, an attitude that they noticed. Eventually, Henry spent more and more time with the kids of the school, taking lunch with them, sitting with them during assemblies, and playing basketball with them after school. He rarely interacted with teachers or administrators.

One day, things came to a crisis. Henry was not maintaining professional balance when it came to problems between the students and the school. What started as a cool attitude toward the principal and teachers emerged as full-blown animosity—Henry laughed at the administration during assemblies, made disparaging comments about the teachers to the students, and openly and aggressively argued on their behalf with the administration.

Henry was proud of the fact that he has always been on "their" side, that helping troubled kids was his mission in life. "What's wrong with that? I'm alive because someone helped me when I was in trouble. The school counselor literally saved my life by being my advocate after everyone else had given up on me. All I want to do is give that back, to help kids see that not all adults are jerks. The kids will never trust me if I bail out on them now!" (adapted from Dollarhide & Mickelson, 2000).

Challenge Questions

What do you see as Henry's major challenges? Did he go into school counseling for the right reasons? What gifts does he bring to the school? What problems does he bring to the school? How would his preprofessional experience help him as a school counselor? How would that experience hinder him as a school counselor? If you were Henry, what would you see as your choices? Observing from outside Henry's reality, what do you see as Henry's choices? Reflecting on your own source of motivation, why are you interested in pursuing school counseling?

Overview

There is no "magic bullet" for the problems encountered by our students, our schools, or our communities. There is no cookbook that contains all the programs and approaches for all the problems our students will bring to us. We venture into this profession ready to contest those elements that deprive our young people of their vitality, imagination, and creativity, but our good intentions alone are not enough. We need training, reflection, and practice in those skills that will make school counselors effective in tomorrow's schools.

Professional Standards

In preparing to be effective school counselors, we must be prepared to demonstrate various professional skills and abilities and various personal qualities. According to the 2001 Standards of the Council for Accreditation of Counseling and Related Educational Programs (CACREP, 2000), school counselors must be able to demonstrate significant professional skills. These competencies comprise the essence of comprehensive school counseling, and with each competency, you will find the chapters in which that competency is addressed in this book.

- School counselors must demonstrate the ability to provide counseling, developmental curriculum, information, and skills training to assist students in maximizing their academic, career, and personal/social development. This competency is addressed in Chapter 6 on the domains of academic development, career development, and personal/social development; in Chapter 7 on counseling with students; in Chapter 8 on the developmental curriculum (education and advocacy); in Chapter 9 on consulting with students, and Chapter 10 on leading and coordinating events with students. In addition, Chapter 7 provides a discussion of the use of peer facilitators for peer helping.
- School counselors must demonstrate knowledge and skill in multicultural counseling issues including culture, stereotyping, family, socioeconomic status, gender/sexual identity, language, values, and social equity issues. In addition, school counselors must be aware of the dynamics and effects of the various systems in which students live. These competencies are addressed in Chapters 2, 3, and 4 on the developmental issues of adolescents, and in Chapter 6 on identity development for persons of diversity.
- School counselors must demonstrate methods and techniques for prevention and early intervention to maximize school success for students, and they must be aware of issues that may affect the development and functioning of students. School success is addressed throughout Chapters 4, 5, 6, 7, 8, 9, and 10, which focuses on our work with students. Furthermore, Chapters 17, 18, 19, 20, and 21 provide insights into issues of school violence, alternative sexual orientation, spirituality, substance abuse, and careers.
- School counselors must demonstrate knowledge and skill in the consultation process, effectively teaming, partnering, and consulting with teachers, administrators, parents, students, community groups, and agencies as appropriate, empowering them to work

on behalf of students. In response to this competency, Chapters 9 and 13 are devoted to the role of consultation in secondary school counseling.

- School counselors must be knowledgeable in conducting programming for the education of teachers, parents, caregivers, families, and communities to enhance student development. Chapter 12 specifically addresses this competency.
- School counselors must demonstrate the ability to coordinate and develop programs and services that enhance school climate for effective student learning, including the use of technology and data for needs and outcomes assessment (student and adult competencies) and program improvement. You will find that Chapter 5 presents various models and a discussion of comprehensive school counseling programming, Chapters 10 and 14 address leadership and coordination of programs for all the partners in the school counseling program for data gathering, and Appendixes B and C present competencies for students and adults. Technology is discussed in Chapter 16.
- School counselors must demonstrate knowledge of legal enablements and constraints and demonstrate skill in applying these to specific counseling situations impacting school counselors and students. Furthermore, school counselors are expected to demonstrate knowledge of the ethical standards and practices of the school counseling profession, as well as skill in applying these standards to specific counseling situations. Chapter 15 addresses the moral, ethical, and legal issues in school counseling; Appendix A contains the Code of Ethics for the American School Counselor Association (ASCA).
- School counselors must demonstrate effective advocacy for student access to school and community programs. Chapters 8 and 12 will present discussions of advocacy for students with all educational partners.
- School counselors must demonstrate the ability to carry out a comprehensive developmental school counseling program, including organizing and leading groups; designing, planning, delivering, and assessing the developmental curriculum; and providing counseling interventions. To facilitate your understanding of this competency, Chapter 5 discusses comprehensive school counseling, Chapter 7 is devoted to the role of individual and group counseling in the secondary school setting, and Chapter 8 examines the comprehensive issues of the developmental curriculum.
- School counselors must demonstrate skill in working collaboratively with all members of the educational community. Collaborative relationships with other members of the school environment are discussed in Chapters 1, 11, 12, 13, and 14.

Reflection Moment

Where are you in the development of these professional competencies? Would the design of a professional portfolio (a compilation of your work that documents your mastery of these professional competencies) assist you in demonstrating these skills and abilities? If you were told that a professional portfolio could contain anything you wanted, how would you demonstrate your mastery of these competencies?

Structure of the Book

To understand young people, schools, and counseling in schools, we must understand each separately, then bring them together to examine their interaction. It is impossible to understand the forest if we do not understand plant life (botany), the habits of animals and insects (biology), the nature of weather patterns (meteorology), and the characteristics of the soil (geology). But after understanding each of those discrete elements of the forest, we still must venture into the forest to observe and appreciate the interaction among the plants, animals, insects, weather, and soil that culminate in what we experience as "forest." So it is with school counseling.

As school counselors, we must understand the nature of our profession (counseling), the persons for whom we are in the profession (students), the context in which we will practice our profession (schools), and then put that understanding to work for us in the shape of professional comprehensive school counseling programs. We will briefly examine counseling and schools in this chapter. We will then seek to understand adolescents and their development in Chapter 2; in Chapter 3, we will explore how adolescents develop in a systems context. In Chapter 4, we will reexamine schools in light of our new understanding of adolescents to explore what is meant by "developmentally appropriate" schools for adolescents. Starting with Chapter 5, we will discuss comprehensive school counseling programs and present our model of a comprehensive school counseling program. This model serves as a template with which we will examine each element of a comprehensive secondary school counseling program, focusing on our partnership with students in Chapters 6, 7, 8, 9, and 10. In Chapters 11, 12, 13, and 14, we will discuss our partnership with parents, colleagues in the schools, and colleagues in the community. In Chapter 15, we will discuss the moral, ethical, and legal issues of school counseling, then contemplate professional issues and the future of secondary school counseling in Chapter 16. The final chapters address salient issues in the lives of students: violence, sexual orientation, substance abuse, spirituality, and career choice.

Personal Qualities of the School Counselor

There are also many personal qualities that school counselors must possess. As mentioned in the Preface, effective school counselors function with both intellect and intuition, with both objectivity and passion. What are the personal qualities that contribute to intuition? An exhaustive list would be impractical, but below are some of the most notable qualities.

Creativity and Imagination

Students, parents, teachers, administrators, and other professionals will bring questions, perspectives, issues, experiences, and challenges to us that we have never before encountered. Furthermore, as society changes over time, the needs of our students will change. We must have the creativity to be able to respond to their various needs in an appropriate, ethical, and effective manner, and the ability to imagine and design new approaches to address old problems.

Flexibility

School counselors must be flexible in how they view their time, their activities, their clients, and their clients' needs over time. In the schools, counselors move from one activity to the next with little time to regroup. This means that school counselors need to move fluidly from one role to the next and from one activity to the next. Furthermore, school counselors address the needs of many different kinds of people (students, parents, teachers, administrators, school board members, and community members to name a few), each with his or her own unique cultural, intellectual, emotional, and developmental signature. School counselors with high flexibility will be more fluid in response to those various needs. As needs change over time, flexible counselors will find themselves more comfortably adapting to new ways of looking at school situations.

Courage and Faith

School counselors address situations every day that challenge their courage and faith, from students who are engaging in dangerous risk-taking, to irate parents who don't understand why the counselor can't fix their child, to school board members who threaten to cut the counseling program because they don't understand what counselors do. Having courage and faith in the face of these challenges comes from knowing that counselors make a difference, and that, while the larger pattern of meaning might not be immediately visible, all things do happen for a reason. This is not to say that school counselors must adopt a fatalistic worldview. A good example of courage and faith is found in the story of the young girl who, when the tide was out, threw stranded starfish back into the sea. She knew she couldn't save them all, but she did what she could to make a difference for one at a time. She had the courage to try to help and the faith to know that it mattered that she try. School counselors can't "save" any students, but they know they make a difference for those whose lives they touch. Knowing that school counselors make a difference in the lives of students is a powerful antidote to apathy and burnout.

Passion

Passion is not a word that is used in many counseling books. However, passion is a wonderful word that describes the feeling of profound commitment, the type of commitment and meaning described in existentialism (Frankl, 1984). The best counseling professionals are passionately and profoundly committed to clients, to the clients' best interests, and to their own personal and professional excellence. For counselors who work in the schools, this means that they are passionately committed to their students and to education. For some professionals, this might be a daunting challenge: If you've never worked in a school or around young people, how do you know you have that passion for kids and for schools? The answer: Find a way to work with students in schools to see if there is "passion" in working with those clients in that setting.

If professional competencies are addressed in this book, are the requisite personal qualities addressed in these pages also? Where do creativity, flexibility, courage, faith, and passion come from? We hope that after reading this book, thinking about the counselors you will meet in each chapter, reflecting on the questions posed throughout the text, and integrating the text with insights from your own life and experience, you will have the answers to those questions.

Reflection Moment

How would you rate yourself on the preceding personal qualities? Reflect on the most important task or accomplishment of your life. In the completion of this task, how did each of the listed personal qualities manifest themselves? In what ways did you demonstrate your creativity, flexibility, courage, faith, and passion? How did each quality help you in your task or accomplishment?

Philosophies of Counseling

Imagine yourself outside on a cold, clear, moonless winter night, far from the lights of a city. When you look up, you see millions upon millions of points of light. How would you describe what you see?

Astronomers would talk about black holes, galaxies, and light years of distance as related to time, while historians would contemplate how mariners navigated using the stars. Classical Greek scholars would describe the mythical origins of various constellations (Zimmerman, 1964), astrologers would talk about those same constellations as related to personalities and birth signs, and the Onondaga people would tell you that the stars are the Spiritual Beings of the Sky World (Wall & Arden, 1990). Poets would find divine inspiration, while physicists would find inspiration from the possibility of discovering life somewhere else in the universe. And each of these persons would recommend that, to truly understand the points of light in the midnight sky, you need to study, as they have, in their philosophy, their discipline, and their culture.

We can use the example of how various people describe the stars to understand how various people describe counseling. In this culture, it is generally agreed that the points of light in the sky are stars (as opposed to the belief that the lights are millions of spacecraft, or evil demons, or campfires on the roof of the world). Similarly, we agree on certain qualities of a helping relationship that we call counseling (Brammer & McDonald, 1999; Corey, 1996; Cormier & Hackney, 1987; Hutchins & Cole, 1992; Kottler, 1991, 1993; Krumboltz & Thoresen, 1976; Meier & Davis, 1997; St. Clair, 1996). These qualities bind various theories of the counseling process into a constellation that we can map and navigate.

Counseling is a helping relationship, in which the primary focus is on the psychological healing, growth, change, and development of the client, with the goal that the client will be able to establish and maintain healthy relationships with self and others. The relationship is intentional, meaning that the counselor engages the client in activities that are thoughtfully chosen for their potential to help the client heal, grow, and develop.

Counseling is a unique profession. It shares some common theoretical underpinnings with other disciplines such as psychology, psychiatry, and social work, but it is unique in its focus on developmental issues, interpersonal and intrapersonal relationships, and therapeutic milieu (Hanna & Bemak, 1997). As a profession, counseling is ethical, meaning helping behaviors are exhibited that adhere to moral, ethical, and professional guidelines as defined by the profession and the law (American Counseling Association, 1995; American School Counselor Association, 1998; Blackwell, Martin, & Scalia, 1994; Canon & Brown, 1985; Christopher, 1996; Corey, Corey, & Callanan, 1993; Herlihy & Corey, 1996; Huber & Baruth, 1987; Van Hoose & Kottler, 1988).

Counseling is both an art and a science, requiring intellect and intuition (Nystul, 1993). Intellectually, counselors need to understand various theories of change and the stages of development and maturation. Intuitively, counselors need to listen to the inner voice that whispers when to speak, when to be silent, when to intervene, and when to let go. Furthermore, to be ethical and effective, counselors must be sensitive to the values of the client's contexts of significance, as defined by the client and suggested by the client's culture, family system, gender, generation, abilities, health, and other diversity and values markers (Dollarhide & Haxton, 1999; Nichols & Schwartz, 1991; Sue & Sue, 1990).

Recall the various descriptions of the stars. Every time a counselor meets a client for the purpose of engaging in an intentional helping relationship, what will best facilitate change can be described in a variety of contexts based on theoretical orientation or philosophy. Some counselors would describe what they do in spiritual or intuitive terms, and other counselors would describe what they do in scientific or intellectual terms. Each theory describes change and those strategies that facilitate change: behavioral (Ellis, 1973), existential (Frankl, 1984). Rogerian (Carkhuff, 1987), Alderian (Dinkmeyer, Dinkmeyer, & Sperry, 1987), reality therapy (Glasser, 1965), and others.

How you see counseling is determined by your theoretical orientation, the lenses of your philosophy. While we can generally agree that the points of light in the night sky are indeed stars, how the stars are described varies widely. The profession of counseling generally agrees that the goal of counseling is to facilitate psychological healing, growth, change, and development to empower clients to experience healthy relationships with self and others. To be an effective counselor, you must have a method of bringing that healing, growth, change, and development to fruition with the client.

One useful way to conceptualize how to facilitate change with the client is to use the principles of learning, dealing with ambiguity, and reflective judgment. These are the same principles of learning described by Social Learning Theory (Bandura, 1977) and epistemological development (Dollarhide & Scully, 1999; Kegan, 1982; King & Kitchener, 1994; Perry, 1981). These theories constitute a description of counseling that includes a model of both the process of counseling and the process of change and growth; in using the language of learning, this description lends itself well to the educational setting.

In essence, both Social Learning Theory and counseling based on epistemological development begin at the same point: that counseling and learning are parallel constructs. If the point of counseling is to help clients learn how to develop and maintain healthy relationships with themselves and with others, then counseling strategies that utilize learning paradigms will be successful. In Social Learning Theory, that learning is the result of direct experiences, observation of models and vicarious experiences, and verbal persuasion (Bandura, 1977), which modifies the client's perception of self-efficacy and expectations of outcomes. From more positive perceptions of self-efficacy and more accurate expectations of outcomes, clients can choose more healthy behaviors and attitudes. In counseling based on epistemological theory (Dollarhide & Scully, 1999), clients learn how to choose more healthy behaviors and attitudes when they are allowed to encounter, struggle with, and resolve ambiguous life questions that have no clear answers. The counseling process entails allowing the client maximum freedom to explore existential questions such as: What is the meaning of my life? What is my life direction? How do I establish healthy relationships? The counselor helps the client move from looking outside oneself for the answers to these questions, to looking within oneself for the answers, to, ultimately, understanding how to look within for future answers.

Reflection Moment

What is your theory of counseling? How adaptable is that theory for use with adolescents and young adults? How adaptable is that theory for use in the schools? What can you foresee as challenges in using your theory? What can you foresee as advantages in using your theory?

Philosophies of Education

To understand education, we must first understand the rationale for the design of educational experiences. These experiences are defined by the philosophy of education of state departments of education, superintendents, principals, parents, teachers, and district personnel. The style of the educational experience could be characterized by two basic camps on either side of a "pedagogical and philosophical divide" (Olson, 1999, p. 25): progressive versus traditional education. According to Olson, in its simplest form, traditional philosophy holds the primacy of subject matter, mastery of content, and preservation of the existing national cultural heritage. Progressive philosophy, on the other hand, has been characterized by primacy of the child, active learning, recognition of students' individual differences, the drive to relate school to real life, the "broad mission to address health, vocational, social and community issues" (p. 26), and an agenda that includes transforming the national cultural heritage. There are significant problems and significant strengths of each approach.

What we see in schools today are the various combinations of a number of subtexts within the progressive movement, as well as the swing of the cultural values pendulum back and forth between progressive agendas and return-to-basics traditionalism (Olson, 1999). From 1873 through 1918, the pedagogical progressive movement was in full swing, emphasizing learning environments that were more informal and pupil-oriented and pedagogical approaches emphasizing active learning through meaningful, comprehensive projects and interdisciplinary teaching. Progressive professionals believe that schools should fit the natural development and interests of children, and should encourage self-expression through the arts—that children are "creative beings" who should be "nurtured, rather than disciplined, shaped, and controlled" (Olson, 1999; p. 26).

The next educational movement came to its own during the Great Depression and was called the social progressive, or social reconstructionist, movement. The educational reform agenda at this time included addressing the social ills created by laissez-faire capitalism and by the perceived inability of the family or community to provide for the basic needs of children. According to Olson, the legacy of this movement manifests in professionals who bring health and other social services into the schools and in the move to involve schools in community issues (p. 29).

The third strand in the progressive movement also has had a long-reaching influence on education. Called the administrative progressive movement, this philosophy arose from the need to organize education to be more cost-effective in times of rapid growth in enrollment (Olson, 1999). It falls into the progressive philosophical camp because its proponents' rationale was to help students adapt to society, rather than transforming society, by scientifically measuring students' abilities, grouping students based on ability, and then individualizing instruction by those groupings. Scientific testing and ability grouping (also known as tracking) were the legacies of this movement.

During the Korean War and the McCarthy era, progressive schools were criticized heavily for creating school environments without goals or educational standards in which low performance was excused and from which students emerged without demonstrable social morals (Olson, 1999). Critics charged that without a solid academic foundation, students from disadvantaged backgrounds would remain disadvantaged and social inequities would be perpetuated. With the launch of Sputnik in 1957, progressive education was given less emphasis as the call arose for more math, science, and foreign language education. Also known as academic rationalism (Eisner, 1985), this criticism emerged in the belief that the major purpose of schools is to "foster intellectual grown of the student in those subject matters most worthy of study" (p. 66).

In the 1960s and 1970s, the progressive movement enjoyed a temporary resurgence, with many notable contributions to the debate about pedagogy, including Bruner's article on discovery learning (Bruner, 1961). However, the pendulum swung back toward traditional educational approaches in the late 1970s with the back-to-basics movement, which brought minimum competency testing, increases in course requirements, and a reliance on standardized tests (Brown & Peterkin, 1999; Olson, 1999).

As you can see, the debate over educational reform has been a topic for over a century, with conversations continuing about the best environments and pedagogy for educating young people. Current thinking about learning and the educational process has emerged from various disciplines. From psychology and counseling came Adlerian schools (Dubelle & Hoffman, 1984, 1986), the application of Reality Therapy to schools and adolescents (Glasser, 1965), and personality styles translated into education (Berens, 1988). The constructivist movement from psychology was brought into schools, holding that students need to construct meaning for themselves in order to learn. The implications of this educational strategy have been explored from kindergarten to college teaching (Palmer, 1998). From learning styles literature came various ways of conceptualizing learning: Gardner's Multiple Intelligences (Gardner, 1983; Lazear, 1999), various models of learning preferences (Dunn & Griggs, 1988), and various ways of understanding thinking, including gender as a learning construct (Clinchy, 1989; Golderberger, Clinchy, Belenky, & Tarule, 1987).

Many educators have examined various pedagogical approaches espoused by various educational traditions and have opted to incorporate teaching methods that energize both teaching and learning. Cooperative learning, where students are encouraged to work together on projects (Gibbs, 1995; Slavin, 1994), and learning centers, where students move physically to a location in the room designed for group activities, have transformed many classrooms into highly mobile, interactive learning environments. New strategies for helping students acquire knowledge include manipulatives for math and abstract concepts, extensive creative writing strategies such as mindmapping and clustering (Rico, 1983), and socially reinforcing strategies such as Tribes (Gibbs, 1995), all of which are designed to assist students in the acquisition and retention of knowledge, skills, and attitudes.

As we will see in the next section of this chapter and in Chapter 4, the research into effective schools suggests some ways to think about which educational philosophies, in which combinations, have implications for helping students learn what they need to know as adults.

Reflection Moment

Think back on the various classrooms you've been in. Have you ever been in a traditional classroom? How did it feel? Have you been in a more nontraditional, more informal classroom? How did that feel? In which class did you feel more motivated to learn?

What is your description of what schools are supposed to do? What, exactly, is your philosophy of education? Based on that philosophy of education, describe what a school would look like that followed that philosophy. What would that school do? What would teachers do? What would counselors do?

Effective Schools

Occasionally, educators want to infuse progressive learning strategies into their schools and classrooms, only to find parents, caregivers, community or school board members have different educational philosophies—different ideas of how learning should be designed (Lewis, 1994). Our jobs as counselors involve helping these stakeholders to understand the development of young people, learning and education, and what constitutes excellent schools. Understanding how to facilitate excellent schools can only come from understanding how schools function as organizational entities and what qualities culminate in effective schools.

Professionals in schools today have tremendous expectations and are faced with tremendous challenges. Usually, school districts are governed by an elected body from the community, which makes all policy, financial, and educational decisions (Simon, 1999).

Funding for schools comes primarily from state and local taxes; taxes paid by the community or communities in the school district for school support must be approved by the voters in that community or communities (Newman, 1994). School district board members are accountable to those voters for expenditures and outcomes for all school programs.

Education professionals are accountable to the parents/guardians of the students of that school and to the school board. With certain variations, professionals in schools are expected to:

- Interact positively with the community.
- Maintain high educational expectations.
- Maintain test scores in crucial academic areas.
- Provide special assistance to students with special physical, academic, and emotional needs.
- Provide early screening and intervention for young students entering kindergarten.
- Provide transportation to and from the school to within a reasonable and safe distance from the student's residence.
- Communicate with parents/guardians/caregivers regularly.
- Respond to parents' and caregivers' concerns.
- Provide a safe, exciting, fun, invigorating learning environment.
- Provide language assistance as needed.
- Provide limited health services and screening for problems.
- Provide limited mental health services and screening for problems.
- Instill respect for the traditions and symbols of the country, state, and /or community.
- Instill core values that transcend cultures, such as honesty, caring, respect, responsibility, and justice.
- Provide education in fundamental behaviors such as problem solving, friendship building, and decision making.
- Other requirements as determined by local school boards, state law, federal mandate, the community, and society as a whole.

If these expectations are not met, it is easy to blame others. Parents and caregivers blame teachers, teachers blame parents and schools, schools blame the school board, the school board blames the community and parents, and everyone blames society, movies, music, and the media. If it takes a village to raise a child, then we are all accountable for the education our young people do or do not receive in our schools. Communities must be willing to fund excellent schools; schools must be willing to listen to the needs of the students, families, and the community; and parents and caregivers must be willing to participate in the educational processes of all children. Counselors can be a crucial link in the chain of excellence and achievement, facilitating communication and understanding among all stakeholders in the process of educating young people.

A broad synthesis of research, incorporating ideas emerging from youth development and resiliency literature, protective factors research, and developmental assets literature, yields eight outcomes desired by society for young people. According to UCLA's School Mental Health Project/Center for Mental Health in Schools [SMHP](1999; p. 5), these eight outcomes are:

1. Academics, which includes connection to and commitment to learning, motivation for learning and self-learning, and feelings of academic competence.
2. Healthy and safe behavior, which includes the ability to make good decisions about how to establish and maintain good physical health and a healthy lifestyle, solve interpersonal conflicts and problems as a means of managing stress, delay gratification, and resist impulses and unhealthy peer/social pressures.
3. Social-emotional functioning, which includes the ability to relate interpersonally in a culturally appropriate manner; understand, express, and manage emotions; experience generally positive feelings about oneself, others, and the world; experience a sense of social and emotional competence and connection with others; and experience a sense of hope for the future.
4. Communication, which includes basic communication skills and the ability to understand social cues and the perspectives of others.
5. Character/Values, which includes personal, social, and civic responsibility, honesty and integrity, and the ability to monitor one's own choices to maintain congruence between values and behaviors.
6. Self-direction, which describes the ability to evaluate life situations and make effective long-term decisions that are appropriately autonomous and self-responsible.
7. Vocational and other adult roles, which include those skills and attitudes that facilitate locating, securing, and maintaining employment, community involvement, intimate adult relationships, and other adult roles.
8. Recreational and enrichment pursuits, which include engaging in behaviors and activities that improve quality of life, permit expression of creativity, and reduce stress.

Given these eight outcomes as desired for young people, an effective school would provide the environment in which progress toward these outcomes is evident. According to Travers, Elliott, and Kratochwill (1993), effective schools are characterized by connections among staff, teachers, students, and caregivers, consistently fair decision making and discipline, an environment of encouragement for academic and personal achievement, teaching that blends both the basics and methods that facilitate discovery, realistic but high expectations for all, and high accountability for learning (p. 16). In this effective school setting, two principles emerge of primary importance: a caring environment and an emphasis on holistic development (SMHP, 1999; p. 5).

These two conditions are the result of collaborative efforts among schools, communities, and caregivers to provide a school environment in which young people feel welcome and respected, in which there are opportunities to make connections with caring adults and peers, in which information and counseling is provided to help them determine what it means to care for self and others, and in which opportunities and expectations are present that encourage them to contribute to the community through service and advocacy (Pittman, undated). These caring conditions and holistic factors do not appear magically; they are the result of hard work, determination, and the focus of the school and community on those elements that nurture young people. Counselors are instrumental in advocating for environments of respect and caring, and counselors share enormous responsibility for the holistic development of students.

Relationships with School Professionals

Take a moment to reread "A Day in the Life of a Counselor: The Hurdle for Henry." Imagine yourself as Henry. Now consider that Henry is the only counselor for 758 students. Does knowing that student/counselor ratio affect your reaction to his choice to distance himself from other professionals in the school?

School counselors, as we will see in Chapter 5, are charged with a large task: the academic, social/emotional, and career development of students (Dahir, Sheldon, & Valiga, 1998). While it is natural that new professionals will feel tremendous professional pride, when such pride results in the belief that "the counselor is the only one who works with kids" or "the counselor only conducts one-on-one counseling," the counselor is creating a situation that is fraught with problems.

The national average student-to-counselor ratio is 561 to 1 ("$20 Million Set Aside," 2000). With that ratio, no one person alone (emphasis on "alone") can attend to all the academic, career, and personal/social needs of all the students in any school, even a small school. Not only does it take an entire community to raise a child, it takes an entire community to educate a child.

Community, in this context, refers both to the community outside a school and the community within a school. Essential elements of students' lives—including the primary support system, caregivers, and family—exist outside of school. To be effective on behalf of students, school counselors must be able to engage caregivers and families—to develop rapport, develop trust, make referrals, educate, consult, and counsel, if need be. In many schools, school counselors provide direct services to caregivers, teaching parenting and communication skills, economic survival skills (such as resume writing and interviewing), consulting on the needs of students, and providing direct counseling through one-on-one sessions and support groups.

In addition, counselors must be able to work effectively with other members of the outside community. For example, counselors must have effective working relationships with social agencies, health providers, and other mental health providers to facilitate referrals. Since counselors are also charged with the career development of students, effective relationships with employers will facilitate career exploration programming. Effective relationships with community leaders will enable the counselor to be an effective advocate for schools and for children and may facilitate the exploration of external funding for schools and for school counseling programs.

The school system itself is also a community, and within that community are professionals with whom partnerships are essential. Effective partnerships with school board and central administration members, as well as with building-level administrators such as principals and directors, result in an increased districtwide awareness of and appreciation for the school counseling program. These partnerships yield trust, communication, resources, and more effective services for students.

Other pupil services professionals (or student services professionals, depending on local terminology) are also essential. Adelman and Taylor (1997) have written extensively on the need for greater collaboration among pupil services professionals such as school psychologists, school social workers, school counselors, and school nurses. Together, the pupil services team of counselors, psychologists, social workers, and nurses represent the expertise and training needed to support the learning of young people. Called "enabling factors" by Adelman and Taylor, the elements of good physical health, good psychological health, and solid support systems enable young people to be successful—to become healthy and resilient learners. The pupil services team facilitates the personal/social development of students. (Chapter 14 will present more information on the need for collaboration to reach all students.)

Finally, no discussion of effective partnerships within schools would be complete without a discussion of the need to partner with teachers. Counselors are experts in both the change process and the learning process—these processes are the foundation of each theory of counseling. Using our expertise to help students learn can only go so far without the primary partner in the learning process: the teacher. Many teachers are already aware of and appreciate the role that counselors play in schools, but not all. It is essential that counselors work with teachers to facilitate effective referrals, problem solving, and communication with students, families, and administrators about students, their lives, and their challenges.

Reflection Moment

What are your perceptions of the professions of school administrator, school psychologist, school social worker, and school nurse? Have you had any experience with members of these professions? Were those contacts positive or negative? What will you do to learn more about these professions to enable you to interact effectively with the professionals you will meet in the future?

General Issues of Concern for School Counselors

Up to this point in the chapter, we have prompted you to reflect on your philosophy of counseling, your philosophy of education, the nature of effective schools, and the critical need for collaboration and partnership with other school professionals. To heighten your awareness of the important issues that school counselors address, we now turn to a discussion of issues that confront our schools and our students. It is impossible to give a comprehensive overview of each issue facing school counselors (as that would necessitate numerous volumes to accomplish); however, it is important that you have a basic understanding of some significant challenges as defined by professionals in the field. It is also important that you begin *now* to seek additional information about these issues; additional reading, reflection, interviews with professionals, and additional coursework can enhance your ability to deal with these issues as a professional school counselor.

School Issues

Accountability of Professionals   There is a movement to make professionals in education more accountable for their time and efforts (Olson, 1999). In some states, there are discussions of linking teachers' salaries with test scores (Lubman, 1995); while it is not likely that this will happen at a national level, it is indicative of the mood of the public and many school districts. Most professionals in education agree that schools need to be more accountable, but there is little agreement on how to accomplish this. In school counseling, discussions of accountability are increasingly crucial as funding issues become more critical (Wittmer, 2000). It is hard to argue that you need more resources when you cannot demonstrate the need for or impact of the resources you've been allocated. Needs assessment, outcomes assessment, and resource allocations go hand-in-hand; if you are unable to demonstrate that you are providing programs that are needed and that you attain outcomes that are deemed appropriate and valued, then your pleas for more human and fiscal resources will fall on deaf ears. Counselors are essential for schools, but our efficacy must be documented.

Student Competency Testing   In many states, students are promoted to the next educational level based on their ability to demonstrate their mastery of certain educational goals (Olson, 1999). Whether you agree with this form of assessment or not, many schools are effected adversely by reliance on testing as the only measure of students' learning. Problems such as teaching to the test, overreliance on verbal and computational learning, and lack of stimulation of creativity are the results of overemphasis on testing (Eisner, 1985). Counselors are often relied upon to monitor the school environment for such dehumanizing forces.

Funding   Funding for schools continues to be an issue. First, securing sufficient funding to maintain and improve schools is a significant challenge. The many reasons why additional funding is difficult to secure from voters include already high taxes that overburden citizens, growing numbers of retirement-age adults who resist paying additional taxes for the education of other people's children, and the public's perception that schools are not functioning effectively (Lewis, 1994; Simon, 1999). Second, schools are experiencing tremendous increases in costs (Simon, 1999). These additional costs come from increasing demand for specialized services for special needs students; increasing mandates from federal and state departments of education that do not come with independent funding; and ever-increasing costs of energy, building maintenance, human resources, and the technology and resources to teach young people in today's world. Counselors can articulate the ways in which our children benefit from better schools that can result from increased funding.

Adequacy of Facilities   In many parts of the country, school facilities are deteriorating at an alarming rate. Many schools were built for the post–World War II baby boom. As birth rates have declined, these buildings have fallen into disrepair. Furthermore, population movement has been out of the Rust Belt of the Northeast to the Sun Belt of the South and Southwest, causing further decay as the tax base moves away. Adding to this is student-caused damage to buildings and grounds through misuse or acts of vandalism. It all adds up to a general climate of decay and neglect—which translates directly into an environment that conveys to young people "We don't care about you." In other parts of the country, namely the Sun Belt, there is a boom in population, causing new schools to become too small between the time the blueprints are drawn and opening day. This results in the use of temporary modules or hastily converting building space previously allocated to other purposes into classrooms. Raising additional funds so soon after major capital expenditures such as required with new construction is almost impossible, leaving brand-new schools understaffed, underequipped, overfull, and clearly under stress. Again, because of skills in communication and advocacy, counselors can help schools express their needs to various stakeholders.

Crisis Planning   Schools, once considered safe havens for learning, are now aware of their vulnerability. Lethal violence has entered the schools, usually through the front door, and has walked unchecked through the halls. Most school professionals are aware that they cannot remain complacent in their illusion of safety. It is policy in many schools to lock all exterior doors except one, which is watched during the day, and many have enacted policies requiring all visitors to check in with the central office for an identifying pin, sticker, or badge. Many school administrators have installed metal detectors, hired armed security guards, and conducted drills in the event of armed assault. And these safeguards are not only designed to deter intruders from the street—we are now also afraid of our children. Counselors help design crisis plans; help young people learn skills in empathy, impulse control, and nonviolent conflict resolution; and help schools deal with tragedies that occur in the building or in the community.

Careers for All—Noncollege Options   Many schools are hearing from caregivers and students that not enough is being done to meet the career needs of non-college-bound students. If one of the desired outcomes of education is that students leave our schools with the ability to engage in adult roles, then schools must be more aware of noncollege occupational and career options. It is a legacy of the belief that "success = college" that schools promote college as the best post–high school option, but in reality, college right after high school might not be the best option for many young people who have not yet found their direction in life. The wide range of options includes community college or technical education and training, military service, community service and volunteerism, apprenticeships, full- or part-time employment, or becoming a family caregiver. In the interest of allowing all students to discover for themselves what their life direction will be, school counselors are challenged to help diverse students with diverse callings in life to find their own paths.

Student Issues

Family Problems   No one can deny the effect of families on our students, positive and negative. As families change, emotional support for children often becomes uncertain. Chaos in the family results in chaos in the student's life, and traditional support systems of extended family members are not always ready, willing, or available to pick up the slack. As a result, young people are often adrift emotionally, seeking significance and safety from others like themselves. The result is affiliation with other disenfranchised youth—a gang (McWhirter, McWhirter, McWhirter, & McWhirter, 1998). To counteract the effects of nonfunctional families or gangs, counselors can help young people find a connection with positive role models in the school or in the community.

Aggression and Violence   Many young people witness violence daily in their own homes (McWhirter et al., 1998; Tolan & Guerra, 1998). In fact, the violence that is witnessed most often by young people is relationship violence, in which one family member or "loved" one assaults another. Furthermore, violence is a part of young people's everyday lives: from newscasts, to video games, to movies, music, and television "talk" shows such as Jerry Springer and Sally Jessy Rafael. In fact, Rollo May draws parallels between the social malaise of our society and the art of the culture, finding that in art we see "symbols galore of alienation and anxiety" (1975, p. 23). Does art imitate life, or does life imitate art? Counselors can help young people find their way through the chaos that the media presents as "real life."

Sexuality   As will be discussed in Chapter 2, adolescence is the time for sexual development and experimentation. School counselors need to be prepared for conversations about sexuality with young people, even though it is generally agreed that the primary responsibility for teaching young people about sexuality and sexual morality rests with the family. Nonetheless, many young people struggle with appropriate forms of sexual expression, health-related issues, unplanned pregnancy, and/or sexual orientation issues, and it is to the school counselor that they may come for information, counseling, and support. The seriousness of these concerns cannot be underestimated: McFarland (1998) reports that research has found strong correlations between nontraditional (gay, lesbian, and bisexual) sexual orientation and suicidal ideation and attempts. Our personal and professional experiences with clients and students of nontraditional sexual orientation suggests that this correlation is indeed very strong. It is imperative that school counselors become aware of their own attitudes, values, and beliefs about sexual expression and sexual orientation. Through awareness and a balanced approach to sexual issues, counselors can effectively work with young people in a way that (1) preserves the dignity and autonomy of the student; (2) meets the student's needs for information, counseling, and support; and (3) preserves the authenticity and congruence of the counselor.

Mental Health Issues   School counselors report that the frequency with which they encounter students with mental health issues is increasing at an alarming rate. Students with emotional disabilities, such as problems with depression, anger management, posttraumatic stress, reactive attachment disorder, autism, and oppositional defiance are being increasingly diagnosed at all educational levels. It is crucial that counselors become knowledgeable about these issues to assist in the early assessment, identification, and referral of these students to school and community resources. Furthermore, school counselors must be able to provide counseling and support services for these students to facilitate their academic, social and emotional, and career development. A student's DSM-IV diagnosis doesn't eliminate the counselor's vital role in promoting school success. School counselors must understand special education terminology, legislation, and issues, since they must facilitate educational responses to a student's mental health status.

Crisis Counseling   Counselors must be able to work effectively with students who are in crisis, and they must be able to act decisively in cases of suicidal risk. In a recent study of 186 secondary school counselors, researchers found that 87 percent of them felt that suicide work was part of the job, but only 38 percent of them felt they had the skills to be effective with suicidal students (King, Price, Telljohann, & Wahl, 1999a, 1999b). Yet, according to the National Mental Health Association, "the incidence of teen suicide has reached near epidemic proportions, with over 5000 suicides annually among our nation's youth ages 15–24.

At a rate of nearly 14 per day, suicide is the second leading cause of death among adolescents . . ." ("ASCA and Ronald McDonald House," 2000). School counselors must have skills in the assessment of suicide potentiality. Furthermore, it is crucial that counselors know the answers to the following questions:

1. What are the expectations of the district and the school administrators in terms of notification of caregivers and school administration?
2. What are the processes and roles of social services, law enforcement agencies, school professionals, and counselors in terms of getting the student to a safe location?
3. How do you access local mental health emergency services? What is the location, address, phone, and placement procedures of the local mental health facility if a commitment becomes necessary?
4. What are the implications of transportation, information sharing, and notification of all parties (caregivers, administrators, law enforcement, and mental health professionals)?

Unhealthy and Self-Destructive Behaviors Along with mental health issues, school counselors are reporting increasing instances of unhealthy and self-destructive behaviors. According to McWhirter and colleagues (1998), young people are engaging in high-risk behaviors, such as intake of alcohol and other drugs, in alarming numbers. Along with these unhealthy and high-risk behaviors, some students express their pain in self-destructive behaviors such as self-mutilation, cutting, and burning. Furthermore, counselors need to understand their own reactions to some nontraditional ways of self-decoration, such as tattooing, piercing, branding, and carving, to be able to understand when self-marking is self-destructive and when it is self-decoration. Responses to these behaviors range on a continuum of prevention/intervention/treatment, according to severity and systemic issues (McWhirter et al., 1998), and counselors must be able to move within this continuum to meet the needs of the students.

Economic Realities Regardless of family income, in this competitive, capitalistic society, it's not enough. Our market-driven, advertisement-saturated culture makes everyone feel inadequate; the goal of the marketing profession is to make us want things we don't need (Fox, 1994). It's little wonder that young people, who are painfully status- and self-conscious, feel the effects of peer pressure to have bigger, more, better, newer, biggest, newest, best. It's a race with no winners (except in the corporate world), and young people are played for all their worth, since marketing an image to young people is big business. School counselors need to understand this race for the best and most expensive luxuries and need to be able to work with students whose income doesn't match their wish list.

Technology Computers are both a gift and a curse in modern society. We can communicate around the world, access information, transact holiday shopping, and produce volumes of work in a fraction of the time it took a short decade ago. However, it is also a dangerous toy in the family den: Through it, pedophiles access new victims, threats of violence are delivered, young people withdraw further from meaningful human contact, and new addictions are fostered. As new technologies become more affordable, more students will need help understanding the power and the dangers of the computer: how to use it as an effective and efficient tool for learning and how to avoid the problems that new technologies might bring. Counselors are often the best resource for teachers and students to help humanize the school environment, to facilitate conversations among all persons in the school setting.

Reflection Moment

What are your experiences and feelings about these issues? What are your attitudes, values, beliefs, or biases about each of these issues? Go back through the issues discussed in this chapter and write a personal reaction to each. How can you develop a better understanding about these issues?

Chapter Summary

In this chapter, we have introduced the "big picture" of school counseling through a discussion of the professional standards and personal qualities that are essential for all school counselors and where each of those competencies and qualities may be developed. Next, we explored counseling, because we believe that it is important that you consider your own philosophy of counseling and through it, find and develop mastery of your theoretical orientation. School counseling is, at its core, a counseling activity.

In the next section of the chapter, we discussed schools, starting with an overview of various philosophies of education. These various philosophical orientations to education have led to various school environments; with each philosophy, there are advantages and disadvantages. From there, we discussed effective schools and looked at those qualities that culminate in effective schools. The two crucial factors are a caring environment and an emphasis on holistic development, which cannot be created without collaboration with other school professionals. We then explore those professionals with whom school counselors must develop those collaborative connections.

Finally, in an attempt to sensitize you to the important issues facing our schools and our students, we have provided snapshots of critical issues, in the hope that you will begin now to explore additional readings in these areas.

A Day in the Life Revisited: Integration

Now that you've read the chapter,

1. What are Henry's hurdles?
2. What do you see as Henry's philosophy of helping? Of education? How has his philosophy of education contributed to this situation?
3. How does he see his role relative to other professionals in the school? If you were advising Henry, what role would you encourage him to develop?
4. How would you describe a healthy relationship with other professionals in the school? How would you help Henry move toward establishing those healthy relationships? What specifically can he do to improve those relationships?

Application

1. In this chapter, you have been challenged to think about the development of a professional portfolio to document your professional competencies and personal qualities that will make you an employable school counselor. Outline what you would insert into such a portfolio.

2. What is your philosophy of counseling and your theoretical orientation? Do you need to adapt that orientation for use in the schools? How, specifically, will you accomplish that? Where can you go to get additional information and/or practice in using your theory?

3. Schools don't have signs on them that identify their philosophy of education, but you can make some educated guesses about which philosophy or philosophies guided the design of the school and its programs. Make an appointment and visit your local high school. See if you can identify the legacy of each of the educational philosophies discussed in this chapter. Interview the principal and the school counselor and see if you can identify their philosophical orientation(s) in their answers to the question, "What does this school provide to its students?"

4. Outline a plan for learning more about each of the professions presented in the discussion about collaboration. What distinguishes school counselors from school social workers and from school psychologists? Why do some schools hire one professional over another? Obtain job descriptions and identify those job duties that are unique to each.

5. Take each issue discussed at the end of the chapter and outline your stand on each. How do you think and feel about accountability? School testing? Funding for schools? The importance of facilities and the message it sends to young people? School security and fear of outside or student violence? Should we be afraid of our children? Is college the "best" choice for everyone? How do you view appropriate sexuality? What are your views on alternative sexual orientation? How do you feel about suicide? Do you use alcohol? What are your beliefs about drug use? Are some drugs better than others? How do you see self-decoration? What is the line between that and self-mutilation? To what extent do you pursue economic status? How do you view technology?

6. Outline a plan to obtain additional education in each of the issues presented. As a professional in education, you are expected to be a role model in the pursuit of lifelong learning. Here's your chance to demonstrate your commitment to education!

7. Conduct an Internet search using "education" and "schools" as keywords. How many responses do you get? Outline a strategy for selecting descriptors that will help you access more meaningful sites. Visit those sites and record the web addresses for future access. Why did you select the sites you did? What does that say about your philosophy of education?

8. Look at the student quote that opens this chapter. How does it relate to the content of the chapter?

Suggested Readings

Hahn, T. N. (1991). *Peace is every step*. New York: Bantam.

Hoff, B. (1982). *The Tao of Pooh*. New York: Penguin.

Hoff, B. (1982). *The Te of Piglet*. New York: Penguin.

These three resources are recommended to help the reader to think outside the box of linear, Western society, with the hope that reflection on these readings will increase flexibility, creativity, and access to intuition.

McWhirter, J. J., McWhirter, B. T., McWhirter, A. M., & McWhirter, E. H. (1998). *At-risk youth: A comprehensive response for counselors, teachers, psychologists, and human service professionals*. Pacific Grove, CA: Brooks/Cole. A must-read for school counselors, this book provides wonderful insights about risk factors, issues facing youth, and issues facing educational professionals who work with youth.

References

$20 million set aside for school counseling. (2000, January). *Counseling Today, 42,* 1, 19.

Adelman, H. S., & Taylor, L. (1997). Addressing barriers to learning: Beyond school-linked services and full service schools. *American Journal of Orthopsychiatry, 67,* 408–421.

American Counseling Association (ACA). (1995). *Code of ethics and standards of practice.* Alexandria, VA: Author.

American School Counselor Association (ASCA). (1998). *Ethical standards for school counselors.* Alexandria, VA: Author.

ASCA and Ronald McDonald House Charities team up to battle teen depression. (2000, January/February). *The ASCA Counselor, 37,* 19–20.

Bandura, A. (1977). *Social learning theory.* Englewood Cliffs, NJ: Prentice-Hall.

Berens, L. V. (1988). *Please understand me: Empowering students of the 90's.* Huntington Beach, CA: Temperament Research Institute.

Blackwell, T. L., Martin, W. E., Jr., & Scalia, V. A. (1994). *Ethics in rehabilitation: A guide for rehabilitation professionals.* Athens, GA: Elliott & Fitzpatrick.

Brammer, L. M., & McDonald, G. (1999). *The helping relationship: Process and skills* (7th ed.). Boston: Allyn and Bacon.

Brown, O. S., & Peterkin, R. S. (1999). Transforming public schools: An integrated strategy for improving student academic performance through districtwide resource equity, leadership accountability, and program efficiency. *Equity and Excellence in Education, 32* (3), 37–52.

Bruner, J. S. (1961). The act of discovery. *Harvard Educational Review, 31,* 31–32.

Canon, H. J., & Brown, R. D. (Eds.). (1985). *Applied ethics in student services.* San Francisco, CA: Jossey-Bass.

Carkhuff, R. R. (1987). *The art of helping* (6th ed.). Amherst, MA: Human Resource Development Press.

Christopher, J. C. (1996). Counseling's inescapable moral visions. *Journal of Counseling and Development, 75,* 17–25.

Clinchy, B. (1989). On critical thinking and connected knowing. *Liberal Education, 75* (5), 14–19.

Corey, G. C. (1996). *Theory and practice of counseling and psychotherapy* (5th ed.). Pacific Grove, CA: Brooks/Cole.

Corey, G. C., Corey, M. S., & Callanan, P. (1993). *Issues and ethics in the helping professions.* Pacific Grove, CA: Brooks/Cole.

Cormier, L. S., & Hackney, H. (1987). *The professional counselor, a process guide to helping.* Englewood Cliffs, NJ: Prentice-Hall.

Council for Accreditation of Counseling and Related Educational Programs (CACREP). (2000). *The 2001 standards: CACREP accreditation standards and procedures manual.* Alexandria, VA: Author.

Dahir, C. A., Sheldon, C. B., & Valiga, M. J. (1998). *Vision into action: Implementing the National Standards for School Counseling Programs.* Alexandria, VA: American School Counselor Association.

Dinkmeyer, D. C., Dinkmeyer, D. C., Jr., & Sperry, L. (1987). *Adlerian counseling and psychotherapy* (2nd ed). Columbus, OH: Merrill.

Dollarhide, C. T., & Haxton, R. (1999). Generations Theory: Counseling using generational value systems. *The CACD Journal, 19,* 21–28.

Dollarhide, C. T., & Mickelson, D. J. (2000, February). *So you're a counselor supervisor: What now?* Paper presented at the meeting of the Wisconsin School Counselor Association, Stevens Point, WI.

Dollarhide, C. T., & Scully, S. (1999). The counseling/learning model: Using epistemological theory in college counseling. *The Journal of the Pennsylvania Counseling Association, 2,* 3–18.

Dubelle, S. T., & Hoffman, C. M. (1984*). Misbehavin': Solving the disciplinary puzzle for educators.* Lancaster, PA: Technomic.

Dubelle, S. T., & Hoffman, C. M. (1986). *Misbehavin' II: Solving more of the disciplinary puzzle for educators.* Lancaster, PA: Technomic.

Dunn, R., & Griggs, S. A. (1988). *Learning styles: Quiet revolution in American secondary schools.* Reston, VA: National Association of Secondary School Principals.

Ellis, A. (1973). *Humanistic psychotherapy: The rational emotive approach.* New York: McGraw-Hill.

Eisner, E. W. (1985). *The educational imagination: On the design and evaluation of school programs* (2nd ed.). New York: Macmillan.

Fox, M. (1994). *The re-invention of work: A new vision of livelihood for our time.* San Francisco, CA: Harper.

Frankl, V. E. (1984). *Man's search for meaning* (revised). New York: Washington Square.

Gardner, H. (1983). *Frames of mind: The theory of multiple intelligences.* New York: Basic.

Gibbs, J. (1995). *Tribes: A new way of learning and being together.* Sausalito, CA: Center Source Systems.

Glasser, W. (1965). *Reality therapy: A new approach to psychiatry.* New York: Harper & Row.

Golderberger, N. R., Clinchy, B. M., Belenky, M. F., & Tarule, J. M. (1987). Women's ways of knowing. In P. Shaver & C. Hendrick (Eds.), *Sex and gender*. London, UK: Sage Publications.

Hanna, F. J., & Bemak, F. (1997). The quest for identity in the counseling profession. *Counselor Education and Supervision, 36*, 194–206.

Herlihy, B., & Corey, G. (1996). *ACA ethical standards casebook* (5th ed.). Alexandria, VA: American Association for Counseling and Development.

Huber, C. H., & Baruth L. G. (1987). *Ethical, legal, and professional issues in the practice of marriage and family therapy*. New York: Merrill.

Hutchins, D. E., & Cole, C. G. (1992). *Helping relationships and strategies* (2nd ed.). Pacific Grove, CA: Brooks/Cole.

Kegan, R. (1982). *The evolving self: Problem and process in human development*. Cambridge, MA: Harvard University Press.

King, K. A., Price, J. H., Telljohann, S. K., & Wahl, J. (1999a). How confident do high school counselors feel in recognizing students at risk for suicide? *American Journal of Health Behavior, 23*, 457–467.

King, K. A., Price, J. H., Telljohann, S. K., & Wahl, J. (1999b). Preventing adolescent suicide: Do high school counselors know the risk factors? *Professional School Counseling, 3*, 255–263.

King, P. M., & Kitchener, K. S. (1994). *Developing reflective judgment*. San Francisco, CA: Jossey-Bass.

Kottler, J. A. (1991). *The compleat therapist*. San Francisco, CA: Jossey-Bass.

Kottler, J. A. (1993). *On being a therapist* (revised ed.) San Francisco, CA: Jossey-Bass.

Krumboltz, J. D., & Thoresen, C. E. (Eds.). (1976). *Counseling methods*. New York: Holt, Rinehart and Winston.

Lazear, D. (1999). *Eight ways of teaching: The artistry of teaching with multiple intelligences* (3rd ed.). Arlington Heights, IL: SkyLight Training & Publishing.

Lewis, A. C. (1994). Expectations for schools. *Education Digest, 60* (4), 72–74.

Lubman, S. (1995, March 10). Schools tie salaries to pupil performance. *The Wall Street Journal*, pp. B1, B3.

May, R. (1975). *The courage to create*. New York: W. W. Norton.

McFarland, W. P. (1998). Gay, lesbian, and bisexual student suicide. *Professional School Counselor, 1*, 26–29.

McWhirter, J. J., McWhirter, B. T., McWhirter, A. M., & McWhirter, E. H. (1998). *At-risk youth: A comprehensive response for counselors, teachers, psychologists, and human service professionals*. Pacific Grove, CA: Brooks/Cole.

Meier, S. C., & Davis, S. R. (1997). *Elements of counseling* (3rd ed.). Pacific Grove, CA: Brooks/Cole.

Newman, J. W. (1994). *America's teachers: An introduction to education* (2nd ed.). New York: Longman.

Nichols, M. P., & Schwartz, R. C. (1991). *Family therapy concepts and methods* (2nd ed.). Boston: Allyn and Bacon.

Nystul, M. S. (1993). *The art and science of counseling and psychotherapy*. New York: Merrill.

Olson, L. (1999, April 21). Tugging at tradition: Lessons of a century. *Education Week*, 25–29, 30–31.

Palmer, P. (1998). *The courage to teach: Exploring the inner landscape of a teacher's life*. San Francisco, CA: Jossey-Bass.

Perry, W. G., Jr. (1981). Cognitive and ethical growth. In A. Chickering (Ed.), *The modern American college*. San Francisco, CA: Jossey-Bass.

Pittman, D. (undated). *Preventing problems or promoting development: Competing priorities or inseparable goals*. Online: www.iyfnet.org/document.cfm/22/general/51. Accessed: November 30, 1999.

Rico, G. L. (1983). *Writing the natural way: Using right-brain techniques to release your expressive powers*. Los Angeles: Tarcher.

School Mental Health Project/Center for Mental Health in Schools [SMHP]. (1999, Fall). Promoting youth development and addressing barriers. *Addressing Barriers to Learning*, 1–8.

Simon, C. A. (1999). Public school administration: Employing Thompson's Structural Contingency Theory to explain public school administrative expenditures in Washington State. *Administration and Society, 31*, 525–542.

Slavin, R. E. (1994). *A practical guide to cooperative learning*. Boston: Allyn and Bacon.

St. Clair, M. (1996). *Object relations and self psychology*. Pacific Grove, CA: Brooks/Cole.

Sue, D. W., & Sue, D. (1990). *Counseling the culturally different* (2nd ed.). Somerset, NJ: Wiley and Sons.

Tolan, P., & Guerra, N. (1998). *What works in reducing adolescent violence: An empirical review of the field*. Boulder, CO: Center for the Study and Prevention of Violence.

Travers, J. F., Elliott, S. N., & Kratochwill, T. R. (1993). *Educational psychology: Effective teaching, effective learning*. Madison, WI: Brown & Benchmark.

Van Hoose, W. H., & Kottler, J. A. (1988). *Ethical and legal issues in counseling and psychotherapy*. San Francisco, CA: Jossey-Bass.

Wall, S., & Arden, H. (1990). *Wisdomkeepers: Meetings with Native American spiritual leaders*. Hillsboro, OR: Beyond Words.

Wittmer, J. (2000). Implementing a comprehensive school counseling program. In J. Wittmer (Ed.), *Managing your school counseling program: K–12 developmental strategies* (2nd ed.; pp. 14–36). Minneapolis, MN: Educational Media.

Zimmerman, J. E. (1964). *Dictionary of classical mythology*. New York: Bantam.

2

Celebration of the Adolescent

Kelli A. Saginak

"What do I like least about high school? People do tend to make judgments about others by the way they act or look. If it's not "in," they look down on you."

Brooke, age 16

Learning Objectives _____

By the end of this chapter, you will:

1. Gain an understanding and appreciation of "normal" adolescent development.

2. Understand adolescent identity development from the standpoint of sexual identity in terms of biological identity, role identity in terms of social identity, and self-identity in terms of psychological development.

3. Integrate and apply developmental theory to your understanding of normal adolescent development.

4. Recognize specific issues and concerns faced by today's adolescents.

A Day in the Life of a Teenager: Mandy's Manic Monday

"Mom! Where are my blue capris?! I can't find them and want to wear them today. Everyone is wearing their blue capris! I can't go to school without them! Mom!" Frantic, hair wet, half dressed, and running late for school, Mandy rushed through each room in the house, paying no attention to the chaos she was leaving behind, in search of one article of clothing that would determine her fate on this rainy, dreary Monday. All her friends promised to wear capri pants to school today! And it was just days before the homecoming dance and Mandy still didn't have a date. She had to look perfect today! Jason, or someone, had to ask her to the dance. Needless to say, the zit forming on her chin wasn't helping matters either. "Go on! I can't believe I have a zit! Everyone will see it!"

Distraught, Mandy appeared at her mother's bedroom door holding a dirty pair of blue capri pants, red-faced, and on the verge of exploding. Mandy's mom quickly cut her off, "Don't start with me, Mandy. I have to get to work and you have to get to school. Just wear something else. It's not my fault that you didn't get all your dirty clothes to me to wash this weekend." Mandy turned and yelled, "I hate you! You have no idea how important this is to me!" as she slammed her bedroom door, rattling just about everything in the house.

The ride to school was quiet, except for the mindless chatter of Mandy's little brother Joey, sitting in the back seat. Mandy jumped out of the car without a word of goodbye to her mother and rushed to class as the first bell rang, thinking, "I'm dead meat! My hair's ruined! I look horrible! I hate my life!" Her mother, just as distraught, punched the gas and squealed off, hoping that she wouldn't be late for her morning meeting as she went over the grocery list in her head.

Once in class, Mandy slid into her seat, hoping that no one noticed her hair, her clothes, or her in general, especially the zit on her chin, which was now starting to feel the size of a grape. Her sort-of-on-and-off boyfriend, Jason, who caught a glimpse of her out of the corner of his eye, didn't even notice what she was wearing or that her hair was wet. "I really want to ask Mandy to the homecoming dance, but like wow, what will the guys say? They're going to expect us to 'do it' that night, and I know Mandy's not into that. I should probably ask Sue. Oh man! I forgot to study for the test today! I hope I lost enough weight for the wrestling match today . . ." As the tardy bell rang, the atmosphere of the classroom quieted to a low, dull hum as class began . . . and minds wandered. . . .

Challenge Questions

As you entered Mandy's world, what were some of your reactions? What feelings came up for you? As an adult, what did you notice about yourself as you experienced Mandy and Jason? What do you struggle with the most? What is it you do not understand about teenagers? How does that influence your relationship with teens?

Growth and Development: What Is "Normal"?

"Adolescence is not planned. It happens" (Mercer, 1997, p. 60), and most, if not all, of the annoying, unpredictable behaviors that frustrate and alarm many of us are essential to the natural evolution from childhood to young adulthood. This natural evolutionary process, a period of "reaching out, gaining life experiences, making mistakes, and testing . . ." (Gabriel & Wool, 1999, p. 2), wreaks havoc within families and the lives of adults attempting to ride out the storm of adolescence. Few understand this period of development, many even fear it, and even fewer accept, nurture, and celebrate it. Pipher (1994) profoundly reminds us:

> Adolescents are travelers, far from home with no native land, neither children nor adults. They are jet-setters who fly from one country to another with amazing speed. Sometimes they are four years old, an hour later they are twenty-five. They don't really fit anywhere. There's yearning for a place, a search for solid ground. (p. 52)

If we look at human development from a life-span perspective, one that takes into account that individuals grow toward a sense of autonomy all within a context of constant relations and interactions (Ivey, 1993), the few years allotted to prepare for adulthood could only be chaotic and confusing. Flooded with physical, emotional, sexual, intellectual, academic, and vocational changes, adolescents have the challenge of pulling all these pieces together in preparation for adulthood. Yet, today's society gives little thought to the immediate experience of the adolescent and the obstacles that lie in the path toward adulthood. Instead, society focuses on the next achievement, the next accomplishment, the next feat, often forgetting about the adolescent, the person—and in many ways, still the child. When we take the time to step back and look at our young people, see all they are and are capable of, find the unique and special qualities they bring, and embrace all that they can become, we can then perhaps relish in and celebrate the experience of adolescence. If not, we risk the possibility of losing an exciting and very "normal" stage of life. In the words of Rousseau (as cited in Crain, 2000):

> The wisest writers devote themselves to what a man [sic] ought to know, without asking them what a child is capable of learning. They are always looking for the man [sic] in the child, without considering what he is before he becomes a man [sic]. (Crain, 2000, p. 1)

With the exception of infancy, no other stage of development experiences such rapid amounts of change in such a short amount of time. Relationships with family members change as adolescents strive for autonomy and separate from their families while creating new attachments with peers and significant others in their lives, all while learning to love and accept themselves and who they are becoming. The question "What will I be when I grow up?" lingers in the forefront of all teenagers' minds as they prepare to enter the world as full-functioning, highly responsible, competent, and capable adults. Not that they have a clue what that means!

Growing up in the twenty-first century and the numerous challenges it brings make it especially difficult on today's adolescents. Environmental challenges and economic concerns, all within the evolving social and cultural makeup of the United States, have a significant effect on how teens see themselves and their world today. Cultural values and beliefs and attitudes about gender, life, and death are significant influences on the formation of adolescents' identities (Carter & McGoldrick, 1999).

Many youth today manage to "make it" through their adolescent years with few to no real problems to speak of; however, many do not, continuing to struggle well into their adult years. These issues and challenges permeate the world of the school and scream for the assistance and support of educators, administrators, and school counselors. School counselors especially are in unique positions to reach out to youth, their families, their schools, and their communities and awaken society to the realities that teens encounter every day.

Chapter 1 introduced you to the professional competencies and personal qualities school counselors develop through years of professional education and training. Yet, when faced with the reality of adolescents, their array of developmental issues, combined with the reality of our world and the secondary school, competencies and personal qualities go out the window. Secondary school counselors find themselves not only working in the world of the teenager but also working within the world of the school where theories, competencies, domains, and educational standards compete with piles of phone messages, paperwork, administrative tasks, and crises.

Immersed in adolescent development, secondary school counselors eager to use their professional training find in reality very little time for actual counseling. Developmental programming falls by the wayside as graduation requirements and college applications take precedence. Squeezed into twenty minutes of lunch or study hall, group counseling rarely finds its place in a cram-packed academic schedule. Counselors reluctantly rely on career guidance and the registration process, hoping for some sort of interpersonal connection with students. Amidst today's schools and modern society's view of the teenager, the essence behind theories of adolescence and the meaning of developmental guidance has been often forgotten and frequently lost.

This chapter reintroduces you to the adolescent and "normal" adolescent development, the foundation on which developmentally appropriate schools, developmental curriculum, and programming rest. Here adolescent development is explored through the use of theory and celebrated by creating a sense of normalcy for this exciting yet challenging stage of life. Theory is used as a general guideline and framework from which to view development and analyze the world of the adolescent, not as a means to judge what is normal or abnormal based on the traditional universal patterns of development (Berger & Thompson, as cited in Vernon, 1993). Opportunity for reflection on your own teenage years is also provided in order to remind you that yes, you were once a teenager too, and probably felt anything but "normal."

Reflection Moment

Stop and reflect on your own developmental transition from adolescent to adulthood. What images come to mind? What feelings best describe this period in your life? What specific situations stand out for you? What patterns do you see? How did those years of transition affect the person you are today? The school counselor you are becoming?

Adolescent Development: So What Does "Normal" Look Like?

Adolescence comes from the Latin *adolescere,* meaning "to grow up"; it is the period of development starting roughly around 12 years of age with the beginning of puberty and ending around the age of 19 with the entrance into young adulthood (Rice, 1997). In today's modern society, with its unique set of challenges and hurdles, there are those who believe that adolescence continues until around age 21 (Pipher, 1994), a period of development referred to as "youth" (Kotre & Hall, 1990). Growing up and the experience of adolescence today may not necessarily end with earning a high school diploma; in fact, it may continue well into the college years for many.

Adolescence is a highly transitional stage of development characterized by extreme and rapid physical, intellectual, and relational growth and change, and accompanied by tremendous emotional upheavals. Adolescents question all that is happening to their bodies and their minds, demanding to know if any of this is normal. According to Schave and Schave, cognitive and moral reasoning capabilities explode as adolescents begin to identify who they are and develop a sense of self separate from that of their families and friends (as cited in Vernon, 1993). Relationships with childhood friends and family suddenly look and feel different as teens begin to explore issues of intimacy, autonomy, separation, and attachment.

Combine these external changes with those occurring internally, and one can begin to understand why this period of development is often described as storming, turbulent, challenging, and, sometimes, out of control. It is so much out of control that often adults have little to say about adolescence that is positive, instead viewing it as a troublesome time filled with unpredictable risk-taking behavior, raging hormones and moodiness, limit testing, deviance, and rebelliousness. This less-than-positive view unfortunately also seeps into the field of education and human services, and even though our intentions are good, our inability to fully embrace the world of the adolescent often results in the stifling of our youths' imagination, creativity, and vitality.

Reflection Moment

How do you define "normal?" How do you define "normal" adolescent development? In what ways do you pathologize "normal" adolescent development? How can you embrace adolescent development and approach it more positively in your work as a school counselor?

Identity Development: "Who Am I?"

"For indeed, in the social jungle of human existence there is no feeling of being alive without a sense of identity" (Erikson, as cited in Rice, 1997, p. 130). "Who am I?" is the eternal question pondered by each of us at many points in our lifetime. However, the question of "Who am I?" has special significance for the adolescent. The *achievement of identity*, the most important psychosocial task of adolescence, asks individuals to question and explore issues of identity achievement versus identity confusion (Erikson, as cited in Rice, 1997). In a few short years, teens are expected to discover who they are, what they want to do with their lives, and with whom they want to do it all—a task not easy for most of us, much less a novice, inexperienced teenager.

Typically, we think of identity development as only "Who am I?" Yet, Rogow, Marcia, and Slugoski found that the creation of identity encompasses so much more, such as sexual, social, physical, psychological, moral, ideological, and vocational characteristics, all of which make up the total self (as cited in Rice, 1997). According to Gabriel and Wool (1999), adolescents are trying to establish three forms of identity: *sexual identity*, *role identity*, and *self-identity*, each of which overlaps and becomes integrated with the other in the overall achievement of identity.

Knowing "who I am" involves defining self as a sexual being and through the portrayal of gender roles. It involves knowing the self through social interactions, group memberships, relationships, and intimacy with others, as well as acceptance of body, build, and physical attributes and capabilities. It entails an expression of self through religious, spiritual, and political affiliations; the alignment with morals, values, and philosophies that govern life; the achievement and success in a career; and through the awareness of ethnic and cultural heritages, "personality characteristics, psychological adjustment, and mental health" (Rice, 1997, p. 379). One might view these tasks as an individual's journey toward self-actualization, a stage usually not accomplished during adolescence (Vernon, 1993), and for some of us, not crystallizing until well into the adult years, if ever at all (Rice, 1997).

Reflection Moment

Think back to your adolescent years. How many of these components of identity were you successful at completing? Which ones still remain works-in-progress?

Sexual Identity: Biological Development

". . . [F]ew situations in life . . . are more difficult to cope with than an adolescent son or daughter during the attempt to liberate themselves" (Freud, as cited in Crain, 2000, p. 276). Puberty, which begins around the age of 11 for girls and age 13 for boys, marks the point at which teenagers begin the task of freeing themselves from their parents, a painful emotional experience that most of us never completely accomplish (Crain, 2000). Relationships at home transform as adolescents begin the process of separating from their parents in hopes of discovering who they are independently. This transformation is seen as boys and girls begin to look outside the comforts of home for intimacy and closeness and break away from the structure and control of the family (Freud, as cited in Crain, 2000).

This process of breaking away and finding intimacy with others varies among teens, yet general stresses and patterns of behavior typically coincide with sexual identity development. According to Anna Freud, previous Oedipal feelings and impulses emerge once again, often creating feelings of resentment toward parents. As sexual energies evolve from mere fantasies to conscious desires, adolescents suddenly experience tension and anxiety accompanied by the need to "bolt" and get away from their parents (as cited in Crain, 2000). This impulse to "take flight" sends teenagers retreating into the privacy of their rooms, the comfort of friends, and, for some, to the danger of the streets.

Sometimes taking flight reveals itself in the form of contempt for parents by casting aside any feelings of love and affection. The all-too-familiar "I hate you!" comes to mind as the defense of choice necessary to push parents away. Behaviors aimed at preventing any resurgence of feelings and impulses such as intellectualizing and rationalizing and shying away from dances, dates, and school functions that symbolize fun and pleasure are natural occurrences. Unfortunately, some of these natural feelings of defense can be taken to the extreme through such means as strict dieting and compulsive exercising.

Unexplainable sexual urges and aggressive tendencies are often reconstructed into abstract theories that allow adolescents to analyze Oedipal issues from a distance (Freud, as cited in Crain, 2000). This reminds me of nights spent writing in my diary attempting to explain and rationalize the feelings I had as a teenager, or long involved conversations with close friends trying to figure out and understand love, sex, and relationships. Yet even just a mere twenty years ago, contemplating sex mostly focused on "not doing it," even though the curiosity and interest was there. Today's teens are taking a more active role in exploring these issues.

Adolescents today face much more than normal sexual desire, impulses, and feelings. Teens are now having sex earlier than in previous generations, and issues of sexually transmitted diseases, AIDS, and pregnancy continue to wreak havoc on families as adolescents attempt to maneuver through the issues surrounding sexual identity. For gay, bisexual, and lesbian teens, the process of sexual identity is filled with additional challenges as they not only seek to understand their own sexual orientation (Carter & McGoldrick, 1999), but at the same time desperately reach out in hopes of finding acceptance from their peers and society.

Reflection Moment

Think back to your first sexual urges, those feelings and excitement, those tingling sensations experienced in private or in the company of others. What was it like living at home then? What were some of the feelings and impulses you remember having?

"Whose Body Is This Anyway?"   Looking back on my middle school years, what I remember most is towering over most of the boys in my seventh- and eighth-grade classes.

Since I was taller than just about everyone, or that was my perception, I felt I stuck out like a sore thumb. (Not to mention that my shoe size exceeded what I thought to be normal, causing me to hate the frequent trips to the shoe store. "I'm not wearing those! They look like boats!") Relief came the first day of 9th grade when, miraculously, all the boys had grown, developed, and now towered over me. Unfortunately, when comparing myself to the other girls in my class, I had little relief. Their bodies had transformed into what looked to me like fashion models and cover girls. So what happened to me? If I could just blend in, not be noticed, and by some miracle, wake up from this bad dream, everything—well, almost everything—would be fine. To say I was a late bloomer is an understatement, and yet what brings about laughter for me now was quite humiliating and painful to me as a teenager.

The physical changes that take place during the adolescent years are of such magnitude that many, if not all, adolescents feel overwhelmed and question whether the transformations taking place in their bodies are normal. Dangling arms, gangling legs, acne, body odor, body hair, and other new and extreme body changes leave teens running for the mirror time and time again, desperately trying to grasp who that person is staring back at them. Initial growth spurts of adolescence mark the ending of childhood. The years of slow, steady, and manageable changes are lost in an overwhelming surge of hormones (Schickedanz, Schickedanz, Forsyth, & Forsyth, 2001).

Puberty for girls and boys starts and stops at various times and shows itself in distinct and different ways. The most visible signs of puberty for girls begin around the age of 10 or 11. Possibly breasts will begin to bud, body hair will emerge, and hips will start to spread a little bit; a general sense of "filling out" may be noticed. Yet it is usually around the age of 12 or 13 when girls typically experience the most visible growth spurt that means the first menstrual cycle is not far behind (Kotre & Hall, 1990). It is typical at this time to see girls' bodies "blossom" so to speak, into more mature woman-like figures. During this period of development, girls may become frustrated enough with their bodies to resort to unhealthy means of "controlling" what nature is intending. Often adolescent girls will attempt to control their natural developmental growth through dieting and/or inadequate nutrition, extreme amounts of exercise, or through the use of over-the-counter drugs and remedies.

For boys, the onset of puberty is generally later; and by about the age of 12, boys begin to show visible, physical signs of puberty (Kotre & Hall, 1990). At this point, boys will begin to grow taller, muscles may become more pronounced or defined, chests and shoulders will expand, and there appears to be an overall filling out and/or lengthening of the body. Facial and body hair may start to grow, and voices may begin to change. Yet for both males and females, the rapid physical growth they experience will often cause them to eat more and sleep longer. They may also show spurts of physical energy and then plummet into periods of lethargy (Carter & McGoldrick, 1999).

The experience of such rapid physical changes is not only confusing to adolescents but is also a challenging variable in their quest for sexual identity. With body image being everything to many teens and the media making sure they do not forget it, the development of a healthy self-image and self-esteem is quite a hurdle for today's teens. Adolescents are continually reminded of society's ideal body image, and only those teens with the highest self-esteem and self-acceptance can defend themselves in the battle between culture's ideal body image and their own (Schickedanz et al., 2001). Both females and males compare their bodies to those portrayed by the media, striving, or even starving, at any cost to meet societal standards, which for most are unattainable. Often the result is a crushed self-esteem that leaves young people feeling horrible about their bodies, causing their self-image and sexual identity to teeter on the edge. The question for them is, "If I don't feel good when I look in the mirror, how can I feel good when you look at me?"

Adolescents rarely can depend on their bodies to grow at a so-called "normal" rate, thus intensifying their feelings of confusion and inadequacy. The experience of early development or later development dumps additional challenges on the shoulders of many teenagers. Girls who mature early often face the possibility of teasing, harassment, and avoidance by their peers because of sticking out and looking different—whispers of, "Oh, she must date" as an early maturing young teenage girl enters the library hoping that no one notices her. The late maturing boy whose stomach aches as he enters the boy's locker room to change for gym class is already bracing himself for the teasing and bullying he will endure once inside. On the contrary, early maturing boys typically do not experience the same ridicule and embarrassment as early maturing girls. They instead are looked up to, seen as the "jocks" of the school, and are held in high esteem by their peers. However, later maturing girls may also experience teasing like late maturing boys, yet typically report feeling okay about themselves in later adolescence (Kotre & Hall, 1990; Schickedanz et al., 2001).

Physical development places early adolescents' identity on shaking ground amidst raging hormones, growing pains, and extreme emotions. "Fitting in" is paramount for teens as they seek reassurance from their peer group that they're okay, still cool, and worthy of being included. Unfortunately, if you do not look "right," being accepted is often more difficult to achieve. Adolescents' self-esteem is much more than "I feel good about myself." The perception of others is equally (if not more) important in adolescents' quest for overall identity development.

Reflection Moment

Think back on your physical development as an adolescent. What experiences to you remember and how were those experiences related to your quest for identity? How did your physical development affect your relationships with peers? How did your peers react to your physical development?

Role Identity: Social Development

"Human development never occurs in a 'context-free situation' but always in a specific ecological setting—a unique family, a specific neighborhood, school, and community—a social context" (Muuss, 1988, p. 312). For adolescents today, identity problems are much more a social matter (Crain, 2000). According to Crain, today's adolescents struggle more with how they look in the eyes of others and meeting others' expectations than the challenges of physical growth and sexual impulses. Today's youth are finding a greater sense of identity through the intimacy found in "close, meaningful, and loving relationships" (Rice, 1997, p. 385) and gravitating to their peers in order to feel safe. In general, it is the relationships with peer groups and friends that adolescents today value most and that provide a sense of direction toward the person they are becoming.

According to Sullivan (as cited in Muuss, 1988), it is only through these relationships with others that a true sense of personality can be established and maintained, only through our interactions between self and others can one's identity actually evolve. It is the eruption of sexual urges that kicks off the need to enter into more intimate relationships with others. Adolescents depend on these important relationships in their development, and they are a crucial and normal part of healthy identity development. Social interactions and relationships are vital to teens and throughout life they will continue to experience a need to be with others. When this need is not fulfilled, anxiety emerges and their sense of security falters.

Social learning theory and its emphasis on the socialization process through which individuals learn provides additional understanding of the social development of adolescents. Relying on behavioral assumptions and a belief that environmental, situational, and social factors are primary for learning and development, social learning theorists believe that it is the rewarding of imitative responses that is paramount in the socialization process (Muuss, 1988). Simply put, the learner observes the model's behaviors and then imitates the observed behavior, with the prevailing notion of "if he can do it, I can do it" (Bandura & Walters, as cited in Muuss, 1988). Throughout childhood, the models of choice are generally parents, teachers, and other significant adults. Children copy and integrate many of the behaviors demonstrated by these models. Models provide a foundation from which one's individual identity begins to emerge.

Parents and significant adults are still essential role models in the lives of young people, yet during adolescence, relationships with parents and other adults change or shift, and the creation of new, increasingly mature relationships or attachments develop. Teens begin to converse on a more mature level with adults, take on new roles within the family, school, and community, and begin to have opinions. This change naturally brings about resistance, conflict, and lots of emotions. Parents fight to hang on to the children they once knew and their parental roles. Other relatives and significant adults feel the tension as their roles begin to alter. It is true that adolescents have the unique ability to remind all of us of our own developmental transitions. Instead of accepting our adult developmental challenges and moving forward, we fight the one person who *is* doing what he or she is supposed to be doing developmentally: the adolescent.

How important is the influence of parents and peers on the adolescent? According to Kandel (as cited in Muuss, 1988), parents play a vital role in helping adolescents sort through issues concerning basic values, such as religious and spiritual beliefs, future aspirations, educational endeavors, and relationships with the opposite sex. Parents also model intimacy and relationships, how conflict is managed and decisions are made, and, perhaps most important, parents model how emotions are expressed and dealt with. In other words, the social and emotional interactions that take place in the home of the adolescent have a profound influence on how he or she interacts socially and emotionally outside the home.

Peers, on the other hand, play an important role in the everyday life of the adolescent. For example, peer influence becomes instrumental when making decisions concerning drugs and alcohol, styles of dress and music, how to maneuver socially in and out of friend- ships and groups, and involvement in co-curricular activities within school and out in the community. Keep in mind that different peer groups promote different values, some of which are more accepted and approved of by parents than others. For example, most parents and adults view groups known as "druggies" negatively, whereas groups identified as "brains" usually are viewed positively (Muuss, 1988, p. 316). In either case, peer groups and friends serve a significant purpose in adolescent's development. Adolescent friendships and peer groups will be explored in more detail in Chapter 3.

Just how do adolescents influence each other? According to Kandel (as cited in Muuss, 1988), two psychological constructs based on social learning theory exist that help explain the influence that teens have on each other. *Imitation* or *modeling* suggests that if one adolescent accepts, likes, and values the behavior or attitude of another adolescent, he or she will imitate that particular behavior or attitude. *Social reinforcement*, however, implies that the adolescent will go along with a particular attitude or behavior of another adolescent or peer group merely for the social benefit received in return, perhaps in "status, praise, recognition, or peer group admiration" (p. 317). The overall process of social influence between adolescents seems to be similar for both females and males; yet some gender differences may exist. Girls typically form intimate relationships and are more aware of interpersonal influences than boys; they are more sensitive and perceptive to social cues and social pressures (Brown, Lohr, & McClena- han, as cited in Muuss, 1988), regardless of whether peers or parents are doing the influencing. Peer influence also tends to peak around ninth grade for girls and begin to decline throughout the remaining high school years (Muuss, 1988).

Cross-cultural differences exist in the development of friendships and peer group rela- tionships. Bronfenbrenner (as cited in Muuss, 1988) noted a definite divergence between the values of peer groups and those of adults here in the United States compared to other countries such as Russia or China, where values of both adults and peer groups come together around a common political core. Coming from cultures based on rigid standards creates a challenging dynamic for youth attempting to acculturate and assimilate to the often ambigu- ous norms of the United States. Bronfenbrenner warns, however, that because our nation is one promoting pluralistic, egalitarian, and democratic values, we may have encouraged peer group autonomy to the extreme and failed at using peer groups pro-socially to influence "responsibility, considerations for others, social skills, and mental health" (Muuss, 1988, p. 318).

As a society, have we pushed autonomy and independence to the extent of leaving our young people out in the cold, alone with their friends and peer groups to develop their own sets of sense of self, morals, values, and personal ethics? Western society does an adequate job of pushing the adolescent out the door while shouting, "Go out there and make a life for yourself. You're on your own now." Yet, have we abandoned our teens at a time when they need us the most? We advocate and promote independence, autonomy, take care of yourself and do-it-on-your-own, yet we are able to demonstrate over and over the power and influ- ence of social support structures, interactions, intimacy, and relationships on the develop- ment of the adolescent's identity and sense of self.

Reflection Moment

Who influenced you as a teenager? Who were your role models? Who were your heroes? How is that different for youth today? What are schools, communities, and societies modeling for youth today? In what ways are you influencing the youth in your life? What are you modeling for them?

"Can't You See Things from My Point of View?"   We assume that most adolescents can. As adults, we often operate under the assumptions that our youth (1) see the world through adult eyes, (2) will make decisions according to adult standards, and (3) will act and behave in adult ways. This is a mistake that adults continually make—so much so that often it is adults who add stress to the lives of adolescents instead of the reverse!

As adults, we generally reason and make decisions through a process that involves balancing the needs of others with our own wishes and desires. This process may include looking at a situation through the eyes of others—or what we refer to as social cognition. Adolescents typically do not reason at this level, due to a natural state of self-absorption. As adolescents grow to understand themselves and who they are distinct and separate from others, they eventually mature to a level where they are able to consider the needs of others and direct their behaviors and actions in a pro-social manner (Schickedanz et al., 2001).

In general, *social cognition* involves the ability to think about a situation from another person's point of view (Schickedanz et al., 2001), the process of how we come to understand others. According to Muuss (1988), it involves role and perspective taking, empathy, moral reasoning, interpersonal problem solving, and self-knowledge. It also involves the ability to make inferences about others, a process referred to as *social perspective taking*.

Selman (as cited in Muuss, 1988) focused much of his work on the development of interpersonal understanding and social perspective taking. Greatly influenced by Mead's theory of self, Piaget's theory of cognitive development, and Kohlberg's theory of moral development, Selman described role taking as a form of social cognition intermediate between logical and moral thought (Muuss, 1988). It rests on the assumptions that social role taking is a skill requiring advanced levels of cognitive ability, differentiating between one's perspective of self and others, and accurately perceiving the thinking of others. Selman's model is detailed here in order to provide the reader with a continuum of how children proceed through the levels of social perspective taking.

1. *Stage 0: Egocentric.* Up to around the age of 6, children can differentiate self and others, but not their points of view or perspectives, believing instead that everyone feels the way they do. *"Sally and I are friends. I don't like Erica. Sally doesn't like Erica. If I don't want to play with Erica, Sally doesn't want to play with Erica."*
2. *Stage 1: Social-Informational.* From the age of 6 to around the age of 8, children begin to realize that people feel differently because they have different experiences and information, yet they still believe that their perspective is the correct one. *"Yes, I know I hurt Sally's feelings by not playing with her and Erica. She likes Erica and I don't. Erica is too bossy and so Sally shouldn't like her either."*

3. *Stage 2: Self-Reflective (ages 8–10).* Children begin to understand that people can have different points of view and that no one perspective is necessarily right. *"Yes, I know I hurt Sally's feelings by not playing with her. She likes Erica and I don't. Erica is too bossy, but if Sally wants to play with her then she can play with her. I'm not."*

4. *Stage 3: Mutual.* Children from about age 10 to early adolescents around the age of 12 begin to talk about different perspectives and can put themselves in someone else's shoes to see it through their eyes. *"Yes, I know I hurt Sally's feelings by not hanging around with her. She likes Erica and I don't. Erica is too bossy and I don't like being around her, but I can see why Sally is upset and if I were Sally I'd be mad at me too."*

5. *Stage 4: Social and Conventional.* Adolescents around the ages of 12 to 15+ begin to use principles of the larger social society to analyze and evaluate their points of view and the perspectives of others. *"Yes, I know I hurt Sally's feelings by not going to the mall with her and Erica. She likes hanging with Erica and I don't. Erica is too bossy! I can understand why Sally is upset with me, and perhaps I need to give Erica a break. Heck, maybe she doesn't know any better. Maybe if we all sat down and talked we could figure out a way to get along better. I know Sally would like that, and I do miss hanging with Sally. Maybe if we talked about it we could all end up being even better friends."*

According to Byrne (as cited in Muuss, 1988), there exists a definite relationship between logical, moral, and role-taking stages. Simply stated, a certain level in logical thinking and social role taking appear to be necessary before the corresponding stage of moral judgment can be reached. However, cognitive abilities may mature without having developed the equivalent moral and social role taking stage, yet the later stages are rarely accomplished without the equivalent stage of logical thinking. In other words, teens just beginning to develop the ability to think abstractly may not have the capacity to put themselves in someone else's shoes and may still rely on moral judgment based on serving their own needs or interests. For example, we could say that the youth who designed and implemented the massacre at Columbine High School were cognitively advanced in their studies and creative abilities, yet we are reminded daily of their lack of moral judgment and appropriate social role-taking abilities. One can read the paper to find continued and ongoing evidence of adolescents caught in the cross-fire of self-serving, immoral acts of violence, where teens think of their own needs first without consideration for the person being harmed or violated. Evidence also demonstrates that many adults never fully develop their moral and social role taking perspectives and continue to put their needs first and rarely step into someone else's shoes. Where then lie the role models for today's youth?

Reflection Moment

Think back to your adolescence. Do you remember circumstances in which you put yourself in someone else's shoes? Was this something that came easy for you or was it more difficult for you? What about others around you? Where are you in your own development of social perspective taking today? What is missing in our work with teens that enables them to fully develop appropriate moral judgment and social role taking responsibilities?

"Tell Me Again How You Came to That Decision?"   Piaget (as cited in Muuss, 1988) theorized that the moral development of children follows closely along the patterns of cognitive development, meaning that an individual's view of morality has a lot to do with his or her level of cognitive ability: how he or she perceives and organizes the world. *Moral autonomy*, the highest level of moral development, begins at puberty. Adolescents begin the process of shifting their interest to not only the rules of the game but all the possible alternatives in which these same rules might apply. Abstract thought is now possible, yet it is far from being fully developed or consistently attained. Ethical and moral responsibility can begin to develop based on abstract principles of what is right or wrong, a task only possible through involvement and participation in a variety of situations and modeling (Berk, 1999; Muuss, 1988). Again, it is developmentally appropriate and necessary that teens take risks and engage in situational dilemmas and decision-making circumstances in order to strengthen their abstract and moral reasoning capabilities.

Kohlberg (as cited in Muuss, 1988) viewed the adolescent years as the most critical for the development of advanced levels of moral reasoning. He further emphasized that it is "the way an individual reasons," or the process of reasoning, not the resulting action, that determines an individual's level of moral maturity (Rice, 1997, p. 611). During adolescence, a *conventional* level of moral reasoning creates a strong, yet egocentric desire to maintain support, seek conformity to social conventions, and justify the existing social order. While still deriving their moral constructs from individual needs, adolescents have the ability to base this justice orientation on an acceptance of an existing social order and recognition of the rights of others (Berk, 1999; Gilligan, 1982; Muuss, 1988). In other words, moral decisions are generally made to gain approval from significant others; for the adolescent, this approval often comes from the peer group.

Most adolescents, and some adults, function at the conventional level where they find themselves in constant turmoil as they attempt to make "big" decisions that will gain the approval of others. Decisions surrounding smoking, drinking, sex, drugs, and even abortion confront teens daily, and in today's society are not simple or easy to make. Developmentally, the way adolescents go about making such decisions has a tremendous impact on the resulting outcome. Making the "right" decision and gaining the approval of others can have profound and potentially lethal consequences for all those involved. Interestingly, Gilligan, Kohlberg, Lerner, and Belenky (as cited in Muuss, 1988) concluded that decisions involving sex actually depressed adolescents' ability to reason at a level comparable to that of other moral issues.

Gender also plays a definite role in moral development. Gilligan (1982) looked at moral development by comparing how males and females approach morality. For women, moral development typically takes place through the care and responsiveness found within relationships. The morality of females tends to emphasize care, concern, sensitivity, empathy, and attachments to others. Females tend to function from a more conventional level where doing the "right" thing to gain approval from others is paramount. However, doing what is "right" many times places young females in vulnerable and dangerous situations, such as the adolescent (and adult) female who struggles to find a sense of identity in a relationship where making the partner or boyfriend happy is of the utmost concern. Developmentally, young females are making decisions appropriate for their age, yet the way they go about making those decisions is not always in their best interest.

Males tend to view the world from more of a one-sided, masculine, justice orientation (Berk, 1999; Gilligan, 1982; Muuss, 1988), leaving out the care and relational aspect of moral decision making. Gilligan maintains that justice and care must be given attention when making moral decisions. The ways in which both males and females go about making moral decisions are critical, and without integration of the two orientations, people can never reach their fullest potential in moral and general development (Muuss, 1988).

Reflection Moment

When you were a teenager, what process did you go through when making decisions? Did you make them for yourself or for others? How did you perceive decisions that were made in your home? Did you notice any gender differences?

Self-Identity: Psychological Development

". . . [O]nly through conflict can maturity be attained . . ." (Blos, as cited in Muuss, 1988, p. 98). Adolescence, the journey toward self-identity, creates conflicts as teens begin the process of separating from their families and childhood friends. They struggle to evolve as one, able to stand alone announcing to the world, "I am independent. I am unique. I am special. I am capable of giving and receiving love. I am a productive member of society."

According to Ivey (1993) the journey toward identity is an abstraction that can only be clearly identified through concrete action. For example, the child who finds success in mastering a task feels a sense of accomplishment and competency, a building block to healthy identity development. These concrete actions or tasks more often than not fall under the demands and expectations of families, schools, and society.

"Who Am I and What Makes Me Tick?"   Havinghurst (as cited in Rice, 1997) outlined eight *developmental tasks* that combine these demands and/or expectations with the needs of the individual. They are: (1) accepting one's physique and using the body effectively, (2) achieving emotional independence from parents and adults, (3) achieving a masculine or feminine social-sex role, (4) achieving new and more mature relations with agemates of both sexes, (5) desiring and achieving socially responsible behavior, (6) acquiring a set of values and an ethical system as a guide to behavior, (7) preparing for an economic career, and (8) preparing for marriage and family life. These eight developmental tasks comprise the necessary components for effective functioning as a mature adult. However, in today's world, it is often difficult to accomplish many of these tasks, which often leaves teens wandering aimlessly with little sense of direction.

Erikson (1968) agreed that the primary task facing adolescents is the establishment of a new sense of ego identity, a feeling of who I am and who I am in the larger social order—*identity versus identity confusion*. Identity achievement involves the domains of occupation, sexuality, values, and politics, not necessarily in that order or all at the same time (Schickedanz et al., 2001). It asks adolescents to answer "Who am I, where did I come from, and who do I want to become?," integrating all four domains into a general sense of completeness. Individuals who fail at this task generally lack direction and do not have a sense of identity.

Adolescence also marks a time when individuals begin to process information significantly different than from when they where children. Life as a child can now be reflected upon, analyzed, and internalized. Reality now becomes much more than concrete objects (Berk, 1999), what Piaget (1952) terms *formal operational thinking.* The world of teenagers becomes a laboratory where they hold the title of "scientist," where they not only come up with hypotheses, but test their hypotheses through exploration, analysis, and experimentation. Elkind (as cited in Muuss, 1988) best described this stage as the *conquest of thought,* and this pattern of constructing and testing of theories typically continues on throughout adulthood. Simply stated, adolescents are developmentally programmed to take risks.

As adolescents seek to establish a sense of identity, they engage in the ongoing process of exploring, analyzing, and experimenting with a variety of roles before committing to those chosen roles in life, what Erikson (1968) calls *psychosocial moratorium.* Ultimately, this process leads to the achievement of identity—unfortunately, a path not free from crisis or conflict. Adolescents are destined to enter into a variety of situations and experiences that challenge them with new roles and expectations. Social feedback from others provides a mirror in which the adolescent can see self. Through peer involvement, adolescents can experiment with certain roles, receive feedback on those roles, choose what fits or does not fit, and eventually reach a sense of commitment.

The variables of crisis and commitment are expanded upon through the work of James Marcia (as cited in Rice, 1997) and his model of *identity statuses.* According to Marcia (as cited in Muuss, 1988), "Crisis refers to times during adolescence when the individual seems to be actively involved in choosing among alternative occupations and beliefs. Commitment refers to the degree of personal investment the individual expresses in an occupation or belief" (Muuss, 1988, p. 66). The model states that: (1) the formation of ego identity involves establishing firm commitments in such basic identity areas as vocational choice or selection of a mate; (2) the task of forming an identity demands a period of exploration, questioning, and decision making, referred to as *identity crisis*; and (3) Western society fosters a period of *psychosocial moratorium*, during which adolescents may experiment with roles and beliefs so as to establish a coherent personal identity (Bilsker, as cited in Rice, 1997).

Based on these assumptions, Marcia (as cited in Rice, 1997) recognized four *identity statuses* that generally characterize adolescents as they move through the process of identity development. *Identity diffusion* describes the adolescent who has not experienced an identity crisis or established any firm commitment to a personal belief system or a vocation in life. *Identity foreclosure* refers to the adolescent who has not experienced an identity crisis but instead has chosen to accept the "ready-made" values of their family and/or other authority figures without any question or exploration. *Moratorium* describes the adolescent who is in an acute state of crisis, actively exploring and searching, yet has either only vaguely committed or has not made any commitments. *Identity achievement* refers to the adolescent who has experienced moratorium and committed him- or herself to an occupation, a religious belief, a personal value system, and has resolved his or her attitude toward sexuality (Muuss, 1988).

It is important to keep in mind that these statuses are far from linear, and adolescents will typically experience any one or more of these statuses, even some consecutively, shifting back and forth from one status to the other until identity is achieved (Berk, 1999; Rice, 1997). This speaks to the importance of providing teens with continued opportunities for exploration throughout high school and allowing them more time in moratorium instead of asking them to commit when perhaps they are not ready. In addition, most adolescents move through these statuses as psychosocial maturity increases, suggesting that the late adolescent years from 18 to 21 are the most crucial years for identity achievement (Marcia, as cited in Berk, 1999), the years most often devoted to college, technical training, and entering the world of work.

Reflection Moment

Identify periods during your adolescence that characterize one or more of Marcia's identity statuses. What did your process of moving through the various identity statuses look like? Feel like? What images come to mind as you reflect back? When did you reach a level of identity achievement? Are we asking our teens to enter adulthood before they are developmentally ready?

"What Do You Want to Be When You Grow Up?"   "In general it is the inability to settle on an occupational identity which most disturbs young people" (Erikson, 1968, p. 132). A crucial piece of identity development focuses on the establishment of a career or vocation. Late adolescence is a time most often devoted to college, vocational training, military training, and entering the world of work. Identity achievement does not necessarily coincide with high school graduation, and exiting from high school does not always mean teens have completed the developmental tasks associated with adolescence. Instead, identity development may continue well into the young adulthood years (Chickering & Reisser, 1993; Pipher, 1994).

Chickering and Reisser (1993) maintain that identity achievement is the core developmental issue facing the individual experiencing late adolescence but not yet entering young adulthood. According to this perspective, an individual's overall sense of individuation develops through the discovery of his or her uniqueness and connection with others and society at large. The seven vectors of this theory resemble a growth spiral dealing with the developmental tasks of: (1) developing competence, (2) managing emotions, (3) moving through autonomy toward independence, (4) developing mature interpersonal relationships, (5) establishing identity, (6) developing purpose, and (7) developing integrity. Individuals tend to move through these seven vectors at different rates, with varying amounts of overlap, yet with similar themes: "gaining competence and self-awareness, learning control and flexibility, balancing intimacy with freedom, finding one's voice or vocation, refining beliefs, and making commitments" (Chickering & Reisser, 1993, p. 35).

Josselson (as cited in Chickering & Reisser, 1993) used the term *anchoring* to describe the processes of staying connected during periods of development separation. Staying connected or anchored to family, careers, or friends is a vital component in how adolescents come to feel about themselves. These anchors provide adolescents with the necessary interactions from which to tackle the developmental challenge of shifting from basing decisions on the approval of others (superego) to that of self-approval (ego) or personal value (Chickering & Reisser, 1993).

Connections are at the core of surviving adolescence and developing a healthy ego. In order for individuals to develop a sense of reality, autonomy, and independence, they must stay connected to significant anchors. Giving adolescents space and room to grow, test the waters, and experience life requires that parents and significant adults maintain strong connections. That may mean being just as visible in the middle and high schools as in the elementary schools. Based on theory, we can expect our teens to balk at such an idea—they're supposed to! Yet we have to trust that deep down inside, our being present and visible in their lives provides them with the sense of support and connection that will allow them to feel safe, supported, and connected as they enter life and strive to find their place in the world.

Reflection Moment

Reflect back on your process of exiting high school and entering college. What themes and patterns do you recall? What developmental issues were you dealing with at the time? Describe your process of attaining Chickering's seven vectors. How were you prohibited or limited from attaining these vectors? How can you apply developmental theory to help explain this period of your development? Describe your sense of identity and how it related to your career choices and/or aspirations. Where did you find support? Who were your connections? What allowed you to feel safe as you took risks and experienced life?

"That Will Never Happen to Me"   As discussed previously, adolescence is a time when the "mastery of thought processes" is achieved (Muuss, 1988, p. 268). Not only are teens now able to think about their own thinking, but they can also think about others' thinking: the emergence of *adolescent egocentrism*. Different from the egocentrism characteristic of the elementary school years where young children believe that the world sees things the way they do, adolescent egocentrism operates under the assumption that other people's thoughts and beliefs are centrally focused on them, the adolescent, at all times and under all circumstances. The young boy who comes to school with a zit on his chin sincerely believes that all eyes are upon him, especially on his zit!

We can generally agree that adolescents are intensely preoccupied with their bodies, their physical appearance, and their behavior. As a result, there emerges this overwhelming belief that others are just as occupied as they are with their bodies, their hairstyles, and what they are wearing. Whereas the young child in elementary school is generally unable to take the point of view of others, the adolescent takes the views of others to an extreme, to the extent that the adolescent often loses sight of his or her own perspective (Muuss, 1988).

Adolescent egocentrism can also be noticed in adolescents' need to be the center of attention, for others to "notice" them. Where once the middle school preteen would do anything NOT to be noticed (while at the same time longing to fit in), the budding adolescent is caught in the wake of egocentrism and sulks and pouts when not given the full attention expected. This form of thinking is directed to what Elkind (as cited in Muuss, 1988) characterized as the *imaginary audience*. Adolescents spend a great deal of time performing to their audience of peers with hopes of earning approval and respect. However, since this audience is created specifically for and by the adolescent, it is the adolescent who determines what the audience wants to see with regard to physical appearance, body image, clothes, hairstyles, and so on (Muuss, 1988). It is as if the audience becomes the adolescent's mirror, with the reactions of the audience meant to affirm or confirm how the adolescent feels about him- or herself.

Since the imaginary audience is made up of teens also performing to their own imaginary audiences, adolescents are actually paying less attention to each other than assumed. For example, before going out, adolescents will spend countless hours trying to look just right for their dates. The other person more than likely engages in the same rituals, both with anticipation of the other's reaction. According to Elkind (as cited in Muuss, 1988), when the moment comes that the two lay eyes on each other, each one is actually "more concerned with being observed than being the observer" (p. 270). Eventually, adolescents realize that others are generally not being as critical as imagined and adolescent egocentrism eases (Muuss, 1988).

Adolescents not only act out their egocentrism to imaginary audiences, they also perform under the assumption that they are unique in who they are and that no one can even remotely see what they see, feel what they feel, and experience what they do. This belief in individual uniqueness is what Elkind (as cited in Muuss, 1988) refers to as the *personal fable*. Teens may seek refuge in diaries and close, intimate friends to share their innermost beliefs, ideals, images, values, and convictions, believing that no one else could possibly understand how they feel (Muuss, 1988). Adults and parents many times feel the pangs of the personal fable through the slamming of the bedroom door and the shouts echoing, "You have no idea how I feel!"

For adults and parents, however, the most frightening aspect of adolescent development is adolescent's belief in his or her own invincibility or *indestructibility*. According to Blos (as cited in Muuss, 1988), this notion of indestructibility impairs adolescents' judgment, especially in critical situations, causing them to end up in life-threatening or dangerous situations. This false sense of power is played out repeatedly in traffic accidents and fatalities involving teens drinking and driving. "It will never happen to me" clearly sums up adolescent thinking, which is directly related to the actions they take.

Reflection Moment

Reflect back on your own adolescent egocentrism. What do you recall? In what ways did you perform to your imaginary audience? What assumptions were you performing under? How did your personal fable influence your relationships with others, especially family members? In what ways were you indestructible?

Identity achievement for adolescents who belong to minority groups can be especially challenging as youth attempt to discover who they are within their own subculture, and seek to find identity within the dominant culture. For example, minority youth whose family values are not consistent with mainstream U.S. culture can experience "intense identity exploration" (Berk, 1999). For many minority adolescents this process is especially painful and confusing, causing them to feel "diffused or foreclosed" with the task of developing an ethnic identity (Markstrom-Adams & Adams, as cited in Berk, 1999, p. 608). They either fail to create a sense of who they are within their subculture, dismissing their ethnic and racial heritage, or choose to accept those values of their subculture with little to no exploration. Other minority teens construct a *bicultural identity*—identity achievement that involves exploring and adopting values from their subculture as well as from the dominant culture. Based on interviews with mixed-race teens, Clemetson (2000) discovered the key to acceptance is "claiming your own sense of identity no matter what other kids want to make you" (p. 72).

In today's society, cultural identity does not rest merely on physical appearance. Cultural identity has evolved from only relying on skin color to now include one's social circle as well. Due to the increased number of mixed-racial marriages and resulting families, teens are growing up in households of more than one culture and selecting peer groups and friends of yet other cultures, all while living under a dominant culture. The message is "I'm myself and if they don't like me, that's too bad" (Clemetson, 2000, p. 74). As more and more mixed-race and biracial teens take their place in society, they are reporting fewer feelings of isolation. These youth see a better world, one in which they are actively confronting issues of racism, homophobia, and sexism that previous generations shied away from (Clemetson, 2000).

Chapter Summary

Today's modern teenager: a precious, unique, and wonderful creation all wrapped up in ideals, hopes, dreams, and hormones. Adolescence is not the most comfortable place to be, for teenagers or the adults in their lives. By gaining an understanding and acceptance of the challenges and hurdles of this stage of development and knowing that most of what is experienced is "normal," perhaps the period of adolescence can be embraced and nurtured.

The adolescent mind is ripe for stimulation as abstract thinking takes flight and teens are ready to challenge themselves and the world they live in. The process of theorizing, exploring, analyzing, and integrating allows adolescents to challenge the boundaries of childhood and eventually break through them, hopefully feeling self-confident with who they are and all they are becoming. Without the opportunity to take risks and test the waters, teens are left to wander and wonder, with little sense of identity and their place in the world.

As adults, we have a responsibility to work toward a better understanding of our young people, their needs, their hopes and dreams, as well as their fears. We are their role models, their idols, and their heroes. Adolescents not only soak up and integrate what they learn from us, they are also eager to gain our acceptance and win our approval. They perform for us, prove they are indestructible, and lather us with their individual uniqueness. At times they can actually fool us into believing they are grown up!

We assume so often that teens are fully wired for the adult world, already knowing who they are, what they will become, and how to make the right decisions to get there. Adolescents are good at fooling us into thinking they are all grown up and can handle the world, a trait that is developmentally normal. Yet in many ways teenagers are still children. Children, as well as adolescents, depend on the supportive, nurturing structures of families, other significant adults, and social institutions. These supports provide a sense of safety in a world that often feels and looks unsafe, while allowing adolescents space to build a sense of competence and identity in the world in order to realize their full potential.

A Day in the Life Revisited: Integration

Return to Mandy's Manic Monday.

1. Now that you have had the opportunity to rediscover normal adolescent development, what are your reactions to Mandy and Jason?
2. How has developmental theory normalized some of the interactions occurring in the scenario?
3. How does developmental theory provide acceptance and understanding of adolescents you know and/or have worked with?
4. How will you integrate and use these theories of development in your work as a school counselor?

Application

1. Spend the day observing adolescents at a local middle school or high school. Take notes on the interactions you see them engaging in. Apply developmental theory to your observations. What do you notice?

2. Interview adolescents about what it's like to be a teenager in today's society. Integrate in your interview the three aspects of identity: sexual, social, and psychological. Apply what you find to developmental theory. What discoveries do you make?

3. Interview parents and other adults about their feelings concerning today's adolescents. What themes come up? What feelings do you hear most? How can developmental theory be integrated into your findings?

4. Explore your own adolescence. Pay specific attention to the three aspects of identity: sexual, social, and psychological. What themes and patterns do you recognize? Use developmental theory to explain what you discover.

References

Berk, L. E. (1999). *Infants, children, and adolescents* (4th ed.). Boston: Allyn and Bacon.

Carter, B., & McGoldrick, M. (1999). *The expanded family life cycle: Individual, family, and social perspectives* (3rd ed.). Boston: Allyn and Bacon.

Chickering, A. W., & Reisser, L. (1993) *Education and identity* (2nd ed.). San Francisco, CA: Jossey-Bass.

Clemetson, L. (2000, May 8). Color my world. *Newsweek*, pp. 70–74.

Crain, W. (2000). *Theories of development: Concepts and applications.* Upper Saddle River, NJ: Prentice Hall.

Erikson, E. H. (1968). *Identity: Youth and crisis.* New York: W. W. Norton & Company.

Gabriel, H. P., & Wool, R. (1999). *Anticipating adolescence: How to cope with your child's emotional upheaval and forge a new relationship together.* Collingdale, PA: Diane Publishing.

Gilligan, C. (1982). *In a different voice: Psychological theory and women's development.* Cambridge, MA: Harvard University Press.

Ivey, A. E. (1993). *Developmental strategies for helpers: Individuals, family, and network interventions.* Pacific Grove, CA: Brooks/Cole.

Kotre, J., & Hall, E. (1990). *Seasons of life: The dramatic journey from birth to death.* Ann Arbor: University of Michigan Press.

Mercer, M. E. (1997). *The art of becoming human: Patterns of growth, the adventure of living, love and separation, limitless possibilities.* Amherst, NY: Prometheus Books.

Muuss, R. E. (1988). *Theories of adolescence* (5th ed.). New York: Random House.

Piaget, J. (1952). *The origins of intelligence in children.* New York: W. W. Norton & Company.

Pipher, M. (1994). *Reviving Ophelia.* New York: Ballantine Books.

Rice, F. P. (1997). *Child and adolescent development.* Upper Saddle River, NJ: Prentice Hall.

Schickedanz, J. A., Schickedanz, D. I., Forsyth, P. D., & Forsyth, G. (2001). *Understanding children and adolescents* (4th ed.). Boston: Allyn and Bacon.

Vernon, A. (1993). *Developmental assessment and intervention with children and adolescents.* Alexandria, VA: American Counseling Association.

3

A Systems View of Adolescents: The Student in Context

Kelli A. Saginak

*"What is the single most important problem I see in the lives of my friends?
Living up to society's standards, parent's standards, and their own standards
of what they think they should be. This ranges from image, to grades, to at
times personality. A lot of kids don't know who they are."*

Margaret, age 18

Learning Objectives

By the end of this chapter, you will:

1. Understand general systems theory and family systems theory as a context for adolescent development.
2. Be introduced to the family lifecycle and its influence on the adolescent.
3. Gain an understanding of adolescent's social systems as it pertains to peer groups, cliques, crowds, peer clusters, and gangs.
4. Have the opportunity to apply and integrate a systems perspective into your work as counselor.

A Day in the Life: Susan's System Situation

Susan is one of four school counselors at Independence High School. During eighth grade orientation Susan noticed Camille, an eighth-grade girl who looked very sad and disconnected from the rest of the students. Susan made a mental note of Camille and decided she would make contact with her to see how things were going for her during the transition.

Susan noticed Camille again in the halls during assemblies and tried to catch her eye to say "hello." This proved unsuccessful in that Camille made no eye contact with Susan or anyone else in the halls. She talked to no one and didn't seem to have any friends. She kept her head down as she slowly made her way to her classes. Curiously, Susan checked her school records to find that Camille was passing all her classes—no shining star academically yet no trouble either. She was a solid B/C student. In conversations with her teachers, Susan discovered that Camille sits quietly in her seat, speaks to no one in her classes, and makes no eye contact with any one. The teachers weren't concerned—so much of their time was spent dealing with behavioral problems and disruptions that they were grateful for Camille's quiet presence. No one seemed concerned about her.

Eventually, Camille landed in Susan's office on a smoking violation. During their session Susan discovered numerous cigarette burns on Camille's forearms. Camille confided in Susan how she wants to be invisible at school. She has no friends and wants it to stay that way. At home, Camille, her father, mother, and little sister live in the semirural fringes of what is considered a very affluent district. They live in a mobile home next to her paternal grandmother's house, a ramshackle farmhouse barely standing. Her father was raised in the farmhouse. Her grandmother is supposed to watch out for the kids when they come home from school yet usually falls asleep in the rocker on the front porch. Camille thinks she passes out from sipping on too much whiskey all day. Camille's mom works as a waitress and her dad does odd jobs around the neighborhood. Mostly, he just watches television all day and drinks beer. Money is very tight. According to Camille, he sits around and drinks just like her grandmother. When Camille's mom gets home from work the fighting begins. Camille tells Susan that the fighting is getting worse and she's now afraid for herself and her little sister. Recently, Camille and her mother have even started fighting with each other. "Mom just won't let me alone. She's always on my back, telling me to do this and do that."

With Camille's permission, Susan called Camille's mother to discuss the family's situation and offer some assistance. On the verge of hysterics, Camille's mother confirms the trouble at home, but that she can handle it. Camille's mother states that she has been trying to get a restraining order filed against her husband and that a divorce is imminent. She has to work, but because she's not getting enough sleep, she's been messing up on the job lately and is afraid she may be let go. She realizes the burden this is placing on the girls, yet she needs them to "grow up!" At the same time she has nowhere to turn, is doing the best she can, and . . . no, they can't afford nor will they attend counseling.

Challenge Questions

What are the out-of-school issues in Camille's situation? Parental? Sibling? Extended family? Financial? Occupational? Community? What school issues do you see? How do these out-of-school issues lead to school issues for Camille? What are your options for helping Camille? What are your options for helping the family? What kinds of interventions would you recommend with this student? Family? School? Community? Why?

General Systems and Family Systems Theory

General systems theory emerged in the 1940s as a result of the work of biologist Ludwig von Bertanlanffy (as cited in Brown & Christensen, 1999). His work, along with that of other scientists, set the stage for a paradigm shift that would influence the way the world was viewed and accepted. This new systems perspective, based within a social context, viewed individuals in relation to their families and the other social systems around them. No longer were individuals viewed in a vacuum. The emergence of general systems theory influenced the counseling profession by dramatically changing the way counselors viewed human nature, conceptualized issues and problems, and thus worked with clients (Goldenberg & Goldenberg, 1998).

When we think of "system," we have a complex entity comprised of interacting parts. How these interacting parts communicate and relate with each other, the rules and patterns that decide how the parts relate to one another, and how these parts ultimately interact with the other systems around them are the focus of general systems theory (Goldenberg & Goldenberg, 1998). No longer are individuals viewed from "a one-person paradigm," but instead are viewed as part of a larger social system (Peeks, 1993), meaning that "the pattern of relationships within a system or between systems became the focus instead of studying parts in isolation" (Goldenberg & Goldenberg, 2000, p. 59).

The language of general systems theory, sometimes referred to as *cybernetics*, has grown into an invaluable way of understanding the world of families. Sit in a room with a group of family systems therapists and you will quickly become familiar with such terms as homeostasis, open and closed systems, linear and circular causality, organization, wholeness, positive and negative feedback loops, and permeable and rigid boundaries. These terms, used to explain the complex relationships, interactions, and communication patterns between family members, comprise *systems theory*, which combines concepts from general systems theory and cybernetics. It is the overall shift in thinking that has opened up a whole new way to view individuals and families (Goldenberg & Goldenberg, 2000).

Systems thinking and family systems theory has also made its way into public education. Those responsible for school policy, educational practice, and educational reform are recognizing the importance of relationship and interaction between students, families, and schools (Maerhoff, 1990). School counselors today are being trained in systems theory as well as family systems theory, changing the face of educational programming. The practice of targeting only the student is transforming into what Lusterman (1988) calls "mapping the ecosystem"—that is, assessing the family and the school before developing a course of treatment for the child.

Emerging is the understanding that schools, families, and communities must work together collaboratively to support the educational process for students to be successful (Peeks, 1993). Students are no longer viewed as a single unit, but instead as part of larger system: the family. In other words, first and foremost, students are "members of a family" (p. 9). Today's adolescents are not only members of a family, they are also part of larger social systems. Adolescents' families, schools, peer groups, and communities are important systems affecting the life of today's teens.

Family Systems and Adolescence

"Interdependence, not independence, is the reality of the world" (Peeks, 1993, p. 8). This basic premise has permeated the field of counseling by way of the family therapy movement with its emphasis on the *family* rather than on the *individual*. Family therapy focuses its attention on the interactions of family members and how those interactions and relationships influence individual family member's adjustment and functioning (Sabatelli & Anderson, 1991). According to Peeks (1993), "family systems theory teaches that the unit of intervention is not the individual but the social context" (p. 245). As such, family systems theory operates under the assumption that families organize themselves and create boundaries that ultimately determine how individuals within the family and those outside the family will relate and interact with each other (Whitechurch & Constantine, as cited in Henry, Sager, & Pluckett, 1996).

Within a family system, individuals interact, influencing each other, and in turn, being influenced by others. This interaction produces a *whole*, or a system that is greater than the sum of its interdependent parts. In other words, a system can only be understood as a whole entity, not by its individual parts. From a systems perspective, the adolescent can only be understood in the context of the family in which he or she lives.

In the words of Jay Haley (1971), "a smile in one family member might initiate an action response in another, and this initiates a reverie about a dream in another, which is followed by a change-the-subject joke in another" (p. 172). Each individual in a system is affected by whatever happens to any other individual within the system. If one member of the family changes, then all the other members of the family change as well, much like a ripple effect (Brown & Christensen, 1999). Take, for instance, the alcoholic family. The situation might look something like this: One partner's drinking grows out of control. The other partner compensates for the drinker's behavior by taking on a different role in the family. The children then compensate by taking on various roles in order to cope with the drinker's and the nondrinker's behavior. In this example, the entire family system is affected by what started out as one person's out-of-control drinking. In systems terms, we might say that the family has altered its original structure or reorganized in order to compensate for the drinker's behavior.

Family structure and organization also change during the adolescent years. As stated in Chapter 2, adolescence generally brings a sense of turmoil, stirring up not only the teenager living through adolescence, but also the family. The old saying "hormones are raging" is felt by all as individuals negotiate for new roles and the family takes on a new shape. Yet, on a positive note, the changes in structure and organization that families typically experience through the stage of adolescence are normal developmental adjustments, even though at the time they may feel quite uncomfortable. Systems theory holds that eventually the family system will find a comfortable sense of balance once again.

According to Nichols and Everett (as cited in Horne, 2000), the basic structure of a family is defined by how it *organizes* itself. Families can be organized in a variety of ways. Some families organize themselves around a rigid, dominating parental figure with those beneath behaving subserviently, whereas other families organize more democratically where everyone's voice is heard and respected. However a family chooses to organize itself, it is the consistent patterns of interaction that ultimately describe how a family system maintains its sense of structure and balance (Brown & Christensen, 1999).

How a family organizes itself can greatly influence how a family maneuvers through adolescence. Chapter 2 reminded us that adolescents need a healthy balance between structure, limits, and freedom to fully explore the world around them. Families that maintain too rigid a structure may not allow the adolescent to do the very exploring and experimenting that is so vital for the development of a healthy sense of identity. On the other hand, a family that organizes itself too loosely may not provide the teenager with the safety of knowing exactly what the limits are and where the boundaries lie. Finding an appropriate balance is key.

The way in which a system organizes itself also depends on the rules it imposes on members. *Family rules* are the predictable and persistent patterns of behavior that define each individual's roles and duties within a family. These rules become the family's "governing principles," and in a sense its "way of life" (Jackson, as cited in Goldenberg & Goldenberg, 2000, p. 63). For example, "Children are to be seen and not heard," "No interrupting," "You must eat everything on your plate," "Girls play with dolls," "Boys don't cry," "Dad has the last word," and "No dating until 16" are just a few of the family rules that have trickled down through generations. Family rules also come in the form of rituals, traditions, inside jokes, and other patterns of interaction that make them unique from other families and social groups (Horne, 2000).

Family rules often shed light as to how open or closed a family system is. According to Goldenberg and Goldenberg (1998), family systems may be open or closed depending on how much contact they have with the larger social systems around them. An *open system* maintains contact with its surroundings and allows new information to enter freely. Open systems typically have what is referred to as *permeable boundaries*, which allow for communication to flow freely back and forth between systems.

In contrast, a *closed system* shuts itself off to the outside world, offering little interaction or contact with other systems. Such a system would be said to have *rigid boundaries* where little to no communication or interaction is allowed to flow back and forth between systems. *Boundaries*, those invisible lines that separate individuals within the family, also serve to separate families from the flow of information from other systems as well. Permeable flexible boundaries respect each family member as an individual while supporting the need for support and protection. Rigid boundaries strangle an individual's need for closeness and connection (Brown & Christensen, 1999), a detriment to all family members—including the adolescent.

Sometimes boundaries can become excessive on either end of the spectrum, resulting in *enmeshment* and *disengagement* within the family system. Boundaries described as enmeshed are too permeable, meaning too much information flows between individuals. For example, the mother who opens her teenage daughter's mail, goes through her things in her room, and overinvolves herself with her daughter's private life demonstrates enmeshed boundaries. Such boundaries can result in teens who leave home at the first chance, never looking back. They feel so smothered and invaded that they cannot wait to leave. Disengagement would describe the family who functions with little to no interaction or communication, almost as separate little islands. Meals are rarely shared together, there is little to no organized family time, and communication is very limited. Adolescents growing up within a disengaged family enter the adult world alone and isolated, with no real sense of a support system or love.

According to Brown and Christensen (1999), how family members communicate with each other is referred to as *feedback*. It is not so much what is communicated but how it is communicated that determines feedback. *Positive feedback* produces change in the family structure, whereas *negative feedback* works to maintains stability. You might think of negative feedback as something much like a thermostat, regulating the amount of deviation from what is set as the norm. Feedback flowing in and out of a system has the tendency to either create change or maintain the status quo, or *homeostasis*. A homeostatic state depends on stability within the family system and keeping things as they are. For example, when adolescents begin the process of breaking away as they prepare to leave home, suddenly the status quo is threatened. The structure of the family is on shaky ground, and individuals scramble to find stability within a system on the verge of change. The expectations, patterns, and roles that once existed within the family, and on which individual members came to rely, are spinning out of control. These patterns of behavior are usually unconscious, and family members do not realize the purpose these behaviors serve in the overall workings of the family system (McWhirter, McWhirter, McWhirter, & McWhirter, 1998).

Feedback, in the form of communication, events, and interactions, are generally related through a series of repeating cycles, or *circular causality*. These repeating cycles do not simply move in a straight line, but instead develop into a circular pattern with "each influencing and being influenced by each other" (Goldenberg & Goldenberg, 1998, p. 22). Let's take the case of Camille. Systems theorists would suggest that the behaviors taking place within the family (i.e., the drinking and the fighting) are not related merely to cause and effect; instead, they are maintained by the system as a whole. Systems theorists would argue such questions as "How does the behavior of each family member maintain the disruption in the family?" instead of simply blaming everything on her father's drinking.

Maintaining a homeostatic balance is the goal for most families (Brown & Christensen, 1999). Change any one behavior within a family system and the family's state of homeostasis changes. Suddenly, family members no longer know what to expect, what their roles are, and how the family operates. For instance, if Camille's father suddenly stops drinking and fighting with Camille's mother, what happens to the rest of the family members' behaviors? A certain amount of comfort exists in knowing what to expect, even if it is unhealthy and dysfunctional. Changing roles and behaviors can be frightening for individuals and families. Many of us have heard how in alcoholic families, it is often the nondrinking partner or spouse who has a difficult time adjusting when the alcoholic gets treatment and stops drinking. What becomes of that role in the family now that it does not depend on managing the drinking family member?

Change in family roles can also take place during the adolescent years as teens strive toward independence and autonomy. As adolescents developmentally separate from the family, not only do *they* experience the awkwardness of new and different roles, so do their family members. At the same time, as families feel the push and pull of adolescence, they also feel the challenges facing parents coping with middle age, as well as extended family members working through their own developmental crises. Within the context of the family system lie the answers to who we are, where we come from, and what we will come to be (Carter & McGoldrick, 1999).

Reflection Moment

> Using some of the principles of systems theory, explore your own family system and the negotiation of certain developmental tasks. What do you notice?

The Family Life Cycle

Basing his studies on the work of Milton Erickson, Jay Haley (as cited in Brown & Christensen, 1999) first presented a view of the family life cycle from a systems perspective. He proposed that families, like individuals, meet with crises as they transition between developmental stages. More recently, the family life cycle has been expanded through the work of Carter and McGoldrick (1999), who gave special attention to the developmental transitions that disrupt the life cycle of the family. According to Carter and McGoldrick, "symptoms and dysfunction are examples within a systemic context and in relation to what the culture considers to be 'normal' functioning over time" (p. 1). The *family life cycle* is the natural context within which individuals develop (Carter & McGoldrick, 1999).

Families are comprised of people who share histories and futures, making up multiple generations, each with its own sets of boundaries, roles, functions, patterns of interactions . . . and relationships. It is in these relationships where families find their true value and meaning. The emotional ties that bridge families and bond them together add complexity to a system that is continually moving through time and history. The historical eras and cultures in which families develop influence members' world views and attitudes, which in turn effects the relationships and interactions of members. The families of "days gone by" are just that, gone by, and families today are evolving at a rate that few social institutions are able to understand, much less support. As generations unfold, those before continue to shape and mold those generations of families that follow (Carter & McGoldrick, 1999).

In general, families go through fairly predictable developmental stages throughout the course of the family life cycle (Brown & Christensen, 1999). These stages include the beginning family, the school-age family, the adolescent family, the launching family, and the post-parental family. Renegotiation is a central theme in each of these stages and is crucial for successful negotiations for each stage to come (Brown & Christensen, 1999).

Like previous generations, the first stage of the life cycle, the beginning family, is created through the uniting of two individuals. Both individuals bring with them generations of history consisting of rules, boundaries, patterns of behavior, and cultural and family-of-origin issues that will need to be negotiated and resolved. This stage of the life cycle will last until the first child is born, adding the role of "parent" to the list of roles already developing within the family (Brown & Christensen, 1999).

As children are added to the family, parents continue to renegotiate roles, expectations, parenting styles, boundary issues, as well as family-of-origin and extended family issues. The attainment of puberty for the first child is generally the onset of what is referred to as the *adolescent family*. Typically, this stage will continue until the last child leaves home. For some families, this stage can last for more than the usual seven to eight years dealing with teenage pubescence, depending on the number of children being raised in the household. As parents continue to practice renegotiations, mainly in the areas of autonomy and control ("How much do I hang on?" and "How much do I let go?"), parents are entering their own crisis—midlife. This period of time can place additional stress on the family system. One particular challenge is that of identity development. As teenagers struggle to find their own sense of identity, parents suddenly are beginning to question their own. Adolescents feel the pull to let go, and often parents are fighting to hang on. Family life cycle theory might tell us that perhaps it is really not the *adolescent* that parents facing midlife are hanging on to.

Within the family life cycle, successful negotiations and resolutions in previous stages set the stage for successful completion of following stages. Successful completion of the adolescent family stage depends mainly on the completion of two developmental tasks: separation and individuation (Brown & Christensen, 1999). As stated by Carter and McGoldrick (1999), it is essential that families shift parent-child relationships to allow adolescents to move freely in and out of the system. Such a shift requires reorganization within the family and increased flexibility with regard to established boundaries. Helping teens separate from the family and embrace their individuality is of utmost importance during this stage of the family life cycle.

The process of separation and individuation, however, is not without its challenges and hurdles. Not only are adolescents assertively testing rules and boundaries and renegotiating relationships within the family system, but the parental system and the extended family system are also dealing with their own developmental issues. Parents are often facing their own midlife crises, possibly renegotiating their relationships with each other. Issues with extended family may also develop as the generational family life cycle experiences the turmoil and stress of adolescence (Brown & Christensen, 1999). As teens grow in independence, grandparents grow more dependent. These simultaneous developmental occurrences support the belief that adolescence does not happen in a vacuum and that an entire family system is in operation, all changing, growing, influencing each other.

Reflection Moment

> Consider your family history and the generations before you. What influence did your family of origin have on your development as an adolescent? As an adult? The family you live in today?

Peer Groups, Cliques, Crowds, Peer Clusters, and Gangs

The family is only one of several influential systems in the life of the adolescent. The additional social systems that make up the world outside of the family have great influence on today's adolescents. As stated in Chapter 2, adolescents need to experience the outside world as part of the process of individuating from the family. Peer groups provide adolescents with valuable experiences as they emerge into adulthood (Sabatelli & Anderson, 1991).

According to McWhirter and colleagues (1998), involvement with peers provides young people with opportunities to "develop age-related skills and interests, control their social behavior, and share their problems and feelings" (p. 74). It is through interactions with these peer groups in addition to the family system that adolescents develop a sense of identity, acquire the ability to reason morally, and learn how to function as independent adults in society separate from their families.

Stimulation, belongingness, loyalty, devotion, empathy, and resonance are essential supports generally made available to adolescents by their families. They are crucial components to healthy psychological development, and it is important that they not be lost during an adolescent's move to individuate. As stated by Blos (as cited in Muuss, 1988), separating from parental dependencies and "familial love objects" is a critical task for normal adolescent development (p. 90). Through the process, teens establish a "personal, social, and sexual identity" (p. 90).

As part of the separation process, adolescents turn away from their parents and, because of still insufficient autonomy, turn toward peers. Peer groups help adolescents resolve internal conflicts and reduce anxiety by serving as sounding boards without arousing guilt or anxiety, respecting competencies as seen in social and athletic skills, and providing honest and critical feedback about behaviors and personal attributes (Blos, as cited in Muuss, 1988). According to McWhirter and colleagues (1998), "the peer group represents the transfer vehicle for transition from childhood to adulthood," and through relationships with peers, adolescents learn "to relate to different roles and to experiment with interpersonal interactional skills that will eventually transfer to the world of adults" (p. 75).

According to Sabatelli and Anderson (1991), peer relationships especially play a crucial role in the healthy overall development of adolescents. Parents and families influence those "bigger" decisions in an adolescent's life such as education, occupation (Sebald & White, as cited in Sabatelli & Anderson, 1991), and moral/religious choices. Peers, on the other hand, are influential in day-to-day decisions, such as choices in clothes, music, leisure activities, and intimacy and sexual relationships—a "reference group" so to speak for identity development (Sabatelli & Anderson, 1991, p. 364). In addition, however, Piaget (1932) stated that peers provide a constructive force in influencing moral and cognitive development. The quality of adolescents' family *and* peer relationships is related to their overall psychological development and adjustment. From a systems perspective, the whole is much greater than even the individual members of the family system—the concept of the whole must also include peer influences.

The peer group is extremely important in the development of the adolescent (Dunphy, as cited in Muuss, 1988) but it is difficult to define in today's society. The structure and organization of today's adolescent peer groups are a result of modern society and go beyond that of classroom friends appearing at sleepovers, parties, athletic events, dates, and social events. Today's peer groups take the shape of cliques, crowds, peer clusters, and gangs. The differing values and influences of these groups affect their interaction with the systems with which they come in contact (i.e., the family, the school, community). Families, schools, and communities see some peer groups in a positive light, whereas other peer groups are not viewed positively. This clash in values has a tremendous impact on teens and their relationships in and outside their families and other social systems.

Let us first consider cliques. According to Dunphy (as cited in Muuss, 1988), *cliques* are small, socially cohesive groups of friends who share similar ages, socioeconomic statuses, interests, attitudes, and preferences. These are tight-knit groups whose members stick closely to one another. Their similarities often form the rules of the group, which can serve to dictate some fairly rigid boundaries. For instance, I recall a clique of preadolescent girls that insisted that one "never" wear the same outfit twice in a two-week period. Every morning before classes began, members would size each other up making sure that a particular outfit had not been worn in the previous two weeks.

Cliques have the ability to exert extreme pressure on their members in order to maintain their structure and organization. This pressure can create so much anxiety for those trying to fit in that the clique serves to upset most of what balance the family and school are trying to maintain. School counselors are familiar with tales of adolescent girls flocking in and out of their offices, emotions running high, desperate to fit it.

Crowds, on the other hand, are larger social groups, usually made up of a several cliques. Crowds are typically not as cohesive as cliques, individuals are not necessarily friends, and their value structures tend to be more varied than those of cliques. Yet, Dunphy notes they share some common interests (as cited in Muuss,1988). Crowds typically describe the last stage of peer group development before late adolescence when dating and the desire to form a couple emerge. From a developmental standpoint, cliques serve to transition adolescents into crowds, and crowds make way for the next stage of development, young adulthood, where intimacy and the couple become "the basic unit of social interaction" (Muuss, 1988, p. 319).

Reflection Moment

> Reflect back on the peer groups you associated with as a teenager. What influenced you to "hang out" with these groups? What did these groups provide you as an adolescent? What reactions did your family members have to your association with these groups?

Peer groups model behaviors, teach values, and develop attitudes, all of which are important to the developing teenager. Yet the underdeveloped identity of the adolescent makes him or her vulnerable to the peer pressure that groups exert on those who choose to join them. According to Blos (as cited in Muuss, 1988), "security is found in the shared code of what constitutes adequate behavior and in the dependency on mutual recognition of sameness" (p. 188). In the quest to free themselves from the structure and boundaries of their families, adolescents often find themselves "fallen prey to the tyranny of peers who require conformity to their standards in return for the security they provide" (p. 90). Just as peer groups can exert positive peer pressure such as leadership skills, they can also exert negative peer pressure in the form of deviance and antisocial behavior. It is interesting that youth who tend to engage in deviant, antisocial behavior have a tendency to gravitate toward each other, forming peer clusters.

Peer clusters are smaller subsystems of the larger peer group, yet they have a much greater influence on the teens who associate with them (McWhirter et al., 1998). Whereas the larger peer group may have an established set of beliefs and values, within the peer cluster each member is active in determining the group's norms and making sure they are carried out. As determined by Oetting and Beauvais (as cited in McWhirter et al., 1998), peer clusters are highly organized, maintain rigid boundaries, and are highly resistant to change. They organize and operate as an interactive whole and as a whole decide the attitudes, beliefs, values, and behaviors of the entire cluster. Peer clusters differ from cliques in that peer clusters are often antisocial and enforce compliance through physical intimidation, eventually developing into gangs.

As defined by Lal, Lal, and Achilles (as cited in McWhirter et al., 1998), *gangs* are organized structured groups of young people who form an allegiance for a common purpose, usually involving unlawful or criminal behavior. The term "gang" provokes thoughts of fear, violence, crime, and drugs, and they are usually not the kinds of groups with which we want our adolescents to associate. Yet adolescents are meeting specific developmental needs through gang membership that they are not able to find within their families, schools, or communities. According to the Maxson and Klein (as cited in Omizo, Omizo, & Honda, 1997), it is the breakdown of homes, schools, and communities that has led to the prevalence of gangs in today's society. Many teens feel isolated within their families, misunderstood within their school buildings, and disengaged from their communities, and they are seeking connections elsewhere. In a study conducted by Omizo, Omizo, and Honda (1997), results indicated reasons adolescents join gangs and the benefits to being a member of a gang included an increased self-esteem, a sense of belonging, feelings of protection and safety, and social and recreational aspects. In other words, teens are meeting their needs in systems outside of their families, their schools, and their communities, but not without a price. The system of the gang does not easily allow normal adolescent separation; this particular system strongly resists any change that might upset the status quo, meaning getting out is often detrimental, and sometimes fatal, to the teenager involved.

Whether these and other social systems interacting on the adolescent are viewed as positive or negative, the fact remains that they are part of the adolescent system and should no longer be ignored. School systems must first consider the family system in order to create a successful environment for students to thrive while being open to and considerate of the numerous other social systems influencing adolescents. We must be careful not to give in to the temptation to devote all our energies toward the adolescent and forget all the other social systems operating within the adolescent's life. A systems perspective suggests that in order to understand a student's behavior, counselors need to be familiar with the multiple interrelated systems that are an ongoing part of a student's life. For example, the school counselor operating from a systems perspective searches for patterns or connections. *What* maintains the behavior becomes more important than *why*. Remember there are elements in place that are of vital importance to maintaining the status quo or homeostatic balance within systems. The "what" that maintains the behavior exists among the interrelated systems that are in continuous interaction.

Chapter Summary

Systems theory states that since a system, as a whole, is more powerful than the individuals within it, when an individual attempts to change, the system may operate against that change. The system's tendency toward maintaining the status quo, or homeostasis, may be more powerful than the individual's attempt to change. In other words, it is not uncommon for a school counselor to expend a considerable amount of energy helping a student develop new ways of thinking, feeling, or behaving only to become discouraged when changes are not sustained by the family system, neighborhood system, classroom system, or larger school system. Systems can get quite comfortable with their present state of interaction and functioning. Roles are clearly defined and everyone knows what is expected of them. Change causes disruption in a system's organization, structure, and stability. Individuals no longer know what is expected of them and roles are no longer clearly defined. This can be a very threatening situation for many systems.

However, remember that change in one member of the family system results in change in the other members as well. And even though we cannot always see the changes taking place within a family system, if we believe in the essence of family systems theory, we will trust that the family is capable of adapting, reorganizing, and changing its structure with the goal of reaching a homeostatic state. Even within those families who resist services or are violent and abusive, any positive feedback that enters the system will ultimately serve to "stir up" the status quo, forcing the family to reorganize itself in what we hope is a healthier, more functional way. From a systems perspective this is the ultimate goal.

Adolescents are first and foremost members of a family system. Relationships with parents, siblings, and extended family members play crucial roles in adolescents' overall development. Other social systems are also highly influential forces in the lives of adolescents. In particular, peer groups play an important role in that they often help bridge the gap between adolescence and adulthood, a time when teens are developmentally separating from their families. Cliques and crowds take the place of families and extended families as the social networks of choice and serve a developmental function in supporting teens through the transition of adolescence to adulthood (Muuss, 1988). Even deviant peer clusters and gangs provide a sense of safety and support to alienated teens.

Systems thinking is replacing working only with the adolescent; we have to reach out beyond the walls of our school counseling offices if we are going to effect long-lasting change with our teens. Working with families is a crucial first step (as we will see in future chapters), and yet even they should not be our last effort. Peers and peer groups can be as equally important. In instances where families cannot be reached, peer networks can be an important focus for interventions and strategies (Sabatelli & Anderson, 1991). To truly intervene in the lives of youth, we need to embrace all the systems interacting with adolescents and address our programming accordingly.

A Day in the Life Revisited: Integration

Return to Susan's System Situation.

1. Now that you have been introduced to the systems philosophy as it relates to family systems and the world of the adolescent, how might you conceptualize the case of Camille?
2. How might family life-cycle theory add to your conceptualization of Camille's family?
3. What systems do you see interacting in Camille's world?
4. How might you integrate systems work into your philosophy of school counseling?

Application

1. Observe the day-to-day operations of a school. Based on your observations, conceptualize your findings from a systems perspective. What do you notice? How do students influence the school? How does the school influence the students?

2. Extend this activity out into your community. Based on your findings, how do you see what goes on in and around your community influencing what happens in your building? How do you see your school influencing your community?

3. Recall a counseling situation with a student. Attempt to conceptualize that case from a sys-

tems perspective by taking into account the student's relationships with his or her family, peer groups, the school, the community, and any other systems involved in the student's life. What do you notice? How have your intervention strategies changed as a result?

4. Explore prevention programming from a systems perspective. Develop a prevention program for a secondary school that involves students, peer groups, families, and communities. What assets do you see with such a program? What was most difficult about designing such a program? What challenges do you see in implementing such a program?

Suggested Reading

Carter, B., & McGoldrick, M. (1999). The expanded family life cycle: Individual, family, and social perspectives (3rd ed.). Boston: Allyn and Bacon. This is an extensive exploration of family systems insights and research; it can be valuable for school counselors to understand families.

References

Brown, J. H., & Christensen, D. N. (1999). *Family therapy: Theory and practice* (2nd ed.). Pacific Grove, CA: Brooks/Cole.

Carter, B., & McGoldrick, M. (1999). *The expanded family life cycle: Individual, family, and social perspectives* (3rd ed.). Boston: Allyn and Bacon.

Goldenberg H., & Goldenberg, I. (1998). *Counseling today's families* (3rd ed.). Pacific Grove, CA: Brooks/Cole.

Goldenberg H., & Goldenberg, I. (2000). *Family therapy: An overview* (5th ed.). Pacific Grove, CA: Brooks/Cole.

Haley, J. (1971). *Changing families*. New York: Grune & Stratton.

Henry, C. S., Sager, D. W., & Plunkett, S. W. (1996). Adolescents' perceptions of family system characteristics, parent-adolescent dyadic behaviors, adolescent qualities, and adolescent empathy. *Family Relations*, 45(3), 283–293.

Horne, A. M. (2000). *Family counseling and therapy* (3rd ed.). Itasca, IL: F. E. Peacock.

Lusterman, D-D. (1988). Family therapy and schools: An ecosystemic approach. *Family Therapy Today*, 3(7), 1–3.

Maehroff, G. (1990, May 21). Three missing keys to public-school reforms. *The Wall Street Journal*, p. A10.

McWhirter, J. J., McWhirter, B. T., McWhirter, A. M., & McWhirter, E. H. (1998). *At-risk youth: A comprehensive response* (2nd ed.). Pacific Grove, CA: Brooks/Cole.

Muuss, R. E. (1988). *Theories of adolescence* (5th ed.). New York: Random House.

Omizo, M. M., Omizo, S. A., & Honda, M. R. (1997). A phenomenological study with youth gang members: Results and implications for school counselors. *Professional School Counseling*, 1(1), 39–42.

Peeks, B. (1993). Revolutions in counseling and education: A systems perspective in the schools. *Elementary School Guidance and Counseling*, 27(4), 245–252.

Piaget, J. (1932). *The moral judgment of the child*. London: Kegan Paul.

Sabatelli, R. M., & Anderson, S. A. (1991). Family systems dynamics, peer relationships, and adolescent psychological adjustment. *Family Relations*, 40(4), 363–369.

4

Developmentally Appropriate Schools for Adolescents

Colette T. Dollarhide

"What do I like least about high school? The way that some teachers teach. They know that kids in their class don't do very well in their class but don't do much about changing the way they teach."

Rebecca, age 18

Learning Objectives _____

By the end of this chapter, you will:

1. Identify and be able to challenge those elements of the educational environment that impede the development of young people.

2. Understand the concept of developmentally appropriate education.

3. Identify and be able to advocate for those elements of the educational environment that enhance the development of young people.

4. Understand developmentally appropriate high school experiences and articulate implications for post–high school life choices.

5. Understand and articulate the importance of respect in the development of young people.

6. Identify and discuss the counselor's role in environmental assessment.

A Day in the Life of a Counselor: Mrs. Ross's Choices _____

It's the summer of 1998, and a new student and her mother arrive at school to meet with the high school counselor, Mrs. Ross. Not only is the new student concerned about entering high school, but she also is concerned about fitting in. Her family has just moved to this small, midwestern town from a large community on the west coast, and she knows that, while her middle school was very large and diverse, this school is very small. She is feeling culture shock and is overwhelmed with all the changes in her life.

As they walk through the hall toward the office, they stop to notice the photographs in the hallway. The pictures are of graduating classes, each consisting of about a dozen people, and the dates go back to the early 1900s. The walls are covered with signs that state "No talking in the halls," "No loitering in the halls," "No shouting or loud noises in the halls."

They become lost in the hallways, since there are no signs directing newcomers to the office. Either school officials don't expect visitors, or they don't expect anyone who doesn't already know the school. Finally, they stumble on the office. As they enter, a surly woman looks up from her typing to demand "What do you want?" The principal walks through the office grumbling something to the secretary, then slams the door on his way out. They are told to wait for Mrs. Ross.

Mrs. Ross, the school counselor, greets the student and mother and offers to take them on a tour. She leads them into the home economics room, where, she explains, all the girls take cooking, sewing, and domestic science. When the student asks about computers, the counselor responds with "You're kidding, of course. You're not going to need to worry about computers."

They return to the office, where the counselor fills out the student's schedule. "Don't worry about a thing. I chose all your courses." When the student tries to indicate that she's interested in certain subjects, perhaps to go into business someday, Mrs. Ross stops her with "We have our way of doing things here, dear, that you don't understand. If you just go along with our system, you'll fit in just fine. You're here to get educated, and it's my job to be sure that you do just that. You have no idea what interests you. When you're an adult, then you get to call the shots. Until then, you just do what you're told. There's a good girl."

Challenge Questions

Do you have any concerns about anything Mrs. Ross said? Do you believe that adults should make all choices for young people? What are appropriate choices for young people to make for themselves, and within those choices, when do adults need to step in? What additional issues did you notice in terms of the school environment? What messages are sent to students about the school and their place in it? How inviting do you think the school feels to students? What role do you think the counselor plays in that feeling? What role should the counselor play in evaluating the school environment?

Schools

Imagine that you are in a school. What do you see around you? What do you smell, hear, see? Take a moment to experience that school.

When students in a graduate Introduction to School Counseling class are asked to imagine a school, the responses typically include the sound of young peoples' voices, laughter, bright colors of clothes and bulletin boards, and the smell of peanut butter, apples, crayons. These images are evoked by elementary schools; the emotions generated by these images are usually positive. In contrast, when asked to imagine a high school, the images are darker, more somber, less vibrant. Typical responses include crowded hallways, darker colors, angry voices, slamming lockers, a dusty-smoky smell. Why? Secondary school students are no less vibrant, no less creative, no less happy than elementary students—or are they?

To understand school counseling, we must understand schools. We must be able to understand what contributes to—and what impedes—the development of our students. Since counselors are charged with facilitating the academic, career, and personal/social development of students, it is essential that counselors be willing to confront, as appropriate, those elements that impede students' development. Conversely, counselors need to empower themselves to advocate for those elements that contribute to students' development. You will be able to understand why those images of high school darken in comparison to elementary school if you understand the extent to which schools respond to the developmental needs of their students.

A Tale of Two Schools

School counselors see the full spectrum of students, with a wide range of needs. Some students seem to sail through school. They love going to school; they love learning; they feel energized by their teachers, their peers, the subjects they study. Their lives are blessed with strong families, strong career goals, and strong social skills. For these students, the school counselor may be the person who challenges them to stretch, encourages their potential, and cheerleads for them for scholarships and college entrance. But such students are rare.

Other students don't fare well, struggling with social skills, academic skills, or life challenges. After reading Chapters 2 and 3, you have some ideas of the developmental issues of adolescents, and you can see how young people's physical, social, or emotional needs may not always be met. But many education professionals still struggle with why students fail. Don't all schools meet the educational needs of their students? Just as family systems research has found that the way you were parented can determine, to a large extent, the way you will parent, so it is with education. The way we were schooled, if unquestioned, translates into the way we school our young people.

The problem is that not everyone learns the same way. If you're one of those unfortunate students whose learning needs do not match what the school can provide, school after school, teacher after teacher, year after year, failure after failure, you learn one thing. You might not learn math, or reading, or history, but you'll learn one lesson very well—that you don't belong in school, that you're stupid, useless, worthless, a waste of time for everyone. So you find ways to avoid being there, or ways to avoid facing yet another failure, or ways to make everyone think you know when you don't. Then perhaps you will find ways to make other people pay for making you feel bad, ways to settle the score a little, ways to make others wish they weren't there, either.

Does this sound familiar? It should. We read about these students in the newspapers every day. Their pain becomes more obvious as time passes, their spirits more subdued each year as their self-esteem wears down. The person who started out as an energetic, bubbly kindergartner has come to high school expecting to fail.

What can counselors do to help? The answer may be found in the literature about developmentally appropriate schools, but to understand what is developmentally appropriate, let's first look at what dehumanizing schools look like.

Dehumanizing Schools   Schools, as a reflection of the society in which they were created, evolved ways of dealing with children based on models used in other sectors of society—namely, business. The model of efficiency of the 1860s through the 1930s was the factory, and schools evolved classrooms where everyone did the same thing at the same time (sat in rows, no talking, eyes forward) (Perry, 1992; Sheldon & Biddle, 1998), and everyone was expected to progress at the same rate based on chronological age (Morrison, 1997). The expressed goals of schooling, as described in the Cardinal Principles of Secondary Education (written in 1918), were to teach health, a command of fundamental processes, worthy home membership, citizenship, ethical character, vocational preparation, and worthy use of leisure time (as cited in Morrison, 1997). The unexpressed goal of schooling was to instill a common morality, which came to mean nondenominational Christian (Newman, 1994, p. 149).

The process of learning involved rote memorization (Newman, 1994) of information deemed appropriate by the social mores of the time (Morrison, 1997). The relevance of the data was unquestioned—it was in the book, so it must be learned. Recitation, drills, and evaluation of recall in the form of objective tests were the norm (Shaffer, 1999).

Classes were controlled by the adult, in what is known as teacher-centered instruction. Teachers were required to maintain order, cover a body of material, and demonstrate that students have learned (Newman, 1994). A significant advantage of teacher-centered instruction is control, and as class sizes got bigger in the post–World War II baby boom, control became more and more important. In the eyes of school boards, schools were measured by test scores and cost-effectiveness (Newman, 1994).

What drove the factory model was competition: To establish and maintain the United States as the industrial giant of the world, we needed to train factory workers. What drove the need to control was fear: fear of the sheer numbers of students, fear of losing our competitive edge, fear that young people could not be trusted to make sound decisions. What drove education-by-memorization and teacher-centered classrooms was the "banking" model of learning (Sheldon & Biddle, 1998): that the learner was an empty vessel, passively awaiting wisdom from the all-knowing expert in the front of the classroom who was the exclusive source of knowledge. Knowledge could not be gained by discovery, self-teaching, or intuition, but only after such grace was earned by many hours of hard work, sacrifice, and discipline.

The implicit curriculum of the factory model of education, according to Eisner (1985), is compliance with authority rather than initiative, dependence on others to provide answers, extrinsic motivation, and competitiveness with classmates. The intellect is nurtured at the expense of the affect; learning about the arts is no more than play that one earns when the serious endeavor of schooling has been finished. He likens the school to a hospital environment, stamped with routine, sameness, sterility, and lack of privacy. "Schools are educational churches, and our gods, judging from the altars we build, are economy and efficiency. Hardly a nod is given to the spirit" (Eisner, 1985, p. 97).

It is easy to see how the schools described above would create places where the spirit, if not outright crushed, is at least substantially bruised. These are dehumanizing institutions, and young people who have endured twelve (or more) years of such institutionalization do not usually emerge whole. The price they pay is their creativity, initiative, flexibility, autonomy, and trust in themselves as change agents for tomorrow's world.

Yet, if we agree that schools are charged with helping students to become citizens of tomorrow's world, we need workers who possess those very characteristics that factory-model schools are designed to eradicate (Sheldon & Biddle, 1998). Recall from Chapter 1 that the two most salient features of effective schools are a caring environment and a holistic orientation to the development of students. It is from the synthesis of the needs of tomorrow's world with the research into effective schools that the concept of developmentally appropriate education has emerged.

Developmentally Appropriate Schools   It would be inaccurate and unfair to claim that there was nothing of educational value to be gained from traditional schools. Among some positive lessons that are learned in a structured setting are punctuality, persistence, and delayed gratification (Eisner, 1985), and the need to obey the rules, respect authority, and become good citizens (Shaffer, 1999). It is also true that some lessons, such as abstract concepts, are easier to learn in a structured, lecture-oriented setting (Shaffer, 1999). As we shall see, developmentally appropriate education incorporates these benefits of structured education and extends the range of learning experiences to reduce structure, as determined by students' developmental needs.

First coined to describe educational strategies for use with preschool-age children (Travers, Elliott, & Kratochwill, 1993), developmentally appropriate education (also known as open classrooms [Eggen & Kauchak, 1994]) refers to educational experiences that are tailored to the developmental needs of students in terms of social skills, emotional maturation, and academic strengths and challenges. According to Eggen and Kauchak (1994), developmentally appropriate education provides balance among academic, social, and emotional goals, in a well-organized classroom that includes an emphasis on peer and teacher interaction, active learning strategies, and intrinsically interesting learning activities. They characterize developmentally appropriate methodology as utilizing discovery, group projects, independent thinking, and reflection; motivation is intrinsic and based on curiosity; classroom organization is designed for individualized instruction and small group interaction; and the educator's role is perceived as that of director and facilitator, rather than exclusively that of presenter (p. 111).

The key to understanding what makes these educational strategies "developmentally appropriate" is that the entire learning environment and all learning activities within that environment are designed based on what is most conducive to the learning of *those particular* students. Balanced consideration is given to the students' social, emotional, and academic needs; cooperation, rather than competition, drives peer interactions, and initiative, rather than blind compliance, is fostered.

According to Eggen and Kauchak (1994), open classrooms were criticized when educators misunderstood how to apply these concepts and allowed students to do whatever they wanted in class. The quality of learning suffered in those classrooms. As school counselors, we must be concerned for the holistic development of the student, so we must know: How well do students learn in developmentally appropriate classrooms?

Research into the academic efficacy of various pedagogies suggests that students will actually learn *more* in a developmentally appropriate learning environment (Charlesworth, 1996; Schickedanz, Schickedanz, Forsyth, & Forsyth, 1998; Travers, Elliott, & Kratochwill, 1993). The reasons students learn better involve *how* and *why* students learn. Since developmentally appropriate education allows for natural curiosity and intrinsic motivation to be expressed, students may learn better because they enjoy what they are learning. Studies have shown that intrinsically motivated learners retain memorized material longer, demonstrate a stronger understanding of both memorized and more complex material, and demonstrate greater creativity and cognitive flexibility (Sheldon & Biddle, 1998, p. 166). Furthermore, open classrooms allow students to learn in the way that is most natural to them, as "active, autonomous agents who learn better by being actively involved in education" (Shaffer, 1999, p. 611).

There is evidence that developmentally appropriate education, or open classrooms, provide additional developmental benefits in the social and emotional domains (Shaffer, 1999). Students in such classrooms expressed more positive attitudes about school, they were more self-directed, they displayed greater ability to cooperate with their classmates, and they exhibited fewer behavioral problems.

Recall from Chapter 1 our discussion of effective schools. In any well-functioning academic setting, academic expectations and accountability for learning are high, but there is also a connection between educators and students, an environment of encouragement, and teaching that blends structure and discovery (Travers, Elliott, & Kratochwill, 1993). It would appear that developmentally appropriate education fits these conditions for effective schools. Given the preponderance of evidence in support of developmentally appropriate educational strategies, it is hard to argue for a return to factory-model schools.

Reflection Moment

Recall a class in your graduate or undergraduate experience in which the professor operated from the factory model of education. In this classroom, how did you feel? Did you feel connected to the teacher or other students? If you were graded on a curve (competition with your peers for grades), how did that effect the way you interacted with fellow students? Was the professor the ultimate expert? If so, who determined that expert status: you or the teacher? If you gave him or her that expert status, how did that feel? If the teacher gave him- or herself that expert status, how did that effect your relationship with him or her?

Now recall a class in your graduate or undergraduate experience in which you experienced a more developmentally appropriate approach. How did that classroom feel to you? How did the teacher express his or her awareness of your social, emotional, and academic developmental needs?

In which classroom did you learn more? In which classroom did you feel more connected? More respected? How does that connection and respect effect the way you perceive your education?

Developmentally Appropriate Secondary Schools   So what does developmentally appropriate education look like in high school? In order to move to a discussion of developmentally appropriate secondary education, we first need to recall what you learned in Chapters 2 and 3 on the developmental challenges of adolescents. In a nutshell, adolescence is defined by the following developmental tasks and characteristics (Pipher, 1994; Pollack, 1999; Schickedanz, Schickedanz, Forsyth, & Forsyth, 1998; Travers, Elliott, & Kratochwill, 1993):

1. The need to resolve issues of identity and future direction
2. The need to establish a healthy and balanced sense of self-esteem
3. The need to develop mature relationships with authority figures, while concurrently trying to differentiate and individuate from adults
4. The need to learn responsibility
5. The need to see connections between discrete elements of their existence (school, work, personal relationships)
6. The need to learn through relationships
7. The need to be active

An examination of the literature on school reform helps us to weave the developmental needs of adolescents into the fabric of educational strategies. To help young people with these developmental tasks, given their social, emotional, physical, and intellectual realities, developmentally appropriate secondary education would:

- Provide exploratory courses (Pollak, 1995), which would facilitate self-knowledge, identity, autonomy, and self-esteem.
- Allow student class groupings that emphasize academic and ability diversity rather than conformity (Comfort & Giorgi, 1997; Fisher & Sax, 1997; Heron, 1990), which

would provide greater connections between students, reduce situations in which students' self-esteem is lowered, and foster self-appreciation.

- Provide settings in which all students are challenged to achieve at meaningful, challenging, and complex tasks (Midgley & Edelin, 1998), which will enhance self-awareness and self-esteem.
- Provide settings in which students are grouped based on academic or life interests (Comfort & Giorgi, 1997; Midgley & Edelin, 1998), which would allow for connections between students, facilitate exploration of life direction, and reduce situations in which students' self-esteem is lowered.
- Provide small-group learning environments and extended scheduling blocks where students and teachers can get to know and appreciate each other (Comfort & Giorgi, 1997; Lipsitz, 1984; Morrison, 1997), which will enable students to see adults as complete human beings, not instruments of inauthentic authority. This will also reinforce a sense of community.
- Provide facilities where students are able to express themselves artistically and where that expression is valued by the school (Lipsitz, 1984) to help students learn about responsibility, community, and themselves.
- Provide organic, fluid organizational structures that flow from a shared vision of pupil development, to school philosophy, to organizational policies and procedures (Lipsitz, 1984), which will enhance opportunities for students to witness how authentic authority functions and how responsible adults navigate change.
- Provide choices in electives, opportunities for decision making, self-scheduling, and self-regulation in the form of negotiated discipline (Comfort & Giorgi, 1997; Fay & Funk, 1995; Lipsitz, 1984; Midgley & Edelin, 1998), which will give them greater responsibility for their own learning (Comfort & Giorgi, 1997) and foster a sense of autonomy, identity, and individuality.
- Involve students in dialogues about assignment of grades, grading for progress as well as product, allowing students to redo work, and practices that encourage academic risk-taking (Fay & Funk, 1995; Midgley & Edelin, 1998; Travers, Elliott, & Kratochwill, 1993), which will help students assume greater academic responsibility, foster self-esteem, and build life-work habits.
- Provide integrated, thematic academic experiences in terms of multidisciplinary courses provided by interdisciplinary teams (Comfort & Giorgi, 1997; Fisher & Sax, 1997; Heron, 1990; Kling & Zimmer, 1999; Midgley & Edelin, 1998; Pollak, 1995), which will help students see connections among the subjects they study.
- Provide academic connection to real-life problems (Comfort & Giorgi, 1997; Fisher & Sax, 1997), which will help students understand how their learning connects to real life and life direction, increase their responsibility for learning, and actively involve them in learning.
- Provide caring, mutually respectful relationships with teachers, staff, and administrators (Comfort & Giorgi, 1997; Morrison, 1997; Pollak, 1995) through an advisory system (Comfort & Giorgi, 1997; Heron, 1990; Pollak, 1995), which helps establish relationships through which students learn, helps students deal more effectively with authority, provides a sense of community and safety, and enhances self-esteem.

- Foster student tutoring (Heron, 1990; Midgley & Edelin, 1998), cooperative learning (Midgley & Edelin, 1998), and thematic student teaming (Comfort & Giorgi, 1997), which will help establish relationships, a sense of community with and responsibility to other students, and a venue through which to explore various life directions.
- Foster community-school connections and a sense of community within the school through community and campus improvement projects (Comfort & Giorgi, 1997; Fisher & Sax, 1997), which will provide connections between discrete areas of the students' lives, establish community, and provide relationships within which students can learn.
- Provide counseling and developmental curriculum lessons to foster direct learning about self, cultures, relationships, conflict resolution, and social skills building (Comfort & Giorgi, 1997; Morrison, 1997; Pollak, 1995), which helps students establish their sense of identity, self-esteem, responsibility, community, autonomy, and life direction.
- Engage learners actively in the learning process (Comfort & Giorgi, 1997; Fay & Funk, 1995; Kling & Zimmer, 1999; Lipsitz, 1984), which will increase their responsibility for learning, self-knowledge, and self-esteem.
- Look at students' lives to find what's right or what's working, look for untapped resources to empower them to look within for their answers, and focus on cooperation, which will affirm their internal locus of control.
- Utilize new technologies and alternative instructional environments (Comfort & Giorgi, 1997; Morrison, 1997, Travers, Elliott, & Kratochwill, 1993) that coordinate with career choices, which provides active involvement with learning and enhances self-esteem.

While developmentally appropriate education is not a guaranteed panacea for all the ills of schools and society, it does hold the promise of helping young people find their way to functional adulthood (Paisley & Peace, 1995). Recall from Chapter 1 that we discussed the eight outcomes desired by society for young people. The outcomes are enjoyment of and commitment to lifelong learning; healthy and safe behaviors; effective socioemotional functioning; basic communication skills; character and values including responsibility, self-direction, and autonomy; vocational and adult roles; and recreational and avocational pursuits. As we saw in Chapter 2, the most essential task in the development of the adolescent is the development of identity—the ability to make one's own decisions. The essence of developmentally appropriate education for adolescents is summarized by Fay and Funk (1995), "All effective systems allow people to learn from the results of their own decisions" (p. 26). It is only through making decisions—and learning from the results—that young people attain the eight desired outcomes of education.

Without the ability to make decisions and learn from that process, young people leave secondary education ill equipped to deal with adult decisions, yet society expects—and demands—that they do so. In the eyes of the law, when young people reach the age of 18 years, they have attained the age of majority, or adult, status, in terms of contracts, marriage, voting, and criminal sanctions. School counselors are in a unique position to help schools teach young people, incrementally, about responsibility, decision making, and learning from mistakes.

Reflection Moment

Can you imagine what a school would look like that incorporated all the above developmentally appropriate strategies? What is the mental image you experience when you imagine such a school? How would it feel to be a student in such a school? How would it feel to be a counselor in that school? How does it feel to know that, as a school counselor, you will be in a position to help such a school become reality?

Schools as Systems   Recall from Chapter 3 that all young people are shaped developmentally by their environmental systems or context. It is in these contexts that young people learn the rules of living; these contexts are where values are acquired and explored and where attitudes are shaped. It is also in these contexts that young people learn the rules of relating: to themselves, each other, their families, and society as a whole.

In a systemic, holistic view of development, it is essential that school counselors be mindful of the fact that *schools are systems*. Two important points need to be made relative to this concept:

1. All actions within a system affect all members of that system. Much like all elements of a mobile move when one element is touched, all parts of a system resonate with disturbance anywhere in the system.
2. Young people can be profoundly affected by the values and attitudes that are directly or indirectly taught through that system.

The messages that are taught to young people through the system of formal education need to be more thoroughly explored. What values, messages, attitudes, and rules are taught in our schools? How are young people taught to relate to each other and themselves? We believe that developmentally appropriate schools provide healthier systems for nurturing young people because the central premise of the system is profoundly simple: Respect.

Respect as a Guiding Philosophy

As Lipsitz (1984) pointed out, "Schools are peculiar social agencies, charged by society with socializing youth into that society *while excluding them from it* (emphasis added)" (p. 7). She goes on to add that, in schools for adolescents, teachers and administrators substitute for other adults while adolescents act out their ambivalence about adults, one another, and themselves. Perhaps it is this acting out that causes society to exclude adolescents from society. The search for identity, the struggle between dependence and independence, the quest for a life vision—all these developmental tasks are painful to watch. Yet school counselors are in a unique position to be able to support young people's journey toward adulthood.

In their book about educational psychology, Travers, Elliott, and Kratochwill (1993) educate new teachers who will be working with adolescents. To help students attain psychosocial maturity, they recommend "treating them as *almost adults* (emphasis authors'); that is, providing them with independence, freedom, and respect" (p. 105). Fox (1994) also addresses "important questions about how readily we trivialize our young, render them passive and dependent, create consumer monsters of them, or make them into carbon copies of our own adultist fantasies and unresolved adolescent urges" (p. 182). The *Grolier-Webster International Dictionary* defines respect as "to hold in high estimation or honor; to treat with consideration; to avoid interfering with or intruding upon" (p. 817). As counselors, you are trained to respond to other people with unconditional positive regard and respect for their values, attitudes, and experiences. Is it possible to hope that an entire institution can view students with respect?

The answer is a resounding "yes." Secondary students need all professionals who work in schools to view them with positive regard and respect. We may not accept individual behavior within the boundaries of responsibility, accountability, and mutually respectful choices in a community, but we value each young person as a human being, with all the creativity, potential, beauty, and hope that any human being possesses. We respect their potential and their reality, and, as counselors, we hold onto our belief in their potential in the face of sometimes very painful reality. Recall from Chapter 1 that the necessary personal qualities of school counselors were described as creativity and imagination, flexibility, courage, faith, and passion. Here is where your faith and courage will be called into play.

As professionals working with secondary students, school counselors must be able to maintain faith that young people will rise to our high expectations, and if they don't, that it is their life path to learn their life lessons another way. In any case, we must respect them as having a right to their opinions, talents, interests, and feelings—AND help them learn appropriate and responsible ways to express those opinions, talents, interests, and feelings (Fay & Funk, 1995) in the context of a learning community. This is how we educate our young people into responsible citizenry in our society.

If we do not respect young people, we fall back into the factory model of schools, back into teacher-centered education, and back into the trap of the banking model of learning. Without respect, we revert to the "adult control—adolescent acting out—more control—more acting out" cycle of interaction with young people. When we demonstrate respect for young people and their developmental needs, we break that cycle and opt instead for a more responsible and responsive school environment. We build a more holistic system, teaching healthier values, attitudes, and ways of relating.

Environmental Assessment and Educational Quality

In reflecting on the role of the school counselor, it is clear that school counselors are uniquely aware of the general environment of the school. School counselors interact with many students (hopefully, with all students) and many teachers (again, hopefully, with all teachers) within the school community. As we will see in more detail in Chapter 13 on coordinating programs and services for colleagues in the schools, the counselor is charged with observing and assessing the educational environment to help students achieve in their academic, social, and career development. It is within the roles of observer and assessor that another of the school counselor's personal qualities will be required: that of courage. It is essential for the school counselor to not only observe the general school environment in terms of respect and developmentally appropriate education, but to also advocate for those educational elements that are conducive to respect and developmental appropriateness.

Environmental assessment is both an informal and formal process, depending on the needs of the institution. On an informal level, counselors can be sensitive to messages that are sent to students throughout the school. On a formal level, counselors can systematically assess the extent to which elements of the school are respectful or disrespectful to the needs of students, teachers, and other members of the school community.

One way that counselors can formally assess the respectful nature of the environment is through assessing the extent to which the school is practicing developmentally appropriate educational strategies as outlined in this chapter. Counselors can be instrumental in helping schools become more responsive to the developmental needs of students and, in so doing, can substantially improve the quality of the education provided to young people.

Another environmental assessment tool is the concept of "inviting" (respectful) and "disinviting" (disrespectful) elements within a school as described by Purkey and Schmidt (as cited in Schmidt, 1997, 1999). According to Schmidt, "invitational counseling advocates for school counseling programs that incorporate beneficial human relationships, improved physical environments, and respectful systems in which students can thrive" (Schmidt, 1999, p. 158). Designed as a means of identifying and assessing those "factors that contribute, or detract from, student development" (p. 159), invitational counseling examines the *people*, *places*, *programs*, *policies*, and *processes* that a student encounters in a school.

Using this concept, the assessment involves determining the extent to which the **people** are "inviting": friendly, welcoming, respectful, consistently sending the message that students, parents, teachers, and staff are "valued and worthwhile" (p. 159). **Places** are also evaluated: Are the facilities (building, classrooms, lockers, hallways, bathrooms, lockers) clean? Well cared for? Well designed? Well supplied? "Places that show disrespect by being unclean or unsafe dissuade students and others in deceptive, yet powerful, ways" (p. 159). An assessment of **programs** would explore the extent to which programs are inclusive (respectful and inviting) versus exclusive or needlessly competitive (disrespectful and disinviting). To evaluate the inviting nature of **policies**, an assessor would ask: Are fair policies designed with the best interests of the students in mind? Or are policies designed for the convenience of some other entity (or entities)? Finally, in terms of how policies are implemented, are the **processes** designed to facilitate cooperation and compliance, or are they unnecessarily obtuse or arbitrarily enforced? "Programs that neglect cultural or individual differences, or processes adopted for the convenience of an elite few, may be perceived as disinvitations by people who feel slighted or set apart from the rest of the school population" (p. 159).

The answers to these questions directly impact the way students perceive the school, and through that perception, they way they interact with the school. It is true that we are more likely to respond with respect toward others when we feel respected, just as we are more likely to respond with disrespect when we do not feel respected (Schmidt, 1997). The school counselor, as advocate for developmentally appropriate secondary education and for respect for all persons in the school environment, can use the concept of invitational counseling, with its "unwavering regard for human respect and dignity" (Schmidt, 1999, p. 159), to engage in a dialogue about respect with the school community. Within these conversations, counselors can advocate for staff development, discuss policies, help to create new programs, and work to change aspects of the school that inhibit relationships or discriminate against or alienate groups or individuals (Schmidt, 1999, p. 160).

Similar to a physician's need to monitor the health of the patient, the school counselor must monitor the emotional health of the school's environment. In this way, school counselors directly influence the quality of the educational experience of all students. This holistic concern for students is further refined in the specific activities of school counselors. As we will see in the next chapter, comprehensive school counseling programs at the secondary level include a wide variety of tasks and roles.

Reflection Moment

How do you react when you don't feel respected? What specific behaviors would you describe as being respectful? What specific behaviors would you describe as being disrespectful? Think of examples in your own experience in which adults were behaving respectfully toward adolescents. How did the adolescents behave in response? Now think of examples in which adults were behaving disrespectfully toward adolescents. How did the adolescents behave in response?

Think of how you would help a school administration think about the level of respect or disrespect that is communicated through its people, places, programs, policies, and processes. How do you feel about being an advocate? Do you feel you would be up to the challenge? If your answer is no, what can you do now to start feeling more empowered to be an advocate for respect and developmentally appropriate education?

Chapter Summary

In this chapter, we discussed what can go wrong in a school, examining how fear, control, and various models of education culminate in a school setting that fosters competition, conformity, and resentment. In contrast to that model, we then examined the concept of developmentally appropriate education, and found academic, social, and behavioral benefits from such educational approaches.

We next juxtaposed developmental insights we gained from Chapters 2 and 3 with the concept of developmentally appropriate education. With literature on the topic of high school reform, we described various educational strategies that would be developmentally appropriate for secondary school students. This will enable high school counselors to understand what developmentally appropriate education would look like when it is practiced in the high school classroom and school. It is important to remember that schools are systems, a vital human context in which young people learn values and attitudes about living, learning, and relating to self and others. They are more likely to learn respect when they are treated with respect.

We then discussed respect as a guiding philosophy in schools, outlining why respect is so vital to a healthy, responsive, and responsible school community. Strategies such as informal observation, formal assessment of developmentally appropriate educational strategies, and formal assessment of inviting and disinviting aspects of the school can help the counselor address aspects of the school that are not respectful. Through environmental assessment, school counselors empower themselves to address disrespect in the school and advocate for more respectful treatment of all members of the school community.

A Day in the Life Revisited: Integration

Take a minute and reread Mrs. Ross's Choices. This conversation was not made up; it really happened. Now that you've read the chapter:

1. What specifically did the school counselor say that was characteristic of a dehumanizing school environment?
2. What specifically did the school counselor say that was contrary to the concepts of developmentally appropriate education?
3. What messages did you see in the school environment? Were those messages inviting or disinviting?
4. Evaluate what was described of the school environment in terms of people, places, programs, policies, and processes. To what extent were those elements of the school inviting or disinviting?
5. If you were the school counselor of this school, what changes would you recommend to the administration that might help students feel more respected?

Application

1. Given what you know about developmentally appropriate education, select your favorite high school subject and design a developmentally appropriate classroom, describing how each developmentally appropriate strategy would be woven into your "ideal" classroom.

2. Visit one or two local high schools. When you walk through the halls, see if you can identify the following:
   a. What remnants of the factory model still exist in the school?
   b. What evidence of teacher-centered education and the banking model of learning did you see?
   c. What evidence of developmentally appropriate education did you see?
   d. What evidence of respect for students did you see?
   e. What evidence of respect for faculty, staff, and administration did you see?
   f. Evaluate the school environment in terms of the following:

People
Places
Programs
Policies
Processes

3. We believe that one important function of the school counselor is that of effective advocacy. Design a plan for advocacy within the schools for something you think is very important. Now think about the following questions:
   a. What are the personal qualities of an effective advocate? Outline those qualities. Which of those qualities do you currently possess? Outline a plan to develop or refine those qualities.
   b. What are the skills of an effective advocate? Which of those skills do you currently possess? Outline a plan to develop or refine those skills.

4. Look at the student quote at the start of this chapter. How does it relate to the content of the chapter?

Suggested Readings

Fay, J., & Funk, D. (1995). *Teaching with love and logic: Taking control of the classroom.* Golden, CO: Love & Logic Press. A practical book that provides important insights into developmentally appropriate ways to work with students.

Pipher, M. (1994). *Reviving Ophelia: Saving the selves of adolescent girls.* New York: Ballantine. Provides a comprehensive overview of the developmental issues of young women.

Pollack, W. (1999). *Real boys: Rescuing our sons from the myths of boyhood.* New York: Henry Holt & Co. Provides a comprehensive overview of the developmental issues of young men.

Schickedanz, J. A., Schickedanz, D. I., Forsyth, P. D., & Forsyth, C. A. (1998). *Understanding children and adolescents* (3rd ed.). Boston: Allyn and Bacon. This book describes the development of children and adolescents and is very useful for school professionals.

Wisconsin Association for Middle Level Education (1999). *Elements of an exemplary middle level school.* Waunakee, WI: Author. This publication provides an overview of early adolescence (transescence) providing a useful perspective about students who are entering high school.

References

Charlesworth, R. (1996). *Understanding child development* (4th ed.). Albany, NY: Delmar.

Comfort, R. E., & Giorgi, J. (1997). In a different voice: A student agenda for high school reform. *High School Journal, 80* (3), 179–184. Retrieved on March 9, 2000, from EBSCO database on the World Wide Web: http://www.ehostvgw3.epnet.com.

Eggen, P., & Kauchak, D. (1994*). Educational psychology: Classroom connections* (2nd ed.). New York: Merrill.

Eisner, E. W. (1985). *The educational imagination: On the design and evaluation of school programs* (2nd ed.). New York: Macmillan.

Fay, J., & Funk, D. (1995). *Teaching with love and logic.* Golden, CO: Love & Logic Press.

Fisher, D., & Sax, C. (1997). Including all students in the high school reform agenda. *Education & Treatment of Children. 20*(1), 59–68. Retrieved March 9, 2000, from the EBSCO database on the World Wide Web: http://ehostvgw3.epnet.com.

Fox, M. (1994). *The reinvention of work: A new vision of livelihood for our time.* San Francisco, CA: Harper.

Grolier-Webster international dictionary of the English language. (1975). New York: Grolier.

Heron, B. (1990, September/October). High school reform: Playing not to lose. *Clearing House. 64*(1), 13–16. Retrieved March 9, 2000, from EBSCO database on the World Wide Web: http://www.ehostvgw8.epnet.com.

Kling, D., & Zimmer, K. G. (1999). *Weaving curriculum strands together: Data driven results on the implementation of an interdisciplinary/integrated model for high school reform.* (Report No. FL 025 809).

No location given. (ERIC Document Reproduction Service No. ED 429 457).

Lipsitz, J. (1984). *Successful schools for young adolescents.* New Brunswick, NJ: Transaction Books.

Midgley, C., & Edelin, K. C. (1998). Middle school reform and early adolescent well-being: The good news and the bad. *Educational Psychologist, 33*(4), 195–206.

Morrison, G. S. (1997). *Teaching in America.* Boston: Allyn and Bacon.

Newman, J. W. (1994). *America's teachers: An introduction to education* (2nd ed.). New York: Longman.

Paisley, P. O., & Peace, S. D. (1995). Developmental principles: A framework for school counseling programs. *Elementary School Counseling & Guidance, 30*(2), 85–93.

Perry, N. (1992). *Educational reform and the school counselor.* (Report # EDO-CG-92-25). Washington, DC: Office of Educational Research and Improvement. (ERIC Document Reproduction Service No. ED 347 491). Retrieved April 18, 2000, from EBSCO database on the World Wide Web: http://webnf2.epnet.com.

Pipher, M. (1994). *Reviving Ophelia: Saving the selves of adolescent girls.* New York: Ballantine.

Pollack, W. (1999). *Real boys: Rescuing our sons from the myths of boyhood.* New York: Henry Holt & Co.

Pollak, J. P. (1995, January/February). Caring in the middle school classroom. *Clearing House, 68*(3), 185–187. Retrieved February 15, 2000, from EBSCO database on the World Wide Web: http://www.ehostvgw8.epnet.com.

Schickedanz, J. A., Schickedanz, D. I., Forsyth, P. D., & Forsyth, C. A. (1998). *Understanding children and adolescents* (3rd ed.). Boston: Allyn and Bacon.

Schmidt, J. J. (1997). Invitational counselling: An expanded framework for comprehensive school counselling programs. *Canadian Journal of Counselling, 31*(1), 6–17.

Schmidt, J. J. (1999). *Counseling in schools: Essential services and comprehensive programs* (3rd ed.). Boston: Allyn and Bacon.

Shaffer, D. R. (1999). *Developmental psychology: Childhood and adolescence* (5th ed.). Pacific Grove, CA: Brooks/Cole.

Sheldon, K. M., & Biddle, B. J. (1998). Standards, accountability, and school reform: Perils and pitfalls. *Teachers College Record, 100*(1), 164–180.

Travers, J. F., Elliott, S. N., & Kratochwill, T. R. (1993). *Educational psychology: Effective teaching, effective learning.* Madison, WI: Brown & Benchmark.

Comprehensive School Counseling:

The Domains/Activities/Partners Model

ACTIVITIES	DOMAINS					
	Academic Development	Career Development	Personal/Social Development			
Counseling	1a	1b	1c	5	6	7
Educating and Advocating	2a	2b	2c	8	9	10
Consulting	3a	3b	3c	11	12	13
Leadership and Coordination	4a	4b	4c	14	15	16
	Students			Parents and Caregivers	Colleagues in Schools	Colleagues in Community

PARTNERS IN THE PROCESS

5

Comprehensive School Counseling Programs and the Domains/Activities/Partners Model

Colette T. Dollarhide

"What do I think should be done to address problems with kids? School programs should bring kids to jails and low income areas and help show kids what happens with poor choices."

Erik, age 19

Learning Objectives

By the end of this chapter, you will be able to:

1. Understand how the profession of school counseling evolved.

2. Identify the traditional emphasis on careers as the focus of school counseling and understand why that is no longer the primary focus.

3. Identify the traditional emphasis on guidance as the primary activity of school counselors and understand why that is no longer the primary activity.

4. Identify the origin of the emphasis on mental health in schools and understand why that is no longer a school counselor's primary emphasis.

5. Describe developmental guidance and identify some of the reasons that it does not adequately describe all the important tasks of school counselors.

6. Describe comprehensive school counseling, including the ways that the American School Counselor Association (ASCA) defines the role of the school counselor and the National Standards of school counseling.

7. Understand the unique qualities of school counseling at all levels of schooling.

8. Outline the Domains/Activities/Partners model of school counseling and describe how it fits comprehensive school counseling.

9. Identify the domains of school counseling and give examples of each domain.

10. Identify the activities of school counselors and give examples of each activity.

11. Identify the partners of school counselors and give examples of each partner.

12. Understand the process of designing a comprehensive school counseling program.

A Day in the Life of a Counselor: Marcia's Meltdown

Marcia came briskly into the counselor's office and sat on the edge of the large chair. After exchanging pleasantries, the counselor asked Marcia what she could do for her. Taking a deep breath, Marcia began. "I've been a school counselor for four years now, and I'm not sure I can stay with it. It's always been something I wanted to do, but now, I don't know."

With a minimum of encouragement, Marcia tearfully described her job. "I come to school before 7:00 A.M., hoping to get some work done before students arrive. But every day, I find myself buried before school even starts. I've got students who are failing, students who are depressed and suicidal. I've got reports that need to be filled out, and I'm asked to be on every special education committee in the school. My desk is piled so high with paper that I haven't seen the top of the desk in months!

"I'm supposed to help students with college applications, scholarship applications, test dates, and college requirements. I'm expected to handle all the building-wide testing. I'm supposed to know the career software the school just bought, but I haven't had time to learn it yet. Now the teachers want me to demonstrate it.

"I have at least five students a day who need to change their schedule, who need to add a class, take a study hall with a friend, drop a class. That doesn't even include registration for new students to the school. I have full responsibility for registration for all the students—

even incoming freshmen. Teachers yell at me if their classes are too full and they yell if their classes are too empty and get canceled. I have all the senior graduation checks still to do—and this is February! I have parent phone calls from people who don't know what to do with their kids—Bob's in jail, Sally's in trouble with drugs, Jennie's pregnant, Steve just got a DUI, Tom has ADHD and can't I just help him get a tutor?

"I have teachers who don't understand why I can't coordinate career day for the school, a principal who insists that I have lunchroom and hall duty, and no secretary. The phone interrupts me all day long.

"A local employer calls to tell me that one of our students didn't show up for work. The corner quickmart calls to tell me that students are hanging around the market trying to get customers to buy cigarettes for them. The local doctor calls to tell me that he's worried about a student who is a star athlete. I'm the advisor of the prom committee, and the caterer called to change his price for the third time. I'm also involved with the state professional association, and I promised the newsletter editor that I would write an article for the next newsletter, which is due in one week.

"As it is now, I never get to bed before midnight. When I get home, I have about a half hour to eat some dinner, then I have to be back at school for some game or event. On weekends, I open my email at home to find dozens of messages from students, parents, teachers, every one wanting me to do something for them.

"How am I supposed to do all this? I have 566 students in the school, and I'm expected to do everything for all of them, their parents, and the teachers? Take on committees for the school? Employers, too? I can't, I just can't . . . I want to quit before it makes me crazy. I really need some career counseling."

Challenge Questions

How did you feel while reading about Marcia's life? Did you feel her sense of being overwhelmed? What sorts of things did you think about while you were reading? Did you experience a sense of impending doom in her life? What do you see as the cause of her "meltdown"? What suggestions do you have for her? If you were her counselor, what would you say to her?

The Historical Context of School Counseling

If you pick up a book, open it to the middle, and begin reading, you will get to the end of the book never truly understanding the relationships among the characters, the depth of the story, or the journey of the main character. The drama and characters are seen in a smaller frame of time and understanding, becoming flattened and two-dimensional in the process. Without context, events, people, and places become oversimplified stereotypes, seen though a lens focused on current experience. However, if you read the entire book and spend time reflecting on the story, you would have the context within which to understand the ending, and you might better understand the insights within the story that could help you in your own life journey.

In the same way, it would be a mistake to attempt to understand school counseling as it is today in this country without also examining school counseling of yesterday.

Guidance/Careers Emphasis

The development of school counseling is linked to the development of secondary education. Until the late 1800s in the United States, education was defined in terms of reading and writing, necessary to achieve pious living through reading the Bible. Education about life—learning about jobs, relationships, and duty to one's community—was seen primarily as the responsibility of the family (Hine, 1999). Organized education was more common at the elementary ages than in adolescence, since the work produced or wages earned by older children often was needed for family survival (Hine, 1999). However, with the advent of the Industrial Revolution, the nature of education changed.

The Industrial Revolution brought the need for higher level skills. Awareness of these skills was articulated in the mission of the first high school in this country, Boston English High School, established in 1821 "to give a child an education that shall fit him [sic] for an active life, and shall serve as a foundation for eminence in his [sic] profession, whether Mercantile or Mechanic" (Hine, 1999, p. 144). But the social ills that came with the Revolution—poverty, ethnic slums, corruption, and moral decay—generated awareness of the power of the schools as a tool for social remedies (Olson, 1999; Schmidt, 1999), which fueled the birth of the school counseling profession in the early 1900s.

Two primary persons are credited with the emergence of school counseling, then known as vocational guidance. Jesse B. Davis, principal of a high school in Grand Rapids, Michigan, in 1907, began a program in his school to include guidance lessons in English composition classes to "help students develop character, avoid problem behaviors, and relate vocational interests to curriculum subjects" (Schmidt, 1999, p. 7). A year later, Frank Parsons, who is credited as the "father of guidance," issued a report from his Vocational Bureau, in which the terms "vocational guidance" first appeared. In this report, Parsons called for vocational guidance to be provided by "trained experts" and offered in all public schools (Gysbers & Henderson, 2000, p. 4). In response, Boston elementary and secondary schools hired vocational counselors from their teaching staff, and charged them, in addition to their regular teaching duties, with gathering and maintaining occupational information, presenting lessons in occupations, interviewing pupils who are failing and suggesting a remedy, and conferencing with parents (Gysbers & Henderson, 2000).

It is easy to see the connection between these duties and the duties of current professionals in school counseling. For the nascent profession, this was the genesis of professional identity, training, and definition. Vocational guidance in schools grew around the country (Gysbers & Henderson, 2000). The emphasis of the secondary school as preparation for vocations, college attendance, and productive citizenship emerged as the rallying point for the passage of compulsory attendance legislation. This served to maintain focus on careers as the outcome of schooling and directive guidance as the activity by which those outcomes were guaranteed (S. B. Baker, 2000). Many school administrators, teachers, and counselors still hold these beliefs.

Further reinforcing the directive guidance function of school counselors was the need to classify young men into various activities within the military during World Wars I and II.

Educational and vocational psychometrics, or mental measurement, grew in importance with the development, widespread validation, and acceptance of group-administered intelligence tests (S. B. Baker, 2000). "Psychometrics offered school guidance not only the tools for assessment but also corresponding respectability because the tools seemed so precise and scientific" (S. B. Baker, 2000, p. 4). Bolstered by the administrative progressive movement (Olson, 1999) discussed in Chapter 1, advising students on ways to reach their potential by identifying their limitations became the cement that hard-set advisement and directive guidance as the role of counselors during the 1930s and 1940s. Called "trait-and-factor" guidance, this approach was characterized by testing students' intelligence, interests, and abilities, then using that information to advise them about vocational and adjustment issues (S. B. Baker, 2000).

Challenged as too narrow, too restrictive, and inadequate to address students' developmental issues, emphasis on test-and-tell directive guidance waned in popularity during the late 1940s and 1950s.

Mental Health Emphasis

As criticism mounted concerning the emphasis on "guidance" and "advisement," conversations were occurring in the educational and psychological arenas that would culminate in the second direction of school counseling. The writings of John Dewey in the 1920s caused many education professionals to reexamine their philosophy based on a more student-centered, progressive view of the role of education (Olson, 1999), and the writings of Carl Rogers in the 1940s and 1950s caused many mental health professionals to reexamine their philosophy based on a more holistic view of the relationship between guidance counselors and students (Schmidt, 1999). According to Schmidt (1999), "This focus moved the profession away from the counselor-centered perspectives of earlier times and emphasized a growth-oriented counseling relationship as opposed to an informational and problem-solving one" (p. 11). At this time, mental health services and counseling became "the central secondary school guidance function, with all other functions in supplementary roles" (S. B. Baker, 2000, p. 6).

The agenda of the social progressive movement in education was welcome, because it gave counselors greater awareness of their role in facilitating the development of all students in terms of their social, emotional, educational, and vocational needs. The emphasis on the role of the counselor as the mental health provider of the school was incorporated into the training of many school counselors during the 1950s and 1960s—the time when the National Defense Education Act of 1958 was funding the training of record numbers of school counselors (S. B. Baker, 2000, p. 6). However, in the 1960s, conversations emerged in the professional counseling literature challenging the focus of counselors on the limited number of students who needed crisis counseling and therapeutic services (S. B. Baker, 2000; Schmidt, 1999). It is the legacy of the mental health emphasis of this era that many counselors still hold the view that their primary role is to be the mental health provider for the school (Smith & Archer, 2000).

In a reevaluation of the profession, and in discussions about the role of elementary school counselors, there was increased advocacy for "developmental rather than remedial goals for elementary and secondary school guidance" (S. B. Baker, 2000, p. 8), leading to the third wave in defining what school counselors do: developmental guidance.

Developmental Guidance

During the late 1960s and through the 1970s, school counselors became increasingly aware of the need to prevent problems by providing educational activities that promote healthy adjustment, social awareness, interpersonal problem solving, and vocational development (Wittmer, 2000). And if the foundation unit of education is the classroom, what better venue to provide this preventive programming than in the classroom itself? As Wittmer stated,

> The question becomes, who does the most good? The school counselor who works with 25 children (using a large group guidance approach) in a six-week, one hour per week unit on improving self-concept, or the school counselor who spends six hours with one child in crisis? Although the latter is important (and may even be more fun for some), it is obvious that the school counselor using the former approach meets the needs of more students and does much more good in the long run. (Wittmer, 2000, pp. 4–5)

While some authors use the term "developmental guidance" to refer to all activities of a school counselor (Gysbers & Henderson, 2000), other authors cite the terms "guidance" and "development" as archaic (S. B. Baker, 2000). According to Baker, the term "developmental guidance" is limited, denoting a focus on classroom interventions that is more often associated with elementary school counseling programs. Furthermore, the strong association between the term "guidance" and the role of the counselor (Schmidt, 1999) suggests that the responsibility for guiding young people is the sole purview of the counselor, a fallacy that continues to trap counselors in inappropriately directive relationships with students (such as overreliance on test results) and in inappropriate administrative tasks (such as enrollment management). Hoyt (1993) also found that, when surveyed, the American School Counselor Association leaders expressed the preference for the term "counseling" rather than "guidance" when referring to the program offered by the school counselor.

Reflection Moment

Take a moment and reflect on your experience as a student interacting with your school counselor. Based on what that person did and said, can you identify her or his philosophy of school counseling? Did that person adopt an "expert" stance, provide directive guidance, and focus more on your career development than on your personal, social, or academic development? Or did that person assume a more therapeutic posture toward you, focusing more on your mental health? Did your school counselor(s) come to the classroom to present lessons and facilitate discussions about personal adjustment, academic success, or career development? Can you see the connection between when a counselor was trained in school counseling, and his or her philosophy of school counseling?

Comprehensive School Counseling

So, what's the correct way of defining school counseling? There is no one absolute way of defining school counseling. What we see in today's school counseling is a field manifesting a "number of themes, all having varying degrees of influence across training programs and among counselors. The newer activist, developmental, service-oriented, and eclectic themes mixed with remnants of the trait and factor, adjustment, administrative, and counseling themes that were [are] still very much alive" (S. B. Baker, 2000, p. 9).

However, in the mix of various philosophies, it is possible to articulate a path that outlines what school counselors need to be able to know, feel, and demonstrate. It is called *comprehensive school counseling* (or developmental school counseling [Paisley & Hubbard, 1994; Paisley & Peace, 1995]), and it brings together various roles and responsibilities with which school counselors are charged.

ASCA Role Statement and National Standards

School counselors have joined together in a national association of school counselors, the American School Counselor Association (ASCA), which has defined the role of the professional school counselor.

> The professional school counselor is a certified/licensed educator who addresses the needs of students comprehensively through the implementation of a developmental school counseling program. . . . They are specialists in human behavior and relationships who provide assistance to students through four primary interventions: counseling (individual and group); large group guidance; consultation; and coordination. (American School Counselor Association [ASCA], 1999)

ASCA (1999) goes on to define each of the four functions. Counseling is defined as "a confidential relationship in which the counselor meets with students . . . to help them resolve or cope constructively with their problems and developmental concerns." Large group guidance is defined as "a planned, developmental program of guidance activities designed to foster students' academic, career, and personal/social development" provided for all students. Consultation is defined as "a collaborative partnership in which the counselor works with parents, teachers, administrators, school psychologists, social workers, visiting teachers, medical professionals, and community health personnel in order to plan and implement strategies to help students be successful in the educational system." Finally, coordination is defined as "a leadership process in which the counselor helps organize, manage, and evaluate the school counseling program."

To further describe what school counselors do, ASCA states that "Above all, school counselors are student advocates who work cooperatively with other individuals and organizations to promote the development of children, youth, and families in their communities. . . . They work on behalf of students and their families to insure that all school programs facilitate the educational process and offer the opportunity for school success for each student" (ASCA, 1999).

This begs the question "What is school success?" The National Standards established by ASCA present guidelines for school counseling programs across the country (Campbell & Dahir, 1997). These standards outline goals for school counseling programs for the twenty-first century, establish school counseling as essential and integral to the educational mission of schools, promote access by all students, and describe the key competencies all students should be able to demonstrate by the end of their K–12 experience. (See Appendix B for the complete text of the Standards and Student Competencies.)

As presented in Figure 5.1, the National Standards highlight three content areas that summarize the developmental themes of schools. There are reasons behind the order in which these content areas are presented. Competencies in academic development, as the primary mission of education, confirm that school counselors are integral to the mission of the school and district in which the counselor functions. Competencies in career development, the transition from school to contributing member of society, represent outcomes of education as defined by society. Competencies in personal and social development answer the need for young people to function in an informed citizenry addressing the challenges of the twenty-first century.

Each Standard is accompanied by student competencies that define the Standard as outlined in Appendix B. For example, Standard A under Academic Development states that "Students will acquire the attitudes, knowledge, and skills that contribute to effective learning in school and across the life span." In Appendix B, you can see that this standard involves three global competencies: improve academic self-concept, acquire skills for improving

---

I. ACADEMIC DEVELOPMENT

Standard A: Students will acquire the attitudes, knowledge, and skills that contribute to effective learning in school and across the life span.

Standard B: Students will complete school with the academic preparation essential to choose from a wide range of substantial postsecondary options, including college.

Standard C: Students will understand the relationship of academics to the world of work, and to life at home and in the community.

II. CAREER DEVELOPMENT

Standard A: Students will acquire the skills to investigate the world of work in relation to knowledge of self and to make informed career decisions.

Standard B: Students will employ strategies to achieve future career success and satisfaction.

Standard C: Students will understand the relationship among personal qualities, education and training, and the world of work.

III. PERSONAL/SOCIAL DEVELOPMENT

Standard A: Students will acquire the attitudes, knowledge, and interpersonal skills to help them understand and respect self and others.

Standard B: Students will make decisions, set goals, and take necessary action to achieve goals.

Standard C: Students will understand safety and survival skills.

FIGURE 5.1 *National Standards for School Counseling Programs*

learning, and achieve school success. Each global competency is then further specified in language that allows counselors to evaluate the success of their students and their program in terms of attaining that competency. Dahir, Sheldon, and Valiga (1998) provide implementation strategies for the Standards. They describe the entire *process* for implementing the Standards, building a comprehensive school counseling program from the ground up. The five steps in this process include discussion with all stakeholders in the process, awareness of current school counseling activities and how successful each activity is in terms of students' competencies, designing the actual service components and activities that will meet the Standards, implementation of the service components and activities, and then evaluation of the students' success in the demonstration of the competencies. This mirrors the process we will propose at the end of this chapter.

In the design phase of the process, the authors list activities, services, and program delivery methods that "can be directly or indirectly linked to the student competencies for the nine standards and are based upon the academic, career, and personal/social developmental school counseling domains" (Dahir, Sheldon, & Valiga, 1998, p. 58). The activities include:

1. Individual counseling: Academic program planning (annual reviews), intervention, and academic and attendance intervention.
2. School counseling curriculum (content): Classroom guidance activities.
3. Responsive services: Group counseling, peer mediation programs, and special events, such as career fairs, college nights, and multicultural events.
4. System support: Afterschool academic support programs, honor societies and student recognition activities, and co-curricular and extracurricular activities that encourage student success. (p. 58)

Neither the Role Statement nor the National Standards mandate that all counselors must do all things for all students, parents, teachers, administrators, and community members. These documents outline a system of student competencies by which school counselors can prioritize, design, and evaluate the counseling activities in the school. It is vital that school counselors become knowledgeable about the how the profession defines its role and the standards of effective programs, and then apply those standards to design, implement, and evaluate the school counseling program in their schools and districts.

School Counseling across Elementary, Middle, and Secondary Schools

Until now, we have been discussing school counseling as a whole, without making local distinctions or distinctions among the three educational levels. It is important to note that many states address the time school counselors spend in different activities, and you need to consult your state department of education for those regulations or legislation to understand local requirements and expectations.

While the distinctions among school counseling activities between grade levels are hard to identify, we can see distinctions between the three *levels* of educational progression: elementary, middle school, and secondary school. Gysbers and Henderson (2000) identify time allocations at the three levels, suggesting that counselors at different levels allocate time differently to each of the four activities of curriculum work, individual planning, responsive services, and system support. In order to understand secondary school counseling, we have to discuss school counseling at all levels. However, it is important to remember what we discussed earlier in this chapter about the evolving nature of the school counseling profession; as the needs of students, families, and communities change, so will our role.

Recall from Chapter 4 the concept of developmentally appropriate education. The foundation of that concept is that schools should be built around an understanding of the development of young people and that this understanding should include balanced consideration of academic, social, and emotional needs. It is on this basis that we begin our discussion of developmentally appropriate, comprehensive counseling at the three levels of elementary, middle, and secondary schools (Myrick, 1993).

Elementary counseling encompasses the largest span of a young person's development. This span of development requires counselors to be sensitive to the needs of primary grade students (prekindergarten through third grade) as well as the needs of intermediate grade students (fourth through sixth grades). Elementary students in the primary grades are characterized by their strong ties to primary caregivers, the development of social skills, adjustment to non-home environments and challenges, high need for physical activity, and rapid cognitive development (Charlesworth, 1996). Elementary students in the intermediate grades are characterized by the development of same-sex peer relationships, integration and solidification of prior learning, development of fine motor skills, and exploration of non-family adult relationships (Schickedanz, Schickedanz, Forsyth, & Forsyth, 1998). From these insights into development, it is easy to see why counselors at the elementary grades focus on building healthy self-concept, learning to get along with peers, developing morality and values, achieving personal independence, and developing healthy attitudes toward social groups (Snyder, 2000).

Both the focus of each activity and the amount of time devoted to each activity change according the developmental level of the student. Overall, elementary counselors provide a) behavioral counseling, with an emphasis on play and art in counseling, b) small group counseling focusing on issues and skills specific to elementary development, c) classroom guidance in self-concept and adjustment issues, and d) consultation for parents and teachers (Schmidt, 1999). The focus is more on personal/social development and academic development than on career development (Dollarhide, 2000). According to Gysbers & Henderson (2000), elementary counselors ideally spend approximately 35 to 45 percent of their time in developmental guidance delivered in the classroom, with individual responsive services (counseling, consultation, and referrals) comprising approximately 30 to 40 percent of the counselor's time. Within this broad framework, elementary counselors adjust the amount of time providing individual counseling, depending on the level of language development and capacity for insight of the child (Schmidt, 1999). This would suggest that counselors generally spend more time counseling with intermediate students than with primary graders, due to the older students' greater abilities to understand themselves and their choices.

The middle school student is characterized by "transescence," being caught between childhood and adolescence (B. B. Baker, 2000). This educational phase involves multiple transitions: the transition from small neighborhood elementary schools to larger, more diverse middle or junior high schools, and the transition from childhood to adolescence. Young people at this stage of development struggle with their self-esteem, focus on their status relative to peers, begin to experiment with various behaviors, and develop formal thought processes (Schickedanz, Schickedanz, Forsyth, & Forsyth, 1998). It is at this point that many young people begin to exhibit the signs of troubles to come: eating disorders; unhealthy sexual choices; smoking, drug, and alcohol use; and lack of interest or motivation in schools (Schickedanz, Schickedanz, Forsyth, & Forsyth, 1998), increasing the need for counselors to be proactive and aware of each student's unique challenges.

To address these developmental needs, middle school counselors have to be as flexible and spontaneous as their students are. Typical activities include insight-oriented and rational individual counseling; group counseling (which, given the transescent's focus on peers, is usually highly effective); peer helping and mediation programming; transitional services to ease students from elementary to middle school and then from middle to high school; developmental curriculum on change, sexuality, healthy choices, and conflict resolution; and consultation with teachers, and to a lesser degree, with parents (Schmidt, 1999). Middle school counselors generally distribute their time equitably across issues addressing personal/social development, career development, and academic development (Dollarhide, 2000). Other ways that middle school counseling varies from elementary school counseling include more emphasis on crisis counseling and management and more developmental curriculum involving drug and alcohol education and prevention (B. B. Baker, 2000), realities shared by secondary school counselors.

As you will recall from Chapters 2, 3, and 4, the developmental issues of young people in secondary schools involve the search for identity, independence, self-definition, meaningful relationships, and ways to make a unique contribution to the world. In response, school counselors need to become more aware of their roles as student advocate and environmental assessor, working to enhance the climate of mutual respect in secondary schools. Coy and Sears (2000) identify the primary activities for secondary school counselors as individual counseling, group guidance, group counseling, career development and information services, placement, consultation, and coordination. Similarly, Schmidt (1999) found that counseling, decision making about postsecondary options, providing college information, and helping with class schedules were the most important counseling services as identified by students, parents, and teachers. The focus of secondary counselors often shifts away from personal/social development, to focus instead on career and academic development (Dollarhide, 2000). An evaluation of a counselor's time will help you to understand the implications of these trends.

The priorities of a job can often be inferred from how time is allocated to certain tasks performed by the worker in that job, and studies into how secondary school counselors allocate their time reveals some troubling trends. Secondary school administrators, more than those of elementary or middle schools, seem to impose noncounseling, administrative activities on counselors (Coy & Sears, 2000; Schmidt, 1999). These administrative duties divert time from the comprehensive counseling program activities, and consist of duties most representative of a registrar, vice principal, testing coordinator, special education coordinator, or attendance officer. These duties constitute what Partin (1993) found to be the largest "wasters" of time for secondary counselors: paperwork, scheduling, and administrative tasks.

As we will see in future chapters, administrative tasks need to be evaluated carefully before accepting them as part of the school counseling program. When a comprehensive school counseling program is delineated, the extent to which these duties detract from a focus on students will be a deciding factor in how many, if any, of these duties will be incorporated into the school counseling program. Studies into the actual allocation of time by secondary school counselors suggest the need for careful consideration of activities. Partin (1993, p. 278) found that counselors indicated the following distribution of their time, expressed as a percentage of their day, listed in descending order:

30.96%	—	Individual counseling
17.27%	—	Administrative and clerical tasks
11.47%	—	Guidance activities
11.32%	—	Consultation
8.77%	—	Group counseling
6.68%	—	Testing, appraisal
6.11%	—	Resource coordination
4.55%	—	Professional development
3.98%	—	Other nonguidance activities

These findings are hard to comprehend unless you understand what these time allocations mean to students. How do students feel about the time counselors spend in administrative duties? Wiggins and Moody (1987) found that school counseling programs rated by students as most effective also devoted the highest percentage of time to individual and group counseling. In fact, counselors in the counseling programs rated best by the students were found to spend 71 to 72 percent of their time providing individual and group counseling, and only 11 to 12 percent of their time in administrative and clerical tasks. Conversely, in programs rated as below average by students, the amount of time in administrative tasks rose to 24 to 43 percent of the counselors' time. In a study of students' needs, Hutchinson and Bottorff (1986) found that 89 percent of students reported needing career counseling; only 40 percent reported they received it. Similarly, 60 percent reported needing counseling for personal issues; only 21 percent received the counseling they needed. It is clear from these insights that counselors' time is precious and needed by students, but that without a clear, coherent program that provides the conceptual frame for the counselors' efforts, school counselors' time can be siphoned off into other activities.

Reflection Moment

Can you see the different ways that school counselors function at various levels? With which age group do you see yourself functioning most effectively? How much does the work of a secondary school counselor appeal to you? Why?

The Domains/Activities/Partners Model of Comprehensive School Counseling

Overview

One consistent theme in each of the models of comprehensive school counseling is that school counselors must have a systematic way of understanding their work in order to design programmatic interventions, prioritize conflicting demands on time, and evaluate both their effectiveness and that of their program (S. B. Baker, 2000; Coy & Sears, 1993; Gysbers & Henderson, 2000; Schmidt, 1999, Wittmer, 2000). To that end, we have designed a model that serves a variety of purposes: It increases the emphasis on students while concurrently reducing the emphasis on nonstudent-focused activities and provides a systematic way of thinking about the work of the school counselor.

Called the Domains/Activities/Partners (DAP) Model, the model outlines the domains of student competencies that focus the work of the counselor and the program, the activities in which school counselors engage to facilitate the students' success in those competencies, and the partnerships that are crucial to the success of our students, our programs, and our schools. (See Figures 5.2 and 5.3.) As you can see, the Domains define our work

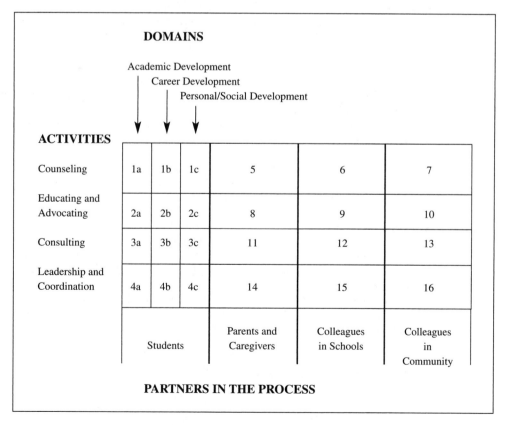

FIGURE 5.2 *Domains/Activities/Partners Model*

1a: Academic counseling with students
1b: Career counseling with students
1c: Personal/Social counseling with students

2a: Educating students about academic issues (developmental curriculum) and advocating academic excellence with students
2b: Educating students about career issues and advocating pursuit of career dreams
2c: Educating students about personal/social issues and advocating personal/social excellence

3a: Consulting with students about academic issues (e.g., how to work with certain teachers)
3b: Consulting with students about career issues (e.g., using computer career software)
3c: Consulting with students about personal/social issues (e.g., how to get along better with family members)

4a: Coordinating academic events for students (e.g., study skills workshops or presentations)
4b: Coordinating career activities for students (e.g., career fairs, school-to-work programs)
4c: Coordinating personal/social activities for students (e.g., serving as the advisor of a student group)

5:     Counseling with parents and caregivers, as appropriate, then referrals
6:     Counseling with colleagues in schools, as appropriate, then referrals
7:     Counseling with colleagues in the community, as appropriate, then referrals

8:     Educating parents and caregivers about students, school, careers, and advocating on behalf of students
9:     Educating colleagues in schools about developmental issues of students and advocating on behalf of students
10:     Educating colleagues in the community about developmental issues of students and advocating on behalf of students

11:     Consulting with parents and caregivers about problems with students and/or school
12:     Consulting with colleagues in schools about developmental issues of students
13:     Consulting with colleagues in the community about developmental issues of students

14:     Leadership in making the school a respectful place for parents and coordinating services for parents as appropriate (e.g., assisting with a parent resource room)
15:     Leadership in making the school a respectful place for students and coordinating information for the school and district administrators about the school counseling program; administrative tasks as appropriate
16:     Leadership in making others aware of the needs of the school community and coordinating efforts of community colleagues who support the school (e.g., coordinating the mental health staffing for students who are in therapy in the community)

FIGURE 5.3   *Domains/Activities/Partners Model, Detail*

with students, but each activity is nonetheless applicable to each of the Partners in the model. Figure 5.3 gives a description of each unit in the model, based on how the model would be used in a secondary school, to help you conceptualize how each unit of the model would appear in practice.

Domains (Academic, Career, and Personal/Social Development) Consistent with the ASCA National Standards (Campbell & Dahir, 1997), the Domains of the model consist of the student competencies promulgated in that document. Counselors designing programs for their school and district would insert those competencies (see Appendix B), and those prioritized within their district, to define the primary focus of their comprehensive school counseling program (see pages 97–99 on the process of designing your comprehensive school counseling program). Even though these Domains only pertain to work done directly with students, the Domains within the Student Partner column are the most important priority of the comprehensive school counseling program.

Activities (Counseling, Educating and Advocating, Consulting, and Leadership and Coordination) Appropriate school counselor activities have been described as counseling, developmental curriculum programming, consulting, referral, coordinating, providing information (advising), enhancing transitions, assessment/appraisal, and system support of public relations, committee service, and community outreach (ASCA, 1999; S. B. Baker, 2000; Gysbers & Henderson, 2000; Schmidt, 1999). We have tried to synthesize these insights into four activities: Counseling, Educating and Advocating, Consulting, and Leadership and Coordination. We believe that these four terms incorporate the activities of the other models, in that:

1. *Counseling* refers to individual and group counseling, as well as making referrals as a means of bringing closure to counseling relationships. It is listed first as the foundation of the comprehensive school counseling philosophy, and as the most essential activity that students indicate they want from the school counselor (Hutchinson & Bottorff, 1986; Wiggins & Moody, 1987).
2. *Educating* refers to developmental curriculum, facilitating transitions, advisement, placement, and assessment and appraisal. In addition, this term, more than the term "guidance," accurately describes what counselors do in the schools, as well as clearly describes how comprehensive school counseling allies with the mission of the school. *Advocating* refers to activities that educate with passion, those activities that enhance others' affective understanding of, and empathy for, students, schools, families, the comprehensive school counseling program, and better human relationships. It includes, as ASCA (1999) points out, championing what is best for students, their families, schools, and the community.
3. *Consulting* refers to problem solving, referring, enhancing communications, and mediation. We feel this activity is a hybrid between counseling and educating, requiring specialized skills that are unique.
4. *Leadership* involves several areas: developing and maintaining the vision of the comprehensive school counseling program and promoting the importance of a

developmentally appropriate learning environment. *Coordination* refers to the management of logistics to bring programs to the partners of the school counselor. These two activities are connected in that they both include management activities to provide information to the school and the district about the program, general outreach and public relations, school/professional/community committee service, and programs that reach a large audience of students, such as career fairs.

Partners (Students, Parents, Colleagues in the School, and Colleagues in the Community)   It is vital that you understand why we have chosen the concept of "partnership" in discussing the people involved in the comprehensive school counseling program. First, it is important to reinforce the collegial, collaborative, and egalitarian nature of the relationships counselors must develop with everyone in the school setting. Second, we hope to reinforce the active nature of the participation in school counseling programs; counseling, educating/advocating, consulting, and leading/coordinating are all active, intentional behaviors, both for the counselor and for others in the process. Third, it is important that the counselor remember that, as stated in Chapter 1, it takes a whole community to raise a child. Similarly, it takes an entire community to educate healthy and resilient young people; no one person can do it alone. So no one school counselor, no matter how talented and dedicated that person may be, can be the only helping professional for our students. We must reach out and establish these broad, inclusive partnerships for the students' benefit. None of the work of the school counselor could happen without our partners in the process.

Our primary partner is the student. At its most fundamental level, school counseling would not occur without the students; their development is the very essence of the comprehensive school counseling program. By calling them a partner in the process, we hope to convey that they, too, are stakeholders in the program; their involvement in the program, in many cases, is voluntary, and so we can't take for granted that they will avail themselves of the services we have to offer. We must actively solicit their continued involvement.

Our second partners are parents and caregivers. While the nature of the work we do with parents is unique (as we will see), we also must remember that they, too, have a stake in the school counseling program (Schmidt, 1999). Involvement of the student is contingent on parental approval (depending on the age and circumstance), so we cannot forget that, by extension, parents impact whether we have students with whom to work. Their involvement is essential (Colbert, 1996).

Our third partners are our colleagues in the schools. Teachers, administrators, school social workers, school psychologists, school nurses, and the administrative staff are very involved with how our program functions and how effective we can be. By extension, this includes professionals from other schools, at the district level, and in the school counseling profession as a whole.

Finally, we have partners in the community. From the mental health professional who provides therapy, to the physician who provides medication, to the local businessperson who provides jobs, these stakeholders need to be included in the school counseling program.

As we will see in upcoming chapters, this model is useful in understanding comprehensive school counseling programs for secondary schools.

Designing Your Comprehensive School Counseling Program

A template or model from which to shape your program is incomplete without having the process by which to implement it. The DAP model forms the skeleton of your program, and your individual school process will flesh out priorities within the program. The process for designing your comprehensive school counseling program involves the following steps.

Step One: Select members of an advisory committee. The size of the group will need to be carefully considered to maximize the ability for members to meet as a group over several meetings. This advisory committee should consist of representatives of each group of partners:

1. Students: Select student representatives from all areas, not just the areas that are already well represented in school structures. For example, select students from honors groups, athletics, the vo-tech program, frequent detention attendees, music, theater, and other student venues.
2. Parents and caregivers: Select parent and caregiver representatives from all economic strata of your attendance area, including those who are in shelters and/or homeless (Strawser, Markos, Yamaguchi, & Higgins, 2000).
3. Colleagues in the schools: Select representatives from teachers, aides, administrators, and other pupil services professionals. Go outside your school building to invite counselors from your feeder middle schools and counselors from other high schools in your area. In addition, you will want to invite representatives from the district level of administration, perhaps including the director of pupil services and even a representative from the school board itself.
4. Colleagues in the community: Invite representatives from employers, community mental health providers, counselors from postsecondary educational options, and representatives from trades-training options (such as apprenticeship programs and the armed services).

There are several purposes of this group. First, they will assist you in the design of the comprehensive school counseling program. Second, they will guide you as you implement the program as designed. Third, they will assist you in the assessment and evaluation of your program as time passes, so it is imperative that your advisory group is comprised of people who are committed to and understand developmentally appropriate schools, young people, and school counseling.

Step Two: In consultation with your advisory committee, conduct a comprehensive needs assessment to assess current needs of all stakeholders in the program. The assessment instrument would be administered to all partners: students, parents, colleagues in the school, and colleagues in the community, through random sampling and mailing to parents and the community, and administration to students and staff in the school (Scruggs, Wasielewski, & Ash, 1999). In the assessment instrument, respondents would be asked to rate *both student and adult competencies* in three ways: (1) currently, (2) at the minimum level, and (3) at the ideal level. Using predefined competencies will help you in the design of this assessment instrument; both student and adult competencies are described in appendices included for your reference. For student competencies, the ASCA National Standards for School Counseling Practice are presented as Appendix B. For adult competencies, a suggested list of goals is presented as Appendix C.

Focus groups (Scruggs, Wasielewski, & Ash, 1999) comprised of each group of partners within the advisory committee (students, parents, colleagues in the school, and colleagues in the community) would provide you the opportunity to gather additional information relative to ranking each of the competencies. Furthermore, the focus groups provide you with the opportunity to educate members of these focus groups about counseling, educating and advocating, consulting, and leadership/coordinating activities. Once you feel they understand the four activities of the model, you can ascertain how each group ranks the four activities as priorities. Compile the results of the needs assessment in terms of each of the partner groups.

Step Three: Using small-group discussion both within their partner sphere and as a larger group, allow the advisory committee to design a mission statement for the new program (Gysbers & Henderson, 2000). Within this mission statement, the advisory committee will articulate the role of your counseling program relative to the academic mission of the school, a statement of the purpose of your program in terms of academic, career, and personal/social development of students, and the professional and ethical standards by which the program will be operated.

Your role with this group is as educator and facilitator. The first item on your agenda for your first meeting will be to provide them with information relative to comprehensive school counseling, the Domain/Activities/Partners model, and the nature of high school students. Realistically, the advisory committee will struggle if it is asked to create such a comprehensive statement without any input from you, so plan to provide a draft with some basic ideas to begin discussions. Allow the discussions to follow their own course, but it is important to remember that you are the professional school counselor; you will need to facilitate the design of a document that reflects your professional training, ethics, and philosophy.

Step Four: Once the mission statement is completed, the advisory committee will now factor in the results of the needs assessment process from Step One. The desired results of this step would be a profile of the needs of each partner group, as seen through the lens of the mission statement. The advisory committee will now help you to articulate your program priorities in terms of each square of the DAP model. These priorities will be stated in terms of what you will do in each block of the DAP model—it is a list of activities for each partner in the model. As an example, consider Figure 5.3: Domains/Activities/Partners Model Detail. For your program design process, you would ask the advisory committee to prioritize the list of activities in Figure 5.3.

It might be helpful to address the model in two phases for this process: have the committee prioritize the activities and domains for students first, then address the activities relative to the other three partner groups as a secondary focus. This reinforces the consistent message that students should come first as you design your program. This also reduces the chance that the advisory board will overfocus on one domain over the others (for example, careers) or that the administrative tasks of coordinating activities for colleagues in the school will be overemphasized.

Step Five: Now that the program priorities have been established, you and the advisory board will design the goals for each aspect of the program. Your goals for your students will address academic, career, and personal/social competencies, such as those described in the National Standards found in Appendix B of this book. As you can see in Appendix B, each goal is stated in terms of standards, which are then broken down into individual student competencies. (For a comprehensive discussion of student competencies, see Gysbers & Henderson, 2000, pp. 327–334.) Furthermore, Appendix C is a similar list of goals, but these goals are stated in terms of the adult partners in the DAP model. Using Appendix B (the National Standards for Student Competencies) and Appendix C (Goals for Adult Partners), you and the advisory board can design the goals for each block of the DAP model as prioritized in the preceding step.

Step Six: Once each goal is articulated, you and the board will outline a basic outcomes assessment plan. The means of collecting outcomes information needs to be built into your program and will be discussed in more detail in Chapter 14.

Step Seven: Once the advisory board has helped you identify the program priorities, goals, and outcomes assessment strategies, the budget and resource discussions will begin. This is often a very difficult part of the process, and involves allowing the priorities emerging from the advisory group to guide in the construction of a new budget. Try to focus the committee on building a new budget based on need (called a "zero-based budget"), not on adjusting the old budget. Once the new budget has been established, then talks can take place within the district on ways to meet this ideal budget, or on plans to move toward that ideal budget incrementally. If it is clear that there is no way to fund the new budget, then the committee needs to know that so that it can reprioritize activities on the basis of the actual budget.

Step Eight: You will now compile all this input and synthesize it into five parts: a comprehensive mission statement, a program overview stated in terms of priorities within the DAP model, the goals for each part of the program, an outcomes assessment strategy for each part of the program, and the budget and resources to meet those priorities.

Step Nine: You will now present this final product to the advisory committee for its final input and approval. Exceptions and reactions to your program will be noted and will become part of the guiding process for the next year's advisory committee meeting. You will need to collect data on outcomes measures (evaluating program goals for each partner in the DAP model and assessing student competencies) throughout the year, which will then become part of the improvement process for your program discussed in Chapter 14.

Step Ten: Once you have the approval of the advisory committee, these documents should be presented to the administration of your school and district. Even if you have involved administrators and district representatives on your advisory committee, you must present your findings to the formal leaders of your district and secure their support.

Chapter Summary

Comprehensive school counseling comes from a rich heritage comprised of various ways to work with young people to enhance school success. Historically, school counseling developed to facilitate young people's transition into careers, and the primary activity to accomplish that goal was advisement, which came to be known as guidance. As mental health counseling theory evolved, school counselors became focused on providing therapeutic services in the schools; however, school counselors then found themselves critical of the limitations that one-on-one counseling created in terms of time. Prevention soon emerged as more effective than intervention and remediation, and awareness of developmental needs and schoolwide education in academic, career, and emotional issues resulted in the emergence of the developmental guidance movement. From this movement, school counseling has now emerged as comprehensive school counseling as defined by the American School Counselor Association (ASCA). An examination of ASCA's role statement and National Standards help define what school counselors do and what the outcomes of their efforts should be.

To fully appreciate the complexities of comprehensive school counseling, you must also understand how counseling programs change at each educational level. At the elementary level, counselors often spend more time in classroom developmental guidance and consultation than is spent in individual counseling, addressing issues of social skill development and the building of appropriate academic habits and skills. At the middle school level, counselors often increase the amount of time they spend in individual and group counseling and in classroom developmental guidance, addressing issues of healthy choices, behaviors, and transitions. Middle school counselors usually address all three domains equally. At the secondary school level, school counselors are often challenged to find time to enter classrooms, finding group and individual counseling, administrative duties, postsecondary decision making, and advisement to be their most common activities. While many current counselors report that they spend more time in activities related to career and academic development than they do in activities related to personal and social development, there is a strong argument that secondary students need counselors to focus on all three domains. There are often large discrepancies between the realities of an individual counselor's day and the ideal amount of time recommended in each activity. The better educated you are in appropriate ways for counselors to spend their time, the better prepared you will be to articulate how your comprehensive school counseling program should be structured.

The Domains/Activities/Partners model was introduced as a way to define comprehensive school counseling. In this model, the Domains are academic, career, and personal/social development; the Activities are counseling, educating and advocating, consulting, and leading and coordinating; and the Partners are students, parents or caregivers, colleagues in the schools, and colleagues in the community.

Finally, a step-by-step process was provided to assist you in the design of your own comprehensive school counseling program, which will produce your mission statement, a program overview, program goals stated in terms of student competencies and goals for the adult partners in the DAP model, outcomes assessment strategies for each part of the program, and the budget for the program, all of which will be used in the management of your program.

A Day in the Life Revisited: Integration

Now that you've read the chapter,

1. What would you say is Marcia's most pressing challenge? Does she need career counseling, more counselors to help her, or a model of school counseling to help her make sense of the conflicting demands on her time?
2. What three questions would you ask Marcia to facilitate her thinking about her job in a more healthy, balanced way?
3. Given what you know about school counseling at the other levels of school counseling, would you see her as being happier at another educational level? What does she say that makes you think she might be happier as an elementary counselor? What does she say that makes you think she might be happier as a middle school counselor?
4. Compare her description of her job with the Domains/Activities/Partners model of comprehensive school counseling. How would the use of that model help her?

Application

1. This chapter addresses various philosophies of school counseling, from career guidance, to mental health, to developmental guidance, to comprehensive school counseling. Which one is most consistent with your own philosophy of school counseling? In what ways? Which one is the least similar? In what ways?

2. School counselors allocate time to various activities for a variety of reasons. Contact an elementary school counselor, a middle school counselor, and a high school counselor and ask them how they allocate their time while they're at work. Find out not only what they spend their time doing, and how much time they spend doing it, but also why they spend that amount of time on that activity. When there are conflicting demands on their time, how do they prioritize their efforts? What criteria do they use to determine high priority activities?

3. Review Figure 5.3, the Domains/Activities/Partners Model Details. Can you think of example activities in an elementary school to fit each of the units? Can you think of example activities in a middle school to fit each of the units?

4. Again using Figure 5.3, the Domains/Activities/Partners Model Details, what will be your favorite activities? Why? What will be your least favorite activities? Why? What will you do to help you cope with your least favorite activities (assuming that opting out of those activities is not an option for you as a professional)?

5. Search the Internet using "school counseling" as your keyword. How many hits do you get? Visit several of those sites, recording them for sharing with the class. What did you find there? How well did those sites fit the picture you have in your mind about school counseling? How well did they fit the DAP model? Visit the website of a local high school. What message does that site send about what they do? In other words, how would you describe their school counseling program based on their website?

6. Design a website for the perfect comprehensive school counseling program, using the DAP model as your template.

Suggested Readings

American School Counselor Association (1999). *The role of the professional school counselor.* Alexandria, VA: Author. Retrieved May 31, 2000, from the World Wide Web: http://www.schoolcounselor.org/role.htm. This resource, provided by ASCA, outlines the role and expectations of professional school counselors.

Campbell, C. A., & Dahir, C. A. (1997). *Sharing the vision: The national standards for school counseling programs.* Alexandria, VA: American School Counselor Association. Every school counselor must be aware of the national standards for counseling programs and should use these standards in designing their programs.

Dahir, C. A., Sheldon, C. B., & Valiga, M. J. (1998). *Vision into action: Implementing the national standards for school counseling programs.* Alexandria, VA: American School Counselor Association. The companion resource for the implementation of the national standards.

Gysbers, N. C., & Henderson, P. (2000). *Developing and managing your school guidance program* (3rd ed.). Alexandria, VA: American Counseling Association. This resource addresses the programmatic concerns of initiating change in the school system to move toward coherent school counseling programs.

References

American School Counselor Association (ASCA). (1999). *The role of the professional school counselor.* Alexandria, VA: Author. Retrieved May 31, 2000, from the World Wide Web: *http://www.school counselor.org/role.htm.*

Baker, B. B. (2000). Middle school counseling in the new millennium: A practitioner's perspective. In J. Wittmer (Ed.), *Managing your school counseling program: K–12 developmental strategies* (2nd ed.; pp. 49–55). Minneapolis, MN: Educational Media.

Baker, S. B. (2000). *School counseling for the twenty-first century* (3rd ed.). Upper Saddle River, NJ: Merrill.

Campbell, C. A., & Dahir, C. A. (1997). *Sharing the vision: The national standards for school counseling programs.* Alexandria, VA: American School Counselor Association.

Charlesworth, R. (1996). *Understanding child development* (4th ed.). Albany, NY: Delmar.

Colbert, R. D. (1996). The counselor's role in advancing school and family partnerships. *School Counselor, 44* (2), 100–104.

Coy, D., & Sears, S. (2000). The scope of practice of the high school counselor. In J. Wittmer (Ed.), *Managing your school counseling program: K–12 developmental strategies* (2nd ed.; pp. 56–67). Minneapolis, MN: Educational Media.

Dahir, C. A., Sheldon, C. B., & Valiga, M. J. (1998). *Vision into action: Implementing the national standards for school counseling programs.* Alexandria, VA: American School Counselor Association.

Dollarhide, C. T. (2000, April). *How do school counselors allocate their time?* Paper presented at the meeting of the Tri-County School Counselors Consortium, Whitewater, WI.

Gysbers, N. C., & Henderson, P. (2000). *Developing and managing your school guidance program* (3rd ed.). Alexandria, VA: American Counseling Association.

Hine, T. (1999). *The rise and fall of the American teenager.* New York: Bard.

Hoyt, K. B. (1993). Guidance is not a dirty word. *The School Counselor, 40,* 267–273.

Hutchinson, R. L., & Bottorff, R. L. (1986). Selected high school counseling services: Student assessment. *The School Counselor, 33,* 350–354.

Myrick, R. D. (1993). *Developmental guidance and counseling: A practical approach* (2nd ed.). Minneapolis, MN: Educational Media Corporation.

Olson, L. (1999, April 21). Tugging at tradition: Lessons of a century. *Education Week,* pp. 25–29, 30–31.

Paisley, P. O., & Hubbard, G. T. (1994). *Developmental school counseling programs: From theory to practice.* Alexandria, VA: American Counseling Association.

Paisley, P. O., & Peace, S. D. (1995). Developmental principles: A framework for school counseling programs. *Elementary School Counseling & Guidance, 30*(2), 85–93.

Partin, R. L. (1993). School counselors' time: Where does it go? *The School Counselor, 40,* 274–281.

Schickedanz, J. A., Schickedanz, D. I., Forsyth, P. D., & Forsyth, C. A. (1998). *Understanding children and adolescents* (3rd ed.). Boston: Allyn and Bacon.

Schmidt, J. J. (1999). *Counseling in schools: Essential services and comprehensive programs* (3rd ed.). Boston: Allyn and Bacon.

Scruggs, M. Y, Wasielewski, R. A., & Ash, M. J. (1999). Comprehensive evaluation of a K–12 counseling program. *Professional School Counseling*, *2*, 244–247.

Smith, S. L., & Archer, J. (2000). The developmental school counselor and mental health counseling. In J. Wittmer (Ed.), *Managing your school counseling program: K–12 developmental strategies* (2nd ed.; pp. 68–74). Minneapolis, MN: Educational Media.

Snyder, B. A. (2000). Managing an elementary school developmental counseling program: The role of the counselor. In J. Wittmer (Ed.), *Managing your school counseling program: K12 developmental strategies* (2nd ed.; pp. 37–48). Minneapolis, MN: Educational Media.

Strawser, S., Markos, P. A., Yamaguchi, B. J., & Higgins, K. (2000). A new challenge for school counselors: Children who are homeless. *Professional School Counseling*, *3*, 162–171.

Wiggins, J. D., & Moody, A. H. (1987). Student evaluations of counseling programs: An added dimension. *The School Counselor*, *34*, 353–361.

Wittmer, J. (2000). Section One: Developmental school counseling: History, reconceptualization, and implementation strategies. In J. Wittmer (Ed.), *Managing your school counseling program: K–12 developmental strategies* (2nd ed.; pp. 1–34). Minneapolis, MN: Educational Media.

6

The Domains

Colette T. Dollarhide

"What scares me most about my future? I don't know what I want to do. I'm extremely afraid of failure and not being able to achieve my goals."

Angie, age 15

Learning Objectives _____

By the end of this chapter, you will be able to:

1. Understand the reason school counselors must know how to navigate the developmental domains on behalf of students.

2. Understand the developmental domain of academic development, with a comprehensive understanding of the presenting issues and several models of academic functioning.

3. Understand the developmental domain of career development, with a comprehensive understanding of the presenting issues and several models of career functioning.

4. Understand the developmental domain of personal/social development, with a comprehensive understanding of the presenting issues and several models of personal/social functioning.

A Day in the Life of a Counselor: Mr. Paulson Counseling Ty

Mr. Paulson was finishing up some paperwork before the bell rang to start the day, when Ty came into the office. "Mr. Paulson, can I see you today?" he asked.

"Yeah, Ty. Sure. What's up? Do you want to meet now?" He gestured to the chair by his desk when he saw Ty's face. "Have a seat."

He paused to keep himself from swearing. "What happened to your face? Who did this to you?" Instinctively, he began to reach up to the young man's face, but withdrew his hand when Ty pulled away.

"You know, man. The streets are a bitch." Ty paused. "That's not why I'm here. I'm getting pressure at home to get another job to help out more with the bills. I hate working at the burger place, but I do it to help out Momma. Now how'm I gonna get the grades to get into college if I'm working two jobs? I'm already struggling in my science class and Miss Epps tells me I'm barely pulling a C. Now this.

"Maybe I should just give up the college thing anyway. Everyone tells me that I won't make it, because I don't know what I want to study. They think it's a waste of time. But I wanted to go just to get the hell out of the city. I don't think I'll have any life at all if I stay here—just end up selling drugs like everybody else does. There aren't any jobs here, the ones that are here don't pay anything, and I don't want to live with my mom the rest of my life.

"And then there's this," he says as he points to the cuts and bruises on his face. "I'm sick of being called a 'nigger.' I'm just not going to take it any more. My momma wants me to turn the other cheek, but how can I ever call myself a man if I don't stand up for myself and what I believe in?"

Challenge Questions

What are your reactions as you picture Ty? What questions came to your mind? What would you like to say to Ty? Where would you begin in your conversation with him? What do you think Mr. Paulson should do? What do you see as Ty's biggest challenges? What will be the most helpful for him right now? In the long run? Are those different issues or not? What grade level did you assume Ty to be? What would your reaction be if Ty is a senior? A junior? How would your reaction be different if Ty were a freshman?

Comprehensive School Counseling and the Domains

As we saw in Chapter 5, school counselors are charged with an awesome task: facilitating the academic, career, and personal/social development of young people in our schools. To help clarify how you can accomplish this, the Domains/Activities/Partners (DAP) model was presented. This model suggests that your work with students will be focused on the three domains of academic development, career development, and personal/social development.

As you recall from Chapters 2, 3, and 4, the overall development of young people depends on so many factors: biological, social, familial, and educational. Now we need to take the insights you gained from those chapters and apply them to young people in secondary schools to breathe life into what is meant by academic development, career development, and personal/social development. In order to facilitate a student's development, you must know what issues are unique to secondary schools in each domain. Then, you need to know what the experts say about those issues.

We would like you to think of this chapter as a roadmap. In Chapter 1, we discussed the outcomes of excellent education: That is our destination. To get to that destination, our students must maximize their personal potential in each area: academic success, career success, and personal/social success. This chapter is designed to help you understand where students are headed with their development and how to help your students achieve the most within each domain. (See the chapters at the end of this book for an in-depth discussion of problems that arise when development does not go well for students.)

Academic Development: The "a" Column of the Domains

There is no doubt that the mission of the school is academic development—the lifelong ability to acquire and use new information, new insights, and new ways of seeing and interacting with the world. Addressing academic development as the first domain is a confirmation of the partnership between secondary school counselors and the educational mission of the institution.

Why is a counselor expected to be knowledgeable about academic issues? Being an effective partner in the educational process requires that counselors be able to effectively help students with the mission of the institution. This begs the question: To be effective, must the school counselor also have teaching experience? The perception has been (and in some states, continues to be) that former teachers make the best school counselors (Farwell, 1961; Fredrickson & Pippert, 1964; Hudson, 1961; Rochester & Cottingham, 1966; Tooker, 1957). In studies of the perceptions of administrators, recent studies suggested that teaching experience was not a predictor of a counselor's success (Beale, 1995; Dilley, Foster, & Bowers, 1973; Olson & Allen, 1993). However, teachers themselves might still perceive counselors with teaching experience as more effective (Quarto, 1999). Rather than accept this conclusion fatalistically, school counselors should accept that it is their expertise in *academic issues* that will establish their credibility in the school, and they should be willing to develop this expertise in response.

The following issues are representative of the kinds of problems raised by students as they struggle in this domain.

Issues

Learning Success   One of the many academic issues that students bring to school counselors involves their levels of success in academics. Academic success brings many blessings to students: access to scholarships, extracurricular activities, special programs such as tutoring and being a teacher's assistant, and many nontangible benefits such as mentoring relationships with teachers. The lack of academic success, on the other hand, can result in institutional punishment: denial of extracurricular activities, threats of repeating courses and/or graduating late, and shaming, indifference, or outright hostility in the classroom. For some students, this outcome feeds into an antischool peer values system, reinforcing academic failure. For other students, this outcome causes frustration and concern, which then manifests in a variety of presenting problems that brings them into the counselor's office. As dropout rates increase with increased academic failure (McWhirter, McWhirter, McWhirter, & McWhirter, 1998), counselors are often called upon to help students who are at risk for failure, retention, and/or dropout. Knowledge of academic development helps counselors monitor for academic success and to assist students who are at risk.

Academic Advisement and Postsecondary Options   One of the duties assigned to many secondary counselors involves academic advisement (Herr, 1996; Isaacson & Brown, 1997; Schmidt, 1999). In this context, the counselor is responsible for helping students select appropriate courses that will culminate in graduation. Further expectations in this area include appropriate advisement for postsecondary academic options. Knowledge of academic development helps counselors to understand the nature of learning, assist students to become aware of learning styles, and help students maintain progress toward graduation.

Academic Mediation   Many problems are brought to the counselor that involve dissonance between teaching style and learning style. This dissonance in styles usually results in the impending academic failure of the student. In these cases, the counselor serves as a mediator in an attempt to help both the teacher and the student understand the style of the other. Counselors help students understand their learning style in an attempt to improve their academic performance. To help teachers understand students better, counselors advocate for students and consult with teachers. More will be said about these counseling functions in Chapter 12 (Educating and Advocating with Parents, Colleagues in the School, and Colleagues in the Community) and in Chapter 13 (Consulting with Parents, Colleagues in the School, and Colleagues in the Community).

Assessment   Baker (2000) believes that "assessment remains an important school counseling function" (p. 271), but he laments the use of assessment for what he considers nonlegitimate (namely, noncounseling) purposes (p. 272). Many high school counselors are charged with the responsibility for conducting the achievement tests that are increasingly mandated by school districts (Baker, 2000; Schmidt, 1999). Whether appropriate or not (we will address the extent to which this responsibility is appropriate in Chapter 14), the fact remains that the ability to understand and make use of the assessment results depends on the extent to which counselors understand academic development. Just as in the case of learning success, students are at greater risk of dropping out of high school if they do not perceive themselves as academically successful.

Time Management, Life Management   Some academic issues are really issues of time management and life management, not academic issues per se. If a student is failing, it might not be due to poor study habits or learning styles that are inconsistent with the teacher's teaching style. Sometimes the academic problems are a result of other priorities that take precedence over academics: work, sports, social time, or extracurricular activities. Young people in high school have many competing demands on their time, and academics might not be their highest priority at that point in their lives. It's also important to recognize that not all students come to counselors because they are failing. Sometimes they come with academic issues that stem from being too driven to succeed or too perfectionistic. While presenting as an academic issue, these issues are, underneath, issues of personal/social development.

Models

The following models are presented to give you an overview of ways to think about the learning of young people. They are not the only ways to conceptualize academic development, but are presented as a means of thinking about how young people learn and ways to help young people be more successful academically.

Learning Styles   In the most basic models of learning, academic success or failure is a result of input (the relative efficiency of various ways individuals acquire and attend to information to be stored) and output (the relative efficiency of various ways individuals recall and communicate the information they have stored). Notice the almost mechanical "feel" to the model; this is not accidental. The closest metaphor for these models is the computer: Intellectual processes that allow information to be acquired, stored, and retrieved with minimal loss are considered the most elegant and efficient.

One way of conceptualizing learning preferences involves internal versus external orientation. For some students, information about the world comes from external reality as accessed through the five senses of touch, taste, sight, sound, and smell. For others, information about the world comes from the internal world of perception, intuition, and connections. Both the Myers-Briggs Type Indicator (Briggs & Myers, 1998) and the Keirsey-Bates (Berens, 1988; Keirsey, 1974) capture this most basic orientation to learning in the S/N continuum. In this score, the "S" represents "sensing," the external orientation, in which the student trusts information that comes from the external world through the five senses. Conversely, the "N" represents "iNtuition" [sic], in which the score represents a preference for information that is discovered, intuited, or inferred. Implications for helping students involve an understanding of how the student orients him- or herself to what is to be learned. For those with an external orientation, information that is outside of self and acquired from an expert other would be more readily accepted. Conversely, for those students with an internal orientation, discovery and intuitive insights are more trusted and valued.

Another way of thinking about learning is described by Dunn, Dunn, and Price (1996) and Dunn and Griggs (1988). Providing a comprehensive inventory of learning modalities, their Learning Styles Inventory (LSI) assesses a wide variety of conditions in which learning takes place. First, the assessment gives students a chance to reflect on the physical environment in which their learning is maximized: ambient noise level, lighting, temperature, physical environment (formal with chair and table or informal with places to recline), preferences of intake of food during studying, the time of day that they prefer to study, and the amount of mobility they need to feel alert while studying. Second, students are assessed on their qualities, such as their motivation level, persistence level, responsibility for learning, and need for structure in directions and assignments. Third, students are asked to reflect on social influences that affect their learning, in terms of whether they learn better alone or with peers, and whether they learn better with authority figures present (and if so motivated, whether they are parent-motivated or teacher-motivated). Next, students respond to preferred sensory input(s) to define the unique sensory constellation to which they ascribe effective learning: auditory, visual, tactile, or kinesthetic (also known as experiential, where the whole body is used to learn), and if they prefer variety or consistency of stimuli. In the LSI, each score is represented on a continuum. Furthermore, group summaries can be generated to give counselors, teachers, and administrators information relative to the learning styles and needs of groups, classes, or entire schools.

The purpose of presenting this information is not to promote the use of the LSI; rather, Dunn, Dunn, and Price (1996) and Dunn and Griggs (1988) present an important way to help students think about their best learning by reflecting on a variety of factors that enhance their ability to perform academically.

Multiple Intelligences   The traditional definition of intelligence as a univariate construct, the "individual's capacity or innate potential for learning," has been challenged for a number of years (Travers, Elliott, & Kratochwill, 1993, p. 231). What has replaced this elementary definition of a complex construct are various models, both psychometric and practical (Esters & Ittenbach, 1999).

Based on the work of Howard Gardner (Gardner, 1983; Gardner & Hatch, 1989; Lazear, 1999), one practical and useful model for understanding academic development involves understanding the concept of multiple intelligences. According to Gardner, an intelligence involves the ability to solve a problem or create something that has meaning in a particular context, and it is this view of intelligence as related to *context* that is unique and powerful. Gardner asserts that individuals possess the full spectrum of intelligences as identified in his writings, but that individuals have natural strengths that bring one or more of these strengths into use more often than the others. Furthermore, the issue of context becomes important in that individuals choose to access certain intelligences based on context and situation.

This perspective on intelligence is particularly useful for understanding why a student learns (motivation and predilection for learning), how a student learns (acquisition and retention of information), as well as how a student manifests that learning has taken place (performance on academic tasks). In other words, when you understand an individual's unique constellation of intelligences, you can understand why that student is interested in certain subjects, how the student learns, and how the student might prefer to demonstrate her or his understanding of the subject learned.

As you can see from Figure 6.1, the intelligences include verbal/linguistic intelligence, logical/mathematical intelligence, visual spatial intelligence, bodily/kinesthetic intelligence, musical/rhythmic intelligence, interpersonal intelligence, intrapersonal intelligence, and

Verbal/linguistic intelligence is responsible for the production of language and all the complex possibilities that follow, including poetry, humor, storytelling, grammar, metaphors, similes, abstract reasoning, symbolic thinking, conceptual patterning, reading, and writing. This intelligence can be seen in such people as poets, playwrights, storytellers, novelists, public speakers, and comedians.

Logical/mathematical intelligence is most often associated with what we call scientific thinking or inductive reasoning, although deductive thought processes are also involved. This intelligence involves the capacity to recognize patterns, work with abstract symbols (such as numbers and geometric shapes), and discern relationships and/or see connections between separate and distinct pieces of information. This intelligence can be seen in such people as scientists, computer programmers, accountants, lawyers, bankers, and of course, mathematicians.

    The logical/mathematical and verbal/linguistic intelligences form the basis for most systems of Western education, as well as for all forms of currently existing standardized testing programs.

Visual spatial intelligence deals with visual arts (including painting, drawing, and sculpting); navigation, mapmaking, and architecture (which involve the use of space and knowing how to get in it); and games such as chess (which require the ability to visualize objects from different perspectives and angles). The key sensory base of this intelligence is the sense of sight, but also the ability to form mental images and pictures in the mind. This intelligence can be seen in such people as architects, graphic artists, cartographers, industrial design draftspersons, and of course, visual artists (painters and sculptors).

Bodily/kinesthetic intelligence is the ability to use the body to express emotion (as in dance and body language), to play a game (as in sports), and to create a new product (as in invention). Learning by doing has long been recognized as an important part of education. Our bodies know things our minds do not and cannot know in any other way. For example, our bodies know how to ride a bike, roller-skate, type, and parallel park a car. This intelligence can be seen in such people as actors, athletes, mimes, dancers, and inventors.

Musical/rhythmic intelligence includes such capacities as the recognition and use of rhythmic and tonal patterns, and sensitivity to sounds from the environment, the human voice, and musical instruments. Many of us learned the alphabet through this intelligence and the A-B-C song. Of all forms of intelligence, the consciousness altering effect of music and rhythm in the brain is probably the greatest. This intelligence can be seen in advertising professionals (those who write catchy jingles to sell a product), performance musicians, rock musicians, dance bands, composers, and music teachers.

FIGURE 6.1 *Multiple Intelligences*

From *Eight Ways of Knowing: Teaching for Multiple Intelligences,* Third Edition, by David Lazear. © 1991, 1999 by SkyLight Training and Publishing, Inc. Reprinted by permission of SkyLight Professional Development. www.skylightedu.com

Interpersonal intelligence involves the ability to work cooperatively with others in a group as well as the ability to communicate, verbally and nonverbally, with other people. It builds on the capacity to notice distinctions among others such as contrasts in moods, temperament, motivations, and intentions. In the more advanced forms of this intelligence, one can literally pass over into another's perspective and read his or her intentions and desires. One can have genuine empathy for another's feelings, fears, anticipations, and beliefs. This form of intelligence is usually highly developed in such people as counselors, teachers, therapists, politicians, and religious leaders.

Intrapersonal intelligence involves knowledge of the internal aspects of the self, such as knowledge of feelings, the range of emotional responses, thinking processes, self-reflection, and a sense of or intuition about spiritual realities. Intrapersonal intelligence allows us to be conscious of our consciousness; that is, to step back from ourselves as an outside observer. It involves our capacity to experience wholeness and unity, to discern patterns of connection within the larger order of things, to perceive higher states of consciousness, to experience the lure of the future, and to dream of and actualize the possible. This intelligence can be seen in such people as philosophers, psychiatrists, spiritual counselors and gurus, and cognitive pattern researchers.

Naturalist intelligence involves the ability to discern, comprehend, and appreciate the various flora and fauna of the world of nature as opposed to the world created by human beings. It involves such capacities as recognizing and classifying species, growing plants and raising or taming animals, knowing how to appropriately use the natural world, its creatures, weather patterns, physical history, etc. In working with and developing the naturalist intelligence one often discovers a sense of wonder, awe, and respect for all the various phenomena and species (plant and animal) of the natural world. This intelligence can be seen in such people as farmers, hunters, zookeepers, gardeners, cooks, veterinarians, nature guides, and forest rangers.

FIGURE 6.1 *Continued*

naturalist intelligence (Lazear, 1999). Information about the individual's unique intelligence constellation can be obtained through conversation with the student, through discussions of what the student finds interesting, how the student learns things, and what he or she does for fun. You don't need a formal assessment to understand which intelligences the student possesses and uses.

There are many ways that multiple intelligences can be helpful when students struggle with academic issues. Counselors could use multiple intelligences as a context in which to mediate conversations between students and teachers about ways to individualize learning and teaching strategies. Furthermore, we will visit multiple intelligences again when we discuss counseling in Chapter 7 and developmental curriculum delivery in Chapter 8.

Higher Processing Skills: Critical Thinking and Reflective Judgment   In the interest of developmentally appropriate education, we must not only be aware of how students are *currently* learning, but also of how students need to move to the next level of functioning. So not only should counselors be in tune with how students are learning today, we should also be concerned with how students are maturing intellectually to ensure their continued growth.

For many years, the highest level of intellectual functioning was thought to be Piaget's formal operations stage, which is generally obtained at age 14 to 15 and involves the ability to generalize from specific to abstract, to hypothesize, and to imagine ideal solutions and futures (Piaget, 1954). However, continued exploration of adult development has resulted in various ways of understanding adolescent-to-adult cognitive growth. Two models of higher processing skills are critical thinking (Brookfield, 1987) and reflective judgment (King & Kitchener, 1994).

Critical thinking involves more than deconstructing what others have said (also known as critical analysis; Clinchy, 1989). According to Brookfield (1987), critical thinking is a productive and positive activity, triggered by both positive and negative life events and involving both the emotive and rational realities of the learner. In this view of critical thinking, the learner is engaged in a growth process that involves four components. First, the learner is involved in identifying and challenging assumptions and values, becoming self-aware in the process. Second, the learner is able to identify and challenge contexts in which those assumptions are based, becoming context-aware. Third, the learner is actively involved in imagining and explore alternatives, becoming intentional in finding solutions to the learning challenge. Finally, the learner is able to identify and challenge given conclusions, becoming reflective in the process.

An overview of this process, according to Brookfield (1987), involves several phases. First, the learner is confronted with a trigger event that provides undeniable evidence that is in direct contradiction with currently held worldviews and beliefs. Second, the learner engages in appraisal of the situation, brooding over the perplexing contradiction, attempting to minimize the cognitive dissonance (Festinger, 1957), and finally engaging in self-examination. In the third phase, the learner explores ways to explain or cope with the contradiction, testing out new ways of thinking and/or acting. Next, the learner develops alternative perspectives, becoming comfortable with new ways of being that make sense with the new situation and developing confidence in new roles. Finally, the learner solidifies those changes into new ways of seeing old assumptions, new ways of understanding old contexts, new ways of expressing one's identity, and new ways of defining solutions.

Brookfield (1987) identifies specific ways that learners can be facilitated through this process. Some of the strategies for developing critical thinking are already a foundation of the counselor's skills: affirming the learner's self-worth, supporting efforts at self-exploration, reflecting and mirroring new ideas and actions, and listening attentively. In addition, Brookfield suggests that educators provide a thinking stimulus by posing meaningful, open-ended questions that introduce dissonance and contradiction, then look for assumptions through role playing, debates, and discussion. He further suggests that educators create networks in which critical thinkers can interact, building bridges between prior experiences of critical thinking and current contradiction to help learners building on learning strengths. For educators, he suggests that classrooms become forums for critical dialogue and reflection, giving learning to the learners, and modeling critical thinking qualities like courage, risk-taking, intellectual humility, and developing contextual clarity. Finally, he charged educators with providing practice for open-ended resolution by using brainstorming, developing scenarios, and allowing students to use esthetic triggers like art, music, and prose to communicate about possible solutions.

The process of developing reflective judgment (King & Kitchener, 1994) is similar to that of critical thinking, in that the learner arrives at a personally validated solution at the end of the process. However, there are substantial differences in how evidence is used to support new thinking, and in the way the model describes the process of developing "voice," or internal authority. In developing reflective judgment, the learner moves through seven levels of relationship with knowledge. In the first and most elementary level, the learner believes that all knowledge is known, concrete, and absolute. Other perspectives are not acknowledged. From there, the learner moves to a belief that any knowledge that isn't absolutely certain can be obtained from authority figures or directly through the senses. Further development will lead the learner to believe that knowledge is uncertain and that all knowledge claims are idiosyncratic to the individual and situation, based on the rationale that evidence is only used to justify an already established opinion. From there, the learner develops the ability to see that knowledge is contextual and subjective, but the learner is limited by the view that only personal interpretations of evidence may be known. In the final stages, the learner is able to understand that knowledge is constructed into individual conclusions on the basis of evaluation of evidence across contexts, to the final realization that knowledge is the "outcome of a process of reasonable inquiry in which solutions to ill-structured problems are constructed. The adequacy of those solutions is evaluated in terms of what is most reasonable or probable according to the current evidence, and it is reevaluated when relevant new evidence, perspectives, or tools of inquiry become available" (King & Kitchener, 1994, p. 15).

Strategies to assist learners at each level are articulated by King and Kitchener (you are urged to read their book for more in-depth discussion; see the Suggested Readings section of this chapter), but will not be addressed in detail here. In general, the suggestions to educators would involve being supportive of learners at each level of the model as they navigate the uncertainty of developing their own ability to identify competing perspectives, locate evidence for each viewpoint, evaluate that evidence, then construct their own perspective.

For students in high school, these levels of reflective judgment resonate in terms of how accepting they are of the authority and expertise of the teacher in the classroom. Counselors can use this model to understand not only students, but the reflective judgment levels of faculty also, knowing that the ways we learn are also the ways we teach. It is possible to facilitate communication between students and teachers by understanding where teachers and students differ in their levels of critical thinking and reflective judgment.

Reflection Moment

What were your academic issues during high school? What were your grades like? Did you study hard or did you play hard? What were your life priorities? What were your "easy" subjects and which ones really challenged you? Ask significant others what they remember from their high school days. Compare their "easy" courses with your own. Now compare your hardest courses with theirs. Talk about what made those courses seem hard and what made them seem easy. See if you can identify their intelligence constellation. How would you have wanted to be treated if you came to someone for help with a hard course that he or she thought was easy? What are the implications for your counseling style?

Career Development: The "b" Column of the Domains

As we saw in Chapter 5, this domain has been the historical "home" of the school counselor, especially at the secondary level. It is an important part of what school counselors do, and you will find that much of your day as a high school counselor will be spent dealing with career issues.

Issues

According to Fox (1994), "There must be a reason more heart attacks occur between 8:00 and 9:00 A.M. on Monday mornings than any other time during the week. There is; it is returning to work that one hates" (p. 14). Many adults will tell you that they wish they had received more career counseling as they were growing up, yet it is clear that career decision making is a lifelong process that improves with trial and error (Brown, Brooks, & Associates, 1996; Dollarhide, 1997; Gysbers, Heppner, & Johnston, 1998; Hansen, 1997; Isaacson & Brown, 1997). There is tremendous pressure on young people to make the "right" decisions early, because the "cost" of exploration is high, and the "cost" of making "mistakes" is even higher. More than ever before, society is becoming aware that "career" and "job" are not synonymous (Hansen, 1997), yet as a society, we continue to pressure young people to choose wisely—a task that most *adults* would say is *their* biggest life challenge.

The Career Moratorium   One of the biggest challenges to young people during this time of life is their own developmental agenda: The development of identity is the primary focus, with career direction being just one of many subsets of the manifestation of that identity (Craig, 1996). The struggle to crystallize identity, not make career decisions, is the focus of this time of life. Marcia (as cited in Craig, 1996) labeled this a career "moratorium," characterized by an ongoing or prolonged identity crisis or decision-making period. In fact, according to Isaacson and Brown (1997), "Identification of specific career options should not be expected for most high school students, and those students who are likely to pursue a baccalaureate degree may be least inclined to engage in career planning. The refining of choice to the point of naming a specific goal is not a function of age, grade level, or ability, but rather should be directly related to the imminence of entry into the world of work or into a specific preparatory program" (p. 261).

Dreams and Pressure from Peers and Parents   Talking to young people about what they want to do with their lives can be a joyous activity, because their dreams are so big and limitless. It isn't uncommon to hear a wide variety of high-profile occupations listed by one person: "I want to be an astronaut, a drummer in a rock band, a professional ball player, and help homeless people." And not a brain surgeon? "Well, yeah, that too." This dreaming-of-big-dreams was described in Super's Exploration stage of career development, in which 14- to 24-year-olds "turn to daydreaming about possible selves they may construct" as a means of exploring possible futures (Super, Savickas, & Super, 1996, p. 132). However, the pressure to "get real" usually comes from peers and parents. Peers are threatened because "watching someone else reach for his or her greatness reminds me of my potential, and that scares me." Parents are often concerned about their children's ability to make it economically in the world, and so their message is often "Play it safe. Go where the money and the jobs are." For better or worse, these two groups shape people in high school more than anyone else in terms of identity formation and occupational choices (Craig, 1996; Isaacson & Brown, 1997; Wahl & Blackhurst, 2000).

When young people base their identity and occupational choices on those of parents or others without going through their own identity development and decision-making period, they are experiencing "foreclosure" (Marcia, as cited in Craig, 1996). While it may appear that the young person has made all the right choices from an adult perspective, it is probable that he or she has circumvented a necessary stage of his or her own development and may come to regret the shortcut.

Rate of Change in the World   The world is changing exponentially in all facets of our lives: in work, families, education, organizations, leisure, demographics, politics, and technology (Hansen, 1997). The speed of change and the extent of change cannot be anticipated or projected, even for short periods of time into the future. When faced with making career choices that might extend out numerous years into the future (after high school graduation and some postsecondary training), young people need the ability to be creative and proactive, not reactive (Gellatt, 1991; Herr, 1996).

Narrowing or Expanding Options   The process of career exploration is not one of linearity and predictability; it is unique to each person, dictated by interests, abilities, gifts, challenges, family setting, parental occupations and expectations, timelines, resources, and focus (Kraus & Hughey, 1999). In the throes of this process, some students will come to the counselor to discuss their overwhelming range of options, while others will come to discuss their depressingly narrow range of options. This expansion/contraction cycle of exploration, focus, widening view, more exploration, more focus, and so on, is a natural part of decision making. Counselors can help students understand the process, since it is the *process* (learning decision making skills in general, and career decision-making skills in particular), not the *product* (the career decision), that is important.

Not Everyone Goes to College   School counselors need to be aware that noncollege-track students are not given the same attention, resources, or opportunities as college-track students. Parents, school administrators, and teachers want students to go to college and so push students in that direction, but the fact remains that not everyone needs to go to college and not everyone will be successful in college. The decision not to go to college is not a failure, but many adults will react as though it is. What has evolved is a two-tiered system of courses: college prep courses and noncollege prep. The results of being in the noncollege track are often negative (Hotchkiss & Borow, 1996), "being cut adrift from either school-based or community-based support services" (Herr, 1996). It is important to recognize that, as college-educated, graduate-level professionals, school counselors may be biased in favor of college for young people; we need to resist the urge to pressure students to go to college and should honor their journey wherever it takes them.

There is a wide range of postsecondary options that can help prepare young people for productive adult roles (Wahl & Blackhurst, 2000). These options include two-year and technical colleges and private schools, the military, apprenticeships, full employment, starting a family or fulfilling a family role, religious missions, volunteer work, or travel. The wisdom and efficacy of each of these options vary depending on the individual, but each person has the right to choose his or her own destiny. Perhaps the individual needs time to learn about him- or herself before deciding on a career direction.

McJobs and the Value of Part-Time Employment   Most authors agree that part-time work is valuable for young people: It teaches work behaviors and ethics, it allows for some independence, it provides a chance for person/environment/task fit analysis (Dawis, 1996), and it provides socialization into the work environment (Herr, 1996; Hotchkiss & Borow, 1996; Isaacson & Brown, 1997). However, that conventional wisdom needs to be balanced with some cautions about part-time work during high school. Time spent at work may decrease time spent with parents (Hotchkiss & Borow, 1996) and may detract from time needed to devote to academic endeavors, resulting in lowered grades, poor academic performance, and an increased dropout rate (Ritzer, 1996). Furthermore, some critics charge that these jobs do not contribute to the adolescent's psychological growth and development, since they do not allow for unstructured, personal expression (Hotchkiss & Borow, 1996). The most scathing criticism is leveled by Ritzer (1996): "It is important that we see McJobs for what they are . . . low status, poorly paid and dehumanized jobs that tend to offer dead-end careers that serve to a large degree as impediments to one's ability to acquire the higher-status, higher-paying, more complex and more human post-industrial jobs" (p. 211).

How can these jobs be contrary to the future career development of adolescents? The concern is that they will provide financial incentives that, *in the short run*, will be more valued by the young person than long-range career goals. A young person who may not be adept at delayed gratification may see the independence of employment, even in a dead-end job, as more important than obtaining training for some eventual career. The result? More potential heart attack victims, trapped by bills and family demands, trudging along on Monday morning to jobs that they hate.

Models

Overview of the Career Process   What does the career decision process look like, both in terms of the process itself and in terms of the outcomes? From a lifelong perspective, the process of making viable career decisions involves seven steps (Dollarhide, 2000):

Step One: Understanding of self (knowledge of one's likes, dislikes, abilities, skills, gifts, challenges, values, needs, dreams, lifestyle goals, personality, interests)

Step Two: Understanding of the world of work (knowledge of career paths, job titles, salary levels, employers, employment environments, occupational projections, training requirements)

Step Three: Reality testing (firsthand experience through employment, volunteering, internships, cooperative education jobs, lab experiences, job shadowing)

Step Four: Commitment (making a decision, with relative confidence, in the face of uncertainty)

Step Five: Career preparation (accessing formal or informal training for the job or occupation)

Step Six: Placement/Career entrance (utilizing job-seeking skills, filling out applications, writing cover letters and resumes, participating in interviews, then accessing opportunities in the chosen occupation)

Step Seven: Evaluation and renewal (As the individual matures throughout life, the core self changes in terms of likes, dislikes, values, and other variables outlined in Step One. Concurrently, there are changes in the work world. Individuals continuously evaluate their level of career satisfaction, and will begin again at Step One when their level of career satisfaction reaches a low-point threshold of tolerance. If they still like the tasks of the occupation, they may decide to change employers. If they dislike the tasks, they may decide to change occupations entirely.)

In terms of outcomes, Henderson (2000) studied persons who were happy at work and found striking similarities among those studied. The first finding was that they were "notably similar in their particularly dogged commitment to follow their interests, their competencies, and what they enjoyed doing. Consequently, their careers tended to follow a *positive meandering path*" (emphasis added) (p. 309). This metaphor feels particularly empowering, and will help students and families feel less pressure to make the right choice right now.

Henderson's (2000) second finding has implications for our discussion of the personal/social domain; she found significant attributes that characterized the study participants who were happy at work. These attributes include:

1. A positive sense of self (defined as self-confidence, self-understanding, intuition, and imagination, among others).
2. Self-determination (defined as "independent strategies in choice and action that determine successful . . . approaches to experiences, all characterized by measures of rational thinking and self-responsibility," p. 315).
3. Energy (defined as enthusiasm, goal-directed motivation, and forward focus).
4. Strength of character (defined as the ability to tolerate ambiguity and uncertainty, self-advocacy, resilience, and tenacity).
5. Positive relationships with others (defined as strategies of behavior and communication, such as humor, open-mindedness, and active listening, that build positive relationships with others).
6. Positive orientation to the world (defined as positive attitude, optimism, and curiosity that provides a "hopeful and practical approach to functioning in the world," p. 315).

These individuals are persons who, because of their overall positive life orientation, would be well equipped to make life work, no matter how inconvenient some details of life might be. The point is not that these people had perfect jobs or perfect lives; the point is that these findings can help students and families understand what personal qualities and characteristics could lead students to find their "bliss," no matter what life has in store for them.

Positive Uncertainty   Gellatt (1991, 1996) presents one response to the dilemma of decision making in times of uncertainty and rapid change. He suggests a personal, decision-making philosophy or paradigm, dubbed "positive uncertainty," to help people both "imagine and create possibilities" (1996, p. 391). In this paradigm, people are urged to balance two opposing perspectives simultaneously. To maximize adaptability and flexibility while maintaining focus on a desired life/career outcome, Gellatt would urge being "focused and flexible" about life and career goals (p. 391). To maximize learning while maintaining awareness of career information, this philosophy would maintain being "aware and wary" about what is known, since "facts" change all the time (p. 391). To maximize the power of dreams while remaining grounded, people are urged to "be objective and optimistic" about one's beliefs (p. 391). Finally, to maximize the power of creativity while engaging in reality testing, Gellatt would suggest being "practical and magical" in one's career behavior (p. 391). In essence, Gellatt (1996) sums it up:

> Developing future sense involves becoming a dreamer and a doer, combining pie-in-the-sky and feet-on-the-ground strategies, balancing achieving goals with discovering them, balancing useful facts and fantasy, balancing reality testing and wishful-thinking, balancing responding to change and causing change. This involves a reinvention of career development. (pp. 392–393)

The implications for high school students? Keep dreaming those big dreams, and never eliminate the possible to settle for the probable.

The Career Portfolio   One tool for facilitating the career development process is the career portfolio, in which students systematically explore their career ideas and understanding of self. There are a variety of ways such portfolios can be constructed, from highly individualized to highly structured. One model for a comprehensive, schoolwide portfolio project is distributed by the American School Counselor Association (ASCA) and the National Occupational Information Coordinating Committee (NOICC) (n.d.).

In this portfolio, students first document their self-knowledge in terms of personal qualities, personal skills, decision-making processes, descriptions of self-discoveries, things they do well, and various competencies. Next, they document their life roles in terms of acceptance of self and others, family influence, leisure activities, and various competencies. They then document their educational development, including things they know about their own learning, their plans for after high school, and various competencies. Finally, they document the results of their career exploration and planning, including the results of any career assessments taken and various career competencies. The final document is a personal career plan, in which students synthesize their self-knowledge, awareness of the world of work, career assessment information, career exploration, training options, and skills into a viable list of career and training *options* that seem workable. The emphasis is on the word "options." The goal isn't to force students to make a career choice; the goal is to empower students to identify options that will focus further *exploration*.

Reflection Moment

Recall your career journey. Were you intentional, focused, and deliberate, or did your career follow a "positive meandering path"? Do you know, with certainty, how your career path will unfold? (What do you want to do when *you* grow up?) What is the most empowering thing anyone said to you about your career path? What is the most destructive thing anyone said to you about it? What can you do now to avoid ever inflicting that same disappointment and disillusionment on any of your students?

Personal/Social Development: The "c" Column of the Domains

The third domain that forms the foundation of comprehensive school counseling programs is the development of personal and social skills. This is an area where many counselors feel especially comfortable, because it is the domain in which counseling itself is focused. At the high school level, personal/social concerns can be addressed proactively (prevention and early intervention efforts) or reactively (later intervention and treatment efforts). While students will come to counselors with a wide range of personal/social developmental needs, it is easy to see that proactive efforts are more efficient.

Issues

Me as Young Adult: Identity   Let's start with the most common of adolescent problems: the identity crisis (Erikson, 1968). It is safe to say that 99 percent of your student population, at any given moment, is suffering pangs of anxiety, frustration, and angst from their natural need to crystallize their identity. It is also safe to say that the other 1 percent of your population will be suffering in the next five minutes. The birthing of a viable identity is a long, painful process; it starts in late childhood, and for most people, will not be resolved until early adulthood (which research suggests is now being pushed into late twenties; Howe & Strauss, 1993; Loeb, 1994; Potter, 1996). In its most common form, the sufferers of this affliction exhibit a wide variety of styles and behaviors within relatively stable parameters. Here is a metaphor that might help. Think of the students' search for identity as driving down a deserted street. The quest for an identity may lead to driving from curb to curb, but they are still on the road to finding themselves. The curbs represent those relatively stable parameters, boundaries beyond which they will not go because they know at least that much about themselves. "Drugs are not me," or "Piercing that part of my body grosses me out." Proactive prevention programming can help these students.

Now imagine that some students have jumped the curb and are driving across people's lawns. This is a red flag; you don't know where they are going. They are suffering from what Marcia (as cited in Craig, 1996) described as "identity diffusion," in which the young person lacks a sense of direction or motivation to determine a life direction. To avoid dealing with their identity crises, these young people seek activities that provide immediate gratification, or they experiment "in a random fashion with all possibilities" (p. 439). These students don't know who they are, who they want to be, or where they belong. Counselors will see them as a result of their lack of motivation (excessive absenteeism or chronic truancy), as a result of their method(s) of immediate gratification (unwanted pregnancy, substance abuse and/or addiction, poor impulse control in the classroom, excessive risk-taking), or as a result of their bizarre behaviors as they experiment with the style of the month. Intervention can help these students.

Now imagine that some students are driving their cars straight toward a brick wall and the accelerator is to the floor. For these students, the identity crisis has been resolved; the problem is that they despise the self they have found. These students engage in seriously self-destructive behaviors, such as self-cutting, self-mutilation, eating disorders, suicidal behaviors and risk-taking, and substance abuse. The differences between identity diffusion and identity loathing are the intensity of the self-inflicted damage and the intentionality of the act of self-destruction. Treatment is warranted for these students. More will be said about these counseling responses in Chapter 7.

Cultural Identity   Cultural identity comes from areas of diversity in a student's life, defined as any factor in the student's life that makes him or her different from her or his peers. If you listen to students, you will hear, over and over, "I just want to be *normal*!" Anything that makes them different causes them extreme anxiety, and while this is a natural part of cultural identity development (which we will discuss in the next section), it is still a difficult process. The argument here is that cultural identity comes from the full constellation of human uniqueness: intellectual ability (straight-A students, special education students), ethnicity (racial diversity), sexual orientation (straight, gay, lesbian, bisexual), gender (female, male, transgendered), color of hair (blondes as dumb, redheads as hot-tempered), body shape and weight (full-bodied or model thin), height (especially for males), religion (strong Christian bias in this country that borders on anti-Semitism), physical ability ("jocks," students with physical challenges), health status (any range of physical illnesses, both chronic such as diabetes and asthma and acute such as mononucleosis), amount of hair (especially desirable is facial hair for males, especially undesirable is body hair for females), language and accent (persons for whom English is not the native language are perceived as unintelligent), region of birth (a Southern accent is perceived as unintelligent), socioeconomic status (rich kids, poor kids, who has the designer tennis shoes), and the list could go on. Adolescents have internalized all of society's messages about the "perfect" body, skin, hair, background, ethnicity, resources, family, and possessions—and they use those messages to find themselves, and everyone around them, woefully inadequate. Called "social comparison" (Craig, 1996), it is thought that this activity allows teens to identify those "like me" from those "not like me" to aid in identity development and refinement. However, this mechanism is often taken to extremes and can lead to intolerance, harassment, and violence (Pollack, 1998).

Relationship Development   Most adolescents develop the ability to generate deeper and more lasting friendships during high school (Craig, 1996). In addition, young people are exploring more adult couple relationships (Craig, 1996; Davis & Benshoff, 1999) and using those insights to learn about self and self-in-relationship. Knowing that the development of intimate friendships and intimate couple relationships is an integral part of adolescence, counselors should be aware of the potential for problems and the potential for "learning moments" that can come from those problems. There is a need to be aware of the problem of interpersonal violence among adolescents in general (Elliott, 1998; Guerra & Williams, 1996; National Institute of Justice, Office of Justice Programs, 1998; Tolan & Guerra, 1998), the rise in interpersonal violence among dating couples (Davis & Benshoff, 1999), and a need to proactively address such violence (Davis & Benshoff, 1999).

Rites of Passage into Adulthood   Another problem faced by youth today involves how we acknowledge that a young person has "arrived"—namely, rites of passage into adulthood (Hine, 1999). Anthropologists have studied what it means to become a responsible, contributing member of a society in other cultures and can point to dramatic ceremonies that identify adults in that context. In our society, however, the age of adulthood is indeterminate; ceremonies like senior prom and high school graduation are milestones toward chronological maturation that say nothing about emotional, financial, or civic maturity. Laws have been passed to move driving age up (suggesting later maturity), while other laws have been changed to prosecute and punish adolescents as an adult at younger ages (suggesting earlier culpability). As Hine (1999) noted,

> Perhaps because most American adults see themselves as still young, we are particularly reluctant to acknowledge the maturity of our children. An ironic result is that age limits established to keep young people from endangering themselves—such as minimum ages for drinking liquor, smoking cigarettes, and gambling legally—become important passages to maturity. *The mark of adulthood in America is the license to indulge in bad habits* [emphasis added]. (p. 45)

Most adults would argue that steady gainful employment, establishment of a home and family, and following the rules of society constitute adulthood. Since these things don't usually occur until late twenties or early thirties, young people see this as too distant to worry about now, resulting in their feeling too young to be responsible, but too old to be irresponsible—basically, in a state of liminality, literally on the threshold, until adult society accepts their claim to adulthood (Hine, 1999).

Models

Identity Achievement   Marcia (as cited in Craig, 1996) referred to the resolution of the adolescent identity crisis as "identity achievement" (Craig, 1996, p. 439). This was defined as people who have made commitments to their careers and their own "individually formulated moral code" (p. 439). It is easy to see how this development of personal identity, morality, and definition resonates with the concepts of reflective judgment, critical thinking, and careers discussed in the previous sections. Working to help young people develop higher cognitive skills concurrently helps them to think critically about their choices and to reflect on their responsibility for choice. It also puts into perspective the risk-taking and experimentation with expression that young people exhibit during identity exploration (Craig, 1996, p. 453). Since experimentation is an essential part of choice, it might behoove school counselors to discuss the concept of safe risk-taking with families and school professionals. In this context, safe risk-taking would involve allowing young people safe expression of individuality without adult boundaries. For example, what does it hurt to allow a young person to wear a black shirt in the summer sun rather than a white one? That young person will learn that black shirts do indeed get hot in the summer sun and will choose the white one next time. If indeed life lessons are really only learned the hard way (Fay & Funk, 1995), then allowing young people to experience the consequences of their choices is the best way we can help them learn about choice.

Identity Development for Students of Difference   Since identity development depends on how young people see themselves and how others see them, those qualities that cause them to see themselves as "less than" are intensely painful and embarrassing. While adults tell young people to be proud of their unique qualities, the reality is that such appreciation comes much later in life. The journey toward accepting oneself and others can begin, however, in high school, and the struggles of young people to accept their own Difference can be resolved in a way that allows for the appreciation of many Differences. (Since "diversity" has been used rather narrowly to refer to only racial difference, we will use "Difference" to refer to the full spectrum of uniquenesses: race, gender, religion, sexual orientation, ability status, culture, etc.) Many authors have addressed the unique challenges of one group of nondominant values holders, such as racial identity development (Atkinson, Morten, & Sue, 1989; Helms, 1994), disability identity development (Scheer, 1994), female identity development (Pipher, 1994), male identity development (Pollack, 1998), and gay and lesbian identity development (D'Augelli, 1994). Each of these models has made a significant contribution to the understanding of the struggles of that particular population, and school counselors are urged to become familiar with the identity development models that address the challenges of their students.

While each model reflects the struggles of that particular population, many of these models reflect some common experiences. In general, these models of identity development share these five common stages:

1. *Unawareness of Difference:* The Different person sees him- or herself as the same as others; is unaware that others think of him or her as different.
2. *Awareness of Difference:* The person begins to see that others view her or him as different and becomes aware that those of other groups are treated preferentially.
3. *Anger at Other Groups:* The person is now fully aware that others treat him or her prejudicially. This can result in tremendous anger, frustration, and rejection of those who are a part of the "dominant" culture. At this stage, people of Difference will often associate with, and identify themselves exclusively with, others of their Difference category.
4. *Awareness of Commonalities:* At some point, the Different person recognizes that there are some similarities between his or her views and the views of others in the "dominant" culture.
5. *Integration of Both the Different and Dominant:* At this stage, the Different person sees that there are ideas, persons, and concepts of value from other perspectives and is able to integrate the best of the Different culture with the best of the dominant culture to become self-defining and tolerant of the Difference of others.

School counselors who are aware of the Differences of their students and who understand the models of Different identity development can better understand the painful aspects of the process of identity development, such as rage, isolation, and the need to associate with those of their Difference category. Furthermore, knowing about identity development can help counselors communicate with students by knowing when to help students connect with positive role models of their own Difference culture. Finally, counselors who use the insights gained from knowing identity development models can help students integrate the best of both perspectives, teaching tolerance toward others in the process.

Goleman's Emotional Intelligence   In helping high school students to maximize their personal/social development, school counselors often struggle with how to help them learn emotional stability. Goleman (1995) addressed this using the construct of emotional intelligence.

> In the dance of feeling and thought, the emotional faculty guides our moment-to-moment decisions, working hand-in-hand with the rational mind, enabling—or disabling—thought itself. Likewise, the thinking brain plays an executive role in our emotions—except in those moments when emotions surge out of control and the emotional brain runs rampant. In a sense, we have two brains, two minds—and two different kinds of intelligence: rational and emotional. How we do in life is determined by both—it is not just IQ, but *emotional* intelligence that matters. Indeed, intellect cannot work at its best without emotional intelligence. (Goleman, 1995, p. 26)

In essence, Goleman described emotional intelligence in terms of five domains: (a) knowing one's emotions; (b) managing one's emotions; (c) motivating oneself, or "marshaling emotions in the service of a goal" (p. 43) to enable sustained attention, management of stress, and delayed gratification; (d) recognizing emotions in others primarily through empathy; and (e) understanding and managing relationships effectively, or understanding and managing the emotions of others. It is through these five elements of emotional intelligence that people learn about themselves, acquire goal-directed behaviors and attitudes, learn about others, and acquire leadership skills and interpersonal effectiveness. Goleman further discussed emotional intelligence in terms of "schooling the emotions" (p. 261) and identified ways that classroom guidance can address cooperation, problem solving, conflict resolution, empathy training, and impulse control through a curriculum called Self Science (Stone & Dillehunt, 1978).

Snyder's Concept of Hope   Snyder (1994) provided a powerful model for helping us understand how to help young people with a new definition of hope. This new definition states that "Hope is the sum of the mental willpower and waypower that you have for your goals" (Snyder, 1994, p. 5). In this context, goals are those objects or accomplishments that we desire that serve as "mental targets for our thoughts" (p. 5). To serve effectively as a motivating target, goals should be meaningful, important, and clearly articulated. To reach our goals, we access our willpower, which is defined as a "driving force" toward our goals, the "reservoir of determination and commitment that we can call on to help move us in the direction of the goal to which we are attending at any given moment" (p. 6). The final piece of the puzzle is waypower, defined as the mental roadmap that guides hopeful thought (p. 8). It is waypower, or planfulness, that is the "mental capacity we call on to find one or more effective ways to reach our goals" (p. 8).

In order to have hope, then, one would need (1) clearly articulated, meaningful goals, (2) a sense of willpower or energy to move us toward those goals, and (3) high waypower, or the mental flexibility needed to find alternative routes should our path be blocked. Snyder also addresses ways that hope can be nurtured in children, or, if hope is already mortally wounded, ways that hope can be rekindled (pp. 189–205). Some of these suggestions include:

- Teach kids to have positive mental tapes.
- Help them formulate clear short- and long-term goals.
- Praise them for determination.
- Help young people accentuate strengths.

- Discuss roadblocks as a normal part of life.
- Help them articulate paths around roadblocks.
- Help them see cause and effect to increase their planfulness.
- Help them break a long path to a goal into smaller, doable parts.
- Help them see failures as learning experiences to improve future planning.

It is possible that the concept of hope as presented by Snyder can help students to understand how to move forward with their lives. It also gives counselors new language to discuss goals, goal-related planning, and the energy or commitment needed to attain goals.

Reflection Moment

What were your most significant challenges in these areas when you were in high school? Do you remember struggling with your identity? What sorts of things did you do to express your individuality? What was the reaction of adults to your forms of self-expression? What would be "safe" risk that you could allow in your school?

In what ways were you Different? How did that feel?

How did the events of your life affect your emotional intelligence and hope? How did school impact your development of emotional intelligence and hope?

How did you know you had attained adult status? When did that happen for you? (Pardon the assumption that it has happened—there is always the chance that you are still searching for that status! Sometimes I know I'm still looking . . .)

Prevention, Intervention, and Treatment

Now that you have an understanding of the Domains, we need to discuss the concepts of prevention, intervention, and treatment. To understand what is meant by the terms of prevention, intervention, and treatment, high school counselors must understand the concept of being "at risk." McWhirter, McWhirter, McWhirter, and McWhirter (1998; p. 7) define at risk in terms of risk from "dangerous future events" (substance use, abuse, and addiction; early sexual behavior and/or unplanned pregnancy; early departure from school; criminal and/or violent behaviors).

Counselors working with all high school students must be able to see the connection between risk, impediments to learning, and comprehensive counseling programmatic responses. These responses are categorized into three levels: prevention, intervention, and treatment (Adelman & Taylor, 1998; McWhirter et al., 1998) and can be defined as:

Prevention: Programmatic responses that are designed to enhance resilience and prevent the onset of at-risk characteristics. Examples of prevention efforts are schoolwide programs for excellence, classroom lessons on developmental topics, and working toward an environment of respect and inclusion.

Intervention: Programmatic responses that are designed to arrest the deterioration of existing at-risk characteristics or to mitigate against the effects of psychosocial or educational stressors. Examples of these responses include individual counseling, group counseling, family interventions and home visits, consultation with teachers, consultation with parents, and conflict mediation between teachers and students.

Treatment: Programmatic responses that are designed to address fully developed at-risk behaviors. In some cases, counselors can adequately address the treatment needs of students through groups and one-on-one counseling, but often, students who need treatment are best served by mental health professionals in the community. Outside counseling for students who need treatment does not imply that counselors are not trained to provide such assistance to students. Rather, outside therapy for students who need treatment reflects the intensity of treatment (often students in treatment need several sessions each week), and the necessity of medications to assist with the therapeutic process (which counselors are not authorized to prescribe).

Now that you have some familiarity with the issues and models for development in the domains let's look at how we address these issues through the activity of counseling with our students in the next chapter.

Chapter Summary

In this chapter, we presented the three domains of development: academic development, career development, and personal/social development. Within academic development, we outlined several problems that face high school students, in terms of learning success and potential for dropout, academic advisement and postsecondary options as an important focus of high school counseling, academic mediation to help students learn about teaching and learning styles, assessment of student learning, and time management/life management as a significant challenge for secondary school students. We then discussed several models to help you understand ways to help students with these issues. We discussed learning styles in terms of ways students can understand and modify their academic style, and we covered multiple intelligences to help explain why students enjoy learning certain subjects, how they learn, and how they express that learning. In addition, we discussed the higher processing skills of critical thinking and reflective judgment to help you see where secondary students are going in terms of epistemological development, and we outlined ways counselors can help students move toward those higher level skills while still in high school.

In the next section of the chapter, we addressed career development in terms of the career challenges of secondary school students. The career moratorium describes why career decisions are challenging in high school, and discussing dreams, peer pressure, and the rapid rate of change in the world help to round out an understanding of how career images develop and morph into various shapes and configurations. The process of narrowing or expanding options is a common problem faced by secondary students, because as we discussed, there are many expectations that might not be accurate about going to college and about some of the benefits and problems of obtaining part-time employment.

To help you work with students in this domain, several models are presented. First, we discussed an overview of the career process, describing the lifelong sequence of events that repeatedly cycle throughout life. In the face of rapid change, the model of Positive Uncertainty was presented. Finally, the career portfolio was discussed as a way of helping students organize and integrate their K–12 experiences and competencies into a meaningful career plan of explorable options.

In the final domain of personal/social development, we discussed identity as the central theme of development during this life phase. Specifically, we discussed Difference, cultural identity, and the emphasis on relationship development that is a natural part of adolescence. In addition, because our society has no clear rites of passage into adulthood, young people have additional challenges asserting themselves as adults in our culture.

We then discussed identity development, using the metaphor of a car to help you understand which counseling approach is indicated ("driving down the street within the curbs" suggests prevention efforts; "driving across lawns" suggests the need for intervention; and "driving straight into a brick wall" demands treatment). The concept of identity achievement was presented, and we then outlined a model for identity development for students of Difference to help you work with students who are struggling with who they are. Emotional intelligence and hope were presented and discussed in terms of their application in educational settings, important concepts that can help counselors understand and work with students more effectively.

Finally, we discussed risk for dangerous future events and introduced the concepts of prevention, intervention, and treatment. As school counselors, you will need to understand which level of programming response is required when you encounter students who are at risk for unhealthy behaviors.

A Day in the Life Revisited: Integration

Go back and reread Mr. Paulson's conversation with Ty. Now that you've read the chapter:

1. There are examples in this conversation of Ty's struggle in all three domains. Find an example of each.
2. What model(s) from the chapter would you employ to talk with Ty about his struggles?
3. What are the most significant areas of concern for you as you read the conversation?
4. Because there are several issues with which Ty needs help, you might feel conflicted about where to begin with him. Where would you begin and why?
5. In this chapter, we did not get a chance to discuss what to do when a student is a victim of violence. Does it matter if the violence takes place on the street or in the school? In what ways does that alter what you would do?
6. Ty is caught between the pacifism of his mother and the "tough it out" message from society and the streets. What does "being a man" mean to you? What does it mean to Ty? How can you help Ty honor his sense of emerging manhood (dignity) and increase his ability to ask for help dealing with the harassment and violence?
7. How do you feel about college attendance for Ty? How do you feel about his getting a second job? Here is a chance for you to examine your own values and assumptions!
8. How would you work with Ty if he were a senior? How would that be different if he were a freshman?

Application

1. Using a real adolescent or a fictional adolescent from a movie or book, practice identifying that young person's life challenges. Outline a prevention-intervention-treatment plan for that young person.

2. Take each one of the models presented in this chapter and apply it to someone you know well: a relative, your significant other, or yourself. Interview that person to see if you can determine which of the models seem to "fit" the life of the person you interview.

3. Enroll in a big brother/big sister program or volunteer to mentor a high school person. As you get to know the young person, examine the student's life to ascertain her or his level of development in each of the domains. Then see which of the models would help you to understand ways that this young person might benefit from your mentoring relationship.

4. Expand your understanding of these models by acquiring the recommended readings and enjoy!

5. It is often hard to discuss certain things with young people, such as dreams, hope, and their identity. Young people want to be noticed, but they find it very hard to talk about their internal experiences (beware, however, because they can talk for *days* about events and people!). Think of ways that you could comfortably engage a young person in a conversation about his or her identity, risk-taking, career dreams, and hope (goals, willpower, and waypower).

6. There are many additional models to address each of the three domains. Go to a local bookstore and peruse the shelves to find additional resources to address these domains.

7. Expand your own multiple intelligences. Take each of the multiple intelligences and look for lessons that address the three domains. For example, what lessons can be gleaned from social insects that might provide a model for a problem in the personal/social domain?

8. Look at the student quote that opens this chapter. How does it relate to the content of the chapter?

Suggested Readings

Brookfield, S. D. (1987). *Developing critical thinkers: Challenging adults to explore alternative ways of thinking and acting.* San Francisco: CA: Jossey-Bass. This book contains wonderful insights into ways to help young people develop their critical thinking skills. While not written as a counseling manual, this book has many implications, both for counseling and for the developmental curriculum.

Brandan, N. (1994). *The six pillars of self-esteem.* New York: Bantam. This book defines self-esteem in terms of intentional practices that reinforce a healthy life direction. Many practical suggestions for developing self-esteem are provided that can help school counselors design counseling and curricular experiences to foster self-esteem in students.

Gellatt, H. B. (1991). *Creative decision making using positive uncertainty.* Los Angeles, CA: Crisp. Many school counselors are faced with helping students make important decisions in the face of uncertainty, and Gellatt offers ideas for reframing this stressful situation into one that is intuitively engaging for both counselor and student.

Goleman, D. (1995). *Emotional intelligence: Why it can matter more than IQ.* New York: Bantam. This book helps counselors understand and articulate to faculty and staff why the developmental curriculum is important. It provides a holistic perspective of what constitutes a well-functioning person in this society.

Hansen, L. S. (1997). *Integrative life planning: Critical tasks for career development and changing life patterns.* San Francisco: CA: Jossey-Bass. This author writes about life-career planning from a holistic, existential view; this philosophy can help counselors to retain that holistic foundation while engaging students in discussions about their future.

Hine, T. (1999). *The rise and fall of the American teenager.* New York: Avon. For anyone who wants to understand "why teens are the way they are" and "why it was different in my day," this author offers a historical overview of what youth, teenage, and adolescence meant in America's past.

King, P. M., & Kitchener, K. S. (1994). *Developing reflective judgment: Understanding and promoting intellectual growth and critical thinking in adolescents and adults*. San Francisco, CA: Jossey-Bass. Since intellectual development and academic maturity are goals of the comprehensive school counseling program, counselors will benefit from an understanding of what their students are working to attain. This book provides many insights that can help counselors design counseling and curricular experiences to help students develop intellectually.

Lazear, D. (1999). *Eight ways of teaching: The artistry of teaching with multiple intelligences*. Arlington Heights, IL: SkyLight Training and Publishing. This book offers educators practical ideas for engaging students of all ages in the learning process by designing learning experiences tailored to each student's individual intelligence constellation.

Pipher, M. (1994). *Reviving Ophelia: Saving the selves of adolescent girls*. New York: Ballantine. This book describes the challenges of growing up female in this culture.

Pollack, W. (1998). *Real boys: Rescuing our sons from the myths of boyhood*. New York: Henry Holt. This book outlines the challenges of growing up male in this culture.

Snyder, C. R. (1994). *The psychology of hope*. New York: Free Press. Detailing research into the concept of hope, this author provides a model of hope that is teachable to students. Each component is then discussed in detail, providing insights that can help when counseling and educating students, faculty, and parents.

References

Adelman, H. S., & Taylor, L. (1998). Reframing mental health in schools and expanding school reform. *Educational Psychologist, 33* (4), 135–152.

American School Counselor Association (ASCA) and the National Occupational Information Coordinating Committee (NOICC). (no date). *Get a life: Your personal planning portfolio for career development*. Alexandria, VA: Authors.

Atkinson, D. R., Morten, G., & Sue, D. W. (1989). *Counseling American minorities: A cross-cultural perspective*. Dubuque, IA: Brown.

Baker, S. B. (2000). *School counseling for the twenty-first century* (3rd ed.). Upper Saddle River, NJ: Prentice-Hall.

Beale, A. V. (1995). Selecting school counselors: The principal's perspective. *School Counselor, 42,* 211–217.

Berens, L. V. (1988). *Please understand me: Empowering students of the 90's*. Huntington Beach, CA: Temperament Research Institute.

Briggs, K. C., & Myers, I. B. (1998). *Myers-Briggs Type Indicator* (3rd ed.). Palo Alto, CA: Consulting Psychologists Press.

Brookfield, S. D. (1987). *Developing critical thinkers: Challenging adults to explore alternative ways of thinking and acting*. San Francisco: CA: Jossey-Bass.

Brown, D., Brooks, L., & Associates. (1996). *Career choice and development* (3rd ed.). San Francisco, CA: Jossey-Bass.

Clinchy, B. (1989). On critical thinking and connected knowing. *Liberal Education, 75* (5), 14–19.

Craig, G. J. (1996). *Human development* (7th ed.). Upper Saddle River, NJ: Prentice Hall.

D'Augelli, A. R. (1994). Identity development and sexual orientation: Toward a model of lesbian, gay, and bisexual development. In E. J. Trickett, R. J. Watts, & D. Birman (Eds.), *Human diversity: Perspectives on people in context* (pp. 312–333). San Francisco, CA: Jossey-Bass.

Davis, K. M., & Benshoff, J. M. (1999). A proactive approach to couples counseling with adolescents. *Professional School Counseling, 2,* 391–394.

Dawis, R. V. (1996). The theory of work adjustment and person-environment-correspondence counseling. In D. Brown, L. Brooks, & Associates (Eds.), *Career choice and development* (3rd ed.; pp. 75–120). San Francisco, CA: Jossey-Bass.

Dilley, J., Foster, W., & Bowers, I. (1973). Effectiveness ratings of counselors without teaching experience. *Counselor Education and Supervision, 13,* 24–29.

Dollarhide, C. T. (1997). Counseling for meaning in work and life: An integrated approach. *Journal for Humanistic Education and Development, 35,* 178–187.

Dollarhide, C. T. (2000). Career process and advising: Tools for the advisor. *NACADA Journal, 19* (2), 34–36.

Dunn, R., Dunn, K., & Price, G. E. (1996). *Learning Styles Inventory*. Lawrence, KS: Price Systems, Inc.

Dunn, R., & Griggs, S. A. (1988). *Learning styles: Quiet revolution in American secondary schools*. Reston, VA: National Association of Secondary School Principals.

Elliott, D. S. (1998). *Prevention programs that work for youth: Violence prevention.* Boulder, CO: Center for the Study and Prevention of Violence.

Erikson, E. H. (1968). *Identity, youth, and crisis.* New York: Norton.

Esters, I. G., & Ittenbach, R. F. (1999). Contemporary theories and assessments of intelligence: A primer. *Professional School Counseling, 2,* 373–376.

Farwell, G. F. (1961). The role of the school counselor. *Counselor Education and Supervision, 1,* 40–43.

Fay, J., & Funk, D. (1995). *Teaching with love and logic: Taking control of the classroom.* Golden, CO: Love & Logic Press.

Festinger, L. (1957). *A theory of cognitive dissonance.* Stanford, CA: Stanford University Press.

Fox, M. (1994). *The reinvention of work: A new vision of livelihood for our time.* San Francisco: CA: Harper.

Fredrickson, R. H., & Pippert, R. R. (1964). Teaching experience in the employment of school counselors. *Counselor Education and Supervision, 4,* 24–27.

Gardner, H. (1983). *Frames of mind: The theory of multiple intelligences.* New York: Basic.

Gardner, H., & Hatch, T. (1989). Multiple intelligences go to school: Educational implications of the theory of multiple intelligences. *Educational Researcher, 18* (8), 4–10.

Gellatt, H. B. (1991). *Creative decision making using positive uncertainty.* Los Angeles: Crisp.

Gellatt, H. B. (1996). Developing a future sense. In R. Feller & G. Walz (Eds.), *Career transitions in turbulent times: Exploring work, learning, and careers* (pp. 387–394). Greensboro, NC: ERIC Counseling and Student Services Clearinghouse.

Goleman, D. (1995). *Emotional intelligence: Why it can matter more than IQ.* New York: Bantam.

Guerra, N. G., & Williams, K. R. (1996). *A program planning guide for youth violence prevention: A risk-focused approach.* Boulder, CO: Center for the Study and Prevention of Violence.

Gysbers, N. C., Heppner, M. J., & Johnston, J. A. (1998). *Career counseling: Process, issues, and techniques.* Boston: Allyn and Bacon.

Hansen, L. S. (1997). *Integrative life planning: Critical tasks for career development and changing life patterns.* San Francisco: CA: Jossey-Bass.

Helms, J. E. (1994). The conceptualization of racial identity and other "racial" constructs. In E. J. Trickett, R. J. Watts, & D. Birman (Eds.), *Human diversity: Perspectives on people in context* (pp. 285–311). San Francisco, CA: Jossey-Bass.

Henderson, S. J. (2000). "Follow your bliss": A process for career happiness. *Journal of Counseling and Development, 78,* 305–315.

Herr, E. L. (1996). Career development and work-bound youth. In R. Feller & G. Walz (Eds.), *Career transitions in turbulent times: Exploring work, learning, and careers* (pp. 245–256). Greensboro, NC: ERIC Counseling and Student Services Clearinghouse.

Hine, T. (1999). *The rise and fall of the American teenager.* New York: Avon.

Hotchkiss, L., & Borow, H. (1996). Sociological perspective on work and career development. In D. Brown, L. Brooks, & Associates (Eds.), *Career choice and development* (3rd ed.; pp. 281–336). San Francisco, CA: Jossey-Bass.

Howe, N., & Strauss, B. (1993). *13th gen: Abort, retry, ignore, fail?* New York: Vintage.

Hudson, G. R. (1961). Counselors need teaching experience. *Counselor Education and Supervision, 0,* 24–27.

Isaacson, L. E., & Brown, D. (1997). *Career information, career counseling, and career development* (6th ed.). Boston: Allyn and Bacon.

Keirsey, D. (1974). *Please understand me.* Del Mar, CA: Prometheus Nemesis.

King, P. M., & Kitchener, K. S. (1994). *Developing reflective judgment: Understanding and promoting intellectual growth and critical thinking in adolescents and adults.* San Francisco, CA: Jossey-Bass.

Kraus, L. J., & Hughey, K. F. (1999). The impact of an intervention on career decision-making self-efficacy and career indecision. *Professional School Counseling, 2,* 384–390.

Lazear, D. (1999). *Eight ways of teaching: The artistry of teaching with multiple intelligences.* Arlington Heights, IL: SkyLight Training and Publishing.

Loeb, P. R. (1994). *Generation at the crossroads: Apathy and action on the American campus.* New Brunswick, NJ: Rutgers University.

McWhirter, J. J., McWhirter, B. T., McWhirter, A. M., & McWhirter, E. H. (1998). *At-risk youth: A comprehensive response for counselors, teachers, psychologists, and human service professionals.* Pacific Grove, CA: Brooks/Cole.

National Institute of Justice, Office of Justice Programs. (1998). *Preventing crime: What works, what doesn't, what's promising.* Washington, DC: U.S. Department of Justice.

Olson, M. J., & Allen, D. N. (1993). Principals' perceptions of the effectiveness of school counselors with and without teaching experience. *Counselor Education and Supervision, 33,* 10–21.

Piaget, J. (1954). *The construction of reality in the child.* New York: Basic Books.

Pipher, M. (1994). *Reviving Ophelia: Saving the selves of adolescent girls.* New York: Ballantine.

Pollack, W. (1998). *Real boys: Rescuing our sons from the myths of boyhood*. New York: Henry Holt.

Potter, A. E. (1996). Working: A perspective for a new generation. In R. Feller & G. Walz (Eds.), *Career transitions in turbulent times: Exploring work, learning, and careers* (pp. 285–291). Greensboro, NC: ERIC Counseling and Student Services Clearinghouse.

Quarto, C. J. (1999). Teachers' perceptions of school counselors with and without teaching experience. *Professional School Counseling, 2*, 378–383.

Ritzer, G. (1996). McJobs. In R. Feller & G. Walz (Eds.). *Career transitions in turbulent times: Exploring work, learning, and careers* (pp. 211–218). Greensboro, NC: ERIC Counseling and Student Services Clearinghouse.

Rochester, D. E., & Cottingham, H. F. (1966). Is teaching experience necessary? Counselor educators speak out. *Counselor Education and Supervision, 5*, 175–181.

Scheer, J. (1994). Culture and disability: An anthropological point of view. In E. J. Trickett, R. J. Watts, & D. Birman (Eds.), *Human diversity: Perspectives on people in context* (pp. 244–260). San Francisco, CA: Jossey-Bass.

Schmidt, J. J. (1999). *Counseling in schools: Essential services and comprehensive programs* (3rd ed.). Boston: Allyn and Bacon.

Snyder, C. R. (1994). *The psychology of hope*. New York: Free Press.

Stone, K. F., & Dillehunt, H. Q. (1978). *Self science: The subject is me*. Santa Monica, CA: Goodyear.

Super, D. E., Savickas, M. L., & Super, C. M. (1996). Life-span, life-space approach to careers. In D. Brown, L. Brooks, & Associates (Eds.), *Career choice and development* (3rd ed.; pp. 121–178). San Francisco, CA: Jossey-Bass.

Tolan, P., & Guerra, N. (1998). *What works in reducing adolescent violence: An empirical review of the field*. Boulder, CO: Center for the Study and Prevention of Violence.

Tooker, E. D. (1957). Counselor role: Counselor training. *Personnel and Guidance Journal, 36*, 263–267.

Travers, J. F., Elliott, S. N., & Kratochwill, T. R. (1993). *Educational psychology: Effective teaching, effective learning*. Madison, WI: Brown & Benchmark.

Wahl, K. H., & Blackhurst, A. (2000). Factors affecting the occupational and educational aspirations of children and adolescents. *Professional School Counseling, 3*, 367–374.

Partnering with Students

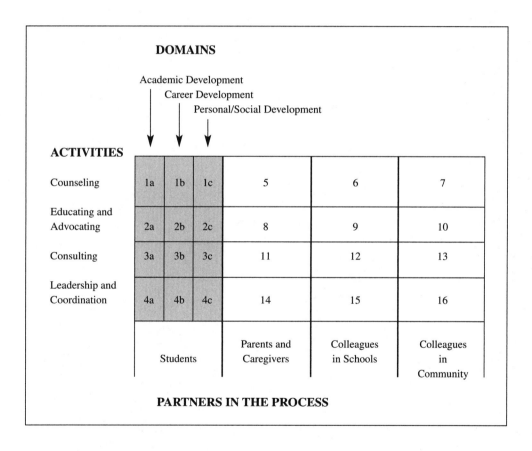

DOMAINS

Academic Development
  Career Development
    Personal/Social Development

ACTIVITIES

	Students			Parents and Caregivers	Colleagues in Schools	Colleagues in Community
Counseling	1a	1b	1c	5	6	7
Educating and Advocating	2a	2b	2c	8	9	10
Consulting	3a	3b	3c	11	12	13
Leadership and Coordination	4a	4b	4c	14	15	16

PARTNERS IN THE PROCESS

7

Partnering with Students: Counseling in the Three Domains (Blocks 1a, 1b, 1c of the DAP Model)

Colette T. Dollarhide

"What is the single most important problem I see in my friends' lives? Their peers, and truly feeling loved by someone, and not having enough self-confidence. What can be done about the problem? Listen."

Rebecca, age 18

Learning Objectives _____

By the end of this chapter, you will:

1. Understand how counseling may be perceived by colleagues in the school setting; design ways to communicate with them about the nature of counseling and how important it is for students.

2. Understand the concept of developmentally appropriate counseling with high school students.

3. Understand how to use multiple intelligences when developing theoretically congruent counseling interventions.

4. Evaluate when counseling is warranted for effective intervention and when referral is warranted for effective treatment.

5. Be familiar with the presenting issues of high school students, so that assessment strategies will be more effective. Develop commitment to increase your familiarity with these issues through additional training and education to make your interventions more meaningful.

6. Understand some of the factors that school counselors need to consider when evaluating when to conduct groups.

7. Be able to evaluate the advantages and disadvantages of group counseling.

8. Be able to articulate the conditions under which it is viable to provide group counseling.

9. Discuss the ethical issues of using assessment instruments in counseling and identify various assessment instruments for counseling in each domain.

A Day in the Life of a Counselor: A Rose for Shellay _____

Yolanda had been a school counselor for only two years when Shellay came to the school. Shellay was a girl from a small town whose family moved to follow her dad's factory job, but things weren't working out well for the family. Yolanda knew that Shellay, her parents, and brother were all living in a small two-bedroom apartment in a very industrial part of town.

It was November, and Yolanda had been concerned with Shellay's transition to the school. Even though she was a junior, Shellay was quiet and shy, not willing to get involved in the new school. It was overwhelming, Yolanda knew, for Shellay to come from a small, 400-person high school to this new place with over 1200 students. Shellay wasn't connecting with anyone in the school.

One day Shellay came in to see Yolanda about her classes. After some hesitation, she said, "I've been thinking about something that I want to talk to you about, but I'm not sure where to begin."

Yolanda put down her pen and closed Shellay's folder. She sat back in her chair and said, "Just start wherever you need to. I'm here to listen."

A deep sigh. Shellay fidgeted with her rings, not meeting Yolanda's eyes. "I've got a secret. Something I haven't told anyone." Again, she sighed.

After a long silence, Shellay continued. "You're the only person I can talk to. You've been so nice, helping me to feel OK at this school. I don't know if you want to hear this, though." She took a deep breath. "I'm not sure if I'm looking for help, not sure anyone can help, really. I'm not sure about whether this is a problem . . . maybe it is for me alone."

Yolanda was concerned she would get up and leave. "You don't have to tell me, but I'd like to help if I can. I can't know unless you tell me what the problem is, though."

Shellay continued to look at her rings, seeming to make up her mind. "OK. Here's the thing. I've been pretty lonely since we moved here. No one talks to me, and I don't have much to say to anyone here. People leave me alone and I leave them alone. Everyone except one person. This person talks to me, seems to care about me. I have feelings for this person, strong feelings, like I've never had before. I had feelings for someone at the old school, but when I said something to that person, I got laughed at, and they told the whole school. No one talked to me after that. I can't take that risk here.

"Now I come to school today, and here, on my locker door, is a rose. It's this beautiful red rose, and it's got my name on it. I open the card, and sure enough, it's from the person I love." She stopped.

Yolanda was glad for her. "That doesn't sound so bad! Here you care about someone, and it seems they care about you. I'm not sure I understand why this is a problem . . .?"

Shellay looked miserable. "I know, I know. I should be thrilled, huh? But the problem is . . ." She raised her eyes to watch Yolanda's reaction. "The problem is that my rose is from Kelli."

"Kelly Thomas, the senior in your chem class?"

No, Kelli Upham, the head cheerleader. A girl. I think I'm gay. Can you help me?"

Challenge Questions

Can you picture yourself working with Shellay? With which counseling theory (or theories) do you feel most comfortable? What are the assessment strategies your theory utilizes? What are the intervention strategies? Imagine that you have known Shellay for several months, and you know that she is very intellectual, rational, and logical. How will you counsel her so that she taps her own unique strengths and ways of interacting with her world? Imagine now that she is highly emotional, very connected to other people, and very verbal. What would you do differently given those strengths?

What do you know about the struggles of gay and lesbian youth? What do you know about homophobia and the process of coming out? What factors of Shellay's background provide some insight into the challenges she faces as she struggles with her sexual identity and orientation?

What do you know about transition issues? What are the implications you notice in her transition to this new school?

Now imagine that your administration has indicated that students who need more than three counseling sessions should be referred to an outside counselor. How will you meet Shellay's needs and address the administration's directive?

Counseling with Students

The work we do with students is a partnership—a symbiotic relationship that exists because our work helps them to achieve the outcomes of education and their full cooperation gives our profession its unique position as a member of the education team. Our partnership with students begins with the foundation of our profession: counseling. We are school counselors, not registrars, not bus monitors, not vice principals. As the basis of everything we do, the profession of counseling provides guiding philosophies, ways of viewing students, and ways of working to help students.

The importance of counseling as an essential part of a counselor's job is reinforced when examining student needs. Recall from Chapter 5 that students were surveyed to measure how they perceived school counselors. When students from several schools were asked to rate their school counseling programs, the counselors in schools with the highest ratings reported that they devoted 71 percent to 72 percent of their time in individual and group counseling (Wiggins & Moody, 1987). Furthermore, when students were asked what services they needed in high school, 89 percent responded that they needed career counseling, and 60 percent indicated that they needed personal counseling (Hutchinson & Bottorff, 1986). Sadly, only 40 percent said they received career counseling, and only 21 percent said they received any personal counseling. These studies serve as reminders that students value counseling.

Counseling is not just for students who are "troubled," nor does counseling *only* enhance a student's personal/social functioning. According to ACT, "students who see themselves a competent and effective, with a realistic view of themselves and their abilities, are more than three times more likely to be high achievers as low achievers . . . Students who have a low level of motivation to succeed, or who have a high level of anxiety about their schoolwork or home environment are five to six times as likely to be low achievers as high achievers" (Noble, 2000, p. 15). The domains of academic development, career development, and personal/social development resonate with each other, so counseling for concerns in one area can improve a student's functioning in all areas. But there are many misconceptions about counseling, so this is where we will begin in our discussion of counseling across the domains.

Misconceptions of Counseling

It is easy to see how misconceptions about counseling could exist: For many adults, their only experiences with counselors were the career guidance counselors or the mental health counselors they knew in their high school days. (Refer to Chapter 5 to recall the historical context of school counseling.) Because of that training in either the career guidance or mental health models of school counseling, school counselors functioned very differently than counselors of today—but our colleagues and the parents of our students don't know that. Adding to this misunderstanding are movies and public events that portray counselors in general as charlatans (or worse, criminals), and counseling as ineffective, manipulative, or brainwashing. Therefore, the closed door and closed lips of our profession (privacy and confidentiality) that are designed to protect our student-clients may be misunderstood. It is important that counselors are sensitive to the questions and concerns that arise about counseling and are pro-active in helping others understand the nature of counseling.

Letters to parents and teachers at the beginning of each year help to introduce the nature and scope of the comprehensive school counseling program in general and school counseling activities specifically. Follow-up communication reminds them of the work you do with students, parents, colleagues in the school, and colleagues in the community. Furthermore, professional accountability demands that school counselors communicate regularly with administrators, both at the building and the district levels, about the activities of the comprehensive school counseling program. (This will be discussed in depth in Chapter 14.)

Even for those who understand and appreciate comprehensive school counseling in general and counseling with students specifically, the pressure on teachers to ensure that students meet performance standards for graduation may cause teachers to be extremely reluctant to allow students out of class to come for individual or group counseling. Counselors need to be creative in designing time for appointments: Some ideas for counseling appointments that won't interfere with class time include scheduling appointments before and after school, during lunchtime, and during study halls.

Developmentally Appropriate Counseling

Most counseling training programs teach basic counseling skills using the template of adult clients to help counselors-in-training learn about empathy, unconditional positive regard, active listening, and other counseling competencies. It is up to counselor trainees to generalize those skills to the unique populations with which they will practice those skills in a professional counseling context. This means that now is your opportunity to take the foundation counseling skills you know and modify those skills to counsel high school students.

As we discussed in Chapters 2 and 3, adolescents have unique developmental and contextual realities. And as we discussed in Chapter 4, schools for adolescents can be configured in ways to foster their development. And as we saw in Chapter 6 on the three domains of comprehensive school counseling, young people have issues relative to academic, career, and personal/social development. To apply all these insights to counseling with adolescents, we should be mindful of the following guidelines:

1. Young people need to be active because they possess a shorter attention span than most adults.
2. Young people are still developing their own moral compass and intellectual, critical thinking skills. This means they are still developing their ability to tap their inner reality or insight.
3. Young people may not have the emotional intelligence to be able to identify their emotions, the source of their emotions, or words to describe their experience of their emotions.
4. Young people need to feel significant and respected.
5. Young people need to feel free to choose, while concurrently needing help articulating their *framework* (value system) by which to evaluate alternatives.
6. Young people need help developing *strategies* for generating and evaluating alternatives, making a commitment to an identifiable alternative, and then understanding the consequences of the choices they make. They are still refining their ability to draw cause-and-effect connections.

These important insights into the developmental realities and needs of adolescents yield implications for both the *manner* in which we counsel young people and the *content* of our counseling. In terms of the manner in which we counsel high school students, we need to be aware of their activity level and attention span. We also need to be aware that they may have limited ability to understand themselves—limited insight. They may not be able to identify their feelings, or they may not have language to describe what they are experiencing.

Most importantly, counselors must understand adolescents' need to feel in charge of their own lives; high school counseling clients must feel that their counselor trusts them to make good decisions and believes in them.

In terms of the content of counseling, high school counselors must be aware that young people may need help articulating their own value system (the framework for evaluating alternatives) before conversations can take place about the alternatives themselves. The autonomy this dialogue teaches, and the respect this conveys, goes far in developing trust between the counselor and the client.

In addition, high school clients are still learning how to make decisions, practicing the process of identifying goals, articulating alternatives, evaluating alternatives, making a choice, then designing a plan to implement that choice. Developing a counseling approach that emphasizes and teaches the *process* of decision making, in addition to the focus on the *product* of the decision making, helps high school students develop an important adult competency.

Furthermore, it is very important that counselors understand that young people need help evaluating the consequences of their choices. These young clients are still developing their abilities to understand cause and effect, so evaluating alternatives in terms of possible consequences is particularly challenging. For example, many researchers believe that adolescents engage in high-risk behavior because they see themselves as invulnerable, living the myth of "It won't happen to me" (Craig, 1996, p. 453). Helping young clients understand that it *can* happen to them may be a hard sell, but without addressing this, young people are not effectively or realistically assessing the consequences of their choices (Ponton, 1997). While the outcome of some choices have nonlethal consequences (i.e., Should I go out for cheerleading?), the consequences of others are life and death or are life altering (i.e., Should I wear a condom if I'm going to have sex?).

This means that high school counselors need to be able to assess:

- The client's attention span
- The client's level of insight
- The client's level of emotional intelligence (ability to identify emotions, the source of emotions, or their experience of emotions)
- The client's clarity of values
- The client's level of decision-making strategies
- The client's ability to understand cause and effect relative to his or her choices

Reflection Moment

Recall a time when you needed help making a decision. If the alternatives were clear, how did it feel if the person you asked for help doubted your ability to evaluate your alternatives? Conversely, if your alternatives weren't clear, how did it feel to have a helper who assumed it was all so clear and so simple? These are common experiences. The point is to become more sensitive to how you help young people in terms of their decision making.

Prevention, Intervention, and Treatment: When to Counsel and When to Refer

As you will recall from Chapter 6, prevention efforts are often associated with classroom developmental curriculum and schoolwide efforts to improve the school environment. Intervention efforts are often associated with individual counseling, group counseling, and parent-student-teacher-administration consultation and mediation. Treatment is called for when the student's issues are chronic, deeply traumatic, or deeply seated in the personality, such as issues of chronic depression, survival of abuse or violence, or severe anger management. In terms of this chapter, we are focused on counseling, which is usually classified as intervention.

In general, counselors try to enhance the positive elements of a student's life and mitigate the effect of negative elements through prevention efforts. Counselors work primarily with developmental issues that arise for students through intervention, referring for treatment as needed. Intervention involves short-term issues that may be addressed in four to eight counseling meetings (which could last from 10 to 30 minutes, depending on the situation) and usually involve predictable developmental issues (such as relationship issues, transition issues). Medium-term issues could require a counselor's involvement (counseling, consulting with teachers, acknowledging the student with an encouraging smile) for a semester and involve issues that often resolve themselves as the student matures and as time passes (such as careers, grief). Deep-level issues are those for which the student may require lifelong recovery work and are those issues for which the counselor would provide immediate intervention and support, with referral for treatment (such as substance addition, suicidal behaviors, depression).

Treatment consisting of in-depth, intensive, or medication-assisted therapy, however, is most often *not* conducted in schools. When students are in need of treatment, most school counselors refer those students to mental health therapists in the community (Smith & Archer, 2000). As mentioned above, counselors provide intervention and referral, then, with permission, contact the community therapist to coordinate school efforts with the student's therapy. The school counselor and the community therapist work together to facilitate the student's education and development, often with the counselor providing counseling, education, consultation, and coordination of services to assist the student with educational and developmental concerns. For example, if it is discovered that a student is severely depressed due to years of sexual abuse, that student may need medications, frequent sessions, and intensive recuperative therapy to address the depression and begin healing old scars from the abuse. The community therapist and the school counselor would collaborate so that the school counselor:

1. Knows what medication(s) the student is taking.
2. Would be available if the student experienced a crisis during school.
3. Would assist in the coordination of IEP (individualized education plan) meetings or other efforts aimed at assuring academic, career, and personal/social success.
4. Would provide individual counseling for academic, career, and personal/social issues.
5. May want to include the student in any groups currently meeting for students with similar issues.

Further discussion of school-community collaboration will be presented in Chapter 14.

The quality of intervention offered through counseling, however, should not pale in comparison with quality of therapy obtained from a community mental health professional (Smith & Archer, 2000). In schools, the delivery of high-quality, wellness-directed, non-pathological, context- and systems-aware counseling is essential to help students address academic, career, and personal/social issues, since students continue to come to school with issues that will impede their abilities to be successful (Baker, 2000; Keys, Bemak, & Lockhart, 1998).

As an extension of this prevention-intervention-treatment continuum, many districts are moving to limit the number of individual counseling meetings with any one student. We feel it is a serious mistake for districts to impose seemingly arbitrary limits on school counseling activities. We believe that it is important that the professionally trained counselor be the one to identify when a student needs intervention and provide that intervention—and when a student needs treatment, provide that referral. We believe that honest conversations with administrators about these limits constitute the only way to educate them about the services a professional school counselor provides—and to help them understand that counseling success cannot be guaranteed within a time limit.

Districts or schools that impose time limits on counseling seriously compromise the efficacy of the school counselor and only through tireless advocacy will administrators understand this fact. (This is why we devote two chapters to a discussion of leadership: Chapters 10 and 14). If it is hard for them to understand your position, consider other resources to assist you. Consider contacting the state's counseling association, or the state's school counseling association. Also consider taking your message to other decision makers to secure their support: the school board, the parents, local mental health providers, and the local community at large. Invite an outside review of your program to discuss the priorities of your comprehensive program or invite your advisory committee (described in Chapter 5) to discuss your program priorities. Conduct action research to determine how many students you have seen successfully with how many sessions, or collaborate on such a study with other high schools to collect data to support your position. If, in spite of your best efforts to change the policy, the district maintains its stand in limiting counseling, then you need to think about how you will meet the needs of your students.

Functioning as a Professional, Ethical Counselor

Just as we saw in the Day in the Life vignette at the beginning of this chapter, many students will use an "acceptable" reason for coming to see the counselor so that they are not exposing their concerns to anyone but the counselor. In Shellay's case, she asked if she could see the counselor to talk about her schedule. Often, students will use scheduling, careers, or minor academic concerns to mask their real reason to talk to the counselor. As an ethical professional counselor, you must be aware of this and be prepared to work with student clients on a deeper level if their issues warrant it. The general rule is to be open to all issues, be sensitive to nonverbal cues, and be constantly assessing all areas of the student's functioning to be aware of those times the student needs more attention than was given as the presenting issue. It is crucial that counselors give the time and attention needed to students who come to see them; not providing adequate care is unethical and unprofessional (Refer to Ethics in

Chapter 15). Furthermore, not devoting adequate time and attention to student clients will damage the trust that the students need to have in the counselor to make effective use of the counselor's time and expertise.

For the school counselor, trust is essential. If the students do not trust the counselor, the counselor's ability to be effective will be seriously compromised. There are many things to fear about going to see a counselor: Many students do not know about confidentiality and have concerns about their "secrets" being told to teachers, administrators, friends, or parents, or they fear being labeled "weird" or "sick." In particular, students of color might find the counselor's office to be a very threatening place, especially if the counselor represents a different culture or socioeconomic background than the student (Wittmer, 2000). As the student establishes trust in both the person of the counselor and the process of counseling, the real reasons for the visit will be revealed.

Students also need to know that the counselor has a breadth of knowledge about student issues and what it means to be an adolescent, called "withitness" (Gordon, 1997). Students need to know that you're not going to "freak out" when you hear their problems. No counselor can know everything there is to know about every issue of every client, but counselors need to be knowledgeable enough about most issues to listen effectively for underlying themes and concerns, facilitate effective assessment and intervention, and help put the student-client at ease that help is possible. The case of an unplanned pregnancy can illustrate the embarrassment of sharing the "secret," the need for the counselor to be able to deal rationally with the "emergency," the need for the counselor to understand his or her own personal perspectives on the issue of teenage sexuality and parenting, and the need to be informed about options available in the community (Kiselica & Pfaller, 1993).

To be effective, you need to understand both the process of helping your student clients (your theoretical orientation and strategies) and the product of healing that you hope for your student clients (your insights into the client's issues). All of this is interrelated: How issues relate to each other and how you address various issues is shaped by your theoretical orientation. Let this serve as another reminder that you must, as an ethical counselor, be able to articulate, and practice within, your theoretical orientation.

Furthermore, an ethical school counselor must be sensitive to multicultural issues. Wittmer (2000) points out that culturally skilled counselors know how crucial culture is to a student's identity development and know how to preserve the dignity of both the student client and his or her culture. Since most counselors are trained in the traditional Euro-American worldview, there are often large gaps in the understanding of different cultures that need to be identified and addressed, either by additional professional development and training, or by addressing it explicitly with the student client ("I don't know what it has been like to grow up in your culture. Tell me what growing up has been like for you . . ."). Even what we *think* we know about another culture must be respectfully explored with each student client of that culture.

Common Issues Addressed in Counseling Secondary School Students

An exhaustive list of student issues would not be possible in one book, but as a school counselor, you need to be aware of counseling intervention strategies that address the following issues. You are urged to expand your professional library by acquiring resources to help you understand and counsel young people struggling with these issues.

Academic Issues:
Failure and/or fear of failure
Performance issues: Overachievement and underachievement
Test anxiety
Stress management
Learning issues and future careers
Relationships with teachers, administrators
Learning problems (ADHD)
Academic self-efficacy

Career Issues:
Career indecision that causes anxiety
Career choice in conflict with pressure from others
Perceived inadequacy for desired career
Career indecision while receiving pressure from others

Personal/Social Issues:
Dependence, independence, and interdependence
Sexual orientation
Sexual activity and morality
Pregnancy (for both mother and father)
Parenthood (for both mother and father)
Relationship choices
Violence in home and/or dating relationships
Crisis issues
Suicidal ideation
Grief: loss of parents, siblings, friends, other loved ones
Identity issues
Diversity issues
Stress
Substance use/abuse/addiction
Family issues with substance abuse and addiction
Dysfunctional families
Friendships
Relationship with parents, siblings, family
Loss of illusion of safety and/or victimization (violence, crime, or natural disaster)
Living with or history of abuse: emotional, physical, sexual
Health issues (acute or chronic; AIDS, STDs)
Mental health issues (depression, anger management)
Violent and semiviolent behavior (criminality, bullying, gang membership)
Self-esteem
Self- and body-image (eating disorders, steroid use)

Peer pressure
Normal versus unhealthy risk taking
Family issues (divorce, blended family issues)

Reflection Moment

What are your experiences with these issues? Do you know someone who is living with problems or questions about these areas of life? Personal experience with an issue isn't always the best way to learn about how to help others who struggle with the same issue— but relying solely on learning from books isn't ideal either. Balance what you learn from books with what you can learn from others who have lived with the issue, and then blend that with your own insights.

Individual Counseling

Every counselor will select the theoretical orientation that works for him or her, so you will want to focus on those theories that lend themselves well to the school environment. Given that students don't often have much time for one-on-one sessions and that schools are not perceived to be the best setting for intensive psychotherapy, school counselors usually adopt a theoretical orientation that works well within time constraints (Smith & Archer, 2000). Three counseling approaches that are often practiced by school counselors are Adlerian therapy, solutions-focused or brief therapy, and reality therapy. You are urged to find out more about these approaches.

Using Multiple Intelligences in Counseling

Additional insights into how to work effectively with high school clients can be found in the concept of multiple intelligences. Recall from Chapter 6 that Gardner and Lazear described each learner as a unique constellation of eight intelligences (Lazear, 1999). These intelligences include verbal, mathematic/logical, artistic, musical, naturalist, interpersonal, intrapersonal, and kinesthetic strengths. Recall also that we discussed these intelligences as providing insights into why a person learns (motivation and predilection for learning), how a student learns (acquisition and retention of information), and how a student manifests that learning has taken place (performance on academic tasks). In other words, multiple intelligences can explain why students have interests and abilities in some areas and not in others. Grades can be a good indicator of an intelligence strength, but grades alone are not sufficient indicators of intelligences. Some students can get good grades in subjects they hate through hard work and perseverance, but there is a big difference between hard work and a labor of love.

If you know a student's strengths, you have important information that can be very useful in designing counseling interventions. For example, the use of journaling, art, music, and poetry has been advocated for years as effective ways to work with counseling clients, regardless of theoretical orientation (Cormier & Hackney, 1999; Hutchins & Vaught, 1997). Effective counselors would naturally look for counseling methods that fit with the strengths of the client. Using Lazear (1999; pp. 142–145) and Corey (1999) as a springboard, the following list suggests some counseling strategies based on multiple intelligences and theoretical foundations.

1. Verbal/Linguistic Intelligence:

    Journaling of feelings and events.

    Making up jokes about negative beliefs, events, or concerns (Rational Emotive Behavior Therapy).

    Poetry.

    Storytelling (telling own story, writing about ideal life, and/or writing about own problems in the third person; Contextual therapy).

    Debate between opposing sides (Gestalt therapy).

    Metaphor analysis to discern underlying themes.

2. Logical/Mathematical Intelligence:

    Creating formulas to show relationships between events (such as A → B → C from Rational Emotive Behavior Therapy).

    Creating logic/pattern games (show the client the events and ask him or her to create the pattern or logic that connects the events).

    Syllogisms: Creating If . . . Then deductions from choices (Systematic Problem Solving; Harrison, 2000).

3. Visual/Spatial Intelligence:

    Guided Imagery: Imagining oneself solving the problem, acting on new choices, or living out the consequences of choices (Multimodal therapy, Image Psychology [Parker, 1998]).

    Art therapy: Drawing, painting, sculpting, creating a collage, wood carving to represent the problem, the client's feelings, the ideal solution (Kahn, 1999).

    Mind mapping: Creating a web of connections on paper to elicit connections between events, feelings, behaviors.

4. Bodily/Kinesthetic Intelligence:

    Situation sculpting: Using people or props, the client designs a setting or stage in which conflicts are depicted and acted out under the direction of the client (Psychodrama, family sculpting).

    Acting: Using the client's own body, the client acts out his or her experiences (Gestalt therapy, "behavior rehearsal" in behavior therapy, "acting as if" in Adlerian therapy).

    Dance, gymnastic movement: The client uses movement to express feelings.

    Sports: The client uses sports as a metaphor for his or her life.

Model building: The student invents something or creates a physical model to illustrate conflict or problems.

Charades: The client mimes the situation to help with expression of the event or problem.

Role playing.

Ropes courses and outdoor challenge experiences.

5. Musical/Rhythmic Intelligence:

Using music or sounds to tell the client's story, either music written or played by the student, or existing prerecorded music.

Rapping.

Singing new words to an existing song (Rational Emotive Behavior Therapy).

Practice hearing tonal differences to convey emotions in the human voice.

6. Interpersonal Intelligence:

Insight counseling, using other people's experiences to gain perspective on own issues (Adlerian therapy, Gestalt therapy, Person-Centered counseling).

Telling about the situation using pictures of others feeling certain emotions.

Group counseling.

Using cooperation to solve problems.

Ropes courses and outdoor challenge experiences.

7. Intrapersonal Intelligence:

Insight counseling, to gain perspective on issues (Adlerian therapy, Gestalt therapy, Existential logotherapy, Person-Centered counseling).

Anxiety and stress reduction using meditation.

Metacognition techniques: Helping the client think about his or her own thinking to recognize relationships between beliefs, events, emotions, and consequences (Rational Emotive Behavior Therapy).

Mindfulness exercises: Helping the client to focus on the present and live intentionally (Existential therapy, Person-Centered therapy).

Emotional awareness: Using the client's insight to identify, name, and deal with emotions.

8. Naturalist Intelligence

Archetypal pattern recognition: Helping the client identity patterns and themes that emerge in human nature.

Caring for plants and animals: Stress reduction and anxiety management using pets and other living things (Adlerian counseling).

Natural world insights: Using examples from the natural world to discuss the human condition (e.g., social animals, pack behavior, insect colonies, flocking of birds and schooling of fish; rock formations and geologic forces; plants, weather phenomena).

Ropes courses and outdoor challenge experiences.

Counseling outdoors while taking a walk with the client.

Listening to natural sounds during counseling.

This list is by no means exhaustive. As a counselor, you will develop your own ideas of counseling strategies that will be helpful with your clients, but these ideas might help you identify strategies that will engage the student more fully in the counseling process.

Reflection Moment

What is your theoretical orientation? Can you see yourself counseling Shellay using one of the multiple intelligences outlined in this section? Which one?

Group Counseling

Research into the efficacy of group counseling indicates recent changes in the ways counselors perceive group counseling in the schools. In 1993, Carroll found that elementary school counselors did not feel that they had adequate skills in group counseling; they would have liked more training in groups in their graduate programs. By 1996, Dansby found that counselors generally felt "that small group work should be a vital part of any counseling program, that their programs would be more effective if they led more groups, and that they felt adequately trained to implement group counseling" (pp. 233–234). More specifically, Dansby found that high school counselors were more emphatic than elementary or middle school counselors that their counseling programs should involve group work and that they should lead more groups.

It is important to define group counseling. According to Johnson and Johnson (2000), groups are "two or more individuals in face-to-face interaction, each aware of positive interdependence as they strive to achieve mutual goals, each aware of his or her membership in the group, and each aware of the others who belong to the group" (p. 20). Group counseling involves primary intervention (Dansby, 1996), and for some student clients, it may be the most therapeutic intervention they will experience. The intent of conducting group counseling is that participants will be able to learn about themselves, other people, life tasks, and authentic ways of relating in a safe, confidential setting. While there are similarities between group counseling and group educating, we will emphasize that group counseling, as we mean it in this chapter, has a therapeutic and intervention focus. Educating a large group (15+) of students can have intervention effects, but since the emphasis of that activity is teaching rather than introspection and values clarification, that activity will be considered in Chapter 8 as a prevention activity.

For many counselors, group counseling is the primary mode of delivery of counseling services. For others, group counseling represents a way to segue student clients from individual counseling to full termination. Used in this way, group counseling is a "halfway house" between more intensive counseling and fully autonomous functioning of the student client. The group is a support platform, allowing the student client to cement insights and behavior changes.

The importance of group counseling in schools cannot be overemphasized (Fleming, 1999). In fact, Keys, Bemak, and Lockhart (1998) suggested that group counseling is more effective than individual counseling to address the needs of students, most especially at-risk students. This contention is supported through research into violent youths, which suggests that peer-group interventions are effective in redirecting peer values, confronting antisocial behaviors, teaching problem-solving skills, and encouraging prosocial behaviors (Bemak & Keys, 2000; Tolan & Guerra, 1994).

If you refer back to the list of common issues of students in high schools, you will notice that any of these topics could constitute a meaningful group experience. These topics can be addressed in structured or process group formats.

Structured versus Process Groups

To understand group counseling, it is important to understand that there is a difference between structured groups and process groups. Structured groups refer to group experiences in which the counselor takes direct leadership of the group, including identifying goals, presenting material with an assumed values orientation, selecting activities, and directing interaction. Often, structured group exercises (i.e., role playing, behavior rehearsal, didactic experiences) and curricular materials are utilized to move the group intentionally toward certain conclusions and insights involving a psychoeducational goal (Goldstein, 1999). For this reason, structured groups are often criticized for being too prescriptive (Keys, Bemak, & Lockhart, 1998). Examples of structured group topics for secondary schools would include decision making; stress management; communication skills; learning new behaviors (such as anger management, parenting skills, prenatal care); drugs, tobacco, and alcohol resistance; test taking; study skills; planning for college; and career exploration. As you can see from each of these topics, the outcome of the group is predetermined; each topic has a clear learning goal.

In contrast, process groups rely on the learning that emerges from the group interaction and spontaneous experiences that occur as the members learn to negotiate the natural progression of all relationships: *forming* (working through trust issues), *storming* (working through authenticity issues and interpersonal dissonance), *norming* (creating shared norms and rules for the group), *performing* (addressing the therapeutic topic or issue that brings members to the group), and *adjourning* (saying goodbye at the end of the experience) (Tuckman & Jensen, as cited in Kline, 2003). Furthermore, process groups do not have a clearly predetermined goal; each member comes to the group to explore her or his own choices, and there is often a greater emphasis on the support that groups can provide. In fact, what is commonly referred to as "support groups" are process groups. Examples of such process groups would include groups for sexual orientation (Street, 1994), career counseling, learning issues such as attention deficit disorder, self-concept or self-esteem, changing families (divorce, blended families, nontraditional families), loss and grief, self-discipline, fears, addiction recovery, diversity support, and suicide/depression.

The extent of structure or the extent of process within the group is best conceptualized as a continuum, with highly structured on one end and highly process-focused on the other. In the middle are groups that are blended: Perhaps the counselor has structure in the overall view of the group, but allows processing to be the main vehicle for change within each meeting. An excellent example of a blended group is presented by Muller (2000), in which she describes a group counseling experience for African American high school females to foster positive identity development. For each meeting, the facilitators have a stimulus experience or question to start the session, but then allow group interaction to guide the processing of that experience. Examples of such stimulus experiences include the words "It's Not Fair!" written on the board to focus discussion on instances of discrimination and presentation of the life story of a successful African American woman to focus on qualities that foster success (p. 266). It is always advisable that group leaders have activities planned for each meeting, in case the members are uncomfortable with sharing feelings or ideas (Posthuma, 1999). While silence is not a problem per se, some adolescents might find extensive silence disconcerting, and chances of acting up increase as dissonance increases.

Our hope is that you will be able to see how that many topics could be presented as either a structured group or a process group. For example, a topic like truancy could be a process group if the group is designed to allow members to clarify their values relative to attendance, explore their own attendance challenges, make choices about future behavior, and support each other in continuing those new behaviors. The same topic could be presented as a structured group if the intent is to teach the importance of regular attendance, emphasize strategies for reducing truancy, and then support members in truancy-reducing behaviors. Another example is a group about sexual activity: As a process group, members would clarify their values relative to sexual expression, discuss their options, and support each other in their choices; as a structured group, members would learn about issues involved with sexual expression and what to do about them if encountered.

Which kinds of groups are most often conducted in high schools? Dansby (1996) asked counselors what topics were addressed in their groups and found that high school counselors responded with more structured topics than counselors at the other two levels; the top five topics were "planning for college," "careers," "decision making," "self-concept/self-esteem," and "study skills" (Dansby, 1996, p. 234). One possible explanation for the structured group emphasis at the high school level involves demographics: Dansby reported that years of counseling experience increased with grade level, with 58 percent of the high school counselors having more than ten years of experience (1996; p. 233). Recall from our discussion about school counseling philosophy that there is a historical emphasis on career and college guidance at the high school level. These counselors were providing programs that fit within that historical philosophical orientation; you may have the opportunity to help your school examine its guidance emphasis to allow for more counseling focus in *your* comprehensive school counseling program.

Advantages of Group Counseling

There are numerous advantages to providing services to student clients through a group counseling format. Primarily, these advantages involve the developmental appropriateness of groups for students who are peer-oriented, the efficiency of groups in terms of the counselor's time, and the systemic nature of groups.

Since adolescents are peer-oriented at this developmental stage of life, it makes sense that counseling formats involving peers will meet with success (Ball & Meck, 1979). As we have seen in Chapters 2, 3, and 4, peer interaction is essential for effective identity development. Group counseling harnesses that natural peer orientation to interest student clients in becoming involved in a group, engages them in values exploration and clarification, motivates them to attend, empowers them in the change process, and supports them while they try new behaviors.

A second advantage of group counseling involves efficiency: Conducting group counseling allows counselors to reach more student clients than is possible through one-on-one counseling. This does not mean that group counseling is "easier" than individual counseling, it only means it is more efficient—student clients with similar issues will learn together, brainstorm ideas for growth for each other, and support each other as they struggle together. Furthermore, it connects students who may otherwise have little contact with each other and assures students who feel isolated by their problems that they are not alone in their suffering, providing significant therapeutic benefits. Studies into the efficacy of groups have documented significant benefits for members in general (Zinck & Littrell, 2000) and in terms of specific counseling strategies such as solution-focused group counseling (LaFountain & Garner, 1996) and adventure counseling (Nassar-McMillan & Cashwell, 1997).

Finally, there is a call in the literature for more systems-awareness in our work in schools (Bilynsky & Vernaglia, 1999; Dansby, 1996; Fontes, 2000; Geroski & Knauss, 2000; Keys, Bemak, & Lockhart, 1998; Taylor & Adelman, 2000). Students come to schools as both products of, and producers of, change within the multiple systems of their existence. Working with students in group counseling allows counselors to expand their awareness of each student client: What better way to see how students interact in their systems than to witness it firsthand? Group counseling opens the perspective of both client and counselor to include awareness of our webs of interaction within systems.

Disadvantages of Group Counseling

Group counseling is not for all students, nor is it for all issues. One of the most important limitations of group counseling is the issue of confidentiality: No matter how emphatically the counselor insists that all members respect confidentiality, some breeches may occur. Additional concerns involve the special relationship between schools, parents and other caregivers, and the school counselor in terms of the limits of confidentiality for health, safety, and legal reasons. In some cases, mandated reporting and/or informing parents of the problems of student clients could result in serious trust issues with members of a group if those situations are not addressed in advance.

Furthermore, scheduling difficulties can seriously interfere with a counselor's ability to schedule groups, especially if there is no schoolwide study hall or period for such student-driven activities. Dansby (1996) found that lack of time and scheduling problems/difficulty getting students out of class were the top two sources of interference that hindered group counseling efforts.

Often, other school professionals do not understand the importance of group counseling, representing another limitation of groups. Dansby (1996) reported that 50 percent of the counselors in her study identified "some teachers" as interfering with the implementation of group counseling, followed by 22 percent citing the principal, and 17 percent citing some parents (p. 234). This highlights that clear communication about group counseling is a necessity for successful group counseling activities.

Logistics of Groups

Groups take planning and forethought to be successful. Dansby (1996) asked counselors what they needed to implement more effective group counseling, and the answer was a resounding "more time" cited by 64 percent of high school counselors (p. 234). When asked to elaborate, most high school counselors replied with "too much paperwork" or "too many administrative duties" (p. 234). At best, this suggests that these counselors are reactive in their approach to student clients, waiting until there are serious problems, then addressing them with individual counseling. At worst, this suggests that these counselors might be sacrificing time they need to spend with students to complete paperwork and/or administrative tasks. In either case, what these counselors express is a reality of group counseling: While an essential part of any comprehensive school counseling program, group counseling takes time to design. The crucial insight here is that this is time well spent, because the benefits of group counseling have a ripple effect that goes beyond the individual members. Early planning is essential.

Additional logistical issues come from planning group counseling in a typical high school. Since releasing students from class is a challenge, the best suggestion is to schedule meetings during study halls or before or after school. Recognizing that there are transportation issues for many students, there may be no options outside the normal school operating hours, and those logistical challenges must be met creatively. Many school counselors will schedule group meetings that rotate through the day, so that students are not pulled from the same class for each meeting. If the school has a rotating schedule (in which the subjects rotate through the day so that each day starts with a different subject), then the group sessions are scheduled at the same time each day to accomplish the same goal: that the students do not miss the same subject for every group meeting.

As with any group counseling planning, the number of members, the issues with which they are struggling, and the duration of the group must all be considered holistically. For some topics, such as dealing with ADD or ADHD, smaller groups are recommended (perhaps four to five members); meetings should be scheduled around awareness of the effects of possible medications (when medications take effect, when they wear off and the rebound effect occurs); and the length of each meeting should be developmentally appropriate based on attention span. Do not forget that it is critical that every member is interviewed and screened for appropriateness for every group, as this element of planning is often skipped in the crush of time and responsibilities. In general, you do not want the members to vary too widely in age or developmental level (Posthuma, 1999).

In addition, you need to consider how you will advertise the group: how you will present it to students, parents, teachers, and administrators. To do this, you must consider what you will call the group. For example, if you are advertising a group for gay, lesbian, and questioning students, calling it the "Gay, Lesbian, and Questioning" group will seriously compromise your ability to secure students (who may not be ready to label themselves or may not be ready to come out) and may cause serious objections from parents, teachers, and administrators who do not believe such a lifestyle is healthy or appropriate. Perhaps a better name would be a Lifestyle group. By the same token, a group for Concerned Others might be a better way to promote a group for those who use alcohol, tobacco, and other drugs (ATOD) and those who are concerned about someone who is using. A Changing Families group might be more acceptable for students and others than a group for children of divorce, since families might be concerned that family issues will be aired in public. A group for career issues might sound boring to students; a group called "Dreams of Your Future" might elicit more interest. Another consideration might be to secure interested students from informal interaction, teacher referrals, or individual counseling referrals, then allow the group to name itself to enhance cohesion and identity (Muller, 2000).

Group counseling will never replace individual counseling, nor should it. But effective planning, creative ways of thinking about conducting groups, and conscientious follow-through can make group counseling one of the most powerful interventions available to high school counselors.

Reflection Moment

Have you ever had a group counseling experience as a member? As a facilitator? As a leader? Most counselors have a course in group counseling in their graduate program, but one course may not give you a chance to fully explore your group leadership/facilitation skills. How comfortable are you with groups? For which issues would you be motivated to design a group experience? With which issues would you be comfortable leading a group? Would you feel more comfortable with group members of your gender and ethnicity? If so, how can you expand your comfort zone? How many members would you find comfortable? What is your personal style: Are you a leader or are you a facilitator?

Peer Facilitators

We must not neglect the powerful benefits that result when young people are actively involved in the counseling program. By this, we do not mean involvement as a student client—we mean involvement as a peer helper (Foster-Harrison, 1995). In this program, young people would be selected and trained to act as peer facilitators, assisting the counselor in the logistics and management of a variety of services, including peer tutoring, peer mediation, peer helping, peer programs to help orient new students to the school, and peer facilitation of groups. Peer facilitators would need to be carefully screened for appropriateness with the counseling program, persons to be helped, the specific counseling topic (academic subject, careers, adjustment issues for new students), and other factors. Special training would be provided in the helping process, listening, the basics of confidentiality, and facilitation of interaction. Most importantly, special attention would be paid to teaching peer helpers about the limits of their competence, so that the professional counselor would be involved immediately if there were any problems. It is crucial that these peer helpers are carefully supervised and monitored; even a well-trained peer facilitator is not qualified to conduct a group alone (Fleming, 1999).

A program of peer facilitation, with carefully selected, trained, and screened peer facilitators, can provide benefits for the counselor, the peer facilitator, and other students. For the counselor, the benefits of having peer facilitators are numerous: The peer facilitator can provide feedback about the progress of students being helped, serve as a role model to other students, and assist with some of the logistics of running the program, such as helping with scheduling and publicity. For the peer facilitator, this provides an opportunity to develop helping and leadership skills—a powerful way for the young person to "try on" roles connected with school-related and helping professions. One of the important ways that young people can develop and extend their "social interest" (to use an Adlerian term) is to help others, a powerful intrinsic motivator. Finally, there are benefits to the student population as a whole: Peer helpers provide a safe method of connecting with the counselor in cases where trust is an issue, and it empowers students to see themselves, like the peer facilitator, as capable. In a recent study, students who had worked with a peer counselor were found have a decrease in discipline referrals, improved attitudes toward school, improved school attendance, and improved grades ("Peer Counselors Help Kids . . . ," 2000).

Assessment in the Counseling Process

Many authors agree that assessment and appraisal of students are important counselor functions (Baker, 2000; Gysbers & Henderson, 2000; Loesch & Goodman, 2000; Schmidt, 1999). But the extent of the counselor's involvement with student assessment and appraisal is a subject of debate in the profession. Some authors would consider assessment and appraisal to be major activities in the comprehensive school counseling program (Loesch & Goodman, 2000; Schmidt, 1999), while other authors argue that school counselors use assessment and appraisal as components of other, more important activities, such as counseling (Baker, 2000) and individual planning (Gysbers & Henderson, 2000). In this text, we will address assessment in terms of its application within the activities of the DAP model of counseling and educating.

First, it is essential that you obtain an in-depth understanding of assessment instruments and concepts; this is usually accomplished by the completion of a discrete course in assessment or appraisal in the graduate program. As you will note in the ethics statements of both the American Counseling Association and the American School Counseling Association (Appendix A), you are required to know the purposes, nature, results, reliability, validity, limitations, and appropriateness of any instrument you administer, and you must be able to communicate those clearly to your student-clients. Furthermore, you must be able to understand the differences between formal and informal assessment strategies, so that you are able to use informal assessment strategies, like card sorts, case histories, and behavioral observation checklists as professionally as the formal assessment instruments. A comprehensive discussion of these important concepts will not be attempted here; rather, the purpose of this discussion is to help you integrate information from that appraisal course with the comprehensive school counseling program as outlined in this text.

Second, it is important that school counselors are aware of the criticisms of certain instruments that are often used in the schools. For example, instruments that are not presented in a student's native language will yield results that are highly suspect. Similarly, instruments that are administered in adverse conditions, such as overcrowded, noisy rooms, or under conditions contrary to those of the norming population are suspect. The use of assessment instruments in ways for which they are not designed (such as confusing aptitude tests for achievement tests) will invalidate the results. And counselors must maintain a healthy skepticism about some dear and long-held myths of education, such as the concept of intelligence as a hard-and-fast, measurable characteristic (when, in fact, the concept of intelligence should be viewed as very plastic and fluid and might better be understood in terms of multiple intelligences presented in Chapter 6).

School counselors are not psychometrists (usually paraprofessionals who are trained in the administration of certain tests) or school psychologists (who are trained in the administration and interpretation of psychological assessments for diagnostic purposes). School counselors often use assessments in the counseling function within the three domains.

Within the academic domain, assessments can help students to know their learning styles and strengths, which can then be helpful in academic planning. One such example is the Learning Styles Inventory (Dunn, Dunn, & Price, 1996), which provides information about individual students as well as for an entire group of students (as discussed in Chapter 6). Aptitude tests, purportedly measuring a student's ability to achieve in certain areas, might also be helpful in a student's academic development. Such instruments would include the General Vocational Aptitude Battery (available from the U.S. Employment Service), the Armed Services Vocational Aptitude Battery or ASVAB (available from the U.S. Department of Defense), the Differential Aptitude Test or DAT (available from The Psychological Corporation), and the Scholastic Aptitude Test or SAT. Tests that can be used to help assess a student's verbal and nonverbal functioning include the Peabody Picture Vocabulary Test and the Slosson Intelligence Test (but these instruments must be carefully considered in terms of appropriateness with a high school student since they are designed for use with younger clients).

Within the domain of career development, there are many instruments and computer programs that can help students further their self-knowledge and match that self-exploration with information about the world of work. These instruments include the Self Directed Search (available from Psychological Assessment Resources), the Strong Interest Inventory (available from Consulting Psychologists Press), and the Kuder General Interest Survey (available from Science Research Associates). Computer programs such as DISCOVER and SIGI are also designed to help students evaluate and understand their interests, lifestyle choices, and possible career options.

In the personal/social domain of development, counselors often use assessments to help students understand themselves better. One such instrument is the Myers-Briggs Type Indicator (MBTI, available from Consulting Psychologists Press), which yields information about preferences in sources of energy (being energized by contact with others or by internal reflection), sources of information (external senses or intuition), primary decision-making criteria (personal and social values or rational thinking), and need for structure (preferring structure or spontaneity) (Isaacson & Brown, 1997). This instrument comes with a high school form and is often used to help students with career decision making.

In addition to these formal assessment instruments, high school counselors also derive important information to be used in the counseling process from informal methods, such as observations, interviews with student-clients (Schmidt, 1999), family histories, card-sorts, student journals, checklists, classroom observations, and reports from teachers, administrators, parents and caregivers, and other school and community professionals.

Chapter Summary

In this chapter, you have had an opportunity to think about a variety of issues related to counseling in high schools. First, we outlined some general observations about counseling. We discussed the many misconceptions of counseling held by students, parents and caregivers, and school professionals, and highlighted the need to provide clear information to all concerned about the nature of counseling in general and the nature of our school counseling program in particular. We introduced the concept of developmentally appropriate counseling as a way of thinking about how to conduct counseling in ways that show respect for our students' developmental realities.

In a further exploration of counseling, we then revisited the prevention-intervention-treatment continuum, and discussed when to counsel a student and when to refer that student for more intensive treatment to a mental health professional in the community. We explored the issues of professionalism in terms of trust, assessment, and commitment to continuing education and professional development. We provided an overview of many of the counseling issues presented by high school students, with the hope that you will identify those areas in which you need additional training.

In the next section of the chapter, we juxtaposed counseling and multiple intelligences, arguing that counseling might engage students more holistically when their own natural strengths are tapped.

Finally, we discussed group counseling. A comprehensive definition was provided, along with the role of group counseling as an intervention tool. We then examined structured groups and process groups in terms of a continuum of structure provided by the leader. Group counseling provides numerous advantages for members and the school counselor, and these were presented in terms of support for members, developmental appropriateness, and efficiency. Several disadvantages of group counseling were then identified, with the logistical issues of scheduling groups addressed in terms of planning and scheduling.

One controversial way of addressing the needs of heavy student loads is the use of trained peer facilitators. The concept of peer facilitators was presented as one possible way of increasing the efficacy of counseling professionals, providing assistance in peer helping (with close supervision and contact with the counselor), including peer tutoring and peer mediation.

Assessment in the counseling process was outlined, with cautions about the need for a course in appraisal and assessments, the ethical use of assessment instruments, and the ambiguity of concepts being measured. We then outlined how assessment is used in counseling across the three domains, providing some examples of instruments that are applicable in academic counseling, career counseling, and personal/social counseling. Finally, some examples of informal assessment strategies were provided.

A Day in the Life Revisited: Integration

As you return to the Day in the Life section of this chapter, picture yourself as Yolanda working with Shellay.

1. What new insights do you have into possible ways to work with her?
2. What are the issues you identified that Shellay is struggling with?
3. Where would you place your work with Shellay in the prevention-intervention-treatment continuum? More importantly: *Where does each issue fall on that continuum?*
4. If the district had a three-session limit on your counseling services, how would you address that limit with Shellay? With your administrator? How will you meet her needs?
5. What is your professional comfort level with Shellay's issues?
6. Do you need more training in sexual orientation issues?
7. Do you need more training in transition issues? Self-esteem issues?
8. What are the trust issues that you see in this situation?
9. What theory of counseling would you use to address her concerns?
10. What multiple intelligence strategies would you employ with her?
11. Would you design a group experience with other gay, lesbian, and questioning youth to support her while she thinks about her sexual orientation? Would it be a process group, a structured group, or a blending of the two styles?

Application

1. Identify some resources from the Suggested Readings list or from the References to include in your professional library.

2. Identify issues in which you need additional training from the list of common counseling issues. Use the Internet to research journal articles on these topics.

3. Volunteer to co-lead or facilitate a group for your local high school.

4. Revisit the class you took in counseling theories and review the textbook for that class. Find the theory you would like to use with your student clients and write up a detailed treatment plan for Shellay. Imagine that you will have eight meetings with her. For each meeting, identify your process goal (your goal for each meeting in terms of steps of the counseling process) and your therapeutic goal (your goal for each meeting in terms of steps toward her healing, usually defined by your theory).

5. Imagine that you are limited to four sessions with her. Design a treatment plan for her in four sessions. Does this cause you to rethink your theory?

6. Imagine you work for a school that limits counseling to a certain number of meetings. Outline a plan to explore community support for your school counseling program. What data about your program would be helpful to take to the community to solicit their support? How will you collect that data?

7. Design a structured group experience for gay, lesbian, and questioning youth. Now design a process group for the same issue. Which plan seems more comfortable for you? Now design the "perfect" group. What is your theory of group counseling? How would you apply that theory in this group?

8. For the perfect group from question 7, outline how you would advertise the group, how you would screen members to determine membership of the group, and how you would communicate with those not selected for the group. Detail how many members, how many meetings, the length of the meetings, the location,

and any other factors that are critical to plan. How would you describe this group to teachers, administrators, parents, and community members?

9. Outline a plan for the selection and training of peer helpers. What qualities would you look for in a peer helper?

10. Identify at least one formal assessment instrument for each of the domains about which you want more information. Conduct an Internet search to find all the information you can about each instrument. When would you use each instrument and why?

Suggested Readings

Dansby, V. S. (1996). Group work within the school system: Survey of implementation and leadership role issues. *The Journal for Specialists in Group Work, 21,* 232–242. This article provides an excellent overview of how counselors view the challenges and benefits of group counseling.

Dinkmeyer, D. C., & Losconcy, L. (1996). *The skills of encouragement: Bringing out the best in yourself and others.* Delray Beach, FL: St. Lucie. For Adlerian counselors, this book helps to structure meaningfully encouraging experiences for others.

Harrison, T. (2000). Brief counseling in the K–12 developmental counseling program. In J. Wittmer (Ed.), *Managing your school counseling program: K–12 developmental strategies* (2nd ed.; pp. 85–94). Minneapolis, MN: Educational Media. An excellent overview of several models of brief counseling in the schools.

Keys, S. G., Bemak, F., & Lockhart, E. J. (1998). Transforming school counseling to serve the mental

health needs of at-risk youth. *Journal of Counseling & Development, 76,* 381–388. This article challenges many traditional assumptions of the school counseling field, a refreshingly holistic view of what school counselors can do to help all students.

Ponton, L. E. (1997). *The romance of risk: Why teenagers do the things they do.* New York: Basic. This author's mental health experience provides a frame for understanding why teens often engage in "crazy" risk-taking.

Pryor, D. B., & Tollerud, T. R. (1999). Applications of Adlerian principles in school settings. *Professional School Counseling, 2,* 299–304. For the Adlerian counselor, a wonderful primer of how Adlerian counseling works in the school setting.

Sklare, G. B. (1997). *Brief counseling that works: A solutions-focused approach for school counselors.* Thousand Oaks, CA: Corwin. For the solutions-focused counselor, a wonderful primer of how brief counseling works in a school setting.

References

Baker, S. B. (2000). *School counseling for the twenty-first century* (2nd ed.). Upper Saddle River, NJ: Merrill.

Ball, J. D., & Meck, D. S. (1979). Implications of developmental theories for counseling adolescents in groups. *Adolescence, 14,* 528–534.

Bemak, F., & Keys, S. (2000). *Violent and aggressive youth: Intervention and prevention strategies for changing times.* Thousand Oaks, CA: Corwin.

Bilynsky, N. S., & Vernaglia, E. R. (1999). Identifying and working with dysfunctional families. *Professional School Counseling, 2,* 305–314.

Carroll, B. (1993). Perceived roles and preparation experiences of elementary counselors: Suggestions for change. *Elementary School Guidance and Counseling, 27,* 217–224.

Corey, G. (1999). *Theory and practice of counseling and psychotherapy* (5th ed.). Pacific Grove, CA: Brooks/Cole.

Cormier, S., & Hackney, H. (1999). *Counseling strategies and interventions* (5th ed.). Boston: Allyn and Bacon.

Craig, G. J. (1996). *Human development* (7th ed.). Upper Saddle River, NJ: Prentice Hall.

Dansby, V. S. (1996). Group work within the school system: Survey of implementation and leadership role issues. *The Journal for Specialists in Group Work, 21,* 232–242.

Dunn, R., Dunn, K., & Price, G. E. (1996). *Learning Styles Inventory.* Lawrence, KS: Price Systems.

Fleming, V. M. (1999). Group counseling in the schools: A case for basic training. *Professional School Counseling, 2,* 409–413.

Fontes, L. A (2000). Children exposed to marital violence: How school counselors can help. *Professional School Counseling, 3,* 231–237.

Foster-Harrison, E. S. (1995). Peer helping in the elementary and middle grades: A developmental perspective. *Elementary School Guidance and Counseling, 30*(2), 94–104.

Geroski, A. M., & Knauss, L. (2000). Addressing the needs of foster children within school counseling programs. *Professional School Counseling, 3,* 152–161.

Goldstein, A P. (1999*). The Prepare curriculum: Teaching prosocial competencies* (revised ed.). Champaign, IL: Research Press.

Gordon, R. L. (1997). How novice teachers can succeed with adolescents. *Educational Leadership, 54*(7), 56–58.

Gysbers, N. C., & Henderson, P. (2000). *Developing and managing your school guidance program* (3rd ed.). Alexandria, VA: American Counseling Association.

Harrison, T. (2000). Brief counseling in the K–12 developmental counseling program. In J. Wittmer (Ed.), *Managing your school counseling program: K–12 developmental strategies* (2nd ed.; pp. 85–94). Minneapolis, MN: Educational Media.

Hutchins, D. E., & Vaught, C. C. (1997). *Helping relationships and strategies* (3rd ed.). Pacific Grove, CA: Brooks/Cole.

Hutchinson, R. L., & Bottorff, R. L. (1986). Selected high school counseling services: Student assessment. *The School Counselor, 33,* 350–354.

Isaacson, L. E., & Brown, D. (1997). *Career information, career counseling, and career development* (6th ed.). Boston: Allyn and Bacon.

Johnson, D. W., & Johnson, F. P. (2000). *Joining together: Group theory and group skills* (7th ed.). Boston: Allyn and Bacon.

Kahn, B. B. (1999). Art therapy with adolescents: Making it work for school counselors. *Professional School Counseling, 2,* 291–298.

Keys, S. G., Bemak., F., & Lockhart, E. J. (1998). Transforming school counseling to serve the mental health needs of at-risk youth. *Journal of Counseling and Development, 76,* 381–388.

Kiselica, M. S., & Pfaller, J. (1993). Helping teenage parents: The independent and collaborative roles of counselor educators and school counselors. *The Journal of Counseling and Development, 72,* 42–49. Retrieved December 8, 2000 from the EBSCO database.

Kline, W. B. (2003). *Interactive group counseling and therapy.* Upper Saddle River, NJ: Merrill Prentice Hall.

LaFountain, R. M, & Garner, N. E. (1996). Solution-focused counseling groups: The results are in. *The Journal for Specialists in Group Work, 21* (2), 128–143.

Lazear, D. (1999). *Eight ways of teaching: The artistry of teaching with multiple intelligences.* Arlington Heights, IL: SkyLight Training and Publishing.

Loesch, L. C., & Goodman, W. J. (2000). The K–12 developmental school counselor and appraisal. In J. Wittmer (Ed.), *Managing your school counseling program: K–12 developmental strategies* (2nd ed.; pp. 204–210). Minneapolis, MN: Educational Media.

Muller, L. E. (2000). A 12-session, European-American-led counseling group for African American females. *Professional School Counseling, 3,* 264–269.

Nassar-McMillan, S. C., & Cashwell, C. S. (1997). Building self-esteem of children and adolescents through adventure-based counseling. *Journal of Humanistic Education and Development, 36,* 59–67.

Noble, J. (2000). Students' educational achievement: What helps or hinders? *The ASCA Counselor, 38,* 14–15.

Parker, L. J. (1998). *Mythopoesis and the crisis of postmodernism: Toward integrating image and story.* New York: Brandon House.

"Peer counselors help kids with problems, study shows." (2000). *The National Certified Counselor, 16,* 16.

Ponton, L. E. (1997). *The romance of risk: Why teenagers do the things they do.* New York: Basic.

Posthuma, B. W. (1999). *Small groups in counseling and therapy: Process and leadership* (3rd ed.). Boston: Allyn and Bacon.

Schmidt, J. J. (1999). *Counseling in schools: Essential services and comprehensive programs* (3rd ed.). Boston, MA: Allyn and Bacon.

Smith, S. L., & Archer, J. (2000). The developmental school counselor and mental health counseling. In J. Wittmer (Ed.), *Managing your school counseling program: K–12 developmental strategies* (2nd ed.; pp. 68–74). Minneapolis, MN: Educational Media.

Street, S. (1994). Adolescent male sexuality issues. *School Counselor, 41,* 319–325.

Taylor, L., & Adelman, H. S. (2000). Connecting schools, families, and communities. *Professional School Counseling, 3,* 298–307.

Tolan, P., & Guerra, N. (1994). *What works in reducing adolescent violence: An empirical review of the field.* Boulder, CO: Center for the Study and Prevention of Violence.

Wiggins, J. D., & Moody, A. H. (1987). Student evaluations of counseling programs: An added dimension. *The School Counselor, 34,* 353–361.

Wittmer, J. (2000). Counseling the individual student client. In J. Wittmer (Ed.), *Managing your school counseling program: K–12 developmental strategies* (2nd ed.; pp. 95–110). Minneapolis, MN: Educational Media.

Zinck, K., & Littrell, J. M. (2000). Action research shows group counseling effective with at-risk adolescent girls. *Professional School Counseling, 4,* 50–59.

8

Partnering with Students: Educating and Advocating in the Three Domains (Blocks 2a, 2b, 2c of the DAP Model)

Colette T. Dollarhide

"In high school in general I look at and think about actions that my peers take that I do not agree with. By not thinking before they act, they put everybody in danger. Sometimes if kids would just think logically they will not get themselves in trouble. Sometimes I look at their actions and think to myself, 'How could one be so different?'"

Heidi, age 16

Learning Objectives _____

By the time you finish this chapter, you should be able to:

1. Define the relationship between educating and advocating.
2. Discuss the importance of student competencies in terms of educating and advocating.
3. Identify several student competencies that could be included in a comprehensive developmental curriculum.
4. Describe the process of writing a lesson for the developmental curriculum.
5. Write a developmental curriculum lesson that employs multiple intelligence strategies.
6. Write a developmental curriculum lesson that encourages creative thinking strategies in students.
7. Identify curricular areas within which developmental curriculum could be delivered.
8. Outline effective teaching strategies, including how to demonstrate respect for students' personal and intellectual integrity.
9. Outline a strategy of classroom management that is respectful and developmentally appropriate.

A Day in the Life of a Counselor: Jack and the "Beanstalk"

Jack never wanted to be a teacher; he just wanted to work with kids on their problems. The high school that hired him was a large urban school, where over 70 percent of the students were diverse in culture and heritage: Many of the students were first-generation Americans whose families originated in Asia, the Pacific Rim, South America, and the Middle East. The rest of the students represented diversity among U.S. cultures: African American, Hispanic American, and Asian American. The one thing all the students had in common was their poverty. Jobs were few, and the industrial employers of the area were moving out of the Rust Belt to other states and countries.

As a first-year school counselor, Jack found himself the only male counselor of a counseling staff of five women, and his African American heritage represented the only diversity among the counselors. He was acutely aware, however, that his middle-class background meant that he did not know "the streets" the way his students did. He hated to admit that he felt a little intimidated by the students; times had changed even since he was a teen, and he never had to grow up fighting for survival the way these kids did. He felt tremendous pressure to reach the young men of the school, especially those of African American heritage; he hoped he could be a positive role model for them.

He chose to focus on his athletic background to connect with the toughest of his students and challenged a couple of kids to a game of basketball in the afternoons. After a few weeks, he had up to thirty students coming in after school. As they shot hoops in the gym, he would talk to the kids about their lives, their decisions, their problems, and their concerns. For him, those informal talks opened the door to respect and trust.

One of the most difficult kids to reach during those afternoon hoops was a tall, lanky young man whom everyone called the Beanstalk. He was a star on the basketball team, a junior who believed that he was marked for stardom as a pro basketball player. He was confident and self-assured as a basketball player and as a ladies' man, but he was barely passing academically, chose to be truant at will, and was well known for disrupting his classes. Jack was able to keep up with him on the court, but Beanstalk seemed to be determined to show him up at every opportunity. Respect was going to be hard to earn.

Jack was aware that the other counselors would occasionally make classroom presentations, but he had so far managed to "dodge the bullet." He was intensely fearful of making public presentations and hoped that the classroom assignments would be handled by the other counselors. He knew he was making his connections after school hours in the gym.

His hopes did not last long. In the middle of January he found a note in his mailbox asking him to make a class presentation on alcohol and drug issues in health education class. At first he tried to convince the director of counseling to assign someone else, but these opportunities to present in classes were so rare that the director was not interested in trying to reschedule so that someone else could present. No, Jack was on deck for that class, and he needed to get prepared.

Jack was there at the assigned time and place, one page of illegible, scribbled notes written at the last minute, smeared by the nervous perspiration of his hands. The teacher met him at the door, wished him well, and said he'd be down the hall in his office. Jack could dismiss the students when the class was over.

As soon as the door closed after the teacher, Jack looked at the room. To his dismay, the back row was full of many of the kids from the gym—and there, in the middle of all his friends, a big grin on his face, was Beanstalk. Jack tried a joke: no response, no smiles. He tried another joke; again, silence and blank faces. One of the kids in the back made a rude noise. Then things started to go bad.

"OK, children, here we go," Jack said, and he started to read his notes, trying to survive the experience. The noise in the room grew louder and louder; he just read louder to drown it out. Soon, he realized he was shouting. He stopped reading and looked up, just in time to see Beanstalk at the door. Jack was overwhelmed with anger at the act of disrespect and ordered him to stop and to return to his chair. With a derisive snort, Beanstalk mimicked Jack in a high falsetto, " 'OK, children, here we go.' What a loser!" And then he was out the door and gone.

Challenge Questions

There are many layers of dynamics here. First, consider the cultural dynamics. What role did culture play in Jack's situation? What role did gender issues have in this scenario? What are some possible issues from the athletic culture? Were there additional cultural pressures that you noticed? What is the relationship between Jack's success with students on the basketball court and Beanstalk's behavior?

What effect did Jack's first words have on the situation? What effect did Jack's emotions have on the situation? Do you think he handled his stress effectively? What would you have done to manage the situation more professionally?

Imagine that you are Jack, experiencing that classroom. What are the skills Jack needs to learn? How would you suggest that he learn those skills?

Are good teachers born or made? What are the qualities that will enable you able to lead a classroom of high school students? What are the skills that will enable you to inspire students?

What is the relationship between educating and advocating?

Definition: Educating, Advocating, and the Developmental Curriculum

Counselors educate clients in new ways of dealing with relationships with self, others, and the world, either by direct instruction or by allowing clients to discover and evaluate their life lessons. In this chapter, we will consider when school counselors are more intentional about that instruction, in what we consider to be the second most essential function of school counselors: that of educating students.

We have carefully chosen the word *educate* rather than *teach*. According to the *Grolier-Webster International Dictionary* (1975), *teach* means "to give instruction to, to guide the studies of" (p. 1007), while *educate* means "to advance the mental, aesthetic, physical or moral development of; to qualify by instruction for the business and duties of life" (p. 313). The difference is subtle, but important. *Teaching* implies the traditional model of instruction, complete with all the connotations of the factory-model of schools as described in Chapter 4. On the other hand, *educating* implies development, discovery, relatedness—all the qualities of developmentally appropriate education that was also discussed in Chapter 4. We believe that school counselors should not view themselves as masters-level teachers, because this implies competition. However, school counselors should view themselves as educators, a role that, as has been proposed in earlier chapters, cements our connection and vitality within the school system (Coy & Sears, 2000; Cuthbert, 2000; Gysbers & Henderson, 2000; Wittmer, 2000).

The connection between educating and advocating is also important (Clark & Stone, 2000). The *Grolier-Webster International Dictionary* (1975, p. 17) defines *advocate* as "to plead in favor of, as of a cause, policy, etc.; to recommend publicly; to support." We believe that educating with passion means to plead in favor of, to recommend, and to support. It is our hope that as counselors, you will educate your students with passion; this form of education *is* advocacy. Counselors advocate for healthy choices when they communicate the importance of healthy development.

The emphasis on educating and advocating for healthy development has increased with discussions about character education, humanistic education, and values clarification (Kirschenbaum, 2000; Robinson, Jones, & Hayes, 2000; Williams, 2000), violence prevention (Elliott, 1998; Guerra & Williams, 1996; Sherman et al., 1998; Tolan & Guerra, 1994), and helping all youth function more effectively in today's world (Goldstein, 1999; Goleman, 1995; McWhirter, McWhirter, McWhirter, & McWhirter, 1998; Rak & Patterson, 1996). These discussions have emphasized that school counselors must employ strategies to reach every student in the school, and the classroom has been the primary venue for that outreach effort. It is clear that counselors can no longer afford to be reactive, waiting for students to come to them with their concerns (Gysbers & Henderson, 2000; Wittmer, 2000).

Furthermore, the discussions of character education, violence prevention, risk reduction, and resiliency enhancement have also sensitized counselors to the fact that they play a crucial role in prevention and early intervention efforts. Recall that prevention activities are designed to mitigate the effect of internal and external realities that can cause students problems as they mature, whereas early intervention efforts are designed to help curb current unhealthy risk factors (McWhirter, McWhirter, McWhirter, & McWhirter, 1998). As we encounter young people who struggle with self-esteem, family problems, abuse issues, learning problems, low impulse and emotional control, poor social skills, and a host of other concerns, we must be aware that developmental curriculum delivered in the classroom provides students with critical survival skills that are the essence of prevention and early intervention (Goldstein, 1999; Goleman, 1995; McWhirter, McWhirter, McWhirter, & McWhirter, 1998; Rak & Patterson, 1996). In fact, research suggests that these classroom interventions can be as meaningful, and can provide intervention as powerfully, as small group counseling (Nassar-McMillan & Cashwell, 1997; Shechtman & Bar-El, 1994; Shechtman, Bar-El, & Hadar, 1997). To ensure that these skills are being addressed, counselors must carefully develop and evaluate the content of their developmental curricula to meet the student competencies defined by their comprehensive school counseling program and the American School Counselor Association (ASCA).

Student Competencies

As you will recall from Chapter Five, comprehensive school counseling programs are designed to meet the standards for school counseling programs in terms of the National Standards promoted by ASCA. (Refer to Appendix B for the complete text of the National Standards.) To accomplish the goal of helping all students to maximize their academic, career, and personal/social development, school counselors structure their comprehensive program around the student competencies articulated in the National Standards. (Recall from the Program Development discussion of Chapter 5 that the National Standards are the foundation of the needs assessment that informs the advisory committee's recommendations for the design of the comprehensive school counseling program.)

Moreover, many state departments of education and school districts have used the National Standards to refine their school counseling programs by articulating specific grade-level competencies, as recommended by Gysbers and Henderson (2000). Counselors need to know national, state, district, and local standards to understood which competencies to address in what order.

For the purpose of this chapter, we will continue to use the National Standards as the template of our discussion. Reviewing Appendix B, you can see that students need specific knowledge, skills, and attitudes to be successful in their academic, career, and personal/social development.

To help students to develop these competencies, it is easy to see that a comprehensive developmental curriculum addresses a wide range of developmental topics. There are many resources to help counselors to understand, develop, and present developmental lessons to high school students on these areas. (See Paisley and Hubbard [1994] for examples of lessons.) A brief list of these topics would include:

- Anger management
- Conflict resolution
- Emotional intelligence
- Academic survival skills
- Respect for diversity
- Boundary building
- Perspective taking and empathy
- Friendships and relationships

- Stress management
- Time management
- Critical thinking skills
- Decision making
- Planning
- Goal setting and perseverance
- Career process skills
- Employment acquisition skills, such as resume writing, interviewing
- Gratification delay strategies and skills
- Crisis management skills
- Personal safety
- Alcohol, tobacco, and other drug resistance education
- Healthy sexual choices
- Transition issues
- Values clarification
- Leadership
- Character education

(Brookfield, 1987; Cuthbert, 2000; D'Andrea & Daniels, 1996; Division of Violence Prevention, Centers for Disease Control and Prevention, 2000; Elliott, 1998; Goldstein, 1999; Goleman, 1995; Grevious, 1999; Guerra & Williams, 1996; Kirschenbaum, 2000; Lewis, 1998; McWhirter, McWhirter, McWhirter, & McWhirter, 1998; Nelson & Galas, 1994; Rak & Patterson, 1996; Robinson, Jones, & Hayes, 2000; Sherman et al., 1998; Street, 1994; Tolan & Guerra, 1994; Williams, 2000)

Reflection Moment

What are your personal experiences with these topics? What insights do you currently have into the dynamics of these issues?

Imagine that you're in a thirty-person class and someone is lecturing you about one of these issues. How does that feel? What insights do you have into ways to present these discussions to young people that are engaging, interesting, and dynamic? Imagine yourself in that thirty-person class in which someone is *interacting* with you and your classmates about one of these issues. You now have a chance to express how you view this topic. How does that feel? In what way(s) is the first scenario effective? In what way(s) is the second scenario effective? Which format would you find more engaging and respectful?

Designing Learning Experiences for the Developmental Curriculum

Intent

Where does change begin—with change in thoughts, feelings, or behavior? Think about a significant change you made in your life, such as stopping smoking, starting exercise, or starting graduate school. What process did you go through before you actually made the change in your behavior?

The answers to these questions aren't just an exercise in mental gymnastics: They are designed to help you think about where to begin when designing learning experiences. This insight is useful for you, your counseling clients, and your students: *Most people know what they need to do to make their lives better. The reason people don't act on this knowledge is that something needs to happen to move that knowledge from their intellect (cognition) into the external world (behavior). What is that something?* The answer to that question is the key to help young people move from "Yeah, yeah. I've heard this all before. I can spout all the conflict resolution/drug resistance/delay-of-gratification nonsense . . ." to "OK. I can do that. I will do that." Here's a clue: We think that missing link between cognition and behavior is feeling, or affect.

This is where the passion of the counselor will be tapped. To be effective with our students, we have to know, deep in our souls, that what we teach has value, has meaning, and has the ring of human truth to it. Without that conviction from our "bones," we will teach from the intellect only, distancing ourselves from our feelings and knowing of that truth. Palmer (1998) accurately captures what occurs in the classroom when that artificial rift between intellect and intuition is reinforced in the classroom.

> What we teach will never "take" unless it connects with the inward, living core of our students' lives, with our students' inward teachers . . . We can speak to the teacher within our students only when we are on speaking terms with the teacher within ourselves . . . Deep speaks to deep, and when we have not sounded our own depths, we cannot sound the depths of our students' lives. (p. 31)

What happens when intellect and intuition are joined, when the teacher's inner teacher speaks to the students' inner teacher, is the creation of a community of truth, where students and teacher alike are able to examine the subject as both knowers and learners (Palmer, 1998). The implications for pedagogy, for designing and presenting topics in the developmental curriculum, are consistent with the core concepts of developmentally appropriate classrooms—respect, conversation, discovery, and inclusion (D'Andrea & Daniels, 1996). Within this context, developmental curriculum is carefully planned and thoughtfully executed to establish and enhance the learning community of the classroom.

This does not prevent the counselor from presenting material to students for their consideration, nor does it mean that the class becomes free-for-all, 35-people-all-talking-at-once bedlam. To design developmentally appropriate learning experiences that invite students into the conversation (with you, with each other, with the subject), you would begin with the *intent* to create a developmentally appropriate lesson. This is the first step: Look for ways to engage students in experiences that facilitate discovery and in conversations that allow them to process their existing and emerging truths.

Instructional Purpose

Next, you will articulate your overall purpose within the framework of the student competencies of academic, career, or personal/social development. You will answer two questions: (a) What is it that you want them to know, be able to do, and/or feel by the end of the instructional time? and (b) Is your goal prevention or intervention? The answers to these questions will help you allocate adequate time to delivering the topic.

Instructional time is usually defined in terms of lessons (defined as a single classroom visit, usually one instructional hour or "period") or units (defined as several lessons). Depending on the topic (what you want them to know, do, or feel) and the goal (prevention or intervention), you will extend or shorten the amount of time needed to accomplish your purpose.

For example, if your overall purpose is to help students who fight a lot to learn anger management techniques, you will design a unit consisting of several lessons, each one addressing one topic. In this example, one topic would consist of learning anger triggers; the next would be relaxation techniques; the next would be options to anger; and the last would be role playing and practice. The reason you would want to allot adequate time for each of the four topics is that your goal is early intervention, since these students are already choosing unhealthy behaviors. These behaviors must be unlearned before new behaviors are learned. However, if your students are not already engaged in physical fighting, your goal is prevention, and you might decide that one lesson would enable you to remind students of these anger management skills to prevent future problems. Generally, the less time you spend on a topic, the less "deep" the learning will go.

Learning Objectives

The next step is to create learning objectives for the student, which can be configured for each lesson or for the entire unit. These objectives should be related to *outcomes for the student* (not the process of presenting the material), specific, and measurable (Mager, 1997). From these objectives, you will have a basis for selecting the materials and instructional strategies for the lesson; you will have structure within which to be flexible and creative; you will have measurable results of your instruction; and you will have a basis for understanding and evaluating your instructional efficiency (Mager, 1997, p. 19). Examples of learning objectives might include:

- Students will be able to write down at least three healthy responses when someone challenges them to a fight.
- Given a copy of the Sunday employment section from the city newspaper, students will (a) generate a list of five career paths from the ads they find, (b) describe the lifestyle they anticipate from each career path identified, and (c) write a one-page essay on what they discovered they would like in their future lifestyle.
- After watching a professional sporting event, students will write down at least ten jobs related to sports, excluding the job of professional athlete.

Instructional Methods, Multiple Intelligences, and Creative Thinking

Once you have identified the overall purpose and objectives of the lesson or unit, you are now free to design the instructional methods that will best meet those objectives within a developmentally appropriate context. It is important to remember that students need to be actively involved, both mentally and physically. Consider how to incorporate the insights gained from the concept of multiple intelligences: How can you address students with a variety of different intelligence strengths?

Too often, lessons within the developmental curriculum are targeted to students who think like we do—in other words, for students who are verbal, interpersonally intelligent, and intrapersonally intelligent. This means that those from the other *five* intelligence orientations are unable to benefit from the insights we hope to offer—left in their confusion, frustration, and perhaps, rejection of the developmental curriculum. There are a variety of instructional strategies that tap each intelligence area, and we should expand our instructional methodology to include all students in the class (Lazear, 1998, pp. 142–145). These include:

1. *Verbal/Linguistic Intelligence:* Writing, speaking, humor, poetry, storytelling, and debates.
2. *Logical/Mathematical Intelligence:* Symbols, formulas, codes, logic and pattern games, outlining, problem solving, and syllogisms.
3. *Visual/Spatial Intelligence:* Imagining, drawing, painting, collage, fantasies, mind mapping, sculpting, guided imagery.
4. *Bodily/Kinesthetic Intelligence:* Physical movement, dance, body sculpting, inventing, role playing, sports, dramatic enactment.
5. *Musical/Rhythmic Intelligence:* Instrumental and environmental sounds, music, percussion vibrations, rhythmic patterns, vocalization.
6. *Interpersonal Intelligence:* Cooperative activities, giving feedback, group projects, intuiting other's feelings, person-to-person communication, sensing other's motives, empathy.
7. *Intrapersonal Intelligence:* Altered state of awareness practices, emotional processing, focusing and concentration, independent projects, awareness of self, silent reflection, metacognition (thinking about own thinking).
8. *Naturalist Intelligence:* Natural pattern recognition, caring for plants/animals, environmental awareness, laboratories, natural observations, natural phenomena modeling, species organization and classification, sensory stimulation.

Common developmental curriculum delivery methods include presenting information, discussions, debates, quiet reflection and writing, artwork, journaling, role playing, demonstrations, experiments, and field trips. But don't let this list confine you—be innovative! Include discussions about what is important to the students, to their lives and their culture. Consider bringing contemporary music, movies, cultural events, and current events into the classroom. Go where the students are: to the movies they watch, the TV shows they enjoy, the music they listen to, the stores they frequent, the events they attend. Who are their heroes and stars? Pull insights from their lives for the students to consider.

Furthermore, current delivery methods of classroom instruction can be substantially enhanced by encouraging creative thinking. If one of the outcomes of education is to help young people think creatively about the problems of the world, then it behooves us to examine the ways we encourage creative thinking in our students. It is possible to examine the creative thinking of world leaders in science, the arts, and the humanities to understand the tools that encourage creativity (Root-Bernstein & Root-Bernstein, 1999). Many of

Root-Bernsteins' ideas resonate with those of multiple intelligences, but they merit consideration in detail. The thirteen ideas for sparking creative genius in students are:

1. *Observing:* Encourage students to observe the world around them; foster curiosity and an intense desire to know.

2. *Imagining:* Unlike the "wisdom" of yesteryear, young people should be encouraged to imagine, to daydream. Help students use visual, aural, kinesthetic, olfactory, and gustatory images to think and to communicate. Help them practice connecting images from one sense to those of others, such as "hearing" the scream in Edvard Munch's classic painting.

3. *Abstracting:* Pulling the essence of any concept or thing helps to distill that concept or thing into its purest form. Encourage students to identify the most essential elements of what you're teaching.

4. *Recognizing Patterns:* Students who can find patterns in life will be able to connect ideas from one area of life to other areas, such as finding patterns of behavior in social animals that resemble those of humans and vice versa.

5. *Forming Patterns:* Encourage students to express themselves through juxtaposition of various patterns to create something new: in communication, the arts, music, or science. "Juxtaposing one element or operation with another in a consistent way yields a synthetic pattern that may be much more than, and far different from, the sum of its parts" (Root-Bernstein & Root-Bernstein, 1999, p. 115).

6. *Analogizing:* Communicating through metaphor and analogy is the essence of learning, giving us the ability to generalize from learning in one area to learning in another. Helping students find their own pearls of wisdom and express them allows students to construct and express their unique view of the world.

7. *Body Thinking:* Using the sense of "muscle movement, posture, balance, and touch" (p. 161), body thinking allows students to focus and acknowledge that body and mind are connected. Solutions can be worked out, tested, and manifest in physical ways, as effectively in dance and body language as in the laboratory. In fact, tools that extend human consciousness (such as prosthetics and virtual reality) are expressions of body thinking.

8. *Empathizing:* As counselors, we have been trained in this way of creative thinking, raising it to a fine art in our profession. For students, the act of imagining oneself living in the shoes of another could be a transformative experience, allowing them to experience viscerally what another person is feeling.

9. *Dimensional Thinking:* Encourage students to practice spatial imagery, or thinking in three dimensions (width, length, and depth). Including issues of scale, dimension, perspective, and power, dimensional thinking expands students' views of the world. "The scale of a sculpture of a car or a building has social, psychological, and political ramifications. Massive buildings, for instance, connote power; small rooms connote privacy and intimacy" (p. 214).

10. *Modeling:* This allows students to "see" both the minute details and the wider scope of problems or issues. Models can be realistic or abstract, but they provide a simulation of the problem that allows students to manipulate and problem solve.

11. *Playing:* Play and problem solving has been linked in animal and human terms, yet we consistently forget this in education. Play is the intersection between work and leisure, strengthening various mental skills in the process. What better way to learn than while having fun?

12. *Transformation:* Encourage students to translate insights from one form of creative thinking into other forms—for example, to transform dimensional thinking into a model or to transform an empathic connection with a dancer's movements into a verbal image or story.

13. *Synthesizing:* "The inevitable result of tranformational thinking is synthetic understanding, in which sensory impressions, feelings, knowledge, and memories come together in a multimodal, unified way" (p. 296). In this creative strategy, students are encouraged to express found knowledge in holistic fashion, making externally manifest their inner insights. In the classroom, this could mean giving students permission to express their learning in a variety of ways: models, stories, plays, music, games, poems, pictures, sculptures, architecture, to name a few.

Materials Needed

Based on your instructional methods, identify the materials you will need for each lesson. For example, books, paper, overheads, worksheets, permission slips for the field trip, predesigned roles for role playing, films, music, art materials would appear on this list. Again, be creative in selecting your materials, looking for contemporary resources. The importance of timeliness cannot be overemphasized. You may remember a movie made in the 1950s called *Reefer Madness*, in which the evils of marijuana are presented. If you used that movie today, students would laugh. Of course, if your intent of the lesson is to provide them with a juxtaposition of "old" ideas of drugs with "new" ideas of drugs, this movie would provide a humorous way to accomplish that goal.

Procedure

In this phase of building your lesson or unit, you will identify the specific activities for each lesson. It is helpful to know how each topic will be presented in terms of introduction, activity, processing, and closure (Cuthbert, 2000). Remember that each topic needs to be presented or experienced, processed in terms of how each student will apply the learning or insights gained from the lesson, and closed in terms of what new choices the student will make as a result of the learning. To neglect any of these phases will cause the lesson to be incomplete and fragmented. In the section of this chapter on Delivering the Curriculum (beginning on page 173), you will see detailed suggestions about how to structure the delivery of each lesson.

Evaluation

It is very important that you have a means of evaluating both the effect of the lesson or unit as well as your effectiveness in the presentation of that lesson or unit. In terms of evaluating the effect of the lesson, you can use the student objectives to assess the extent of their learning. If your lesson involves homework, this provides you with tangible evidence of learning (in theory). Remember: If you ask for homework from your students, always give feedback on those efforts. It isn't respectful to drop the "conversation" without follow-up. In terms of evaluating your effectiveness in the design and/or presentation of the learning experience, solicit student feedback with an anonymous survey at the end of the class. This process can be informal, such as distributing notecards at the end of the class and asking students to tell you what they liked most and liked least about the lesson they just experienced. This way you will know what to adjust in future lessons.

Reflection Moment

What experiences do you have in designing learning experiences? Are there steps you have found to be important to include in this process? For example, would you feel it necessary to practice the presentation of material before you take it into the classroom with real students? Rewrite the steps listed above, including any steps you feel would be helpful for you in the design and presentation of the developmental curriculum.

What creative thinking strategies do you use currently? Which ones would you like to enhance or practice more often? Many of the intelligence strengths resonate with the strategies for creative thinking. If you create a grid with the multiple intelligences on one side and the creative thinking strategies across the top, what insights could you glean from thinking about each intelligence in terms of creative thinking? What implications for presenting developmental curriculum do you perceive in that grid?

Integrating the Curriculum Using Multiple Intelligences

One of the biggest challenges to secondary school counselors involves how to schedule the developmental curriculum. Informal conversations with high school counselors reveal that many feel they are not able to deliver a developmental curriculum because increasing pressure on teachers from high-stakes graduation testing means more reluctance to surrender precious classroom time. This conflicts with a recent study that surveyed eighty K–12 counselors, which concluded that seventy-eight of the eighty were able to deliver group/classroom guidance, varying from once or twice a week, to monthly, to variable scheduling (Burnham & Jackson, 2000). The key to access to the classroom is in curricular integration, meaning that the developmental curriculum supports the academic standards and benchmarks of learning. To accomplish this integration, counselors need to think about how their lessons dovetail with academic subjects.

Curricular integration involves two levels of effort: practical and conceptual. The practical efforts involve developing and maintaining an advisory cadre of teachers who will assist in the articulation, refinement, and implementation of your comprehensive school counseling program. This ongoing support and advisory cadre should be comprised of teachers who believe in the comprehensive school counseling program and who are willing to meet regularly to facilitate the holistic development of students through promotion of the program. Through their insights, you can survey other teachers to determine who is already presenting topics that satisfy the developmental curriculum and who is open to your presenting topics that satisfy the developmental curriculum. It is also with the input of this cadre that you can address the conceptual considerations of curricular integration.

The conceptual aspects of integrating the developmental and academic curricula are, once again, facilitated by the concept of multiple intelligences. Many lessons about human nature, relationships, human challenges, and other topics within the developmental curriculum can be explored through experiences associated with other intelligences. As previously mentioned, counseling is a highly verbal, interpersonal, and intrapersonal activity, but five other intelligence strengths are not tapped if all developmental curriculum lessons are focused on the first three. So if you are able to develop a lesson using the naturalist intelligence, it makes sense that you could approach science teachers, especially of a subject like earth science, to see if the developmental curriculum might be integrated there. For example, a science class might be exploring chemicals in the body. What better place to conduct a discussion of the effect of toxic chemicals from drugs, especially contaminated street drugs? The lessons relative to the alcohol, tobacco, and other drugs (ATOD) curriculum would be integrated into the science class, rather than presented as a separate lesson that they have heard over and over again.

Figure 8.1 presents other ideas for curricular integration using the multiple intelligences. Expand this list to consider other teachable moments that exist in extracurricular activities, such as student government, dances, the school newspaper, the yearbook, athletics, and school clubs. What about integration with the school-to-work curriculum? With community service? The possibilities are endless, and you are only bound by the limits of your imagination.

FIGURE 8.1 *Curricular Integration: Developmental Curriculum and Academic Curriculum by Multiple Intelligence Themes*

Intelligence	Academic Curriculum	Developmental Curriculum	Instructional Method
Verbal/Linguistic	English composition	Self-knowledge Self-understanding Self-acceptance Career dreams Job search skills	Journaling Poetry Concept papers Humor Creative writing Resume writing

	Literature	Relationships
		Character flaws:
		   Addiction
		   Obsession
		   Insanity
			Study of characters
			Storytelling
			Debate of characters

(Continues)

FIGURE 8.1 *Continued*

Intelligence	Academic Curriculum	Developmental Curriculum	Instructional Method
Logical/Mathematical	Mathematics	Decision making Problem solving Pro-con graphing Generation and evaluation of alternatives Calculating lifestyles	Syllogisms Outlining Login/pattern games Calculating the cost of various lifestyles
Visual/Spatial	Art Drawing Sculpture Photography	Career dreams Future family Lifestyle Self-concept Current family Emotional insight Emotion/behavior connections	Painting Drawing Imagery Mind mapping Collage Sculpture
Bodily/Kinesthetic	Physical education	ATOD resistance Relaxation training Health awareness Trust Self-protection Nonaggressive, self-assertive training	Exercise Physical experience Ropes or challenge experiences Martial arts
	Mechanical arts Home economics	Career decision making Goal setting Planning	Working through a problem Career experience
	Theater	Emotional expression Seeing emotions	Acting Role playing
Musical/Rhythmic	Music Band	Career imagery Relationships Stress management	Evaluting songs for 1. career messages 2. emotional messages Relaxation sounds
Interpersonal	Psychology Sociology Social studies History Political science	Social skills Cooperation Relationships Trust Self-esteem Diversity appreciation Social implications of poverty	Group experiences Conversation Empathy World court Jury duty Role playing Motivation exercises Trust exercises

FIGURE 8.1   *Continued*

Intelligence	Academic Curriculum	Developmental Curriculum	Instructional Method
Interpersonal (continued)		Compassion Social responsibility Emotional communication	
Intrapersonal	Psychology	Knowing emotions Critical thinking skills Career decisions Personal values Relaxation	Self-reflection Emotional processing Metacognition techniques Personal application Meditation Journaling

Naturalist	Earth science
	Chemistry
	Biology, botany
	Astronomy
	Health education
		ATOD resistance
		Healthy choices and
		  disease
		Social responsibility
		Family planning
		  choices
			Effects of toxins on
			  the human body
			Diseases (HIV, AIDS)
			Pollution
			Resource depletion

Reflection Moment

What are your intelligence strengths? Think about your favorite classes in high school. Now imagine your least favorite classes. If you could take the excitement of learning through your intelligence strengths into those least favorite classes, what would your learning have been like?

Delivering the Curriculum

Exactly who delivers the developmental curriculum is an important question. In keeping with the concept that colleagues in the schools are our partners in the education of all students, it would be entirely appropriate that teachers would be as involved in the delivery of the developmental curriculum as they would be of the academic curriculum (Myrick, 1993). In many cases, teachers are already presenting topics from the developmental curriculum, but they may or may not recognize it as such. For example, a teacher who coordinates the School-to-Work program would logically teach resume writing and interviewing skills to those students. The problem is that not all students would be able to take that class, and so not all students can benefit from that instruction. Meeting with the teacher advisory cadre will help you to determine where students are already learning the developmental curriculum and where additional efforts are needed to reach all students. Whether presented by the teacher alone, a teacher/counselor team, or the counselor alone, the developmental curriculum must be provided to all students.

Teaching Strategies and Lesson Planning

Effective classrooms are founded on respect, both personal and intellectual. Personal respect has been presented in terms of respect for each person and his or her perspective. Let's turn our attention to intellectual respect. What does this mean? You respect someone intellectually when you take the time to understand that person's level of intellectual functioning and then address him or her in terms that effectively match that level. Unfortunately, this is a common problem area for persons who are new to the classroom. Anyone who comes into a high school classroom and talks to students as if they were small children is doomed to failure (Valde, 2000). It is disrespectful to patronize or talk down to anyone, especially to high school students, who are sensitive to threats to their emerging adulthood and/or autonomy.

Furthermore, intellectual respect also involves informing people about what is going to happen and inviting their consent, either tacit or explicit. For example, a physician who does not inform the patient that a shot will be administered, but administers it anyway, is not respecting the patient's right to choose or consent to the treatment. (Imagine how you would feel to be suddenly jabbed with a needle without consenting!) In the same way, a presenter in a classroom who does not inform students of what the class entails is not respecting the student's right to choose whether to pay attention and thus, with that assumption, increases the likelihood that the student will choose to "check out." In the classroom, this means informing students of the major areas of learning they will experience and asking them to join in the conversation. Getting their agreement up front that what you're presenting is meaningful, interesting, or important will increase their attention and decrease distracting classroom behavior.

There are a variety of models that address effective teaching and classroom management, but they all start from the same premise: When students are engaged in learning because you have structured the learning experience in a developmentally appropriate way, you will have a minimum of interruptions (Travers, Elliott, & Kratochwill, 1993). In general, the qualities that define a well-structured learning experience include:

- Having a meaningful, interesting lesson.
- Getting the lesson started on time.
- Having a clear idea of what you're doing from moment to moment.
- Knowing what you want students to do and how they are to do it.
- Establishing a respectful relationship with students.
- Being aware of what students are doing.
- Keeping the group focused on the topic.
- Being able to design and manage transitions from topic to topic.
- Being able to communicate expectations for appropriate behavior and consequences for inappropriate behavior.

- Classroom rules are clear, explicit, and concrete.
- The classroom rules are basic but global (Example: We will respect all opinions in here. We will communicate that respect by not using any put-downs.)
- Rules are enforced fairly.
- Inappropriate behavior is addressed immediately.
- Corrections of behavior are made incrementally: proximity (getting closer to the unfocused student), subtle reminders (looking directly at the student, pointing at the work), verbal reminders (saying the student's name, asking him or her to focus), directions (telling the student to stop what they are doing and return to work), removal for a private conversation (asking the student to step into the hall where you can ask if he or she can work or if he or she needs to go somewhere for time out), to direct removal (telling the student to go to the office) (Eggen & Kauchak, 1994; Goetz, Alexander, & Ash, 1992; Travers, Elliott, & Kratochwill, 1993).

Since prevention of behavioral distractions is more effective than remediation, useful strategies that are consistent with developmentally appropriate classrooms include those proposed by Cuthbert (2000, pp. 128–129):

- Cohesion should be enhanced within the class, reminding everyone that we are all working together toward the same goal.
- Cooperation should be explained and modeled by the counselor, including taking turns, listening to others, respecting each other, and working together.
- Communication should be emphasized as the key to success for students. Allow students to express their feelings; use active listening, responding, and linking strategies to allow each student to feel heard and respected.
- Coaching allows you to help students learn new behavior by direct instruction and practice. Encouragement will help students feel safe taking risks as they practice.
- Contribution focus allows each student to feel that he or she has helped the group to reach its goals, either through ideas, respectful quiet listening, or volunteering.
- Control issues are important to manage so that you lead the group without dominating it, yet maintain your role as the person responsible for content and delivery.
- Configuration refers to how the physical arrangement of the classroom is managed. Varying the layout of the room can add interest to the lesson and can help students break out of more passive learning modes.
- Closure, a summary of what is to be learned in the lesson, is important to remember. This allows the group to feel that the topic is finished and that it now "belongs" to them.
- Confidentiality, as the hallmark of the counseling profession, is important to address in large groups. Establishing a safe, inviting environment for conversation and learning could inspire students to share more than they intended. You need to remind the group that as listeners, everyone should be respectful of maintaining confidentiality; as speakers, everyone should carefully choose what they share with the group since confidentiality cannot be guaranteed.

Translating these insights into effective instruction involves knowing something about how to deliver instruction to a group of students. Hunter and Russell (1981) describe the seven steps of effective instruction, to which the insights of this chapter have been added. This constitutes what is known as a lesson plan.

1. Review previous learning and focus students' attention on what is to be learned. Example: "You already know that some relationships work over years and others do not last. Do you ever wonder why some marriages last and other don't? What are some of the reasons you've seen or heard that describe why relationships fail? What are the effects on people—adults and kids—when a marriage fails?"

2. Inform students about what they should be able to do at the end of the lesson and why it is important that they learn the material. Example: "Well, I don't want to see any of you live with those effects (insert what the class answered to the last question in the example above: loss of income, loss of home, loss of children, loss of self-esteem). So let's talk today about relationships, what makes them healthy, what helps them last, so that you can think about the relationships that you choose. By the end of today's time, I'd like you to know what makes a healthy relationship and how to evaluate your relationships in terms of whether they are healthy."

3. Provide the lesson, using multiple intelligences and strategies for creative thinking. Example: Counselor talks about the qualities of healthy relationships and how to evaluate relationships, showing a clip of a popular movie that depicts a couple in a healthy exchange of ideas, agreement and disagreement, and compromise. The counselor asks "What qualities did these people show that illustrate healthy relationships?"

4. Model what you want the students to know. Example: "Here is a description of a relationship. Let's evaluate what is healthy and unhealthy about it. What do you notice about communication style?"

5. Throughout the lesson, check that students understand what you're presenting. Example: "How are we doing? Everyone understand?" If there are questions, address them.

6. Provide time for guided practice. Example: "Here's another description of a relationship. You can work independently or quietly with one other person (providing choices, see Teaching with Love and Logic on page 177), and we'll talk about it in 10 minutes. Answer each question about the healthy and unhealthy aspects you notice. I'll walk around and answer any questions you have."

7. Review the major concepts of the lesson, then provide independent practice in the form of homework or a paper. Example: "OK, today we talked about healthy and unhealthy relationships in terms of . . . , took a look at some examples of each, and applied those to an evaluation of some relationships. Now I want you to go home and think of a relationship—either one you have been in or one that someone else (a friend, a relative) has been in. Don't tell me whose relationship it is, because that's not what's important. I want you to do two things. I want you to write out a description of that relationship, and then I want you to evaluate that relationship, using the questions on the case studies we talked about here in class today. Any questions? Then I'll see you tomorrow."

Finally, there is one personal quality that must be addressed that comes from literature for beginning teachers: the concept of "withitness." According to Gordon (1997), "Beginning secondary teachers need more than knowledge of content and teaching strategies. Insight into adolescent culture is critical to success in managing a classroom" (p. 56). Withitness involves social insight, or knowing what is going on with their students in the classroom. This means that effective educators understand how students communicate, both verbally and nonverbally; they know what students value and why; they know how students identify with others, whom they identify with, and why. Gordon proposes five strategies for developing and maintaining this connection with students (p. 58):

1. Become familiar with adolescent culture (but don't feel you have to become a part of it). Leave the latest fashions to the adolescent.
2. Affirm the reality of students' concerns. If there is a prom coming up, their attention will be focused on that event. Use the event in your lesson!
3. Relate content to students' outside interests: games, music, sports, fashions, trends.
4. Know your students: their names, their interests, their social connections.
5. Share your humanity with students as appropriate. Let them get to know you as a human and they will be more open to those times when your humanity shows. This includes some self-disclosure, humor, and your own "weather."

Classroom Management

Teaching with Love and Logic   Teaching with love and logic derived from a system developed by Foster Cline (Fay & Cline, 1986), in which student misbehavior in the classroom is viewed as ways to avoid the pain of loss of self-esteem and autonomy (Fay & Funk, 1995). An artful blend of Adlerian natural and logical consequences with Control Theory/ Reality Therapy's focus on choices (Glasser & Wubbolding, 1997), this approach highlights how young people test the limits of their environment. When this testing is brought into the classroom, an adult's natural reaction is to try to assert control. This sets up a cycle of testing, reacting, punishing, more testing, more extreme reacting, more rigorous punishing, and so on. Rather than perpetuate this system of control and punishment, Fay and Funk believe that people learn best from their own decisions and their own mistakes (p. 26).

First, the love and logic system challenges three "myths" of classroom management. To the myth that students must be warned in advance of the consequences for violating rules, Fay and Funk (1995) argue that each situation and each person is unique and should be treated as such. To the myth that consequences must follow immediately after the infraction, Fay and Funk contend that this means the teacher and student are both upset while trying to deal with the situation, instead of "cooling off" before addressing the problem. To the myth that students don't need to like their teachers, Fay and Funk counter that if students like their teachers, they will work harder to please them. In place of a discipline system built on fear, these authors believe that adults should build a system based on both love and logic.

In place of these myths, Fay and Funk (1995) propose that professionals in the classroom use the following three rules with young people:

1. Use enforceable limits. This means that rather than tell students how to run their lives, you tell them how you're going to run yours. This means that the limits are set within how you, as the professional, will be handling your job. Rather than ordering, "Don't

you dare talk to me with that tone of voice!" you could say, "I'll be glad to listen to you when your voice sounds like mine" (p. 27).

2. Provide choices within limits. Because everyone strives for autonomy, we all want choices in our lives. These choices need to be acceptable on your terms, not dangerous or life threatening, involve only that student's choice about his or her own behavior, and offered without sarcasm or anger. The more choices you can offer students about little things, the more you can call upon that goodwill when you need to take control of a situation that requires you to make the choice. An example of choices within limits would be "This assignment needs to be completed this week. Would you rather make the deadline Thursday or Friday? You decide." Another example would be "Today you have your choice of working alone or with a friend. It's up to you" (p. 30).

3. Apply consequences with empathy (p. 26). This allows the young person to focus on the consequences of the mistake, not on anger or fear (yours or theirs). "A mistake can be a great teacher, provided the child is allowed to experience the consequences of the mistake. However, it is the empathy of the adult that drives the pain of the consequence into his or her heart and turns experience into long-term memory and wisdom" (p. 39). Fay and Funk report the story of a father who decided to use love and logic as an example of the use of empathy. After many years of yelling at his daughter about poor grades, the father put his arm around her and said, "This must feel awful for you, getting grades like this. I can't imagine how much it must hurt. I tell you what, you go to school tomorrow and tell everyone that I will love you no matter how many years it takes you to get through seventh grade." His daughter looked up and him and screamed, "Years??? I don't have years to get though seventh grade! My friends are going on to the eighth grade!!" To which Dad replied, "I know, but maybe they won't dump you because you're a year behind them in school. Besides, you don't need them. You have me for a friend" (p. 39). The empathy reinforced that the choice was hers and that the consequences would be hers, also.

The love and logic system consists of six steps. First, you build a relationship with students by noticing the students' likes and dislikes and quietly commenting on them to the students. These comments would not be judgmental or manipulative (not "I like the way you're doing that," but "I see you like skateboards"). Once these positive relationships are built, you set enforceable limits through enforceable statements of what you are willing to do. (Not "I will deduct ten points for each day late," but "I give full credit for papers turned in on time"). Third, you share control with students in terms of "small" decisions (not "I have to have all these papers in today," but "You can turn these in now or after lunch"). Fourth, if there are discipline problems, you implement disciplinary interventions that stop the undesirable behaviors, utilizing empathy and sorrow to connect with the student and to allow them to focus on the consequences ("Janet, I'm sorry that you are unable to work without talking. You can finish your work sitting over here or you can finish your work quietly at your desk. You decide."). Fifth, you would delay consequences to allow the student to think about her or his choices and to decide what he or she can do about the situation, such as that in the following scenario:

> *Teacher:* "Tom, seems hard for you to concentrate on your work today. What do you think might happen if you keep talking instead of working?"
>
> *Student:* "I might get a low grade."
>
> *Teacher:* "That's a possibility. What else?"
>
> *Student:* "I might have to stay after school."
>
> *Teacher:* "That's another possibility. Anything else?"
>
> *Student:* "You might not let me sit next to my friends."
>
> *Teacher:* "That's another possibility. Tell you what. I'll come back in a couple of minutes. If it seems you're still having trouble concentrating, I'll pick one of those suggestions." (Fay & Funk, 1995, p. 166)

Finally, as you can see in the above example, you give the same assignment the student initially had, underscoring your belief that they will learn from the consequence and make a better decision in the future.

This approach takes practice, since it takes unlearning the test-reaction-punishment cycle and replacing that with the connection-choice-empathic consequence cycle. For counselors who are delivering the developmental curriculum, the principles of this approach are intuitively engaging, since counseling involves the same choices, empathy, and working through consequences. The practice and reflection involved in becoming comfortable with this approach is well worth it, however, since becoming comfortable in the classroom determines how successful your teaching will be. And being an educator is an essential part of every counselor's job.

Reflection Moment

Think about when you were young. Can you remember being in trouble at school? Was that experience handled in a way to allow you to learn, or were you yelled at? Imagine that situation again, recalling as many details as possible. Knowing what you know now, what should have been done to make that a learning experience? Imagine yourself as the person who imposed the punishment; what do you think he or she was feeling as the situation unfolded? If you could go back to that moment and take all these wonderful ideas of classroom management with you, what would you do to enhance the learning of that young person?

Chapter Summary

In this chapter, we discussed the connection between educating and advocating, that educating young people with passion, enthusiastically supporting their learning about healthy choices, constitutes advocacy. The importance of being an effective educator and advocate cannot be understated; counselors who are delivering a comprehensive school counseling program must be able to reach all students, and the best way to do this is through the classroom.

Delivering the developmental curriculum allows you to reach those students, whether the intent is prevention or early intervention.

We next discussed the process of designing learning experiences in terms of several steps. First, we clarified our intent of the curriculum as that of inviting students into a conversation about important topics. Second, we described the instructional purpose as the topic of the lesson or unit. Third, we outlined the process of writing learning objectives in terms of student outcomes, which will help in the design of the lesson. Fourth, we presented what you need to consider when selecting instructional methods in terms of eight multiple intelligences, the use of current events, and the thirteen creative thinking strategies. Fifth, materials were discussed in terms of timeliness and appropriateness for your audience. Sixth, the actual procedure for each lesson is written. Finally, a plan for evaluation is included in each learning experience.

Often, counselors are challenged to find ways to integrate the developmental curriculum into the academic curriculum. An advisory cadre comprised of teachers who support the comprehensive school counseling program can help you determine where you can infuse the developmental curriculum as a support of the academic curriculum. To accomplish this infusion, multiple intelligences provides a useful template from which curricular ideas could be generated. Such a template is represented in Figure 8.1.

Delivering the curriculum effectively involves the acquisition of skills that may be new to counselors. Each counselor needs to evaluate his or her own preferences in these areas to determine the presentation format that works best.

Effective classroom presentations are based on respect for students' personal and intellectual integrity and autonomy. In general terms, this respect translates into effective classroom strategies of planning, awareness of students, focus, and communication about classroom behavior. A model of effective instruction describes the elements of an effective lesson plan, consisting of creating interest in the lesson, informing students of the expected outcomes of instruction, providing the instruction, modeling the learned behaviors, checking for understanding, guided practice, then independent practice. An example was provided that illustrates what each step might include with a developmental topic.

A model of classroom management, Teaching with Love and Logic, outlines the connection-choice-empathic consequences cycle of working with students, so that students learn from their choices in a way that empowers them and reinforces better choices. What better way to help students understand the process of lifelong learning than to model it during a lesson in the developmental curriculum?

A Day in the Life Revisited: Integration

Let's return to the story of Jack and the "Beanstalk." Can you see what some of the problem areas were?

1. First, what were the sources of Jack's sense of inadequacy? Evaluate each aspect of Jack's background, in terms of culture, socioeconomic issues, and professionalism. How did his self-view and his worldview interact with his perceptions of the lives of his students that increased his stress?

2. Next, consider the role of athletics in this scenario. What are some of the advantages and disadvantages of connecting with students on the basis of athletics? How did the competitiveness of athleticism affect Jack's relationship with the Beanstalk?
3. What did Jack do or not do that fateful day in the classroom that created the potential for failure? Consider the following:
   • How prepared was he?
   • How did he make his feelings of fear clear to the class?
   • What effect did his first words have on the class?
   • What effect did his reaction to Beanstalk have on Beanstalk? On the class?
4. You are Jack's supervisor. What will you do to help Jack? What does he need to learn? How will you help him learn those skills?

Application

1. Inventory your current teaching skills. What are your strengths and what are your challenges? Outline a professional development plan, including strategies for both skill acquisition and practice.

2. Ask the local high school counselor(s) for the name of a teacher who is known for being both effective and beloved in the classroom. Interview this person about effective instructional methodology, favorite teaching strategies, and classroom management. Observe this person in the classroom. Write up your insights and compare them to this chapter. How do your insights inform your own presentation style?

3. Examine the list of developmental curriculum topics in this chapter. Select the most important fifteen topics and rank order them. Time consuming, isn't it? If you only have a limited number of opportunities to make presentations in the classroom, you need to think about which topics you feel are most important to present.

4. Take the top five topics from the list you generated above and design a lesson or unit on them. How will you communicate your passion for these topics? Make sure to include each step from the Designing Learning Experiences part of this chapter.

5. Take one topic from your assignment above and design an instructional method for each of the eight intelligence strengths.

6. Take the same topic from assignment 5 and write one instructional method each of the thirteen creative thinking strategies.

7. Take the same topic and write three instructional methods that use current events or persons as the central theme.

8. Write an evaluation instrument for a classroom presentation. What do you want to know from your students?

9. Interview a local high school counselor about which academic area(s) that person wishes to present developmental guidance. Using what you know about multiple intelligences, Figure 8.1, and your imagination, design a strategy for infusing developmental curriculum into the academic curriculum. Use at least three creative thinking strategies in your plan. Now present this plan to the counselor you interviewed.

10. One of the ideas for Jack in the Day in the Life scenario would have been to discuss his concerns with the teacher before the class met, to invite that teacher to co-present. This would have allowed Jack to observe the students'

behavior and the teacher's interaction with the class. Write up a script for Jack inviting the teacher to co-present. Write up a different script asking the teacher for pointers to help with classroom interaction.

11. Look at the student quote that opens this chapter. How does it relate to the content of this chapter?

Suggested Readings

Fay, J., & Funk, D. (1995). *Teaching with love and logic.* Golden, CO: Love and Logic Press. An extensive look at the effective use of choice in a school and classroom setting, this book provides useful strategies for working with students. The key to these strategies is that students learn to want to act better, reducing the need for adults to force them to behave.

Goldstein, A. P. (1999). *The Prepare curriculum: Teaching prosocial competencies.* Champaign, IL: Research Press. Based on Social Learning Theory, this book is the result of the author's training experiences with youth who needed retraining in aggression reduction, stress reduction, and prejudice reduction. Structured small and large group experiences are outlined to enable the reader to use these lessons with prevention and intervention developmental curricula.

Mager, R. F. (1997). *Preparing instructional objectives: A critical tool in the development of effective instruction* (3rd ed.). Atlanta, GA: The Center for Effective Performance. A comprehensive discussion of how to establish the foundation of any well-developed learning experience.

O'Connor, K. (2001). The principal's role in report card grading. *NASSP Bulletin, 85*(621), 37–46. Although intended for a high school principal, this article outlines strategies for grading that could be very useful for counselors who must grade the work of students in the developmental curriculum.

Paisley, P. O., & Hubbard, G. T. (1994). *Developmental school counseling programs: From theory to practice.* Alexandria, VA: American Counseling Association. A compilation of developmental curriculum ideas and modules.

Palmer, P. (1998). *The courage to teach: Exploring the inner landscape of a teacher's life.* San Francisco, CA: Jossey-Bass. A powerful discussion of what constitutes teaching with passion, combining pedagogy and learning into a "community of truth."

Root-Bernstein, R., & Root-Bernstein, M. (1999). *Sparks of genius: The thirteen thinking tools of the world's most creative people.* Boston: Houghton Mifflin. These authors present their ideas on creative thinking and the tools to enhance creativity in very practical terms, with many quotes and examples from science, the arts, and the humanities. Any classroom would be enriched by applying these ideas to modern education.

References

Brookfield, S. D. (1987). *Developing critical thinkers: Challenging adults to explore alternative ways to thinking and acting.* San Francisco, CA: Jossey-Bass.

Burnham, J. J., & Jackson, C. M. (2000). School counselor roles: Discrepancies between actual practice and existing models. *Professional School Counseling, 4,* 41–49.

Clark, M. A., & Stone, C. (2000). The developmental school counselor as educational leader. In J. Wittmer (Ed.), *Managing your school counseling program: K–12 developmental strategies* (2nd ed.; pp. 75–82). Minneapolis, MN: Educational Media Corporation.

Coy, D., & Sears, S. (2000). The scope and practice of the high school counselor. In J. Wittmer (Ed.). *Managing your school counseling program: K–12 developmental strategies* (2nd ed.; pp. 56–67). Minneapolis, MN: Educational Media Corporation.

Cuthbert, M. I. (2000). Large group developmental guidance. In J. Wittmer (Ed.), *Managing your school counseling program: K–12 developmental strategies* (2nd ed.; pp. 123–134). Minneapolis, MN: Educational Media Corporation.

D'Andrea, M., & Daniels, J. (1996). Promoting peace in our schools: Developmental, preventive, and multicultural considerations. *School Counselor, 44,* 55–64.

Division of Violence Prevention, Centers for Disease Control and Prevention. (2000). *Best practices of youth violence prevention: A sourcebook for community action*. Atlanta, GA: Author.

Eggen, P., & Kauchak, D. (1994). *Educational psychology: Classroom connections* (2nd ed.). New York: Merrill.

Elliott, D. S. (1998). *Prevention programs that work for youth: Violence prevention*. Boulder, CO: Center for the Study and Prevention of Violence.

Fay, J., & Cline, F. (1986). *The science of control*. Golden, CO: Cline/Fay Institute.

Fay, J., & Funk, D. (1995). *Teaching with love and logic*. Golden, CO: Love and Logic Press.

Glasser, W., & Wubbolding, R. (1997). Beyond blame: A lead management approach. *Reaching Today's Youth, 1*(4), 40–42.

Goetz, E. T., Alexander, P. A., & Ash, M. J. (1992). *Educational psychology: A classroom perspective*. New York: Merrill.

Goldstein, A. P. (1999). *The Prepare Curriculum: Teaching prosocial competencies*. Champaign, IL: Research Press.

Goleman, D. (1995). *Emotional intelligence: Why it can matter more than IQ*. New York: Bantam.

Gordon, R. L. (1997). How novice teachers can succeed with adolescents. *Educational Leadership, 54*(7), 56–58.

Grevious, S. C. (1999). *Teen smart: Ready to use activities to help teens build positive relationships with peers and adults*. West Nyack, NY: Center for Applied Research in Education.

Grolier-Webster international dictionary of the English language. (1975). New York: Grolier.

Guerra, N. G., & Williams, K. R. (1996). *A program planning guide for youth violence prevention: A risk-focused approach*. Boulder, CO: Center for the Study and Prevention of Violence.

Gysbers, N. C., & Henderson, P. (2000). *Developing and managing your school guidance program* (3rd ed.). Alexandria, VA: American Counseling Association.

Hunter, M., & Russell, D. (1981). Planning for effective instruction: Lesson design. In *Increasing your teaching effectiveness*. Palo Alto, CA: The Learning Institute.

Kirschenbaum, H. (2000). From values clarification to character education: A personal journey. *Journal of Humanistic Counseling, Education and Development, 39*, 4–20.

Lazear, D. (1998). *Eight ways of teaching: The artistry of teaching with multiple intelligences* (3rd ed.). Arlington Heights, IL: SkyLight Training and Publishing.

Lewis, B. A. (1998). *What do you stand for? A kid's guide to building character*. Minneapolis, MN: Free Spirit.

Mager, R. F. (1997). *Preparing instructional objectives: A critical tool in the development of effective instruction* (3rd ed.). Atlanta, GA: The Center for Effective Performance.

McWhirter, J. J., McWhirter, B. T., McWhirter, A. M., & McWhirter, E. H. (1998). *At-risk youth: A comprehensive response for counselors, teachers, psychologists, and human service professionals*. Pacific Grove, CA: Brooks/Cole.

Myrick, R. D. (1993). *Developmental guidance and counseling: A practical approach* (2nd ed.). Minneapolis, MN: Educational Media.

Nassar-McMillan, S. C., & Cashwell, C. S. (1997). Building self-esteem of children and adolescents through adventure-based counseling. *Journal of Humanistic Education and Development, 36*, 59–67.

Nelson, R. E., & Galas, J. C. (1994). *The power to prevent suicide: A guide for teens helping teens*. Minneapolis, MN: Free Spirit.

Paisley, P. O., & Hubbard, G. T. (1994). *Developmental school counseling programs: From theory to practice*. Alexandria, VA: American Counseling Association.

Palmer, P. J. (1998). *The courage to teach*. San Francisco, CA: Jossey Bass.

Rak, C. F., & Patterson, L. E. (1996). Promoting resilience in at-risk children. *Journal of Counseling and Development, 74*, 368–373.

Robinson, III, E. H., Jones, K. D., & Hayes, B. G. (2000). Humanistic education to character education: An ideological journey. *Journal of Humanistic Counseling, Education and Development, 39*, 21–25.

Root-Bernstein, R., & Root-Bernstein, M. (1999). *Sparks of genius: The thirteen thinking tools of the world's most creative people*. Boston: Houghton Mifflin.

Shechtman, Z., & Bar-El, O. (1994). Group guidance and group counseling to foster social acceptability and self-esteem in adolescence. *The Journal for Specialists in Group Work, 19*, 188–196.

Shechtman, Z., Bar-El, O., & Hadar, E. (1997). Therapeutic factors and psychoeducational groups for adolescents: A comparison. *The Journal for Specialists in Group Work, 22*, 203–213.

Sherman, L. W., Gottfredson, D. C., MacKenzie, D. L., Eck, J., Reuter, P., & Bushway, S. D. (1998). Preventing crime: What works, what doesn't, what's promising. *National Institute of Justice Research in Brief*. Washington, DC: U.S. Department of Justice.

Street, S. (1994). Adolescent male sexuality issues. *School Counselor, 41*, 319–325.

Tolan, P., & Guerra, N. (1994). *What works in reducing adolescent violence: An empirical review of the field*. Boulder, CO: Center for the Study and Prevention of Violence.

Travers, J. F., Elliott, S. N., & Kratochwill, T. R. (1993). *Educational psychology: Effective teaching, effective learning*. Madison, WI: Brown & Benchmark.

Valde, G. (2000). [Student reactions to the approach of educators]. Unpublished raw data.

Williams, M. M. (2000). Models of character education: Perspectives and developmental issues. *Journal of Humanistic Counseling, Education and Development, 39*, 32–40.

Wittmer, J. (2000). Developmental school guidance and counseling: Its history and reconceptualization. In J. Wittmer (Ed.), *Managing your school counseling program: K–12 developmental strategies* (2nd ed.; pp. 1–13). Minneapolis, MN: Educational Media Corporation.

9

Partnering with Students: Consulting in the Three Domains (Blocks 3a, 3b, 3c of the DAP Model)

Colette T. Dollarhide

"What do I think should be done to address the problems in the school? Give a social time or do more group activities with the whole school. Make students feel needed by fellow students."

Sandra, age 16

Learning Objectives

By the end of this chapter, you will:

1. Understand what is meant by consultation.
2. Be able to enumerate reasons why consultation is such an effective way of working in schools.
3. Be able to describe differences between consultation and other forms of helping.
4. Understand ways in which consultation can be used to help students.
5. Be able to identify several models of consultation.
6. Identify which model of consultation will fit best with your personal philosophy of helping.

A Day in the Life of a Counselor: Joleene's Future

It was 4 o'clock, and Lisa was on her way out the door. She was the last counselor left in the office that day. She had turned out the lights in the counseling office and was slipping on her coat when she heard someone call her name. "Ms. Rangel, can I talk to you for a minute?"

As a senior, Joleene was the editor of the school newspaper for this year, and she was putting in long hours of her own with the student staff of the paper. She was a good student who worked hard at her education; she wanted to attend a prestigious East Coast university, but needed scholarships to be able to afford the tuition. Lisa had been working with Joleene on scholarship applications in journalism. So far, neither admission to the university nor scholarships were assured, and Lisa knew that if this year's school paper won any awards, Joleene's applications would be viewed more favorably.

"What's up, Joleene?"

"We just had another production meeting for the paper, and I guess I'm ready to throw in the towel and call it quits. No one is willing to do anything! I've been working on the paper basically by myself. I've got five people—three reporters and two section editors—but no one is interested in writing anything, no one gets advertising, no one helps with layout. I have to write all the stories, I have to contact advertisers, I have do layout myself. The others just get together to hang out. This is the pits! How will I ever get into a journalism program if I can't get a decent paper out?"

Lisa wanted to help in some way. "Mr. Hine is the advisor for the paper? What does he say about this?"

"Oh, he's been home with the new baby. He'll be out of the school for the next two months. They haven't found a replacement yet."

"I'd like to help, Joleene, but I don't see how. I'm not the advisor for the paper; I'm the counselor. I'm happy to talk with you about your feelings of frustration, but I'm not sure I'm the one you need to talk to about this. I don't know where to go from here. Perhaps you should talk with the assistant principal about Mr. Hine's replacement. I'm sorry; I just don't know what else to say."

Joleene sighed, shrugged her shoulders, and gave a wry smile. "Oh well. OK. Never mind then. You're just the counselor. Whatever."

Challenge Questions
What was your reaction to Lisa's response to Joleene? What were all the possible options for Lisa to help Joleene? In what way(s) would counseling have been effective? For what issues? In what way(s) would counseling have been ineffective?

What was your reaction to Joleene's situation with her staff? What were all the possible options you see for Joleene to pursue? If you would have urged Lisa to help Joleene find a solution to her problem with her staff on the school paper, you are thinking along the lines of consultation.

Introduction to Consultation

As we saw in Chapter 1, the premier organization that accredits counseling programs, the Council for the Accreditation of Counseling and Related Educational Programs (CACREP) (1997), requires school counselors to demonstrate knowledge and skill in the consultation process, effectively consulting with teachers, administrators, parents, students, community groups, and agencies as appropriate. In Chapter 5, we discussed the ways that the national professional association, the American School Counselor Association (ASCA), defines the primary interventions provided by school counselors. In that list of interventions, ASCA identifies consultation as "a collaborative partnership in which the counselor works with parents, teachers, administrators, school psychologists, social workers, visiting teachers, medical professionals and community health personnel in order to plan and implement strategies to help students be successful in the educational system" (American School Counselor Association, 1999). For these reasons, consultation is an important part of the Domains/Activities/Partners model that forms the organizer for this book.

As you can see from the ASCA statement above, consultation is a systemic intervention strategy. Unlike counseling, which is characterized by one-to-one intervention, consultation is, by its nature, an intervention that addresses improving relationships and interaction *within a system*, whether a family system or a school/building system.

Recent research has established the amount of time that counselors spend in consultation in the schools. Burnham and Jackson (2000) found that counselors spend from 1 to 80 percent of their time providing consultation, with a majority spending about one-fourth of their time consulting. These results suggest that more than just a theoretical aspect of school counseling, consulting is a crucial part of the counselor's job.

Most counselor preparation programs will address consultation as part of school counselor training; in fact, many CACREP-accredited programs will offer a course in consultation. This chapter is not meant to suffice as your only exposure to consultation but as a supplement to focus and refine your consultative skills relative to comprehensive secondary school counseling.

Definition of Consultation

When we examine consultation, we can see why it is such a useful way for counselors to accomplish their many duties. There are various approaches to consultation, but all define consultation as interaction between the counselor and another person with the primary focus of assisting that other person to function more effectively with a third person or group within a work, school, or interpersonal system. Dougherty (1990) defines consultation as "a process in which a human services professional assists a consultee with a work-related (or caretaking-related) problem with a client system, with the goal of helping both the consultee and the client system in some specified way" (p. 8). Other common characteristics of consultation involve a professional, voluntary, tripartite, and temporary relationship, in which the consultant provides *direct service* to the consultee in problem solving and *indirect service* to the client by improving the situation for both (Dougherty, 1990). The relationship is confidential, collaborative, and collegial, without power differential or supervisory implications, where the consultee maintains responsibility for implementing the insights and outcomes of the consulting relationship (Dougherty, 1990; Dustin, 1992; Kahn, 2000; Kurpius & Rozecki, 1992; Mauk & Gibson, 1994). This definition maintains a focus on the consultee as being another professional or adult (Dougherty, Dougherty, & Purcell, 1991; Erchul & Conoley, 1991; Hall & Lin, 1994; Kahn, 2000; Kurpius & Rozecki, 1992; White & Mullis, 1998) who works with the consultant on behalf of the client system. In schools, "client" means the student or the student's family.

For our purposes, we will use a broader definition of consultation provided by Brown, Pryzwansky, and Schulte (1998), while maintaining all the characteristics, conditions, and caveats of the relationship and goals of consultation outlined above.

> Human service consultation is defined as a voluntary problem-solving process that can be initiated and terminated by either the consultant or the consultee. It is engaged primarily for the purpose of assisting consultees to develop attitudes and skills that will enable them to function more effectively with a client, which can be an individual, group, or organization for which they have responsibility. Thus, the goals of the process are twofold: enhancing services to third parties and improving the ability of consultees to function areas of concern to them. (p. 6)

As we shall see from our examination into the models of consultation, the way consultants approach the consultee's issues is from a position of respect for the autonomy and independence of the consultee to see problems, generate alternatives, evaluate alternatives, and independently select appropriate change strategies.

Inherent in these definitions are three parties: the *consultant* (the school counselor), the *consultee* (the person who approaches the consultant for assistance), and the *client* (the third person, usually not present during the consultation, about whom the consultee has concerns). In this chapter, we will focus on the *student* as the *consultee*. (Chapter 13 will address the other partners of the Domains/Activities/Partners model to examine how consultation is used when they are the consultee and the student is the client.) The identity of the *client* in consultation can be other students, the student's family, or the larger school system (however, some experts in consultation would disagree that this last client group would be possible, since the student does not have direct responsibility for the larger school system). We believe that the school counselor, through consultation, has the tools to facilitate systemic change for schools by providing consultation to students about the larger school system.

Consultation provides many benefits to school counselors, the consultees, and the client/system. First, consultation is an efficient use of time, providing an opportunity for the counselor to intervene in a holistic, systemic way with the school, whole classrooms, students, and their families (White & Mullis, 1998). Furthermore, consultation empowers the consultee to address his or her own problems and work them through, providing long-term benefits to both the consultee and those with whom the consultee interacts (Hall & Lin, 1994). These benefits accrue to all parties, whether the counselor is consulting with students, families, teachers, administrators, or community members.

While it is possible to see many similarities between counseling and consulting, the two processes are distinct and separate. In terms of their similarities, both counseling and consulting are predicated on a helping, genuine, respectful relationship, and both are focused on the goal of an independent, fully functioning helpee/consultee (Brown, Pryzwansky, & Schulte, 1998). Both may employ one-on-one meetings or group education as interventions, and both maintain confidentiality. However, there are substantial distinctions between them. Counseling is dyadic, involving only two parties, and is focused on the intrapsychic, personal problems of the client (Dougherty, 1990) with the goal of altering the behavior, feelings, or beliefs of the client in the deeply interpersonal counseling relationship (Brown, Pryzwansky, & Schulte, 1998). Consultation, on the other hand, is always triadic, involving the consultant, the consultee, and the client (the person or group *for* whom the consultee has some responsibility [Brown, Pryzwansky, & Schulte, 1998; Dougherty, 1990] or *toward* whom the consultee feels some responsibility). Furthermore, consultation focuses on systemic or work issues, not on the personal issues of the consultee (except as they may interfere with work issues) (Brown, Pryzwansky, & Schulte, 1998; Dougherty, 1990; Kurpius & Rozecki, 1992).

Another helping process that is often confused with consulting is advice-giving. Just as there are important distinctions between *counseling* and advice-giving, so too are there important distinctions between *consulting* and advice-giving (Brown, Pryzwansky, & Schulte, 1998). While popular use of the term "consulting" is often used synonymously to mean advice-giving, the process of advice-giving is not consulting. Because the advice-giver assumes the role of an expert, there is no collegial relationship (if, indeed, there is any relationship at all). In addition, there is no assumption of respect or confidentiality. Finally, the goal of giving advice is not to improve the functioning of the helpee; it is on solving problems in the most expedient way possible. Advice-giving is a casual, problem-focused, expert-to-neophyte interaction focused on expediency and convenience. Consultation is an intentional, professional, respectful, collegial, problem-focused *and* process-focused interaction focused on enhancing the functioning of both consultee and client/system. When these processes are juxtaposed, it is easy to see the unique qualities of consultation.

Consulting with Students

The reason for expanding our definition of consultation is to allow that counselors do indeed consult with students as an appropriate part of the job (CACREP, 1997), in spite of what more traditional definitions of consultation might suggest. In fact, Burnham and Jackson (2000) found that counselors consulted with students more than with parents (p. 45).

In terms of the classical definitions of consulting, it is difficult to distinguish when a counselor is consulting with students about a third person for which the student feels responsible, and when the counselor is problem solving with the student about a third person. In traditional definitions, problem solving with the student about a third person would not meet the criteria for consultation, since there is no responsibility for the third person; however, this issue does not diminish the counselor's ability to enhance the functioning and interaction of the consultee or the client. In fact, we would argue that, as an appropriate extension of the advocate role of the counselor, consulting with students about ways to improve the school environment/system or the family environment/system is an appropriate use of consulting skills. In this view, the student is not responsible *for* the school or family system, but rather, is responsible *to* that system, and student efforts to make change in that system takes tremendous courage. Using this perspective, consulting with students about ways to facilitate positive change in family systems or school systems is not an option; it becomes a mandate. One example of this mandate would include sexual harassment (Stone, 2000) where a student may need consultation to understand how to address this serious issue.

Let's examine several situations to see understand how consulting works with students:

Scenario One: A student comes to the counselor because the student is not getting along well with a group of friends. The counselor provides counseling to help the student decide if he wants to continue with the friendship, then helps the student acquire better communication skills to confront the friends about the problems in the friendship. This is counseling, not consultation. If, however, the counselor and the student work together to strategize ways to improve the interaction and environment within the friendship *group,* without delving into the intrapsychic dynamics of the student who came for help, this is consultation.

Scenario Two: A student comes to the counselor because the student is not getting along well with others in the student council. Rather than a friendship, this relationship with the other students is "work" related—addressing the work of the student council. The counselor consults with the student, helps him understand the context of student government, allows him to examine his interaction style relative to the group, and then asks him to let her know how it goes with the council. This is consultation, not counseling. If, however, the counselor and student examine why the student feels he must always have the approval of others, this is counseling.

Scenario Three: A student comes to the counselor because her family is dysfunctional, with alcohol addiction in both parents. The counselor provides counseling to the student to allow her to process her feelings of despair, grief, and frustration, then they brainstorm ideas for helping her make healthier choices for her own future. This is counseling, not consultation. If, however, the student wants to understand the implications of organizing a family intervention with the goal of helping her parents into treatment, this is consultation. There is no direct or sustained attention paid to the student's feelings about her parents' addiction.

Scenario Four: A student comes to the counselor because her parents are overly strict. The student asks for help in showing her parents that she is trustworthy. The counselor provides consulting in a systems context: helping the family "work" more effectively from the student's perspective. The counselor helps the student understand families, and then they brainstorm ideas for proving her trustworthiness to her parents. In this way, it is hoped that the parents will allow the student to take on more responsibilities and privileges, thereby improving the functioning of the family. This is consultation, not counseling. If, however, the student wants to talk about her feelings of being smothered, and the only goal is to help the *student* change, then that is counseling.

Scenario Five: A student comes to the counselor with a problem with one of the teachers. The counselor provides counseling for the student to help him understand his feelings about the teacher's actions, they talk about perspective-taking to help the student understand the teacher's perspective better, then they brainstorm ways that the student can adjust his behavior to allow better interaction between teacher and student. This is counseling, not consulting. There are situations, however, in which the counselor may function as a consultant to the student. If, for example, the behavior of the teacher becomes one of intimidation, or if the behavior of the teacher suggests serious impairment, the counselor may strategize with the student about how the student could take these concerns to the administration, with the goal of empowering the student to address his concerns directly. Indirectly, the school system may benefit from helping this teacher change his or her behavior. IMPORTANT NOTE: This situation must be handled *very* professionally and carefully to avoid serious negative consequences to the student, the teacher, and the counselor.

Scenario Six: A student comes to the counselor with a problem with the assistant principal. The counselor tells the student to get over it, because the assistant principal is a powerful administrator, and the student only has two years to graduation. The counselor suggests that the student get a hobby to help with stress management. This is advice-giving, neither counseling nor consulting.

Reflection Moment

Can you think of a situation in which you have already provided consultation according to the definition of professional consultation outlined above?

When consultation is not done appropriately, serious ramifications can result. Can you think of what some of those consequences might be? At what point does poorly done consultation become unhealthy triangulation? (Triangulation occurs when one person becomes involved in a problem between two others, taking sides in the conflict instead of encouraging direct communication between the two with the problem.)

On Academic Development

In addition to the examples provided above, the following are examples of consultation with students about academic issues:

- Consulting with a student to develop better study skills, which will then facilitate better interaction between the student and the teacher (school system), or between the student and the student's family system.
- Consulting with a student to develop different classroom behaviors to be more appropriate in the classroom, which will then facilitate better interaction between the student and the teacher (school system).
- Consulting with a student to strategize about communication with the administration about academic problems or issues that effect the school as a system.
- Consulting with a student to strategize about communication with administration, the school community, parent groups, and/or community members about an academic program that will improve the academic environment of the school.

On Career Development

The following are examples of consultation with students about career issues:

- Consulting with a student about an employer who has created an intimidating environment at the workplace, empowering the student to address these environmental issues directly with the employer.
- Consulting with a student about improving work-related behaviors, such as positive attitude and motivation, that will improve the relationship between the student and potential employers.

On Personal/Social Development

In addition to the examples provided above, the following are examples of consultation with students about personal/social issues:

- Consulting with a student about the student's family system, to help the student understand how to relate more positively with the family.
- Consulting with a student about the student's relationship with a significant other, to help the student develop communication skills to interact in a healthier way in that relationship system.
- Consulting with a student about the student's peer or friendship relationships, to help the student develop communication skills to interact in a healthier way in that relationship system. One example might include concern over substance abuse.
- Consulting with a student about an occurrence or situation at school that made the student feel unsafe or anxious, to help the student feel comfortable reporting the situation to administration and to parents, with the goal of eliminating the intimidating or unsafe situation and improving the school environment as a result. One example might include sexual harassment or verbal threats in the school.
- Consulting with a student about community activism, to help the student strategize ways to address a societal problem or need (such as eliminating a drug house or establishing a new afterschool program), with the goal of improving the community system in which the student lives.

Reflection Moment

What are some additional examples of consultation for academic issues? For career issues? For personal/social issues?

Models of Consultation

General Issues: Expertise and Resistance

In our discussion of the traditional definitions of consultation, we focused on the relationship between the consultant and the consultee as equal and collegial. When working with students in a school setting, it is likely that counselors might need to be flexible in how their expert status is factored into the relationship, to acknowledge the consultee's expectations of the counselor's expertise. To address these expectations, Schein (as cited in Dougherty, 1990, p. 196) described three models of consultation in terms of the expectations of the consultee relative to the expert status of the consultant. Schein labeled these models as the purchase of expertise model, the doctor-patient model, and the process model of consultation.

In the *purchase of expertise model,* the consultant is an expert who is expected to provide a solution to a previously determined problem. In the *doctor-patient model,* the consultant is again an expert, but in this model the consultant is expected to provide both a diagnosis of the situation and the solution. In contrast, the role of the consultant in the *process model* is not expert as in the other two models, nor is the consultant expected to provide a diagnosis or the solution. Rather, the role of the process consultant is egalitarian, and the consultant's job is to monitor and provide insights into the process of problem solving. In this model, the focus is on helping the consultee formulate his or her own solutions to the problem. Schien's process model has been the primary structure upon which the other authors constructed the traditional definitions.

These models provide useful perspectives from which to understand consultation in schools, where students come with varying levels of insight into the problem, the solutions, and the process to resolve any given dilemma. Many students come to the school counselor because they acknowledge the counselor's expertise in certain issues and will engage in consultation with the counselor on the basis of that expert status. Often, students want the counselor to provide some insights into the problem, the solutions, and the best process for problem resolution. Schein's insights allow counselors to accept that status as needed to facilitate the growth of the consultee and improvement of the client system.

Understanding the expectations of the consultee is only one way to address consultee resistance. Throughout consultation, there is always the possibility that the consultee will resist the consulting efforts of the school counselor. There are a number of strategies to reduce resistance (Dougherty, Dougherty, & Purcell, 1991). First, counselors should recognize that resistance is normal and not unhealthy (Dougherty, 1990; White & Mullis, 1998). Second, helping the consultee to understand the process of consultation, the role of the consultant, and the appropriate role of consulting within the professional purview of the counselor can increase cooperation. Third, establishing an open, respectful, and confidential relationship that fosters trust will provide greater comfort to consultees, which, in turn, will help them deal with the stress of change and fears of loss of control or loss of status. Fourth, counselors can increase cooperation by focusing on the positives of the situation and expressing support for the consultee (White & Mullis, 1998). Furthermore, consultants will find greater success when they remain objective, refrain from engaging in power struggles, use encouragement, and emphasize the control of the consultee in the implementation of the solution (Dougherty, Dougherty, & Purcell, 1991; White & Mullis, 1998).

Generic Model of Consultation

There are a variety of models that outline the process of consultation, each with its own strengths and limitations. Similar to the search for a good match between a counselor's personal theory of change and various counseling theories, school counselors have a variety of consulting approaches that may match their personal styles. As an introduction to these various models, let's examine a generic model of the process of consultation (Hall & Lin, 1994). In this model, Dougherty (1990) identified four major phases of consultation: entry, diagnosis, implementation, and disengagement. Adapted for school counselors, corresponding activities for each stage would include:

I. Stage One: Entry
    A. Establish a professional helping relationship with the consultee.
    B. Explore the needs of the consultee.
    C. Set tentative goal(s) with the consultee.
II. Stage Two: Diagnosis
    A. Gather information about the situation, the consultee, and the system about which the consultee has concerns.
    B. With the consultee, define the problem.
    C. Confirm goal(s) with the consultee.
    D. Generate possible interventions.
III. Stage Three: Implementation
    A. Facilitate consultee's selection of an intervention.
    B. Facilitate the consultee's creation of a plan of action.
    C. The consultee implements the plan.
    D. Together, the consultant and consultee evaluate the plan.
IV. Stage Four: Disengagement
    A. Formulate a contingency plan with consultee.
    B. Reduce involvement.
    C. Invite consultee back as needed to provide follow-up and support.

Now that you've had an overview of the process of consultation, you will be able to understand the differences in process, focus, and orientation of the theoretical models for Adlerian consultation and solution-focused consultation.

Adlerian Consultation

One popular model of consultation in the schools (also a popular counseling approach in schools) comes from the Adlerian tradition. Adler's Individual Psychology is predicated on the foundation that all behavior has social meaning; that belonging and significance are the goals of all persons; that all behavior must be viewed and understood holistically; and that change occurs as people understand that their private logic, or system of assumptions about the nature of the world, was formed on incomplete information and can be amended to better reflect their current existence (Dinkmeyer, Dinkmeyer, & Sperry, 1987). Adlerian consultation is described in detail by Dinkmeyer, Carlson, and Dinkmeyer (1994), Brown, Pryzwansky, and Schulte (1998), and White and Mullis (1998). In this text, these models have been modified to focus on consulting with high school students.

    1. **Developing the Relationship.** In this stage, the consultant works to establish an egalitarian, collaborative, respectful relationship with the consultee. Encouragement is an important part of this process, in which the consultant focuses on the effort of the con-

sultee, not on the results. In this way, the consultee is made to feel more comfortable taking risks to facilitate change. When students are consultees, the conditions of the relationship defined above are especially challenging if the counselor has not communicated, from the first day on the job, profound respect for, concern about, and faith in students.

2. **Problem Identification and Goal Setting.** Without judgment and without blame, the consultant now moves to explore the issue(s) with the consultee. The Adlerian consultant, consistent with the Adlerian counselor, maintains the phenomenological framework of the consultee, examining the situation from the consultee's perspective. Even if the consultant sees the situation differently from the consultee, the focus remains on the consultee's view of the problem. In this step, then, the student-consultee would be encouraged to share his or her concerns, and the consultant would carefully attend to all aspects of the problem. Goals emerge from a clear definition of the problem.

3. **Exploration.** In this phase of consultation, the consultant conducts a systemic, holistic, structured exploration of the situation with the consultee. Using an Adlerian frame, this exploration includes assessment of all the social interaction surrounding the problem, the nature and context of the relationships of those involved, the private goals (attention, power, revenge, or helplessness) of those involved, any previous attempts to resolve the situation, and the results of those efforts. Since Adlerians are also interested in logical and natural consequences, any consequences of actions would be explored. For many student-consultees, this part of the process seems tedious and unnecessary; some explanation might help them understand why it is essential to understand all these aspects of the problem. Encouragement is used to empower the consultee to address his or her concerns.

4. **Intervention and Planning.** The consultant will now assist the consultee in the selection of an appropriate intervention within an Adlerian framework. There are a variety of options available as interventions. Primary interventions involve helping the consultee understand social interest as a motivator, democratic decision making and autonomy, encouragement, private logic, goals of behavior, inferiority and superiority issues, family dynamics (family values, styles, and atmospheres), and birth order. Additionally, the consultant may help the consultee understand logical and natural consequences and their effects on behavior. (While a student-consultee will not be in a position to impose consequences on parents and other adults, an understanding of the dynamics of consequences is helpful for students.) The student-consultee selects an intervention, and together, the consultant and consultee devise a plan to implement the intervention as outlined and then to follow up with the consultant after the plan has been implemented. In this stage, encouragement is used to help increase the consultee's resolve.

5. **Follow-up and Termination.** Once the plan has been implemented, the consultant and consultee meet to evaluate the effectiveness of the intervention, address any new or emerging concerns, and to terminate as appropriate. In this final stage, the consultee is encouraged to continue with efforts and to contact the consultant as needed.

Adlerian consultation can provide a comfortable, natural structure from which to practice consultation. Because this consultation approach focuses on encouragement, a holistic and systemic worldview, and the improvement of the consultee's understanding of and skills in dealing with others, many high school counselors use an Adlerian consultation model.

Solution-Focused Consultation

Solution-focused counseling is described as oriented toward problem solving (not diagnosis), positive growth (not remediation), and goals and solutions (not the nature of the problem) (Kahn, 2000).

> Solution-focused approaches propose that one can choose to disregard the difficulty or problem entirely and instead focus on how one would like things to be and how one has successfully approached that desired state in the past. . . . Evidence suggests that focus upon the desired condition or goal creates a positive reality that is reinforced by even minute indications of movement toward that desired goal. (Kahn, 2000, p. 249)

Kahn (2000) described solution-focused consultation as being more fluid than traditional models, in that the phases of consultation may flow into one another or occur simultaneously. There are five basic steps in solution-focused consultation (Kahn, 2000):

1. **Presession and Initial Structuring.** The primary goals of this stage involve helping the consultee understand the change process and the language of solution-focused work, articulating the strengths and resources of the consultee and determining initial consultation goals. The consultee uses language that presupposes that change will occur, that the problem will be resolved using the consultee's existing strengths, and that goals are essential for success. This prepares the consultee for a discussion of goals.

2. **Establishing Consultation Goals.** Unlike the Adlerian model, solution-focused consultation does not involve extensive assessment before establishing goals. In the consultee's own words, the ideal situation is described, and then from this ideal situation, goals are generated. These goals are expressed in positive terms (presence, not absence, of behavior), are measurable, concrete, and behavioral.

3. **Examining Attempted Solutions and Exceptions.** "Exploration of the past focuses on exceptions, times in which the problem did not occur" (Kahn, 2000, p. 250). Possible solutions stem from an exploration of exceptions, giving the consultee hope that a solution is possible and attainable. Since the solutions are derived from the consultee's own resources, they fit more naturally into the consultee's existing behaviors and do not require learning new skills.

4. **Helping Consultee Decide on a Solution.** Solutions are defined behaviorally and concretely (as goals are) and are based on the exceptions identified by the consultee. This empowers the consultee to pursue more consistent change that will move the consultee and the client toward the positive goals. The focus must be on situations that are under the control of the consultee, specifically the consultee's behavior. Consider the following scenario: A student is a representative on the student council. She comes to you, troubled that the student council is inconsistent in its decisions, always favoring the needs of student athletes. As a solution-focused consultant, you help her identify her goal for consultation in terms of more balanced decisions of the student

council and discuss that exceptions occur when strong voices remind the council of the need for fairness. You then explore one possible solution for this consultee in terms of empowering herself to speak up for fairness when the student council is making important decisions. According to Kahn (2000, p. 251) "The initial solution may not be where the consultee wants to be at the end of the consultation, but it should be a small step in that direction."

5. **Summarizing and Complimenting.** In this final step, the consultant summarizes the situation, the goal(s), and the identified solution, and provides support for the consultee by acknowledging the courage, resolve, and energy it takes to bring about change for the client. This complimenting and encouraging also involves congratulations for beginning the change process already manifest in the exceptions identified by the consultee and places the locus of control with the consultee for addressing future problems by reminding him or her of the personal resources that brought about the exceptions.

Solution-focused consultation may be the most useful orientation to use with student-consultees who are interested in seeing systemic change occur in their schools. While Adlerian consultation focuses on the individual characteristics, behaviors, and intrapsychic functioning of consultees and clients, solution-focused consultation can help consultees understand their role in bringing about change, no matter how systemic that change might be. By focusing on the exceptions, solution-focused consultation highlights individual contributions to the solution and empowers consultees to draw upon personal resources to move toward their ideal situation or condition.

Reflection Moment

Which of the models presented here can you see yourself using? Which one fits best with your view of your work with students to help them address individual issues? Which one fits best with your view of your work with students to help them address systemic issues?

Chapter Summary

This chapter is an overview of consultation, designed to help you apply the skills of consultation to your work as a secondary school counselor. Consultation is an essential skill for school counselors as defined by ASCA and CACREP, enabling counselors to work with students in ways to facilitate change for individuals, families, schools, and even entire communities. As a problem-solving approach, consultation is defined as a tripartite, voluntary, respectful, confidential process where the consultant assists the consultee (in this chapter, a student) to address problems with a client (a third person or entity) for whom the consultee has responsibility or to whom the consultee feels responsible. While traditional definitions of consultation do not acknowledge consultation with students, we argue that consultation is very appropriate with students as a means of helping them address issues within the three domains of academic development, career development, and personal/social development.

Consulting is not the same thing as counseling or advice-giving. Counseling and consultation are similar in the confidential and respectful nature of the work, but consultation always involves three parties (the consultant, the consultee, and the client) and does not focus on the intrapsychic dynamics of the consultee. Advice-giving and consultation are often used interchangeably in common parlance, but advice-giving does not allow for interaction, confidentiality, or respect—three essential aspects of consultation.

With this understanding of consultation, we provided several scenarios to help you see how consultation works with students in academic development, career development, and personal/social development. In many of these scenarios, either counseling or consultation would be appropriate counselor responses to the issues presented by the student, but you can see how consulting provides for systemic change.

To help you understand consulting better, we then discussed two important issues of consulting: the expectation of expertise and resistance. Since many consultees come to the consultant with expectations of expert help, Schein (as cited in Dougherty, 1990) outlined three ways that consultants could work with their consultees: the purchase of expert model (in which the consultant-as-expert provides the solution), the doctor-patient model (in which the consultant-as-expert provides both the diagnosis of the problem and the solution), and the process model (in which the consultant-as-equal facilitates the consultee's own process of problem solving and solution). Additional insights were discussed in terms of overcoming resistance, which necessitates an in-depth understanding of the consultative relationship and strategies to support the consultee as change is explored.

Various models of consultation were outlined. In the generic model of consultation, the stages include entry, diagnosis, implementation, and disengagement. In the Adlerian model of consultation, the stages are developing the relationship, problem identification and goal setting, exploration, intervention and planning, and follow-up and termination. In solution-focused consultation, the stages are presession and initial structuring, establishing consultation goals, exploration of attempted solutions and exceptions, helping the consultee decide on a solution, and summarizing and complimenting. Details of each model are provided to allow you to determine the extent to which the model "fits" your ideas of how to best help your student-consultees and their client systems change.

Day in the Life Revisited: Integration

Now that you've read the chapter, go back and reread the interaction between Joleene and Lisa.

1. Lisa proposed a counseling solution to address Joleene's frustration. In what way(s) was that solution too limited?
2. How would you recommend that Lisa address Joleene's problem with the newspaper staff? Outline a plan based on consultation with Joleene.
3. Which of Schein's models would you use: purchase of expertise, doctor-patient, or process model?
4. Which of the models of consultation would you use: the Adlerian model or the solution-focused model? Why would the one you chose work better than the other?

Application

1. Reread Scenario Six on page 191, about the problem between the student and the assistant principal. What would you have done if you had been the counselor? Reflect on your solution: Is that consultation or counseling? Think of a counseling response to that scenario. Now think of a consulting response. Which response would be more effective? In what ways and for whom? Which response would be more time efficient? In what ways?

2. Identify a time in your recent experience in which you provided some problem-solving assistance for someone about a problem with another person. Was that consultation? Imagine yourself back in that conversation with that person and now imagine you will consciously choose to conduct consultation with that person. Outline a plan for consulting with that person.

3. Talk to a high school counselor about the problems the students have brought to the counseling office recently. Pick one of those problems and outline a consultation based on that situation.

4. Interview a high school counselor about the last time she or he provided consultation. Identify which of the three models the consultation most closely resembled: the generic model, the Adlerian model, or the solution-focused model of consultation.

5. Interview a high school student about positive changes that person wishes were in place in the school. Outline a plan for consulting with that student about how to generate that positive change.

6. Interview a high school student about positive changes that person wishes were in place in his or her family. Outline a plan for consulting with that student about how to generate that positive change.

Suggested Readings

Brown, D., Pryzwansky, W. B., & Schulte, A. C. (1998). *Psychological consultation: Introduction to theory and practice* (4th ed.). Boston: Allyn and Bacon. A seminal text that outlines the variables and implications of the models, styles, skills, ethics, and legalities of consultation.

Dougherty, A. M. (1990). *Consultation: Practice and perspectives.* Pacific Grove, CA: Brooks/Cole. This text provides a generic model of consultation as well as an overview of models of consultation.

References

American School Counselor Association (ASCA). (1999). *The role of the professional school counselor.* Alexandria, VA: Author. Retrieved May 31, 2000, from the World Wide Web: http://www.school counselor.org/role.htm.

Brown, D., Pryzwansky, W. B., & Schulte, A. C. (1998). *Psychological consultation: Introduction to theory and practice* (4th ed.). Boston: Allyn and Bacon.

Burnham, J. J., & Jackson, C. M. (2000). School counselor roles: Discrepancies between actual practice and existing models. *Professional School Counseling, 4,* 41–49.

Council for Accreditation of Counseling and Related Educational Programs (CACREP). (1997). *The 2001 standards (draft 1). CACREP accreditation standards and procedures manual.* Alexandria, VA: Author.

Dinkmeyer, D. C., Jr., Carlson, J., & Dinkmeyer, D. C., Sr. (1994). *Consultation: School mental health professionals as consultants.* Muncie, IN: Accelerated Development.

Dinkmeyer, D. C., Sr., Dinkmeyer, D. C., Jr., & Sperry, L. (1987). *Adlerian counseling and psychotherapy* (2nd ed.). Columbus, OH: Merrill.

Dougherty, A. M. (1990). *Consultation: Practice and perspectives*. Pacific Grove, CA: Brooks/Cole.

Dougherty, A. M., Dougherty, L. P., & Purcell, D. (1991). The sources and management of resistance to consultation. *The School Counselor, 38,* 178–186.

Dustin, D. (1992). School consultation in the 1990s. *Elementary School Guidance & Counseling, 26,* 65–76. Retrieved November 13, 2000, from EBSCO database available on the World Wide Web: http://webnf1.epnet.com.

Erchul, W. P., & Conoley, C. W. (1991). Helpful theories to guide counselors' practice of school-based consultation. *Elementary School Guidance & Counseling, 25,* 204–212. Retrieved November 13, 2000, from EBSCO database available on the World Wide Web: http://webnf1.epnet.com

Hall, A. S., & Lin, M. J. (1994). An integrative consultation framework: A practical tool for elementary school counselors. *Elementary School Guidance & Counseling, 29,* 16–28. Retrieved November 13, 2000, from EBSCO database available on the World Wide Web: http://webnf1.epnet.com.

Kahn, B. B. (2000). A model of solution-focused consultation for school counselors. *Professional School Counseling, 3,* 248–254.

Kurpius, D. J., & Rozecki, T. (1992). Outreach, advocacy and consultation: A framework for prevention and intervention. *Elementary School Guidance & Counseling, 26,* 176–189. Retrieved November 13, 2000, from EBSCO database available on the World Wide Web: http://webnf1.epnet.com.

Mauk, G. W., & Gibson, D. G. (1994). Suicide postvention with adolescents: School consultation practices and issues. *Education and Treatment of Children, 17,* 468–484. Retrieved November 13, 2000, from EBSCO database available on the World Wide Web: http://webnf1.epnet.com.

Stone, C. B. (2000). Advocacy for sexual harassment victims: Legal support and ethical aspects. *Professional School Counseling, 4,* 23–30.

White, J., & Mullis, F. (1998). A systems approach to school counselor consultation. *Education, 119;* 242–253. Retrieved November 13, 2000, from EBSCO database available on the World Wide Web: http://webnf1.epnet.com.

10

Partnering with Students: Leadership and Coordination in the Three Domains (Blocks 4a, 4b, 4c of the DAP Model)

Colette T. Dollarhide

"What is the single most important problem I see in my friends' lives? Among myself and my friends I see the ongoing dilemma of competition. Sometimes all people think about is themselves and not how they are hurting others."

Heidi, age 16

Learning Objectives

By the time you finish this chapter, you will be able to:

1. Understand the definition of leadership and its role in effective comprehensive secondary school counseling.
2. Be able to challenge common myths about leadership to see how anyone can develop leadership skills.
3. Understand and identify the personal qualities of a good leader.
4. Understand and identify the professional skills of a good leader.
5. Be able to apply a model of leadership to school counseling.
6. Understand the definition of coordination and its role in effective comprehensive secondary school counseling.
7. Identify opportunities for leadership with students.
8. Identify opportunities for coordination of events and activities with students.

A Day in the Life of a Counselor: Curious Kate

Kate was the first of her family to go to school for her bachelor's degree, majoring in early childhood education. After graduation, she decided to pursue her master's degree in school counseling so that she could help young people in high schools, believing that this age group would be able to make independent choices for their lives. She earned excellent grades in her graduate program because her sense of being on a mission energized her studies; she wanted to reach as many students as she could to help them make these crucial life decisions. Furthermore, she felt that she carried the dreams of her family with her; they had sacrificed a lot to send her to school, and she wanted them to be proud of her.

After graduation, she interviewed and was hired at a small rural high school. That summer she rented a little house and moved to her new town.

Finally, the first day arrived for staff meetings before the school year. Kate was excited to get in there, roll up her sleeves, and get to work in her new life. She was going through the files left by the previous counselor when she noticed a disturbing trend. She went to the assistant principal to discuss her discovery.

"Betty, if you have a minute, I'd like to ask you something. I'm curious about this . . ." Kate began. Betty smiled and waved for her to come in to her office.

"In looking at the files left in the counseling office, I noticed that there have been five counselors in the past seven years. I also noticed that there is no school counseling program to speak of, or at least no record of one. I'm a little concerned about this. Do you have any insights that I need to be aware of?"

"Good heavens, no. You don't need to be worried about that," Betty assured her. "I've been the assistant principal here for twelve years, and Mr. Foster's been the principal for almost twenty. I can assure you that you don't need to worry about the guidance program here."

"Oh, I'm glad." Kate was relieved. "I was afraid that the high turnover meant there was a problem!"

"No problem that I know of!" Betty laughed. "Our guidance program's been solid since Mr. Foster arrived, and it'll be solid long after we're both retired!"

"Wait . . . you said the program's been here for twenty years? Surely you don't mean that!" Kate's smile faded. "Do you?"

"Well, what's wrong with that, dear? Mr. Foster will tell you everything that you need to do. He's had the program clearly laid out and knows exactly what you need to do when. All you have to do is what you're told. Here, let me get a copy of the guidance program for you." She stood to open a file drawer behind her desk, looking through the papers for what she wanted. "Let me see, the last copy I remember getting was in 1985. Yes, here it is . . ."

Betty turned around to hand Kate the file. "Kate, where'd you go? Kate? Kate!" she called. "Hmmm!" she mused, as the door to the office softly closed.

Challenge Questions

What are some reasons you might guess to explain why there were five counselors in seven years? Where do you think Kate was headed? To the principal's office to give her notice? To her house to pack up her things and move back in with her parents? Perhaps she went to find her files from 1985. Or, maybe she was headed to the phone to call her master's advisor to look for a new job or to the local bar for a drink. In a moment of horror like this, where would you go?

Seriously, what do you see as the options for Kate, assuming that she will stay in this new school? Remember, she is passionate about her new profession and reluctant to disappoint her family. Again, assuming that she will remain on this job, what do you think she should do first? What would you do under similar conditions?

School Counselor as Leader

Imagine that you're on a plane and there's engine trouble. But in our imaginary world, there is no captain or co-pilot on the plane, no one who is designated to make decisions about how to handle problems or to be responsible for the welfare of the passengers. How safe would you feel? There may be 300 very nice people on board that plane, and you could all talk about how to come to a decision by consensus, but you would likely have 300 different ideas about what to do, each one as uninformed as the next. Without a trained, competent person to focus, coordinate, and lead those 300 nice people, there is likely to be a crash.

Schools are like that plane. The principal is responsible for the academic mission of the school, in a sense, the captain of the plane. But the co-pilot, while responsible to the captain, has responsibilities also—for many technical aspects of the flight, for communication with the ground, for helping the captain remain on course. The co-pilot advises the captain, problem solves with the captain, but is also a leader in the eyes of the passengers and the flight crew. We believe that the school counselor is, in essence, the co-pilot of the school, responsible for the comprehensive school counseling program, the developmental curriculum, and the academic, career, and personal/social development of students. This means that the school counselor must also be aware of and prepared to accept the roles, duties, and responsibilities of being a leader.

Think about the metaphor of school-counselor-as-co-pilot, as there are many parallels. First, just as the co-pilot is responsible for advising, problem solving, communication, and direction for the pilot, the school counselor advises the principal, problem solves with that professional, communicates up and down the chain of command and to external constituencies, and helps the school remain "on course" in terms of developmental education, school climate, and the developmental needs of students and families. Second, the co-pilot is perceived by the passengers as part of the flight crew, as a leader in his or her own right, responsible to and for them. Third, the co-pilot acts within his or her own professional duties, ensuring that her or his own unique tasks are accomplished to keep the flight in the air, on time, and on course—in essence, a coordinator of his or her professional activities.

These professional activities for school counselors form the foundation of most graduate programs in counselor education. Typically, counselors are taught in graduate school how to build consensus, how to facilitate others' finding their own answers, how to foster communication within and between groups, and how to empower clients to embrace their own intuitive life direction while simultaneously evaluating their alternatives. With that training, you are now being asked to integrate a new way of viewing yourself as a professional: a leader. This might be a paradigm shift for you. But consider this: If there is no leader for the comprehensive school counseling program of a secondary school, how will you know what your course is, much less whether you're still on it? Who will attend to the communication of constituencies and be responsible for the developmental agenda for students and families? Who will lead the "heart" of the school?

Many authors agree that school counselors must accept a leadership role in the school. Clark and Stone (2000a, 2000b) call for school counselors to accept the need for leadership in developing a professional image, accepting certain organizational roles in the school, and providing staff development. Furthermore, they cite the need for counselors to lead the school in advocacy for student success, by leading various committees in terms of external constituencies (i.e., parent groups), multicultural awareness, pupil assistance committees, mentoring programs, student leadership, and political involvement (Clark & Stone, 2000a, 2000b). In a similar vein, Bemak (2000) "focuses on a critical redefinition of the future school counselor as a leader in promoting educational reform and meeting national and state educational objectives inclusive of creating healthy safe school environments. . . ." (p. 324).

Other authors have called for school counselors to become leaders in advocating for specific constituencies (partners in the terms of this book) or for certain issues. For example, Kurpius and Rozecki (1992) suggested that school counselors should take leadership in advocating for students, families, and teachers and in advocating for general school improvement within the building and in the district by collaborating with mental health agencies and the community at large. Smaby and Daugherty (1995) called for school counselors to become leaders in the effort to have schools free of drugs and violence. Cole and Ryan (1997) called for school counselors to take leadership in portfolio development and authentic assessment for students. All these authors agree: School counselors cannot be complacent in passively maintaining the status quo. School counselors must be leaders in championing students, families, issues of social justice, schools, and most of all, the developmental agendas of students and families.

In fact, lack of leadership has been cited as one of the central problems of school counseling programs. O'Dell and Rak (1996) found that the literature they examined cited the piecemeal nature of school counseling programs as indicative of a lack of leadership, noting that decisions about counseling programs often came from principals and central office administrators who have little knowledge of counseling. Interviews with school professionals indicated that poorly conceptualized, poorly communicated, and poorly administered programs caused a school guidance program to be labeled ineffective. Lack of quality programming, the erosion of counselor time devoted to students, and the intrusion of administrative tasks into the counseling agenda (Hutchinson & Bottorff, 1986; O'Dell & Rak, 1996; Partin, 1993; Wiggins & Moody, 1987) are further indicators that counselors are not effectively leading their programs.

O'Dell and Rak did find that "strong leadership from the local board, the state department of education, a nearby university, or the counselors employed in the school," "time set aside for counselors to act as middle managers to plan, implement, and evaluate their programs," and "a strong commitment to organize the counseling program to address student competencies" (1996, online document) were all identified as factors that contributed to effective guidance programs. This is the purpose of this chapter: to explore what is meant by leadership, how this concept applies to school counselors, and further, to extend leadership into the realm of implementation to discuss coordination of program activities.

Definition of Leadership

In a synthesis of what other authors have proposed as definitions of leadership, Hersey, Blanchard, and Johnson (1996) defined leadership as "the process of influencing the activities of an individual or a group in efforts toward goal achievement in a given situation" (p. 91). Kouzes and Posner (1995) take the definition one step further, defining leadership as "the art of mobilizing others to *want* to struggle for shared aspirations" (emphasis authors', p. 30). Their point in adding emphasis to the voluntary nature of the struggle is important. While a person with extrinsic power can motivate someone to do something with the promise of rewards or the threat of retribution, this is not leadership according to their definition. Only when the leader is able to tap *intrinsic* motivators will there be true leadership. This is important to our discussion of comprehensive school counseling, since most school counselors do not have the power to reward or punish in most school organizations. For school counselors, the issue of choice has important implications for their leadership: There must be attention paid to methods for tapping intrinsic motivators.

The methods for motivating others vary, depending on the context of leadership and the goals that are to be accomplished (Bolman & Deal, 1997; Gardner, 1995; Hersey, Blanchard, & Johnson, 1996). In fact, Bolman and Deal (1997) have identified four leadership "frames" or contexts of leadership: *structural leadership,* involving the building of viable organizations; *human resource leadership,* involving the empowerment and inspiration of followers; *political leadership,* involving the distribution of power; and *symbolic leadership*, involving the interpretation and reinterpretation of meaning within our society. Each of these frames has implications for leadership within school counseling.

The first frame or context, structural leadership, involves technical mastery, strategizing for change and growth, and implementation (Bolman & Deal, 1997). The insights from this leadership frame suggest that school counselors must be effective at their jobs and up to date with the "science" of counseling and education. For example, school counselors must be informed about innovations in counseling (new theories and strategies, new medications), informed about innovations in school counseling (new programs, new approaches to student issues), aware of the status of student issues (changing families, new drugs on the street, new ways students express their pain), and innovations in schools (new programs and approaches to teaching and learning). School counselors must also be able to plan effectively for changes, both within the comprehensive school counseling program and in the school as a whole. Finally, school counselors must be accountable for implementation; all the good intentions in the world will not make change happen. Change only happens when action is taken in the desired direction.

The second frame, human resource leadership, involves believing in people and communicating that belief, being visible and accessible, and empowering others (Bolman & Deal, 1997). These are the strengths of most school counselors, so leading using these qualities is very comfortable. For school counselors, our belief in our students, families, and colleagues is one of the reasons for being a counselor and a source of passion and joy. Being visible and accessible, being around others, is also a natural part of being a counselor: being in the halls, out at the buses, in the lunchroom with the students. (Incidentally, we call this "counseling by walking around," a play on "management by walking around." The idea is that by being with the students and teachers, the school counselor is available for conversations with those who may not want to make an appointment, but who need to talk with the counselor.)

The third frame, that of political leadership, addresses an area in which many counselors report high levels of anxiety and stress. This leadership context involves being realistic about what the leader wants and what she or he can get, being able to assess the distribution of power, building linkages to important stakeholders, and using persuasion and negotiation (Bolman & Deal, 1997). These four strategies for political leadership directly relate to the realities and politics of any organization, including those of a school district and building. School counselors need to be realists, aware that change is incremental and often comes with a price. School counselors also need to know who is in both formal and informal positions of power in the school and the district, knowing what those in power want and knowing how to overcome opposition by trading on the basis of those interests. School counselors need to know who important stakeholders are and how to connect with them on behalf of the school and the comprehensive school counseling program. Finally, school counselors need to be able to persuade others and to negotiate for benefits to the program, the school, and the students.

The fourth and final leadership frame is symbolic leadership. Within this leadership context, leaders use symbols to capture attention, they frame experience in meaningful ways for the follower, and they discover and communicate a vision (Bolman & Deal, 1997). In addition, leaders have a relationship with and a conversation with the community they represent (the school, families, students) and they embody the story of healthy choices they seek to tell (Gardner, 1995). When a school counselor is an effective leader, the counselor symbolizes many things: mental health, the profession of counseling, the ombudsman for students, to name a few. We can use these symbols to help others understand our position in the school and our comprehensive programs. We can help others frame their experiences in a larger context, perhaps a spiritual context or a historical context. School counselors can lead others by articulating a vision of healthy, resilient students, and by maintaining faith in that vision. School counselors must remember that leadership involves a constant conversation with all partners in the process. We must also always remember that we embody the story we tell about our students, our schools, and our profession, and as such, we are role models.

Another way to understand leadership is to examine the roles that are a part of leadership. In a discussion of leadership roles within character education programs, DeRoche (2000) listed the following, which have been adapted to address the roles of leaders of comprehensive school counseling programs:

- Visionary for future directions for the program, the school, and the students.
- Designer and author of the mission statement for the school counseling program.
- Consensus builder for the importance of the school counseling program, the developmental domains, and the values and content of the developmental curriculum.
- Information provider about the program, the school, the developmental issues of students and families, and current innovations in the field of education, counseling, and school counseling.
- Standard bearer for the quality of the comprehensive school counseling program, including methods to "guide and judge the effectiveness of the implementation, maintenance, and evaluation of the program" (p. 43).
- Architect of implementation plans for the program.
- Role model for the values and lessons of the developmental curriculum, comprehensive school counseling, and the counseling and mental health professions.
- Risk taker and advocate for the development of all students. As stated by DeRoche: "The leader has to take a stand and bear witness to the proposition that there is more to educating children and youth than increasing their test scores" (2000, p. 44).
- Communicator, the voice of the program, to inform all partners about the program, the students, the school, and counseling as a profession.
- Collaborator in efforts to implement the comprehensive school counseling program.
- Resource provider, which may take the form of materials or ideas for ways to integrate the developmental curriculum into the classroom (see Chapter 8).

Myths of Leadership

Kouzes and Posner (1995) described the outdated myths about leadership that discourage capable people from seeing themselves as leaders. Contrary to popular belief, leaders arise not from maintaining the status quo, but from finding new ways to address old problems. They are not renegades who attract a lunatic following, but attract followers with their deep faith in the abilities of others. Rather than focus on the short term, they are able to maintain a long-term approach to problem solving, knowing that change is incremental and slow. But their future orientation is not superhuman; it evolves, as all good ideas, from original thinking or the inspiration of someone else.

According to Kouzes and Posner, the "most pernicious myth of all is that leadership is reserved for only a very few of us" (p. 16). Are good leaders born, or are they made? Most authors agree that it is a combination of innate qualities and leadership skills that make an effective leader (Bolman & Deal, 1997; Gardner, 1995; Hersey, Blanchard, & Johnson, 1996; Kouzes & Posner, 1995), but that anyone can become a leader with training and practice.

Leadership is an "observable, learnable set of practices" (Kouzes & Posner, 1995, p. 16) that enhances certain qualities. So what are those qualities and those skills?

Personal Qualities of Effective Leaders

In Chapter 1, we talked about personal qualities and professional skills that are needed by effective school counselors. In that discussion, we listed both intuition and training as necessary to this profession, and we defined intuition in terms of creativity and imagination, flexibility, courage and faith, and passion. It is interesting to note that the *qualities of effective leaders include the same list* (Bolman & Deal, 1997; Gardner, 1995; Hersey, Blanchard, & Johnson, 1996; Kouzes & Posner, 1995).

In addition, many other qualities are necessary: vision, strength, commitment (Bolman & Deal, 1997); adaptability, social awareness, achievement-orientation, assertiveness, cooperation, decisiveness, dependability, energy, persistence, self-confidence, tolerance for stress, responsibility, intelligence, creativity, diplomacy and tact, persuasiveness, ability to be organized (Yukl, as cited in Hersey, Blanchard, & Johnson, 1996, p. 102); charisma, originality (Kirkpatrick and Locke, as cited in Hersey, Blanchard, & Johnson, 1996, p. 104); honesty, forward-looking (visionary), ability to be inspiring, competence, fairness, supportiveness, credibility, and broad-mindedness (Kouzes & Posner, 1995).

It is important to note that this list is not exhaustive. It is not a list of qualities that only leaders possess, it is not a list of qualities that someone aspiring to be a leader *must* have, and it's not a list of qualities all leaders have. These qualities, however, are those that will serve any counselor or any school counselor well; in fact, we believe that we see these qualities in most school counselors in our training programs. The purpose of presenting this list is to challenge you to think about which of those qualities you currently possess and which qualities you might further develop as you move into leadership in your school.

Reflection Moment

What are the qualities you see in yourself? What qualities do others see in you? Which qualities would you like to develop more fully? What can you do now to begin your development in that area (or in those areas)? See Exercise 10-1 for a structured way to think about your professional development in this area.

Professional Skills of Effective Leaders

This list of professional leadership skills will also be familiar in many ways. You will notice a direct overlap with many of the skills you have been challenged to develop in this book. According to Bolman and Deal (1997, pp. 297–298) the following are the most effective leadership skills:

- Establishing a vision for the program
- Setting standards for performance of tasks or excellence of endeavors
- Creating focus and direction for collective efforts

EXERCISE 10.1 *Leadership Qualities Survey*

Use the first column to rate yourself on the following qualities, then fold the paper to hide your responses and ask a colleague, mentor, or other professional to rate you on the same qualities. Compare the responses and design a plan for your "leadership growth" based on areas in which you see a need.

Use the following scale for your responses: 1 = Always, 2 = Often, 3 = Sometimes, 4 = Rarely, 5 = Never

	Your Responses						*Other Responses*				
	fold						**fold**				
Creativity	1	2	3	4	5		1	2	3	4	5
Imagination	1	2	3	4	5		1	2	3	4	5
Flexibility	1	2	3	4	5		1	2	3	4	5
Courage	1	2	3	4	5		1	2	3	4	5
Faith	1	2	3	4	5		1	2	3	4	5
Passion	1	2	3	4	5		1	2	3	4	5
Vision	1	2	3	4	5		1	2	3	4	5
Strength	1	2	3	4	5		1	2	3	4	5
Commitment	1	2	3	4	5		1	2	3	4	5
Adaptability	1	2	3	4	5		1	2	3	4	5
Social awareness	1	2	3	4	5		1	2	3	4	5
Achievement-orientation	1	2	3	4	5		1	2	3	4	5
Assertiveness	1	2	3	4	5		1	2	3	4	5
Cooperation	1	2	3	4	5		1	2	3	4	5
Decisiveness	1	2	3	4	5		1	2	3	4	5
Dependability	1	2	3	4	5		1	2	3	4	5
Energy	1	2	3	4	5		1	2	3	4	5
Persistence	1	2	3	4	5		1	2	3	4	5
Self-confidence	1	2	3	4	5		1	2	3	4	5
Tolerance for stress	1	2	3	4	5		1	2	3	4	5
Responsibility	1	2	3	4	5		1	2	3	4	5
Intelligence	1	2	3	4	5		1	2	3	4	5
Diplomacy	1	2	3	4	5		1	2	3	4	5
Tact	1	2	3	4	5		1	2	3	4	5
Persuasiveness	1	2	3	4	5		1	2	3	4	5
Ability to be organized	1	2	3	4	5		1	2	3	4	5
Charisma	1	2	3	4	5		1	2	3	4	5
Originality	1	2	3	4	5		1	2	3	4	5
Honesty	1	2	3	4	5		1	2	3	4	5
Forward-looking (visionary)	1	2	3	4	5		1	2	3	4	5
Ability to inspire	1	2	3	4	5		1	2	3	4	5
Competence	1	2	3	4	5		1	2	3	4	5
Fairness	1	2	3	4	5		1	2	3	4	5
Supportiveness	1	2	3	4	5		1	2	3	4	5
Credibility	1	2	3	4	5		1	2	3	4	5
Broad-mindedness	1	2	3	4	5		1	2	3	4	5

- Caring deeply about whatever the organization or group does
- Believing that doing the group's work well is important
- Inspiring trust
- Building relationships
- Communicating the vision with passion to others

According to Hersey, Blanchard, and Johnson (1996, p. 97), the following are the most essential leadership skills:

- Monitoring, refining, and establishing the vision, mission, and [organizational] ideas in light of the organization's environment
- Energizing, attuning, and aligning the strategic initiatives and the culture
- Connecting, unifying, and focusing teams toward their goals
- Empowering, engaging, and enabling people for their tasks

While the terminology of "strategic initiatives" and "teams" might be a little foreign to counselors, it is important to note that the essence of these skills are many of the professional skills of counselors. In establishing a vision, counselors are articulating what they see their school can do for students and how their comprehensive school counseling program moves the school toward that goal. In setting standards, counselors establish an expectation for excellence and identify their accountability. By creating and maintaining focus on students and their development, counselors communicate that they care deeply about how students grow and about all partners in the school and the community.

By our belief that the developmental work we do is important, we serve to inspire others to trust in students and in the school. When school counselors build effective and healthy relationships with all constituents, we have the means to communicate our vision with passion. By being sensitive to environmental issues in the school, we are able to remove barriers to learning and foster healthy development. By energizing and aligning the school counseling program within the culture of the school, we connect our students with the school community. By providing the energy and vision to connect, unify, and focus students, families, and colleagues toward the goal of healthy development for students, we reinforce the positive contributions that schools make to students and the community. Finally, by empowering, engaging, and enabling people for their tasks in the education and development of our students, we provide leadership in creating a cycle of healthy and respectful appreciation for all members of the school community and beyond.

Accepting that school counselors are leaders is not so much of a stretch when you think of the professional skills that you have developed and are currently developing. These skills and leadership skills are not so different after all. Complete Exercise 10-2 and see how you rate yourself on these skills.

Reflection Moment

Have you used any of these skills? If so, where and when? How did that feel? If not, where are there opportunities for you to observe someone model these skills? Can you see yourself as a leader?

EXERCISE 10.2   *Leadership Skills Survey*

Rate yourself on the following skills, using the following scale:

1 = underdeveloped, never used   2 = seldom used   3 = sometimes used
4 = often used, well developed   5 = used consistently, very well developed skill

Conceptualize and organize a school counseling program.	1	2	3	4	5
Counseling	1	2	3	4	5
Listening	1	2	3	4	5
Consulting	1	2	3	4	5
Educating others	1	2	3	4	5
Advocacy	1	2	3	4	5
Collaboration.	1	2	3	4	5
Manage resources of a program and coordinate efforts.	1	2	3	4	5
Communicate belief in others.	1	2	3	4	5
Be open and inviting to others.	1	2	3	4	5
Empower others.	1	2	3	4	5
Understand power dynamics in relationships.	1	2	3	4	5
Understand power dynamics in your environment.	1	2	3	4	5
Communication	1	2	3	4	5
Negotiation	1	2	3	4	5
Persuasion	1	2	3	4	5
Envisioning symbols and metaphors	1	2	3	4	5
Understanding change.	1	2	3	4	5
Putting experience into meaningful context.	1	2	3	4	5
Communicating a vision.	1	2	3	4	5
Connecting with your community:	1	2	3	4	5
School boards	1	2	3	4	5
School community	1	2	3	4	5
Parents	1	2	3	4	5
Students	1	2	3	4	5
Be a role model in professional activities.	1	2	3	4	5
Develop a professional identity.	1	2	3	4	5
Caring about the work you do.	1	2	3	4	5
Creating focus and consensus in the work of others.	1	2	3	4	5
Inspiring trust.	1	2	3	4	5

A Model of Effective Leadership

Kouzes and Posner (1995) have described their "commitments of leadership" (p. 318) that outline five steps for leaders to follow, which is presented as Figure 10-1. This model will help you to conceptualize the process of leadership as each "practice" can be seen as one step in the process. These five steps are:

- Challenge the process
- Inspire a shared vision
- Enable others to act

Leaders challenge the process.
They *search for opportunities* to change the status quo. They look for innovative ways to improve the organization. They *experiment and take risks.* And since risk taking involves mistakes and failure, leaders accept the inevitable disappointments as learning opportunities.

Leaders inspire a shared vision.
They passionately believe that they can make a difference. They *envision the future,* creating an ideal and unique image of what the community, agency, or organization can become. Through their strong appeal and quiet persuasion, leaders *enlist others* in the dream. They breathe life into the shared vision and get people to see the exciting future possibilities.

Leaders enable others to act.
They *foster collaboration* and build spirited teams. They actively involve others. Leaders understand that mutual respect is what sustains extraordinary efforts; they strive to create an atmosphere of trust and human dignity. They *strengthen others* by sharing information and providing choice. They give their own power away, making each person feel capable and powerful.

Leaders model the way.
They create standards of excellence and then *set an example* for others to follow. They establish values about how constituents, colleagues, and customers should be treated. Because complex change can overwhelm and stifle action, leaders *achieve small wins.* They unravel bureaucracy, put up signposts, and create opportunities for victory.

Leaders encourage the heart.
Getting extraordinary things done in organizations is hard work. To keep hope and determination alive, leaders *recognize contributions* that individuals make in the climb to the top. And because every winning team needs to share in the rewards of team efforts, leaders *celebrate accomplishments.* They make everyone feel like a hero.

FIGURE 10.1   *Five Fundamental Practices of Exemplary Leadership*

Source: Kouzes, J. M., & Posner, B. Z. (1995). The leadership challenge: How to keep getting extraordinary things done in organizations. Copyright © 1995 Jossey-Bass. Reprinted by permission of John Wiley & Sons, Inc.

- Model the way
- Encourage the heart

These steps are not specific to the business world; according to Kouzes and Posner (1995), they are the means to make a difference in the world.

> Beyond the horizon of time is a changed world, very different from today's world. Some people see beyond that horizon and into the future. They believe that dreams can become reality. They open our eyes and lift our spirits. They build trust and strengthen our relationships. They stand firm against the winds of resistance and give us the courage to continue the quest. We call these people *leaders.* (emphasis authors', p. 317)

As we hope you have learned from this book, school counselors can be, and must become, leaders in the domains of student growth: of academic development, career development, and personal/social development.

Definition of Coordination

In the personal statement at the beginning of this chapter, the observation was made that to implement and nurture your school counseling program, you must have skills in coordination, cooperation, and collaboration. These are essential skills for school counselors and deserve careful consideration.

To understand why this coordination is essential for effective school counseling programs, we must explore what is meant by "coordination." Harrison (2000) summed it up best in his definition: "Coordination is a *counselor initiated leadership process* in which the counselor helps *organize* and *manage* the comprehensive guidance program and related services" (emphasis added, p. 190). Within this definition are embedded several important concepts. First, coordination activities are connected to leadership. Second, coordination activities are counselor initiated, therefore not a passive or second-rate function of the comprehensive school counseling program. Third, coordination is essential for the organization of the program and, finally, coordination is essential for the management of the program. Let's examine each of these observations separately.

The connection of leadership and coordination is important. Good leaders are involved in the day-to-day activities of their work, and so coordination of work, services, and programs is a natural part of effective leadership. This technical mastery increases trust in the professional skills of the leader, and the willingness to actually "get your hands dirty and work" increases everyone's trust in the credibility of the leader.

The fact that coordination is not a passive, but an active, part of the school counselor's job is also important. As previously mentioned, good intentions alone do not get the job done; only active, goal-directed movement will lead to progress toward goals.

Furthermore, counselors utilize coordination in the organization and management of the program. Organization activities include coordinating ideas, resources, materials, and personnel to bring about the design and creation of the program, then coordinating all those ideas, resources, materials, and personnel to make the program happen. Counselors also use coordination skills to manage the program: the oversight, supervision, evaluation, and redesign of the program based on feedback. In this view, the work counselors must do with personnel involves intense collaboration and cooperation to foster the coordination of personnel resources for the school counseling program. More will be presented on this aspect of the school counseling program in Chapter 14.

In case this all sounds very conceptual, rest assured, it's not. Much of the work of coordinating the comprehensive school counseling program is very practical. To provide a more concrete view of coordination, examples of mundane activities might include scheduling meetings (with counseling groups, advisory boards, teachers and parents), scheduling appointments (with students, teachers, parents), creating budgets, writing grants, documenting activities and achievements, evaluating the program, evaluating events within the program, scheduling facilities for events, arranging for refreshments, securing donations for a program or event, typing flyers and creating brochures, stapling, sealing envelopes, and affixing stamps. Don't assume you will have clerical help in the school; many counselors do their own typing and answer their own phones.

Another important concept must be presented in the discussion of coordination: that of using coordinating (administrative) activities as a smoke screen to avoid doing more personal (counseling) work with students (Myrick, 1997). Harrison (2000, p. 191) also noted that some school counselors become involved in "noncounseling, administrator-driven" activities inappropriately. This situation may arise when the school counselor is not the leader of the comprehensive school counseling program, when the counselor's time and energies are defined by noncounselors. Out-of-balance administrative tasks will be discussed more in Chapter 14.

Leading and Coordinating Events and Activities for Students

Leadership and coordination are important activities with each of the partners in the DAP model. In terms of leadership with students, the school counselor is looked to as the professional and personal leader of and advocate for programmatic efforts that focus on mental health, nurturing, care, respect, and healthy development. As we have discussed, these are important aspects of the learning students must do in order to become healthy, functional adults in the community, to become healthy parents, significant life partners, contributors to the community in terms of work and/or employment, and community builders. As a visible leader in the school, the school counselor is the role model for students through his or her work in the school and in her or his own personal life and interactions with others.

As the leader of these programmatic efforts, school counselors coordinate programs and events for students in the three domains. While not intended as an exhaustive list of events all counselors must coordinate, specific examples of possible programs and events in each domain might include the following (Bemak, 2000; Burnham & Jackson, 2000; Clark & Stone, 2000a, 2000b; Cole & Ryan, 1997; Fazio & Ural, 1995; Harrison, 2000; Smaby & Daugherty, 1995):

Academic Development

Academic excellence award programs

Peer tutoring

Academic Olympic games

Learning styles workshops

Debate teams, forensics

New student orientation and transition programs

College fairs and information sessions

Academic intervention for nonpassing students

Portfolios and authentic assessments

Career Development

Mentoring programs in professions and trades

Career days and events

Interviewing workshops

Career interest testing programs

Informational interviewing in professions and trades

School-to-work programs

Personal/Social Development

Individual and group counseling

Developmental curriculum infusion and/or delivery

Advisor for student groups

Peer mediation programs

Peer mentoring programs

Community service programs

Student recognition for campus/ community service

Mental health issues (for example, National Depression Screening Day)

Support groups, crisis and loss groups

Substance abuse prevention, intervention, and referral programs

Referrals for therapeutic intervention and treatment

While many counselors also coordinate administrative functions, the following are examples of some activities that have potential for contributing to out-of-balance conditions (Burnham & Jackson, 2000) and will be discussed more in Chapter 14. Since they each involve a student program or service, they are presented here for your consideration.

1. *Scholarship applications, college applications, and letters of recommendation for college.* It is our view that expecting secondary school counselors to funnel students into colleges is unethical. Imposing a college-oriented agenda on counselors and students skews the relationship between the counselor and the student, compromising the counselor's impartial stance with students and infringing on the counselor's ethical duty to allow students to explore their future without pressure to accept one path over another. If counselors are responsible for the choices of students after high school, then they should also be responsible for filling out job applications for students who choose to work after high school, an equally ludicrous expectation. If secondary school administrators choose to be responsible for getting students into college, then that activity should lie with the administration as the academic leadership of the institution, not with the comprehensive school counseling program leadership.

2. *Student records maintenance and transfer, preparation and evaluation of student transcripts, preparation of curriculum booklets and materials, and student registration.* These are purely academic functions and should be housed with the academic administration. It is appropriate that counselors help students choose their courses based on some life-career counseling that has occurred, but it is important to remember that progress toward graduation is a shared responsibility between academic professionals, the counseling professionals, the parents of the students, and the students themselves. Registrars are the appropriate professionals to manage academic records, evaluate transcripts, prepare materials to help students understand the curriculum of the school, and enroll students into their classes on the computer. These responsibilities do not require a graduate degree in counseling (Gysbers & Henderson, 2000).

3. *Student academic assessment, building assessment coordinator.* The administration of academic achievement and graduation tests seems a purely academic function that does not require a master's degree in counseling and seems outside the boundaries of the comprehensive school counseling program (Burnham & Jackson, 2000).

Reflection Moment

> What are your reactions to the administrative functions discussed above? Do you believe these functions should be done by counselors? If so, which one(s)?

Chapter Summary

In this chapter, we discussed the functions of leadership and coordination as essential aspects of a comprehensive school counseling program. While little formal training is usually provided in leadership in most graduate programs in counseling, it is clear from research that school counselors must be prepared to lead their program, and by extension, to lead the "heart" of the school.

Leadership was defined as tapping the intrinsic motivation of people to want to work toward shared goals. Four contexts of leadership were outlined to help define what leadership could be: structural leadership, human resource leadership, political leadership, and symbolic leadership. Next, we shared the roles that leaders fill to further illustrate how the school counselor, functioning as the leader of the comprehensive school counseling program, also functions as a leader in the school.

Several myths about leadership were explored and contradicted. These myths, depicting leaders as superhuman, isolated, distant, omnipotent, and omniscient, keep people from believing they are capable of leadership. Our conclusion, consistent with research, is that leadership is based on certain personal qualities and learned skills.

These personal qualities resonate with the personal qualities of effective counselors. Qualities such as creativity, imagination, honesty, trustworthiness, energy, passion, and others were listed, and you were challenged to explore how many of those skills were already a part of your own personal reservoir of skills. The learned skills of leadership were outlined next and also resonate with many skills of professional counselors. These skills include communication, coalition-building, establishing a vision, setting standards for excellence, caring deeply, believing that doing the work is important, and inspiring others. A model of leadership was presented that takes these skills and structures them into a way of conceptualizing the process of leadership, so that you can apply them to the school setting.

We then discussed coordination in terms of four issues: the connection between leadership and coordination, the active nature of coordination of events in a school, the role of coordination in the organization of the comprehensive school counseling program, and the role of coordination in the management of the comprehensive school counseling program. Collaboration and cooperation were also discussed as components of coordination of the human resources available to the program. Some of the more routine activities that are inherent in coordinating a program of comprehensive school counseling were outlined.

Finally, we gave some examples of programs and events that the school counselor might coordinate in each of the three domains. We also shared some administrative functions that often are subsumed under the job responsibilities of the school counselor and outlined why those functions might be more appropriately housed in the academic administration of the school.

A Day in the Life Revisited: Integration

Reread the Day in the Life section at the beginning of this chapter. Based on what you now know about your role as a leader in the school, what would you have done if you were Kate?

Think of how you would address this situation. First, what questions would you ask a principal or interviewing committee about the school counseling program to help you understand who "leads" the program?

How would you establish yourself as the leader of your program? How would you blend the insights from each of the four contexts of leadership to maximize your ability to lead? What did you see in Kate's situation that provides you some feeling of the four contexts in her school?

What functions do you see as appropriate in the coordination of your program? How would you go about establishing your leadership in terms of what programs and services you would coordinate within the structure of your program?

Application

1. Take the Leadership Qualities Survey and Leadership Skills Survey in Exercises 10.1 and 10.2 on pages 209 and 211. Create a plan for self-development based on the results of these instruments.

2. Watch a contemporary popular movie or TV show about a school. As you watch, see if you can document:
   - Who the leaders are
   - What the leadership context or frame is (structural, human resources, political, or symbolic)
   - What roles they fill in the school
   - What the formal and informal power structures are
   - The qualities of the leader(s)
   - The skills of the leader(s)

3. Read a book about a leader whom you admire. What insights into your own leadership style did you glean from your reading?

4. Look at times in your life when you assumed leadership of a group. What was that experience like for you? What can you learn from that experience now in your professional training and development?

5. How do you feel about the conceptual nature of the coordination function of school counseling? How do you feel about the hands-on nature of the coordination function of school counseling? How prepared do you feel for these roles? Outline a plan to increase your abilities to be effective in both these areas.

6. At the end of the chapter, several functions were presented that could belong in academic administration. Assume that you agree with the arguments that the functions belong in academic administration. Outline your arguments to move those functions into the principal or vice principal's office. Structure a plan that addresses each of the four contexts or frames of leadership: structural, human resource, political, and symbolic.

7. Interview a high school counselor. Ask that person to list all the events and programs he or she coordinates. Which ones does that person feel are appropriate and which are inappropriate? Why? Which ones do you feel are appropriate and which ones are inappropriate? Why?

8. Look at the student quote that opens this chapter. How do you feel it relates to the content of the chapter?

Suggested Readings

Bolman, L. G., & Deal, T. E. (1997). *Reframing organizations: Artistry, choice, and leadership* (2nd ed.). San Francisco, CA: Jossey-Bass. These authors examine the four frames or contexts of leadership, applying these typologies to a variety of organizations and institutions. They also provide excellent ideas for developing leadership skills.

Burnham, J. J., & Jackson, C. M. (2000). School counselor roles: Discrepancies between actual practice and existing models. *Professional School Counseling, 4,* 41–49. A current study that describes the work that school counselors do (providing wonderful insights into how counselors actually spend their time), then compares the findings to two existing models of comprehensive school counseling.

Kouzes, J. M., & Posner, B. Z. (1995). *The leadership challenge: How to keep getting extraordinary things done in organizations.* San Francisco, CA: Jossey-Bass. This book is full of exciting ways of viewing leadership that can help the reader understand the many skills that leaders employ in getting things done in organizations. An inspired and inspiring reading for anyone who hopes to get things done in this world.

References

Bemak, F. (2000). Transforming the role of the counselor to provide leadership in educational reform through collaboration. *Professional School Counseling, 3,* 323–331.

Bolman, L. G., & Deal, T. E. (1997). *Reframing organizations: Artistry, choice, and leadership* (2nd ed.). San Francisco, CA: Jossey-Bass.

Burnham, J. J., & Jackson, C. M. (2000). School counselor roles: Discrepancies between actual practice and existing models. *Professional School Counseling, 4,* 41–49.

Clark, M. A., & Stone, C. (2000a). The developmental school counselor as educational leader. In J. Wittmer (Ed.), *Managing your school counseling program: K–12 developmental strategies* (2nd ed.; pp. 75–82). Minneapolis, MN: Educational Media Corp.

Clark, M. A., & Stone, C. (2000b, May). Evolving our image: School counselors as educational leaders. *Counseling Today, 42,* 21, 22, 29, 30, 46.

Cole, D. J., & Ryan, C. W. (1997). Leadership in portfolio development: The school counsellor's [sic] role. *Guidance & Counselling* [sic], 12(4), 10–14. Retrieved November 28, 2000, from the EBSCO database available on the World Wide Web: wysiwyg://bodyframe.9/http://ehostv.

DeRoche, E. F. (2000). Leadership for character education programs. *Journal of Humanistic Counseling, Education, and Development, 39,* 41–47.

Fazio, T. J., & Ural, K. K. (1995). The Princeton peer leadership program: Training seniors to help first year students. *NASSP Bulletin, 79*(5), 57–60.

Gardner, H. (1995). *Leading minds: An anatomy of leadership.* New York: Basic.

Gysbers, N. C., & Henderson, P. (2000). *Developing and managing your school guidance program* (3rd ed.). Alexandria, VA: American Counseling Association.

Harrison, T. C. (2000). The school counselor as consultant/coordinator. In J. Wittmer (Ed.), *Managing your school counseling program: K–12 developmental strategies* (2nd ed.; pp. 183–191). Minneapolis, MN: Educational Media Corporation.

Hersey, P., Blanchard, K. H., & Johnson, D. E. (1996). *Management of organizational behavior: Utilizing human resources* (7th ed.). Upper Saddle River, NJ: Prentice-Hall.

Hutchinson, R. L., & Bottorff, R. L. (1986). Selected high school counseling services: Student assessment. *The School Counselor, 33,* 350–354.

Kouzes, J. M., & Posner, B. Z. (1995). *The leadership challenge: How to keep getting extraordinary things done in organizations.* San Francisco, CA: Jossey-Bass.

Kurpius, D. J., & Rozecki, T. (1992). Outreach, advocacy, and consultation: A framework for prevention and intervention. *Elementary School Guidance and Counseling, 26,* 176–190. Retrieved November 13, 2000, from the EBSCO database on the World Wide Web: http://webnfl.epnet.com.

Myrick, R. D. (1997). *Developmental guidance and counseling: A practical approach* (3rd ed.). Minneapolis, MN: Educational Media.

O'Dell, F. L., & Rak, C. F. (1996). Guidance for the 1990s: Revitalizing the counselor's role. *Clearing House, 69*(5), 303–308. Retrieved on November 28, 2000, from the EBSCO database on the World Wide Web: wysiwyg://bodyframe.9/http://ehostv.

Partin, R. L. (1993). School counselors' time: Where does it go? *The School Counselor, 40,* 274–281.

Smaby, M. H., & Daugherty, R. (1995). The school counselor as leader of efforts to have schools free of drugs and violence. *Education, 115,* 612–622.

Wiggins, J. D., & Moody, A. H. (1987). Student evaluations of counseling programs: An added dimension. *The School Counselor, 34,* 353–361.

IV

Partnering with Parents, Colleagues in the School, and Colleagues in the Community

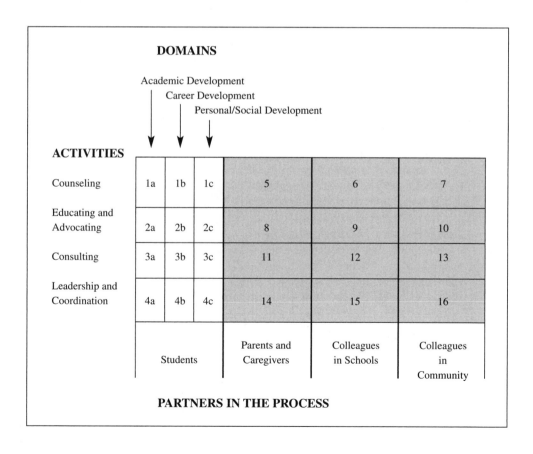

DOMAINS

Academic Development
Career Development
Personal/Social Development

ACTIVITIES						
Counseling	1a	1b	1c	5	6	7
Educating and Advocating	2a	2b	2c	8	9	10
Consulting	3a	3b	3c	11	12	13
Leadership and Coordination	4a	4b	4c	14	15	16
	Students			Parents and Caregivers	Colleagues in Schools	Colleagues in Community

PARTNERS IN THE PROCESS

11

Counseling with Parents, Colleagues in the School, and Colleagues in the Community (Blocks 5, 6, 7 of the DAP Model)

Colette T. Dollarhide

"What would I like to say? Just that people need to realize that in order to pass in life as a person you have to be yourself and not anyone else or what anyone wants to make you."

Sandra, age 16

Learning Objectives _____

By the end of this chapter, you will:

1. Understand systems perspectives and be able to articulate why school counselors need to work with the adult partners of the DAP model.

2. Understand various perspectives on adult development in terms of career development.

3. Understand various perspectives on adult development in terms of personal/social development.

4. Understand the developmental cycle of systems using a model of family system development.

5. Be able to apply those perspectives when assessing the situation to determine whether to provide counseling for adult partners.

6. Understand the counseling implications and strategies for addressing the needs of families of students.

7. Understand the counseling implications and strategies for addressing the needs of colleagues in the school.

8. Understand the counseling implications and strategies for addressing the needs of colleagues in the community.

A Day in the Life of a Counselor: Mr. Paulson Meets Ty's Mother _____

(Go back to Chapter 6 and reread Mr. Paulson's conversation with Ty.)

Later that day, Mr. Paulson called Ty's house to make an appointment to meet with Ty's mother. She was able to come to the school on her lunch break, so Mr. Paulson arranged to have the conference room at noon so that they could talk while they ate lunch. After exchanging greetings and getting settled with their sandwiches, Mr. Paulson explained why they were meeting.

"Thank you for coming in, Mrs. Bonté. I'm Calvin Paulson, Ty's counselor. Please call me Calvin. Ty came in this morning with some bruises on his face and concerns about school. I'd like to see what we can do together to help Ty deal with things."

Mrs. Bonté nodded. "I've been concerned about him. He's not been himself lately, more moody and irritable with everyone. What do you think's going on?"

"Well, he seemed upset with his needing to work more to help out at home. He said his grades are slipping, and he's not sure he can get into college. What can you tell me about what you see at home?"

Mrs. Bonté's eyes grew moist as she thought about her son. "He's such a good boy, always helping out with everything. He's my oldest, and he took over after his daddy died three years ago, helping out with his two younger brothers. I'm working all I can at my job, but I don't earn a lot. Ty watches his brothers, and that's no easy task—they like to needle him and pick fights with each other. Last week they had a big fight, and when Ty tried to break it up, they all got into it. Ty's littlest brother ended up with a sprained wrist and the middle one got a black eye. Nobody will talk about what happened that night, so I don't know who did what, but I do know that Ty has his hands full until I get home.

"Ty usually starts dinner, then when I get home, he goes to his job. When he gets home from his work, he does his homework and studies until all hours of the night, because he wanted to get into college. Now he doesn't know what he wants to do, go to college or stay home and take care of me and the boys.

"I was sick for a couple of weeks and lost some hours at work; now I owe the doctor some money and all the bills are late. Ty insisted that he could work more hours or get a second job to help pay those bills, even though I told him I didn't want him to. His dad and I put some money aside so that he could go to college if he wanted. If I save that money for his schooling, I need his help for the bills, which means he won't be able to study as much and may not even get into college. If I use that money now for the bills, there won't be anything for his tuition." She sighed, feeling the weight of her worries.

"He's really having a tough time in his science class," she continued. "I don't know what it is about that teacher, that Ms. Epps. She seems to ride Ty pretty hard. He said that she seems mad at him all the time, but he's not sure what he did to cause it. Then there are problems with some of the kids on the block—some name-calling and pushing. I'm not sure what that's about, because he won't talk about that, either.

"I see him sinking, Calvin, and I don't know what to do about it. Look at all the things he's having trouble with—his brothers, the money worries, his job, his grades, Ms. Epps, the kids on the street. I don't know what to do to help him. I don't even know where to begin."

Challenge Questions

Think about what you heard from Ty and now you've heard from his mother. Do you understand Ty better, now that you see the context of his life? When you first heard from Ty that he needed to work more to help his family with the bills, did you jump to any conclusions about his parents? (Be honest!) Now that you know more, do you feel more compassion for him and his family?

What do you think about the need for family counseling here? Should Calvin provide family counseling for Ty and his family? Would you see yourself providing family counseling? Why or why not?

What about the situation with the science teacher? What do you see as the options with Ms. Epps? Should Calvin intervene here? Would you see yourself providing counseling, consultation, or avoiding the situation and not saying anything to Ms. Epps? What are the reasons for your choice?

What can you do about the situation in the community—the other kids who caused Ty's bruises? How would you intervene in the community to foster more tolerance? (Remember, Ty reported that the kids are using racial slurs.)

If you recall a basic truth, that each of us has power to influence the world, then what are the costs to all involved if you do nothing to intervene in these systemic problems?

Systems Thinking: Families, Schools, and Communities

It should come as no surprise to hear that there is a lot of pain in the world. You only have to open a newspaper or watch the evening news to see evidence of that pain. Recall the story in Chapter 1 of the little girl who threw stranded starfish back into the sea. It is true that we can help individual starfish by putting them back in the ocean, but if the water is polluted or poisonous, the starfish won't survive, in spite of our best efforts. Our work with students has to incorporate the environment and context in which our students live, otherwise the poison from that context will render our best efforts moot. The next four chapters address the ocean of the starfish: the context of our students' lives.

As a whole, educational professionals know the environmental factors needed for healthy development. We touched on these in Chapter 3, in which we outlined the systems in which students live, and in Chapter 4, in which we discussed schools as systems. Those factors that support students in their development have been called *developmental assets* (Search Institute, 1996). The top six support assets are identified as family support, positive family communication, supportive adult relationships, a caring neighborhood, a caring school climate, and parental involvement in schooling.

When those developmental assets are missing, we have good documentation of the negative effects (McWhirter, McWhirter, McWhirter, & McWhirter, 1998). Communitywide economic instability, stagnation, intolerance, poor healthcare (mental and physical), poor childcare, and a host of other problems can cause increased stress in the home. This stress often resonates with stress and vulnerability in the family system, increasing the risk for divorce, family violence, neglect, substance abuse and addiction, and mental health problems, which then resonate with increased stress on the children living in the home. This increased stress in the children then resonates with the stressors of the schools: overcrowding, insufficient funding, anxiety over testing, unhealthy school environments, unhappy staff, and other problems. All these problems can erode students' efforts to learn, grow, and prosper (McWhirter, McWhirter, McWhirter, & McWhirter, 1998).

These problems have a direct correlation with academic achievement, career development, and personal/social life functioning. For example, Noble (2000) found that students whose parents earn less than $36,000 a year or who have experienced three or more major problems at home (e.g., parental unemployment, chronic health problems, death, separation or divorce, or the need to work to help support the family) are more than twice as likely to be low academic achievers as high academic achievers (p. 15). These stressors also have a direct correlation with more serious behaviors, such as school dropout, substance abuse and addiction, teenage pregnancy and risky sexual behaviors, delinquency, violence, and suicide (McWhirter, McWhirter, McWhirter, & McWhirter, 1998).

As you will recall from Chapter 3, systems thinking is a way of seeing and addressing these problems from a holistic, naturalistic perspective. It views all students as members of interlocking and dynamic systems of social interactions, which then informs intervention efforts aimed at those systems. Providing counseling from a systems perspective involves counseling families, parents, members of the school community, and members of the larger community to effect change on behalf of students, as needed.

Does this mean that school counselors provide counseling for anyone who walks through the door? *Most emphatically, no.* Does this mean that school counselors provide family systems counseling? *No, family systems counseling is a therapeutic treatment approach that requires specialized training.* Does this mean that the school counselor is responsible for events in the community and should conduct counseling with homeless persons, criminals, or others who are not functioning well in the community? *Again, no.* But we cannot ignore the pain of our families, schools, or communities. *There are ways we can help, and problem-solving, intervention-level counseling for families, school colleagues, and community colleagues might be appropriate, depending on the situation.* We will explore various situations in which counseling *might* be appropriate, but first, let's look at developmental issues of adults to better understand how to evaluate those situations.

The Developmental Stages of Adulthood

We have focused this book on the developmental issues of adolescents to understand appropriate ways to facilitate their academic, career, and personal/social development. If we continue the developmental theme with our adult partners, we can better understand what interventions might be effective with them also. Since Chapter 12 addresses educating and advocating with adults, we will save our discussion of intellectual (academic) development for Chapter 13 and will focus our discussion here on the career development and personal/social development of adults.

Career Development

We live in a capitalist society, where our very survival depends on our ability to make a living. For adults, earning a living to support oneself and one's family, or connecting with meaningful efforts in an existential sense, anchor us to each other and to society (Fox, 1994; Hansen, 1997). Conversely, the loss of the ability to support oneself and family, or the loss of that connection with meaningful effort, can result in personal and societal decay (Fox, 1994; Hansen, 1997).

There are a variety of ways to understand career development, but Super, Savickas, and Super (1996) and Hansen (1997) provide us with holistic views of adult career development. In their approach, Super, Savickas, and Super use time (life stages of childhood, adolescence, adulthood, middle adulthood, and senescence) and space (life roles of child, student, leisurite, citizen, worker, and homemaker) to understand how people mature in a career and life context.

Using their construct, the Life-Career Rainbow (p.127), Super, Savickas, and Super (1996) describe how various life roles take on increased emphasis during certain life and career stages. They outline these career stages as follows:

- *Exploration* (Adolescence: ages 14 to 24, approximately) is the stage in which individuals engage in the career development tasks of crystallizing their ideas of appropriate careers, specifying the career direction that most fits their personality and lifestyle choices, and implementing occupational choices.
- *Establishment* (Adulthood: ages 24 to 44, approximately) involves the career development tasks of stabilizing, consolidating, and advancing in an occupational position. Stabilizing involves the assimilation of the rules, culture, and expectations of the place of employment and performing job tasks satisfactorily. Consolidating involves the long-term demonstration of positive work attitudes, habits, and productivity, which then may result in career advancement.
- *Maintenance* (Middle adulthood: ages 45 to 65, approximately) represents a decision point for many adults. If adults do not enjoy their work, they cycle back through exploration and establishment. If they do enjoy their work, they move into the maintenance

stage of career development, in which they continue their productivity, learn new skills, innovate new approaches to old problems, or discover new challenges.

• *Disengagement* (Senescence, ages 65 plus) involves deceleration, retirement planning, and retirement living. This involves "slowing down on the job, starting to turn over tasks to younger colleagues, and contemplating retirement" (p. 134).

Describing a more circular and less linear view of career development, Hansen (1997) challenges counselors to expand their ideas about careers, life, and work. From roots in traditional career theory and adult development, multicultural counseling, gender studies, and systems thinking, Hansen (1997) has developed her approach, called Integrative Life Planning. Hansen suggests that career development and life development are not separate constructs, but must be integrated. This integration involves two phases. First is the integration of factors within the individual: identity dimensions (race, ethnicity, gender, ability, class, sexual orientation, religion, and others), developmental domains (social, intellectual, physical, spiritual, emotional, and career/vocational), life roles (love/family, labor/work, learning and leisure), and contexts (society, organization, family, and individual). Then, once the individual understands him- or herself in these terms, holistic life/career choices emerge as the individual explores the six critical tasks of:

1. Finding work that needs doing in changing global contexts.
2. Weaving lives into a meaningful whole.
3. Connecting family and work.
4. Valuing pluralism and inclusivity.
5. Exploring spirituality and life purpose.
6. Managing personal transitions and organizational change.

To fully understand how career and work-related problems in the home or community can affect your students, consider the situation in which a major employer in your community has announced it will close its facility and all employees will be laid off. Such an event has tremendous implications for your students (who may have to move when parents look for new employment or have to adjust to a different lifestyle than the one they currently know), the school (that may have to scale back programs, facilities, and curriculum as students leave), and the community (that may have to suffer loss of programs and services as the tax base erodes). From this example, you can see how the employment realities of individual families or entire communities have a direct impact on your students, their families, the school, and the community.

Reflection Moment

Think about these two approaches to career development for adults. Where are you in your career development? How would you proceed with the parent of a student who comes to your office to talk about her unemployment? What would you say?

Personal/Social Development

There are many models of personal and social development of adults, but we will focus on two: one that gives a sequential view of adult life and one providing a holistic sense of challenges all adults face.

This is a sequential and epigenetic (one stage building on the previous one) view of adult development provided by Erikson (as cited in Craig, 1996). As Craig notes, however, even Erikson redefined the theory to label it a "normative life event" model (Craig, 1996, p. 490), meaning that each stage recycles back into focus in the event of major life transitions such as the death of a spouse, the loss of employment or the establishment of a new position, or relocating to a new community.

According to Erikson, adult stages are timed and characterized as follows:

Early Adulthood
Identity achievement versus identity confusion, in which the young adults work to establish a sense of continuity within adult experiences, to "define and redefine themselves, their priorities, and their place in the social world" (Craig, 1996, p. 490), and *Intimacy versus isolation,* in which young adults work to establish mutually satisfying relationships in which the two identities join but do not merge.

Middle Adulthood
Generativity versus self-absorption, in which adults feel that they are making viable contributions to the world, are challenged intellectually, contribute to the training of new professionals, and tend to the needs of the next generation. Peck (as cited in Craig, 1996, p. 577) expanded this stage to include:

1. Valuing wisdom versus valuing physical powers
2. Socializing versus sexualizing in terms of relationships
3. Emotional flexibility versus emotional impoverishment
4. Mental flexibility versus mental rigidity

Older Adulthood
Integrity versus despair, in which older adults examine their lives to determine if they have fulfilled their youthful expectations. "Those who can look back and feel satisfied that their lives have had meaning and that they have done the best they could with life's circumstances will have a sense of integrity" (Craig, 1996, p. 645) Again, Peck (as cited in Craig, 1996, p. 577) expanded this stage to include:

1. Ego differentiation versus work-role preoccupation (which helps adults deal with impending retirement)
2. Body transcendence versus body preoccupation (which helps adults deal with the aches and pains of old age)
3. Ego transcendence versus ego preoccupation (which helps adults deal with impending death by becoming involved in sharing with younger generations)

Contrasted with the previous sequential, stage-focused model is the following holistic model. Called *developmental tasks* by Upcraft, Finney, and Garland (as cited in Upcraft,

1985) and *vectors of young adult development* by Chickering and Reisser (1993), these are holistic challenges faced by all adults throughout their lifetimes. You will notice that many themes continue from adolescent development into adulthood (and you may recall this model from Chapter 2).

1. Achieving competence in terms of intellectual skills, social skills, and manual skills that help establish confidence in one's ability to face life challenges successfully.
2. Managing emotions in terms of decision making and adult functioning (also called emotional intelligence by Daniel Goleman; see Chapter 6).
3. Becoming autonomous in terms of emotional independence (freedom from the need for constant reassurance of support) and instrumental independence (freedom from the need to secure help from others to cope with problems and being geographically mobile in relation to one's needs).
4. Establishing identity and internal/external continuity based on an understanding of one's needs, characteristics, personal appearance, sexual identification and orientation.
5. Freeing interpersonal relationships, which provides a means of expressing trust, interdependence, respect, tolerance, and individuality in relationships.
6. Establishing and integrating one's purpose in life in terms of career goals, leisure activities, lifestyle, and community citizenship.
7. Developing integrity, making one's values internally and externally consistent and compassionate.
8. Maintaining personal health and wellness.

What makes these developmental issues relevant for all adults are the ubiquitous realities of transition and change. With change in various life realities—family, work, location, health—adults are in constant transition. With each transition, adults must renegotiate their growth in each of the preceding eight developmental tasks. For example, the launching of a young adult means that the parents are learning new social skills in the relationship with the child-turned-adult, they are learning new emotional responses in trying to let the new adult learn his or her own mistakes, and they are learning how to adjust to their own aging process and identities as middle-to-late adults.

This overview of the developmental stages of adults in terms of careers and personal/social development may provide a reminder about the importance of context when interacting with others. As you can see from these theories, career and personal development overlap and interact. It is important to note that these stages of adult development happen in conjunction with family and systemic changes, as we will see in the next section outlining the developmental cycle of families and systems.

Reflection Moment

What stage(s) of adult development describe(s) your life right now? What would you say to the parent of a student who comes in to talk about his son, but shares that he is overwhelmed right now with his job and the needs of three teenagers, his mother, and his mother-in-law, all of whom live in his home and depend on him for support?

The Developmental Stages of Systems

Just as individuals experience the cycle of life, so do systems, as we discussed in Chapter 3. Using a description of the life cycle of families, we can generalize to other systems to gain greater understanding of the systemic dynamics within schools and, to a more limited extent, within communities.

According to McWhirter, McWhirter, McWhirter, and McWhirter (1998), the following summarizes the family life cycle:

1. **Unattached young adult stage:** The young adult separates from his or her family of origin, establishes a work environment, and establishes a significant relationship.
2. **Establishment stage:** The couple marries, makes new rules, defines roles within the marriage, and adjusts relationships with friends and family.
3. **New parent stage (infant to 3 years):** The couple must adjust to parenthood and new roles. The marital dyad adjusts to include children.
4. **Preschool stage (oldest child 3 to 6 years):** Work and family roles are priority, with the major challenges involving the development of effective parenting skills.
5. **School-age stage (oldest child 6 to 12 years):** Parents become more involved in school and community activities as children grow.
6. **Teenage stage (oldest child 13 to 20 years):** The couple must address their own aging parents at the same time there is increasing demand for time and energy for personal, work, and parenting issues. Adolescent children are challenging rules and boundaries as they struggle to establish their own identities.
7. **Launching stage (departure of children):** Members of the family disengage emotionally from each other as children leave the home. Related tasks involve renegotiating the marital dyad and establishing relationships with adult children. Death of older family members is common.
8. **Postparental middle years stage:** New roles as grandparents are learned and relationships with adult children and their spouses continue.
9. **Aging family stage:** Now the aging parents themselves, questions of senior care arise. Independence in the final years is an issue.

It is important to mention that some of your students may be married, may be parents currently, or may in the process of becoming parents. It is even more important that you, as the school counselor, understand their unique development. Not only are these young people working on their own developmental issues, but they are also dealing with the additional developmental tasks that come with being a part of a new family.

Are there parallels between the family life stages and the systemic life stages of schools and communities? In a systems context, the basic stages involve creation, establishing rules, performing the work of the organization, disengagement, and termination (similar to the stages of group counseling outlined in Chapter 7: forming, storming, norming, performing, and adjourning). In schools, a new administrator, a new cohort of faculty, or new professionals in the school counseling office can breathe new life into the school, bringing the excitement and energy of creation. As people get to know each other, rules and expectations are established. For a time, the focus is on the work, and the school is highly energized and efficient as everyone gets "on board" with the new agenda. Eventually, some members of the system will, for a variety of reasons, choose to disengage from the school, mentally, emotionally, or physically, changing the nature of the dynamics in the system. As the energy base of the system wanes, the system goes into a decline. This "systemic holding pattern" waits for the next infusion of new ideas, creativity, and enthusiasm, at which time the school will enjoy a resurgence of productivity.

Within communities, neighborhoods also evolve as people move in and out. New families in the neighborhood infuse new energy into making this a good place to live. Eventually, homes age, property values decline, and the neighborhood suffers from a loss of identity and community. But this decline can be reversed: Downtown revitalization projects document that renewal can come to a community just as it can to a school.

Selection of Counseling as an Intervention

Understanding these developmental stages and cycles does not necessarily provide the school counselor with all the answers to families', schools', or communities' problems. It does, however, provide a framework for understanding the system and viewing it with compassion rather than with frustration. It is easy to blame the family for the student's problems, the teachers or principal for the school's problems, or "those people" for the neighborhood's problems. Understanding systems from a developmental perspective can reframe the blame into a plan for action.

The full range of actions available to school counselors vary from counseling, to educating, to consulting, to leadership and coordination. Which of these four responses you incorporate into your intervention plan is based on your own philosophy of counseling, your philosophy of education, your views on comprehensive secondary school counseling, and your professional assessment of the situation. In deciding whether to provide *counseling* as an intervention, these are the most essential issues:

1. A student-focused problem. The time and effort of counseling is justified if you believe that the problem is directly related to the development of your student(s). If you, as a professional, do not believe that the issue you see in the system creates a problem for the student, you might choose to use another activity to address the situation.
2. Time considerations. Some counselor may express concern about the time needed to provide basic counseling support to parents, spouse, family, school colleagues, or community colleagues. While there are scheduling implications for working with these adult partners in the DAP model, there is also support for the efficacy and timeliness of family counseling in the resolution of school problems (Hinkle, 1993; Stone & Peeks, 1986; Wells & Hinkle, 1990).
3. Training in family systems counseling IF you are providing family systems counseling. This is an ethical issue (See Chapter 15) (Hinkle, 1993; Magnuson & Norem, 1998). It is important, however, to distinguish family systems counseling (systemic counseling approach with unique training requirements), from counseling with an individual parent, spouse, teacher, or other adult (individual counseling approach consistent with school counselor training), and from problem-solving counseling for a family (counseling approach consistent with school counselor training). *You do not need specialized*

training to provide counseling for a family member, parent, colleague in your school, or colleague in your community. You do not need specialized training to provide non-systemic problem-solving counseling for the family of a student.

4. Administrative support. There are many studies that document the need, efficacy, and processes of systemic interventions. For administrators, the frame in which you present this part of your comprehensive school counseling program must include:

   a. Needs assessment data that documents the importance of this part of the program for your students.

   b. Program evaluation data that support the effectiveness of this intervention as a contributor to student success.

   c. Processes that highlight *problem solving* rather than *treatment*.

5. Availability of referral support. In some isolated communities, there may be very limited mental health services available. The school counselor may represent the only option for help and may need to expand interventions accordingly (Cowie & Quinn, 1997).

6. The location of the problem on the prevention-intervention-treatment continuum. As with our discussion in Chapter 7 about the prevention-intervention-treatment continuum, there are some issues that are best addressed by community mental health treatment professionals. Chronic issues such as substance addiction, criminality, chronic unemployment, and long-term abuse would be best referred to family systems therapists and treatment professionals in the community. However, issues that fall within the developmental stages outlined in this chapter, such as temporary unemployment or stalled career development, work adjustment issues, family adjustment issues such as parenting a teenager, or the renegotiation of family relationships to reflect healthy development are very appropriate for school counselor intervention.

Once you determine that counseling is an appropriate intervention, you must remember that there are some differences between counseling with adults and counseling with young people. The next section provides some suggestions for counseling with adults and systems.

Counseling with Adults: Individual and System Interventions

All counseling theories highlight the core conditions of the counseling relationship—respect, unconditional positive regard, listening skills, trust, honesty, congruence—and these are no less applicable with adult clients. Many of the insights and counseling strategies we discussed in Chapter 7 apply with adults. For example, counseling with adults may be enhanced by an understanding of the client's intelligence constellation in terms of multiple intelligences. Your individual counseling theory will provide many of the strategies that will inform your work with individual adult counselees.

One unique aspect of counseling with adults may be the ability of many adults to "self-counsel." It is true that many adults can work out their own problems, if they are given the time to reflect and a counselor who is trained to provide active, unbiased listening and feedback. Many adults do not have that time for reflection or contact with someone who can provide caring, respectful, and unbiased listening. When self-counseling, the client seems to be "thinking out loud" about problems and options and, in time, will come to his or her own conclusions about changes that need to be made to resolve the counseling issue. The counselor's role in this experience is to listen, track the path of the client's thinking in case the client gets lost, and offer minimal nudges to help the client remain on a healthy line of thinking with a minimum of interruptions.

If you are working with a family or work group, you will need to expand your counseling repertoire to include systems thinking, even if you are not providing family systems counseling. In a systems view, patterns of actions and reactions by members of the system provide reinforcement of entrenched but unhealthy interactions within the system (Cowie & Quinn, 1997; Evans & Carter, 1997; Hinkle, 1993). And since all behavior exists because it is reinforced, the key is to find the elements within the system that reinforce behavior and interrupt those reinforcements (Cowie & Quinn, 1997; Evans & Carter, 1997; Hinkle, 1993). Interventions are primarily characterized by circular questions, designed to elicit information about the sequence of events in a problem behavior. Circular questioning involves asking each individual in the system to describe what happens first, what happens next, what follows then, in order to fully understand all the actions and reactions that keep unhealthy patterns of behavior in motion. Intervention would target a point of the cycle that can be modified to interrupt the cycle and provide an opportunity for system members to negotiate new patterns of interaction. Ideally, each member of the system would be asked to change her or his role in that unhealthy pattern to allow change to flow from each member and to allow each member a new way of acting within the system.

As we will see in the next section, there are ethical issues involved in providing *family systems counseling.* Doing extensive family systems counseling involves obtaining additional training in family systems, but there are strategies for working with the families of our students that do fall within the school counselor's existing training. We will refer to this approach (for which school counselors are trained) as "problem-solving counseling," to distinguish it from family systems counseling. The next sections will provide some insights into the counseling implications for each of the adult partners in the DAP model.

Counseling with Parents (Block 5)

The professional literature is rich with articles supporting the need for family counseling in the schools (Cerio, 1997; Hinkle, 1993; Kraus, 1998, Peeks, 1993). These perspectives vary in terms of the amount of therapy that should be available in schools, from full mental health services available in schools (Evans & Carter, 1997; Peeks, 1993), to co-therapy sessions with community mental health professionals (Evans & Carter, 1997), to co-therapy sessions with school mental health professionals (Crespi & Howe, 2000). Most, however, argue that school counselors need to be willing to provide family intervention in the school (Kraus, 1998; Lewis, 1996, Nicoll, 1992). In addition, the special needs of certain populations of students and/or families have also been addressed: homeless families (Strawser, Markos, Yamaguchi, & Higgins, 2000), families of divorce (Wilcoxon & Magnuson, 1999), families from Christian fundamentalist backgrounds (Miller, 1995), and families whose students have survived school violence (Juhnke, 1997).

It is important to note that there are two distinct ways to provide services to members of the student's family: individual counseling with one individual of the family and family problem-solving counseling, usually conducted with the parents and the student but may include other family members as needed to effect the desired change. Individual counseling may be provided with one parent or the other to address the individual concerns of that person, with change being facilitated within that individual. On the other hand, family problem-solving counseling is focused on the cycle of action and reaction in that family and involves change for the entire family (Cowie & Quinn, 1997; Kraus, 1998). Examples of change could involve patterns of interaction (communicating with more respect or less fighting), the formal and informal rules of the family, and the ways in which the family expresses support for family members.

It is important to recognize that families function on the basis of values learned from their families of origin, their culture, and their religion. It is not appropriate to impose on a family's value system to create change. Change can be invited, but must not be imposed unethically. With that caution, the following examples are provided. Individual counseling might be provided to help an overprotective mother deal with her anxiety about her daughter's dating at age 18 (if the mother asks for help with this anxiety). In contrast, family problem-solving counseling might be warranted if the rules of the family keep the student from functioning as a emerging young adult at age 18 (not allowed to get a job, not allowed to see friends, mandatory bedtime at 8:00), as long as the family asks for help learning how to parent an 18-year-old. If the counselor provides individual counseling for a member of the student's family, the counselor would use the appropriate individual counseling theory to provide theoretically congruent interventions.

However, if the counselor provides family problem-solving counseling, there are a variety of models available. Those models that fall *within a school counselor's current training and skills* include the "brief intervention model" that highlights problem solving (Bilynsky & Veraglia, 1999), a counseling and consultation model that highlights a behavioral focus (Nicoll, 1992), and a model that blends Brief Counseling with Adlerian concepts (Lewis, 1996). Other authors have outlined school-based *family systems counseling* models that would *require additional training*: solution-focused brief family counseling (Cowie & Quinn, 1997; Evans & Carter, 1997; Hinkle, 1993) and brief counseling using structural and strategic family systems counseling (Cerio, 1997; Kraus, 1998). All of these authors highlight that school counselors would provide assessment and solution-oriented, problem-solving interventions and would provide referrals to community mental health professionals for families who require extensive, long-term treatment for problems.

For those situations in which you provide family problem-solving counseling, a model is helpful (Cowie & Quinn, 1997). The family, usually defined as the parents and the student of concern (but may include more family members if they are directly related to the problem of the student), is welcomed into the school counseling office and made to feel comfortable. Everyone must be given a chance to voice his or her opinions, and so the counselor addresses them equally. The ground rules of respect, listening, and honesty are clarified. The stages of counseling would involve:

1. First, the family is asked to define a positive goal for their work together. Usually this goal addresses the student's behavior.
2. The second stage is the miracle question, or how they would know their problem was solved. The answer to this question must be as specific as possible, couched in terms of the target behavior.

3. The third stage of the process involves identifying where the problem has already faded or improved or environments in which the problem doesn't exist. For example, is the student's behavior the same at home as it is at school? Is it a constant behavior, or does it vary? Under what conditions does the behavior vary?

4. In the fourth stage, the family is asked to identify, on a 1 to 10 scale, where they are now in terms of attaining the goal. The family and the counselor brainstorm ways to move up the scale, using insights gained from the exception question above. As with individual counseling, stumbling blocks are identified and strategies for overcoming them are outlined. Circular questions might be helpful here to highlight those entrenched patterns of problematic behaviors, so that these stumbling blocks might be addressed.

5. The final stage involves a message to the family, congratulating them for their courage in addressing their problems and providing directives for their work at home.

6. The counselor would maintain contact with the student to determine how effective the problem-solving counseling was. If it is clear that the family needs more extensive treatment, a referral is made to a community family systems therapist.

If this approach appeals to you, consider obtaining additional training in family systems counseling. It will help you to better understand family and systems dynamics and will increase your confidence that these tools have tremendous potential to help our students to function better in school and in life.

Counseling with Colleagues in the School (Block 6)

Many colleagues in the school come to the school counselor to seek out professional mental health information. These requests for information increase as trust increases in the counselor's professionalism, discretion, and skills. As with family systems, the health of the school system is determined by the mental health of each member of the system—the more mentally healthy each member is, the more stable, adaptive, and creative the entire system will be. As identified in the list of developmental assets, a caring school environment directly affects students and their ability to function in that system.

Helping to establish and maintain this caring school environment could include providing counseling and/or referral services for staff, teachers, and administrators. Pelsma (2000) suggested that school counselors are in a unique position to help teachers with specific quality-of-life issues and provided a list of solution-focused questions to help teachers assess and address those areas of their worklives that can be improved. This systemic view of schools promotes the premise of this chapter: that school counselors can have a profound impact on the way a system functions by intervening in the system. If there is a condition within the school itself that impedes healthy student development, it is appropriate for the school counselor to intervene.

Just as with counseling with families, counseling with colleagues in the school can take two forms: individual or group. Within the group intervention, there are two approaches: problem-solving counseling or group counseling. An example of individual counseling would be a teacher who comes to you with problems dealing with an impending divorce. You might provide supportive counseling for a limited number of meetings to help your colleague with the transition, using the individual counseling strategies suggested by your counseling theory. These counseling efforts, while focused on an individual, still foster a healthy school system by improving the health of one member of that system.

In a group context, you have two choices: problem-solving counseling with a work group or group counseling. For example, a teacher might come to you for assistance dealing with a communication problem within his or her academic discipline team or department. Systems strategies and insights still apply; circular questions and interventions aimed at stopping unhealthy patterns of behavior have a profound effect on how the system functions (Cowie & Quinn, 1997; Kraus, 1998). To address this concern, you could use the Solutions-Focused Brief Counseling strategies outlined in the previous section.

Another option is group counseling. This scenario might be illustrated by an intervention with a group of teachers who have witnessed school violence or shared some other traumatic event. In this situation, you might decide to offer a group counseling experience similar to that suggested by Juhnke (1997) for parents whose students have survived school violence. Involving some affective and cognitive strategies, group counseling might offer each participant an opportunity to process feelings, thoughts, and behaviors. Again, efforts that enhance the mental health of any member of a system enhance the functioning of the entire system.

One final observation of this activity: As with family counseling, intervention can be provided by the school counselor, but treatment for members of the school community with serious mental health issues would be referred to community mental health professionals.

Counseling with Colleagues in the Community (Block 7)

This is a very nontraditional activity for school counselors, but it is mentioned here as an option if it is deemed necessary to facilitate healthy student development. If there is an individual or group whose issues impede the development of students, counseling with that individual or group could be considered appropriate. For example, if a student is struggling with social services over a foster-care placement, it might be possible for the school counselor to provide problem-solving counseling to facilitate the student's communication with that agency or with that foster family. This could take the form of individual counseling (with the agency personnel or foster family member), problem-solving counseling (with the foster family), or group counseling, depending on the situation, the persons involved, and other considerations.

As before, counseling is appropriate if your intention is intervention not treatment, if counseling is warranted to help students, and if the intervention is short-term in duration. For example, imagine that you are working with a student's community social worker who is frustrated with the school system. You listen to the social worker express his concerns, and based on this new understanding of the situation, move the discussion to problem-solving for the student. Allowing the social worker a safe context in which to vent his frustration could increase his trust that someone in the schools cares about the situation and the student. This cathartic experience is supportive counseling: It is short-term, solution-focused, and warranted because it will directly help the student involved. If the situation involves long-term counseling, is not solution-focused, or may not help the student, then a referral to another professional is warranted.

Admittedly, counseling with colleagues in the community is a rare activity for school counselors. The other options for action—educating, consulting, and coordinating—are chosen more often as interventions with adult partners in the DAP model. The reasons why will be explored in Chapter 12 on educating our partners, Chapter 13 on consulting with our partners, and Chapter 14 on leadership and coordinating services with our partners.

A Day in the Life Revisited: Integration

As you contemplate Ty's situation as described by his mother, consider the following questions:

1. What are the factors in Ty's life that have created this family situation?
2. Which of those factors can be addressed using counseling? Which of those factors would not be appropriate to address using counseling?
3. Ty's family is a good example of why individual counseling would not be very effective. Can you see why? Assume you would conduct family problem-solving counseling with Ty's family. Which family members would be there? What would you want to accomplish with them?
4. With Ms. Epps, would you intervene? Why or why not? If you answered yes to this question, what strategy (counseling, educating, consulting, or coordinating) would you use?
5. With the kids on the block, would you intervene? Why or why not? If you answered yes to this question, what strategy (counseling, educating, consulting, or coordinating) would you use?
6. What do you think Calvin Paulson should do to help?

Application

1. Identify an adult in your life whom you know well. Using the models of adult development, interview that person to determine his or her placement on each model.

2. Take Ty's family situation and write out a detailed problem-solving counseling plan for five meetings using Solution-Focused Brief Counseling as outlined in this chapter. Include who would be involved in the counseling, some suggested counseling goals, and a counseling agenda for each of the five meetings.

3. Interview a family systems therapist or counselor in the community and ask that profes-

sional to describe what he or she would do with Ty's family.

4. Outline a plan for working with Ms. Epps, the science teacher, to address the issues between Ms. Epps and Ty.

5. Conduct a confidential interview with a teacher about the issues that detract from the health of that system. Using no names, ask for specific problems that colleagues or work groups have. Identify a situation appropriate for individual counseling and outline a plan of counseling that individual, detailing your counseling goals and strategies. Identify a situation appropriate for

problem-solving counseling and outline that plan of counseling, detailing your counseling goals and strategies. Identify a situation appropriate for group counseling and outline a plan of counseling that group, detailing your counseling goals and strategies.

6. Identify some community issues that could impede the development of high school stu-

dents. What are some specific things you could see yourself doing to address those issues?

7. Conduct an Internet search of the webpages of family therapists. How do they describe their practices? How do these descriptions vary from family problem solving counseling we outline in this chapter? How are they similar?

Suggested Readings

Bilynsky, N. S., & Vernaglia, E. R. (1999). Identifying and working with dysfunctional families. *Professional School Counseling, 2,* 305–313. This article presents a very practical and user-friendly model of problem solving with families that can assist every counselor to feel comfortable with this process.

Hansen, L. S. (1997). *Integrative life planning: Critical tasks for career development and changing life patterns.* San Francisco, CA: Jossey-Bass. A great book for understanding the career development of adults.

Lewis, W. (1996). A proposal for initiating family counseling interventions by school counselors. *The School Counselor, 44,* 93–99. This article provides two practical approaches to conducting brief family problem-solving counseling that, should a refer-

ral for long-term family therapy be necessary, would provide the counselor with insight into the family's problems.

Nicoll, W. G. (1992). A family counseling and consultation model for school counselors. *The School Counselor, 39,* 351–361. The model presented in this article provides a strategy that allows the counselor to move between counseling and consultation as needed to address the family's problems.

Pelsma, D. M. (2000). School counselors' use of solution-focused questioning to improve teacher worklife. *Professional School Counseling, 4,* 1–5. This article presents solution-focused questions that can help teachers assess the areas of their work system that could be improved.

References

Bilynsky, N. S., & Vernaglia, E. R. (1999). Identifying and working with dysfunctional families. *Professional School Counseling, 2,* 305–313.

Cerio, J. (1997). School phobia: A family systems approach. *Elementary School Guidance and Counseling, 31,* 180–192. Retrieved December 8. 2000, from EBSCO database available on the World Wide Web: http://ehostv…amily%20.

Chickering, A. W., & Reisser, L. (1993). *Education and identity* (2nd ed.). San Francisco, CA: Jossey-Bass.

Cowie, K., & Quinn, K. (1997). Brief family therapy in the schools: A new perspective on the role of the rural school counseling professional. *Family Journal, 5*(1), 57–69. Retrieved December 8, 2000, from EBSCO database available on the World Wide Web: http://ehostv…amily %20.

Craig, G. J. (1996). *Human development* (7th ed.). Upper Saddle River, NJ: Prentice Hall.

Crespi, T. D., & Howe, E. A. (2000, March). Families in crisis: Considerations and implications for school counselors. *Counseling Today, 42,* 6, 36.

Evans, W. P., & Carter, M. J. (1997). Urban school-based family counseling: Role definition, practice applications, and training implications. *Journal of Counseling and Development, 75,* 366–375.

Fox, M. (1994). *The reinvention of work: A new vision of livelihood for our time.* San Francisco, CA: Harper.

Hansen, L. S. (1997). *Integrative life planning: Critical tasks for career development and changing life patterns.* San Francisco, CA: Jossey-Bass.

Hinkle, J. S (1993). Training school counselors to do family counseling. *Elementary School Guidance and Counseling, 27,* 252–258. Retrieved December 8, 2000, from EBSCO database available on the World Wide Web: http://ehostv…amily%20.

Juhnke, G. A. (1997). After school violence: An adapted critical incident stress debriefing model for student survivors and their parents. *Elementary School Guidance & Counseling, 31,* 163–171. Retrieved December 8, 2000, from EBSCO database available on the World Wide Web: http://ehostv…amily%20.

Kraus, I. (1998). A fresh look at school counseling: A family systems approach. *Professional School Counseling, 1,* 12–18.

Lewis, W. (1996). A proposal for initiating family counseling interventions by school counselors. *The School Counselor, 44,* 93–99.

Magnuson, S., & Norem, K. (1998). A school counselor asks: "Am I prepared to do what I'm asked to do?" *Family Journal, 6*(2), 137–140. Retrieved December 8, 2000, from EBSCO database available on the World Wide Web: http://ehostv…amily%20.

McWhirter, J. J., McWhirter, B. T., McWhirter, A. M., & McWhirter, E. H. (1998). *At-risk youth: A comprehensive response for counselors, teachers, psychologists, and human service professionals* (2nd ed.). Pacific Grove, CA: Brooks/Cole.

Miller, D. R. (1995). The school counselor and Christian fundamentalist families. *The School Counselor, 42,* 317–321.

Nicoll, W. G. (1992). A family counseling and consultation model for school counselors. *The School Counselor, 39,* 351–361.

Noble, J. (2000). Students' educational achievement: What helps or hinders? *The ASCA Counselor, 38,* 14–15.

Peeks, B. (1993). Revolutions in counseling and education: A systems perspective in the schools. *Elementary School Guidance and Counseling, 27,* 245–252. Retrieved December 8, 2000, from EBSCO database available on the World Wide Web: http://ehostv…amily%20.

Pelsma, D. M. (2000). School counselors' use of solution-focused questioning to improve teacher worklife. *Professional School Counseling, 4,* 1–5.

Search Institute. (February 1996). *40 Developmental Assets.* Minneapolis, MN: Author.

Stone, G., & Peeks, B. (1986). The use of strategic family therapy in the school setting: A case study. *Journal of Counseling and Development, 65,* 200–203.

Strawser, S., Markos, P. A., Yamaguchi, B. J., & Higgins, K. (2000). A new challenge for school counselors: Children who are homeless. *Professional School Counseling, 3,* 162–171.

Super, D. E., Savickas, M. L., & Super, C. M. (1996). The life-span, life-space approach to careers. In D. Brown, L. Brooks, et al. (Eds.), *Career choice and development* (3rd ed.). pp. 121–178. San Francisco, CA: Jossey-Bass.

Upcraft, M. L. (1985). Residence halls and student activities. In L. Noel, R. Levitz, D. Saluri, et al. (Eds.), *Increasing student retention: Effective programs and practices for reducing the drop-out rate* (pp. 319–344). San Francisco, CA: Jossey-Bass.

Wells, M. E., & Hinkle, J. S. (1990). Elimination of childhood encopresis: A family systems approach. *Journal of Mental Health Counseling, 12,* 520–526.

Wilcoxon, S. A., & Magnuson, S. (1999). Considerations for school counselors serving noncustodial parents: Premises and suggestions. *Professional School Counseling, 2,* 275–279.

12

Educating and Advocating with Parents, Colleagues in the Schools, and Colleagues in the Community (Blocks 8, 9, 10 of the DAP Model)

Colette T. Dollarhide

"What do I like least about high school? All students are forced to take dumb, useless classes that bore them to death or are impossibly difficult and are graded on the same level that everyone else is."

Jeanne, age 15

Learning Objectives

By the end of this chapter, you will:

1. Understand the need for educating our adult partners about:
   a. the development of young people
   b. strategies to foster the development of young people
   c. the nature and issues of student success in schools
   d. the role of the school counselor

2. Understand the need for advocacy with our partners about young people and their developmental issues.

3. Understand and apply a model of adult intellectual development to improve our attempts to educate our partners.

4. Identify examples of ways that school counselors educate others and advocate for students, schools, and the profession of school counseling.

A Day in the Life of a Counselor: Donna's Lunchroom Duty

Donna had been at the school for several years, and in that time, she found that eating her lunch in the faculty lounge provided her with valuable contact with the teachers. She made it a point to eat there at least twice a week and would use that time to talk to teachers about students, listen to their issues, and consult as needed about student issues. She knew that part of her job was to monitor the emotional climate of the school; time in the teacher's lounge was as important as time in the students' lunchroom for taking the emotional "pulse" of the school.

January was the month for mid-year parent conferences, and everyone had been on edge since a car accident in late December in which several students had been injured. The police found marijuana and alcohol in the car; since the driver and all the passengers were students at Donna's school, she had increased her visibility in classrooms providing developmental curriculum about healthy choices. She had communicated with all the teachers about her concerns about the availability of alcohol and drugs in the school.

As she entered the lunchroom, several teachers invited her to sit with them, since they were in a debate about something. "We need you to settle this argument."

"Here's the thing, Donna. I say that the parents of the students in that wreck were at fault for not supervising them better. Where did they get the drugs and booze?" one teacher stated.

"No, you're wrong there. I've had a number of conversations with parents during conferences, and they all blame the school and the school counselor. They say the kids got the stuff here, and that it's the school's fault that they are experimenting with this stuff. They say that the school counselor isn't doing her job because no one is keeping the kids from using drugs; they think no one is addressing this. Sorry, Donna, but that's what I hear from the parents," said another.

"What's wrong with these parents anyway?" interjected a third. "Now we have to *parent* these kids too? Aren't they supposed to monitor their kids' behavior, teach them about right and wrong? I didn't buy the booze those kids had, so why should the school be responsible?"

"Our standards are too slack," posed a fourth teacher. "If we went back to stricter standards, we wouldn't have these problems. They wouldn't have time to mess around with alcohol or drugs—they'd be too busy studying and worrying about exams to get away with partying!"

"So, Donna, what do you think?"

"Yeah, Donna, you're the expert, tell us who's right!"

"I wish I knew," Donna thought, while she pretended to choke on her drink of water to buy time before she answered.

Challenge Questions

What do you think about the opinions expressed around the table? Do parents need to be better educated about the realities of alcohol and marijuana? Do teachers need to be educated about parents? Do parents need to be educated about the school and the role of the school counselor? Do teachers need to be educated about the role of academics in the lives of high school students?

Who is responsible for educating students, parents, teachers, and the general public about young people, families, schools, and the role of the school counselor? Who is responsible for advocating for students, parents, teachers, and schools when there are misunderstandings?

If you were Donna, what would you say?

The Call for Education and Advocacy

Recall that we discussed the career and personal/social development of adults in Chapter 11 to help you understand counseling with our adult partners; in this chapter, we will honor the value of lifelong learning—academic development. In order to educate adults, we must discuss the learning issues of adults.

Learning is shaped by the context of the lesson: We learn about being a teenager from our years as teens, we learn about high school from our years in high school, we learn about what teachers do from our years as a student, and we learn about what parents do from watching our parents. Our insights into these lessons mature over time, so as adults, we look back on our teenage years and wish we had done things differently. These are lessons we hope to pass on to our children, but most people don't know to put these lessons in today's terms.

The problem is that we forget the *context* of these lessons. We forget that our life lessons were a product of that time, that place, and those people, so we generalize those conclusions to all times, all places, and all people. As adults, we know that the world is different today than it was when we were kids, but we don't fully understand *how* it's different, in all the ways it's different. We forget that today's schools are not like our school was years ago. And we forget that not all people parent as we were parented, teach as we were taught, or think as we did, in that time, in that school, in that town.

What this means is that the adults with whom we partner may have unclear images of what it means to be an adolescent, what it means to be in high school, what it means to be a parent, what it means to be an educator or an administrator, or what it means to be a secondary school counselor in a comprehensive school counseling program. Each of these unclear images can have an effect on how successful our students will be and how successful our comprehensive school counseling program will be.

There are many references in the literature to support that counselors need to educate parents, school colleagues, and community colleagues. Many of these authors call for the counselor to be an advocate: to educate with passion. There are calls to provide parent education in almost every issue of professional journals related to school counseling.

Educating parents has been called an essential part of every school counselor's training program (Crespi & Howe, 2000; Ritchie & Partin, 1994) to help counselors address parents' rationalization and learned helplessness (Clark, 1995) and to address systemic problems both within the family and between the family and school (Evans & Carter, 1997). Furthermore, counselors should provide programs to inform parents about the school and to promote parent involvement in the student's education, which can help students feel more connected with the school, address problems with communication, and support at-risk students (Christiansen, 1997; Clark, 1995; Jackson & White, 2000; Peeks, 1993). Finally, it is essential that parents understand the counselor's role in the school so that parental insights can be tapped and parents will support the value of the comprehensive school counseling program (Gibson, 1990; Kaplan, 1997).

The task of educating our adult partners continues with the need to educate our colleagues in the schools. Teachers can benefit from better knowledge about current issues, including family issues such as homelessness, divorce, and custody (Evans & Carter, 1997; Strawser, Markos, Yamaguchi, & Higgins, 2000; Wilcoxon & Magnuson, 1999), and student issues such as ADHD, being an ESL student, being at-risk, sexuality and sexual abuse, and sexual harassment (Christiansen, 1997; Erk, 1999; James & Burch, 1999; McCall-Perez, 2000; Stone, 2000). Teachers can also benefit from training in interpersonal communication skills (Rice & Smith, 1993), dealing with their personal issues (Clark, 1995), and better understanding the role of the school counselor (Gibson, 1990; Jackson & White, 2000). Furthermore, principals can also benefit from a better understanding of the role of the counselor (Burnham & Jackson, 2000; Crespi & Howe, 2000; Gibson, 1990; Kaplan, 1997; Ponec & Brock, 2000) and from better appreciation for school systemic issues (Stone, 2000).

Finally, our colleagues in the community, including school boards, colleges and universities, community mental health providers, employers, and the community at large, could benefit from a better understanding of our students, our schools, and our role in the school (Bemak, 2000; Gibson, 1990; Gysbers, Lapan, & Jones, 2000; Kaplan, 1997; Luongo, 2000; McCall-Perez, 2000; Taylor & Adelman, 2000).

Reflection Moment

Imagine yourself in the role of educating other adults on these subjects. Which of these can you see yourself talking about with parents? With teachers? With administrators? With the public? Which of these topics would you present with the most passion and enthusiasm? Recall that advocacy is educating with passion; for which of these topics, with which partners, would you see yourself as an advocate?

Understanding Learning in Adults

Educating our adult partners is an extension of Chapter 8 on the education of high school students, but we must now understand the intellectual needs of the adult learner. Consistent with the theme of this text that appropriate education is based on the knowledge of development, we must now explore the intellectual development of adults.

Adult intellectual development is known as epistemological development, providing perspectives on the process of learning, the relationship between knowledge and the knower, and the stages of adult cognitive growth (Basseches, 1980; Cheren, 1983; Fleck-Henderson & Kegan, 1989; Golderberger, Clinchy, Belenky, & Tarule, 1987; Kegan, 1982, 1994; King & Baxter Magolda, 1996; King & Kitchener, 1994; McAuliffe, 1993; Perry, 1981; Stage, 1996). It is important to understand that intellectual development does not only come from formal education. Life provides many lessons for adults to learn, but our discussion will focus on what you, as a school counselor, need to know to facilitate the learning of our adult partners.

In general, the process of learning involves movement from *dualistic* thinking ("right and wrong, either my way or the highway") and passive learning, toward *dialectic* thinking ("In this situation, given what I know, this is my decision") and active participation in the learning process. This movement also involves increased tolerance for ambiguity and increased confidence in the search for personal answers, so the relationship between knowledge and the knower becomes personal, coming from informed reflection and not introjection (the automatic adoption of others' perspectives).

The process of moving from one level of development to the next is predicated on numerous conditions that facilitate intellectual development: The learner must be *involved*, must have *sufficient structure*, must be given *feedback*, must be able to *apply* the learning, and must be able to *integrate* new learning with her or his existing view of the world (Schroeder & Hurst, 1996). Given involvement, structure, feedback, application of learning, and integration of learning, the learner has the intellectual tools to learn. The process will not be complete, however, until the learner has two emotional tools essential for movement from one learning level to the next: support and challenge (Kegan, 1994). In the learning context, *support* refers to the connection the learner has with the instructor (or others, in the case of a life lesson), and *challenge* refers to the faith that the instructor has in the learner to grow, change, and attain personal excellence. The learner needs this balance of challenge and support to move from an external locus of control (where others provide all the answers to life's questions) to an internal locus of control (where the learner has the confidence to find her or his own answers to life's questions and the flexibility to understand the need for different answers based on the context of the question).

Taking numerous epistemological theories and synthesizing them, the most basic stage of intellectual development is *dualism* (King & Kitchener, 1994; Perry, 1981), in which the learner uses either/or, right-and-wrong, dichotomous thinking (see Figure 12-1). In addition, the learner looks for an external authority to provide an absolute answer to questions of "good" versus "bad," which is viewed as ultimate truth. A parent at this stage of development might say, "My parents raised me the way they were raised: If you spare the rod, you spoil the child. My parents did a good job keeping me in line. That's all I need to know." In order to progress to the next level, the learner needs a structured learning environment in

FIGURE 12.1   *The Five Stages of Epistemological Development*

Stage	Name	Relationship with Authority	Ability to Deal with Ambiguity
1	Dualism	Unquestioning obedience and acceptance	None; wants simple answers and absolute truth
2	Questioning of Dualism	Begins to notice various authorities have different answers	Disturbed by inconsistencies, but holds onto previous truths
3	Multiplicity	Each "authority" has own opinion opinion of truth	Overwhelmed by various truths; unable to find old beliefs tenable any more
4	Contextual Relativism	Growing awareness of situational variables that contribute to choices or beliefs	Sees that truth is relative to context, but does not yet see pattern to the situations that lead to successful choices
5	Commitment	Able to see self as authority, defend own conclusions, and continue to learn	Sees that all knowledge is temporary pending new learning; continuously open to new learning

which he or she feels support and sufficient challenge to promote involvement and investment in learning.

The second stage is the *questioning of dualism,* in which the learner begins to see that there are multiple ways to define "good" and "bad" (Golderberger, Clinchy, Belenky, & Tarule, 1987; Perry, 1981). At this stage, the learner realizes that there are multiple authorities and multiple truths but holds tightly to previously held truths. A parent at this stage might say, "I know my sister has challenged my parent's philosophy of discipline, and her kids are growing up OK so far. But I'm sure it's just a matter of time before they start to go wild." In order to progress to the next level, the learner needs support in confronting ambiguity and challenge to continue gathering alternative perspectives.

Multiplicity (Perry, 1981) is the next stage, in which the learner loses awareness of those initial, anchoring definitions of "good" and "bad"; all viewpoints are seen as equally valid, since no ultimate truth exists. At this point, learning involves overwhelming ambiguity. A parent at this stage might say, "I just don't know what to do with my son. I've read all the books and listened to all the experts, and they all say something different. I just don't know what to do." The learner needs support to wade through the ambiguity and challenge to begin exploring personal answers and opinions.

The fourth stage, *contextual relativism* (Perry, 1981), consists of awareness of the context of the choice; truth is relative to the context of the situation. Learners at this stage are becoming more aware of the unique qualities of each situation, but they are struggling to understand those uniquenesses to see how they factor into the situation. Based on their ability to understand those situations, they begin to articulate relative shades of personal truth. Parents at this stage might say, "It's weird, but sometimes he listens and other times he doesn't. I'm not sure what the answer is yet, because I don't see what makes him listen to me sometimes and yell at me at other times." Learners need sufficient support to take risks in expressing their own direction and challenge to learn from self-defined erroneous conclusions.

At the fifth stage, *commitment* (Perry, 1981), self-authorizing (Kegan, 1994), or reflective thinking (King & Kitchener, 1994), the learner has access to his or her own voice and tolerance of intellectual ambiguity. This stage involves the ability to define and defend one's own intellectual discoveries; authority resides in the self and in the ability to engage in procedures for testing one's own hypotheses. This is an important and defining characteristic of this stage—that the learner is willing to test her or his own conclusions and continue to learn. A parent at this stage may say, "My response to my son depends on the situation. I've learned that if I really come down hard on him in front of his friends, we end up in a yelling match. If I wait to talk to him when we're alone, he seems to be able to listen better and we actually talk. My dad thinks I'm nuts for not coming down hard on him immediately, but I'd rather wait for the right time than engage my son in a fight neither of us can win. As my son grows, I'm sure we will find new ways to connect and communicate." The learner needs support in dealing with conflicting feedback as a result of those discoveries, and challenge in learning not to rely on previous decisions and assumptions.

Research into chronological maturation, educational attainment, and epistemological development reveals that these learning experiences occur in everyday life but are accelerated in the college experience. Dualism is the most common mode of thinking upon entrance into college, multiplicity is often developed through college, and commitment is often not achieved until graduate school (Baxter Magolda, 1990; King & Kitchener, 1994). *This does not mean that anyone should be stereotyped based on chronological age or educational level!* However, this research might suggest that teachers, administrators, parents, and community members who have a college education might be more open to new ideas proposed in your adult programming than those who have not attended any form of postsecondary education.

It is true, as with any continuum, that the ends of the scale bend to meet each other, as in the example of the "expert." This might describe someone who has developed his or her own answers through careful reflection and research, but who now doesn't listen to anyone else on the subject. This person has come back to dualism: "I've spent years exploring this, and I know everything there is to know on this subject. So what I say is the Truth and you better accept it as your Truth, too!"

Using this overview of intellectual development as a template, we can provide some suggestions for educating our adult partners, parents, teachers, administrators, or community colleagues, in terms of each stage of the model:

1. Dealing with Dualism: Adult learners at this stage look to others for the answers to life's problems, asking the counselor for guidance, advice, and direction. In a group presentation, you would want to validate their autonomy and ability to find their own answers, without undervaluing the expertise you have developed. When you present your program, encourage them to find ways that these new ideas have worked for them already. Let them validate your information with their own experiences. In a one-on-one situation, you would want to be especially careful not to provide quick-fix

solutions for the learner, as dependency may be an issue at this stage. Rather, help learners think about what previous attempts have taught them, and then encourage them to think about the strategies you suggest.

2. Dealing with Questioning of Dualism: Adults at this stage have moved into the awareness that previously defined authorities have conflicting definitions of "the right way" and "the wrong way." This confusion is natural. In a group presentation or one-on-one, allow them to express this confusion. Ask them to think about situations in which what you are presenting has worked for them. Assure them that while there are conflicting opinions on these topics, you are sharing with them what current experts agree on the subject. This anchor to expertise helps give learners some support.

3. Dealing with Multiplicity: As clients become increasingly aware that there is no one absolute authority with ultimate truth, they are overwhelmed with the enormity of finding their own options and owning the selection of the appropriate option(s). In a group presentation, validate the confusion and the contradictory information. Use current information and research to support what you are proposing, again reaffirming learners' autonomy and control over their beliefs or opinions. Remind them that you are asking them to give this new approach a try to see if it works for them. You're not forcing them to accept this, but asking them to look for ways to incorporate these ideas into their work with kids to see if it works better for them.

4. Dealing with Contextual Relativism: Learners at this stage will begin to see that there are situations in which others have chosen their own answers and defined personal solutions. Focus on those situational variables that the learners are likely to encounter so that you can help them understand the situation in which "this works better than that." Give multiple "If this is the situation, then your choice of this action will result in . . ." scenarios. Challenge learners to find a situation when your suggestion worked for them and reinforce the courage to try different approaches to problems.

5. Moving into Commitment: Learners begin to articulate their own answers to life's problems and begin to express greater confidence in those answers. Learners at this stage are more comfortable accepting your program as nonthreatening to their intellectual integrity and are more open to new ideas than learners at the other stages. Support and challenge are more collegial with learners at this stage.

It is important in this discussion that we briefly touch on the concept of "readiness to learn." This concept is as applicable to adults as it is to young students, and the essence is this: You can lead a horse to water but you can't make it drink. You can, however, make it thirsty in the hopes that it will drink because it *wants* the water. Strong (1968) found that clients evaluated counselors on the basis of their expertness, perceived interpersonal attractiveness (similarities), and trustworthiness; when the counselor was found to be sufficiently expert, similar, and trustworthy, the client felt greater investment in the counseling process. These same variables also influence the investment learners have in the learning process when persuading adults that change (in their opinions of students, families, schools, or the counseling profession) is appropriate.

Translated into concrete suggestions, your expertise in academic, career, and personal/social development should be introduced. Your graduate education in school counseling has provided you with unique training and insights into young people, schools, and the processes of education and growth. You will also want to highlight your similarities to those in your audience, since this tends to increase others' perceptions of you as a role model. Furthermore, your trustworthiness needs to be established: that your goal is to foster those conditions that have been proven to be the most conducive to the education, growth, and development of your students. Assuring your audience that you have no ulterior motive, either by example or direct statement of the ethics of the profession, standards of confidentiality, or professional associations, helps them to know that you are not "selling them a bill of goods."

Sometimes, however, in spite of your best efforts, some of your adult partners will refuse to learn anything new. These people are entrenched in their way of viewing the world. They believe that nothing anyone can say is going to change their thinking on a subject. Your approach to these persons would be to assure them that you respect their right to their opinions (as long as those opinions and resulting behaviors fall within the limits of the law) and that, should they ever need to discuss this further, you would be happy to discuss it. At this point, all you can do is hope that they will come to you with questions about students, schools, families, teachers, or the counseling profession, if such questions ever arise.

Putting all these suggestions together for use in educating our adult partners would yield the following suggestions:

1. Know your audience. It is helpful to understand the extent of formal education of the people in the audience.
2. If you cannot know (or deduce) the education of your audience, gear your presentation for those at the first or second stage of intellectual development and adjust for other learners as you gauge the audience's comfort level with your material. Suggestion 6 below outlines a presentation designed for all five levels of development.
3. Remember your training in multiple intelligences and present information in multiple formats: words, examples, graphs, exercises, art, music, or examples from sports, science, food, architecture, television, movies, or other venues.
4. Be informed—do not try to "fake it." If you don't know something, admit it, promise to find out, and arrange to get back to the questioner. Adults are insulted by know-it-alls who are not respectful of the audience's ability to detect false statements. Just one attempt to disguise a guess as a fact will destroy your credibility, trustworthiness, and expertise.
5. Be enthusiastic and passionate. Remember you are an advocate also, and your passion can convince others to consider what you're presenting. Your enthusiasm creates an emotional bond with the audience that enables the learning to have more meaning and long-term impact. Your role as advocate means that you must have a greater sense of social justice and be willing to challenge others in the name of that greater justice. (This also resonates with our discussion of leadership from Chapter 10.)
6. In the presentation, begin with high levels of structure (control) and expertise (for persons in Stage 1 or dualism), then move to an awareness and appreciation of all perspectives on this topic (for persons in Stage 3 or multiplicity), then ask them to think of situations in which they found this to be true for themselves already (for persons in Stage 5 or commitment). Finish with an affirmation of their right as adults to make their own decisions, but indicate the problems that can arise if they do not apply the

insights you are offering (but don't be an alarmist). Remind them that you are happy to consult with them in the future on this topic.

7. Do not lecture your audience. Your audience is comprised of adults, and adults feel insulted when someone scolds them for incorrect behavior and feel patronized when someone talks *at* them in a lecture-hall format. Parents, teachers, administrators, and community colleagues do the best they can with students, based on what they believe students need. Your job is to help them to better understand what students need and to help them design strategies to best meet those student needs—not to shame or embarrass them.

8. Reread Chapter 8 on lesson planning to examine the ways to design the learning experience.

9. Remember that the audience's perceptions of your expertise, similarity to them, and trustworthiness are important. Establish your expertise by sharing your professional training and experience (as appropriate). Establish your similarity to the audience by sharing relevant personal experiences or personal struggles with this topic (as appropriate). Establish your trustworthiness by assuring them that your sole intention is to help them function better in their lives (as appropriate).

10. Do not be surprised or frustrated with resistance to your topic. In every group, there will be those who will not accept what you have to say. Do not dismiss them, but encounter their resistance with calm equanimity. Find value in their contribution and, if you have time, explore those situational variables that made their experience an exception to your point. In this way, their objection becomes additional support for your topic.

Reflection Moment

What have been your experiences persuading or educating adults? Have those experiences been positive or negative for you? What skills would you like to improve to make those experiences more successful? What can you do now to develop or refine those skills? Where are you in terms of *your* epistemological development?

Educating and Advocating with Parents and Families: Parent Programs (Block 8)

What is the current amount of time high school counselors spend educating parents? A recent study indicated that respondents only interacted with parents in terms of consultation, not counseling or educating (Burnham & Jackson, 2000). In another study of a random sample of 100 high school counselors in Ohio, authors found that only 21 percent of respondents provided any parent programming, and 45 percent of those had no training in parent education (Ritchie & Partin, 1994). In spite of this research into the paucity of programming for parents of high school students, there is no shortage of ideas about what such parent programs should include.

When counselors were asked what they thought parent programs should include, they suggested self-concept enhancement, helping students succeed in school, behavior management and discipline, decision making, substance abuse issues, stepfamily issues, moral and values issues, human sexuality, and communication skills (Ritchie & Partin, 1994). These high school counselors rated human sexuality and helping students succeed in school higher than counselors at the other two levels. Other topics that would enhance parenting skills programming include teaching self-control, conflict resolution, understanding other cultures, following directions, nonphysical discipline, and parental teaming (Evans & Carter, 1997), strategies for working with ADHD children (Erk, 1999), dealing with homelessness (Strawser, Markos, Yamaguchi, & Higgins, 2000), foster parenting (Geroski & Knauss, 2000), and using family rituals to ease family traumas and transitions (Parker, 1999). Teaching parents about environmental factors that impede student development would enhance their ability to address those factors more effectively.

Furthermore, parent programs should be used to help parents learn about the school and to increase their involvement with their students' education (Evans & Carter, 1997; Jackson & White, 2000). Such programs could also help parents interact more successfully with the school (Clark, 1995; Evans & Carter, 1997; Peeks, 1993) and could significantly aid at-risk students (Christiansen, 1997; Evans & Carter, 1997). Overall, these programs would include information on strategies for school success, the course selection process and implications, current programs to facilitate the development of students, the process of education, the role of school professionals, and especially the role of the school counselor (Gibson, 1990; Kaplan, 1997).

When Ritchie and Partin (1994) conducted their study of counselors, they found that counselors most often used packaged programs for their presentations to parents (STEP [Dinkmeyer, McKay, & Dinkmeyer, 1997], PET, or Active Parenting). As these counselors became more experienced and comfortable presenting to parents, they designed their own programs. These counselors did recommend that both male and female presenters be involved with the program to model both parenting roles. In addition, other options exist for parent programming, including Cline and Fay's (1990) Love and Logic parent program.

Educating and Advocating with Colleagues in the Schools: In-Service (Block 9)

In-service programs are a valuable venue for educating our colleagues in the schools. Many authors believe that counselors should provide teacher in-services on developmental topics; the counselor's expertise in communication, students' developmental domains, families, and other topics can enhance the teachers' understanding of students and performance in the classroom. To enhance teachers' interpersonal skills, counselors could address rationalization and learned helplessness (Clark, 1995), and the teacher's communication with students. For example, counselors could provide in-service training in interpersonal communication skills: empathy, silence, active listening, genuineness, acceptance, faith in the student, open-ended questions, interpretations, restatement and paraphrase, reflective statements and mirroring, summarizing, and encouragement (Rice & Smith, 1993).

In-service programs could also be tailored to provide teachers with information that will enhance their understanding of their students. Specialized in-service topics focused on students and families would include information on resiliency and protective factors to help at risk students (Christiansen, 1997), ways to work with homeless parents (Strawser, Markos, Yamaguchi, & Higgins, 2000), insights and strategies for working with families on systemic issues (Evans & Carter, 1997), working with ADHD children and families (Erk, 1999), normal sexual development and symptoms and issues of sexual abuse (James & Burch, 1999), issues relative to noncustodial parents' rights (Wilcoxon & Magnuson, 1999), education and advocacy for ELL (English Language Learners) (McCall-Perez, 2000), and issues of sexual harassment (Stone, 2000). Basically, any topic within the developmental domains would be an important and valuable in-service for teachers.

Finally, many teachers will benefit from a better understanding of the role of the school counselor in a comprehensive school counseling program (Gibson, 1990; Jackson & White, 2000). The Domains/Activities/Partners model provides a useful template for that in-service presentation, which would then be focused on those areas that are emphasized in the local needs assessments and outcomes assessments (which will be discussed further in Chapter 14).

But teachers aren't our only colleagues in the schools. Our partners in student services—school psychologists, school social workers, and school nurses—with whom we collaborate on behalf of students also benefit from in-service presentations on our role in comprehensive school counseling programs (Porter, Epp, & Bryant; Taylor & Adelman, 2000). We should include principals in all of these in-service presentations as a way of educating them about comprehensive school counseling programs (Burnham & Jackson, 2000; Crespi & Howe, 2000; Gibson, 1990; Kaplan, 1997; Ponec & Brock, 2000). As with teachers, in-service sessions that address buildingwide systemic issues and problems could be valuable for principals. Examples of these systemic issues are sexual harassment (Stone, 2000), crisis planning, school violence, learning styles literature, school-based resiliency factors, developmental curriculum integration, grants for student success, and outcomes measures for student development.

Educating and Advocating with Colleagues in the Community: Public Relations (Block 10)

Our partners extend well into the community, and programs to educate these partners and advocate for students, schools, and our profession should extend into the community as well. Opportunities to provide these educational programs may be considered public relations, but without these conversations, community partners remain limited in their understanding of young people, schools, and the school counseling profession.

School boards could benefit from education in all the issues mentioned above: issues that enhance and issues that impede student development, family issues, building climate and other building systemic issues, and comprehensive school counseling program issues (Gibson, 1990; Gysbers, Lapan, & Jones, 2000; Kaplan, 1997; McCall-Perez, 2000). Clearly, those who are making decisions about schools' funding, staffing, resources, policies, and procedures must be informed about young people, schools, and resources to enhance school success.

Other community partners, including employers, community mental and physical health providers, public agencies such as probation, parole, welfare, and protective services, postsecondary educational institutions, and others, need a clear understanding of students, schools, families, and school counseling. Whether these individuals and organizations work directly with our students and graduates or indirectly provide support through taxes, efforts to educate them and to advocate for students and schools are invaluable (Bemak, 2000; Luongo, 2000; McCall-Perez, 2000; Taylor & Adelman, 2000).

Efforts to educate our community partners can take the same shape that programs for other adult partners will. School counselors can conduct workshops that are open to the community, connect with community service organizations to make presentations, present at professional conferences from a wide variety of disciplines, and invite the community to brown-bag discussion lunches. Public education can also take the shape of written materials in the form of newsletters for the community and brochures about current issues relevant for families and community members. Counselors can use public media to make public service announcements and write articles for the local newspaper about schools, students, and current issues. Technology could also be used: Counselors can make use of local access television to educate others and use computers to create webpages about developmental issues or start a listserv for community members to discuss their concerns.

A Day in the Life Revisited: Integration

Aren't you glad that Donna went into the lunchroom that day? She was. Now that you've read the chapter, you should be, too. The only chance we have to address problems is when we know the problem exists; if she had not gone into the lunchroom that day, she might never have known of the need to educate her adult partners.

1. What are the misconceptions you heard in the conversation at the table? What are the topics you would see as appropriate to present based on those perceptions?
2. With which partner group would you begin to address the concerns expressed at the lunch table? What would you do next?
3. Recall that tension had been high in the building since the accident and that parent conferences were going on. What is the connection between the accident, the parent conferences, and the tension in the building? Do you see a connection between the adult programming Donna can do and the school climate? To what extent can educational programs for adults alleviate some of that tension?

Application

1. Take a topic from any chapter in this book: a student issue, a family issue, or a school issue. Consulting Chapter 8, design a lesson plan to present to the following audiences, highlighting the learning issues for each audience:
   a. High school seniors

b. Noncollege-educated parents
c. Teachers
d. School psychologists
e. School board members

2. What is the line for you between passionate enthusiasm and overblown emotionalism? With a class colleague, role play an enthusiastic five-minute presentation on your favorite sport, your children, your job, or any other topic about which you feel passionate. Ask the colleague to give you feedback about that presentation. Switch places and listen to a five-minute monologue on a topic about which the colleague is passionate. Note your reactions. Provide feedback to your colleague about your reactions to the presentation. How can you use this experience to better understand your role as an advocate?

3. Interview a school counselor, asking that professional to outline the educational programs he or she provides for adults. Attend a presentation made to one of the adult partner groups. Critique the presentation to develop insights into how you would present to adults.

4. Listen to the comments made in adult conversations to see if you can determine the speaker's level of epistemological development as described in this chapter. Locate the stage the speaker is in and outline a plan to educate that person about a school-related topic.

5. Pick a commercial, news program, or educational program on television. The writers of that program are making assumptions about the viewers' level of epistemological development. Which stage(s) of development is(are) being targeted? In other words, what level of development in the audience is being targeted by the writer of that script? How do you know?

6. Adults are bombarded by attempts to persuade them to buy something, believe something, or try something. What are the strategies adults use to resist these attempts? How can you use that insight to help you make better presentations to adults?

7. Conduct an Internet search for information on a topic of interest to families. Select five topics that you feel would be of interest to parents and caregivers and record those addresses. Create a brochure in which you share those addresses with family members and encourage them to visit those sites.

Suggested Readings

Cline, F. & Fay, J. (1990). *Parenting with love and logic: Teaching children responsibility*. Colorado Springs, CO: Pinon Press. This book is the foundation of the Parenting with Love and Logic program, a very successful and valuable parent program.

Dinkmeyer, D. Sr., McKay, G. D., & Dinkmeyer, D. Jr. (1997). *The parent's handbook: Systematic Training for Effective Parenting (STEP)*. Circle Pines, MN: American Guidance Service. This book is the foundation of the STEP program, also a very successful and valuable parent program.

King, P. M., & Kitchener, K. S. (1994). *Developing reflective judgment: Understanding and promoting intellectual growth and critical thinking in adolescents and adults*. San Francisco, CA: Jossey Bass. This book gives the reader a full discussion of learning issues for adults, providing insights for promoting learning.

MacKinnon-Slaney, F. (1994). The adult persistence in learning model: A road map to counseling services for adult learners. *Journal of Counseling and Development, 72*, 268–275. This article is extremely helpful in articulating the relationship between learning and counseling in adults.

References

Basseches, M. (1980). Intellectual development: The development of dialectical thinking. In E. P. Marmon, B. F. Nodine, and F. W. O'Connor (Eds.), *Thinking, reasoning, and writing* (pp. 23–45). New York: Longman.

Baxter Magolda, M. B. (1990). Gender differences in epistemological development. *Journal of Counseling and Development, 31* (6), 555–561.

Bemak, F. (2000). Transforming the role of the counselor to provide leadership in educational reform through collaboration. *Professional School Counseling, 3,* 323–331.

Burnham, J. J., & Jackson, C. M. (2000). School counselor roles: Discrepancies between actual practice and existing models. *Professional School Counseling, 4,* 41–49.

Cheren, M. (1983). Helping learners achieve greater self-direction. In R. M. Smith (Ed.), *Helping adults learn how to learn.* New Directions for Continuing Education, No. 19. San Francisco, CA: Jossey-Bass.

Christiansen, J. (1997). Helping teachers meet the needs of students at risk for school failure. *Elementary School Guidance & Counseling, 31,* 204–211. Retrieved December 6, 2000, from the EBSCO database available on the World Wide Web: http:///ehostv…teachers.

Clark, A. J. (1995). Rationalization and the role of the school counselor. *The School Counselor, 42,* 283–291.

Cline, F., & Fay, J. (1990). *Parenting with love and logic: Teaching children responsibility.* Colorado Springs, CO: Pinon Press.

Crespi, T. D., & Howe, E. A. (2000, March). Families in crisis: Considerations and implications for school counselors. *Counseling Today, 42,* 6, 36.

Dinkmeyer, D. Sr., McKay, G. D., & Dinkmeyer, D. Jr. (1997). *The parent's handbook: Systematic Training for Effective Parenting.* Circle Pines, MN: American Guidance Service.

Erk, R. R. (1999). Attention deficit hyperactivity disorders: Counselors, laws, and implications for practice. *Professional School Counseling, 2,* 318–326.

Evans, W. P., & Carter, M. J. (1997). Urban school-based counseling: Role definition, practice applications, and training implications. *Journal of Counseling & Development, 75,* 366–375. Retrieved December 8, 2000 from the EBSCO database available on the World Wide Web: http://ehostv…amily.

Fleck-Henderson, A., & Kegan, R. (1989). Learning, knowing and the self: A constructive developmental view. In K. Field, B. J. Cohler, & G. Wool (Eds.), *Learning and education: Psychoanalytic perspectives* (pp. 267–304). Madison, CT: International University Press.

Geroski, A. M., & Knauss, L. (2000). Addressing the needs of foster children within a school counseling program. *Professional School Counseling, 3,* 152–161.

Gibson, R. L. (1990). Teachers' opinions of high school counseling and guidance programs: Then and now. *The School Counselor, 37,* 248–255.

Golderberger, N. R., Clinchy, B. M., Belenky, M. F., & Tarule, J. M. (1987). Women's ways of knowing. In P. Shaver & C. Hendrick (Eds.), *Sex and gender.* (pp. 201–228). London, UK: Sage.

Gysbers, N. C., Lapan, R. T., & Jones, B. A. (2000). School board policies for guidance and counseling: A call to action. *Professional School Counseling, 3,* 349–355.

Jackson, S. A., & White, J. (2000). Referrals to the school counselor: A qualitative study. *Professional School Counseling, 3,* 277–286.

James, S. H., & Burch, K. M. (1999). School counselors' roles in cases of child sexual behavior. *Professional School Counseling, 2,* 211–217.

Kaplan, L. S. (1997). Parents' rights: Are school counselors at risk? *The School Counselor, 44,* 334–343.

Kegan, R. (1982). *The evolving self: Problem and process in human development.* Cambridge, MA: Harvard University Press.

Kegan, R. (1994, June 27). *Adult meaning systems and the demands of school: A constructive developmental approach to adult development.* Unpublished presentation at the 1994 Institute on Adult Learners, Harvard Graduate School of Education, Harvard University, Boston.

King, P., & Baxter Magolda, M. B. (1996). A developmental perspective on learning. *Journal of College Student Development Special Issue: The Student Learning Imperative, 37* (2), 163–173.

King, P. M., & Kitchener, K. S. (1994). *Developing reflective judgment: Understanding and promoting intellectual growth and critical thinking in adolescents and adults.* San Francisco, CA: Jossey Bass.

Luongo, P. F. (2000). Partnering child welfare, juvenile justice, and behavioral health with schools. *Professional School Counseling, 3,* 308–314.

McAuliffe, G. J. (1993). Constructive development and career transition: Implication for counseling. *Journal of Counseling and Development, 72* (1), 23–28.

McCall-Perez, Z. (2000). The counselor as advocate for English Language Learners: An action research approach. *Professional School Counseling, 4,* 13–22.

Parker, R. J. (1999). The art of blessing: Teaching parents to create rituals. *Professional School Counseling, 2,* 218–225.

Peeks, B. (1993). Revolutions in counseling and education: A systems perspective in the schools. *Elementary School Guidance & Counseling, 27,* 245–252. Retrieved December 8, 2000, from the

EBSCO database available on the World Wide Web: http: ehostv…amily.

Perry, W. G., Jr. (1981). Cognitive and ethical growth. In A. Chickering (Ed.), *The modern American college* (pp. 76–92). San Francisco, CA: Jossey Bass.

Ponec, D. L., & Brock, B. L. (2000). Relationships among elementary school counselors and principals: A unique bond. *Professional School Counseling, 3,* 208–217.

Porter, G., Epp, L., & Bryant, S. (2000). Collaboration among school mental health professionals: A necessity, not a luxury. *Professional School Counseling, 3,* 315–322.

Rice, G. E., & Smith, W. (1993). Linking effective counseling and teaching skills. *The School Counselor, 40,* 201–206.

Ritchie, M. H., & Partin, R. L. (1994). Parent education and consultation: Activities of school counselors. *The School Counselor, 41,* 165–170.

Schroeder, C. C., & Hurst, J. C. (1996). Designing learning environments that integrate curricular and co-curricular experiences. *Journal of College Student Development Special Issue: The Student Learning Imperative, 37* (2), 174–181.

Stage, F. K. (1996). Setting the context: Psychological theories of learning. *Journal of College Student Development Special Issue: The Student Learning Imperative, 37* (2), 227–235.

Stone, C. B. (2000). Advocacy for sexual harassment victims: Legal support and ethical aspects. *Professional School Counseling, 4,* 23–30.

Strawser, S., Markos, P. A., Yamaguchi, B. J., & Higgins, K. (2000). A new challenge for school counselors: Children who are homeless. *Professional School Counseling, 3,* 162–171.

Strong, S. R. (1968). Counseling: An interpersonal influence process. *Journal of Counseling Psychology, 15* (3), 215–224.

Taylor, L., & Adelman, H. S. (2000). Connecting schools, families, and communities. *Professional School Counseling, 3,* 298–307.

Wilcoxon, S. A., & Magnuson, S. (1999). Considerations for school counselors serving non-custodial parents: Premises and suggestions. *Professional School Counseling, 2,* 275–280.

13

Consulting with Parents, Colleagues in the School, and Colleagues in the Community (Blocks 11, 12, 13 of the DAP Model)

Colette T. Dollarhide

"What do I like least about high school? Once you are accepted into a certain group, you can never change. You are labeled and you can't change it."

Angie, age 15

Learning Objectives _____

By the time you finish this chapter, you should be able to:

1. Understand Caplan's model for consulting with adults.
2. Apply that model to consultation with parents.
3. Apply that model to consultation with teachers, administrators, and other colleagues in the schools.
4. Apply that model to consultation with partners in the community.

A Day in the Life of a Counselor: An Eye-Opening Lunch for Lupé _____

Lupé and Caroline met for lunch every Friday. They were both high school counselors in neighboring districts; as the only counselor in their individual buildings, they found much-needed support in their lunch meetings. It was wonderful to be able to talk about school-related and counseling issues freely, without fear of unprofessional disclosure. (Being aware of confidentiality, however, they never used names or details.)

Today it was Lupé's turn to talk, and she needed help with a problem with a teacher. "Caroline, you know me. I'm a patient woman—I'm fairly tolerant. But this one teacher this year is driving me nuts! I can't seem to get her to understand that she's crossing the line with these kids."

"Whoa! Back up. What's she doing?"

"She brings me the names of all these kids she wants me to work with. That's a good thing—at least she cares. The problem is that I think she might care too much. She hounds me with 'Did you see her? Did you work with her?' and it's only been two days since she brought me the name."

"You know, Lupé, that doesn't sound like a problem to me . . ." Caroline began.

"Let me finish. That's not the half of it. A couple of the kids have told me that she tries to 'counsel' them after class; she pesters them to give them rides home. She has offered to let a couple of our students come live with her when they have problems with their parents."

"Just to play the devil's advocate, and I hope you won't be offended if I say so, but are you maybe feeling a little threatened? Maybe she's trying to do your job and you don't like it?" Caroline offered gently.

"No, I have already looked at that. She does nice things, but for the wrong reasons. I just have a feeling there's something more to it. A number of students have told me that these same female students invited to live with her are given special favors in class. How weird is that? These special students get higher grades than anyone else. One student brought me his paper and the paper of one of the teacher's favorites, and his complaint that his was better seemed pretty valid to me. But he got a B and she got an A."

"What's your history like with this teacher? Can you talk with her?"

Lupé paused, lost in thought. "I've known her for eight years. She's never done these kinds of things before. You know, I remember when we met, I thought she was the best teacher I'd ever known. And I was so impressed, because she had just had a family tragedy, and she still kept working. That was really something. I had never seen anyone able to bounce back so quickly from such a heartbreak. Her daughter had just died—poor little thing was only 8 years old, and she was killed by a hit-and-run driver. I'll never forget going to that funeral and seeing her picture on the casket. Such a beautiful little girl, gorgeous blond hair. . . . Oh my. That's it." Lupé looked at Caroline like she had seen a ghost.

"That's it, Caroline. That's what's wrong. Her favored students, the ones she has invited to live with her—they all look alike. They're all blonde, slim—they look like her daughter would have. Her daughter would be 16 now."

"Wow." Lupé stopped. "I'm going to have to really give this a lot of thought. Maybe I'm wrong. But what if I'm right? She is too good a teacher to let her credibility as a teacher erode like this."

"But what can you do? Tell her she's nuts? That'll help a lot!" Caroline said.

"No, but there has to be something I can do. This one's going to be tough. I'm going to have to find a good way to approach this."

Challenge Questions
Do you agree with Lupé that she can help in this situation, or do you agree with Caroline that there's nothing Lupé can do?

If you were Lupé, how would you evaluate your hypothesis? How would you go about exploring if you were right or not?

Assuming that Lupé is right, now what? What is the first thing you could do to help? Would you go to the principal? Would you talk to the students? Would you talk to the teacher? What would you say?

If *you* weren't functioning well as a professional, how would *you* want the situation to be handled?

Models of Consultation, Continued

I'm sure you are curious about why the title of this section is "continued." Rather than repeat the definitions and models we discussed in Chapter 9, let's consider this chapter an extension of Chapter 9. Recall that consultation is a three-part helping relationship characterized by confidentiality, mutual respect, and collegiality, focused on helping the consultee function more effectively with the client. In Chapter 9, we defined consultation, discussed it in terms of expertise and resistance, and provided several models of consultation: generic, Adlerian, and solution-focused. But the focus of that chapter was on the use of consultation with our student partners; now we turn our attention to the use of consultation with our adult partners.

True to Dustin's (1992) prediction, consultation does appear to be an increasingly important way for counselors to work with adult partners. The advantages of using consultation as an approach to problems with parents, teachers, administrators, other pupil service professionals, and our community partners are numerous. Consultation provides a systemic intervention, allowing counselors to reach into the students' context and mobilize other persons in the students' support network. It is an efficient use of time, providing reinforcement and collaboration among all partners on behalf of the student, and it is proactive and preventive (White & Mullis, 1998). Furthermore, consultation is an essential element of the advocate function of school counselors, in which the counselor helps parents, teachers, administrators, and community professionals understand students and their issues (Crespi & Howe, 2000). As a direct result of this enhanced understanding, these adult partners can work more effectively with and for students (Kurpius & Rozecki, 1992).

As mentioned in Chapter 9, counselors from all three educational levels reported that they spend an average of 18 percent of their time in consultation (Burnham & Jackson, 2000). Those with whom counselors consulted, in descending rank order, were community agencies (professionals in hospitals, mental health, and social services), teachers, students, and parents (p. 45). The authors of this study expressed concern that "consultation, as an intervention, needs to be more well-defined for counselors . . . [C]onsultation may be a 'catch-all' for services rendered" (Burnham & Jackson, 2000, p. 47). These authors point out that there is overlap between counseling and consulting skills, and that counselors need a better understanding of consulting. To accomplish this, let's look at a model of consultation that outlines various types of consultation.

Because Chapter 9 was focused on consultation with students, we discussed Adlerian and solution-focused consultation. These models of consultation, while possible to expand for use with organizations, were designed originally for use with individual consultees. Caplan's model (1970; Caplan & Caplan, 1993; Erchul & Conoley, 1991) is of particular interest here, since it provides a framework for understanding various dimensions of consultation and strategies for facilitating change both for individuals *and* for organizations. (Note: Caplan's original model was designed for mental health consultation but will be modified here to focus on its application in the school setting.)

It is important to note that Caplan's approaches to consultation all depend on accurate assessment of the consultee's and client's contexts in any consultation. Caplan (1970) cautions consultants to be very sensitive to the norms of the consultee's personal and professional context, so that the consultant does not suggest interventions that are contrary to community, professional, or organizational norms and mores. His insights are relevant for school counselors: Success of the consultation will depend on the extent to which the consultant accurately understands the culture of the family (consulting with parents), the culture of the school (consulting with school colleagues), the culture of the district (consulting with student services partners), the culture of the agency (consulting with community professional service providers), and the culture of the community as a whole (consulting with community members). This is an important reminder to school counselors that the foundation counseling skills are as essential in consultation as they are in counseling.

Caplan's model (1970) begins with two dimensions: focus on the individual (case consultation) versus the organization (administrative consultation), and focus on the single client (client-centered or program-centered) versus the consultee (consultee-centered). As you can see from Figure 13-1, this results in a 2 × 2 grid with four possible consulting approaches, each with its own focus for intervention. Let's explore these four approaches one at a time.

I. Client-Centered Case Consultation

According to Caplan (1970), client-centered case consultation is characterized by direct contact between the consultant and the client in which the consultant's primary goal is to develop a plan for dealing with the client's difficulties. Secondary to this goal is the goal of

Focus on Individual vs. Organization

		Individual (Case Consultation)	Organization (Administrative Consultation)
	Client	I Client-Centered Case Consultation	III Program-Centered Administrative Consultation
Focus on Client vs. Consultee			
	Consultee	II Consultee-Centered Case Consultation	IV Consultee-Centered Administrative Consultation

FIGURE 13.1   *Caplan's Four Types of Consultation (1970)*

helping the consultee improve his or her skills. The consultant is an expert who assesses the environment of the client, the client's level of functioning, and all aspects of the problem in order to arrive at a diagnosis of the problem and a plan that the consultee will then implement. The consultant provides direction to the consultee in the implementation and monitors the progress of the client in this process.

The most common example of this type of consultation is when the school psychologist does assessment for special education referrals, recommending accommodations for teachers to follow. But school counselors also function within this type of consultation when they meet with a student, at the request of a teacher, to determine if a classroom behavior problem is one that should be addressed through counseling or through the disciplinary function of the administration. Similarly, a parent might request that the school counselor meet with a student to determine if counseling or alternative parenting strategies are warranted.

II. Consultee-Centered Case Consultation

This type of consultation is the most sensitive and intricate of the four types presented by Caplan (1970). In this type of consultation, the consultant is assessing and addressing the functioning of the *consultee,* with the secondary goal of improving the interaction between the consultee and the client(s). The consultant rarely meets with the client(s) in this type of consultation, but deals directly with the consultee in the exploration of the problem and determination of interventions. This exploration of the problem centers around conceptual or affective distortions that the consultee exhibits while interacting with the clients.

Caplan (1970) identifies four sources of difficulties that consultees face, with increasing levels of anxiety and resistance: *lack of knowledge, lack of skill, lack of confidence,* and *lack of objectivity*. The first two sources of difficulty, and the easiest to address, are the lack of knowledge and the lack of skill. In these two sources of difficulty, the school counselor can address the challenge faced by the consultee by providing information and/or by providing practice in the missing skill. For example, school counselors may help teachers or parents address the needs of students by providing information relative to the developmental issues of adolescents and may provide role-playing practice with the consultees to improve their communication skills.

The third source of difficulty for the consultee may be lack of confidence. At its least problematic level, the consultant would provide feedback to help the consultee through early professional experiences, such as those experienced by first-year teachers who wish assurance that they are handling classroom management appropriately. Caplan (1970) suggests that consultants (school counselors) support consultees (first-year teachers) in this situation, while also evaluating the extent to which more senior members of the consultee's profession (experienced teachers) would provide long-term support. Another example of this type of situation might include parents who come to the school counselor for assurance that they have handled a rare occurrence, such as the death of their child's friend, appropriately. However, at its most problematic level, serious lack of confidence and resulting anxiety might prevent a consultee from functioning effectively; at this level, the consultant might refer the consultee for more intensive intervention, such as counseling and/or therapy.

The fourth source of difficulty for consultees is the most involved and sensitive. Lack of objectivity involves cognitive and affective distortions that limit the consultee's ability to function professionally. The five distortions described by Caplan (1970) are:

1. *Direct personal involvement.* This occurs when the consultee's professional relationship with the client is transformed into a personal relationship, such as when a teacher becomes romantically involved with a student.
2. *Simple identification.* This occurs when the consultee loses professional perspective because the client represents a struggle in the consultee's personal life. For example, a parent who is ineffective in addressing a student's drinking may be struggling because of her own substance abuse issues.
3. *Transference.* This occurs when the consultee transfers issues from other relationships onto the relationship with the client. An example of this would include a school social worker who has problems working with gay students because he has not yet worked through his own feelings about his gay son.
4. *Characterological distortions.* If, in the above example, the consultee has problems working with gay students because he believes all gays are disgusting, this is an example of the distortions coming from prejudicial attitudes and beliefs.
5. *Theme interference.* "A theme represents an unsolved problem or defeat that the consultee has experienced, which influences his or her expectations concerning a client" (Brown, Pryzwansky, & Schulte, 1998, p. 31). In this case, the consultee expresses hopelessness that the situation with the client can be improved. An example of this type of interference would include a teacher who has problems working with attention-deficit students because she perceives them all as threatening and unpredictable, believing the "theme" that all ADD students will disrupt the classroom.

To address all five of these problems, Caplan (1970) believes that consultants should:

- Model professional objectivity and perspective.
- Refocus the consultee onto the issue(s) of the client.
- Unlink the distortions of the consultee from the reality of the client, so that the consultee can perceive the situation more objectively.
- Dispute the predetermined conclusions and themes by:
    1. Identifying possible outcomes other than those feared by the consultee ("Some ADD students might be disruptive, but let's also look at how much this student could contribute to the class").
    2. Relaying a "parable" about a situation in which the feared outcome did not manifest ("You have had Carlos in your class and you didn't even notice he was diagnosed with ADD").
    3. Relaxing the focus on the situation to diffuse the anxiety ("We can talk any time you want about the situation. I know we won't need to meet that often").

If none of these strategies are successful with the consultee, a referral would be made to allow the consultee to work on these issues with a private counselor or therapist.

III. Program-Centered Administrative Consultation

A parallel to the client-centered case consultation, program-centered administrative consultation occurs when the consultant is called to provide assistance with a specific need or problem in an organization. In this situation, the focus remains on the need or problem and does not broaden to an examination of the entire organization. For example, school counselors might be asked to provide a program review for another high school, so that the review of the comprehensive school counseling program is done by an informed but objective professional. When the parent-teacher organization of the school invites the school counselor to present a program on substance abuse issues to the members, it is an example of program-centered administrative consultation. When the local social welfare agency invites the school counselor to work with its social workers to streamline referrals to the student assistance program in the school, this is also an example of this type of consultation.

IV. Consultee-Centered Administrative Consultation

Caplan's (1970) final type of consultation involves efforts to improve the functioning of the organization as a whole. For example, a school might call in a school counselor from another district to provide consultation for communication problems between the administration and the teachers. (The in-house school counselor would not, in this situation, be the ideal consultant. An outside professional would have the advantage of objectivity, having no history or preconceived ideas about the source of the problem.) In this example, the consultant would enter the system, diagnose the problem, make recommendations to the school administration to resolve the situation, and monitor the success of efforts to facilitate change. Another example of this situation might be a parent-teacher organization that invites the school counselor to provide consultation in the design of an internal structure of officers that can facilitate decision making.

As you can see, Caplan's model and the four types of consultation can be used to conceptualize and plan appropriate strategies for consulting with individuals, groups, or entire organizations of parents, teachers, administrators, pupil/student service professionals, and colleagues in the community. Let's now examine the school counselor's role providing consultation with each of these partners.

Reflection Moment

It's easy to see why many graduate programs in counselor education offer a separate class in consultation. If your program offers such a class, be sure to enroll in it. You are fortunate that you will have more time to absorb these various models. If your program does not offer a class in consultation, consider finding such a class on-line, from another university, or through independent study.

Can you think of examples in your own experience in which you provided consultation in each of Caplan's four types of consultation?

Consulting with Parents (Block 11)

In terms of Caplan's (1970) model, most of the work counselors do in providing consultation to parents is done either as *client-centered case consultation* or as *consultee-centered case consultation*. In these situations, the consultee is the parent or caregiver, and the client is usually the student. (Occasionally, other persons, such as a teacher, might be the client in the consultation.) The most common situation is *client-centered case consultation,* in which the parent approaches the school counselor for help with the student's behavior, attitudes, relationships, or other concern. In this type of consultation, the focus remains on the student, with the counselor meeting with the student and with the parent to assess the problem, identify possible solutions, and help the parent implement recommendations. In the case of *consultee-centered case consultation,* the focus is on helping the parent function more effectively with the student, addressing the parent's problem that interferes with the parent's relationship with the student.

It is with these personal problems of the parent that we see how counseling and consultation can overlap. In fact, some models describe *consultation* with the family in the same terms as *family counseling,* to the point that some authors suggest that if the counselor isn't qualified to provide family counseling, the counselor would apply a model of family consultation and education (Magnuson & Norem, 1998; Nicoll, 1992).

Many of the same topics we outlined as appropriate for parent education are also appropriate for parent consultation. Topics such as student learning, academic achievement, interpersonal relationships, behavioral concerns (Magnuson & Norem, 1998), use of rituals to promote healing and cohesiveness (Parker, 1999), basic communication skills, and developmental information would assist parents with their adolescents.

Consulting with Colleagues in the Schools (Block 12)

Consultation with colleagues in the schools can be focused on individuals (client-centered or consultee-centered case consultation) or on the school as a whole (program-centered or consultee-centered administrative consultation). One of the most common ways that counselors work with teachers and other student service professionals is as a consultant. If a teacher, school social worker, school psychologist, or school nurse is the consultee, a school counselor would use client-centered consultation to help that professional deal more effectively with students' attitudes or behaviors that are deemed problematic. If the problems seem to reside with the professional, a school counselor would use consultee-centered consultation to help that person deal more effectively with all students by working on that person's attitudes or behaviors. If the principal is the consultee, the tasks involved often require administrative consultation: program-centered consultation to design or deliver a specific program (which may overlap with the activity of educating school colleagues discussed in Chapter 12), or consultee-centered administrative consultation addressing overall school issues such as school climate, communication, or morale among the staff.

If the school counselor is partnering effectively with colleagues in the schools, much of that time will involve consulting with teachers. The importance of contact with teachers was highlighted in a study of teacher perceptions of counselors: the highest level of respect for skills and dedication of the counselor was found "in those schools where counselors interacted with every teacher on a one-to-one basis at least once per semester" (Gibson, 1990, p. 254).

Many of the topics of consultation are similar to those topics appropriate for educating school colleagues discussed in Chapter 12. Topics typically addressed in client-centered case consultation would include student behavior and attitudes in general, and more specifically, the needs of special groups of young people in the school, such as the needs of young people in foster care (Geroski & Knauss, 2000), perfectionistic adolescents (Kottman & Ashby, 2000), young people struggling with appropriate sexual expression (James & Burch, 1999), and students whose grandparents have Alzheimer's disease (Magnuson, 1999). Topics for consultee-centered case consultation include any issue or topic that Caplan (1970) identified within the four sources of intra- and interpersonal conflict: lack of knowledge, lack of skill, lack of confidence, or lack of objectivity. For example, teachers might benefit from knowledge and skills that would help them to structure classroom learning environments to promote social skills (Maag, 1994). Topics often addressed through program-centered administrative consultation focus on specific programs in the school, such as student assistance programs addressing substance abuse in the schools (Harrison, 1992). Finally, those topics that could be addressed through consultee-centered administrative consultation include general issues of school climate, staff morale, and student referral process and intervention teams. Examples of appropriate consultation topics would include postvention assistance after a student suicide (Mauk & Gibson, 1994), and the development of school crisis plans (Kaplan, Geoffroy, & Burgess, 1993).

Consulting with Colleagues in the Community (Block 13)

School counselors frequently consult with community partners about schools and about the developmental issues of young people, blurring the lines between education, advocacy, and consultation. If we continue to use Caplan's model (1970) of consultation, we can see the many ways that school counselors consult with colleagues in the community. Individual client-centered or consultee-centered case consultation might take place with a colleague who is a professional in healthcare, mental health, or social services (physician, nurse, psychologist, psychiatrist, counselor, or social worker), who is working with an individual student or family. Program-centered administrative consultation might occur if a community law enforcement, mental health, or social service agency asked the school counselor to present a program on student development or work on ways to coordinate referrals. Consulting with general community members would most often consist of consultee-centered administrative consultation, for example, if the local chamber of commerce or service organization wanted to know how to support school efforts and an educational agenda.

We have seen that the integration of family, community, and school must be accomplished to support young people who have minimal support systems. The most important issues facing education—at risk children and school-community integration, for example—will demand consultation with community colleagues (Dustin, 1992). This requires a very broad focus, the ability to see the big picture of a student's context, and skills in initiating community participation, but the overall benefits are immeasurable (Kurpius & Rozecki, 1992). Improved social and economic conditions can result through voluntary cooperation and self-help efforts (Kurpius & Rozecki, 1992) that can be initiated in the community by mobilizing the community's concern over its young people.

Reflection Moment

Can you see yourself providing consultation to parents, caregivers, teachers, administrators, school psychologists, school nurses, school social workers, community law enforcement, social welfare agency workers, and community healthcare and mental health professionals? Which of these groups will present the most challenge for you? Which one(s) will present the most comfort for you? Why?

Overcoming Resistance with Adult Partners

As Caplan (1970) pointed out, consultants must understand the reality of the family, culture, and community of which consultees and clients are a part. Even with this sensitivity, there are many sources of resistance to consultation. Understanding these sources may help you design approaches to students' caregivers, teachers, and others in ways that reflect your sensitivity to their concerns.

For all of our adult partners, there are many possible sources of resistance to consultation. Specifically, parents and caregivers might fear being blamed, fear a loss of privacy, or fear that the school will take over their authority (White & Mullis, 1998). These parents may have had negative experiences with schools in general or your school in particular or may resist consultation because they believe that everything will work out without intervention (White & Mullis, 1998).

In addition to the above issues, school and community colleagues present a variety of fears and concerns in the face of consultation. These include fear of losing status with students, fear of blame, fear of being perceived as incompetent, fear of success (since success may result in more work), fear of change, and fear of the unknown (White & Mullis, 1998). Other possible sources of resistance include rigidity, discouragement, and hopelessness (White & Mullis, 1998).

Intrapsychic sources of resistance include the possibility that consultees may have serious personal problems impeding their efficacy with students, or they may not be able to overcome *your* racial, educational, or economic background (White & Mullis, 1998). Furthermore, all of the adult partners may experience cognitive distortions that can lead to defensiveness, such as overgeneralizing from past experiences to all new experiences or from one group of students to another, catastrophizing that prior negative experiences will increase or reoccur, and blaming others for one's shortcomings (Dougherty, Dougherty, & Purcell, 1991).

Even with these various impediments to consultation, there are many strategies for addressing the consultee's concerns. With all consultees, effective consultants emphasize the consultee's importance in the process, establish and maintain a positive atmosphere, remain empathic, find areas of agreement, avoid power struggles, and use encouragement (Clark, 1995; White & Mullis, 1998). In addition, consultants should be very sensitive to power issues, and avoid the use of jargon or power statements like a big desk (Dustin, 1992). Through effective interpersonal skills, consultants try to understand the consultees, using active listening to fully explore the consultee's perception of the problem (Dustin, 1992).

In addition to the suggestions above, if you are consulting with parents or caregivers, consider using a structured format that clarifies each step of the process to reduce the mystery and increase their involvement and investment (Downing & Downing, 1991). In a systems context, reframing the problem with the client (student) helps parents to see the issue in a new way, allowing them greater comfort in working to find a solution (Nicoll, 1992). It is essential to establish and nurture the partnership between the caregiver and school (Nicoll, 1992).

When consulting with an organization, the consultant must be aware of systems issues to address resistance. These suggestions also include systems awareness on the part of the consultant. According to Dougherty, Dougherty, and Purcell, (1991), the consultant must obtain high-level support for the goals of the consultation, otherwise change will be impossible. Make the role of the consultant explicit, so that everyone in the organization understands why the consultant is there. As the consultant, you must maintain your objectivity and be aware of organizational power and dynamics. To facilitate change, use social influence, emphasizing the peer nature of consultative relationship (Dougherty, Dougherty, & Purcell, 1991).

These strategies do not guarantee successful consultations, but using these suggestions might help you become more sensitive to the various ways that school counselors are perceived when they offer help to caregivers, school colleagues, and community colleagues.

Reflection Moment

Have you ever been a consultee, asking for help with a problem? How did that feel? What were your most pressing concerns and fears? How can you use that insight to help you become an effective consultant?

A Day in the Life Revisited: Integration

So Lupé's concerns about the teacher in her school were not so far-fetched after all.

1. Should Lupé pursue this issue? With whom? Where would you begin if you were Lupé?
2. Imagine that you have decided to talk to the teacher. Which type of consulting is called for in this situation? What do you see as the source(s) of the problem with the teacher: lack of knowledge, lack of skill, lack of confidence, or lack of objectivity? Assume that you see some elements of the problem from each of the four areas above. What will you do to address each area?
3. Reread the five categories of lack of objectivity. Which of the five categories do you feel explains the situation best? Assume that you see some elements of the problem from each of the five categories. What would you do to address each category?
4. What are all the sources of resistance that you can anticipate? List all of them. What would you do to address each source of resistance, before it becomes a problem?

Application

1. Use the Internet to locate more information on consultation. Prepare a compilation of useful sites for your professional reference.

2. What does the student quote at the beginning of the chapter have to do with the contents of this chapter?

3. Think about your own life. Using the five categories that result in lack of objectivity, catalog examples in your life of potential areas in which you might lose objectivity. Examine each of those areas to determine strategies for preventing those elements from invading your work as a school counselor.

4. Reflect on professionals you've known who exhibit at least one of the four sources of consultee problems: lack of knowledge, lack of skill, lack of confidence, and lack of objectiv-

ity. Outline the results of their deficits on you and others.

5. Interview a high school counselor, describing Caplan's model and asking if the counselor can give you examples of his or her work in each type of consulting. How much time does that professional devote to consulting? After the interview, evaluate what you heard. Do you feel that time is adequate, inadequate, or excessive?

6. Reflecting on the needs of your community, outline a plan for consulting with a community agency or organization to address a problem that exists between the community and the school, or outline a way that the community and school can work more effectively with each other. Provide details of that consultation plan, including who you would approach to propose the consultation.

Suggested Readings

Brown, D., Pryzwansky, W. B., & Schulte, A. C. (1998). *Psychological consultation: Introduction to theory and practice* (4th ed.). Boston: Allyn and Bacon. This book provides an overview of various perspectives relative to consultation, and has specific chapters addressing consultation in the schools.

Caplan, G., & Caplan, R. B. (1993). *Mental health consultation and collaboration.* San Francisco, CA: Jossey-Bass. This book provides a comprehensive and detailed overview of Caplan's model of consultation.

Kurpius, D. J., & Rozecki, T. (1992). Outreach, advocacy and consultation: A framework for prevention and intervention. *Elementary School Guidance & Counseling, 26,* 176–189. Retrieved November 13, 2000, from EBSCO database available on the World Wide Web: http://webnf1.epnet.com. This article outlines a framework for consultation based on the level of intervention needed in schools and communities.

White, J., & Mullis, F. (1998). A systems approach to school counselor consultation. *Education, 119,* 242–253. Retrieved November 13, 2000, from EBSCO database available on the World Wide Web: http://webnf1.epnet.com. This article provides an in-depth discussion of consultation with families.

References

Brown, D., Pryzwansky, W. B., & Schulte, A. C. (1998). *Psychological consultation: Introduction to theory and practice* (4th ed.). Boston: Allyn and Bacon.

Burnham, J. J., & Jackson, C. M. (2000). School counselor roles: Discrepancies between actual practice and existing models. *Professional School Counseling, 4,* 41–49.

Caplan, G. (1970). *The theory and practice of mental health consultation.* New York: Basic.

Caplan, G., & Caplan, R. B. (1993). *Mental health consultation and collaboration.* San Francisco, CA: Jossey-Bass.

Clark, A. J. (1995). Rationalization and the role of the school counselor. *The School Counselor, 42,* 283–291.

Crespi, T. D., & Howe, E. A. (2000, March). Families in crisis: Considerations and implications for school counselors. *Counseling Today, 42,* 6, 36.

Dougherty, A. M., Dougherty, L. P., & Purcell, D. (1991). The sources and management of resistance to consultation. *The School Counselor, 38,* 178–186.

Downing, J., & Downing, S. (1991). Consultation with resistant parents. *Elementary School Guidance and Counseling, 25,* 296–301.

Dustin, D. (1992). School consultation in the 1990's. *Elementary School Guidance and Counseling, 26,* 65–76. Retrieved November 13, 2000, from the EBSCO database available on the World Wide Web: http://webnfl.epnet.com.

Erchul, W. P., & Conoley, C. W. (1991). Helpful theories to guide counselors' practice of school-based consultation. *Elementary School Guidance and Coun-*

seling, 25, 204–212. Retrieved November 13, 2000, from the EBSCO database available on the World Wide Web: http://webnfl.epnet.com.

Fall, M. (1995). Planning for consultation: An aid for the elementary school counselor. *The School Counselor, 43,* 151–156.

Geroski, A. M., & Knauss, L. (2000). Addressing the needs of foster children within a school counseling program. *Professional School Counseling, 3,* 152–161.

Gibson, R. L. (1990). Teachers' opinions of high school counseling and guidance programs: Then and now. *The School Counselor, 37,* 248–255.

Harrison, T. C. (1992). School counseling: Student assistance programs. *Clearing House, 65,* 263–265. Retrieved November 13, 2000, from the EBSCO database available on the World Wide Web: http://webnf1.epnet.com.

James, S. H., & Burch, K. M. (1999). School counselors' roles in cases of child sexual behavior. *Professional School Counseling, 2,* 211–217.

Kaplan, L. S., Geoffroy, K. E., & Burgess, D. G. (1993). Counselors as consultants during a national crisis. *The School Counselor, 41,* 60–64.

Kottman, T., & Ashby, J. (2000). Perfectionistic children and adolescents: Implications for school counselors. *Professional School Counseling, 3,* 182–187.

Kurpius, D. J., & Rozecki, T. (1992). Outreach, advocacy and consultation: A framework for prevention and intervention. *Elementary School Guidance and Counseling, 26,* 176–189. Retrieved November 13, 2000, from EBSCO database available on the World Wide Web: http://webnf1.epnet.com.

Maag, J. W. (1994). Promoting social skills training in classrooms: Issues for school counselors. *The School Counselor, 42,* 100–113.

Magnuson, S. (1999). Strategies to help students whose grandparents have Alzheimer's disease. *Professional School Counseling, 2,* 327–333.

Magnuson, S., & Norem, K. (1998). A school counselor asks: "Am I prepared to do what I'm asked to do?" *Family Journal, 6*(2), 137–140. Retrieved December 8, 2000, from EBSCO database available on the World Wide Web: http://ehostv…family%20.

Mauk, G. W., & Gibson, D. G. (1994). Suicide postvention with adolescents: School consultation practices and issues. *Education and Treatment of Children,* 17, 468–474. Retrieved November 13, 2000, from the EBSCO database available on the World Wide Web: http://webnf1.epnet.com.

Nicoll, W. G. (1992). A family counseling and consultation model for school counselors. *The School Counselor, 39,* 351–361.

Parker, R. J. (1999). The art of blessing: Teaching parents to create rituals. *Professional School Counseling, 2,* 218–225.

White, J., & Mullis, F. (1998). A systems approach to school counselor consultation. *Education, 119,* 242–253. Retrieved November 13, 2000, from EBSCO database available on the World Wide Web: http://webnf1.epnet.com.

14

Leadership and Coordination with Parents, Colleagues in the Schools, and Colleagues in the Community (Blocks 14, 15, 16 of the DAP Model)

Colette T. Dollarhide

"What is the single most important problem for my friends? Stress. Someone should talk to teachers and make them talk to each other and correspond test, project, and paper schedules."

Angie, age 15

Learning Objectives

By the end of this chapter, you should be able to:

1. Understand the importance of effective leadership in managing the comprehensive school counseling program.
2. Identify the activities that characterize effective management of the comprehensive school counseling program.
3. Understand and be able to apply multisystemic coordination and collaboration models, including Adelman and Taylor's model for effective collaboration.
4. Identify leadership and coordination activities with parents.
5. Identify leadership and coordination activities with colleagues in the schools.
6. Evaluate the advantages and disadvantages of various administrative activities often assigned to school counselors.
7. Identify leadership and coordination activities with colleagues in the community.

A Day in the Life of a Counselor: Harmony's District and the Budget

Harmony threw her notes together at the last minute, even though she knew she would be speaking on behalf of school counseling programs in the district. She grabbed her coat and keys as she headed for her front door. "Don't wait up for me, dear. This may be a long meeting," she yelled, then she was off to pick up two other district counselors to attend the school board meeting.

The boardroom was packed, full of teachers, parents, and students. No one was in a good frame of mind; the district had announced a large decline in enrollment for the third straight year, and the budget was to be slashed. Tonight was the only night for any input from the community about the budget, and everyone wanted to have a say in the matter.

As the meeting began, the district announced its position: Money was short for the coming year, and cuts were inevitable. The district had to find positions or programs that would be eliminated, period. They had already explored closing schools, cutting salaries, and a host of other options, but those possibilities had been blocked by overwhelming community reaction to school closings and by union reaction to the salary question. Last year's tax referendum was soundly defeated by the community, so there was no new money coming to the district to support the current buildings and teaching staff. Cuts had to be made.

One by one, programs came up for cutting. And one by one, teachers, parents, students, and administrators spoke on behalf of saving their programs. The vocational education program at the high school was in danger, then was revived; the after-school tutoring program at the middle school was next, but was granted a reprieve. Transportation for after school activities was discussed, but was spared. With each program and each voice, the level of tension increased. Something would be cut.

Finally, comprehensive school counseling was mentioned as a possible program to cut. Harmony braced herself, then asked for a turn to outline the importance of school counseling programs. She talked about the work counselors do with students, she outlined each school's counseling programs, she described how much the students need the developmental curriculum, and she ended by summarizing the administrative work counselors do. Feeling that she had concisely and objectively argued to keep the counseling program, she ended her comments and waited for the Board's reaction.

The members of the Board conferred with each other, then said they all had questions for Harmony. The barrage of questions stunned her.

"Do you have data on how many students the counselors worked with?" "No, that is too hard to compile."

"How do you know you're helping students?"

"We just know."

"You have no data to document your work? Wow! I wish I could work without any accountability!" Laughter in the room.

"You said you work with over 1000 students? How is that possible?"

"We do what we can . . ."

"Do you know why, if the counselors are working so hard with students, there continue to be such high dropout rates, truancy problems, drugs, and discipline problems in the high school?"

"Well, we have so many students, not just those students . . ."

"How much do you actually help kids?"

"I know we help kids, but I don't have numbers to show you."

"Do you know how the teachers feel about your program?"

"No, I haven't asked them but I think . . ."

"You *think*? Are there any teachers here to speak about the counseling program?"

"I'm not sure . . ."

"Are there any parents who are here to speak about the counseling program?"

"I don't know . . ."

"Do you know why so many parents complain that the counselors are misadvising the students?"

"No, I didn't know that was happening . . ."

"Did you know that some parents think that counselors just mess with the kids and interfere with their authority?"

"That's not true!"

"Yes, it is. I talked with a parent group just last month."

"Why should we keep your program when kids have the community mental health center to go to? Those therapists treat all kinds of problems and our taxes already go to support their work. Do you work with them?"

"No, we don't, but we refer students to them."

"Oh, so you know that you can't serve kids the way they do."

"No, it's different . . ."

"Do you realize that the scheduling of students on the computer isn't really necessary? There is a phone system that could handle that job. Or a secretary could do that."

"Yes, a secretary could, but that's always been our job . . ."

"Well, perhaps it's time to revisit that. Thank you, Ms. Burch. That is all we need to know. How much does the counseling program cost again? I think we've found a place to begin cutting. Next on the agenda . . ."

Harmony sat down, and a lump rose in her throat.

Challenge Questions

Do you think this could really happen? Why or why not?

What does your state mandate in terms of student access to school counseling programs and school counselors? Are there mandated or recommended student/counselor ratios? What are those ratios?

What are some of the problems you noticed in Harmony's answers to the Board? What do her answers suggest in terms of managing the school counseling program? In terms of accountability? In terms of leadership? In terms of collaboration? Is this a question of work *style*, or something more?

Based on Harmony's answers to the Board, how would you describe her counseling program? Would *you* have confidence in her program?

Managing the Comprehensive School Counseling Program

As you will recall from Chapter 10, a school counselor is like the co-pilot on a plane, responsible for leadership of his or her program. But what are the specific ways in which the school counselor leads? For what, exactly, is the school counselor responsible? How is this responsibility demonstrated? We will explore how responsibility is manifested through effective leadership and management of the program on a year-round basis.

Many authors discuss the need to be accountable (Baker, 2000; Schmidt, 2000), and there is no question that school counselors must be accountable to their schools, their communities, and to their students for their comprehensive school counseling programs. School counselors are accountable for their time, the quality of their work, and the quality of the program overall evaluated on the basis of needs and outcomes (Hutchinson & Bottorff, 1986). For example, Baker (2000) indicated that school counselors are professionally and morally bound to evaluate (gather information about one's programs and services) and be accountable (report the results of the evaluation) (p. 300). Schmidt (2000) also called upon school counselors to "identify your role in the school, account for the time you allot to specific activities, and measure whether or not these services make a difference in the lives of students, parents, and teachers" (p. 275).

But this is often misunderstood to mean that school counselors must bite the yearly bullet to pull data together and write a self-evaluation, something to be avoided like the plague. We would like to expand accountability to outline a process of effective management, needs and outcomes assessment, reflection, and program improvement. Management of the program is more than being accountable for the *results* of the program—it is a *continuous* process. As a part of understanding leadership and coordinating activities, we need to discuss what counselors need to do to manage, evaluate, and improve a comprehensive school counseling program—in essence, effectively lead the program.

Chapter 10 outlined what is meant by leadership in terms of vision and meaning. But leaders must also provide the day-to-day leadership, or management, of the program. What, exactly, does it mean to "manage" a program? According to Hersey, Blanchard, and Johnson (1996), management consists of the functions of planning, organizing, motivating, and controlling—functions that are consistent across all types of organizations and all levels. Planning is defined as setting goals and objectives and developing "work maps" showing how goals and objectives are to be accomplished. Organizing involves bringing together resources to accomplish the goals and objectives derived from the planning process. Motivating involves working effectively with the human resources available to meet those goals and objectives, and controlling refers to the use of feedback and results "to compare accomplishments with plans and to make appropriate adjustments where outcomes have deviated from expectations" (p. 11).

Are these terms foreign or familiar to you? If all this sounds very businesslike, that's because it is. We are looking at functions that are not the source of passion for most school counselors, functions that may be contrary to the counselor's preference to work with people (not data) and in which counselors seldom receive training (Baker, 2000). We don't know any counselors who jump out of bed in the morning and exclaim, "Yippee! Today I get to plan, organize, and control my school counseling program. Get out of my way, world, here I come!"

So let's translate those four terms into words that we can relate to as counselors. Let's take a look at the both the annual and ongoing process of leading and managing a comprehensive school counseling program, which we will define as planning, organizing, assessment and evaluation, and accountability. The process of motivation, or accomplishing program goals with the human resources of the program, will be further explored in the collaboration section of this chapter.

Planning

According to Hersey, Blanchard, and Johnson (1996), planning is setting goals and objectives and outlining the means by which goals and objectives are to be accomplished. Never doubt for a minute that, as the leader of the program, your vision for the program isn't important—your vision is essential in defining these goals and objectives. In terms of comprehensive school counseling programs, planning needs to be done yearly and is accomplished as an extension of the design process discussed in Chapter 5. As you will recall, the final results of the program design process yielded five products: a comprehensive mission statement, a program overview stated in terms of priorities within the DAP model, the goals of each priority in the program, the outcomes assessment processes to evaluate efforts to meet program priorities, and the budget and resources to meet those priorities. Using those documents, you will now begin the planning process.

Year One
1. Review the national standards of the school counseling profession (ASCA National Standards for School Counseling, Appendix B of this book, which are stated in terms of student competencies).
2. Review the standards for school counseling, or student competencies, that may be in place at the state level. (For a comprehensive discussion of student competencies, see Gysbers and Henderson, 2000, pp. 327–334.)
3. Review the standards for school counseling, or student competencies, that may be in place for your district.

4. Review your comprehensive mission statement and make sure it is consistent with your vision of your program.
5. Review your program overview stated in terms of needs and priorities within the DAP model.
6. Review the goals for your program which were based on the standards for school counseling (based on those in Appendix B) and the goals as designed for the adult partners (based on those in Appendix C).
7. Review the budget and resources to meet program priorities as established in the beginning of the program.
8. Review the outcomes assessment processes to evaluate your efforts to meet program priorities.

Year Two
After a year of implementing the program, planning will also include the following steps:

9. Utilize the outcomes assessments and quality indicators (see "Assessment and Evaluation" section on page 277) to design improvements in the program.
10. Evaluate the budget to determine if the financial resources were adequate.
11. Evaluate time allocations to determine if human resources were adequate.
12. Evaluate space and logistical issues to determine if physical resources were adequate.

All Years:
13. Outline a calendar for the academic year in which time is allotted for each activity with each partner. For Year One schedule, you might use Burnham and Jackson's (2000) research, allotting 24 percent of your time for individual counseling, 10 to 23 percent of your time for group counseling, and 18 percent of your time for consultation (based on Myrick's 1993 model of school counseling). Burnham and Jackson's study did not yield any consensus about the amount of time counselors spent in developmental curriculum delivery, but 10 to 25 percent of your time might be sufficient for this function. Remember that developmental curriculum activities are planned for the entire year, allowing for unpredictable topics that may arise during the year (such as the death of a student). Time for consulting with students, parents, and colleagues is scheduled, as is time for leadership and coordination.
14. Involve the advisory board as needed in the planning process.

Organizing

In management theory, organizing involves bringing together resources to accomplish the goals and objectives derived from the planning process (Hersey, Blanchard, & Johnson, 1996). From the planning process, you have already examined the extent to which resources were adequate. Now you will:

1. Make the formal request for financial resources to continue or improve the program.
2. Make the formal requests for *additional* financial, physical, or human resources to improve the program.

3. Determine where materials and supplies will be housed to allow for access as needed.
4. Organize all materials so that records are kept of activities, outcomes assessments, and needs assessments.
5. Maintain professional responsibility for records and information about the program that must be shared with administrators and with the district.
6. Commit to a calendar of activities that outlines time allocations and resources to meet your program goals and objectives.

Assessment and Evaluation

According to Hersey, Blanchard, and Johnson (1996), controlling refers to the use of qualitative and anecdotal feedback and program results to evaluate accomplishments and to make adjustments where outcomes differ from expectations (p. 11). Because of the negative connotations of the word "controlling" in counseling literature, let's use the terms "assessment" and "evaluation" to refer to the components found in the Hersey, Blanchard, and Johnson definition.

First, an ongoing and comprehensive assessment must be done. This assessment must include:

1. *A full assessment of the needs* of all partners in the DAP model, with primary focus on the needs of students. This process is similar to the process outlined in Chapter 5 in the discussion of program design. The purpose of this needs assessment is to ensure that next year's program will respond to those needs as appropriate. A rolling needs assessment might be recommended: This process involves targeting one or two partner groups each year to conduct an in-depth needs assessment, including surveys, focus groups, and interviews to understand the context in which needs are expressed. In this way, needs are assessed for each group on a predictable schedule.

2. *A full assessment of the outcomes* experienced by all partners in the DAP model, structured in terms of the student competencies outlined in the National Standards (Appendix B) and in terms of the adult competencies suggested in Appendix C. All assessment of students must be related to student learning (Education Trust, 2001; Kaplan, 1997). It is also important to know the perceptions of each of the partner groups in terms of the competencies of each of the other partner groups. In other words, it is important to know how the adult partners see the competencies of the students, and it is also important to know how the students view the competencies of the adult partners. Again, a rolling process might be recommended, in which one or two partner groups are targeted each year for in-depth outcomes assessment. You can alternate the year for outcome assessment with the year for needs assessment, or you might wish to assess both concurrently—collecting data for both needs and outcomes in the same survey, focus group, or interview.

3. *A full assessment of the quality indicators of the program*, including both the quality of the program and the quality of the work done by the counselor. It is essential to know the perceptions of the DAP partners in terms of quality indicators about the counselor and the program (called consumer satisfaction by Schmidt, 2000). The activities of the DAP model itself could form the foundation for the survey, asking respondents to rate the counselor's efficacy in each of the activities with each of the partner groups. Other examples can be found in the literature. For example, the survey could ask respondents to rate the sufficiency of resources for the program, the appropriateness and effectiveness of the roles of the counselor, the appropriateness of the program components and services, the adequacy of crisis responses, the respondent's awareness of counseling programs and activities, and other quality indicators (Scruggs, Wasielewski, & Ash, 1999).

It is essential to recognize that each part of the assessment process will yield distinct, yet essential, information about the program. Needs assessment will allow each respondent to state what he or she would like to derive from the program. Outcomes assessment will address what the respondent sees as the current state of the competencies of the partner group. Quality indicators of the program and the work of the counselor will give feedback about the effectiveness of individual activities and program components.

The assessment process can be time consuming and onerous, or it can be built into the comprehensive program with support from the administration of the school (Trevisan & Hubert, 2001). If it is built in, the opportunities to collect data are planned and predictable, reducing the stress of the process and improving the quality of the data collected. To facilitate the assessment process as a natural and expected part of your program, consider using and/or adapting some of the forms available in the literature (see Schmidt, 2000, Figures 25-1 to 25-7, pp. 284–290, and Daniels & Daniels, 2000, Figures 26-1 to 26-7, pp. 297–305). Furthermore, assessment can be considered an intervention, serving to renew all partners' awareness of the school counseling program's purpose (Lusky & Hayes, 2001).

The evaluation process involves taking the data derived from the assessment process and making meaning out the data in terms of the program. In this part of the process, you would:

1. Compile all the information for that assessment cycle.
2. Categorize the results in terms of program components that require improvement, meet expectations, or exceed expectations.
3. Reflect on the results, consulting with the advisory group to fully understand the results.
4. Design a program for *professional development* for those areas of the assessment process that suggest improvements needed in your skills.
5. Prioritize *program development* areas within each of the following categories:
    a. Program components reflecting high quality (exceed expectations) and strategies to maintain that high quality.
    b. Program components needing minor improvements (meet expectations) and strategies to make those improvements.
    c. Program components needing major improvements (require improvements) and strategies to make those essential improvements.

Accountability

To be accountable for the program, school counselors must now present the results of the assessment and evaluation process to the building administrator (or the professional responsible for evaluating the counselor), to the advisory board, and to the partners of the comprehensive school counseling program. To the administrator, all the information is presented: the results of the assessment process (the report card of the program and the counselor) and the results of the evaluation process (plans for professional development and program improvement determined on the basis of the assessment results that will feed back into the planning process). To the advisory committee, the information presented usually reflects only the outcomes information and evaluation of the program, not the evaluation of the counselor. This means the advisory committee is presented with the overview of how well the program is functioning in terms of needs, outcomes, and quality—and the plan for making changes on the basis of that overview.

Information shared with the partners in the DAP model usually consists of how well the program is functioning and plans for improvement. One idea for disseminating the information could be a newsletter sent to students, parents, teachers, colleagues in the schools, and colleagues in the community. Other ideas include columns in the school and community newspapers, a webpage, articles in counselor journals, and reports for the local school board (Schmidt, 2000). A note of caution: It might be advisable to consult with the advisory committee, your administrator, and other counselors in the district to determine how much information to disseminate. In the early years of the program, while you are still building rapport and creating respect for your program and your professionalism, you might want to be selective in how much you share. Too much "negative press," or public discussion of your struggles to launch your program, might damage your attempts to establish your credibility with your partners. Be judicious with the negative information you send out so that you don't end up compromising your program.

Reflection Moment

Can you think of experience you have had with these functions? Which of these activities (planning, organizing, assessing, evaluating, or being accountable) was the most pleasant for you? Which one was the least pleasant? Why?

Did you have trouble thinking of when you have done these activities? Unless you have a maid who does all your shopping and cooking for you, believe me, you have done each of these functions. When you made out your shopping list, you were planning. When you went to the store, bought your groceries, then brought them home and put them away, you were organizing. When you cooked the meal and thought about whether it tasted good to you, you were assessing. When you decided to cook it again next month or throw away that recipe, you were evaluating and using that information to engage in planning. When you bragged to your friends that you cooked Beef Wellington and it was delicious, you were accounting for your time. Not so frightening now, is it?

Coordination and Collaboration: A Closer Look

Let's now look at how school counselors work with human resources (called "motivation" in the Hersey, Blanchard, and Johnson [1996] model). For this book, the terms *coordination* and *collaboration* will have similar meaning and connotation: Coordinating programs and services assumes the ability to collaborate with our adult partners of parents and care-givers, teachers, administrators, colleagues in the schools, and colleagues in the community. Some view coordination and collaboration as "convincing others to do things my way" or "an unnatural act between nonconsenting adults." Contrary to those views, school counselors must understand how essential it is to coordinate services and collaborate with all partners to help all students develop to their fullest potential. Counselors must practice coordination and collaboration as a professional activity (Baker, 2000; Bemak, 2000; Boes, VanZile-Tamsen, & Jackson, 2001; Colbert, 1996; Jackson & White, 2000; Keys & Lockhart, 1999; Luongo, 2000; Porter, Epp, & Bryant, 2000; Sink, 2000, Taylor & Adelman, 2000).

Coordination and collaboration involves the highest form of collegial dialogue with our adult partners. This manner of interaction assumes equal status, respect, professionalism, and open dialogue between persons seeking the best possible win/win situation for all con-cerned. In a school setting, this activity means that all voices are sought, all perspectives are seriously considered as valid and valuable, and all stakeholders are invested in the process and in the outcome. No one person or profession is assumed to know the answers or to out-vote the others on the team. Like consultation, coordination and collaboration are collegial, but unlike consultation, the partners to coordination and collaboration are many, all meet-ing and interacting at the same time.

In fact, The Education Trust (2001) elevates this function to the highest importance for successful school counseling (as defined by The DeWitt Wallace-Reader's Digest Fund, National Initiative for Transforming School Counseling). Founded to promote "educational equity, access, and academic success for all students K–12," the Trust holds that "the trained school counselor must be an assertive advocate creating opportunities for all students to nurture dreams of high aspirations. . . . The school counselor serves as a leader as well as an effective team member working with teachers, administrators, and other school personnel to make sure that each student succeeds" (The Education Trust, 2001). In the transformation from counseling as ancillary to counselor as leader, the Trust advocates that school counselors focus on the whole school and system concerns by performing the role of leader, planner, collaborator, service broker, and program developer as an integral member of the educational team and champion for creating pathways for all students to achieve.

To move toward this vision of school counselors, let's examine coordination and col-laboration to see how this activity can transform and restructure entire school systems.

Adelman and Taylor Model of Collaboration

Pioneers in the discussion of systemic collaboration among all partners are Howard Adelman and Linda Taylor (Adelman & Taylor, 1994, 1998; Taylor & Adelman, 2000). This researcher/ practitioner team outlined a model of collaboration that effectively involves all stakeholders in the process of educating young people.

The foundation of their approach includes three observations. First, school profession-als do not integrate functions well. The school psychologist, the school social worker, the school nurse, and the school counselor have many overlapping duties and professional goals (helping students function in school). Yet these professional services are fragmented and seldom coordinated. Some professionals feel territorial ownership as the importance of their own role overshadows those of the other school professionals (Adelman & Taylor, 1994). Second, compounding this fragmentation, school professionals often feel threatened by the intrusion of community professionals in the school setting, creating alienation from community resources and isolating school professionals and students (Adelman & Talyor, 1998). Third, the needs of the vast majority of students have not been considered in the design of programs and services. Adelman and Taylor (1998) describe this problem in terms of a normal bell curve representing the needs of students. Imagine that this bell curve describes students' readiness to learn for one hour of one day.

At one end of this bell curve, in the tail (statistically speaking, approximately 2 percent of all students), are those few students who come to school "motivationally ready and able" to learn for that hour (Adelman & Taylor, 1998, p. 146). They have no concerns that prevent them from concentrating, participating, interacting, and learning for that hour. These students experience no barriers to their learning. They engage in the instructional component of the school (defined as classroom teaching and enrichment activities), and consequently experience the desired outcome of the instructional component (learning). Remember, however, that this describes one hour of one day for only 2 percent (one tail) of the total student population.

In the middle of the bell curve, representing approximately 96 percent of students, we find a different story. For that hour, these students are "not very motivated, lacking prerequisite knowledge and skills, possess different learning rates and styles, and experience minor vulnerabilities" such as emotional upsets, concerns about home functioning, minor health concerns, and so on (Adelman & Taylor, 1998, p. 146). For these students, these are barriers to learning that may be addressed in a piecemeal manner by the school professionals who happen to notice, but these services are not designed to address the vast needs experienced by students on a daily/hourly basis.

At the other tail of the bell curve (the remaining 2 percent) are those students whose needs are addressed most regularly by school special service providers. These students are "avoidant, very deficient in current capabilities, have a disability, or major health problems" (Adelman & Taylor, 1998, p. 146). In fact, it is in response to these students that most school support services are designed. But the very intensity of these needs consume much of the school professionals' time, leaving little time for the needs of any other students.

From these premises and student needs, Adelman and Taylor (1994, 1998; Taylor & Adelman, 2000) proposed the need for the "enabling component" that supports and enhances instruction. According to Adelman and Taylor (1998), "such an approach weaves six clusters of enabling activity into the fabric of the school to address barriers to learning and promote healthy development for all students" (p. 146). Pulled from *resources of the district, the school, families,* and *the community,* these six clusters of enabling are:

1. *Classroom-focused enabling,* providing increased teacher effectiveness and an enhanced context of caring in the classroom.
2. *Student and family assistance*, providing support for students, information about available assistance and how to access help, strategies designed to reduce the need for special intervention, and effective case and resource management.
3. *Crisis assistance and prevention*, providing emergency and crisis response and prevention activities.

4. *Support for transitions* from a systems perspective, providing systems for welcoming new arrivals (students, families, staff), ongoing support, articulation strategies at all levels, and enrichment and recreational activities.
5. *Home involvement in schooling*, providing learning support for adults in the home, basic parenting education and strategies, communication within the home and between home and school, enhanced home-school connection and sense of community, and increased home support of the student's learning and development.
6. *Community outreach for involvement and support* of the school, providing outreach to public and private entities, community involvement and support in terms of volunteers, mentors, resources, and incentives, and training and screening of community members involved in schools.

This enabling component is the result of integrating three levels of intervention from schools *and* the community (Adelman & Taylor, 1998). The first level integrates "systems of prevention," including *school programs* in health education, drug and alcohol resistance education, support for transitions, conflict resolution programs, and parent involvement; and *community programs* in public health, prenatal clinics, immunization clinics, recreation, and child abuse education. The second level integrates "systems of early intervention," including *school programs* in the prevention of pregnancy, violence, and dropouts, learning/ behavior accommodations, and work/school programs; and *community programs* in early health intervention, short-term counseling, foster placement, family support, shelters, and job programs. The third level integrates "systems of care," including *school programs* for severe emotional, behavioral, or educational disabilities; and *community programs* for emergency/ crisis treatment, family preservation, long-term therapy, probation/incarceration, disabilities programs, and hospitalization. Taylor and Adelman (2000) suggest that these programs can be integrated to varying degrees (from co-location of community programs on school grounds to fully "meshing" essential services and programs), depending on local emphases in school restructuring.

To implement this concept, schools must rethink how services are provided and programs are designed. Taylor and Adelman (2000) view collaboration as multidisciplinary, interdisciplinary, and transdisciplinary. To them, collaboration entails combining resources, programs, professionals, and volunteers to integrate services and programs to meet the needs of all students. This entails sharing facilities, equipment, and resources; grant writing and funding exploration; information and support; public relations; governance and infrastructure; and responsibility for planning, implementation, and evaluation of programs and services.

Fully restructuring education in this way forces school professionals to think about school counseling in a new way, one that may be challenging at first. Adelman and Taylor took the concept of "partners" and made it fully operational, outlining strategies for sharing governance, creating teams to design new infrastructure, creating leadership processes, managing these systemic collaboratives, securing broadbased funds, and accounting for time, effort, and resources (Taylor & Adelman, 2000).

They call for school counselors to be prepared to carry out new roles in this restructuring process (Taylor & Adelman, 2000). These new roles include increased coordination of programs and services within schools and communities, focus on learner support activities related to broad awareness of barriers to learning, and assuming leadership over the change process. They cite the Memphis School District as one example in which school counselors have been assigned leadership roles in "creating readiness for systemic change; mapping, analyzing, and redeploying relevant school resources; and working to strengthen connections between school, home, and other community resources" (p. 306).

It is clear that this model of coordination and collaboration is holistic. Most schools are not ready for this level of sharing of resources, facilities, and programs. But as a vision of how services can be meshed, how collaboratives can be transdisciplinary, the Adelman and Taylor model provides the best template.

Coordination and collaboration can have a profound effect on the systems in which our students live. As we continue to view the coordinator and collaborative role of school counselors as outlined in the DAP model, we can see the far-reaching and important effects we can have on the lives of students, their families, entire school, and whole communities.

Reflection Moment

What are your reactions as you read about this new vision of schools, school counseling, and systemic change? Think about your feelings right now: Are you enthused? Overwhelmed? Are you able to visualize these new services? Many new counselors report that these models of collaboration and multisystemic services are hard to conceptualize because they don't have a firm grasp on what comprehensive school counseling is, much less this expanded vision of service delivery. If this is the case for you, file this information away in the back of your mind and let it stay there until you're a year or two in a position in the field. Then you can revisit this model and see if it might work for your school.

Leadership and Coordination with Parents (Block 14)

School counselors are directed by professional ethics to, as appropriate, involve the student's family and enlist the family's support when working with students, according to both the American Counseling Association and the American School Counselor Association (ASCA; Appendix A). Many authors call for school counselors to take the lead in coordinating strong connections between schools and parents/caregivers (Bemak, 2000; Colbert, 1996; Jackson & White, 2000; Kaplan, 1997; Keys & Lockhart, 1999; Peeks, 1993).

These parent/family connections vary from coordination of events such as potluck suppers and community building activities (Jackson & White, 2000), to academic interventions involving parents (Kaplan, 1997), to involving parents as a part of the school's organization and structure, such as in curriculum committees and as trainers of other parents (Colbert, 1996), to providing family services such as family health services, employment services, and lifelong training (Peeks, 1993). Bemak (2000) suggests that schools must develop flexible hours to meet the needs of working parents, develop family advocacy programs and parent inclusion programs within the school, and develop a family space within the school where parents and families can go to feel comfortable and safe. The extent of these parent and family connections with the school will be determined by a variety of factors, just as we have discussed in the chapters on counseling with parents/caregivers, educating parents/caregivers, and consulting with parents/caregivers. One thing is clear: School counselors must work extensively with these partners to be successful (Bemak, 2000).

Leadership and Coordination with Colleagues in the School (Block 15)

Just as we have seen in our discussion of leadership and coordination with parents and caregivers, school counselors are often called upon to provide leadership with our partners in the school and in the district. An overview of possible ways for accomplishing these coordinated efforts includes:

1. Collaborative teams to address the systemic issues of students who are at risk or who are not functioning effectively in the school (Bemak, 2000; Keys, Bemak, & Carpenter, 1998). This team approaches the discussion with a focus on cultural, community, and school issues that might interfere with the student's functioning, and brings the support of various school professionals to that discussion (Jackson & White, 2000).
2. Collaborating with special educators and other professionals in the schools to:
   a. Support special education transition services for students who live with disabilities (Sitlington, Clark, & Kolstoe, 2000).
   b. Support the holistic development of students with learning disabilities (Koehler & Kravets, 1998) and at-risk and violent youth (Barr & Parrett, 2001).
3. Integrate services of all school-based mental health providers in school-based health clinics, mental health clinics, and "multiple systems" clinics to provide one-stop access to help. Examples cited include integrating violence prevention, parent training, tutoring, daycare, and bereavement with medical services (Porter, Epp, & Bryant, 2000).
4. Better integrate the services of the school counselor with those of the school psychologist to reduce overlap and to draw on each other's professional expertise (Rowley, 2000).
5. Collaborate more with principals to evaluate the school climate for violence, racism, sexual harassment, and gang activity; to help in the selection of new teachers; to deal more effectively with discipline issues that affect the school by adding a counseling component to the school's discipline policy; to address issues raised by athletic programs in the school; and to assist with the development of the school's crisis plan (Niebuhr, Niebuhr, & Cleveland, 1999).
6. Coordinate employee assistance-like services for school employees (Clark, 1995).

When a counselor is thinking holistically about the best way to help students with their development, it would be impossible to ignore the need to coordinate efforts with partners in the school and in the district. Some counselors may be the only counselor in the school, but there are other counselors in other buildings, and there are other professionals who serve in student services: psychologists, nurses, social workers, and building police or safety officers. Don't let yourself become a "service silo" isolated from other professionals.

Students need everyone in the helping professions to be focused on what is best for the students, and integrated services for students is clearly more effective and more efficient.

Variety as the Spice of Life: Administrative Tasks

The discussion of coordination and collaboration with our colleagues in the schools must also include a discussion of administrative tasks, and this discussion inevitably leads us back to the importance of leadership: the vision of the mission of the comprehensive school counseling program.

Everyone who works in a school will have some administrative tasks to complete. These tasks provide information for the administration, contribute to the well-being and improvement of the school and the district, and enable the building to operate in a safe and orderly fashion. Called *system support activities* by Gysbers and Henderson (2000, p. 75), these duties include many we have already discussed (research and development to evaluate and improve the program and program management activities), but they also describe duties relevant to this discussion such as service on committees and advisory boards, and fair-share responsibilities. When we discuss coordination and leadership within the school and the district, it is essential that we include these activities also.

As you will recall, we touched on some of these issues in Chapter 10, in our discussion of leadership and coordination activities with students. In that chapter, we highlighted several activities that may more appropriately belong with the academic leadership of the school. This is not to imply that all administrative activities must be eschewed by counselors, as there are many activities that on their surface seem to be administrative, but upon closer examination, clearly provide substantial holistic benefits to the school, the students, and to the comprehensive school counseling program.

To help you understand this issue more clearly, let's take a look at the overall advantages of devoting time to these activities. When evaluating the benefits of academic activities such as writing curriculum guides, assessing transcripts, and designing the master schedule, some counselors believe that their participation cements their connection with the academic mission of the school, giving them greater credibility with teachers. When describing activities such as lunchroom duty, hall monitor, chaperoning dances, scheduling students, and serving as advisor for student groups, some counselors believe that they derive enhanced contact with students, allowing for conversation, trust, and greater awareness of student lives and issues. Some counselors simply believe they are "helping out" (Wiggins & Moody, 1987) and may feel more effective as a result.

The disadvantages of these activities are numerous, especially if these activities become out of balance. Counselors might find themselves perceived by teachers and students as being a quasi-administrator, a role that compromises the counselor's credibility and impedes trust (Gibson, 1990). In addition, counselors may believe that they are helping out, but students and teachers may notice the counselor's avoidance of professional tasks (Wiggins & Moody, 1987). But the single biggest problem with out-of-balance clerical and administrative work is time. As Partin (1993) points out, "Particularly for senior high counselors, paper work, scheduling, and administrative tasks are seen as significant time robbers that deter counselors from allotting more time for individual and group counseling" (p. 279). This concern is echoed by Gysbers and Henderson (2000, p. 76): "Care must be taken . . . to watch the time given to system support duties because the prime focus for counselors' time is the direct service components of the comprehensive guidance program." The loss of time to devote to the comprehensive school counseling program can leave counselors exhausted and incapable of responding appropriately to student needs (Burnham & Jackson, 2000).

Each activity in this category must be weighed in terms of its unique advantages and disadvantages to the students and the comprehensive school counseling program. Then these must be weighed against the overall effect *all* these activities have on our ability to meet the goals and objectives of our program.

Committees   There are a variety of committees on which counselors could serve, many of which directly relate to the comprehensive school counseling program. Such direct committees include the comprehensive school counseling advisory board, the building team for school improvement, parent advisory committees, committees that address specific student issues and concerns, and the building team that addresses systemic interventions for students of concern.

Assessment/Testing   As mentioned in Chapter 10, when the counselor devotes time to serving as the testing coordinator for the building, many hours are lost that could more directly benefit the program's main focus (Burnham & Jackson, 2000; Gysbers & Henderson, 2000). Burnham and Jackson (2000) found that schoolwide testing programs were coordinated by 87.5 percent of their respondents. Test interpretation with students and parents, however, would be an appropriate use of the counselor's training and within the scope of the academic, career, and personal/social development of students. In an interesting note, in 1990, Gibson found that *teachers* ranked test administration and interpretation as the third of the top three responsibilities of the school counselor, behind counseling and career information. This would suggest that there are many persons in schools who believe the school counselor should be the testing coordinator for the building; counselors will need to understand the preponderance of opinion they would encounter when they challenge testing as not congruent with their primary role in the school.

Discipline (attendance, hall monitor, conflict resolution, bus duty)   There are good reasons that counselors become involved in helping students with attendance problems, observing student behaviors directly in the halls, and helping with conflict resolution between students. These benefits accrue directly to students when counselors are a part of the building discipline process. The key is for counselors to maintain a role in the prevention and intervention of the inappropriate behavior, but to not be the primary disciplinarian of the school. That role is better handled by the principal, appropriate vice-principal, school police/safety officer, or dean of students, as the case may be. Nevertheless, when Burnham and Jackson surveyed counselors, they found that 38 percent reported having bus duty, 28 percent reported being responsible for attendance, and 26 percent reported having hall, restroom, and lunch duty (2000).

Role of Registrar: Scheduling, Transcripts, and Curriculum Guides   As was discussed in Chapter 10, many counselors are handed the expectation that they will schedule all students, evaluate and maintain transcripts, and prepare curriculum guides. While we do feel that it is appropriate for counselors to provide academic advisement for students and that this role does require an understanding of the curriculum of the school, we do not believe that counselors are responsible for the activities of a registrar. These activities closely relate to the academic mission of the school and should be housed in the offices of academic leadership. Burnham and Jackson (2000) report that, of the *nonguidance duties* identified by counselors, the most often cited activity was requesting and receiving records, the second most cited activity was scheduling, the third was permanent records, the fourth was enrolling students, eighth was withdrawing students, and the eleventh was grades and report cards. In fact, they report that 65 percent of their respondents were charged with student records, 56 percent were responsible for scheduling, 49 percent were responsible for transcripts, and 20 percent were responsible for averaging grades. Clearly, this suggests that many schools are siphoning the time of the counselor away from program duties to perform these inappropriate clerical tasks.

College Entrance Letters, Applications, and Scholarships   Again, as discussed in Chapter 10, school counselors want to promote whatever will maximize the students' potential for success, but this does not always mean that students should be funneled into college. Additionally, is the counselor the best person to write letters of recommendation for students to pursue postsecondary education and scholarships? If the counselor has the time and the desire, due to a personal commitment and knowledge of the student, then certainly that would be appropriate. But, to assume that the counselor must write such letters for all students applying to college is inappropriate. It might be more appropriate for the teachers involved in that student's academic training to write letters of recommendation for admissions and scholarships.

Environmental Assessment   As was presented in Chapter 4 (that seems a long time ago, doesn't it?), school counselors can have tremendous impact on the climate of the school when they are involved in efforts to monitor and improve the emotional environment of the school. In many schools, these conversations take place in committees charged with monitoring the school for "developmental assets," "positive energy," "inviting elements," or other terms. In a nutshell, when school counselors are involved in improving the level of respect, inclusion, and empowerment for all members of the school community, the school as a whole will benefit. We believe that this administrative duty could be an important way the school counselor contributes to the school.

Special Education Case Management and IEPs   School counselors are an important part of the process of educating all students, including those identified as disabled as defined by PL 94-142 and the Americans with Disabilities Act (ADA) (Koehler & Kravets, 1998). In the process of educating students who live with disabilities, school counselors are appropriately involved in the process of referral for evaluation, conversations with parents and caregivers, and meetings to define appropriate accommodations. Counselors are also involved in many Individual Educational Plan (IEP) multidisciplinary meetings that detail the services and programs the student must access to be successful in school. As the professional charged with leadership over the program to secure every student's academic, career, and personal/social development, the counselor must be involved in these meetings. In some cases, however, the school counselor is named the case manager or "lead," and given the responsibility of seeing that the student's IEP is followed and updated yearly. In this situation, the counselor is not the best professional for this role. Those with licensure in special education are specifically trained to understand the needs of students with IEPs, and these professionals are in the best position to handle this responsibility. Burnham and Jackson (2000) report that the fifth most often-cited nonguidance activity was special education referrals and placement, which reinforces how quickly a special education agenda can creep into the counselor's domain to the detriment of the comprehensive school counseling program. For a more in-depth discussion of the school counselor's role with special education students, see Koehler and Kravets (1998).

Addressing Out-of-Balance Administrative Tasks

Researchers have consistently found that counselors are too often pulled away from their professional programs focused on the academic, career, and personal/social development of students to perform nonprogram tasks for the school (Burnham & Jackson, 2000; Gibson, 1990; Partin, 1993; Wiggins & Moody, 1987). It is important to understand the scope and magnitude of these "time robbers."

When Burnham and Jackson (2000) surveyed counselors, they found:

Percent of Respondents	Percent of Time in Nonguidance Tasks
25	10 or less
21	13–20
20	25–30
6	38–40
14	50–88

The average amount of time spent in nonguidance activities was 25.04 percent—slightly over one quarter of the job! This means that out of every week, approximately ten hours, or more than one day, was spent doing tasks not related to the comprehensive school counseling program. And these figures do not include the activity of testing, which we would argue constitute another task that does not belong in the school counselor's list of responsibilities.

The prevalence of such out-of-balance conditions has created the call to transform school counseling. The Education Trust (2001) states, "Large numbers of practicing school counselors are functioning as highly paid clerical staff [and] quasi administrators. . . ." How did this happen?

There are many reasons that these conditions have been allowed to continue. Some counselors allow principals, community pressure, school personnel pressure, or other factors to dictate their jobs. These counselors are not asserting their leadership over their programs (The Education Trust, 2001). It is also possible that, as conjectured by Wiggins and Moody (1987), counselors who spent too much time devoted to administrative tasks "simply did not know how to organize an effective counseling program and lacked effective counseling skills. As a result, they did whatever they could to keep busy. . . ." (p. 359). It has also been our experience that some new counselors, after spending time as teachers, may slip into administrative or academic tasks to maintain their comfort zone, reverting back to areas of experience to mask their stress in a new job. Whatever the reasons, they must address these out-of-balance conditions to ensure a quality comprehensive school counseling program for their students.

How do you engage in a professional conversation about tasks that are not appropriate for the comprehensive school counseling program? There are a number of suggestions to follow, each specific to the situation.

First, if you are involved in the design of a new program, you would be able to challenge the imposition of those administrative tasks during the discussions about the design of the program. As you will recall, the design process of the comprehensive school counseling program as outlined in Chapter 5 included educating the advisory committee about comprehensive school counseling and the DAP model, then addressing the results of the needs assessment in terms of comprehensive school counseling and the model. In this process, you must be able to discuss why certain administrative or noncounseling tasks would not be appropriate in your program, since the priority for time would be focused on meeting the needs of your student partners first. After student partners, the needs of the parents and caregivers would be addressed next. Your stand on how to best meet these competing priorities must be based on the professional literature, your professional judgment, and resources from the profession such as textbooks and expert advice.

If you are employed at a school that has an existing program, Gysbers and Henderson (2000) discuss *displacement* as the means for finding better fit between the tasks and the program (p. 202). They describe the displacement process as specifying the nonprogram responsibilities under discussion, broken down into small tasks, and "either eliminating them or shifting the responsibility for doing them to someone else" (p. 203). They believe that discussing smaller tasks, rather than entire functions, will enable others to accept them within their job duties. Also, they believe that it is the responsibility of the counselor to identify the person to whom the tasks should be assigned, determined on the basis of efficiency.

In some cases, the school will struggle to find the best professional to accept the responsibility. In other cases, the district will need to hire someone to perform the displaced activity. An example of this would be the hiring of a registrar to handle student records, grades, transcripts, enrollment, withdrawal, registration for classes, and scheduling changes (from one section to another or from one time slot to another) that maintain the student's overall educational plan. (The comprehensive school counseling program would retain responsibility for academic advisement, helping students to establish the overall educational plan and program of study for each year, but would no longer be responsible for transcripts, grades, master schedules, or curriculum guides.)

If it is not possible to completely displace the noncounseling program activity, then Gysbers and Henderson (2000) suggest that counselors strive to streamline these activities. In this process, the goal is to reduce the amount of time the counselors spend in the activity. This is useful for those activities in which counselor's involvement at some level is important, but not to the current extent. "Over time, counselors' involvement has become counselors' overinvolvement" (Gysbers & Henderson, 2000, p. 206). One good example is what has happened with testing. Counselors "fell into" this responsibility due to their training in the interpretation of assessment instruments; eventually, this became full responsibility for a horrendous and time-consuming task that belongs with the academic leadership of the school. The solution to this overinvolvement would be the hiring of a professional at the district level to coordinate and conduct the district's testing and academic assessment program, but counselors' involvement would be streamlined to retain responsibility for the interpretation of the testing results.

In the third situation, the counselor might be approached by someone who thinks it would be a good idea for the counselor to accept another responsibility, one that does not already fall in the comprehensive school counseling program. In response, Partin (1993) recommended that counselors should ask " 'In place of what?' Because time is finite, any additional task must be at the expense of something else" (p. 280). He urges counselors to maintain their focus on their program priorities: "If counselors quickly acquiesce to external pressures to take on new projects and duties, others may begin to assume that those counselors must not have had enough to do before or that what they were doing was not important" (p. 280). Clearly, counselors are reminded to focus on their program priorities and to not blindly accept new duties that do not enhance the program.

This is not to imply that new program priorities will never emerge, because new issues and new problems emerge all the time. Remember, though, that you will have an advisory committee that can help you in the case of new program priorities or emerging student issues that must be addressed. If new priorities emerge, they should be discussed with your advisory committee, and the discussions must clearly convey that you are asking for their input in the redefinition of the comprehensive school counseling program.

It is not sufficient for schools to argue that school counselors must continue doing nonprogram activities because they have always done it, or because there is no one else to do it. These are not acceptable reasons. Ultimately, counselors must recognize that they must accept leadership of their comprehensive school counseling programs, and this leadership means setting program priorities to maximize student potential. Counselors are not glorified secretaries, psychometrists, telephone operators, truancy officers, or registrars. They should keep their focus on their program priorities in terms of the developmental domains, the professional activities of school counselors, and their primary partners: students. As a counselor, dare to transform school counseling in *your* lifetime!

Leadership and Coordination with Colleagues in the Community (Block 16)

As we saw in the section on collaboration, powerful interventions result when community professionals join with school professionals to design comprehensive, wraparound services. Programs that utilize community resources to accomplish the goals of the school counseling program include mentoring programs (Brotherthon & Clarke, 1997), interagency collaboration (Price & Edgar, 1995), school/community collaboration (Ponec, Poggi, & Dickel, 1998), and youth services teams for at-risk youth (Hobbs & Collison, 1995).

The extent of school-community collaboration varies with the needs met by the collaborative. In understanding the needs of the community, motivation to collaborate depends on four variables: the way education is envisioned, the ability to integrate diverse systems of care, the ability to implement prevention/intervention programs, and the ability to meet the needs of adults as well as children and youth (Walsh, Howard, & Buckley, 1999). The needs of the school counselor might determine some linkages: Logistics might increase the chance that the school counselor will be compelled to develop strong linkages with community resources. A case in point is the finding that school counselors in isolated rural communities need to collaborate with professionals in the community due to limited resources within the school itself (Morrissette, 2000). In addition, the needs of the student-client are met with school-community collaboration, as evidenced by Luongo's (2000) argument that partnering child welfare, juvenile justice, substance abuse/mental health diagnostic and treatment services, and schools is essential to meet the needs of our most vulnerable youth.

These variables interact to create various models of collaboration. This wide range of school-community linkages (Bemak, 2000; Walsh, Howard, & Buckley, 1999) varies from school-based coordinated referrals to community professionals, to school-based or neighborhood delivery of community services, to completely integrated "community schools" in which is found "comprehensive delivery of education and related health and human services" (Walsh, Howard, & Buckley, 1999, p. 351). This last concept of fully integrated school-community services closely parallels the *systems of prevention, systems of early intervention,* and *systems of care* promoted by Taylor and Adelman (2000). All these authors call for school counselors to assume leadership in conversations about forming these partnerships.

Of particular note, Ponec, Poggi, and Dickel (1998) researched the keys to successful school-community collaboration. They found that communication and personal interaction was crucial to successful collaboration, especially when it allowed each to better understand the roles and responsibilities of the other. This fostered trust and professional relationships, allowing for better referrals and more effective information sharing. Further, the researchers found that developing a sense of professionalism was also important to the collaborators, involving better understanding of each person's area of expertise and the methods of sharing information. Along with this, the researchers found that a shared sense of teamwork improved trust, professionalism, and communication.

It seems logical that school counselors would collaborate with community professionals to meet students' needs, but there are many barriers to such collaboration. Outdated ideas about the role of the counselor and/or the role of schools, site-focused school administrators, turf issues, professional obsolescence, and overloads of "administrivia" are all impediments to moving forward to effect systemic change (Bemak, 2000). But if school counselors are indeed leaders, then it becomes our responsibility to move toward such change.

Reflection Moment

What has your experience been with collaboration across professional lines? Has it been positive or negative? Think about the process you encountered during the collaboration and see if you can outline that process. What are some models presented in this book that parallel the process of collaboration you experienced? Would you see parallels between collaboration and counseling? Collaboration and consultation? Collaboration and leadership?

A Day in the Life Revisited: Integration

Now that you have read the chapter.

1. What do you see in Harmony's answers to the Board that alarm you? If you were on that Board, what other questions would you have for Harmony?
2. How would you feel if you were one of the counselors in the audience listening to this exchange?
3. If you were in Harmony's place, what would you say to the Board?
4. What are some better ways to answer the questions posed by the Board? What does the chapter suggest the Board is looking for?

Application

1. Find two examples in your life in which you demonstrated your skills in:
   a. Planning
   b. Organizing
   c. Assessment and evaluation
   d. Accountability

2. Interview a high school counselor and ask her or him about the program's:
   a. planning process
   b. master calendar for the program
   c. assessment plan and instruments
   d. evaluation from last year
   e. process for distributing that information to parents, teachers, the public, and any others

   Be careful in how you phrase these questions. You might want to ask the counselor to give you an overview of how he or she evaluates his or her work first, then inquire into the pieces of that process based on that answer.

3. Interview a high school principal to learn about that administrator's expectations for the planning and evaluation process. Find out what the district expects in terms of accountability.

4. Reflect on and write about your thoughts and reactions to the Adelman and Taylor model.

5. Reflect on the extent to which you believe that school counselors should collaborate with parents. What are some projects you would propose to foster this collaboration?

6. Create a cost-benefit sheet for each of the administrative tasks addressed in this chapter. After designing the sheet, come to your own conclusion about the appropriateness of that activity.

7. If you were the mayor of a medium-sized town and could mandate collaboration between schools and agencies,
   a. Which agencies would you target to partner with schools? Why?
   b. What level of collaboration/partnership would you mandate?
   c. What would you consider to be the ideal conditions to have in place before these collaborations could take place? (I know, mayors can't do this alone, but work with me! Answer the questions anyway! ☺)

8. Visit the Internet site for the Center for Mental Health in Schools (Adelman and Taylor's organization) at http://smhp.psych.ucla.edu. Consider subscribing to their listserv to receive their monthly electronic newsletter.

9. Visit the Internet site for The Education Trust at http://www.edtrust.org. Decide for yourself whether or not this organization's vision of school counseling is congruent with your vision of school counseling.

10. Reflect on the student quote at the start of this chapter. In what way(s) did this quote relate to the chapter content?

Suggested Readings

Adelman, H. S., & Taylor, L. (1998). Reframing mental health in schools and expanding school reform. *Educational Psychologist, 33*(4), 135–152. This article lays the groundwork for the foundation of Adelman and Taylor's work in coordination and collaboration from a school perspective.

Barr, R. D., & Parrett, W. H. (2001). *Hope fulfilled for at-risk and violent youth: K–12 programs that work* (2nd ed.). Boston: Allyn and Bacon. This book provides examples of programs that have helped at-risk and violent youth to finish their secondary education. Counselors will find many ideas for collaboration with school and community professionals.

Bemak, F. (2000). Transforming the role of the counselor to provide leadership in educational reform through collaboration. *Professional School Counseling, 3,* 323–331. This article passionately presents the need for school counselors to address the needs of young people who are most in danger of making unhealthy choices.

[The] Education Trust. (2001). Working definition of school counseling. *Ed Trust: Transforming School Counseling.* The DeWitt Wallace-Reader's Digest Fund, National Initiative for Transforming School Counseling. Retrieved March 2, 2001, from the World Wide Web: http://www.edtrust.org/main/school_counseling.asp. This organization has challenged school counselors to examine long-held, preconceived ideas of what school counseling should be. There are many important insights into ways that school counselors can improve the quality of the work done in schools.

Keys, S. G., & Lockhart, E. J. (1999). The school counselor's role in facilitating multisystemic change. *Professional School Counseling, 3,* 101–107. In this article, the authors describe the role of the school counselor in collaboration and coordination across the student's subsystems of school, family, and community.

Koehler, M., & Kravets, M. (1998). *Counseling with secondary students with learning disabilities: A ready-to-use guide to help students prepare for college and work.* West Nyack, NY: Center for Applied Research in Education. The title describes this very useful book; a must-have for high school counselors.

Laveman, L. (2000). The Harmonium Project: A macrosystemic approach to empowering adolescents. *Journal of Mental Health Counseling, 22*(1), 17–32. Retrieved December 8, 2000, from the EBSCO database available on the World Wide Web: http://ehostv…community. This article describes the collaboration/coordination process from the community perspective, outlining how those in the community conceptualize their work with their school partners.

Scruggs, M. Y., Wasielewski, R. A., & Ash, M. J. (1999). Comprehensive evaluation of a K–12 counseling program. *Professional School Counseling, 2,* 244–247. This article outlines the process of program evaluation, which will help to operationalize the section of this chapter on the leadership/management process.

Sitlington, P. L., Clark, G. M., & Kolstoe, O. P. (2000). *Transition education & services for adolescents with disabilities* (3rd ed.). Boston: Allyn and Bacon. This book provides an excellent overview of the need for transition services for students with disabilities and will generate many ideas for collaborating with special educators to facilitate the career development of these students.

Taylor, L., & Adelman, H. S. (2000). Connecting schools, families, and communities. *Professional School Counseling, 3,* 298–307. In this article, the Adelman and Taylor model of collaboration and coordination is specifically tied to the work of the school counselor.

Walsh, M. E., Howard, K. A., & Buckley, M. A. (1999). School counselors in school-community partnerships: Opportunities and challenges. *Professional School Counseling, 2,* 349–356. This article outlines many aspects of school-community partnerships, and discusses variables that will improve the chances for these new models of collaboration to succeed.

References

Adelman, H. S., & Taylor, L. (1994). Pupil services and education reform. Paper presented at the "Safe Schools, Safe Students: A Collaborative Approach to Achieving Safe, Disciplined, and Drug-Free Schools Conducive to Learning" Conference, Washington, DC, October 28–29, 1994. ERIC # 383955. Retrieved April 18, 2000, from the EBSCO database available on the World Wide Web: http://webnf2.epnet.com.

Adelman, H. S., & Taylor, L. (1998). Reframing mental health in schools and expanding school reform. *Educational Psychologist, 33*(4), 135–152.

Baker, S. B. (2000). *School counseling for the twenty-first century* (3rd ed.). Upper Saddle River, NJ: Prentice-Hall.

Barr, R. D., & Parrett, W. H. (2001). *Hope fulfilled for at-risk and violent youth: K–12 programs that work* (2nd ed.). Boston: Allyn and Bacon.

Bemak, F. (2000). Transforming the role of the counselor to provide leadership in educational reform through collaboration. *Professional School Counseling, 3,* 323–331.

Boes, S. R., VanZile-Tamsen, C., & Jackson, C. M. (2001). Portfolio development for 21st century school counselors. *Professional School Counseling, 4,* 229–231.

Brotherthon, W. D., & Clarke, K. A. (1997). Special friends: The use of community resources in comprehensive school counseling programs. *Professional School Counseling, 1,* 41–45.

Burnham, J. J., & Jackson, C. M. (2000). School counselor roles: Discrepancies between actual practice and existing models. *Professional School Counseling, 4,* 41–49.

Clark, A. J. (1995). Rationalization and the role of the school counselor. *The School Counselor, 42,* 283–291.

Colbert, R. D. (1996). The counselor's role in advancing school and family partnerships. *The School Counselor, 44,* 100–104.

Daniels, H., & Daniels, D. (2000). Documenting counseling services: A step-by-step method. In J. Wittmer (Ed.), *Managing your school counseling program: K–12 developmental strategies* (2nd ed.; pp. 292–305). Minneapolis, MN: Educational Media.

[The] Education Trust. (2001). Working definition of school counseling. *Ed Trust: Transforming School Counseling.* The DeWitt Wallace-Reader's Digest Fund, National Initiative for Transforming School Counseling. Retrieved March 2, 2001, from the World Wide Web: http://www.edtrust.org/main/school_counseling.asp.

Gibson, R. L. (1990). Teachers' opinions of high school counseling and guidance programs: Then and now. *The School Counselor, 37,* 248–256.

Gysbers, N. C., & Henderson, P. (2000). *Developing and managing your school guidance program* (3rd ed.). Alexandria, VA: American Counseling Association.

Hersey, P., Blanchard, K. H., & Johnson, D. E. (1996). *Management of organizational behavior: Utilizing human resources* (7th ed.). Upper Saddle River, NJ: Prentice Hall.

Hobbs, B. B., & Collison, B. B. (1995). School-community agency collaboration: Implications for the school counselor. *The School Counselor, 43,* 58–65.

Hutchinson, R. L., & Bottorff, F. L. (1986). Selected high school counseling services: Student assessment. *The School Counselor, 5,* 350–354.

Jackson, S. A., & White, J. (2000). Referrals to the school counselor: A qualitative study. *Professional School Counseling, 3,* 277–286.

Kaplan, L. S. (1997). Parents' rights: Are school counselors at risk? *The School Counselor, 44,* 334–343.

Keys, S. G., Bemak, F., & Carpenter, S. L. (1998). Collaborative consultant: A new role for counselors serving at-risk youths. *Journal of Counseling and Development, 76,* 123–133.

Keys, S. G., & Lockhart, E. J. (1999). The school counselor's role in facilitating multisystemic change. *Professional School Counseling, 3,* 101–107.

Koehler, M., & Kravets, M. (1998). *Counseling with secondary students with learning disabilities: A ready-to-use guide to help students prepare for college and work.* West Nyack, NY: Center for Applied Research in Education.

Luongo, P. F. (2000). Partnering child welfare, juvenile justice, and behavioral health with schools. *Professional School Counseling, 3,* 308–314.

Lusky, M. B., & Hayes, R. L. (2001). Collaborative consultation and program evaluation. *Journal of Counseling and Development, 79,* 26–38.

Morrissette, P. J. (2000). The experiences of the rural school counselor. *Professional School Counseling, 3,* 197–207.

Myrick, R. D. (1993). *Developmental guidance and counseling: A practical approach* (2nd ed.). Minneapolis, MN: Educational Media.

Niebuhr, K. E., Niebuhr, R. E., & Cleveland, W. T. (1999). Principal and counselor collaboration. *Education, 119,* 674–679. Retrieved November 13, 2000, from the EBSCO database available on the World Wide Web http://webnf2.epnet.com.

Partin, R. L. (1993). School counselors' time: Where does it go? *The School Counselor, 40,* 274–281.

Peeks, B. (1993). Revolutions in counseling and education: A systems perspective in the schools. *Elementary School Counseling and Guidance, 27,* 245–232. Retrieved December 8, 2000, from the EBSCO database, available on the World Wide Web: http://ehostv…amily.

Ponec, D. L., Poggi, J. A., & Dickel, C. T. (1998). Unity: Developing relationships between school and community counselors. *Professional School Counseling, 1,* 95–103.

Porter, G., Epp, L., & Bryant, S. (2000). Collaboration among school mental health professionals: A necessity, not a luxury. *Professional School Counseling, 3,* 315–322.

Price, L., & Edgar, E. (1995). Developing support systems for youth with and without disabilities. *Journal for Vocational Special Needs Education, 18*(1), 17–21.

Rowley, W. J. (2000). Expanding collaborative partnerships among school counselors and school psychologists. *Professional School Counseling, 3,* 224–228.

Schmidt, J. J. (2000). Counselor accountability: Justifying your time and measuring your worth. In J. Wittmer (Ed.), *Managing your school counseling program: K–12 developmental strategies* (2nd ed.; pp. 275–291). Minneapolis, MN: Educational Media.

Scruggs, M. Y., Wasielewski, R. A., & Ash, M. J. (1999). Comprehensive evaluation of a K–12 counseling program. *Professional School Counseling, 2,* 244–247.

Sink, C. A. (2000). Modeling collaboration through caring community of learners. *Professional School Counseling, 3,* ii–iii.

Sitlington, P. L., Clark, G. M., & Kolstoe, O. P. (2000). *Transition education and services for adolescents with disabilities* (3rd ed.). Boston: Allyn and Bacon.

Taylor, L., & Adelman, H. S. (2000). Connecting schools, families, and communities. *Professional School Counseling, 3,* 298–307.

Trevisan, M. S., & Hubert, M. (2001). Implementing comprehensive guidance program evaluation support: Lessons learned. *Professional School Counseling, 4,* 225–228.

Walsh, M. E., Howard, K. A., & Buckley, M. A. (1999). School counselors in school-community partnerships: Opportunities and challenges. *Professional School Counseling, 2,* 349–356.

Wiggins, J. D., & Moody, A. H. (1987). Student evaluations of counseling programs: An added dimension. *The School Counselor, 34,* 353–361.

V

You as Professional School Counselor

15

Moral, Ethical, and Legal Issues in School Counseling

Colette T. Dollarhide

"What is the single most important problem I see? People who are afraid to take chances, [because of fear of] what people think about you."

Josh, age 16

Learning Objectives _____

By the end of this chapter, you will:

1. Understand the source of our moral standards for counseling.

2. Understand the relationship between those moral standards and the ethical statements of counseling.

3. Understand the importance of knowing the Code of Ethics and Standards of Practice of the American Counseling Association.

4. Be able to identify the major components in the Ethical Standards for School Counselors of the American School Counselor Association (Appendix A).

5. Understand the laws that pertain to school counseling.

6. Understand and apply a model of ethical decision making.

7. Be familiar with several common ethical dilemmas in secondary school counseling.

8. Understand the importance of professional insurance and certification.

9. Be familiar with and able to implement a plan of action for responding to legal action.

10. Be familiar with several resources from which to obtain information in the event of future ethical dilemmas.

11. Know several strategies for practicing in the most ethical manner possible.

A Day in the Life of a Counselor: Jason's Casual Comment _____

Jason was flying through his advising appointments, proud that he had been on schedule all day. His 305-student roster was almost done; the principal would be happy that the counselors had been able to schedule all 1,213 students in the three weeks they were given. The computer hadn't crashed once so far this year, and with luck, he was keeping to his 10-minute scheduling appointments like clockwork. He knew that the director of their counseling program was trying to move the scheduling part of this process to the secretaries in the office, but until then, he was content to do as he was asked. At least it gave him time every year to talk with every one of his assigned students.

Two o'clock, and he was almost done for the day. He'd been on a roll all day, his energy high. "OK, Kim, right? How are you? It's been a long time since we last talked. Do you have your schedule ready?"

Kim was a quiet, withdrawn girl, very petite for her age. She was a sophomore this year, making average grades. She was one of those students who faded into the background in class, in the hallways, in the lunchroom. Jason never saw her in the halls talking to anyone; she was always alone. He wondered why she worked so hard at being invisible. He looked at her file while she came in and sat down.

"I've got a problem, Mr. Whitney," she mumbled, "but I'm not sure who to talk to. I don't want this getting around school."

Jason was thinking about her schedule, and offhandedly said, "Well, you can tell me. You know I won't tell your friends."

"Ok, then. I've been doing some things with my boyfriend that I'm not really proud of, but I don't know how to make it stop without losing him."

Jason's head snapped out of the file when he realized what she had said. "Oh, Kim, I don't know that I can keep that a secret. There are laws about reporting the sexual activity of minors, and your parents should . . ."

"No way! Forget it then! You said you wouldn't tell, just now, you said you wouldn't tell! Damn it—you lied! I'm out of here."

"Don't go, we need to talk about this!"

"No, there's nothing to say. Nothing. I'll deny I said anything. I'll make another appointment to work on my schedule. I'm feeling sick and want to go home. Don't make me puke on your rug to prove it." She looked at him with contempt, grabbed her bookbag, and left.

All he could do was watch her leave. It was going to take him hours to straighten out this mess, and he didn't know if he could ever make it right with Kim. If he reported as he was supposed to do, she would deny everything, she would never trust another counselor, and things could get much more difficult for her all around. If he honored her wishes and didn't report, he could get into legal trouble involving the school, her parents, and heaven knows what else. So much for being on time.

Challenge Questions

There are a variety of internal and external factors that contributed to Jason's problem. What were the internal factors—things about Jason's personality—that affected his actions? What were the external factors?

What is the ethical dilemma? What are Jason's competing concerns?

Reread the scenario. Did Jason jump to a conclusion about what is happening with the boyfriend? Are there other interpretations of her words? What if he reports she is sexually active, only to find out that she wasn't talking about sex at all?

Does Jason have options in ways to proceed? What are those options? Are there ways to address all his concerns? What are they?

What would you do?

School Counseling and Ethics

Counseling graduate students often ask, "How will I know what to do in an ethical dilemma?" And the only answer is, "It depends on what's important to you." A dilemma only exists when there are two or more equally compelling priorities confronting you. You have to know your professional ethics, relevant federal, state, and local laws, and the policies of your district and building, but this is only part of the whole picture. The missing pieces of the puzzle involve obtaining current information, knowing your professional priorities, and knowing how to think through the dilemma. The puzzle, when assembled, reveals a holistic picture of ethical counseling:

1. You have to know ethics, laws, policies and procedures that pertain to your students *very well*.
2. You have to know how to get more information about current issues, laws, and expert advice.

3. You have to know your own professional priorities.
4. You have to know a process by which you can factor these elements together.

In this chapter, we will address all these topics.

In terms of ethics, the school setting is unique in many ways. Because school counselors work with minors, they must have an awareness of the rights of parents and legal guardians. Furthermore, because schools are highly regulated and legislated, counselors must have a sharp awareness of federal, state, and local laws; court decisions; state regulations; and school board policies. (For a detailed discussion of the sources of laws relative to school counselors, see Schmidt, 1999, Chapter 11.) In addition, school counselors must continually update their knowledge about each of these topics, because ignorance of the law is no excuse. This is not to suggest that counselors must become lawyers in order to practice counseling. The point is to know where to go when you have questions about your practice.

This chapter could easily be a course by itself. It is important to note that the discussion in this chapter is not intended to be your only exposure to ethics; you should take additional course(s) in ethics, read in the professional literature about ethics, and be open to professional development opportunities (workshops, conferences) that address contemporary issues and changes in ethics. In this chapter, we will focus on ethical issues that are most relevant to counselors in high schools. Let's begin with a discussion of the source of our ethics: morals and values.

The Moral Vision of Counseling: Our Values

Counseling, as a profession, has evolved a set of moral guidelines that shape our ethics, and, in some cases has resulted in the passage of laws to protect clients and the public (Christopher, 1996). The moral guidelines come from a shared set of assumptions about the therapeutic conditions that facilitate human development—those underlying assumptions of human nature as articulated in theories of counseling.

Everything we do is predicated on the satisfaction of needs, as filtered through our values. These values are interlocking systems of meaning and of significance, providing us with the foundation of our choices: We value one thing more than another, so we choose actions that provide us with what we value. These values are interwoven with our views of the world and provide the structure for defining good, bad, healthy, and unhealthy.

Christopher (1996) argued that, in Western culture, "good" is defined as authenticity, autonomy, and individualism. Counseling as a whole emphasizes self-actualization, self-esteem, autonomy, assertiveness, internal locus of evaluation and control, self-acceptance, and individuation. From this tradition, it is possible to ascertain the source of the counseling values of beneficence (doing good), nonmaleficence (doing no harm), justice (fairness), autonomy (independent decision making), and fidelity (being true to one's word) (Hall & Lin, 1995; Herlihy & Corey, 1996).

It is important to note, however, that not everyone ascribes to this Western values system. In many multicultural traditions, "good" is defined in terms of collectivism, in which the self is viewed in terms of the referent group (family, neighborhood, and culture). In this tradition, emotional maturity is defined in terms of one's ability to uphold one's duty to family, maintain harmony, and demonstrate sensitivity to others' feelings. A person's self-worth comes from the ability to excel in social roles (Christopher, 1996). From this tradition, counseling has now added a sixth value: context and systems-awareness.

Since our values shape our choices, we must think about how our values shape our *therapeutic* choices. As counselors, we promote what we believe helps the client make healthy choices and we discourage what we believe to be unhealthy choices. If we believe that individuation helps clients to make healthy, independent choices, we will encourage clients to individuate: to make choices independent from the undue influence of others. However, if we are not sensitive to non-Western values systems, it would be easy to push a client to make independent choices that could ultimately alienate the client from his or her social and cultural support system, which may not be in the client's best interest overall.

It is important to see that our personal value system and our professional value system will affect our choices as counselors. Students have said, "Then this means that I must not have any values when I'm counseling," as if they could become values-neutral, somehow negating all their values as they counsel. This is not possible, and if it were possible, it is not beneficial. Our values are the essence of our humanity, and we can't, nor would we ever want to, negate that which makes us most human. To do so would negate the very thing that makes us effective counselors. Consider this metaphor. Our values are like a hearing aid that we wear. We attend to the world better as a result of the hearing aid, because it gives us access to the messages that are important to us. But for many, this hearing aid is tuned to only amplify certain frequencies, allowing us to hear only some messages and not others. We don't want to take off the hearing aid altogether—we want to broaden the frequency setting so that we can hear all messages. Rather than strive to become values-neutral (taking off the hearing aid), counselors should examine their values and attempt to make them as broad as possible (tune it to hear as many frequencies as possible), to acknowledge the wide range of various value systems that exist in the world.

According to Christopher (1996), awareness of our personal and professional values and morals leads us to examine our assumptions. Because different moral visions and values exist, we must be able to see the greater common moral strands that bind us together, such as truth, honesty, and the Golden Rule ("Do unto others as you would have done unto you"). Counselors must acknowledge cultural embeddedness and must seek to clarify and question their moral vision. Furthermore, we must ascertain how our moral vision affects our work as counselors and engage in critical dialogue about moral visions and values.

When we examine our values, we become aware of how these values shape our work as counselors. It is only with this continual examination that we are able to truly help our clients to find their own best path to take, because we can see how our values might interfere with the values of the client. Rather than simply assume that individuation is the best way for clients to grow and develop, we must question that assumption and explore with the client her or his view of individuation and potential isolation from cultural supports. As we mature in our ability to see our value system and explore the value system of the client, we become more effective counselors. It is easy to see why we need a deep understanding of our professional ethics: This is the instrument by which we protect the client from harm.

Reflection Moment

> How would you prioritize the six professional values just presented? Rank order them: beneficence, nonmaleficence, justice, fidelity, autonomy, and context and systems awareness. Now justify the rankings. Hard, isn't it?

The Ethics of the Profession

In general, ethics statements are the codification of our shared professional values. They function like curbs on the road: they define the limits of our practice, but within these limits, there is room to express individual preferences in how we practice the art and science of counseling. Some ethical statements mandate those activities that the profession deems important for every counseling relationship (respecting the dignity of the client, fostering the client's positive growth and development, involving the family when appropriate, etc.). Other ethical statements define those activities that the profession deems inappropriate for every counseling relationship (engaging in dual relationships, seeking to meet personal needs, sexual intimacies, etc.). Between the "right" and the "wrong" are immeasurable shades of ambiguous gray. There is no such thing as perfectly ethical practice, and school counselors will be challenged to deal with this ambiguity as will every other counselor.

You will see that the values of the counseling profession are made operational in the codes of ethics (the Code of Ethics and Standards of Practice of the American Counseling Association [ACA] are available at http://www.counseling.org/resources/codeofethics.htm). Several examples will help to illustrate this point. For example, the value of beneficence (do good) is found in the directive to foster the client's positive growth and development (ACA A.1.b.), and the value of nonmaleficence (do no harm) is seen in the directives prohibiting discrimination (ACA A.2.a.), meeting personal needs at the expense of the client (ACA A.5.a.), dual relationships (ACA A.6.a.), and sexual intimacies (ACA A.7.a. and b.). Justice is addressed in the ethical provisions involving appropriate fees (ACA A.10.a., b., c., and d.) and advertising for clients (ACA C.3.a.). The value of autonomy is addressed in the ACA Code's provisions addressing freedom of choice (ACA A.3.b.), respecting differences (ACA A.2.b.), personal values (ACA A.5.b.), and confidentiality (ACA B.1.). The profession's value of fidelity is manifest in the Code's provisions for disclosure to clients (ACA A.3.a.), clients served by others (ACA A.4.), and multiple clients (ACA A.8.). Finally, the newest value, that of context and systems-awareness, is visible in the directive to involve the family as appropriate (ACA A.1.d.), the responsibility to provide socially beneficial pro-bono services (ACA A.10.d.), and the responsibility to inform a third person about a contagious, fatal disease (ACA B.1.d.).

In general, clients have three rights: the right to information, the right to choose, and the right to privacy (Herlihy & Corey, 1996). Under the *right to information*, clients have the right to have information about what the counselor is going to do, how it will work, any limitations to the counseling approach, any risks inherent in counseling, and the limits of confidentiality. The second right is the *right to choose*: for example, the right to engage in or terminate counseling and the right to make personal choices. The counselor will respect the dignity and autonomy of the client to choose what is in the client's best interest, free from the values of the counselor. The third right is the *right to privacy*, which involves two issues: privileged communication and confidentiality.

Privileged communication is a legal concept protecting the content of therapy sessions from compelled testimony in court that must be spelled out in state statute (Herlihy & Corey, 1996). Most states do not name counselors as under the protection of privileged communication. On the other hand, confidentiality is both an ethical and legal concept, addressing the commitment of the counselor to keep confidential what is shared in counseling *within the prescribed limits*. These limitations to confidentiality must be disclosed as part of informed consent and will be discussed in detail later in this chapter. It is important to note at this point that in all states school counselors are mandated reporters in cases of suspected child abuse and/or neglect. This mandate is a higher professional priority than confidentiality (Remley & Herman, 2000).

Codes of Ethics

Both the American Counseling Association (ACA) and the American School Counselor Association (ASCA) have codified standards of ethical practice. The American Counseling Association (1995) has defined a Code of Ethics and Standards of Practice document that outlines the guidelines of the counseling profession as a whole. This document spells out prescribed and prohibited behavior in terms of the general counseling profession. The companion document, the Standards of Practice, outlines the minimal behavior standards as extrapolated from the Code. All counselors, regardless of the setting in which they work, must be familiar with the Code of Ethics and the Standards of Practice. You can obtain this important document from the ACA website at http://www.counseling.org/resources/codeofethics.htm.

The Ethical Standards for School Counselors is not an optional set of standards; it is required of all school counselors. You must follow both the ACA and ASCA ethical codes; a process for working through dilemmas that arise due to conflicting directives in these two documents will be addressed later in this chapter.

As you can see from Appendix A, the Ethical Standards document begins with an important preamble that outlines fundamental beliefs and values of the American School Counselor Association (ASCA). In the first section, it addresses responsibilities to students in terms of priorities, confidentiality, counseling plans, dual relationships, referrals, group work, danger to self or others as a limitation of confidentiality, student records, issues of assessment, computer technology, and peer helper programs. The next section addresses responsibilities to parents, described in terms of the rights of parents and confidentiality. The third section outlines the counselor's responsibilities to colleagues and professional associates, specifically addressing professional relationships and the appropriate sharing of information.

Next, the Ethical Standards address the counselor's responsibilities to the school and the community in terms of protecting the safety of the school and addressing conditions that infringe on the effectiveness of the counselor. In the section addressing responsibilities to self, the Standards discuss professional competence and mandatory multicultural skills. In the section addressing responsibilities to the profession, the Standards outline appropriate behavior in terms of adhering to the Standards, professionalism, research, and contributing to the profession through membership in professional associations. Procedures for addressing the unethical conduct of colleagues is outlined next, followed by resources for further exploration and study in ethics.

You will want to download and print the ACA Code of Ethics keep it and the ASCA Ethical Standards at hand to review regularly. It is easy to lose sight of the nuances of ethics in the busy crush of the day.

Legal Issues

Legal issues of high school counselors become more involved as the student matures toward the age of majority. With attainment of the age of 18 years, the student becomes autonomous in the eyes of the law and is vested with adult status (Remley & Herman, 2000). This is an important milestone in terms of laws.

One of the most important laws is the Family Educational Rights and Privacy Act (FERPA) of 1974, also known as the Buckley Amendment (Remley & Herman, 2000) and its recent modifications in the Grassley Amendment (Sealander, Schwiebert, Oren, & Weekley, 1999). In this legislation, schools receiving federal funds must provide access to all school records to parents of minor students and to the students themselves after they reach the age of 18. Parents and adult students have the right to challenge information in the records (Schmidt, 1999). Schools are prohibited from releasing records to any third party without the minor parents' written consent or the adult students' written consent.

Confidentiality of the records and protection of the identity of any persons receiving drug or alcohol abuse treatment are guaranteed by the Drug Abuse Office and Treatment Act of 1976 (Sealander, Schwiebert, Oren, & Weekley, 1999). In high schools, this act may be important to know because it applies to "all records relating to the identity, diagnosis, prognosis, or treatment of any student involved in any federally assisted substance abuse program" (Sealander, Schwiebert, Oren, & Weekley, 1999, p. 124). This would suggest that the counseling records of any students participating in AODA programs of any organization receiving federal funds would need to be maintained with greater protection than other counseling records; the information is protected even from the student's parents (under applicable state law). According to Sealander and colleagues (1999), the Drug Abuse Office and Treatment Act

> protects any information about a youth if the youth has received alcohol and/or drug related services of any kind including school-based identification . . . When a teacher, counselor, or other school professional identifies student behaviors that could indicate a drug and/or alcohol problem, they can discuss this with the student or other school personnel. However, from the time an evaluation is conducted and/or a student assistance program begins alcohol or drug related counseling, the federal regulations are in effect. (pp. 126–127)

Awareness of this law is essential because it raises issues related to the appropriate and legal release of records and information about whether the student is receiving services.

Another legal area with which you must be familiar is legislation pertaining to the reporting of suspected child abuse or neglect (Remley & Herman, 2000; Schmidt, 1999). The definition of abuse or neglect generally includes physical and sexual abuse, psychological and emotional torment, abandonment, and inadequate supervision. School counselors are mandated *reporters* of suspected abuse, meaning that counselors are not responsible for *investigating* the allegations, but *must report when there is reason to suspect* abuse or neglect (Schmidt, 1999; Sealander, Schwiebert, Oren, & Weekley, 1999). You must obtain a copy of your state legislation and become familiar with its provisions—since these will vary widely from state to state. Procedures for reporting, who must report, and when the report must be made are important variables you must know. In addition, there may be school or district procedures for reporting; for example, the district may require all reports to be made by one designated individual. Reporting to this individual, however, does not absolve you of your legal responsibility to act to protect a child (Tompkins & Mehring, 1993). You must follow up to ensure that the report has been made.

Special education legislation has been increasingly important as instances of lawsuits increase. The Americans with Disabilities Act and Individuals with Disabilities Act (Public Law 101-476), the Education for All Handicapped Children Act (Public Law 94-142), and Section 504 of the Rehabilitation Act of 1973 all address the rights of children to free and appropriate education and services (Erk, 1999; Schmidt, 1999). Counselors must be informed about these laws, since educational services for students are often coordinated with counseling services. Furthermore, as advocates for all students, counselors can educate others (students, parents, colleagues) about rights and responsibilities under the law (Erk, 1999; Schmidt, 1999).

Finally, Title IX of the Education Amendments of 1972 protects students against discrimination on the basis of sex, marital status, or pregnancy (Schmidt, 1999). This legislation guarantees equal access to educational programs, extracurricular activities (such as sports), and occupational opportunities. This law is also the foundation of the sexual harassment guidelines making student-on-student cross-sex and same-sex harassment a violation of the victim's civil rights, and as such, mandates that harassment be reported to school officials who have the responsibility to take appropriate action (Stone, 2000). As Schmidt (1999) points out, counselors are advocates for students and monitors of school policies and programs and are in a unique position to address conditions or situations in the school that are discriminatory.

Moral/Ethical Decision-Making Process

Most ethical decisions are easy: You perform your job duties in a manner that is consistent with the ethics of ACA and ASCA, with the laws of your state, and with the policies of your school and your district. But what if those directives conflict with each other? How do you choose which of those to follow?

Ethical dilemmas are never easy; that's why they are called dilemmas. However, with a decision-making model, you can structure this decision-making process in a way that is professionally accepted. This means that if you are ever required to explain your decision to parents, school administrators, or legal representatives, you have followed a procedure that is supported by others in your profession.

One model is adapted from Herlihy and Corey (1996). In this model, there are seven steps:

1. Identify the problem, obtaining as much information as possible. Do not look for a simplistic solution. If it concerns a legal issue, obtain legal advice.
2. Apply the ACA Code of Ethics and the ASCA Ethical Standards for School Counselors.
3. Determine the nature and dimensions of the dilemma, considering the moral principles, reviewing the professional literature, consulting with professional colleagues and supervisors, and contacting state and national professional associations to obtain other perspectives.
4. Generate potential courses of action.
5. Consider the potential consequences of all actions and determine a course of action. In this step, you are looking for a solution or combinations of actions that best fit the situation and accomplish the priorities you have established.
6. Evaluate the selected course of action to determine if it is fair, if it would be an action you would want reported in the press, and if you would recommend the same actions to another counselor.
7. Implement the course of action.

An alternative model is that adapted from Stadler (1985). Before applying this model, Stadler suggests that you think through the following questions:

- What is legal? Do laws address this situation? If so, what are they?
- What is the policy of my employer?
- What is balanced for everyone involved that will promote a win/win for everyone's needs?
- How will I feel about myself if this becomes public knowledge? How will I feel if my family finds out about my choice?

If at the answer does not become clear in that analysis, you implement the following four-step process.

Step One: Identify competing moral principles that apply to the dilemma. This grounds you in the values of the profession. For review, these values are:

1. Nonmaleficence—Do no harm
2. Beneficence—Promote good
3. Autonomy—Promote self-determination
4. Justice—Be fair; promote fairness
5. Fidelity—Be faithful; keep promises
6. Context and systems awareness

Step Two: Implement moral reasoning strategy. This step consists of several substeps and directives.

1. Secure additional information about the situation, your professional standards related to the situation, any laws that pertain to this situation, and any special circumstances surrounding this situation.
2. Secure additional information about how to obtain more information about the situation. For example, determine who has the information and what the procedures and processes would be for obtaining that information. Is informed consent required? Is a court order required?
3. Rank the moral principles you identified from Step One. This involves the application of your own individual professional judgment. Expect that all ethical dilemmas involve *all* of these values to some extent, so do not be alarmed when you discover that others would rank the principles differently.
4. Consult with colleagues to find out what they would do in your situation. Be sure to maintain confidentiality in this process.

Step Three: Prepare for action. This step also consists of several substeps.

1. Once you have ranked the moral principles and consulted with others, you have a direction from which you will further examine your decision. You will now identify hoped-for outcomes. What is the ideal situation for all parties involved?
2. Brainstorm actions that you believe will lead to these ideal outcomes. List all possibilities, no matter how remote.
3. Evaluate effects of all these possible actions on everyone involved. This means you must consider the student-client, other students, the student's family, the staff with whom you work, the profession of counseling in general and school counseling in particular, the school, the community as a whole, yourself, and your family.
4. Much as we would like to believe that these decisions are grounded in the noble ideals of the profession, often these decisions are influenced by other emotions and concerns, such as power, prestige, reputation, fear of being sued, time constraints, poor time management, revenge, need for love, sexual attraction, and so on. At this stage, identify these competing issues and concerns that will influence your decision. Be honest with yourself. Discard optional actions that are primarily grounded in these issues and concerns.
5. With your prioritized values, consultation, self-awareness, and evaluation of actions on all those involved, you will now choose a course of action that allows you to maximize benefits and reduce risks to everyone involved.
6. Before you act, you must test the action by considering all possible outcomes (intended or not) and all the possible problems that might occur as a result of your choice. Obtain more consultation if needed.

Step Four: At this stage, you are ready to act. To do this, you will:

1. Strengthen your willpower, knowing that taking the action you have chosen may not be easy. Not everyone will agree with your decision. Stadler (1985) suggests:
    a. Maintain your focus on your higher purpose.
    b. Maintain pride in yourself and in your integrity.

     c. Have patience with the process and with the outcomes.

     d. Be persistent with your goals, confident that you are following the best course for all concerned.

     e. Maintain a balanced perspective in hearing feedback.

2. Identify concrete steps necessary to take action.

3. Act.

4. Evaluate the effects of your actions and adjust as needed.

5. Attend to the moral traces that come as a result of your actions. This refers to the residual feelings of regret or pride that you feel as the effects of your actions become manifest. Would you do the same thing again in the future or would you make a different choice? Sometimes the best we can do is resolve to make a better choice in future situations. (Butler, 1993)

You will undoubtedly notice many consistencies between the two models just presented. Both models emphasize consultation, fairness, and careful consideration of all consequences. However, while the Herlihy and Corey (1996) model provides a reminder to consult with state and national professional associations, the Stadler (1985) model makes self-examination and self-awareness an explicit part of the process. Both of these actions are vital to appropriate ethical decision making. Consulting with state and national associations provides you with a broad view of what other professionals would do in your situation, reducing skewed perspectives as a result of local biases. Conducting a thorough and honest self-evaluation highlights your professional priorities and prevents selfish or self-serving motives from influencing your decision. Both the macro and micro levels of examination will help you maintain balance within your choices. We now turn to an examination of the nature of many of these choices.

Reflection Moment

Think back to the last time you confronted an ethical choice. (Can't think of one? Think of a time when you had to resolve a conflict between two people you cared about: two children, two siblings, your parents, two friends in college. That is a similar situation!) What, specifically, did you do about it? How did you resolve it? How similar or dissimilar was your process from those outlined above?

Common Legal/Ethical Problems

Before you read this section of the chapter, reread the ACA Code of Ethics (available at www.counseling.org) and the ASCA Ethical Standards for School Counselors (Appendix A). What is presented below is a discussion of some problematic issues for secondary school counselors, but you will note that no definitive conclusions can be drawn about any of them.

What is most appropriate to do in the face of any of these dilemmas depends on the context and your own professional priorities.

Confidentiality

It would be safe to say that the majority of dilemmas faced by school counselors in general, and secondary school counselors in particular, involve confidentiality (Herlihy & Corey, 1996; Isaacs & Stone, 1999; Ledyard, 1998; Tompkins & Mehring, 1993). When confidentiality should be maintained, when confidentiality must be limited, how to communicate the concept of confidentiality, and how to secure the student's permission to disclose information is highly legalized and problematic.

In general, it is most helpful to think of confidentiality as the need to keep private the details of a counseling session, unless a compelling reason exists to reveal those details. In balance, however, both the ACA and ASCA urge counselors to involve parents and families in the counseling of minor children when appropriate (see ACA A.1.d. and B.3). In addition, the ASCA Ethical Standards devotes an entire section of the ethics to the Responsibilities to Parents in Section B. This provides an excellent reminder to involve parents as appropriate, while concurrently respecting the rights of the counselee. Remley and Herman (2000) issue a reminder that until a student reaches the age of 18, he or she is legally a minor and that, while your professional responsibilities are to minor clients, legal obligations exist to the parents' rights (p. 314). A parent invoking his or her parental rights does not compel revealing the details of counseling conversations, but would suggest that counselors cannot be adamant in the refusal to share any information. The general advice is to help students find ways to share their struggles, as appropriate, with their parents, or to secure their permission when you are asked for information by a parent (ASCA Ethical Standards). It may also be possible to negotiate the request for information with the parent, so that the trust between the counselor and the student is preserved and the concerns of the parent are assuaged (Kaplan, 1996; Remley & Herman, 2000). Only in the case of the Drug Abuse Office and Treatment Act of 1976 is information about the student *not* to be released, even to the parent (Sealander, Schwiebert, Oren, & Weekley, 1999). This may be modified, however, by state statute.

There are various legally mandated situations that require breach of confidentiality, which should be revealed as a part of informed consent. These situations involve a danger to self or others, suspicions of child abuse or neglect (in other words, crimes against a child) (Remley & Herman, 2000; Sealander, Schwiebert, Oren, & Weekley, 1999), when there is an emergency that requires information to protect the safety of the student and others (Sealander, Schwiebert, Oren, & Weekley, 1999), when court ordered (Remley & Herman, 2000), in cases of sexual harassment (Stone, 2000), and in some states, when there is sexual activity, discussions of abortion, or criminal activity on the part of the minor. These state variations provide another reminder that school counselors must know the laws of the state in which they are employed.

In their study, Isaacs and Stone (1999) found that high school counselors would breach confidentiality less often than counselors at other levels, depending on the danger level of the student's activity and the age of the student. "Counselors tend to see serious drug use, abortion, use of crack cocaine, suicide intent, robbery, and sex with multiple partners as areas which are serious enough to warrant a breach of confidentiality, though less so at the high school level" (p. 265). The authors believe that high school counselors breach confidentiality less often because of the view that as students mature, they develop the ability to make independent decisions and become "mature minors" (p. 265).

Furthermore, the issue of confidentiality becomes more diffuse the more contact the counselor has with concerned others. Specifically, school counselors work closely with teachers and administrators, many of whom are interested and concerned about the progress of students. Counselors are often tempted to share too much information in their desire to help students be successful; care must be taken to obtain the student's permission before revealing detailed information to school colleagues (Davis & Ritchie, 1993; Watson, 1990). In addition, school counselors need to function as a part of the school's multidisciplinary treatment team, often involving both in-district and nonschool personnel and specialists. Again, confidentiality becomes an issue and can be addressed by informing students in advance that information may be shared with the team (Strein & Hershenson, 1991). To maintain the student's trust, however, it would be wise to defer revealing details until after securing the student's permission.

Rights of Parents and Informed Consent

Informed consent involves consent for counseling itself, as well as consent for services within the limits and conditions of counseling. Here again we see how parental rights influence the work counselors do with students. Even though parental permission for counseling is not required by law, the legal ability of the student to consent for counseling itself might be an issue (Remley & Herman, 2000). While the law holds that the age of majority is 18, there have been indications that younger persons might be "capable of assuming responsibility for their rights" (Ledyard, 1998). This means that a mature minor might be able to give informed consent for counseling (Isaacs & Stone, 1999; Ledyard, 1998), but counselors should be aware that if parents insist that counseling be discontinued, they "*probably* have a legal right to have their wishes followed" (emphasis authors') (Remley & Herman, 2000, p. 315). Counselors are advised to follow their district's policy about obtaining parental consent for counseling.

The second issue of informed consent involves the information that is shared with students about the limits of confidentiality. In their recent study, Isaacs and Stone (1999) found that 98.1 percent of the high school counselors they studied responded that they inform students about the limits of confidentiality. What is troubling, however, is that they also found that 50 percent of these same counselors indicated they inform students of the limits of confidentiality *only at a time when the discussion turns to the topics that might have to be reported*! While the ASCA ethics are silent on when this information is provided, the ACA Code of Ethics requires that information relative to the limits of confidentiality be discussed as the counseling relationship is initiated and throughout the counseling process as needed (ACA A.3.a). Being respectful of the student's right to informed consent means that the limits of confidentiality are clearly explained to the student early in the counseling relationship.

Defining the "Client": Conflict of Interest between Student and School

Is the counselor foremost a *counselor* or foremost an *employee*? There may be situations in which responsibility to students will conflict with responsibility to the school. While the ASCA Ethical Standards states that the counselor must inform officials of conditions that may be disruptive or damaging, this is couched in terms of concurrently honoring the confidentiality between the counselee and counselor (ASCA D.1.b.). ACA directs counselors to establish clear agreements with employers about the conditions of the work (ACA D.1.b.), but then also indicates that accepting employment implies that counselors agree with the employer's general policies and principles (ACA D.1.l.). If a school policy requires disclosure of confidential information, such as mandating that all employees report all suspicions of intoxicated students, the counselor could be caught in a dilemma. Issues of trust arise (How will students get help if they are afraid of getting into trouble?) as well as credibility (What if all the counselor has is an unsubstantiated rumor?). What if the person spreading the rumor later recants the story, claiming that the report of an intoxicated student was revenge for a lover's quarrel? Does the counselor still have to report? What if all attempts to change the policy are unsuccessful?

Kaplan and Allison (1994) would suggest that confidentiality with the student should be maintained, especially if the limits of confidentiality were not disclosed before the student shared the confidential information with the counselor. However, Remley and Herman (2000) indicate that school counselors must follow the rules, regulations, or policies of the school and the district, even while they work to get them changed. These authors argue that dismissal for insubordination could give you a forum to confront the employer's policy, but the burden of proof would be on you to show that the employer's policy was in violation of the standards of the profession and therefore unreasonable. They propose that educating the employer through information and persuasion would be a more collegial way to approach the situation. Notice in this discussion that even the authors in the field may disagree about the appropriate action to take, reinforcing the need for you to have a process by which you think through professional dilemmas as they arise.

Counselor Competence

Competence refers to both skill areas in which you must be competent, and skill areas in which you are not considered competent without additional, specialized training. Skills areas in which you must be competent include the foundation counseling skills, the ability to encourage client growth and development in ways that foster the client's interest and welfare, the ability to design collaborative counseling plans, and others. These are competencies implied in the Code of Ethics (ACA) and in the Ethical Standards (ASCA) in which the profession defines those minimum performance standards required of all counselors and all school counselors. In addition to these skills, there are specialized issues—such as gender and cultural identity development, psychosocial development, and family development— that are foundation competencies for counselors working with young people (Lawrence & Kurpius, 2000). Counselors not performing in a manner consistent with these minimum performance standards are considered impaired, are required to seek assistance for their problems, and, if necessary, limit, suspend, or terminate their professional responsibilities (ACA C.2.g.).

Conversely, there will also be skill areas in which you will need additional training to be competent. In this book, we have defined school counseling within the parameters of counseling, educating and advocacy, consultation, and leadership and coordination. Within each of these activities, there will be areas beyond which you might be in danger of practicing beyond the scope of your skills. For example, if you do not have a teaching certificate in your state, you cannot call yourself a teacher; if you do not have the professional qualifications, even though some of your work involves social work-like activities, you cannot call yourself a social worker. This is logical. However, are school counselors the same as family therapists? If you have attended a one-hour workshop on the interpretation of the Myers-Briggs, are you "competent" in its administration and interpretation? These are the gray areas in the concept of competence.

In general, there are established standards of proficiency within the counseling profession to help you answer these questions. For example, most graduate programs in counselor education require a class in appraisal procedures and techniques, assessment, tests and measurement, or some other term referring to training in the evaluation, selection, administration, and interpretation of formal and informal instruments used in counseling. Successful completion of this course in your graduate program qualifies you to administer and interpret master's level assessment instruments. Instruments that are required to be administered by a master's-plus or doctoral-level professionals would be beyond the scope of your competence without such training.

Procedures from other specialty areas, such as marriage and family therapy, may also be beyond the scope of the practice of most school counselors, unless they have additional training in that area (Davis, 2001; Magnuson & Norem, 1998). That is why, in Chapter 11, great care was taken to accurately describe the difference between *family systems counseling* (requiring additional training) and *family problem-solving counseling* (within the scope of the training of a school counselor).

As you develop professionally, you would want to remain aware of the lifelong need for professional development, renewal, and training. What you are learning in your graduate program is not all you will ever need to know to be an effective professional counselor. Remaining competent means you must attend conferences, workshops, and classes; you must be up to date in the professional literature; and you must monitor your effectiveness at all times to ensure that you are providing the best possible service for all your partners in the comprehensive school counseling program.

Clinical Notes

Clinical records in the form of private notes kept in the sole possession of the counselor are not subject to the Family Educational Rights and Privacy Act (FERPA), even though administrative records are. According to Remley and Herman (2000), as long as the counselor does not show them to anyone else, these are considered the counselor's private notes. The only access anyone would have of them is through court order, subpoena, or other legal process. Remley and Herman further suggest that counselors document enough information to jog their memory, "to document events that . . . demonstrate [they] have performed [their] responsibilities in an appropriate and professional manner based on 'standards of practice,'" written in a manner that would be appropriate to read in front of the student and his or her family (p. 317). These authors suggest that all public and private clinical notes be put on a record destruction calendar consistent with the destruction schedule for all records held by the district.

Online Counseling

Technology and its effect on the world cannot be denied, and counseling is not immune to these changes in the world. It is entirely possible that school counselors might be contacted by students, parents, and colleagues who need professional services, but their only or best access to their counselor is from the privacy of their homes. In the event that this occurs, you should be aware that there are specific ethical issues involved in online counseling. To address these issues, the National Board for Certified Counselors (NBCC, 2000) has defined Standards for the Ethical Practice of WebCounseling (available from the Internet at http://www.nbcc.org/ethics/wcstandards.htm, updated June 21, 2000).

The NBCC highlights the following issues:

1. Counselors need to remain aware of their professional obligations in terms of local laws and customs regarding age of consent and child abuse reporting.
2. Counselors should inform clients about encryption methods being used to insure the security of communications.
3. Counselors should inform clients if, how, and how long session data are being preserved.
4. Counselors should take steps to address impostor concerns by using code words, numbers, or graphics.
5. Counselors should verify the identity of the consenting adult when counseling minors.
6. Counselors should follow appropriate procedures regarding the release of information and should work to insure the confidentiality of the WebCounseling relationship.
7. Counselors should carefully consider the extent of self-disclosure to the client, providing the same amount of information to the client that would normally be obtained from face-to-face counseling.
8. Counselors should facilitate consumer protection regarding certification and licensing.
9. Counselors should provide information about on-call and emergency services to clients.
10. Counselors should provide instructions for contacting the counselor when he or she is offline by explaining how often email messages are to be checked by the counselor.
11. Counselors should not provide counseling for the presenting issues of sexual abuse, violence, eating disorders, and other disorders that involve distortions of reality, as these are seen as beyond the ability of the counselor to address effectively in a distance technology format.
12. Counselors should explain to clients the possibility of technology failure in terms of calling if problems arise and addressing response delays in sending and receiving email messages.

13. Counselors explain to clients how to cope with potential misunderstandings arising from the lack of visual or auditory cues from the counselor or the client by asking for clarification.

While the technology exists to provide counseling online, there is no reason to believe that counseling must be delivered using the Internet. It may be an option for various students and counselors, but there is no mandate to make online counseling available to your students. If you choose to use this medium, be aware of the issues and questions surrounding its use and potential misuse by being aware of relevant ethics.

Diversity and Values

While it is ethically mandated that counselors are competent in counseling persons of diversity, not all counselors are equally competent in this area. In terms of cultural diversity, recent studies suggest that school counselors still need additional understanding of racial identity development and multicultural within-group differences (Holcomb-McCoy, 2001), as well as a sense of competence to address cross-cultural issues (Constantine & Yeh, 2001). Many counselors do not attend to multiculturalism as an important part of their work, believing that "Students of color would rather work with someone from their own culture, so why should I pursue training in their culture?" It is clear from recent research that ethnicity is not what helps to establish a strong therapeutic alliance; it is the *perceived similarity* between the counselor's and student's attitudes, values, background, and socioeconomic status (Esters & Ledoux, 2001). "After all, a school counselor who shares a student's attitudes and values and a similar background and socioeconomic status will, by most definitions of culture, share more of the culture and will thus be more similar than a school counselor who is simply a member of the same race. This finding should be encouraging to school counselors who find themselves attempting to build a counseling relationship with a student or a group of students with whom they differ in either race, sex, or both" (p. 169). Understanding racial identity development and multicultural dynamics will help counselors understand more clearly those areas of congruence between their values and attitudes and those of their students.

The establishment of a nurturing counseling relationship is the counselor's responsibility under the moral imperative of beneficence, but there is also a moral imperative to protect from harm (nonmaleficence). Issues of diversity may also extend into the rights of students to have a safe, harassment-free educational environment. Not only does this pertain to students of cultural diversity, it also extends to students of values diversity (religious choice, moral choice) and to students of sexual diversity (gay, lesbian, bisexual, and questioning youth). Schools have a legal obligation to address student-on-student sexual harassment, and schools that do not can be held liable for violating the federal civil rights law under Title IX of the Education Amendments of 1972 (McFarland & Dupuis, 2001). By extension, students who are harassed by virtue of their sexual orientation must be protected and nurtured (McFarland & Dupuis, 2001), and their educational experience must not be marred by sexual violence and harassment (Stone, 2000). Recall that school counselors must report instances of sexual harassment to administration under Title IX, but the identity of the victim may be protected by the student's request for confidentiality, even if it hampers the school's ability to respond to the report (Stone, 2000).

Beyond diversity rests the bigger issue of values differences. Counselors are enjoined from imposing their values on their clients, no matter what the age of the client. Both ACA and ASCA address this specifically in their respective ethical documents, mandating that counselors actively respect the dignity of the client and promote the welfare of the client. It is only through careful self-analysis and self-awareness that counselors can come to articulate their own value system and avoid imposing that value system on clients. (Recall the hearing aid metaphor earlier in the chapter?) To examine how challenging this can be for school counselors, consider the following questions:

1. Do you believe in abortion, the right to life, or does it depend on the situation? Under what conditions do you agree with abortion? Under what conditions would you encourage a student to have the baby?
2. Do you believe in corporal punishment? When does a spanking become a beating? When does striking a young person become child abuse?
3. Do you believe that a 14-year-old is old enough to consent to sexual relationships? With a 15-year-old partner? A 17-year-old? A 19-year-old? How old is old enough to give consent for sex? How old is old enough to give consent for marriage? What is the difference between those concepts?
4. What are your attitudes regarding same-sex relationships?
5. What are your attitudes regarding mixed-race relationships?
6. Hard work is a value also. How would you react to a student who wants to go on welfare rather than work? How would you react to a student who wants to contemplate nature rather than work? Who wants to write a great novel, a great play, a symphony, rather than work? Do your answers differ depending on the situation? Why?
7. Your student defines "fun" as drinking to inebriation. Your spouse "relaxes" the same way—sometimes, you do, too. Why is it OK for you and your spouse, but not for the student? Or is it OK for the student? If marijuana were not illegal, would that be OK?

These questions are just the surface of the values questions faced every day by school counselors. If you aren't careful, your values and your attitudes will be communicated in your work, and then you're in violation of the Ethics. Or are you? You have to begin to think of these issues now.

It is important to note that the intent is to advocate for respectful, inclusive, and safe high schools because everyone has the right to be free from harassment and the inappropriate imposition of another's values, *not just because the counselor or school wants to avoid being sued*. The intent is to reinforce our belief that respect, inclusiveness, and safety are the right conditions under which to educate young people, no matter who they are. Our laws and ethics make it our moral imperative to protect all young people and to promote their healthy development.

Professional Liability, Insurance, and Certification

Many school counseling students are surprised and alarmed when they learn that they may be sued in the course of their work as a school counselor. With the rise in student risk behaviors, suicides, and school violence, the duty to warn and protect takes on a much heavier burden than in previous years (Remley & Herman, 2000; Simpson, 1999). School counselors may be held liable for breach of confidentiality, negligence, or malpractice, for providing inadequate services, and for not protecting the student from suicide and/or threats of harm from others.

But aren't school counselors covered by the insurance of the school? Not if the interest of the school and the interest of the counselor are different (Remley & Herman, 2000). If the charges suggest that the counselor acted in contradiction to school policy, the counselor's interests and the district's interests may be very different. To distance itself from fiscal liability, the district may suspend or dismiss the counselor, claiming that the counselor was not acting on behalf of the district when the problem behavior occurred. For example, a counselor is charged with sexual harassment of students. The school has a policy against sexual harassment and will dismiss or suspend the counselor when the complaint is filed. In this way, the school minimizes its liability, and the defense used by the school's attorney will be to locate the blame on the accused, thereby distancing the school from responsibility and reducing the monetary judgment. The counselor must now obtain legal services, paying out-of-pocket for attorney's fees and any judgments against him or her.

It is for this reason that school counselors are urged to obtain their own professional liability insurance ("Personal Liability Insurance," 2000; Remley & Herman, 2000). Such insurance is available through membership in the national counseling professional associations: the American Counseling Association and the American School Counselor Association. (Contact these organizations via the Internet to learn more about professional liability insurance.)

Factors that may mitigate the cost of such liability insurance are professional licenses and certifications. In addition to state certification and/or licensure for school counselors, school counselors may want to consider national certification as a counselor and/or school counselor through the National Board of Certified Counselors (NBCC). This additional level of professional recognition is obtained through successful completion of the National Counselor Exam (NCE), a comprehensive exam offered around the country, and documented postgraduate experience. This qualifies counselors to become Nationally Certified Counselors, or NCCs. With additional documented hours of school counseling experience, counselors can qualify to become Nationally Certified School Counselors, or NCSCs. Continued credentialing with these certifications require additional professional development and education. To obtain more information about these certifications at the national level, you can contact the NBCC through its website: http://www.nbcc.org.

Responding to Legal Action

The first thing most counselors do when they are served with legal papers is become very anxious. But it is not necessary to panic. If you are served with a subpoena for records, information, and/or testimony, the following steps are recommended *before you comply with the court order*:

1. Consult with professional colleagues about the situation.
2. Consult with your administration about the situation.
3. Consult with the school's or the school district's attorney.
4. Consult with your state and/or national professional school counseling association.

5. Review your documents about the situation.
6. Be prepared to protest the subpoena in court, arguing that the information in your possession is not relevant or appropriate. This protects the confidential nature of the counseling relationship.
7. If necessary, obtain legal advice on your own.
8. If the subpoena is for testimony at a custody hearing, Remley and Herman recommend that you do not become voluntarily involved. If you are forced to testify, limit your testimony to only factual information, not your opinions on the competence of one parent over the other. (Remley & Herman, 2000)

Resources and Recommendations for School Counselors

There are a variety of resources pertaining to ethics, laws, policies, and other issues. The end of the ASCA Ethical Standards for School Counselors (Appendix A) lists resources, phone numbers, and web addresses for the American Counseling Association (ACA), the American School Counselor Association (ASCA), the Association for Specialists in Group Work, the National Board for Certified Counselors, and the National Peer Helpers Association, as well as the references for articles and books about ethics from leaders in the profession. In addition, membership in your national and state counseling and school counseling associations entitles you to professional consultation with peers, most often through an ethics committee. Listservs may also be a way of communicating with professional peers to obtain feedback about ethical issues, but due to the public nature of the list discussions, caution would be necessary to protect confidentiality.

Strategies for establishing and maintaining your work as an ethical school counselor include:

1. Obtain supervision periodically from a peer. This involves inviting feedback from a colleague about your counseling, educating and advocacy, consultation, and leadership skills. Most supervision focuses on counseling skills, however. This could be done in a conversational format but is most effective when done with a video or audiotape of your counseling with a student client. Due to confidentiality issues, you would need to ensure that you have permission from the student and the student's parents or guardians to tape counseling for supervision purposes.
2. Read on ethics in the professional literature. For example, take the ethics quiz (Huey, Salo, & Fox, 1995). Check your answers for accuracy in both the current ACA Code and the ASCA Ethical Standards because they have been revised since the quiz was written.
3. Take additional workshops, courses, and/or conference sessions on current issues in ethics.
4. Keep current on contemporary issues in counseling: counseling strategies, new theories and techniques, and client issues. All of these areas are constantly evolving, and you must remain informed in each of them.
5. Obtain professional consultation as needed with peers about national, state, and local issues in schools and in school counseling (Ledyard, 1998). Networking with colleagues is essential.

6. Do not limit yourself to contact with school counselors alone. You need a broader perspective, so become networked with community, college, rehabilitation, and other counselors in your area.

7. You must have an effective referral network in place, so you must know the resources in your community. Learn about these professionals in terms of who they help, how they help, where they are located, how much they cost, and other details.

8. To avoid working in a setting with which you have an ethical difference of opinion, inquire into administrative policy during the interview to determine if you can live with its administrative philosophy (Tompkins & Mehring, 1993). For example, you can ask the interviewer about his or her experiences, positive and negative, with school counseling. Listen for areas in the response that indicate a lack of awareness or appreciation for important counseling issues such as confidentiality, parental consent, and mandated reporting.

9. You must know the laws for your state (Tompkins & Mehring, 1993). This involves some digging on your part, but you have to know what your state requires you to know *before* you step into a school.

10. You must be able to work with persons who hold different values than you do. Research continues to show that the best way to understand diversity is to know diverse persons; get to know people from many walks of life on a personal level. It is only through being open to diversity that you can truly know and become comfortable with various value systems. It is then that you can see, underneath the diversity, those common threads that bind us all.

A Day in the Life Revisited: Integration

Now that you've read the chapter, go back and reread Jason's Casual Comment.

1. What was the comment he made that created the situation?
2. If Kim's comment was related to sexual activity, what do you think Jason should do? What are the questions you would like to ask her? What else do you need to know before you can act?
3. Assume that Kim's comment was not related to sexual activity. Now what are the questions you would like to ask her?
4. What do you believe is the appropriate level of parental involvement in this situation? What is the appropriate level of school involvement? Under what conditions, specifically, would you be mandated to report? List all of them.
5. How have *your* values shaped the answers you gave to these questions?

Application _____

1. Return to the section on values and respond in writing to the questions posed.

2. Go to the Internet and obtain the addresses for the codes of ethics for the ACA, ASCA, NBCC,

and any professional associations in your state that address school counseling. Record these for your files.

3. If your state's statutes are accessible on the Internet, access those that pertain to child protection legislation and record the address for your files.

4. Search the Internet for more information on each of the laws named in this chapter. Print or download what you believe pertains to school counseling. Record those addresses for your files.

5. Interview a high school counselor about her or his experience with ethical dilemmas. Take one of those scenarios and work through the ethical decision making model proposed by Stadler. Did you arrive at the same ethical decision that counselor did? Why or why not?

6. Outline all the situations you can imagine in which you would violate a student's confidentiality. Take that list and organize it into a plan for informed consent that you would use with a high school student. Include in that informed consent document everything that ACA indicates must be included in informed consent.

7. Design a letter that you could send to parents explaining everything needed to meet the ACA criteria of informed consent, asking for their permission to counsel their student.

8. Go to the NBCC website and find out everything you need to be certified at the national level. List all the reasons for and against such certification in a Pro/Con format. Would you pursue additional certifications at the national level? Why or why not?

Suggested Readings

Isaacs, M. L., & Stone, C. (1999). School counselors and confidentiality: Factors affecting professional choices. *Professional School Counseling, 2,* 258–266. This article presents a study in which school counselors at various levels respond to hypothetical situations, involving age- and situation-specific concerns, in which they would break confidentiality. The findings highlight the unique perspectives of high school counselors juxtaposed with those of middle and elementary schools.

Herlihy, B., & Corey, G. (1996). *ACA ethical standards casebook* (5th ed.). Alexandria, VA: American Counseling Association. This book presents the ethics of the ACA with illustrative vignettes and discussion chapters written by experts in the field.

Sealander, K. A., Schwiebert, V. L., Oren, T. A., & Weekley, J. L. (1999). Confidentiality and the law. *Professional School Counseling, 3,* 122–127. This article presents current information relative to the laws affecting confidentiality in schools.

References

American Counseling Association. (1995). *Code of ethics and standards of practice.* Alexandria, VA: Author.

Butler, E. R. (1993, March). *Basic principles for ethical decision making.* A paper presented at the meeting of the National Association for Student Personnel Administrators, Boston, MA.

Christopher, J. C. (1996). Counseling's inescapable moral visions. *Journal of Counseling and Development, 75,* 17–25.

Constantine, M. G., & Yeh, C. J. (2001). Multicultural training, self-construals, and multicultural competence of school counselors. *Professional School Counseling, 4,* 202–207.

Davis, K. M. (2001). Structural-strategic family counseling: A case study in elementary school counseling. *Professional School Counseling, 4,* 180–186.

Davis, T., & Ritchie, M. (1993). Confidentiality and the school counselor: A challenge for the 1990s. *The School Counselor, 41,* 23–30.

Erk, R. R. (1999). Attention deficit hyperactivity disorders: Counselors, laws, and implications for practice. *Professional School Counseling, 2,* 318–326.

Esters, I., & Ledoux, C. (2001). At risk high school students' preference for counselor characteristics. *Professional School Counseling, 4,* 165–170.

Hall, A. S., & Lin, M. (1995). Theory and practice of children's rights: Implications for mental health counselors. *Journal of Mental Health Counseling, 17,* 63–80.

Herlihy, B., & Corey, G. (1996). *ACA ethical standards casebook* (5th ed.). Alexandria, VA: American Counseling Association.

Holcomb-McCoy, C. C. (2001). Exploring the self-perceived multicultural counseling competencies of elementary school counselors. *Professional School Counseling, 4,* 195–201.

Huey, W. C., Salo, M. M., & Fox, R. W. (1995). An ethics quiz for school counselors. *The School Counselor, 42,* 393–398.

Isaacs, M. L., & Stone, C. (1999). School counselors and confidentiality: Factors affecting professional choices. *Professional School Counseling, 2,* 258–266.

Kaplan, D., & Allison, M. C. (1994). Family ethics. *Family Journal, 2*(1), 54–57. Retrieved on February 7, 2001, from the EBSCO database available on the World Wide Web: http://ehost . . .l.

Kaplan, L. S. (1996). Outrageous or legitimate concerns: What some parents are saying about school counseling. *The School Counselor, 43,* 165–170.

Lawrence, G., & Kurpius, S. E. R. (2000). Legal and ethical issues involved when counseling minors in nonschool settings. *Journal of Counseling and Development, 78,* 130–136.

Ledyard, P. (1998). Counseling minors: Ethical and legal issues. *Counseling and Values, 42*(3), 171–198. Retrieved February 7, 2001, from the EBSCO database, available on the World Wide Web: http://ehost . . .

Magnuson, S., & Norem, K. (1998). A school counselor asks: "Am I prepared to do what I'm asked to do?" *Family Journal, 6*(2), 137–140. Retrieved January 23, 2001, from the EBSCO database available on the World Wide Web: http://www.ehostv . . .school.

McFarland, W. P., & Dupuis, M. (2001). The legal duty to protect gay and lesbian students from violence in school. *Professional School Counseling, 4,* 171–179.

National Board of Certified Counselors (NBCC). (2000). *Standards for the ethical practice of WebCounseling.* Retrieved March 27, 2001, from the World Wide Web: http://www.nbcc.org/ethics/wcstandards.htm.

Personal liability insurance: Do you need your own policy? (2000, March/April). *The ASCA Counselor, 37,* 24.

Remley, T. P., & Herman, M. (2000). Legal and ethical issues in school counseling. In J. Wittmer (Ed.), *Managing your school counseling program: K–12 developmental strategies* (2nd ed.; pp. 314–329). Minneapolis, MN: Educational Media.

Schmidt, J. J. (1999). *Counseling in schools: Essential services and comprehensive programs* (3rd ed.). Boston: Allyn and Bacon.

Sealander, K. A., Schwiebert, V. L., Oren, T. A., & Weekley, J. L. (1999). Confidentiality and the law. *Professional School Counseling, 3,* 122–127.

Simpson, M. D. (1999, February). Student suicide: Who's liable? *NEA Today, 17,* 25–26. Retrieved January 23, 2001, from the EBSCO database available on the World Wide Web: http://ehostv . . .school.

Stadler, H. A. (1985). *Confidentiality: The professional's dilemma: Participant's manual.* Alexandria, VA: American Counseling Association.

Stone, C. B. (2000). Advocacy for sexual harassment victims: Legal support and ethical aspects. *Professional School Counseling, 4,* 23–30.

Strein, W., & Hershenson, D. B. (1991). Confidentiality in nondyadic counseling situations. *Journal of Counseling and Development, 69,* 312–316.

Tompkins, L., & Mehring, T. (1993). Client privacy and the school counselor: Privilege, ethics, and employer policies. *The School Counselor, 40,* 335–342.

Watson, C. H. (1990). Gossip and the guidance counselor: An ethical dilemma. *The School Counselor, 38,* 35–39.

16

Professional Issues

Colette T. Dollarhide

"What scares me about the future? I worry most about finding a well-paying job that I like and having time with my family."

Erik, age 19

Learning Objectives _____

By the end of this chapter, you will:

1. Understand the challenges of secondary school counseling in terms of holistic life management.
2. Understand the relationship between personal balance and professional health.
3. Understand the limitations of school counselors and how to deal with those limitations.
4. Have some concrete strategies for addressing the stress of professional school counseling.
5. Discuss the development of professional identity.
6. Identify the need for professional supervision.
7. Understand how consultation and networking can alleviate feelings of isolation.
8. Discuss the need for continued education as a professional school counselor.
9. Understand the role of involvement with professional associations in terms of membership, leadership, conference attendance, and contributing to the profession through conference presentations.
10. Identify the benefits of involvement with action research for district information as well as professional publications.
11. Understand the strategies for locating and engaging a mentor to enhance your professional development, as well as understanding the benefits of serving as a mentor to other professionals.
12. Understand the importance of technology in school counseling and the need to remain current with technological developments.

A Day in the Life of a Counselor: Emilita's Turn to Learn

Emilita's week was not turning out as she had hoped. Here it was, only Wednesday, and she was already looking forward to the weekend; spring break was a distant memory, and the year seemed like it would never end. She came out of the building to go home, only to find she had a flat tire on her car. She waited in her car for the repair truck and thought about her week so far.

On Monday, she had gotten the first bit of bad news: The district was not going to replace Jose's position, so they were going from four counselors down to three. And student needs were higher than ever—their graduation rate for girls was down with so many girls getting pregnant these last two years. Most of them were attending the alternative high school program for young mothers, but those girls weren't counted as part of their graduation rate. Then, with the homeless shelter opening up down the street from the high school, they had several students in and out within weeks—a lot of time spent there with scheduling and transition services, only to have them leave within a couple of days. Every year, the counselors worked with more students with greater needs, but weren't going to have one-fourth of their staff next year.

Then, yesterday, Emilita had gotten her annual professional performance review. She was not pleased with her review. She was supposed to learn email and the new school registration and student record package, but she had not had enough time last year to learn those things. The final report on the grant funds from last year still wasn't done. She was also supposed to conduct an in-service for the staff on the workshop she attended on reactive attachment disorder, but she never got around to that either. And even though she was elected to serve on the state's advisory council for professional school counseling, she had not attended any meetings. Emilita thought she worked hard enough; she deserved the time she took off to relax. Besides, she was trying to spend more time with students, but there were so many other things that got in the way. The director of pupil services for the district had judged her too harshly for these other minor failings. Didn't central office care about the professional counselors at all?

Now this flat. Sighing, she checked her watch. Another twenty minutes before the truck would come. She decided to go back into the building to go to the restroom. Inside, she ducked into the closest girls' bathroom. Within seconds, several girls entered, and Emilita became an unwilling witness to the conversation.

One voice said, "Yeah, she said the counselor didn't really understand anything she was telling her. Ms. Dorado just kept pushing her to tell her mother, tell her mother, you know? She said it really made her mad that Ms. Dorado wasn't listening to her. I thought counselors were supposed to listen to you!"

The second voice laughed. "Maybe it's just a problem with time. I know every time I go to talk to Ms. Dorado, she has about 5 minutes for me, then she has to go to another meeting, or whatever it is that counselors do. No one can ever find her. No one seems to know what the heck she does. You know what I think? I think she's getting it on with Mr. Fenman in math. I see them together in the faculty lounge all the time." Both voices giggled.

"Picture that! Dorado and Fenman! Well, that would explain why she's never around when you need her. No one I know has ever gotten any help from her! They should fire her. Everyone always goes to the other counselors. She's a big joke. She never does what she says she's going to do. You know that new kid? He said she was supposed to get back to him with changes in his schedule, but she never did . . ." The voices moved toward the door, then faded as the conversation moved out into the hallway.

Emilita wanted to cry. She waited until the voices were out in the hall, then she went back out to wait in her car. Deep in thought, she didn't even see the repair truck arrive. She jumped a mile when the driver came to her window and asked, "Are you Emilita Dorado? You called for a tire repair?"

Challenge Questions

What was your reaction as you read the scenario? What conclusions did you come to about the counselor's job performance? What were some areas for potential improvement that you could see?

If you were this counselor, you could choose to ignore the feedback or you could choose to learn from it. What would *your* choice be?

Personal Mental Health: The Search for Balance

Life is a series of choices, and we are all responsible for our choices. We can choose to live life out of balance, either self-focused and self-absorbed (me-first), or other-focused ("I'll give you my soul if you will just approve of me"). Both of these lifestyles are out of balance and unhealthy, causing problems in both work and personal life. One is no better than the other.

"Balance" can be conceptualized as the means by which the needs of the internal reality and the external reality are brought into alignment. It is the boundary between two mutually exclusive realms, the point at which both meet. In creative thinking, this boundary is between imaginary and visceral, between logical and intuitive, between body and mind, between science and art (DeBono, 1992; Gruber, 1993; Morris, 1992; Root-Bernstein & Root-Bernstein, 1999). For the purposes of this book, we will view balance as the need to nurture both the personal needs and the professional needs of the counselor, to the benefit of both aspects of existence. To function well as a counselor, you need to understand how to take care of your personal issues and needs while simultaneously taking care of the needs of your partners in the DAP model. Without balance, your personal needs will be acted out and will drive your professional choices, or your professional needs will compromise your personal self mentally, physically, and/or emotionally. Counselors are the models for mental health in the schools; counselors living with these out-of-balance conditions compromise both their own and other counselors' credibility and ability to function.

In general, there are many sources of stress for a school counselor. Stress comes from the working with others who don't understand the work that counselors do, from struggles of the students, and from budgets that do not keep up with needs. Other stressors include a lack of privacy and anonymity due to heightened visibility as a mental health professional and feelings of isolation resulting from a lack of professional peers within the school setting (Morrissette, 2000). We cannot change the context or realities of the job; what we can do is understand and prepare for ways to counteract these stressors.

In Chapter 1, we discussed the professional competencies for school counselors as outlined by the Council for the Accreditation of Counseling and Related Educational Programs (CACREP), and the rest of this book has been designed to help you to develop those competencies. In Chapter 1, we also outlined the personal qualities that professional school counselors need: creativity and imagination, flexibility, courage and faith, and passion. These are the antidotes for the stressors of working as a secondary school counselor. This chapter is devoted to helping you to evaluate and refine those personal qualities that typify the best secondary school counselors.

Where do these qualities come from? They are partly the result of temperament and they are partly the result of personal and professional health. We can't change temperament, but we can put practices in place to maximize our personal and professional health.

Finding Your Center

The term "center" is used in this context to refer to various aspects of our existence. It is used to refer to a spiritual center, involving our relationship with a higher power or higher purpose, and to a moral center, involving our relationship with our own values and morals.

Our awareness of our own values and morals is a crucial piece of being able to understand ourselves and, by extension, our clients. Since many concepts within our traditional definitions of "mental health" resonate with Western values of individualism, autonomy, environmental mastery, self-acceptance, happiness, and purpose in life, we must understand our own moral center and openly dialogue with clients about the "ongoing interpretive process" between our moral center and theirs (Christopher, 1999, p. 150). This inner work has implications both for helping our student clients and for helping us work on our own issues. It is necessary for our connection with our clients; it is also necessary for our connection with our inner resources. In this context, finding our moral center involves reflection and insight, which requires quiet, compassion, patience, and a commitment to deepening our self-understanding.

Palmer refers to this as "sounding our own depths" (1998, p. 31). The importance of this depth of self-knowledge is reflected in what Palmer believes are truths about our work as educators: "[w]hat we teach will never 'take' unless it connects with the inward, living core of our students' lives, with our students' inward teachers. . . . We can speak to the teacher within our students only when we are on speaking terms with the teacher within ourselves. . . . Deep speaks to deep, and when we have not sounded our own depths, we cannot sound the depths of our students' lives" (Palmer, 1998, p. 31). Palmer reinforces the connection between our inner reality and our outer work and challenges us to develop an ongoing dialogue with our own inner teachers. These inner teachers are the source of our professionalism, our desire to help others grow, and ultimately, our wisdom.

Other authors use the term "spirit" and "wisdom" to describe this sense of connection between self, others, and higher purpose. Fox (1994) suggests that education of the whole person—heart, body, mind, and spirit; books and life; intellect and imagination—should be a part of our curriculum, where students learn awe, wisdom, compassion, and inner growth. This new vision of education would transform the role of counselors, giving additional support to the idea that counselors must know their own center to help students locate and nurture theirs.

In another context, Young-Eisendrath and Miller (2000) examine the connection between spiritual development and health. "[W]e regard spiritual development to be a necessary component of a healthy, effective life as a human being. . . . Mature spirituality is the honing of integrity, wisdom, and transcendence in the service of the question of what it means to be human . . ." (p. 5). As counselors or teachers, educators or human beings, there is support for the idea that being centered fosters the elements needed to maintain balance in life. It is from our "center," or core, that we find the spring from which creativity, imagination, flexibility, courage, faith, and passion flow. If we drain this spring dry, we have nothing left to give others. If we dam the flow to save all these precious qualities, we are no longer of service to our DAP partners. We must be able to dip from the spring as needed to replenish ourselves, while monitoring the flow to ensure enough reserves for the future.

Reflection Moment

Where do you go to get centered? How often do you go there? Do you need to go there more often?

Doing Your Best, Then Letting Go

One of the most difficult lessons for new counselors is learning when to let go. When do you know you've done all you can to help a student, parent, co-worker? When is enough *enough*?

In general, as with any counseling situation, the first step comes with the recognition that each of us is responsible for our own choices in life. As counselors, it is our job to make sure the door to change is open and that the client's movement toward healthy choices is applauded and commended. We can open the door, we can make the "healthy" side of the door attractive and appealing, we can point out the costs of remaining on the other side of the door, but we cannot force anyone to walk through the door. We are only human, with all the limitations that implies. But we are obligated by profession and training to give 100 percent in these efforts to persuade someone to make healthy choices.

With adults, I feel comfortable leaving that much of the choice with the client. However, with young people, I can't help but encourage you to give an extra effort to helping them. In keeping with the metaphor, consider giving 110 percent. School counselors should open the door, encourage student-clients to walk through the door, make the other side of the door very unappealing, and invite them again to walk over that threshold. When does enough constitute enough? Only you can answer that for yourself. What can *you* live with, without compromising your own personal and professional health?

"Letting go" involves an additional concept inherent in counseling in general: that of time. Change takes place when the *client* is ready, and not a moment before. The client needs time to evaluate the risks and benefits of walking through the door to change. If a client, in spite of the counselor's best efforts in giving 110 percent, chooses not to walk over the threshold, "letting go" involves the recognition that the client, for his or her own reasons, is not ready to change yet. Many of the most meaningful conversations counselors have with students are those that take place years after the students have left the school, in which students share with the counselors how meaningful the counselors' interventions were all those years ago.

In this way, there is a strong similarity between counseling and parenting. Often, it's not until we reach our twenties that we realize what our parents were trying to tell us in our teens, that the lessons they were trying to teach us really did have value after all. Just as good parents must let go of their children to allow them to learn their lessons, so too must good counselors. Sometimes the best lessons come from bruised knees or bruised egos, and we can't save them from the lessons life has to teach them.

Reflection Moment

Have you had experience with finding the limit of your professional endurance? Have you had to make the difficult choice to let go? What was that experience like for you?

Stress Management Strategies

As school counselors, you will have many opportunities to talk with your DAP partners about stress. Adolescents and adults alike can benefit tremendously from understanding how stress affects decision making; physical, emotional, and spiritual health; and relationships. Stress compromises performance, erodes stamina, and disables the natural resilience of both body and spirit. But stress cannot be avoided; it is a natural part of our everyday existence and keeps us striving to improve ourselves and our lives (Seaward, 1994). The best we can do is understand and manage stress, since it cannot be eradicated.

First, it is important to understand that stress comes from the way we interpret and internalize events in our lives. Any given event does not cause stress; the emotions we experience as a result of our *beliefs about these events* are the sources of stress. Our beliefs about the "fairness" of life, our "right" to happiness, the way we "deserve" to be treated by life and others often result in anger, frustration, fear, and indignation. Of these, the strongest stress triggers are the emotions of anger and fear (Seaward, 1994). These emotional states, in turn, trigger physiological responses that involve the nervous system and the immune system, which in turn telegraph our internal emotional states into physical reality (Seaward, 1994).

The ultimate anti-stress weapon, according to Seaward (1994), is self-esteem. It is strong self-esteem that allows us to keep fear from hijacking our nervous and immune systems. With strong self-esteem, we are less likely to catastrophize events in our lives, and we are better able to bounce back from life's inevitable disappointments and frustrations. You will undoubtedly notice that many of the strategies for managing stress are designed to enhance this fragile and elusive quality.

Managing stress can be accomplished in a variety of ways. The following stress management strategies are adapted from Seaward (1994).

1. Enhance your spiritual connection with your internal reality. Be centered within all elements of your identity. Get to know yourself well and explore your inner reality with compassion.
2. Enhance your spiritual connections with however you perceive and define the Divine. Seaward provides an excellent reading list, including various perspectives on spirituality—Carl Jung, M. Scott Peck, Black Elk, Matthew Fox, Joan Borysenko, Jesus Christ, Lao Tzu, and Albert Einstein—that are then woven into some common themes of spirituality.
3. Enhance your spiritual connections with loving others, to increase healthy bonding, acceptance, peace, compassion, and respect in your daily life.
4. Explore and define your personal value system, so that you live with greater congruence and authenticity within that value system.
5. Explore and define a meaningful purpose for your life: Have goals to achieve, serve to promote love and respect in the world, or have some purpose to fill. This helps you keep your life in perspective and allows you to better handle disappointments and pain.
6. Explore the connection between your thoughts, expectations, and experiences to determine if you could restructure your cognitions to reduce your experience of stress.
7. Learn and practice assertiveness skills to help you maintain healthy boundaries.
8. Consider journaling as a means of exploring your feelings and experiences.
9. Use art therapy to tap, explore, and/or release your feelings about your experiences.
10. Use humor therapy to cope with disappointments and frustrations. It is important to recognize that there are healthy and unhealthy applications of humor—those that enhance connection, compassion, and relief are healthy, those that ridicule or demean others are not healthy. To foster stress relief, humor used in a healthy way can build

connections with others, reframe experiences, and allow us to view ourselves, others, and our world with more hope and compassion.

11. Use creative problem-solving strategies, such as brainstorming, brainwriting, clustering, and metaphors. Effective problem solving fosters self-efficacy and self-esteem.

12. Enhance your communication skills. Much of the stress of life comes from difficult relationships with others; communicating more effectively can substantially improve our relationships.

13. Improve your time management skills. Having an efficient means of allocating and accounting for time can help you manage the busy schedule of a secondary school counselor. Recall the program definition and prioritization process discussed in Chapter 5 and revisited in Chapter 14.

14. Consider a support group to help you cope with your own unique life situation.

15. Having a hobby can increase your social connections and creativity.

16. Forgiveness and prayer can be a healthy outlet for stress.

17. Taking care of your body is also essential. The primary strategies for taking care of yourself involve a three-prong approach:

> Exercise with a physician's approval
>
> Proper nutrition that supports a healthy lifestyle
>
> Relaxation
>
> The following is a list of possible relaxation strategies:
>
> a. Diaphragmatic breathing.
> b. Meditation.
> c. Hatha yoga (meditation, breathing, and various body postures).
> d. Mental imagery (taking a mental vacation!).
> e. Music therapy.
> f. Massage therapy.
> g. T'ai Chi Ch'uan (movement, breathing, and concentration).
> h. Progressive muscular relaxation.
> i. Autogenic training.
> j. Biofeedback.

These ideas are offered as a means of promoting your holistic well-being and health. After all, if you're not healthy, you will not be of much use to your students or adult partners!

Reflection Moment

How do you know when you're having problems with your stress level? How do you deal with stress? Are there stress management strategies that you can put into place now to help you deal with the stress of graduate school?

Professional Health

A counselor's professional health is also an issue of this chapter. While there is substantial overlap between your personal and professional health, the strategies of this section are designed to help you address the *work-related* challenges of secondary school counselors. Many of the challenges faced by school counselors have already been discussed, but an overview here might help you understand the context of this discussion.

1. Counselors often feel isolated since there are limited numbers of counselors in any given district or building.
2. The role of the counselor is not well understood by parents, students, teachers, or administrators.
3. Counselors are often defined as ancillary services, not central to the functioning of the school.
4. Counselors' time often is eroded by activities that are not essential for the effective functioning of the comprehensive school counseling program.
5. There is little recognition for the hard work counselors do.
6. There may be little privacy for school counselors and their families in communities where school professionals are well known.
7. There are tremendous needs among all the partners—students, families, co-workers, and entire communities look to the school counselor to address a variety of problems.
8. Information about ways of helping, perspectives on new or emerging problems, and technology are always evolving.
9. Burnout is high in the helping professions, and opportunities to "re-charge one's batteries" are few.

Below are some ideas to help you mitigate the effects of these challenges.

Professional Identity

School counselors undergo an identifiable process in the development of a professional identity. It is helpful to have an overview of this process to understand how unique and diverse school counseling programs evolve. According to Brott and Myers (1999), this process involves the slow internalization of external standards and priorities. At first, the school counselor defines his or her role solely in external terms, derived first from graduate training and secondarily from the school and/or district administrators, other counselors, and existing programs. In the middle of this developmental process, school counselors interact with a variety of perspectives that provide feedback about the program as conducted by the school counselor. In other words, the counselor confronts a wide variety of evaluative voices (p. 344). In the final stage of professional development, the school counselor uses personal judgments in the definition of the role of the school counselor and in the design and definition of the comprehensive school counseling program. These personal judgments are now defensible as coming from professional experience and perspective, as professional and personal identities merge, unify, and solidify.

This process explains why it is difficult for new counselors to engage in strong advocacy for the professional identity of all school counselors. For the most part, the development of this professional "voice" does not manifest until the third stage of the process as outlined by Brott and Myers (1999). In spite of how difficult advocacy may be, one of the most important ways school counselors can work to mitigate the problems of the profession is through enhancing the identity and professionalism of the counseling profession in general, and the school counseling profession in particular. Johnson (2000) argues that school counselors must "refine their professional identity as highly trained practitioners, whose goal is to facilitate all students to become effective learners through the provision of a contemporary, integrated school counseling program that promotes the achievement of developmentally based competencies across academic, career, and personal/social domains . . . [T]heir operational identity needs to be shifted from focusing on the individual services they provide to focusing on the integrated school counseling program as a whole. Similarly, their . . . target of services needs to move from being the individual student to the school system as a whole . . ." (p. 32). To accomplish this, school counselors must align their mission as congruent with the academic mission of the school and document ways in which their work helps students to become effective learners (Johnson, 2000). Education of the DAP partners, advocacy for the role of the school counselor, and leadership of the program in terms of leadership teams of the school and district will help provide a common ground from which school counselors can establish their contribution to students and the school.

Documentation of these contributions is also essential, and the professional portfolio provides a venue for that documentation (Boes, VanZile-Tamsen, & Jackson, 2001; James & Greenwalt, 2001; Johnson, 2000). Portfolios are the compilation and maintenance of various "artifacts" (documents, photographs, letters, disks, audio- and videotapes, computer disks—any work-related product) that describe and validate one's work history. James and Greenwalt (2001) refine this definition even further, describing the elements of a "working portfolio" as the documentation of one's entire professional development, and the "presentation portfolio" as a select portion of the working portfolio that is used for a specific purpose (a job interview or a consulting presentation, for example).

Elements of the working portfolio would include (adapted from Boes, VanZile-Tamsen, & Jackson, 2001; James & Greenwalt, 2001; Johnson, 2000):

1. Your philosophy of education.
2. Your philosophy of comprehensive school counseling.
3. Curriculum vita (a comprehensive overview of all work locations, dates, and duties, and all educational experiences, courses, workshops, and conferences).
4. Resume (a summary of those work and educational experiences).
5. Practicum and internship experiences.
6. Results of work projects (such as new programs, surveys, grant proposals, needs assessments, outcomes assessments, reports).
7. Professional credentials, such as licenses, certifications, or endorsements.
8. Continuing education courses, workshops, or presentations you have attended, with dates, locations, and presenters noted.
9. Presentations you've made (including developmental curriculum lessons, workshops, in-services, and/or groups you have conducted).

10. Publications you have authored (including in-house publications such as brochures, flyers, or handbooks for students, parents, faculty, etc.).
11. Professional memberships, including dates and offices held.
12. Service to school, district, and/or community in terms of committee membership, volunteer positions, etc.
13. Results of any counselor efficacy studies or outcomes assessment cycles you've been a part of (refer to Chapter 14 to refresh your memory about outcomes assessments).

Presentation portfolios, as mentioned, are selected artifacts from the work portfolio that serve to document a focused selection of your professional history. For example, if your state has specific competencies that must be documented for licensure, you might use a presentation portfolio for that purpose. Boes, VanZile-Tamsen, and Jackson (2001) suggest that you organize this special portfolio using the National Standards for School Counseling Programs (Appendix B), and include a reflective self-evaluation. A more common example of a presentation portfolio is one that is used for purposes of a job search, in which the applicant takes the presentation portfolio to the interview to share with the search committee. A note of interest: electronic portfolios, those stored to a disk, CD, or available on a webpage, are increasingly viewed as "cutting edge" for counselors who must be able to function in this age of technology.

Supervision

It is clear from the literature that there are problems in the field in terms of supervision of counselors. Supervision can be conceptualized in terms of three functions:

1. *Administrative supervision*, involving accounting for time, daily attendance, communication skills, adherence to school policies; may be provided by building or district administrator.
2. *Program supervision*, involving feedback relative to the progress of the comprehensive school counseling program; may be provided by district pupil services administrator.
3. *Technical, clinical, or counseling supervision*, involving feedback on counseling, intervention, and developmental curriculum delivery skills; best if provided by a more experienced counselor (Roberts & Borders, 1994; Schmidt, 1990).

It is important that you understand that each of the three supervision venues listed above is designed to accomplish a unique purpose. The first is to help you function in the school setting; the second, to help you function in an effective comprehensive school counseling program; and the third, to help you function effectively with students, families, and colleagues.

As a counseling trainee, you will receive supervision from a supervising counselor. As a professional, you will be supervised by a number of supervisors, depending on the way the district designates personnel for the three supervision functions listed above. The most common scenario is supervision by a senior counselor for clinical and program supervision, and supervision by the principal for the administrative supervision. Depending on the district, the district pupil services director may also provide program supervision (which is good if this person has a counseling background). It is a challenge when a noncounselor is designated for any other type of supervision than administrative supervision, for good reason. Noncounselors usually do not have adequate understanding of the counseling profession, and it will be up to you to educate that person about counseling.

While there is no shortage of people in the schools who will give you feedback about how you are doing your job, there is a general hands-off philosophy among counselors in terms of clinical supervision. But this kind of supervision, *especially for new professionals in the field*, can be extremely helpful in your development of a sense of professional efficacy (Crespi, Fischetti, & Butler, 2001). In spite of a lack of supervisors in the field who have received training in supervision (Kahn, 1999; Roberts & Morotti, 2001), you are urged to voluntarily solicit clinical feedback. The ideal situation would involve obtaining this supervision from an experienced counselor, but a study of *peer group supervision* suggested substantial professional advantages accrued to the participants (Agnew, Vaught, Getz, & Fortune, 2000). Specifically, 97 percent of the twenty-nine participants cited positive growth in clinical skills, increased sense of professionalism, increased consultation and referral skills, increased confidence, increased comfort with the job, decreased feelings of burnout, and increased professional validation. In addition, supervision is an important strategy to improve ethical counseling (Herlihy & Corey, 1996).

Colleague Consultation and Networking

There is very little in this world that can help us feel better about our situation than consulting and networking with others. While there may be few formal opportunities to network with your school counseling colleagues, nothing prevents you from initiating a "counselors' lunch" once a month or once a semester. Some counselors take advantage of in-service time provided by the district to call a meeting of the counselors and/or pupil services professionals to discuss issues of importance in the district and community. In this situation, the director of pupil services is usually involved to help design the official agenda.

In addition, one-on-one consultation with your peers can establish resources and expertise that can help you do your job more effectively. This consultation is not limited to counselors; other pupil services professionals, as we discussed in Chapter 14, provide a rich source of perspectives and expertise.

Both formal and informal networks are essential to your professional survival. It is important that you have opportunities to understand the challenges facing the entire community and district—how can you design systemic interventions and build community in your school if you can't build it among your colleagues and peers?

Continuing Education

All counselors are in need of lifelong professional training and education, a position supported in the professional ethics of both ACA and ASCA. School counselors in the field sometimes lament that their districts won't pay for their ongoing educational needs. But take note: Don't wait for your district to pay for your continued education. That is not the district's responsibility—it is *your* professional responsibility to remain up-to-date with the innovations in the field. In addition, new perspectives on important topics, such as multicultural counseling strategies (Constantine & Yeh, 2001) keep skills fresh and enhance self-efficacy.

There are many opportunities for continuing education. These include:

1. In-service topics offered by the district
2. University classes
3. Continuing education programs offered by universities
4. Presentations by local mental health organizations and hospitals
5. Online programs for continuing education
6. Conferences offered by national and state professional associations (American Counseling Association, American School Counselor Association, and their state affiliates)

In addition, you will want to remain up to date with the professional literature from your professional associations. You must read new books that address the issues your students, families, and community are facing. Remain aware of new music, movies, TV shows, and images pervading our culture that send messages to students about how they should be—how they should act, feel, think, and look—and that send messages about how their families, schools, and community should be. You must commit to your own lifelong learning.

Professional Associations

Membership and active involvement in your national, state, and local professional associations will provide you with a number of substantial benefits that will directly enhance the work you do in the schools. Networking with colleagues, professional journals with current perspectives on the field, professional liability insurance, and opportunities for continuing education through conferences are the benefits of membership in professional associations.

In addition, your contribution to those associations in terms of your time and involvement provides you with a greater connection to other dedicated professionals. Service in a leadership capacity in an association can range from being a member of a committee to running for office; a wide range of talents and perspectives is necessary for these associations to function effectively. In addition, professional associations rely on their members to share their expertise in the form of conference presentations. Consider membership, service, leadership, and presentations when you join the professional ranks of school counselors in the field.

Action Research

When you do outcomes assessment, you are collecting important information for yourself, your building, and your district. It is important to note that this information could also be invaluable to your colleagues in other schools, districts, and locations. Action research refers to insights gained by professionals in the field—data collected from students, schools, teachers, programs, activities—any source of information in your job or school. Such information is vital for understanding individual schools in context, providing a basis for locating your situation relative to another's situation. Are your students experiencing something different from those at another school, community, or state? Is there a program that works better than this one to address these issues? How might your students react to this new program? Are the needs of your students and families different from those elsewhere? If so, how are they different? What have others learned about this resource, this counseling strategy, this approach to parents? These questions can only be answered by practicing professionals who are in the field, working directly with students, resources, and parents.

When you initiate a new program, conduct your needs assessments, and compile your data for your outcomes assessments, consider how your data might help others in the field. Don't hide behind "No one would want to read anything written by little ol' me." Consider sharing with others through a district newsletter, state association newsletter or journal, or national association newsletter or professional journal.

Just as geese flying in a V shape benefit from the uplift of the wings of the goose in front, as professionals, we benefit from the wisdom of those who have come before us.

Being Mentored and Mentoring Others

Mentoring provides numerous benefits to both the person being mentored and the mentor. For the mentor, the benefits include opportunities for self-reflection and the positive feelings about making a contribution (VanZandt & Perry, 1992). Overall, mentoring provides an orientation for new professionals that helps them grow in their sense of intellectual competence, sense of purpose, feelings of autonomy, and personal integrity (Bova & Phillips, 1984). It is a forum in which mentees learn:

1. Risk-taking behaviors: dealing with failure, dealing with risk.
2. Communication skills.
3. Political skills: how/where to get jobs inside information about people in power, and the organization's values (a socialization function).
4. Specific professional skills: putting theory into practice, getting the big picture, professional skills, and learning how to put problems into context (Bova & Phillips, 1984)

If mentoring is such a wonderful thing, why doesn't everyone do it? There are a number of reasons that mentoring is not a universal experience. These reasons usually include lack of time, lack of a direct payoff with so many professional priorities, lack of interest in that kind of relationship with co-workers, and lack of knowledge or expertise in mentoring another person. It is important to recognize that locating a mentor is often a challenge, but it must be voluntary. Too much structure can kill the instinctive and voluntary commitment of mentors and the interest of mentees (Bennetts, 1995; Blunt, 1995).

Mentoring is a new way of thinking about a professional relationship. It is a connection between learner and teacher, centering around the teaching of meaning within the context of a professional setting. In this relationship, the goal is to help the new professional develop a professional identity in an environment of support and challenge. To help you understand what makes mentoring unique, consider the following illustrations. In Figure 16.1, various roles are described in terms of support and challenge. In Figure 16.2, the three roles of mentor, consultant, and counselor are located on a continuum describing the focus of the relationship.

Tentoni (1995) outlined a number of activities of mentors. These include sponsoring the mentee's involvement in the environment, supporting the mentee, encouraging and affirming the mentee's independence and professionalism, and inspiring the new professional to

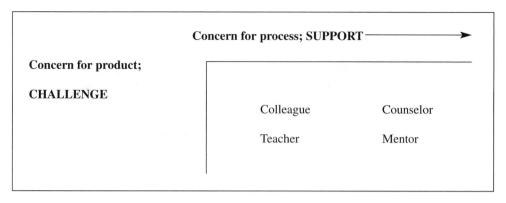

FIGURE 16.1 *Roles of Mentors*

work hard. In addition, mentors provide problem solving, listening, clarifying, and advising, similar to an effective counselor. The mentor also befriends the new professional, accepting new ideas and relating to the new professional. Finally, the mentor is also a teacher, modeling professional behavior and informing the mentee about the job. It is also important to recognize that there are four phases of the mentoring relationship: initiation, cultivation, separation, and ending, in which the relationship is redefined as that of colleagues (Daloz, 1988; Parks, 1990).

To help you determine if you want to seek out a mentor and to help you decide if you would like to mentor others, the following are traditional strategies for mentoring (Borman & Colson, 1984). It is important to note that these strategies about mentoring must be balanced with information about the mentoring needs of women and persons of color (Christopher, 1996; Hawks & Muha, 1991; Heinrich, 1995; Smith & Davidson, 1992). Some of these traditional strategies for mentoring are premised on a male, Eurocentric value system, which may pose certain challenges for women and persons of color who are not necessarily socialized to be comfortable with these behaviors. These potentially challenging strategies are italicized.

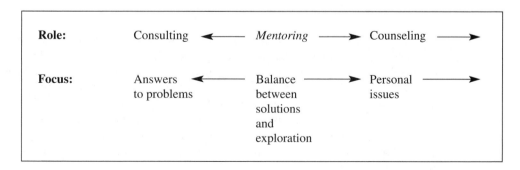

FIGURE 16.2 *Focus of the Relationship*

1. Encourage a positive attitude.
2. Encourage the mentee to establish personal values and goals.
3. Encourage the mentee to maintain an open mind to new ideas.
4. Interactions should be that of sharing, caring, and empathizing.
5. Encourage the mentee to use creative problem-solving processes
6. Encourage the mentee to be an attentive listener and an *assertive questioner.*
7. Encourage the mentee to be an *independent* thinker.
8. Encourage the mentee to recognize *individual* strengths and uniquenesses and build upon them. *Independent thinking and focus on individual strengths presumes an individualistic worldview versus a collectivistic worldview.*
9. Assist the mentee in developing confidence. *This is a different process for those from a more collective worldview.*
10. Stress that the mentee should be aware of the environment, intuitive (*intuition could be culturally or gender-influenced*), problem-sensitive, and ready to make the most of opportunities. *There are implications in terms of competitive versus cooperative cultural norms.*
11. Encourage the mentee to be an active participant, not a spectator. *This may depend on the action orientation of the mentee's culture in a new setting; that is, many Native American cultures stress patient observation of a new environment before becoming actively involved.*
12. Encourage the mentee to be a *risk-taker.*
13. Encourage the mentee to be flexible and adaptable in attitudes and actions, looking for alternatives, and seeing situations/persons from different perspectives.

In addition to these traditional strategies, the following are suggestions for mentoring based on recent research.

14. Encourage your mentee to be flexible in the expectations of the mentoring relationship. Not all mentoring needs can or should be met through ONE mentoring relationship.
15. Strive to minimize dependence. Encourage the mentee to try it on his or her own, just as a good parent's goal is to help a child live his or her own life.
16. Monitor your own attachment to the relationship. Recognize that all mentoring relationships must eventually end to be healthy.

If you decide that you are interested in locating a mentor, you will want to look for a seasoned counselor who is not your direct supervisor. This will reduce dual relationship issues with a supervisor and will enable you to more freely share your concerns and lack of confidence. Trust is an important part of the mentoring relationship (Heinrich, 1995), so you will want to get to know the potential mentor well to determine if you would have a good match between personality, trustworthiness, and personal style. Often you do not need a formal request of the mentor to determine if that person is interested in mentoring you; usually the best mentoring relationships evolve naturally between a novice and an experienced professional.

As you mature in your own professional identity, remember that new, incoming professionals could also benefit from your support in their professional journey. Just as you are being encouraged to consider involvement in research and association leadership, you are also urged to consider mentoring new professionals.

Technology

In a recent survey of ninety-two school counselors from elementary, middle, secondary, and vocational schools, Owen and Weikel (1999) found that 88 percent of the counselors reported that a computer had been assigned to them to support the counseling program. They also found that secondary counselors used computers more in their work than counselors at any other level (an average of 14.5 hours per week), reported the highest level of confidence in their computer skills, and reported the highest level of agreement that their productivity had been enhanced by the use of the computer. However, when asked those activities for which they used the computer, the results revealed that the computer was being used for routine word processing (95%), grade/record keeping (65%), class scheduling (64%), educational programs (30%), email (28%), Internet research (13%), and teaching (5%). The authors lamented the fact that counselors still were not using the computer for activities directly related to student counseling functions.

Numerous authors call for counselors to become more computer-friendly. Some of the ideas to increase the use of the computer include supervision with university, peers, and district professionals, and consultation among counselors (Myrick & Sabella, 1995); listserv discussions (Logan, 2001); instruction (Sampson & Krumboltz, 1991); student advocacy (through an examination of student data and the advocacy for the elimination of barriers to student success) and supervision (Hohenshil, 2000).

In addition, counselors could use the computer to establish connections with students and families through a webpage or could use email with students and families. It is possible that a listserv could be used to conduct discussions with students after a developmental curriculum session or to foster communication with students who are in groups, especially with the advent of live video communication. While there are numerous arguments against relying on computers for communication (confidentiality, security of communication, uncertain identity of communicator), computers are not going to go away. In fact, ACES, the Association for Counselor Education and Supervision, has identified twelve technical competencies that should be expected of counselor education students at the completion of their graduate program (Hohenshil, 2000). Counselors should be able to:

1. Develop webpages, presentations, letters, and reports.
2. Use audiovisual equipment.
3. Use computerized statistical packages.
4. Use computerized testing, diagnostic, and career decision-making programs.
5. Use email.
6. Conduct Internet searches.
7. Subscribe to, participate in, and sign off counseling-related listservs.
8. Access and use counseling-related CD-ROM databases.

9. Know of legal and ethical codes related to counseling services via the Internet.
10. Know strengths and weaknesses of counseling on the Internet.
11. Use the Internet for finding and using continuing education opportunities in counseling.
12. Evaluate the quality of Internet information.

Reflection Moment

Each of these topics for your professional health is important to your professional future. Which ones can you make a commitment to at this point in your training?

A Day in the Life Revisited: Integration

Now that you have read the chapter, consider again Emilita's situation.

1. As you review the topics of this chapter, what activities would help Emilita to do her job better?
2. Apply each of these topics to her situation, one at a time. In what ways would her situation have been different had she followed all the suggestions in this chapter?
3. Do you believe that she can turn this around and salvage her career? To do that, what does she need to do differently with students? With the district administration? With her colleagues in the school?
4. If you were Emilita, what would you do first?

Application

1. What does the student quote at the beginning of this chapter have to do with the lessons of this chapter?

2. Select two or three of the most interesting topics from this chapter and conduct an Internet search on those topics. Compile those sites for sharing with your classmates.

3. Think about the activities or places that make you feel most at peace. How do those relate to your profession? (Or do they?)

4. What are your plans for involvement with professional associations? Interview a secondary school counselor about which organizations that person is a member. Would you ever be interested in service, leadership, or presentations? Outline a plan for that involvement.

5. Outline a plan for your continuing education for the next five years. Determine the financial resources you would need to commit to follow your plan.

6. Outline a plan for action research in a practicum or internship site. Consider a needs assessment of students, parents, teachers, administrators, or other pupil service professionals. What specific information do you think would be of interest to the readers of a state journal of school counseling?

7. Have you ever been mentored? Have you ever been a mentor? Journal those experiences.

8. Where are you in the development of the technology competencies? What do you need to do to improve your technical competence?

Suggested Readings

Boes, S. R., Vanzile-Tamsen, C., & Jackson, C. M. (2001). Portfolio development for the 21st century school counselor. *Professional School Counseling*, *4*, 229–231. This article outlines a very comprehensive approach to the creation of a professional portfolio for school counselors.

Brockman, J. (Ed.). (1992). *Creativity*. New York: Simon & Schuster. This book presents perspectives on creativity written by authors from many different fields, including science, art, medicine, and psychology. These perspectives help the reader consider ways to increase creativity in one's own life.

Brott, P. E., & Myers, J. E. (1999). Development of professional school counselor identity: A grounded theory. *Professional School Counseling*, *2*, 339–348. This article outlines the process and stages of development of a professional identity for school counselors. This perspective can help new counselors understand their feelings of confusion and being overwhelmed by the role ambiguity of school counselors.

Hohenshil, T. H. (2000). High tech counseling. *Journal of Counseling and Development*, *78*, 365–369. This article outlines some important information about computers and counselors, including suggestions of ways that counselors could infuse computers into their work. It also contains an appendix in which the Technical Competencies for Counselor Education Students are presented.

Seaward, B. L. (1994). *Managing stress: Principles and strategies for health and wellbeing*. Boston: Jones & Bartlett. This book outlines the sources and mechanisms of stress and then takes a broad and holistic look at the strategies for managing stress. It is an excellent tool for counselors who are providing developmental curriculum programs and/or group counseling experiences on stress management, as well as a wonderful tool for counselors to manage their own stress.

References

Agnew, T., Vaught, C. C., Getz, H. G., & Fortune, J. (2000). Peer group clinical supervision program fosters confidence and professionalism. *Professional School Counseling*, *4*, 6–12.

Bennetts, C. (1995). The secrets of a good relationship. *People Management*, *1* (13), 38–40.

Blunt, N. (1995). Learning from the wisdom of others. *People Management*, *1* (11), 38–40.

Boes, S. R., VanZile-Tamsen, C., & Jackson, C. M. (2001). Portfolio development for the 21st century school counselor. *Professional School Counseling*, *4*, 229–231.

Borman, C., & Colson, S. (1984). Mentoring—An effective career guidance technique. *The Vocational Guidance Quarterly*, *32* (3), 192–197.

Bova, R. M., & Phillips, R. R. (1984). Mentoring as a learning experience for adults. *Journal of Teacher Education*, *35* (3), 16–20.

Brott, P. E., & Myers, J. E. (1999). Development of professional school counselor identity: A grounded theory. *Professional School Counseling*, *2*, 339–348.

Christopher, J. C. (1996). Counseling's inescapable moral visions. *Journal of Counseling & Development*, *75*, 17–25.

Christopher, J. C. (1999). Situating psychological well-being: Exploring the cultural roots of its theory and research. *Journal of Counseling and Development*, *77*, 141–152.

Constantine, M. G., & Yeh, C. J. (2001). Multicultural training, self-construals, and multicultural competence of school counselors. *Professional School Counseling*, *4*, 202–207.

Crespi, T. D., Fischetti, B. A., & Butler, S. K. (2001, January). Clinical supervision in the schools. *Counseling Today*, *43*, 7, 28, 34.

Daloz, L. (1988). Into the trenches: A case study in mentorship. *Management of Lifelong Education Alumni Bulletin*, *1* (2), 1–3.

DeBono, E. (1992). *Serious creativity: Using the power of lateral thinking to create new ideas*. New York: HarperCollins.

Fox, M. (1994). *The reinvention of work: A new vision of livelihood for our time.* San Francisco, CA: Harper.

Gruber, H. E. (1993). Aspects of scientific discovery: Aesthetics and cognition. In J. Brockman (Ed.), *Creativity* (pp. 48–74). New York: Simon & Schuster.

Hawks, B. K., & Muha, D. (1991). Facilitating the career development of minorities: Doing it differently this time. *The Career Development Quarterly, 39*(3), 251–260.

Heinrich, K. T. (1995). Doctoral advisement relationships between women: On friendship and betrayal. *Journal of Higher Education, 66* (4), 447–469.

Herlihy, B., & Corey, G. (1996). *ACA ethical standards casebook* (5th ed.). Alexandria, VA: ACA.

Hohenshil, T. H. (2000). High tech counseling. *Journal of Counseling and Development, 78*, 365–369.

James, S. H., & Greenwalt, B. C. (2001). Documenting success and achievement: Presentation and working portfolios for counselors. *Journal of Counseling & Development, 79*, 161–165.

Johnson, L. S. (2000). Promoting professional identity in an era of educational reform. *Professional School Counseling, 4*, 31–40.

Kahn, B. B. (1999). Priorities and practices in field supervision of school counseling students. *Professional School Counseling, 3*, 128–136.

Logan, R. (2001, March/April). Creating a listserv—A key to communication. *The ASCA Counselor, 38*, 12.

Morris, J. (1992). *Creative breakthroughs: Tap the power of your unconscious mind.* New York: Warner.

Morrissette, P. J. (2000). The experiences of the rural school counselor. *Professional School Counseling, 3*, 197–108. Retrieved February 7, 2001, from the EBSCO database, available from the World Wide Web: http://ehost . . .

Myrick, R. D., & Sabella, R. A. (1995). Cyberspace: New place for counselor supervision. *Elementary School Guidance and Counseling, 30*, 35–45. Retrieved February 7, 2001 from the EBSCO database, available from the World Wide Web: http://ehostv . . .

Owen, D. W., & Weikel, W. J. (1999). Computer utilization by school counselors. *Professional School Counseling, 2*, 179–182.

Palmer, P. J. (1998). *The courage to teach: Exploring the inner landscape of a teacher's life.* San Francisco, CA: Jossey-Bass.

Parks, S. D. (1990, Fall). Social vision and moral courage: Mentoring a new generation. *Cross Currents*, 350–367.

Roberts, E. B., & Borders, L. D. (1994). Supervision of school counselors: Administrative, program, and counseling. *The School Counselor, 41*, 149–157.

Roberts, W. B., Jr., & Morotti, A. A. (2001). Site supervisors of professional school counseling interns: Suggested guidelines. *Professional School Counseling, 4*, 208–215.

Root-Bernstein, R., & Root-Bernstein, M. (1999). *Sparks of genius: The thirteen thinking tools of the world's most creative people.* Boston: Houghton Mifflin.

Sampson, J. P., Jr., & Krumboltz, J. D. (1991). Computer-assisted instruction: A missing link in counseling. *Journal of Counseling & Development, 69*, 395–397.

Schmidt, J. J. (1990). Critical issues for school counselor performance appraisal and supervision. *The School Counselor, 38*, 86–94.

Seaward, B. L. (1994). *Managing stress: Principles and strategies for health and wellbeing.* Boston, MA: Jones & Bartlett.

Smith, E. P., & Davidson, II, W. S. (1992). Mentoring and the development of African-American graduate students. *Journal of College Student Development, 33*, 531–539.

Tentoni, S. C. (1995). The mentoring of counseling students: A concept in search of a paradigm. *Counselor Education and Supervision, 35*, 32–42.

VanZandt, C. E., & Perry, N. S. (1992). Helping the rookie school counselor: A mentoring project. *The School Counselor, 39*, 158–163.

Young-Eisendrath, P., & Miller, M. E. (2000). Beyond enlightened self-interest: The psychology of mature spirituality in the twenty-first century. In P. Young-Eisendrath & M. E. Miller (Eds.), *The psychology of mature spirituality: Integrity, wisdom, transcendence* (pp. 1–7). Philadelphia, PA: Routledge.

VI

Insights from the Experts

17

Group Counseling with Aggressive Adolescents in the School Setting:

A Cognitive-Behavioral Perspective

Jim Larson, Ph.D., NCSP

Jim Larson is a professor in the psychology department at the University of Wisconsin–Whitewater.

> *"I think it's very important that counselors go to the classroom to talk about violence. A lot of kids use violence toward those who say things about them. Instead, they should go talk to a counselor to talk it out. They just need to feel comfortable talking to the counselor about these things."*
>
> Lyndsey, age 18

Here's an energizing prospect for a Monday morning: Identify the most openly aggressive youth who prowl the hallways of your middle or high school, gather them up into the same room, and then provide counseling services that will significantly reduce their aggressive behavior. Work around frequent truancies, suspensions, court lock-ups, non-compliant behavior, lack of motivation to change, threatening postures, administrator and teacher resistance, slight, absent or antagonistic home support . . . and, by the way, make progress quickly. We can't have these students endangering the safety of other students and staff, now can we?

When I present that challenge to my students or to mental health staff in the school setting at workshops, I can almost visualize the prospect of it dropping to the very bottom of everyone's "to do" file. Make no mistake, working with aggressive adolescents is a daunting undertaking, but as I hope to portray in this chapter, it can be among the most rewarding and worthwhile activities in which counselors and other school mental health professionals can engage.

The recent incidences of targeted violence in schools around the country have heightened fears of students, parents, and administrators and brought the issue of safety in the schools to the forefront (Kaufman et al., 2000). Fear of homicidal violence in school is a legitimate, if somewhat exaggerated, concern when compared to nonhomicidal physical battery. Whereas the likelihood of being victimized by a shooting in the school has been estimated to be in the range of 1 in 2 million (Brooks, Schiraldi, & Zeidenberg, 2000), approximately 15 percent of high school students are involved in a physical fight each year (Kaufman et al., 2000). In fact, the rate of homicide in the school setting has been on a steady downward trajectory for the past decade (Kaufman et al., 2000), while the number of non-fatal physical assaults in that same setting has remained problematic. Very few students are murdered in school each year, but thousands perpetrate and are victimized by aggressive behavior. These data are not meant to underplay the need to prevent future Columbine-type assaults. Instead, they are meant to highlight an often-neglected population of students and emphasize a service delivery option that can have a positive effect on the day-to-day experience of a great number of individuals.

Essential Elements in the Treatment of Adolescent Aggression

Whereas a complete discussion of the many factors that contribute to a successful counseling intervention with aggressive students is beyond the scope of this chapter, I have assembled what I believe to be among the most critical elements. Interested readers are referred to Hanna and Hunt (1999), Furlong and Smith (1994), and Sandhu (2000) for more extended treatments of this and related issues.

Select Student Candidates for Counseling with Care

Identifying the students for aggression management counseling can sometimes be a challenge. In some schools, the number of possible candidates may be overwhelming. One of my interns, who was working in a very large, poorly run middle school, told me that she could "stand in the hallway at passing time, randomly select the first six kids who came her way, and end up with a reasonably good counseling group of students who needed aggression management." In all situations, including those such as this, the counselor must be judicious in the selection process. Factors to consider include one or more of the following: (a) expressed motivation for change; (b) bondedness to the school, perhaps as seen by participation in extracurricular activities and/or possessing mostly passing grades; (c) remorse or regret following an aggressive incident; and (d) active parental support for the effort.

I have worked in high schools in which I knew that there was a group of chronically aggressive, very high negative-profile students, but whom I chose not to treat in a counseling group. Mental health professionals, particularly those in larger schools, must learn to make "triage-type" decisions in order to provide services to those most likely to benefit from them. Counseling is a time- and labor-intensive service, and the professional needs to be confident that the potential for positive outcomes is at least reasonable. Careful screening and selection of students can assist in maximizing this potential. All students deserve mental health support in the school, but not all deserve nor will they all benefit from direct counseling services. In those cases, the school mental health professional's time may be best spent securing alternative education structures and community-based intervention services.

Be Aware of Differing Patterns of Aggression

Research in the area of child and adolescent aggression (e.g., Dodge, 1991; Dodge, Lochman, Harnish, Bates, & Pettit, 1997) has indicated that there are two broad types of aggressive behavior patterns seen in children and youth: proactive and reactive. Very few students fall exclusively into just one type, but many tend to trend in one direction or the other. *Proactive aggression* refers to aggressive patterns that are designed to acquire a desired end for the student—for instance, high peer status, money or material goods, or feared reputation. Proactive aggression is "cool-headed" and calculated. These students either initiate the fight or have others do it for them. They are the elementary school bullies grown older, larger, and sometimes crueler. They are comparatively in control of their emotions and know how to "turn on the charm" with an adult when they see it in their best interest to do so.

Reactive aggressive students are the "hot-headed" types who seem to be always in one scrape or another on a regular basis. They do not initiate fights so much as they "react" to perceived slights, bumps, or other actions of fellow students. "He started it!" is their common cry, and they believe it. The research indicates that, compared to less aggressive peers, reactive aggressive students tend to distort incoming information and hold beliefs that others are behaving in a hostile manner toward them (Dodge & Coie, 1987). This "hostile attributional bias" is often the source of their perceived need to react in an aggressive manner.

Counselors should be alert to the probability that the treatment implications for youth who demonstrate predominately one or the other of these two forms of aggression are quite different and that combining them in the same group may be contraindicated. As a rule, *proactively* aggressive students are more capable of adjusting their behavior to a firm and consistent discipline strategy that encourages nonviolence and provides aversive consequences for aggression in the school setting. However, because of their information processing deficits and distortions, *reactively* aggressive students are the better candidates for treatment intervention with a cognitive-behavioral skills training program.

Establish a Working Relationship in the Student's Area of Concern

It is an understatement to say that most aggressive adolescents who appear in the counselor's office for treatment have not come on their own volition. It usually takes only a cursory examination to find the well-placed footprint of an administrator, parent, or juvenile officer on the youth's backside. How then does the counselor get the essential cooperation and motivation for change with an involuntary client?

Most school mental health professionals can recall the discussions about the importance of "rapport building" from their introductory counseling classes. Building rapport with a student who is in psychological pain and has referred herself for help is one thing; building it with a student who would rather be almost anywhere else on earth than sitting across the room from you is quite another. In such cases, it is the counselor's responsibility to seek out any sliver of "psychological pain" where he or she can find it. Here's a hint: It is almost never what the referring agent says it is.

Presented with objective evidence (report card, scholarship record), these youth may grudgingly acknowledge that they are doing poorly in school, but they will rarely attribute the cause to their own aggressive behavior patterns. Recall that reactive aggressive youth see others as hostile toward *them* and thus attribute their aggression to the behavior of other individuals. In their minds, if the other students and "those blankety-blank teachers" would just stop trying to start it up with them, they'd be fine. Why work on somebody else's problem?

For instance, imagine a youth sitting across the desk from you who was brought in by the administrator following a three-day suspension for his third incidence of fighting. Chances are good that he may be less worried at that time about his own aggression and more angry at the administration for treating him "unfairly." The wise counselor will see that anger as the concern to address first and the issue around which to forge an initial working relationship. Rapport and the working relationship with involuntary clients come through careful probing and listening for the treatment "opening." Where is the youth feeling vulnerable? Fear of academic failure and possible dropout? Inability to tolerate "hostile" teachers? Anger at parent for blaming him? Listen carefully and start there: The link to aggression can be made later.

Talk Therapy Alone Won't Work

Many well-intentioned school mental health professionals have spent long hours with aggressive students trying to educate, cajole, actively listen, reflect, and/or reason them out of their problematic behavior. Unfortunately, chronic aggressiveness is typically not a behavior that can be addressed efficiently through insight-oriented therapy: There is generally no useful "Ah-ha!" that can be uncovered that will lead to effective change.

Rather, therapists should construe their task as "cognitive-behavioral skills building." Much as one might go about the task of teaching some other useful skill—say, learning to drive a car—counselors should similarly approach the needs of most chronically aggressive adolescents. This is not to say that these selfsame students don't have the concomitant array of family, authority, and identity "issues" common to their age or gender that may respond to a more traditional counseling treatment approach. However, physical aggression trumps almost every other manifestation of adolescent adjustment that one is likely to witness in the school setting and always demands a quick and effective response.

Counselors are advised to frame student aggression in the school setting as a maladaptive response to a set of environmental stimuli. Consider these two sets of environmental stimuli: (1) In a car, do you know what to do when a slippery road starts the rear end sliding sideways? (2) In the hallway at school, do you know what to do when someone bumps you from behind? Both demand a set of cognitive-behavioral response skills that the individual may or may not have in his or her repertoire. Slamming on the brakes in a panic or turning to punch the person who bumped you are both maladaptive responses in those individual environments. Chronically aggressive students must learn how to better manage the day-to-day environmental provocations that occur in the school setting or they will surely face the social-academic equivalent of vehicular death.

Moreover, these skills cannot be usefully acquired by the student client through counselor explanation and guided discussion alone. Recall the three most important words in real estate sales: "Location, location, location!" The parallel admonition to cognitive-behavioral skills training is: "Practice, practice, practice!" This means abundant and repeated role-plays in and out of the group room and the utilization of significant "trigger" individuals—administrators, teachers, security guards—when possible and desirable. Remember that just because the youth can tell the counselor what he or she should do in a given situation does not mean that the *skill to perform the behavior* is in the youth's available repertoire.

Expand the Adolescent's Coping Style

Donald Meichenbaum, probably the most influential figure in the field of cognitive-behavioral therapy, wrote nearly a quarter of a century ago that ". . . any coping-skills training approach should be flexible enough to incorporate a variety of cognitive and behavioral strategies that can be differentially employed" (Meichenbaum, 1977, p. 148). That advice is as true today in our work with aggressive adolescents as it was then.

In my work with school professionals and graduate interns who are working with multiple problematic, often highly aggressive, students, the questions often arise, "How does one determine what to do in counseling these students? Where are the starting points?" For the beginning or even more experienced counselor, there are useful, research-supported treatment programs available for guidance (see Feindler & Scalley, 1999; Goldstein, Glick, & Gibbs, 1998; Hammond, 1991; Larson, 1994). These are time-limited, sequenced, group-type interventions that address most of the deficits and distortions of angry, aggressive adolescents, and I recommend gathering experience with one or more of them.

However, the answer to the question about determining the direction and goals of therapy is really quite simple: Ask and answer the question, "What does the youth need to *know and be able to do* to be adaptive in the school environment?" Remember Meichenbaum's directive: Provide the youth with flexible coping skills. The school environment offers a staggering array of potential "trigger points" for students that they must learn to negotiate if they are to be successful. The counselor's job is to (1) engage in a collaboration with the student to identify the most frequently encountered problems and then (2) decide upon the skills necessary to cope them successfully. Once that is accomplished, the skills training begins. The "how to's" of anger management training, attribution retraining, problem-solving training, impulse control training, assertiveness training, and other common coping skills training procedures are beyond the scope of this chapter. The reader is referred to the programs noted above, as well as to Feindler and Ecton (1986), Goldstein (1999), and Kendall (2000) for helpful guidance.

Treating Aggressive Girls May Require Additional Insights

It is considerably more common to have adolescent boys referred for aggression than it is for girls, but some researchers suggest that the gap is narrowing (see Pepler & Sedighdeilami, 1998). To the extent that girls' aggression is similar to that of the boys discussed above—that is, physical, reactive, impulsive, and anger-induced—then the treatment procedures need not vary considerably. Physically aggressive adolescent girls carry a risk status similar to or greater than that of physically aggressive boys. Pepler and Sedighdeilami (1998) found that, compared to nonaggressive girls, aggressive girls were rated as having more emotional problems, lower self-esteem, and more academic difficulties. Additionally, these girls tend to attract aggressive boys as romantic partners and put themselves at significant risk for physical and sexual abuse.

Importantly, however, there is a newer line of research that has implications for the treatment of some girls' aggression. Researcher Nicki Crick and her colleagues (Crick, 1997; Crick & Bigbee, 1998; Crick & Werner, 1998) have formulated a model of girls' aggression that they refer to as "relational aggression." This formulation of aggression is not physical, but rather it often involves using social exclusion, rumor spreading, and mean-spirited teasing as a form of retaliation. Whereas an adolescent male may "get back" at a provocateur through the use of his fists, Crick and colleagues suggest that it is more common for girls to retaliate nonphysically.

As a group, girls place higher value on relational affiliation than on physical superiority. For most females, beating up another peer simply doesn't carry the valence that it does with males. On the other hand, girls know that to really hurt another girl, the place to attack is her reputation and her social acceptance. Have you been "dissed" by another girl? Start an unflattering rumor about her. Exclude her from the group. Have a party and invite everyone but her. Tease her about her looks. Steal her boyfriend.

Whereas most of the current research has centered on younger girls, many readers can attest to the fact that this form of aggression is widespread across age groups and can be inordinately painful for the victim. School mental health professionals need to be cognizant of this behavior and be prepared to work effectively with its victims as well as its perpetrators. As an additional note, early research has suggested that boys and girls who engage in nongender normative aggression (that is, overt for girls, relational for boys) may be at even higher risk for maladjustment (Crick et al., in press).

Conclusion

Aggressive adolescents represent a population of students with genuine and significant treatment needs. Too often, those needs are addressed administratively, not therapeutically. Detention, suspension, or expulsion do not generally have positive effects on the behavior of chronically aggressive students. Despite this, they are among the most common of school responses (Larson, 1993).

And yet, the school is a perfect place for therapeutic treatment of these adolescents: School is where they can be found, where they interact, and where they get in trouble. The critical ability of school-based mental health professionals to have a deep understanding of the problematic context, to control and manipulate environmental variables, to gather information from principal participants, and have access to the students at important moments in the problem manifestation cannot be underestimated. Our colleagues in the private sector can only look on and be envious of our situation.

I cannot conclude this chapter without some mention of the issue of personal physical safety, because it always comes up in my classroom. All of my work in schools for fourteen years was done in a large, major urban school district. At rare times over those years, I have felt unsafe when a fight broke out in a crowded high school hallway or when I was leaving the building after dark, but I have never felt unsafe in a group room full of students referred for aggressive behavior. I believe that this was due to equal parts of careful identification and selection, my willingness to show and expect personal respect, and the absence of an audience of less problematic peers to play to. I never had to break up a fight, nor was I ever concerned that I would have to. The school mental health professional new to this service delivery option should expect to encounter mock aggressive posturing and bragging, an occasional gang rivalry issue between group members, and an ever-present vocal disdain for selected school personnel. He or she will also encounter students who are needy for positive attention, emotionally vulnerable and often depressed to a surprising degree, funnier than expected, and always prepared with abundant recent experiences as fodder for problem solving and role play.

One of my colleagues once told me that she thought working with aggressive adolescents was a calling, and "you either hear the call loudly or you don't: Nobody plays the middle." Maybe she was right, I don't know. I do know, however, that there are many *equally* needy students vying for counselor time, but very few who are *more* needy. Aggressive behavior that extends into adolescence and manifests in the school setting is a powerful risk factor for a host of negative outcomes, including school dropout, drug and alcohol abuse, and prison. With a properly identified group of adolescents and a research-supported style of treatment, it is my opinion that there are few better ways for a school mental health professional to contribute to the betterment of both the school and the community.

References

Brooks, K., Schiraldi, V., & Ziedenberg, J. (2000). *School house hype: Two years later*. Washington, DC: Justice Policy Institute and the Children's Law Center, Inc., Covington, KY.

Crick, N. R. (1997). Engagement in gender normative versus non-normative forms of aggression: Links to social-psychological adjustment. *Developmental Psychology, 33*, 610–617.

Crick, N. R., & Bigbee, M. A. (1998). Relational and overt forms of peer victimization: A multi-informant approach. *Journal of Consulting and Clinical Psychology, 66*, 337–347.

Crick, N. R., & Werner, N. E. (1998). Response decision processes in relational and overt aggression. *Child Development 69* (6), 1630–1639.

Crick, N. R., Werner, N. E., Casas, J. F., O'Brien, K. M., Nelson, D. A., Grotpeter, J. K., & Markon, K. (In press). Childhood aggression and gender: A new look at an old problem. To appear in D. Bernstein (Ed.), *Nebraska Symposium on Motivation*. Lincoln: University of Nebraska Press.

Dodge, K. A. (1991). The structure and function of reactive and proactive aggression. In D. J. Pepler & K. H. Rubin (Eds.), *Development and treatment of childhood aggression*. Hillsdale, NJ: Lawrence Erlbaum Associates.

Dodge, K. A., & Coie, J. D. (1987). Social information processing factors in reactive and proactive aggression in children's peer groups. *Journal of Personality and Social Psychology*, 53, 1146–1178.

Dodge, K. A., Lochman, J. E., Harnish, J. D., Bates, J. E., & Pettit, G. S. (1997). Reactive and proactive aggression in school children and psychiatrically impaired chronically assaultive youth. *Journal of Abnormal Psychology*, 106, 37–51.

Feindler, E. L., & Ecton, R. B. (1986). *Adolescent anger control: Cognitive-behavioral techniques*. Boston: Allyn and Bacon.

Feindler, E. L., & Scalley, M. (1999). Adolescent anger-management groups for violence reduction. In T. Kratochwill & K. Stoiber (Eds.), *Handbook of group interventions for children and families*. Boston: Allyn and Bacon.

Furlong, M. J., & Smith, D. C. (Eds.). (1994). *Anger, hostility, and aggression: Assessment, prevention, and intervention strategies for youth*. New York: Guilford.

Goldstein, A. P. (1999). *The Prepare curriculum* (2nd ed.). Champaign, IL: Research Press.

Goldstein, A. P., Glick, B., & Gibbs, J. C. (1998). *Aggression replacement training: A comprehensive intervention for aggressive youth*. Champaign, IL: Research Press.

Hammond, W. R. (1991). *Dealing with anger: A violence prevention program for African-American youth*. Champaign, IL: Research Press.

Hanna, F. J., & Hunt, W. P. (1999). Techniques for psychotherapy with defiant, aggressive adolescents. *Psychotherapy*, 36, 56–68.

Kaufman, P., Chen, X, Choy, S., Ruddy, S. A., Miller, A. K., Fleury, J. K., Chandler, K. A., Rand, M. R., Klaus, P., & Planty, M. G. (2000). *Indicators of school crime and safety, 2000* (NCES 2001-017). Washington, DC: U.S. Departments of Education and Justice.

Kendall, P. A. (Ed.). (2000). *Child and adolescent therapy: Cognitive-behavioral procedures* (2nd ed.). New York: Guilford.

Larson, J. (1993). School psychologists' perceptions of physically aggressive student behavior as a referral concern in nonurban districts. *Psychology in the Schools*, 30, 345–350.

Larson, J. (1994). Cognitive-behavioral treatment of anger-induced aggression in the school setting. In M. J. Furlong & D. C. Smith (Eds.), *Anger, hostility, and aggression: Assessment, prevention, and intervention strategies for youth* (pp. 393–440). New York: Guilford. (This is a discussion of the *Think First Program*.)

Meichenbaum, D. (1977). *Cognitive-behavior modification: An integrative approach*. New York: Plenum Press.

Pepler, D. J., & Sedighdeilami, F. (1998, October). *Aggressive girls in Canada* (Rep. No. W-98-30E). Applied Research Branch, Strategic Policy, Human Resources Development Canada, Hull, Quebec, Canada. [Online]. Available: http://www.hrdc-drhc.gc.ca/stratpol/arb/publications/research/abw-98-30e.shtml.

Sandhu, D. S. (Ed.). (2000). *Violence in American schools: A practical guide for counselors*. Reston, VA: American Counseling Association.

18

Working with Sexual Minority Youth

Margaret Eichler, M.A., NCC, & Carol Doyle, Ph.D.

Margaret Eichler is a school counselor at Five Oaks Middle School in Beaverton, Oregon, and Carol Doyle is an associate professor of counseling psychology at Lewis & Clark University in Portland, Oregon.

> *"In my school, 'gay' is used to mean 'stupid.' If any of my friends were gay, and anyone hurt them or said things about them, I would stand up for them. I want people to feel OK about themselves."*
>
> Sierra, age 14

> We look forward to the day when models for internalizing self-acceptance will be irrelevant and obsolete because we will have ceased to perpetuate a context that fosters self-loathing— to a day when the word *homosexual* has lost its power to label and stigmatize people and has become merely a descriptor of one wide variety of acceptable forms of loving. (McCarn & Fassinger, 1996, p. 532)

All counselors are keepers of secrets. The therapeutic relationship provides a confidential and safe place for clients to share the stories that affect their lives. We often hear about experiences that are not spoken about in any other contexts. School counselors who know about these experiences are also acutely aware of all the barriers that keep students from feeling good about themselves, enjoying their lives, or achieving success academically. Historically and currently, one of the secrets not discussed in schools are the issues and needs of students who are gay, lesbian, bisexual, and/or transgendered (Anderson, 1994; Fontaine, 1997).

When do we begin discussing these "well-kept" secrets? What can school counselors do to bring their schools closer to the day when the school problems of gay, lesbian, bisexual, and/or transgendered students are perceived no differently than those experienced by the heterosexual students? School counselors can help create the day when these students are merely examples of the many types of diversity that exists in our schools.

As counselors we bring to our work our education, skills, training, our emotional selves, our unique life experiences, our personal beliefs, values, and biases. We are ethically bound by our profession to be aware of our personal values and biases so we do not impose them on clients and students (American Counseling Association Code of Ethics, Section A.5.b, 1995; American School Counseling Association Ethical Standards, Section A.c. 1998).

The school counselor is often the primary confidante, even before friends, when a student is exploring his or her sexual identity or has gay family members. Because of this opportunity to impact these students, especially when there is such a power differential between adult counselors and adolescent students, the path of self-awareness must be well traveled. Our responses to their issues are vital, and if we are aware of our own values and beliefs, then we can focus on hearing students' stories without interjecting our personal biases. Helping adolescents when they have previously been made to feel ashamed of who they are is paramount, particularly during this critical time of identity development and acute self-awareness. Persecution, isolation, and self-hatred can profoundly impact every aspect of a developing child's life. A counselor who can provide a safe haven for students by listening to their stories without prejudice and discrimination can greatly impact their development of a positive and constructive sense of self. A school counselor can intervene, not only to protect students from self-condemning and self-destructive behaviors, but also to generate and support school policies that protect students from the harassment and violence perpetrated on them by others (Fontaine, 1997; Henning-Stout, James, & Macintosh, 2000; Reynolds & Koski, 1995).

The purpose of this chapter is to provide insights into the developmental experiences of lesbian, gay, bisexual, and transgendered youth and how we as school counselors can support these students within the context of the public school setting. It is our belief that through increased understanding of the issues facing sexual minority youth, we can develop ways for fostering supportive interactions and connections.

Sexual Identity Formation and Development

Erikson (1968) proposed that adolescence is a time for exploring issues related to identity and intimacy. The experience of navigating the developmental process of adolescence is daunting enough; merging that monumental task with the unfolding possibility of being gay, and embedding those challenges within the high school culture, can generate an experience fraught with confusion, fear, and isolation (Black & Underwood, 1998; Fontaine, 1997; Hunter & Mallon, 2000). Thus, it is important for counselors working with sexual minority youth to be aware of the developmental issues these students face as they integrate their sexual orientation into their overall identity.

A person's sexual identity is comprised of four separate components, one biological and three psychological (Shively & De Cecco, 1993). It is the interaction of these separate components that determines the development of a person's unique sexual identity. These components are:

Biological Sex. The initial classification of individuals as boys or girls that occurs shortly after birth.

Gender Identity. The psychological process by which girls come to identify themselves as girls and boys identify themselves as boys (Lipkin, 1999).

Social Sex-Role. The process by which children come to behave in the socially/culturally stereotypical ways associated with their gender. It is the extent to which an individual conforms to the societal expectations and exhibits the behaviors and characteristics associated with masculinity and/or femininity as defined by the culture in which they live.

Sexual Orientation. The physical and/or affectional preferences of an individual for persons of the same gender or opposite gender as identified in behavior and/or fantasy.

The separation and identification of these components of sexual identity is especially helpful when trying to understand the developmental trajectories of students. For example, it is often assumed that persons who develop a gay or lesbian sexual orientation also exhibit the social sex role of the opposite gender—that is, all gay men are feminine and lesbians are masculine (Anderson, 1995). This assumption may help to explain why some students, particularly those who do not conform to the norms of behavior associated with masculinity and femininity as defined by our culture, are perceived to be gay when in fact their sexual orientation is heterosexual. By isolating the components of sexual identity, this model makes clear that behaving in a stereotypically masculine or feminine way is not necessarily an indication of a person's sexual orientation. Gay, lesbian, and bisexual students, as well as heterosexual students, can exhibit a broad range of masculine and or feminine behaviors regardless of sexual orientation.

The separation of these components of sexual identity is also helpful in understanding gender atypical youth (Haldeman, 2000) and transgenderism (Lipkin, 1999). For these individuals, a conflict exists between their biological sex and their gender identity. Psychologically, their gender identity is incongruent with their biological sex (Shively & De Cecco, 1993). However, the social sex role and gender identity of transgendered individuals *are* congruent with each other. Thus an adolescent may biologically be a young man, yet may self-identify as female and behave in stereotypically feminine ways.

As same-sex attractions and experiences begin in adolescence (Anderson, 1994), it is also helpful for school counselors to understand the developmental process by which sexual minority persons positively integrate their sexual orientation into their overall sense of identity. Several models have been developed that describe this process of identity development, also called the "coming out" process (Cass, 1979, 1984; Coleman, 1982; Fassinger & Miller, 1996, McCarn & Fassinger, 1996; Troiden, 1988, 1989). These models, which focus on gay/lesbian identity development, similarly describe a process that begins with the recognition of the possibility that one's sexual orientation may be different from one's peers. This leads to feelings of confusion and questioning of one's sexuality. Exploration of same-sex attractions and investigation of what it means to be gay or lesbian is the next part of the process. This exploration leads to a deeper understanding and acceptance of self as a gay or lesbian person. The process concludes with the ongoing integration of sexual orientation into one's overall identity.

McCarn and Fassinger (1996) expanded on previous models of gay/lesbian identity development by suggesting that the development of a gay/lesbian identity simultaneously results in the person becoming a member of a stigmatized minority group. Because of this, McCarn and Fassinger postulate that sexual minority identity formation consists of two separate, yet reciprocal processes—individual sexual identity development and group membership identity development. Their model further specifies four phases of the developmental process: Awareness, Exploration, Deepening/Commitment, and Internalization/ Synthesis. A brief description of the tasks involved in each phase of each aspect of the model follows. (Fassinger & Miller, 1996; McCarn & Fassinger, 1996)

Individual Sexual Identity Development
Phase 1:   Awareness. Awareness of feeling different. Recognition of attractions that are different from the heterosexual norm. Confusion and fear may also be experienced during this phase.

Phase 2:   Exploration. Exploration of sexual feelings and same-sex attractions.

Phase 3:   Deepening/commitment. Increased self-knowledge and crystallization of the individual aspects of sexual identity.

Phase 4:   Internalization/synthesis. Internalization of same-sex desires and sexual minority identity as part of overall identity.

Group Membership Identity Development
Phase 1:   Awareness. A recognition and awareness that there are people in the world whose sexual orientation is not heterosexual.

Phase 2:   Exploration. Actively learning about gays and lesbians as a group and exploring the possibility of belonging to the group. Clarification of attitudes toward gay people.

Phase 3:   Deepening/commitment. Increased involvement with gay/lesbian culture. Understanding of the possible consequences of belonging to a stigmatized minority group.

Phase 4: Internalization/synthesis. Identification of self as a member of a stigmatized minority group and internalization of this identity into overall self-concept.

McCarn and Fassinger's (1996) identification of the two separate aspects of sexual minority identity development is helpful to school counselors because it highlights the fact that at the same time students are dealing with the confusion surrounding their own sexual orientation, they must also come to terms with being a member of a stigmatized group. Dealing with what it means to be gay or lesbian in schools usually means learning to deal with harassment or hiding their identity (Black & Underwood, 1998). School counselors can help students in this developmental process by providing positive information about gays and lesbians, making connections for students with positive role models, and starting support groups and/or gay, lesbian, straight alliances in their schools.

Belonging

A central assumption of Adlerian theory (Adler, 1924) is that people have a need to belong, an important concept when considering the isolation experienced by sexual minority youth. How do these youth deal with and resolve feelings of perceived alienation and isolation? And perhaps more importantly, how do they secure that sense of belonging? How do they move forward to accept themselves, develop a positive self-image, and find their place in the world without internalizing the perceived values of the "norm"?

Sexual minority youth face self-loathing, family rejection, and social rejection as a result of revealing their sexual orientation (Callahan, 2001). School counselors can help gay, lesbian, and bisexual youth to accept themselves, to communicate with others about their emerging identity, and to advocate for equity in their interactions with cultural institutions (Chen-Hayes, 2001). On a systemic level, school counselors can address the barriers in the cultural system that keep a student from experiencing "belongingness" with friends and within the school community in general. We can play a significant role as the conscience of the school, moving the community toward cultural and policy changes that support diversity and make a difference in the life of an adolescent.

On an individual level, school counselors can help these students develop a healthy sense of self. "Self-image and self-concept are a cognitive construct of self-perceived characteristics, while self-esteem is the value we place on those perceptions" (Eliason, 1996, p. 47). Helping a student to understand his or her perceptions of self, then helping that student to *value* those perceptions, is essential for ending isolation. A counselor's support and acceptance of a student during his or her exploration of sexual identity, regardless of how that identity unfolds, is the beginning of self-acceptance. Deep listening, compassion, and empathy create an opportunity for students to explore their own identity in safe and meaningful ways. As self-acceptance and confidence are fostered, the student's identity development is facilitated, paving the way for the student to move to the next level of individual and group identity development: Deepening/commitment (McCarn & Fassinger, 1996). This sense of belonging or identifying with other sexual minority youth allows the adolescent to experience finding his or her place in the world.

Making Connections

The keys to self-awareness for sexual minority youth about any of these issues are (1) unbiased support and (2) meaningful questions that lead them to their own insights. Support means a safe environment with a respectful listener; we must work to understand and, if needed, mitigate our own biases to allow students to freely explore their own identity. Meaningful questions place all power, personal validation, self-esteem, and awareness of feelings in the control of the student, to be explored at his or her individual pace.

In this context, counselors help students to envision their story and their perception of themselves within their world, allowing their exploration and definition of that path. Understanding their timing while conceptualizing their journey through the stages of identity development allows them to address different issues as they arise. Being process oriented, counselors should allow the path to take its own turns and not strive for some idealized version of gay or lesbian identity. If students become familiar with generating their own paths, develop tools for protection and self-advocacy, and refine a sense of recognizing those who support them, these are great achievements. A positive connection with a counselor and the counseling experience can be the paramount difference in a student's life.

Resources

This brief discussion barely scratches the surface of useful information for school counselors who are working with gay, lesbian, bisexual, and transgendered youth. In addition to the references used in the text, the following additional resources provide more specific ideas and interventions for working with these students.

Suggested Readings

Callahan, C. J. (2001). Protecting and counseling gay and lesbian students. *The Journal of Humanistic Counseling, Education, and Development, 40*, 5–10.

Chen-Hayes, S. F. (2001). Counseling and advocacy with transgendered and gender-variant persons in schools and families. *The Journal of Humanistic Counseling, Education, and Development, 40*, 34–48.

Gonsiorek, J. C. (1993). Mental health issues of gay and lesbian adolescents. In L. D. Garnets & D. C. Kimmel (Eds.), *Psychological perspectives on lesbian and gay male experiences* (pp. 469–484). New York: Columbia University Press.

Harris, M. B. (Ed.). (1997). *School experiences of gay and lesbian youth: The invisible minority*. Binghamton, NY: Haworth.

Henning-Stout, M., & James, S. (Guest Eds.) (2000). Lesbian, gay, bisexual, and transgender and questioning youth [Miniseries]. *School Psychology Review, 29*, 153–234.

Henning-Stout, M., James, S., & Macintosh, S. (2000). Reducing harassment of lesbian, gay, bisexual, transgender, and questioning youth in schools. *School Psychology Review, 29*, 180–191.

Lipkin, A. (1999). *Understanding homosexuality, changing schools*. Boulder, CO: Westview Press.

National Education Association. (1999). *Strengthening the learning environment. A school employee's guide to gay and lesbian issues.* Washington, DC: Author.

Lesbian, Gay, Bisexual, and Transgender People and Education. (1996, Summer). [Special Issue]. *Harvard Educational Review.*

Unks, G. (Ed.). (1995). *The gay teen. Educational practice and theory for lesbian, gay and bisexual adolescents.* New York: Routledge.

Web-Based Resources and Fact Sheets

Association for Gay, Lesbian, and Bisexual Issues in Counseling. This site contains competencies for counselors working with GLBT persons, and a resource section with an annotated bibliography. *www:aglbic.org.*

Just the Facts about Sexual Orientation and Youth. A Primer for Principals, Educators and School Personnel. (nd) *http://www.apa.org/pubinfo/facts.html*

Youth Pride. (1997). Creating Safe Schools for Lesbian and Gay Students: A resource guide for school staff. *http://members.tripod.com/~twood/guide.html*

Organizations

GLSEN Gay, Lesbian, & Straight Education Network; 121 W. 27th Street, Suite 804; New York, NY 10001; *www.glsen.org*

Harvey Milk Institute; PMB 451; 584 Castro Street; San Francisco, CA 94114; *http://www.gayglobalsf.com/harveymilk/*

Hetrick-Martin Institute; 2 Astor Place; New York, NY 10003

Project 10; 7850 Melrose Ave.; Los Angeles, CA 90046

Massachusetts Governor's Commission on Gay and Lesbian Youth; Governor's Commission; State House, Room 111; Boston, MA 02113

Parents & Friends of Lesbians & Gays; PFLAG; 1101 14th Street NW, Suite 12030; Washington, DC 20005; *http://www.pflag.org*

References

Adler, A. (1924). *The practice and theory of individual psychology.* New York: Harcourt Brace.

American Counseling Association. (1995). *Code of ethics and standards of practice.* Alexandria, VA: Author.

American School Counselor Association. (1998). *Ethical standards for school counselors.* Alexandria, VA: Author.

Anderson, D. A. (1995). Lesbian and gay adolescents. Social and developmental considerations. In G. Unks (Ed.), *The gay teen. Educational practice and theory for lesbian, gay and bisexual adolescents.* (pp. 17–28). New York: Routledge.

Anderson, J. (1994). School climate for gay and lesbian students and staff members. *Phi Delta Kappan, 76,* 151–154.

Black, J., & Underwood, J. (1998). Young, female, and gay: Lesbian students and the school environment. *Professional School Counseling, 1 (3),* 15–20.

Callahan, C. J. (2001). Protecting and counseling gay and lesbian students. *The Journal of Humanistic Counseling, Education, and Development, 40,* 5–10.

Cass, V. C. (1979). Homosexual identity formation: A theoretical model. *Journal of Homosexuality, 4,* 219–235.

Cass, V. C. (1984). Homosexual identity formation: Testing a theoretical model. *The Journal of Sex Research*, *20*, 143–167.

Chen-Hayes, S. F. (2001). Counseling and advocacy with transgendered and gender-variant persons in schools and families. *The Journal of Humanistic Counseling, Education, and Development*, *40*, 34–48.

Coleman, E. (1982). Developmental stages of the coming out process. *Journal of Homosexuality*, *7*, 31–43.

Eliason, M. J. (1996). Identity formation for lesbian, bisexual, and gay persons: Beyond a "minoritizing" view. *Journal of Homosexuality*, *30*, 31–58.

Erikson, E. H. (1968). *Identity: Youth and crisis*. New York: Norton.

Fassinger, R. E., & Miller, B. A. (1996). Validation of an inclusive model of sexual minority identity formation on a sample of gay men. *Journal of Homosexuality*, *32*, 53–78.

Fontaine, J. H. (1997). The sound of silence: Public school response to the needs of gay and lesbian youth. In M. B. Harris (Ed.), *School experiences of gay and lesbian youth: The invisible minority* (pp. 101–109). Binghamton, NY: The Haworth Press.

Haldeman, D. C. (2000). Gender atypical youth: Clinical and social issues. *School Psychology Review*, *29*, 192–200.

Henning-Stout, M., James, S., & Macintosh, S. (2000). Reducing harassment of lesbian, gay, bisexual, transgender, and questioning youth in schools. *School Psychology Review*, *29*, 180–191.

Hunter, J., & Mallon, G. P. (2000). Lesbian, gay, and bisexual adolescent development. Dancing with your feet tied together. In B. Greene & G. L. Groom (Eds.), *Psychological perspectives on lesbian and gay issues: Vol. 5. Education, research and practice in lesbian, gay, bisexual, and transgendered psychology.* (pp. 226–241). Thousand Oaks, CA: Sage Publications.

Lipkin, A. (1999). *Understanding homosexuality, changing schools*. Boulder, CO: Westview Press.

McCarn, R., & Fassinger, R. E. (1996). Revisioning sexual minority identity formation: A new model of lesbian identity and its implications for counseling and research. *The Counseling Psychologist*, *24*, 508–534.

Reynolds, A. L., & Koski, M. J. (1995). Lesbian, gay, and bisexual teens and the school counselor. Building alliances. In G. Unks (Ed.), *The gay teen: Educational practice and theory for lesbian, gay and bisexual adolescents* (pp. 85–93). New York: Routledge.

Shively, M. G. & DeCecco, J. P. (1993). Components of sexual identity. In L. D. Garnets & D. C. Kimmel (Eds.), *Psychological perspectives on lesbian and gay male experiences* (pp. 80–88). New York: Columbia University Press.

Troiden, R. R. (1988). *Gay and lesbian identity: A sociological analysis*. Dix Hills, NY: General Hall.

Troiden, R. R. (1989). The formation of homosexual identities. *Journal of Homosexuality*, *17*, (1/2), 43–73.

19

Adolescent Spirituality: An Oxymoron?

Gary Koch, Ph.D.

Gary Koch is an associate professor of psychology at Olivet Nazarene University in Kankakee, Illinois. Gary would like to acknowledge the research assistance of Jennifer Sears, a recent graduate of Olivet Nazarene University.

> *"Sometimes I wish for a stronger connection with the world we can't see with our eyes . . . I believe in God and the afterlife, but others don't believe. They are more grounded in 'reality.' "*

Sierra, age 14

Do teenagers have a spiritual nature? If so, how can I, as a school counselor, influence it? Do I want to influence it? How can I talk about spirituality in a public school? Do adolescents really want to talk about spirituality? These are all relevant questions that a school counselor may ask. This chapter is designed as an introduction to the issue of adolescent spirituality, providing a means by which school counselors can consider the above questions.

Numerous surveys have observed or predicted spiritual rejuvenation in our country. One survey predicted a multidenominational religious revival for the year 2000 (Naisbitt & Aburdene, 1990). Gallup (1988) reported an intensified search for meaning in life, involving a rejection of materialism, a bonding with others, and an embracing of spiritual matters. A more recent survey confirmed this in *USA Today* ("Spirituality," 1996), "What has happened in this country is a slow but unmistakable shift from materialism to spiritualism as Americans have come to the end of their emotional resources" (p. 1A). Even though we may hear more about shootings in schools, violence in the workplace, rage on the roads and in the air, there does seem to be a large segment of the population who is searching for a purpose in life and a connection with a higher meaning. This includes adolescents.

In many ways, school counselors already work with spirituality. In the description of a feminist psychospiritual model, Berlinger (1993) equates counseling to "soul healing." A past president of the American Counseling Association (ACA), Joyce Breasure, noted the importance of the mind, body, and soul/spirit connection, stating, "As a counselor I will not separate these. I think the reason we are seeing so many people in disharmony is because the American people have lost their hearts, souls, and spirits" (Breasure, 1996, p. 5). Perhaps school counselors can help address this dilemma.

Spirituality

What Is Spirituality?

For this chapter I will consider spirituality to be a search for higher meaning or purpose in life. Herbert Benson, a physician (as cited by Tolan, 2001), indicates we are biologically predisposed to believe in something or someone divine or greater than ourselves, which is consistent with Jung's philosophy. I believe spirituality is the most defining and significant part of humanness. In other words, spirituality involves "becoming a person in the fullest sense" (Marquarrie, 1972, p. 40). I have heard it said, "We are not human beings having a spiritual experience, but spiritual beings having a human experience." To understand spirituality, it is important to understand that spirituality is innate, involves a transcendence of self, promotes a oneness or connectedness to others, and involves relationships, especially with a Higher Power.

Innate   We are born with a spirit, but it needs development. We need to act spiritually in order to develop this quality. Just like our physical muscles need development, so do our spiritual muscles.

Transcendence   Our behavior has to create movement away from our own ego needs. We paradoxically develop ourselves by giving to others. Included in the concept of transcendence is the ability to find meaning in life's struggles. Maslow (1964) identified these as peak experiences, which produce an heightening of the senses and include an elevation of the spirit.

Connectedness   The need to belong (Maslow, 1964), a sense of social interest (Adler, 1964), and the struggle of becoming and belonging (May, 1983) are examples of connectedness that relate to psychotherapy theories. Practice of spiritual principles produces connectedness with others and emphasizes interdependence over independence. In other words, through practicing spiritual principles we learn a healthy balance of group- and self-dependence. Through this process we learn to appreciate the concept of oneness, that we are all connected to each other and to the environment, an ecological perspective that values all living things.

Higher Power   Higher Power can be anything that is more powerful than oneself and has the characteristics of transcendence and connectedness. This power can be Buddha, Christian God, Jewish God, the Tao, Allah, or even good orderly direction (god). Included in this concept is a conscious effort to contact this Higher Power (Koch, 1997).

In summary, spirituality will be used as a search for a higher meaning or purpose in life, by seeking contact with a Higher Power and practicing spiritual principles. However, the emphasis is on *relationships* in this approach. I will reiterate this throughout the chapter. Humans are relational beings and everything we do in relation to our world, ourselves, and others affects us spiritually.

Are Spirituality and Religion the Same Thing?

Some people do consider spirituality and religion to be the same thing, while others see these concepts as quite different. In a literature review, Koch (1997) found that most researchers found these constructs connected, but different. For the most part, religion was viewed as formal, external/extrinsic, structured, and community based, whereas spirituality was seen as less formal, more internal or intrinsically oriented, less structured, and more personal. Religion was also usually viewed as a component of, or one possible expression of, spirituality.

For this chapter, it will be sufficient to indicate that religion is considered a form of spirituality, although they may be viewed as one and the same by some people. Always use your clients' perspective as a guide and work within their worldview.

Adolescence

Adolescence is a rather modern construct developed in the middle of the twentieth century, and is considered the transition from childhood to adulthood (Coltrane & Collins, 2001). This chapter will view adolescence as the ages of 13 through 19, the teenage years, emphasizing junior high and high school age students. This is a time of not only physical, sexual, social, emotional, and cognitive growth, but of spiritual growth as well.

Although teenagers are attempting to find their identity and create themselves during this life transition, the concept of teens being rebellious and irresponsible can be misleading. Steinberg, as cited in Dacey and Kenny (1997), found that most adolescents admire and love their parents, rely on their parents' advice, embrace many of their parents' values, and feel loved by their parents. However, the preponderance of academic research focuses more on the negative aspects of adolescence. In a review of literature published during the 1990s, Furstenberg (2000) found that most publications focused on such issues as delinquency and violence, substance abuse, academic problems, and mental health issues. Far fewer articles addressed normal adjustment issues and more positive issues such as spirituality.

In fact, many problems faced by teens can be conceptualized as a struggle with spiritual issues. For example, Scott (1998) discusses the significance of spiritual symbols and assumptions in the rite of passage from adolescence to adulthood. He states that a "sense of meaning arising from spiritual values becomes the glue that holds the other pieces together" (p. 323). He emphasizes the importance of reflection during adolescence, not just on academic issues, but also on such issues as the way one lives and one's sense of value and self. This process of reflection is influenced by role models (e.g., parents, teachers, and mentors), who impart what is considered both sacred and moral in the culture (Scott, 1998). He points out that many of the behaviors we consider abnormal in youths are similar to rites of passage (e.g., ritualization, body markings, name and clothing changes, encounters about death, and a search for meaning).

The questions that we, as adults who work with adolescents, must ask are: Have we forgotten essential rituals? Do we pass along our most precious values and standards? Do we practice what we preach? Are we too afraid of the topic of spirituality to listen to teenagers' spiritual dilemmas?

Development of Spirituality

Spiritual Development

Victor Frankl, as cited in Dacey and Kenny (1997), described three interdependent stages in the development of spirituality: somatic, psychological, and noetic. While the somatic stage addresses basic survival, the psychological stage is related to instincts, drives, and needs beginning at birth and developing fully by early adulthood. The noetic stage starts in childhood but primarily develops in late adolescence. This stage includes reasoning, using the conscience, and freedom and responsibility to make choices. This dimension is spiritual, involving a search for meaning in one's life. In another model, Oser (1991) developed a five-stage model based on a study of students in Germany, ages 16 to 22, which provided four distinct views of God and corresponding differing expectations.

There are other such models; however, Fowler's six stages of faith development (Fowler, 1981, 1986, 1991, 1994, 1996; Osmer & Fowler, 1993) are probably the most comprehensive spirituality-oriented stages of development. There are two stages that pertain to the spiritual development of adolescents: the mythical-literal faith stage and the synthetic-conventional stage (Parrott, 1995).

Mythical-Literal Faith   Most adolescents start their spiritual journey here, as they interpret their faith in very concrete ways, consistent with Piaget's concrete operations stage (e.g.,

God in human form in the sky). These interpretations of faith are those that are handed down from authority figures.

Synthetic-Conventional Faith As formal operations thinking develops, teens relate their view with other incompatible views. They acquire the ability to see themselves as others do (Klaczynski & Narasimham, 1998), and a new depth of inner awareness emerges as the adolescent constructs the young man or woman he or she is becoming. This process constitutes to the overall turbulence of adolescence (Osmer & Fowler, 1993). In the corresponding growth of spirituality, the first step is an integration into one *self*, where a sense of identity is developed. The second step is "a drawing together of one's stories, values, and beliefs into a supportive and orienting unity" in which the person struggles with "a sense of the meaning of life generally, and of the meaning and purpose of his or her life in particular" (Osmer & Fowler, 1993, p. 183). Initially, adolescents may see their Higher Power as a personal adviser and guide, but not in a personally constructed manner (Osmer & Fowler, 1993). As they further define who they are, they concurrently mature spiritually and develop a more personal relationship with their Higher Power.

During faith stages, teens' values and actions are changing and must be redefined. "Our very life-meanings are at stake in faith stage transitions" (Osmer & Fowler, 1993, p.182). A Rubik's Cube can be used to metaphorically represent a holistic model of spiritual development. Each colored side of a cube represents a face we show to a specific segment of the population (e.g., family, friends, classmates, etc.). If movement of the tiles simulates adjustments made to interact with different audiences, then a cube of constantly changing colors represents a confused teen seeking to please others. Spiritual maturity would reflect a consistency on each colored side, which unifies the whole (Radcliffe, 1984).

Regardless of your theoretical approach (e.g., Freudian, Jungian, Existential), spiritual development is accelerated according to psychological maturity. In his study of spiritual maturity, Radcliffe indicated that adolescence and early adulthood (ages 12–22), more than any other life stage, was transformed by other developmental issues (physical, intellectual, psychosocial, emotional, social, and moral) (Radcliffe, 1984). Therefore, teens are under heavy construction. In all ways, teens are desperately trying to determine who they are, what they believe and value, and what has meaning and importance in their lives. In this process, spirituality develops most effectively when all areas of one's life are considered dynamic, interactive, and each inextricably affected by the other. Spiritual maturity is viewed as an invariant sequence, each stage progressing only as the former stage is complete. Movement along the maturity continuum is multifaceted and affected positively and negatively by all others areas of one's life (Radcliffe, 1984, p. 45).

Spirituality and Teens

Parrott (1995) cited a recent Gallup Youth survey that reported that 70 percent of U.S. teenagers agreed with the statement that they are a religious person. Nineteen percent of these teens agreed *very* strongly with that same statement; and, of the 30 percent who disagreed, only 5 percent strongly disagreed. Benson (1997) indicated 95 percent of teenagers believe in God or some kind of universal spirit. In a study of pastoral care response to teens, Rowatt

(1989) noted ministers across the country are recognizing the intense needs of adolescents and ministers' inadequate response. The five teenage issues that challenge ministers most are careers, suicide, sex, alcohol and drugs, and depression. All relate to teens' grappling to become, and the latter four can be construed as relational, as a search to fill an emptiness or void. Some drug and alcohol treatment professionals refer to this as a "hole in the soul."

Common questions that reflect teens' personal struggle with spiritual issues include:

Is there a center to life, a coordinate around which I can build my world?

Who and what puts it all together?

How and why is my life important?

What things matter more than others?

What keeps me going when life feels overwhelming?

Is there a foundation for a hopeful future?

In general, junior high students seek a practical, personal religion; want to make their own decisions; have a vision for service/worship; are idealistic about themselves and others; and need their questions and doubts about religion voiced and validated. Senior high students' issues include concern about finding friends and belonging; seeking guidance in moral decisions; establishing priorities in life and for the future; wanting to make a difference; and asking "God" questions and wanting to understand their faith (Evangelical Lutheran Church in America [ELCA] Youth Ministries, 2001). Understanding teenage struggles with these issues may help us better comprehend how adolescents may join a gang or a cult to attain the connection they crave.

Benefits of Spirituality

I am probably preaching to the choir about the benefits of spirituality, so I will include only enough material to provide its legitimacy. For instance, in healthcare, Conco (1995) found a connection between spirituality, reduced anxiety, increased peace, comfort, inner strength, acceptance, hopefulness, calmness, and safety, general well-being, stronger faith, and a positive change in attitude and outlook on life. Some research findings support a decrease in negative symptoms such as depression and loneliness, and an improved feeling of well-being despite acute or chronic physiological problems (Fehring, Brennan, & Keller, 1987).

Teens with personal religious beliefs were found to be half as likely to abuse alcohol or other drugs. This study differentiated between a forced religious affiliation and a personal sense of spirituality, the latter being most effective (Adventist News, 2001). Integrating spirituality into counseling with teens may help them cope better with such issues as identity formation and belonging and help prevent problems such as unplanned pregnancy, involvement with gangs, and suicide (Richards & Bergin, 1997). Lee (1997) notes that the Black Church has traditionally nurtured African American spirituality and Black consciousness, reinforcing the connection between spiritual development and healthy choices. Many other cultures also have strong links to religious organizations (e.g., Latinos with Catholicism, many Asian cultures with Buddhism). In addition, findings from a national longitudinal study on adolescence (Klein, 1997) supported guidelines developed by the American Medical

Association, the Centers for Disease Control and Prevention, and the Maternal and Child Health Bureau, recommending counseling for all adolescents. This opportunity may present a fertile time to discuss spirituality with teens.

Can We Include Spirituality in Counseling?

Spirituality has historically been a part of counseling (Koch, 1997). Jung, as cited in Zinnbauer and Pargament (2000), considered religion an innate, instinctual part of human-ness, connected to an ancestral collective unconscious of spirituality, and an integral aspect of the self. He later stated,

> Religions are psychotherapeutic systems in the truest sense of the word, and on the grand-est scale. They express the whole range of the psychic problem in mighty images; they are the avowal and recognition of the soul, and at the same time the revelation of the soul's nature (p. 168).

Let us recognize, however, that religion/spirituality forced upon teenagers may cause them to avoid discussions of spirituality; however, if adolescents make a free choice to pur-sue a spiritual life, they are less at risk to abuse alcohol and other drugs. Spirituality is the most central theme in an adolescent's life, with or without religion. If spirituality is ignored, teens will search for meaning and communion wherever they can find it (Miller, Davies, & Greenwald, 2000).

Guidelines

The first issue on your minds is probably "How can I do this at school? What about the separation of church and state?" You need to make your own decision about choosing whether to discuss spiritual issues at school, and if so, how to facilitate such a discussion. An important consideration is the supportive nature of the administration: Do the decision makers in the district support holistic counseling, including discussions about the existen-tial decisions of life? It is a professional, and sometimes ethical, decision that only you can make. Corey (2001) encourages counselors to expose their values when appropriate, but to not impose those values.

It is helpful to know that some authors believe that schools already teach values. Rabbi Harold Kushner (Scherer, 1999) stated, "But schools already emphasize a number of spiri-tual values if we would only recognize them as such" (p. 1). He identified examples of these issues, including teaching about truth, responsibility for doing our work and completing it on time, admitting our mistakes, and coming to terms with our limitations. In addition, teach-ing cooperation helps students learn about mutual help and contributing to society. All of these behaviors make the classroom a more spiritual place (Scherer, 1999).

Numerous others have made similar observations. Palmer (1983) discussed the "hid-den curriculum" of schools' systematic rewards and punishments, which have great formative power over the development of learners. He noted, "In a thousand ways, the relationships of the academic community form the hearts and minds of students, shaping their sense of self and their relation to the world" (p. 20). In his book on critical pedagogy in education, McLaren (1994) discusses the issue of transforming others and in the process, ourselves, by connecting to others. Isn't this an apt description of our work as counselors with teens as they struggle to become? We should help develop them so that they grow intra- and interpersonally.

The point here is not to advocate that counselors teach religion. The point is that counselors should be aware of the spiritual needs of students and open to the discussion with students of these existential questions about the meaning of life and their place in it. Based on the student's comfort level and the values taught in the student's home, counselors can help the student to learn how to choose between healthy and unhealthy choices, make a commitment to spiritual development, practice spiritual practices (e.g., forgiveness, humility, altruism, acceptance, praying, or meditation), develop a connectedness with others, and establish a spiritual-centeredness.

In general, a spiritual empowerment philosophy of counseling may be helpful (Koch, 1998). This includes the following guidelines:

1. Spirituality and religion are contributors to our diversity.
2. Spirituality is developed by practicing spiritual principles.
3. It is unethical to *not* attend to spiritual/religious issues identified by students.
4. The most important relationship is between the student and her or his Higher Power.
5. The counselor's spiritual self-awareness is crucial. Be a healthy role model and help students seek healthy role models.
6. Realize their spiritual journey is a process, not an event; expect stops and starts and unsettling adjustments to new insights. This is a time of cognitive turbulence.
7. Expect idealistic thinking that leads to criticism and perhaps cynicism.
8. Adjust to students' emotionality; you may encounter as much emotional as cognitive turbulence.
9. Identify spiritual beliefs that may contribute to the students' distress.
10. Identify spiritual beliefs that may help resolve the students' distress.

Some common errors to avoid would include:

1. *Motivating by guilt*. It can also foster compliant behaviors rather than true growth.
2. *Equating spirituality with youth group activity*. Spiritual programming alone does not develop spiritual growth.
3. *Setting your expectations too low*. It is a mistake and potentially harmful to assume that we can expect little spiritually from teens.
4. *Setting your expectations too high*. We can't expect a teen to be an adult (Parrott, 1995, p. 3). Here's an example: My 2-year-old daughter likes to help her daddy cut the grass. She was helping me rake and throw the cut grass into a lawn bag. I told her to throw the grass into the bag. She threw it and it went all over ME. I started to get mad when I realized she did just what I told her to do. Her 2-year-old aim and understanding just are not very accurate. We have to establish our expectations of adolescents based on their developmental level.

If there are opportunities to discuss the issue of teen spirituality with teachers at your school, you may encourage them to be open to the topic, without necessarily making it one of their goals. For instance, an assignment may be given for students to write about the meaning of life, what is most important in their lives, or what helps them most through the tough times in life. If a student writes about a spiritual/religious topic or figure, help teachers to see it as acceptable.

Exploring and Utilizing a Student's Spirituality

First, you are your best guide; always let that and your own Higher Power guide you in your counseling approach. I am providing some techniques and suggestions that I think you will find useful, but you will decide what to do based upon the situation, the client, and your own being. Hanna, Hanna, and Keys (1999) have some helpful suggestions for working with adolescents, and a review could be helpful.

Spiritual Assessment/History

These questions can open the topic and help gather information about a student's spirituality (modified from Clinebell, 1984, and Peck, 1993):

1. Explore the student's spiritual and/or religious upbringing. What faith community was he or she raised in, and how does he or she identify now? If it has changed, explore the reason(s).
2. Be open to these discussions with atheists and agnostics also.
3. Ask:
    a. What is your concept of Higher Power? Is your relationship close and personal or distant? Has this changed? How has it changed?
    b. Have you had any experiences you would describe as spiritual? Describe them.
    c. What effect do spiritual practices have on you?
    d. How do you understand this issue in light of what's most important in your life?
    e. How does this problem with which you are struggling relate to your personal faith, to your relationship with your Higher Power?
    f. Has this experience changed your faith? In what ways?
    g. What have you learned from this crisis?
    h. What meaning do you attribute to this experience? Could there be a higher meaning in this?
    i. What is the most important benefit you get from spiritual beliefs?

Techniques

In addition to a long list of relaxation techniques (e.g., deep breathing, yoga, Tai Chi, meditation), and prayer (a dialogue between a person and his or her Higher Power), here are some other suggestions:

Creative visualizing

Reframing

Sharing stories, myths, and metaphors

Using metaphors: Use what teens give you. Ask about their metaphors in terms that they can understand. For example: How would you describe what you are experiencing? Can you relate it to anything you have ever experienced or heard about?

Journaling about value issues (e.g. One important relationship in my life is with ___ because . . . ; One way that I live what I believe is . . . ; I believe I am being led to . . . ; To me, spirituality means . . .).

Native American techniques have recently been used in various settings to promote self-discovery, improve behavioral problems, and increase appreciation for ecology ("New, Old Ways," 2001).

Resources

There is no way to do justice to the huge amount of resources about the spirituality of adolescents. I encourage you to consult your local clergy (especially youth ministers), bookstores, libraries, the YMCA and YWCA, as well as other local resources, in addition to those resources listed in Appendix 19-1.

Summary

Porter (1995) reminds us of the importance of our inner compass for meaning making and fulfillment. We need to empower students to recreate themselves with the image of the heart (Porter, 1995). Our role, as counselors, should be to help them discover their heart and soul. Jung, as cited by Zinnbauer and Pargament (2000), stated, "A psychoneurosis must be understood, ultimately, as the suffering of a soul which has not discovered its meaning . . . the cause of the suffering is spiritual stagnation" (p. 163).

Practical guidelines and techniques have been provided to appropriately address adolescents' spirituality in a school setting. A developmental model is suggested. This chapter should serve as a stimulus for further exploration of this subject, rather than a final resource.

References

Adler, A. (1964). *Social interest: A challenge to mankind.* New York: Capricorn.

Adventist News. (2001, April 17). *Teens with personal religious beliefs less likely to abuse drugs, alcohol* [Online], pp. 3–4. Available: *http://www.tagnet.org/ adventist.tm/news1.htm.*

Benson, P. (1997). Spirituality and the adolescent journey. *Reclaiming Children and Youth, 5*(4), 206–209.

Berlinger, P. M. (1993). Soul healing: A model of feminist therapy. *Counseling and Values, 17,* 2–14.

Breasure, J. M. (1996, March). The mind, body, and soul connection. *Counseling Today,* 5.

Clinebell, H. (1984). *Basic types of pastoral care and counseling: Resources for the ministry of healing and growth.* Nashville, TN: Abingdon.

Coltrane, S., & Collins, R. (2001). *Sociology of marriage and the family: Gender, love, and property* (5th ed.). Belmont, CA: Wadsworth/Thomson Learning.

Conco, D. (1995). Christian patients' views of spiritual care. *Western Journal of Nursing Research, 17*(3), 266–276.

Corey, G. (2001). *Theory and practice of counseling and psychotherapy* (6th ed.). Pacific Grove, CA: Brooks Cole.

Dacey, J., & Kenny, M. (1997). *Adolescent development* (2nd ed.). Dubuque, IA: Brown & Benchmark.

Evangelical Lutheran Church in America (ECLA) Youth Ministries Help Sheet (2001, April 17). *Teenage spirituality: Not an oxymoron* [Online], pp. 1–7. Available: *http://www.elca.org/dcm/youth/resource/helpsheets/spirit.html*

Fehring, R. J., Brennan, P. F., & Keller, M. L. (1987). Psychological and spiritual well-being in college students. *Research in Nursing and Health, 10,* 191–198.

Fowler, J. W. (1981). *Stages in faith.* San Francisco: Harper & Row.

Fowler, J. W. (1986). *Faith and structuring of meaning.* Birmingham, AL: Religious Education Press.

Fowler, J. W. (1991). Stages in faith consciousness. *New Directions for Child Development.* 27–45.

Fowler, J. W. (1994). *Moral stages and the development of faith.* New York: Garland Publishing.

Fowler, J. W. (1996). *Faithful change: The personal and public challenges of postmodern life.* Nashville, TN: Abingdon Press.

Furstenberg, F. F. (2000). The sociology of adolescence and youth in the 1990s. *Journal of Marriage and the Family, 62*(4), 896–910.

Gallup, G. (1988). *The 1990's: Decade of the people's religion?* Princeton, NJ: Princeton Religious Research Center.

Hanna, F. J., Hanna, C. A., & Keys, S. G. (1999). Fifty strategies for counseling defiant, aggressive adolescents: Reaching, accepting, and relating. *Journal of Counseling and Development, 77,* 395–404.

Klaczynski, P.A., & Narasimham, G. (1998). Development of scientific reasoning biases: Cognitive versus ego-protective explanations. *Developmental Psychology, 34,* 175–187.

Klein, J. D. (1997). The national longitudinal study on adolescent health. *JAMA, 278(10),* 864–865.

Koch, G. R. (1997). Spirituality and Alcoholics Anonymous: Implications for counselors. *Dissertation Abstracts International, 58,* 09B. (UMI number: 9808830).

Koch, G. R. (1998). Spiritual empowerment: A metaphor for counseling. *Counseling & Values, 43,* 19–27.

Lee, C. C. (Ed.). (1997). *Multicultural issues in counseling: New approaches to diversity* (2nd ed.). Alexandria, VA: American Counseling Association.

Marquarrie, J. (1972). *Paths in spirituality.* New York: Harper & Row.

Maslow, A. (1964). *Religion, values, and peak experiences.* New York: Viking Press.

May, R. (1983). *The discovery of being: Writings in existential psychology.* New York: Norton.

McLaren, P. (1994). *Life in schools: An introduction to critical pedagogy in the foundations of education.* New York: Longman.

Miller, L., Davies, M., & Greenwald, S. (2000). Religiosity and substance use and abuse among adolescents in the national co-morbidity survey. *Journal of the American Academy of Child & Adolescent Psychiatry, 39*(9), 1190–1197.

Naisbitt, J., & Aburdene, D. (1990). *Megatrends 2000.* New York: William Morrow.

New, old ways to teach spiritual values. (2001, June 7). *The Washington Post,* as reprinted in *The Daily Journal,* p. B3.

Oser, F. K. (1991). The development of religious judgment. In F. K. Oser, & W. G. Scarlett (Eds.), *Religious development in childhood and adolescence* (pp. 5–25). San Francisco: Jossey-Bass.

Osmer, R. R., & Fowler, J. W. (1993). Children and adolescents: A faith development perspective (pp. 171–212). In R. J. Wicks, D. Capps, & R. D. Parsons (Eds.), *Clinical handbook of pastoral counseling* (Vol. 1). New York: Paulist Press.

Palmer, P. (1983). *To know as we know: A spirituality of education.* San Francisco: Harper and Row.

Parrott, III, L. (1995, Spring). Adolescent spirituality: What can we expect? *Youthworker* [Online], pp. 1–11. Available: *http://www.youthspecialities.com/ywj/articles/results/adolescent.html.*

Peck, M. S. (1993). *Further along the road less traveled: The unending journey toward spiritual growth.* New York: Simon & Schuster.

Porter, G. (1995). Exploring the meaning of spirituality and its implications for counselors. *Counseling & Values, 40,* 69–79.

Radcliffe, R. J. (1984). Spiritual growth: A developmental approach. *Christian Education Journal, 5*(1), 38–47.

Richards, P. S., & Bergin, A. E. (1997). *A spiritual strategy for counseling and psychotherapy.* Washington, DC: American Psychological Association.

Rowatt, G. W. (1989). A pastoral care response to adolescents in crisis: National survey results. *Affirmations 2, Spring,* 65–74.

Scherer, M. (1999, January). Is school the place for spirituality? A conversation with Rabbi Harold Kushner. *Educational Leadership, 56* [Online], pp. 1–6. Available: *http://www.ascd.org./readingroom/edlead/9812/extkushner.html.*

Scott, D. G. (1998). Rites of passage in adolescent development: A reappreciation. *Child & Youth Care Forum, 27,* 317–346.

Spirituality. (1996, October 15). *USA Today,* p. 1A.

Tolan, S. S. (2001). Spirituality and the highly gifted adolescent. *Spirituality* [Online], pp. 1–8. Available: *http://www.stephanietolan.com/spirituality.htm .*

Zinnbauer B. J., & Pargament, K. I. (2000). Working with the sacred: Four approaches to religious and spiritual issues in counseling. *Journal of Counseling and Development, 78,* 162–171.

Appendix 19.1

Below are some websites that provide meaningful information for helping professionals work-ing with teenagers. For each site, a title, web address, and description of the site are provided.

Articles and Ideas for You to Use with Kids: http://www.teensalive.org/update.html
A Christian website offering information and articles for parents and youth workers.

Focus Adolescent Services: *http://www.focusas.com/CounselingTherapy.html*
This site gives a brief overview of the different types of therapy (i.e., cognitive, behav-ioral, etc.). It includes information about pastoral and transpersonal counseling with links concerning adolescent spirituality.

*Open Directory * Society Religion and Spirituality: http://dmoz.org/Society/Religion_ and_Spiritiuality/*
This is a directory, not a search engine, that provides a list of sites and information related to religious denominations. It is very comprehensive.

Youthwork: http://www.youthwork.com
This website covers an array of issues concerning youth and has some excellent links to search for different issues that may be of interest. Also: activities, games, radio sta-tions, stories of youths, websites for youth, resources, and a humor link. The site is quite comprehensive and includes some good spirituality and diversity information.

Cinematherapy: http://www.ed.uab.edu/cinematherapy
This University of Alabama Birmingham site has a link for school counselors with many movies that are relationship oriented. This site offers a worthwhile visit for some good movie selections that may work with teens.

Parenting Today's Teen: http://www.parentingteens.com
Site includes: Q&A area and links to issues such as humor, spirituality, living with teens, single parenting, and stepfamilies.

Beliefnet: http://beliefnet.com/
Self-described as "The world's leading religious and spiritual e-community." Indicates, "We all believe in something." Provides information and links for many religions. Includes topics such as: religions, spirituality, inspiration, family and life events, and spiritual tools.

Family.org: http://www.family.org/
Site of Christian organization, Focus on the Family. Includes: Focus magazine, infor-mation about children, teens, and collegians, with section for parents and one for pro-fessionals. Good site for Christians.

Innerself Magazine: http://www.innerself.com/
Offers information and articles about topics such as: parenting, relationships, and spirituality and includes a daily inspirational message.

Susan Kramer—Practical Spirituality for Children, Teens, and Adults: http://www.susankramer.com/
Site provides over 100 spiritual-related articles on topics including teen issues, med-itation, and yoga. Includes some links and discussion forums.

20

The Role of the Secondary School Counselor in Substance Abuse Prevention

David Van Doren, Ed.D., LPsy, CPC, CCMHC, NCC, MAC

David Van Doren is an associate professor in counselor education at the University of Wisconsin–Whitewater.

"Is substance abuse a problem? I know a couple of kids who use, drink and smoke weed. The majority don't use at all or they use when it's appropriate. Most don't have a problem with it."

Jessica, age 18

As a beginning counselor at a suburban high school (too many years ago) I was asked by the school administration to counsel a student, whom we'll call Calvin. Calvin had been socially promoted to high school following a physical confrontation with a teacher in the junior high school. He was an interesting student, intelligent and charismatic, yet depressed, surly, and contemptuous. Calvin used alcohol and other drugs, but never presented this as a primary problem during our counseling sessions. He discussed his father's tendency to keep a bottle of whiskey in his truck, his brother's alcohol and other drug abuse prior to imprisonment on theft charges, and his mother's concern that Calvin straighten up, graduate from high school, and escape this family history of alcoholism and drug abuse. I enjoyed counseling Calvin and helped him to identify his positive attributes and increase his self-esteem. He was a very active participant in a group of at-risk youths, often confronting group members on their behavior and lack of openness. Calvin became more actively involved in school and grew much less disruptive in the classroom. Unfortunately, his home situation continued to be extremely difficult, leading to increased depression expressed most often as anger and irritability. The school administration attempted to exert its authority over Calvin's behavior, and it wasn't long until Calvin was suspended for using the F word in a hallway discussion with friends. After much coaxing, I was able to persuade him to return to school after the three-day suspension had been served. Although he attempted to be active in class, he continued to miss a day of school here and there due to suspensions for using inappropriate language, smoking cigarettes in the bathroom (during an era when the atmosphere in the teacher's lounge was also highly carcinogenic), and other violations. This led to difficulties in the classroom. Calvin became less engaged in the academic process and began to refocus on the belief that he couldn't make it in this system. Calvin eventually failed to return after a three-day suspension, even after much coaxing on my part. After more than a year and a half of counseling, Calvin decided that school wasn't going to work for him. I left my counseling position to pursue my doctorate a few months after Calvin quit school. Since those naïve days of my youth, I have learned a lot about alcohol and other drug abuse. I often look back on what I could have done differently to address Calvin's concerns.

The school counselor does not function as the primary treatment provider but plays an essential role in all aspects of prevention. Prevention programs begin in elementary school but must continue into middle and high school with the counselor serving a vital role. Prevention is often broken down into three components: Primary, Secondary, and Tertiary prevention. (You might recognize the parallels with prevention, intervention, and treatment introduced elsewhere in this book.) The school counselor's role varies based on the type of prevention effort. All counseling activities serve as some aspect of the prevention effort.

Primary Prevention

Primary prevention is an effort to address the *precursors* to use and abuse of chemicals in order to decrease the incidence of use and abuse. It is essential to address this aspect of prevention early in the educational process. However, primary prevention also occurs at the secondary level as adolescents make choices about integrating alcohol into their lives. Primary prevention often focuses on education about alcohol and other drugs, as well as programs that enhance self-concept. Education programs by themselves have not proven to be highly successful in changing the behavior patterns of adolescents; however, disseminating information about risk factors and providing counseling programs to address these concerns may be beneficial in decreasing use/abuse.

Risk factors predicting adolescent alcohol and other drug abuse encompass individual, interpersonal, and institutional issues, and each can be addressed through individual counseling, group counseling, and developmental curriculum programming in the high school. Anger, aggressive behaviors, impulsivity, and/or depression are individual factors often linked to substance use/abuse (Wodarski & Smyth, 1994). Interpersonal issues that increase risk for alcohol, tobacco, and other drug abuse (ATODA) include alcohol and other drug abuse in the family; neglectful or abusive parents; parents' marital conflict, separation, or divorce; or the adolescent's membership in a peer group that encourages or tolerates alcohol, tobacco, and other drug abuse (Wodarski & Smyth, 1994). Costa, Jessor, and Turbin (1999, p. 487) indicate that "low self-esteem; a sense of hopelessness and disengagement from social norms; high stress; exposure to friends who use alcohol and other drugs; greater orientation to friends than to parents; poor school performance; and a greater proneness for dropping out of school" are risk factors for problem drinking. Chatlos (1996) describes many of these same antecedents of alcohol abuse and, in addition, implicates insufficient bonding with parents and early initiation of alcohol use. Adlaf and Ivis (1996) identified familial interaction as the most influential factor in determining risk for alcohol abuse. In addition to these individual and interpersonal factors, institutional issues such as poverty, lacking meaningful roles in the community, and impersonal, more anonymous school involvement may increase risk (Wodarski & Smyth, 1994).

Although many of these factors may begin earlier in life, secondary school counselors can identify and address these concerns in primary prevention efforts. Individual and group interventions to address these risk factors can serve as primary prevention. Counselors can identify individuals and provide supportive individual counseling and referrals to attempt to address these concerns. Groups can be formed to help students deal with stress, academic concerns, parental conflict, concerns about another's alcohol or other drug abuse, anger management, increasing positive self-esteem, and so on. Counselors can also identify, counsel, and/or refer adolescents who exhibit academic problems, behavior problems, and/or symptoms of depression.

Furthermore, students who struggle with adolescent developmental issues are likely to be at risk for involvement in negative behaviors such as ATODA. Developmental tasks of adolescence include academic achievement, involvement in extracurricular activities, forming close relationships, and forming a cohesive sense of self (Masten & Coatsworth, 1998). If these are not successfully navigated, the student may be at greater risk. The school counselor attempts to enhance developmental transitions and academic achievement by targeting individuals who are not doing well personally, socially, or academically and providing individual and/or group interventions to address these roadblocks. Establishing significant supportive relationships with these students enables the counselor to identify significant issues and make appropriate referrals to counselors in the community.

By the time I met Calvin in high school, he had already begun to use alcohol and other drugs. Primary intervention efforts should have begun during his elementary years. Calvin's personal history included many factors highly predictive of his use and abuse of alcohol and other drugs. He was a child of an alcoholic and therefore had a greater likelihood of abusing chemicals. Identifying this earlier in his life would have allowed a counselor to help Calvin (individually and/or in a group format) address the impact of alcoholism in his life and help him examine alternative coping behaviors. Externalizing behaviors, such as blaming and projecting one's faults onto others, can also be indicators of alcohol and other drug abuse. A school counselor could have recognized his anger and argumentative behavior in junior high school as a warning sign and provided intervention (a secondary prevention effort). Calvin's negative self-concept and depressive symptoms, such as irritability and feelings of low self-worth and inadequacy, were certainly areas that a counselor could have addressed early in order to decrease the possibility of use or abuse.

The adolescent struggle with self-concept is as prevalent as the recognition that alcohol serves as a temporary solution. From middle school to secondary school the growth trajectory for alcohol use increases, whereas self-esteem declines (Scheier, Botvin, Griffin, & Diaz, 2000). Long-term alcohol use exacerbates the struggle for self-acceptance. Unfortunately, by the time Calvin and I met, he had already learned that chemicals were effective in temporarily numbing these negative feelings. Once use has occurred, the cognition associated with the effects is a determining factor related to frequency and quantity of use (Ellickson & Hays, 1991). Calvin discovered, as many adolescents do, that alcohol does provide an escape. As counselors we need to recognize that chemicals do work to temporarily alleviate the user's pain. The focus on the negative aspects may have benefits in prevention efforts but may be negated by the knowledge that the drug serves as a temporary positive in this person's life. The negative effects we warn about often occur well after the positive effects wear off.

A protective factor that decreases the development of at-risk behaviors (including alcohol and other drug abuse) is a positive parent-child relationship in early childhood. The more supportive adults there are in the child's life, the less likely it is that the child will engage in high-risk behaviors. Although a counselor will never replace a parent, he or she can help students to feel accepted by a significant adult in their lives—a protective factor from many high-risk behaviors. In Calvin's case, he had a very positive relationship with his mother, while having a very negative relationship with his father. I can only hope that our positive counseling relationship provided a sense of acceptance. The counselor, by serving as a supportive adult in the child's life, helps to provide this protective factor.

Secondary Prevention

Secondary prevention occurs after use/abuse has begun and is an attempt on the part of the counselor to decrease the impact of substance use/abuse on the person's life. This entails providing both early intervention into the root causes of the use/abuse and providing support for the adolescent to examine his or her use/abuse and choose a different path. Calvin was a good example of an individual needing secondary prevention, where intervention could have been engaged on a number of levels.

First, Calvin was greatly affected by his father's and brother's alcoholism. Inviting the mother to participate in sessions could have enlisted her aid in acknowledging the impact of Dad's use on the family and allowed Calvin to more openly address his concerns. Although I did meet Calvin's mom, the focus of our discussion was on his grades, not the family issues related to Calvin's personal struggles. Groups for students affected by another's use may have enabled Calvin to effectively find ways to address the impact of alcoholism on his life. It is essential to directly explore this issue. However, many affected students may refrain from involvement in such a group because of the need to maintain the family secret. This acknowledgment of a family problem does not absolve individual responsibility for behavior. However, it provides a context and understanding, which allows the child to acknowledge and express personal feelings.

Another critical factor was Calvin's depressive symptoms, which could have been explored as part of a secondary prevention effort. Counselors need to recognize that mood and anxiety disorders are common dual diagnoses for those who abuse alcohol, tobacco, and other drugs. Support groups could be structured around these symptoms, with a focus on self-esteem and enhancing positive thoughts. During counseling, Calvin could have continued to address self-esteem, increase positive self-statements, and increase feelings of adequacy. At some point, the counselor could have linked these issues with the impact of being a child of an alcoholic and to his own use. Calvin could have benefited from the understanding that alcohol is often used as a way to escape negative feelings.

The third level of concern was Calvin's aggressive behavior, which served as a warning sign of personal and family issues. This could have been a focus of counseling and would have led to additional areas of concern, including alcohol, tobacco, and other drug abuse. Exploration of anger and aggressiveness would uncover conflict resolution approaches learned in his family. Inevitably, this would lead to the hurt and anger related to father's alcoholism and Calvin's inability to effectively express these feelings.

Finally, Calvin's own use needed to be effectively confronted. It would have been beneficial to help Calvin identify how he utilized alcohol and other drugs in his life and examine nonchemical ways to address these issues. Helping Calvin to examine the destructive force alcohol has been in his family and exploring personal damage created by his own ATODA would facilitate a referral for substance abuse treatment.

It is important that school counselors realize that children of alcoholics do not constitute one generic group; some develop more effective coping skills than others. It is true that children of alcoholics are more likely to abuse alcohol and other drugs and/or become dependent (Chassin, Pitts, DeLucia, & Todd, 1999), since "[a]busive drinking by parents may create identifiable adverse effects on both the day-to-day tenor of family life and the overall abilities of the family system. Both of these domains of family functioning contribute to the general atmosphere in which children are raised and the ability of the family to socialize, and protect its members"(Sheridan & Green, 1993, p. 88). No one escapes unscathed from an unhealthy family, but some adaptations are more socially appropriate than others. Calvin's leadership abilities are not uncommon for children of alcoholics. Many children have grown up fast, with parents often providing inappropriate expectations of a child's ability to manage his or her own behavior. Secondary prevention includes counseling the child of an alcoholic who has already begun to use chemicals to intervene in this process as early as possible.

Primary and secondary prevention efforts are served as the counselor identifies and addresses students' mental health issues. It is important for the counselor to have knowledge of the signs and symptoms of common childhood mental health disorders. The counselor will not provide ongoing therapeutic treatment, but can make the necessary referral and provide support. Basic understanding of indicators of anxiety, mood disorders, or disorders first evident in childhood can help address issues prior to involvement with alcohol and other drugs, or be a significant aid in decreasing use.

The counselor can also intervene in substance use/abuse by becoming aware of the warning signs and exploring use with the student. A decline in academic work, increased attendance problems, increased irritability and/or conflict, a shift in friendships (especially toward individuals who are using or abusing chemicals) all can be seen as warnings signs that the student may be using and/or abusing chemicals. Effective intervention includes identifying and effectively confronting these behaviors.

Motivational interviewing approaches (Miller & Rollnick, 1991) can be very useful in confronting these negative behaviors in ways that can be heard by the adolescent. Developing a positive relationship and helping the student to examine his or her behavior is critical to the intervention process. Too often counselors, like parents, want to *mandate* change in students' behavior. However, in order to create lasting change, the source of change must come from within. There are many times when consequences of behavior may facilitate change, and counselors must refrain from shielding the adolescent from the natural consequences of his or her behavior. Only when the adolescent is able to internalize the need to change will it be long lasting.

Miller and Rollnick (1991) identify the following principles of motivational interviewing: (1) express empathy, (2) develop discrepancy, (3) avoid argumentation, (4) roll with resistance, and (5) support self-efficacy. Reflective listening facilitates acceptance and engages the student in the counseling relationship. More than most clients, adolescents struggle with a discrepancy between their goals and how their present behavior will lead to them. Reflecting the discrepancies that the student reveals will help facilitate exploration. "The *client* should present the arguments for change" (Miller & Rollnick, 1991, p. 58). Although counselors and parents may at times be drawn into arguments, it is important to recognize that arguing will lead to increased defensiveness, thereby strengthening the student's resolve. When resistance is met, go with the flow and allow the student's direction to lead to new perspectives and new solutions for present dilemmas. It is crucial to support the students' efficacy for change; no lasting change will occur if the student believes that change is not possible. Helping students to recognize the possibility and their capacity for change in their lives is an essential function of counseling.

Tertiary Prevention

Tertiary prevention (treatment) acknowledges that the best prevention efforts will not eliminate the occurrence of alcohol, tobacco, and other drug abuse and/or dependence. Tertiary prevention attempts to provide treatment to minimize the impact of abuse and dependence, and school counselors, while not usually directly providing this treatment, do have an important role in this process. School counselors can provide significant support to move the adolescent into treatment and provide critical support when the adolescent returns to school. Adolescents are extremely focused on peer relationships. Unfortunately, by the time students enter alcohol and other drug treatment, they have established a lot of peer support for use and abuse of substances and little, if any, support for nonuse. It is critical for counselors to support the students' return to school and help facilitate involvement with different choices of behavior, including peer groups. Much literature suggests adolescents will begin to use to the level of the use of their peer group (Beauvais & Oetting, 1987; Rose, 1999). If an adolescent returns from treatment and maintains this former peer group, continued use/abuse can be anticipated. Of course, parents of adolescents fear for their own child's well being and will often be upset if their child befriends an adolescent who has returned from ATODA treatment.

Treatment would have been very helpful for Calvin. Effective treatment would have addressed the impact of being a child of an alcoholic, as well as Calvin's own alcohol and other drug abuse. Not only would treatment emphasize abstinence, but treatment would also have helped Calvin to identify how he could take care of himself emotionally. This would include helping the adolescent improve social skills; increasing awareness and expression of feelings; developing health habits to take care of one's body through exercise, nutrition, and relaxation techniques; and improving communication skills to effectively interact at home and at school. All of these components of effective treatment can be reinforced and supported by the school counselor. It is important to be actively involved in the student's transition back to school (which is greatly facilitated by the signing of releases so that the counselor can interact with treatment personnel). Returning to school following treatment, Calvin would have been more capable of utilizing his intelligence and charisma toward more positive goals. He may have become a peer leader and been able to discover the intrinsic joy of helping others.

Conclusion

Secondary school counselors serve a significant role in the prevention of use and abuse of alcohol, tobacco, and other drugs. Almost everything we do as school counselors is related to primary, secondary, or tertiary prevention (prevention, intervention, and treatment) of alcohol, tobacco, and other drug abuse. Unfortunately, no school setting is immune from the influence of chemicals. As counselors, we must identify our roles in prevention and effectively address them. Calvin needed to examine his self-concept and self-esteem, but these issues needed to be tied to, and not separated from, his alcoholic family system and his own use/abuse of chemicals. Counseling that failed to integrate ATOD and related concerns with any of his symptoms was doomed to eventual failure. Both the alcoholic family system and Calvin's own use/abuse exacerbated his depression and lowered his self-esteem and academic success, while increasing his irritability and anger. Being caring means not looking away but gently and assertively reflecting the reality that you are witnessing and offering the child and his or her family alternative paths.

References

Adlaf, E. M., & Ivis, F. J. (1996). Structure and relations: The influence of familial factors on adolescent substance use and delinquency. *Journal of Child & Adolescent Substance Abuse, 5*(3), 1–19.

Beauvais, F., & Oetting, E. R. (1987). Peer cluster theory, socialization, characteristics, and adolescent drug use: A path analysis. *Journal of Counseling Psychology, 34*, 205–213.

Chassin, L., Pitts, S. C., DeLucia, C., & Todd, M. (1999). A longitudinal study of children of alcoholics: Predicting young adult substance use disorders, anxiety, and depression. *Journal of Abnormal Psychology*, *108*(1), 106–119.

Chatlos, J. C. (1996). Recent trends and a developmental approach to substance abuse in adolescents. *Child and Adolescent Psychiatric Clinics of North America*, *5*(1), 1–27.

Costa, F. M., Jessor, R., & Turbin, M.S. (1999). Transition into adolescent problem drinking: The role of psychosocial risk and protective factors. *Journal of Studies on Alcohol*, *60*(4), 480–490.

Ellickson, P. L., & Hays, R. D. (1991). Antecedents of drinking among young adolescents with different alcohol use histories. *Journal of Studies on Alcohol*, *52*(5), 398–408.

Masten, A. S., & Coatsworth, J. D. (1998). The development of competence in favorable and unfavorable environments. *American Psychologist*, *53*(2), 205–220.

Miller, W., & Rollnick, S. (1991). *Motivational interviewing: Preparing people to change behavior*. New York: Guilford.

Rose, C. D. (1999). Peer cluster theory and adolescent alcohol use: An explanation of alcohol use and a comparative analysis between two causal models. *Journal of Drug Education*, *29*(3), 205–215.

Scheier, L. M., Botvin, G.J., Griffin, K. W., & Diaz, T. (2000). Dynamic growth models of self-esteem and adolescent alcohol use. *Journal of Early Adolescence, 20*(2), 178–190.

Sheridan, M. J., & Green, R.G. (1993). Family dynamics and individual characteristics of adult children of alcoholics: An empirical analysis. *Journal of Social Service Research*, *17*(1/2), 73–97.

Wodarski, J. S., & Smyth, N. J. (1994). Adolescent substance abuse: A comprehensive approach to prevention intervention. *Journal of Child and Adolescent Substance Abuse*, *3*(3), 33–58.

21

Adolescent Career Development: A Holistic Perspective

M. Alan Saginak, Ed.D.

Alan Saginak is an assistant professor of Counselor Education at the University of Wisconsin, Oshkosh.

"What scares me most about the future? Everyone asks you 'What are you going to do when you grow up? What college are you going to?' And I don't have a clue. I'm afraid I'll go to college, learn something I don't want to do, and be bored my whole life."

Jeanne, age 15

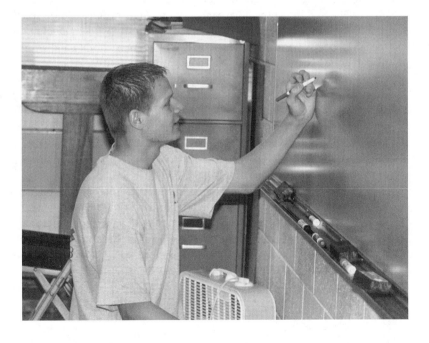

Career development is a lifelong process. Although lifespan career development encompasses and integrates all the roles we fulfill such as worker, student, volunteer, citizen, parent, and leisurite (to name a few), this chapter discusses the concept in relation to work and vocation, including the meaning it has for adolescents during this stage of their developmental journey. In order to gain a better understanding of adolescent career development, we must consider the influence and impact of other developmental challenges with which adolescents are faced.

Adolescence is a crucial time of life in which young individuals are challenged with maneuvering through the transition from childhood to adulthood. An abundance of ongoing research and personal observation suggests that, for most, this is a less-than-smooth period of life. Physiological, cognitive, and emotional changes are impacting the further development and expansion of social, interpersonal, educational, and occupational perspectives simultaneously. Perhaps the essence of this challenge is recognized as a preoccupation with the search for identity as noted by Erikson (1968). He claimed that we typically force adolescents to make career-related choices, decisions, and tentative commitments, often without consideration for the many other factors that are influencing their lives at this stage of development. This experience can significantly impact individuals' identity formation and ultimately influence their lifelong career paths.

Although some may find this challenge to be a positive experience, many others find the search for an appropriate sense of direction overwhelming, resulting in role confusion, difficulty with career decision making, and an unwillingness to commit to various career options. If we embrace the notion that one's relative awareness and understanding of career choice, planning, and implementation may also contribute significantly to identity development and, in turn, that defining one's identity may have a huge impact on one's readiness to pursue career decision making, we begin to view career education and counseling as crucial aspects in effectively working with adolescents. Essentially, developing a personal identity that encompasses various elements of self—including lifestyle, interpersonal, and spiritual (making meaning) components—goes hand in hand with one's ability and willingness to expand overall career perspectives and develop a vocational identity.

However, according to Skorikov and Vondracek (as cited in Scharf, 2002), vocational identity formation often provides a foundation for further development in the other domains. When one begins to identify with a vocational perspective of self, other aspects of identity are more likely to emerge. In addition, as vocational identity development is expanded, adolescents typically display more positive attitudes, an openness to various career options and their exploration, and a higher level of confidence in attaining success in their work (Vondracek & Skorikov, as cited in Scharf, 2002).

Perhaps one of the biggest challenges for adolescents in our own society is developing the ability to manage an unlimited number of career options and choices. Even so, we recognize the importance of vocational career development as it impacts the formation of one's overall identity during the adolescent years. Much of our task as counselors revolves around our ability to help individuals gain a sense of personal meaning in relation to their career/vocational development.

Gaining a Sense of Meaning in Career Development

Most counselors would agree that we seek to enhance the holistic development of individuals, defined as the physical, emotional, intellectual, social, and occupational aspects of the client. This perspective recognizes that becoming whole means that we must address all aspects of our being, including the spiritual domain, the ability to make meaning of our place in the world. This sense of meaning integrates all aspects of our existence, including work and career. Within this context, gaining a sense of meaning in career development suggests that we define, embrace, and pursue what we love, or that which we recognize as our passion. Following our passion relative to interests, abilities, values, personality characteristics, and environmental preferences suggests expressing our true self—essentially, how we see ourselves and who we would most like to become.

Two observations related to the connection between career development and spirituality were explored by Pinder (2000). First, discovering meaning in work offers a more profound purpose behind our motives than the day-to-day attainment of goals or material things. This suggests that there is inherent meaning in vocational pursuits that is unique to each of us as individuals and that provides seeds from which our identity evolves. Second, when we have something unique to offer through our abilities and talents to the larger community, our meaning is enhanced (Peterson & Gonzalez, 2000). This offers us purpose and further contributes to a more complete understanding of how we see ourselves as contributors to a larger cause. In a sense, the process of career development becomes an avenue for discovering more about our true selves. Once we recognize that we have something significant to offer, we begin to sense purpose and self-worth, both of which complement development of identity. Similarly, enabling adolescents to find their own meaning in this process can be significant in helping to build an identity that includes confidence, purpose, and self-worth.

Hansen has proposed another perspective of this concept in her Integrative Life Planning (ILP) model for the career planning process (Hansen & Yost, 1991). ILP is defined as

> a lifelong process of identifying our primary needs, roles, and goals and the consequent integration of these within us, our work, and our family. ILP is interactive and relationship oriented and enables one to achieve greater satisfaction, meaning, and wholeness in one's life. Integrative life planning is a means to empower oneself in shaping the direction of one's life, managing change, and contributing to society at large. (p. 130)

Essentially, this model considers the integration of all our life roles within the context of our values and within which domains we find meaning in our lives. The opportunity exists for expanding how we view our various life roles from a more holistic perspective, where work is recognized as only one of several meaningful aspects.

Hansen and Yost (1991) go on to state that ILP represents "the core of the person—the center from which meaning, self, and life understanding are generated." This definition is expanded to include "the deep integration, wholeness, a sense of the interrelatedness of all of life" (p. 131). Essentially, in today's fast-paced and ever-changing world, both adolescents and adults seem to be searching for something more in their understanding of the essence of life and how they make meaning in the roles they fulfill, including work. This spiritual perspective provides an incentive for integrating this concept into career counseling approaches with adolescents in a manner that may contribute holistically to their overall identity development.

Preparation for Life after High School

It is hoped that by the time adolescents reach their senior year in high school, they have had opportunities and experiences within and outside the educational environment to serve as building blocks for identity formation. At the same time, they are forced to make major life decisions regarding the transition from high school to what comes next. Although the options are varied, for many adolescents the choice of pursuing additional education in a college or university seems to be a common progression. Today more than ever before, parents, employers, and the academic world itself seem to send the message that attending college is the gateway to a successful work life with higher earning potential, more opportunity, and ultimately greater satisfaction.

Despite the fact that postsecondary education overall fosters the above characteristics, two problems emerge with this perspective. First, adolescents are not often given the opportunities to consider a myriad of other options besides attending college, such as applied technical programs, two-year degree programs, apprenticeships, volunteer opportunities, the military, and a wide range of work options that do not require additional education. We have developed the notion in our society that college is the ticket to success and that other options are for those who are not as academically disciplined or talented. The irony emerges when we realize that wonderful opportunities exist for individuals to fill positions in an unlimited number of occupations such as the trades, skilled professional crafts, manufacturing, transportation, and a host of service-related industries. Furthermore, the benefits of pursuing these other avenues of training and employment can be just as rewarding and meaningful, if not more, than certain ambiguous options available for those with four-year degrees. Essentially, we fail to recognize that there are innumerable ways to make meaning and find success in the choices students make regarding work and careers.

Second, as significantly more and more high school graduates have gone on to college in the past two decades, it has become obvious that not all new college freshmen are ready for college. For some, leaving home for the first time and being thrust into a whole new social environment where personal responsibility for day-to-day living is overwhelming, college becomes a very isolated and emotionally draining experience. At the same time that adolescents are experimenting with new options for clarifying their identities, they are asked to take on enormous responsibility for directing their own lives in college. Some adjust well to this challenge, but many struggle with the task. The retention rates of first-year students at many colleges and universities reveal that an alarming number of students drop out and do not return (Noel, Levitz, Saluri, & Associates, 1985).

To understand this problem, it may be valuable to consider what happens to adolescents when they feel forced into going to college as a result of pressure from peers, parents, administrators, and others. If a young person struggles with understanding why he or she is attending college, the investment has little meaning since the dividends may be unidentified. In addition, if one is still facing major personal obstacles with defining his or her own identity, social isolation and withdrawal may affect one's college experience negatively. Although student affairs professionals work hard to develop programs and activities to keep students involved on campus outside the classroom in order to promote and facilitate holistic development of the individual, not all students participate. Finally, the academic experience itself may be more rigorous and demanding than what was experienced at the high school level. As a result, students may feel overwhelmed, isolated, scared, and confused.

Not all adolescents are ready for taking on the challenges of college and its inherent academic, social, and personal responsibilities. At the same time, it is important to recognize that not all professions and meaningful work options require a college education and extensive postsecondary academic training. It is important that we as counselors recognize these realities when we work with young people; otherwise, we do a disservice to our adolescent clients, denying them thorough and effective career counseling.

Biases and Pressures That Impact Career Decision Making

One of the key characteristics of making effective career decisions involves gaining sufficient information with which to make informed career choices. It is true that adolescents are faced with the challenge of learning to make more independent decisions as part of their intellectual growth process as they begin to take more responsibility for their own lives. But when it comes to making career plans, they are often influenced by the input and opinions of individuals to whom they feel closest including peers, parents, grandparents, teachers, coaches, or other significant persons. Sometimes the influence can be quite positive and enable an adolescent to make choices that are based on viable information that is aligned with their own goals and aspirations. At other times, these influences can be misleading to the point that adolescents make career decisions for which they are not ready. Biases of well-intentioned parents, teachers, and administrators can complicate the decision-making process. Additional pressure to pursue career options that are acceptable among one's peers has a huge impact on the decisions that are made.

Part of building identity for adolescents involves being accepted by one's peer group, or fitting in. By the sophomore or junior level in high school, adolescents begin to make decisions regarding what comes after high school and tend to be quite open and interested in their peers' career plans. "Most all of my friends are going to college, so I should, too," may be a common thought. In many cases, this is true for young men and women alike. Unfortunately, many adolescents decide to go on to college because it seems like the thing to do, rather than having a solid reason for making that choice. To not go would exclude them from fitting in with their peers relative to career plans.

Although peer pressure has a huge impact on adolescents' career and educational goals, parents can be even more influential in the choices that their sons or daughters make regarding going to college. In fact, parents can quite possibly become students' most important and resourceful career development partners (Peterson & Gonzalez, 2000). Although parents' and even grandparents' influence can be quite helpful and positive for adolescents making career decisions about college, negative aspects can become a reality when this pressure to succeed becomes more of a demand. Not wanting to disappoint mom or dad, grandma or grandpa, a young teen may decide that going on to college and earning a degree is his or her only option after high school. Unfortunately, parents' and others' good intentions can also limit the number and variety of options available and keep an adolescent from exploring other alternatives. In many cases, this scenario sets the adolescent up for making career and higher education choices that are not congruent with his or her aspirations, skills, abilities, values, and personality. Without a solid beginning in pursuing career interests, the adolescent may go through many years of dissatisfaction before finally making a break toward pursuing his or her own goals, if at all. However, if the parents model good career decision-making skills themselves and become involved, interested in, and encourage the same in their children, it is more likely that the influence will facilitate more positive, confident, and meaningful career choices.

Young adolescents may also feel pressure from teachers, administrators, and even counselors, directly or indirectly, relative to their future career plans. Well-meaning teachers and school officials may talk with adolescents from the perspective that going to college is one of the keys to success in one's work life. Other options are not often the focus of academic coursework and preparation. Although there is some notion that this scenario may be changing today, especially with the technical programs being offered in high school curricula, adolescents could benefit considerably from the recognition that college is just one option in what comes after high school. There are many stories of successful individuals who have and are pursuing very lucrative and meaningful career options in which a four-year degree is not required.

Perhaps one of our most meaningful contributions as counselors to young adolescents is recognition that we do not have to give in to societal pressure to go to college. Not everyone needs to go to college. As resource professionals with knowledge of a variety of options, we can make a significant impact by opening up a broad range of alternatives for adolescents. Furthermore, we empower their decision-making skills and build confidence in making choices that feel right to them despite the various sources of pressure that they may face. It behooves us to reflect on our role and clarify our purpose in working with young adolescents so that our own biases and pressures do not get in the way of effective career counseling.

Career Counseling Perspectives and Roles

When considering the multiple roles and tasks of school counselors today, it seems easy to become overwhelmed with prioritizing those responsibilities so that the greatest number of students are served effectively. Despite the challenges of managing their various tasks, most counselors would agree that there is a critical need for expanded career counseling in the schools. In too many cases, counselors are asked to focus on other priorities, including scheduling, managing crises, dealing with students' academic problems, and addressing issues related to substance abuse, violence, and gangs (Peterson & Gonzalez, 2000).

Although these issues present very real problems and must be addressed, this often means that career-related issues become a low priority. And yet, in various educational reports across the country, professional guidelines, and surveys of parents, a theme emerges that indicates that the public supports and advocates for more career counseling in the schools. In one review that focused on the findings of twenty-nine educational reform reports, increased career counseling and education was viewed as a top priority in the role of the school counselor (Peterson & Gonzalez, 2000).

Perhaps one of the most important roles for school counselors is serving as an advocate for students' ongoing career development. Administrators must be made aware of the critical nature of providing expanded and meaningful career counseling services and skills. Although this may not always be an easy task, seeking this essential support proactively means that students are provided with meaningful services that complement their education and that prepare them for an ever-changing and complex world of work as we know it today.

Educating parents and involving them in career-related dialogue and programming may also open doors for greater communication and decision making relative to career issues that have so much influence on their children's futures. Adolescents want input and support for the career decisions they are being asked to make. Various types of programs, courses, and seminars may serve to educate administrators, teachers, and parents regarding the importance of expanding career development in the schools.

Of all the roles that are fulfilled by school counselors in working with students, perhaps the most important one is to provide the support and encouragement for adolescents to make decisions and choose directions that feel most right to them individually (Peterson & Gonzalez, 2000). Despite the sometimes confusing demands and pressures that are placed on adolescents by peers, family members, administrators, and teachers for making appropriate career decisions, counselors have a unique opportunity to refrain from this pressure, and inquire into what is most meaningful to each individual student with whom they work. Even recognizing that some students may not be ready to make various career decisions is a valuable contribution toward the overall developmental process itself. Students feel support and encouragement for moving through the career development process at their own pace without the feeling that they must make uninformed decisions prior to gaining some understanding of themselves and their desires, aspirations, and goals.

Perhaps the key to effective career counseling approaches involves ongoing introduction, education, involvement, and follow-through with students so that they begin to realize that career counseling is pertinent to preparation for life itself and the variety of life roles that they will fulfill. This role for counselors must also be continually advocated and communicated to parents, teachers, administrators, and other professional and government officials so that the emphasis on career development in the schools will become a priority, and be enhanced significantly.

Choices and Options for the Prospective Graduate

As discussed above, a very high number of high school students make plans to attend college upon graduation. Some go on with relatively clear goals about fields of study they want to pursue, while others may explore via trial and error in the first two years of college, hoping to find a major that aligns with their interests, skills, and goals. Developmental issues that address ongoing identity formation during the late adolescent/early adulthood years influence this process. School counselors can help prepare students for these challenges by working to enhance their decision-making skills while in high school, and providing career counseling approaches that serve to increase self-esteem and self-concept.

One valuable way to gain work-related skills and experience while still in high school is through cooperative education programs such as the School-to-Work Programs sponsored by the U.S. Department of Education and the U.S Department of Labor. Students can develop a wide range of skills by integrating academic subjects and applying them to real work situations, where on-the-job mentors can collaborate to ensure the highest levels of learning. When given the opportunity to pursue these types of experiences, students often develop a foundation for lifelong skills based on knowledge and training that facilitates more successful future decisions. Another advantage is that students learn about a much wider range of employment possibilities by job shadowing various individuals with whom they work in these experiences.

However, in addressing the career development needs of the optimum number of students, school counselors need to have knowledge of a wide range of options for students to pursue upon graduation from high school in addition to college. This may include, but are not limited to, two-year colleges, applied technology programs, apprenticeship programs, military service, volunteerism, going directly to work including family businesses, and even starting a family.

Technical and two-year colleges offer students excellent opportunities to pursue a wide range of degree programs that prepare them for working in various areas, such as skilled trades, mechanical support fields, technical professions, service industry occupations, healthcare, and business. These colleges are becoming better understood and recognized as they strive to integrate rigorous academic preparation with technical training. Efforts have been tireless in attempting to dispel the notion that technical and two-year colleges are better suited for individuals who are not academically inclined. Despite the fact that stereotyping has hindered pursuit of these programs by some students in the past, many students are realizing that the training is demanding and prepares them quite well for an abundance of satisfying opportunities and roles in today's ever-changing workplace. In many cases, students of these programs graduate ready to apply their skills in the work setting and are compensated fairly for their skills and abilities.

Counselors may find it useful and helpful to consider developing initiatives in the schools that offer opportunities to become involved with tech-prep programs. These nationally supported programs integrate academics and technical training for a wide range of students with a focus on integrating curriculums that prepare students for advanced technology positions. Often, these programs are co-sponsored by schools, college and universities, and business and industry representatives, so that on-the-job training can be most thorough and effective. In many cases, some colleges and universities accept completed academic coursework as transfer credits to facilitate students' pursuit of additional education and four-year degrees. Essentially, these programs can become win-win situations for all partners, including the students, when technical training is combined with academic knowledge and skills to enable up-to-date preparation for a changing work world.

Another option that provides a wide range of opportunities is apprenticeship programs. The U.S. Department of Labor supports the expansion of apprenticeship programs designed to enable training under the supervision of a master trainer or worker. These programs have a tremendous advantage in offering students the opportunity to build technical skills that are recognized in the workplace as those of fully trained journeypersons (Zunker, 2002). In other words, students learn skills and receive the theoretical training that provides a solid base for significant contributions to a wide range of trades and craft-related occupations.

In addition, valuable opportunities exist for students interested in pursuing specific skills training, fulfilling a sense of service, and expanding travel through the various branches of the military. Counselors can broaden and foster wonderful opportunities for students by networking with military recruiters. Not only can several years of military service prepare one for various technical and professional civilian jobs and life skills as a whole, but excellent opportunities exist for pursuing military careers that can offer one the satisfaction and lifelong benefits of serving one's country. The military is an excellent occupation for those who have an interest in such a unique and meaningful opportunity.

Another option that students may find meaningful relates to pursuing volunteer opportunities. Typically, these organizations have missions and goals that relate to helping individuals and communities throughout the world. Many individuals who have participated in such opportunities have developed skills, knowledge, and meaningful life perspectives that provide a foundation for future occupational goals. In addition, for those with an adventurous spirit for travel, volunteerism can offer innumerable opportunities for fulfilling this ambition. Such opportunities also provide unique experiences for expanding one's spiritual meaning of contribution and work.

Still others may pursue opportunities within a family business where they can contribute to an established company or organization. These may include manufacturing, retail, or a host of service-related roles where a family name or tradition can be carried on through another generation. For some, a certain pride exists for being able to be part of such an opportunity. Although students with these opportunities may still choose to attend technical, two-year, or four-year colleges and universities to earn a degree, their training may often be more focused and specific relative to their already established goals of going in to the family business.

There are numerous other options for post–high school life. Beginning a family may represent a choice just as much as any of the other options discussed. For others, taking time after high school to travel or work in a job that does not require additional education would be beneficial. Such choices may provide unique experiences that help build a solid base for future life decisions.

In essence, the choices available for students to pursue following graduation from high school are varied and unique in what each offers relative to student's goals. Counselors have a responsibility to expand students' options in a way that offers the optimum in meaning and life satisfaction. Thinking "outside the box" enables expansion of an unlimited variety of career choices that not only contribute to society at large, but also provide meaningful individual expression through work and other activities for adolescents and ultimately impact their identity development positively.

Summary

Although we often still identify work in traditional contexts, in many ways it has changed relative to what we have known over the past century. The workplace and its inherent requirements and demands are changing at a pace unknown in any time past. Technology has exponentially escalated this rate of change. Individuals must adapt and embrace today's world of work, and move forward with enthusiasm toward these new opportunities.

Although work is still a means of providing for oneself and family while contributing to the society as a whole, it seems students could all benefit from a better understanding of the spiritual aspect of why we work. Perhaps counselors could best help students by asking three questions:

1. If there were any occupation, work, or career path that you could pursue, regardless of the skills, abilities, knowledge, required training, or income, what would that be?
2. How could this career goal fit into your overall lifestyle as you would like it to look?
3. How could this career goal fulfill your most meaningful dreams for a satisfying life?

In other words, enabling students to pursue their passion opens unlimited opportunities and excitement for finding one's life mission, sense of purpose, and forming a meaningful identity. This may be the ultimate gift we share as counselors who care about students' well-being, holistic development, and futures.

References

Erikson, E. H. (1968). *Identity: Youth and crisis.* New York: W.W. Norton.

Hansen, L. S., & Yost, M.M. (1991). Preparing youth for changing roles and tasks in society, work, and family. In R. Hanson (Ed.), *Career development: Preparing for the 21st century* (pp. 119–137). Ann Arbor, MI: ERIC/CAPS.

Noel, L., Levitz, R., Saluri, D., & Associates. (1985). *Increasing student retention: Effective programs and practices for reducing the dropout rate.* San Francisco, CA: Jossey-Bass.

Peterson, N., & Gonzalez, R.C. (2000). *The role of work in people's lives: Applied career counseling and vocational psychology.* Belmont, CA: Wadsworth, Brooks/Cole Thomson Learning.

Pinder, M. M. (2000). Spirituality and career development: Using the enneagram. In N. Peterson & R. C. Gonzalez (Eds.), *Career counseling models for diverse populations: Hands-on applications by practitioners* (pp. 150–161). Belmont, CA: Wadsworth, Brooks/Cole Thomson Learning.

Scharf, R. S. (2002). *Applying career development theory to counseling* (3rd ed.). Pacific Grove, CA: Brooks/Cole.

Zunker, V. G. (2002). *Career counseling: Applied concepts of life planning* (6th ed.) Pacific Grove, CA: Brooks/Cole.

22

Epilogue and Fire Drill

Colette Dollarhide

*"What do I look forward to the most after high school? I want to have
complete responsibility of all around me and learn more about myself."*

Eric, age 19

A Day in the Life of a Counselor: What Would You Do?

No one scenario will capture all the complexities of the job of a school counselor. Some of the most difficult situations will emerge as those in which there is a direct conflict among the needs of the student, the needs of the school, the needs of the school counseling program, and perhaps even the needs of the counselor. Every new day will bring new challenges and new triumphs, but the only way to become prepared to face those challenges is to think through your options before they are real. Similar to conducting fire drills, actually walking through a situation and behaving as though the situation were real will help you think about all your options.

Let's now examine a situation that could arise in your school. After you read the situation, read through the questions. Review the book and then answer the questions in writing. Discuss your answers with your professor and classmates. Consider discussing your answers with professional school counselors to get their perspectives.

The Goth versus the Coach: Let's Get Ready to Rumble!

Mike came into Bebe's office in a huff. "I've been a counselor here for ten years," he barked, "and I can't believe how frustrating it can be! I've been trying for three years to get the funds for the peer mediation program, and Coach Heinz waltzes into the meeting and gets all the funds he needs for the football team. How's that for priorities? You're the assistant principal—can't you do anything to help?"

Bebe looked at Mike with patient good humor; they had had this conversation before. "Now Mike," she said, "You know that the coach has led the team to regionals for the past five years, to state for the past two years, and you know that he's well regarded in the school and in the district. You also know that I don't have any say over what he says and does— that's between the principal and him. Heck, he'll outlast both of us here. Go to lunch, get over your pity party, and let's connect next week over some other ways to get that peer mediation program going."

Over lunch, Mike thought it over. It was true what Bebe had said about the power the coach had in the school. It was also true that the coach had been helpful with allowing Mike and the other counselors to come talk to the team about being role models in the school to promote the counseling program in general and the ATODA programs in particular. Heck, the coach had even been instrumental in getting the team members to address the student body during prom week, talking about the dangers of drinking and driving. Perhaps it wouldn't be such a good idea to antagonize the coach over the funding. Mike would talk to the other counselors, and they would meet with Bebe to come up with some other funding source for the program. It would be better not to rub the coach the wrong way, given all the power he seemed to hold.

When he got back to school, Mike felt much better. As soon as he walked into his office, however, he caught sight of a student who he was not happy to see: Morgan. Mike really wanted to like all his assigned students, but Morgan made it hard to like her. She wore the white face paint, black makeup, black clothes, and spike dog collar of the Goth group in the school. She didn't smell as if she bathed or brushed her teeth or hair. Mike just didn't understand the culture or what they were trying to say, so he avoided her and the others of her group. Today was just his lucky day all around. Sighing in resignation, he put his coat away and waved her to come in.

"OK, like, I really need to see you," she began. "I have to get out of my history class or I'm going to blow."

Mike turned to look at her, noting that she really was agitated and upset. "What's going on?"

"Like, it's the History Nazi. He constantly puts me down, commenting on my clothes and hair. He points at me to make the others laugh—he's such a total ass. I can't learn anything from him. I swear he's out to flunk me or get me somehow—I just know it. He hates me and I hate him, so get me out of there."

"The History Nazi? Who's that?" Mike tried to laugh it off.

"Coach Heinz—who else? The God of Football, all champion bully. I get so tired of his tirades about artists, the Goth culture, gays, democrats—anyone who doesn't think just like him and act just like him. You gotta get me out. Get me into another class. Study hall. Anything."

Mike turned to look at her, shook his head. "It's too late to get you into another class, and you don't need another study hall. Maybe it's about time you took some ownership over your life and realized you're not going to like everyone you have to work with. And you're not going to get him to change. Why should he? He's got too much clout around here. You're just going to have to live with it, tough it out. You're a big girl. You'll figure it out. Now go back to class. Bye." He stood up, gestured to the door, and shut it as she left the room, too stunned to protest.

As he returned to his desk, he opened his middle drawer to get his antacid pills. His ulcer was really acting up.

Challenge Questions

1. What do you notice about the situation in terms of power dynamics? Examine the power of each person in this situation. How much power does each person have in terms of the formal power structure of the school? How much power does each person have to effect change in terms of personal choices and in terms of systemic change? (Hint: Each person has tremendous power in terms of personal choice—and each person's personal choices can resonate with systemic change, starting a new way of doing things in an entire system.)

2. What do you see as the goals of each person? What are Bebe's goals? Why do you think these are her goals? What are Coach Heinz's goals? Why do you think those are his goals? What are Mike's goals? Why do you think those are his goals? What are Morgan's goals? Why do you think those are her goals? List all possible goals that could underlie their behaviors. How would you go about exploring the validity of your hypotheses?

3. Focus on the interaction between Mike and Morgan. What are all of the reasons you can see that Mike shut Morgan down? What are the professional reasons? What are the personal reasons?

4. Could Mike have done counseling with her? For what issue(s)? In what way(s) would counseling have been effective? In what way(s) would counseling have been ineffective?

5. Could Mike have done consulting with her? What would be your goal(s) for the consultation?

6. Assume that he was correct and that it was too late to move her to another class. What else could he have done to help?

7. Do you think she will ever come to Mike for help again? Do you think she will ever go to any counselor for help in the future? If so, for what issues or for what kind of help?

8. Focus on the broader situation. Identify the ideal scenario you can envision for this situation. What is the perfect resolution to this situation for *each* person in terms of the health of the *entire* system?

9. What would you like to see each person learn from this situation? What would you like to see Bebe learn? What would you like to see Coach Heinz learn? What would you like to see Morgan learn? What would you like to see Mike learn?

10. Using the DAP model, evaluate each block of the model to determine the helpful strategies suggested in the model. Look for all the *individual* change strategies possible AND for all the *systemic* change strategies. List all the possible intervention points suggested by the model.

11. Create a cost-benefits list for each strategy you found in the model.

12. Identify the top five intervention strategies you would consider appropriate in this situation. Select at least one strategy that would result in *systemic* change. Design a plan for implementing all five intervention strategies.

13. Design a plan for evaluating the effects of each strategy you selected.

14. What does the student quote at the beginning of this chapter have to do with the lessons of the chapter?

15. Identify some Internet sites that could help you work through a situation similar to this one.

Ethical Standards for School Counselors

<small>REVISED JUNE 25, 1998</small>

Preamble

The American School Counselor Association (ASCA) is a professional organization whose members have a unique and distinctive preparation, grounded in the behavioral sciences, with training in clinical skills adapted to the school setting. The school counselor assists in the growth and development of each individual and uses his or her highly specialized skills to protect the interests of the counselee within the structure of the school system. School counselors subscribe to the following basic tenets of the counseling process from which professional responsibilities are derived:

- Each person has the right to respect and dignity as a human being and to counseling services without prejudice as to person, character, belief, or practice regardless of age, color, disability, ethnic group, gender, race, religion, sexual orientation, marital status, or socioeconomic status.
- Each person has the right to self-direction and self-development.
- Each person has the right of choice and the responsibility for goals reached.
- Each person has the right to privacy and thereby the right to expect the counselor-counselee relationship to comply with all laws, policies, and ethical standards pertaining to confidentiality.

In this document, ASCA specifies the principles of ethical behavior necessary to regulate and maintain the high standards of integrity, leadership, and professionalism among its members. The Ethical Standards for School Counselors were developed to clarify the nature of ethical responsibilities held in common by school counseling professionals. The purposes of this document are to:

- Serve as a guide for the ethical practices of all professional school counselors regardless of level, area, population served, or membership in this professional Association;
- Provide benchmarks for both self-appraisal and peer evaluations regarding counselor responsibilities to counselees, parents, colleagues and professional associates, schools, and communities, as well as to one's self and the counseling profession; and
- Inform those served by the school counselor of acceptable counselor practices and expected professional behavior.

A.1. Responsibilities to Students

The professional school counselor:

a. Has a primary obligation to the counselee who is to be treated with respect as a unique individual.
b. Is concerned with the educational, career, emotional, and behavioral needs and encourages the maximum development of each counselee.
c. Refrains from consciously encouraging the counselee's acceptance of values, lifestyles, plans, decisions, and beliefs that represent the counselor's personal orientation.
d. Is responsible for keeping informed of laws, regulations, and policies relating to counselees and strives to ensure that the rights of counselees are adequately provided for and protected.

A.2. Confidentiality

The professional school counselor:

a. Informs the counselee of the purposes, goals, techniques, and rules of procedure under which she/he may receive counseling at or before the time when the counseling relationship is entered. Disclosure notice includes confidentiality issues such as the possible necessity for consulting with other professionals, privileged communication, and legal or authoritative restraints. The meaning and limits of confidentiality are clearly defined to counselees through a written and shared disclosure statement.

b. Keeps information confidential unless disclosure is required to prevent clear and imminent danger to the counselee or others or when legal requirements demand that confidential information be revealed. Counselors will consult with other professionals when in doubt as to the validity of an exception.

c. Discloses information to an identified third party who, by her or his relationship with the counselee, is at a high risk of contracting a disease that is commonly known to be communicable and fatal. Prior to disclosure, the counselor will ascertain that the counselee has not already informed the third party about his or her disease and he/she is not intending to inform the third party in the immediate future.

d. Requests of the court that disclosure not be required when the release of confidential information without a counselee's permission may lead to potential harm to the counselee.

e. Protects the confidentiality of counselee's records and releases personal data only according to prescribed laws and school policies. Student information maintained in computers is treated with the same care as traditional student records.

f. Protects the confidentiality of information received in the counseling relationship as specified by federal and state laws, written policies, and applicable ethical standards. Such information is only to be revealed to others with the informed consent of the counselee, consistent with the counselor's ethical obligation. In a group setting, the counselor sets a high norm of confidentiality and stresses its importance, yet clearly states that confidentiality in group counseling cannot be guaranteed.

A.3. Counseling Plans

The professional school counselor:

works jointly with the counselee in developing integrated and effective counseling plans, consistent with both the abilities and circumstances of the counselee and counselor. Such plans will be regularly reviewed to ensure continued viability and effectiveness, respecting the counselee's freedom of choice.

A.4. Dual Relationships

The professional school counselor:

avoids dual relationships which might impair her or his objectivity and increase the risk of harm to the client (e.g., counseling one's family members, close friends, or associates). If a dual relationship is unavoidable, the counselor is responsible for taking action to eliminate or reduce the potential for harm. Such safeguards might include informed consent, consultation, supervision, and documentation.

A.5. Appropriate Referrals

The professional school counselor:

makes referrals when necessary or appropriate to outside resources. Appropriate referral necessitates knowledge of available resources and making proper plans for transitions with minimal interruption of services. Counselees retain the right to discontinue the counseling relationship at any time.

A.6. Group Work

The professional school counselor:

screens prospective group members and maintains an awareness of participants' needs and goals in relation to the goals of the group. The counselor takes reasonable precautions to protect members from physical and psychological harm resulting from interaction within the group.

A 7. Danger to Self or Others

The professional school counselor:

informs appropriate authorities when the counselee's condition indicates a clear and imminent danger to the counselee or others. This is to be done after careful deliberation and, where possible, after consultation with other counseling professionals. The counselor informs the counselee of actions to be taken so as to minimize his or her confusion and to clarify counselee and counselor expectations.

A.8. Student Records

The professional school counselor:

maintains and secures records necessary for rendering professional services to the counselee as required by laws, regulations, institutional procedures, and confidentiality guidelines.

A.9. Evaluation, Assessment, and Interpretation

The professional school counselor:

a. Adheres to all professional standards regarding selecting, administering, and interpreting assessment measures. The counselor recognizes that computer-based testing programs require specific training in administration, scoring, and interpretation which may differ from that required in more traditional assessments.
b. Provides explanations of the nature, purposes, and results of assessment/evaluation measures in language the counselee(s) can understand.
c. Does not misuse assessment results and interpretations and takes reasonable steps to prevent others from misusing the information.
d. Uses caution when utilizing assessment techniques, making evaluations, and interpreting the performance of populations not represented in the norm group on which an instrument is standardized.

A.10. Computer Technology

The professional school counselor:

a. Promotes the benefits of appropriate computer applications and clarifies the limitations of computer technology. The counselor ensures that: (1) computer applications are appropriate for the individual needs of the counselee; (2) the counselee understands how to use the application; and (3) follow-up counseling assistance is provided. Members of under represented groups are assured equal access to computer technologies and are assured the absence of discriminatory information and values in computer applications.
b. Counselors who communicate with counselees via internet should follow the NBCC Standards for WebCounseling.

A.11. Peer Helper Programs

The professional school counselor:

has unique responsibilities when working with peer helper programs. The school counselor is responsible for the welfare of counselees participating in peer programs under her or his direction. School counselors who function in training and supervisory capacities are referred to the preparation and supervision standards of professional counselor associations.

B. Responsibilities to Parents

B.1. Parent Rights and Responsibilities

The professional school counselor:

a. Respects the inherent rights and responsibilities of parents for their children and endeavors to establish, as appropriate, a collaborative relationship with parents to facilitate the counselee's maximum development.
b. Adheres to laws and local guidelines when assisting parents experiencing family difficulties that interfere with the counselee's effectiveness and welfare.
c. Is sensitive to cultural and social diversity among families and recognizes that all parents, custodial and noncustodial, are vested with certain rights and responsibilities for the welfare of their children by virtue of their role and according to law.

B.2. Parents and Confidentiality

The professional school counselor:

a. Informs parents of the counselor's role with emphasis on the confidential nature of the counseling relationship between the counselor and counselee.
b. Provides parents with accurate, comprehensive, and relevant information in an objective and caring manner, as is appropriate and consistent with ethical responsibilities to the counselee.
c. Makes reasonable efforts to honor the wishes of parents and guardians concerning information that he/she may share regarding the counselee.

C.   Responsibilities to Colleagues and Professional Associates

C.1. Professional Relationships

The professional school counselor:

a. Establishes and maintains professional relationships with faculty, staff, and administration to facilitate the provision of optimal counseling services. The relationship is based on the counselor's definition and description of the parameter and levels of his or her professional roles.
b. Treats colleagues with professional respect, courtesy, and fairness. The qualifications, views, and findings of colleagues are represented to accurately reflect the image of competent professionals.
c. Is aware of and optimally utilizes related professions and organizations to whom the counselee may be referred.

C.2. Sharing Information with Other Professionals

The professional school counselor:

a. Promotes awareness and adherence to appropriate guidelines regarding confidentiality; the distinction between public and private information; and staff consultation.
b. Provides professional personnel with accurate, objective, concise, and meaningful data necessary to adequately evaluate, counsel, and assist the counselee.
c. If a counselee is receiving services from another counselor or other mental health professional, the counselor, with client consent, will inform the other professional and develop clear agreements to avoid confusion and conflict for the counselee.

D.   Responsibilities to the School and Community

D.1. Responsibilities to the School

The professional school counselor:

a. Supports and protects the educational program against any infringement not in the best interest of counselees.
b. Informs appropriate officials of conditions that may be potentially disruptive or damaging to the school's mission, personnel, and property while honoring the confidentiality between the counselee and counselor.
c. Delineates and promotes the counselor's role and function in meeting the needs of those served. The counselor will notify appropriate officials of conditions which may limit or curtail her or his effectiveness in providing programs and services.
d. Accepts employment only for positions for which he/she is qualified by education, training, supervised experience, state and national professional credentials, and appropriate professional experience. Counselors recommend that administrators hire only qualified and competent individuals for professional counseling positions.
e. Assists in developing: (1) curricular and environmental conditions appropriate for the school and community; (2) educational procedures and programs to meet the counselee's developmental needs; and (3) a systematic evaluation process for comprehensive school counseling programs, services, and personnel. The counselor is guided by the findings of the evaluation data in planning programs and services.

D.2. Responsibility to the Community

The professional school counselor:

collaborates with agencies, organizations, and individuals in the school and community in the best interest of counselees and without regard to personal reward or remuneration.

E.   Responsibilities to Self

E.1. Professional Competence

The professional school counselor:

a. Functions within the boundaries of individual professional competence and accepts responsibility for the consequences of his or her actions.
b. Monitors personal functioning and effectiveness and does not participate in any activity which may lead to inadequate professional services or harm to a client.
c. Strives through personal initiative to maintain professional competence and to keep abreast of professional information. Professional and personal growth are ongoing throughout the counselor's career.

E.2. Multicultural Skills

The professional school counselor:

understands the diverse cultural backgrounds of the counselees with whom he/she works. This includes, but is not limited to, learning how the school counselor's own cultural/ethnic/racial identity impacts her or his values and beliefs about the counseling process.

F.   Responsibilities to the Profession

F.1. Professionalism

The professional school counselor:

a. Accepts the policies and processes for handling ethical violations as a result of maintaining membership in the American School Counselor Association.
b. Conducts herself/himself in such a manner as to advance individual ethical practice and the profession.
c. Conducts appropriate research and reports findings in a manner consistent with acceptable educational and psychological research practices. When using client data for research or for statistical or program planning purposes, the counselor ensures protection of the individual counselee's identity.
d. Adheres to ethical standards of the profession, other official policy statements pertaining to counseling, and relevant statutes established by federal, state, and local governments.
e. Clearly distinguishes between statements and actions made as a private individual and those made as a representative of the school counseling profession.
f. Does not use his or her professional position to recruit or gain clients, consultees for her or his private practice, seek and receive unjustified personal gains, unfair advantage, sexual favors, or unearned goods or services.

F.2. Contribution to the Profession

The professional school counselor:

a. Actively participates in local, state, and national associations which foster the development and improvement of school counseling.
b. Contributes to the development of the profession through sharing skills, ideas, and expertise with colleagues.

G. Maintenance of Standards

Ethical behavior among professional school counselors, Association members and nonmembers, is expected at all times. When there exists serious doubt as to the ethical behavior of colleagues, or if counselors are forced to work in situations or abide by policies which do not reflect the standards as outlined in these Ethical Standards for School Counselors, the counselor is obligated to take appropriate action to rectify the condition. The following procedure may serve as a guide:

1. The counselor should consult confidentially with a professional colleague to discuss the nature of a complaint to see if she/he views the situation as an ethical violation.
2. When feasible, the counselor should directly approach the colleague whose behavior is in question to discuss the complaint and seek resolution.
3. If resolution is not forthcoming at the personal level, the counselor shall utilize the channels established within the school, school district, the state SCA, and ASCA Ethics Committee.
4. If the matter still remains unresolved, referral for review and appropriate action should be made to the Ethics Committees in the following sequence:
   - state school counselor association
   - American School Counselor Association
5. The ASCA Ethics Committee is responsible for educating—and consulting with—the membership regarding ethical standards. The Committee periodically reviews and recommends changes in code. The Committee will also receive and process questions to clarify the application of such standards. Questions must be submitted in writing to the ASCA Ethics Chair. Finally, the Committee will handle complaints of alleged violations of our ethical standards. Therefore, at the national level, complaints should be submitted in writing to the ASCA Ethics Committee, c/o the Executive Director, American School Counselor Association, 801 North Fairfax, Suite 310, Alexandria, VA 22314.

H.   Resources

School counselors are responsible for being aware of, and acting in accord with, standards and positions of the counseling profession as represented in official documents such as those listed below:

American Counseling Association. (1995). Code of ethics and standards of practice. Alexandria, VA. (5999 Stevenson Ave., Alexandria, VA 22034) 1 800 347 6647 www.counseling.org.

American School Counselor Association. (1997). The national standards for school counseling programs. Alexandria, VA. (801 North Fairfax Street, Suite 310, Alexandria, VA 22314) 1 800 306 4722 www.school-counselor. org.

American School Counselor Association. (1998). Position Statements. Alexandria, VA.

American School Counselor Association. (1998). Professional liability insurance program. (Brochure). Alexandria, VA.

Arrendondo, Toperek, Brown, Jones, Locke, Sanchez, and Stadler. (1996). Multicultural counseling competencies and standards. Journal of Multicultural Counseling and Development. Vol. 24, No. 1. See American Counseling Association.

Arthur, G.L. and Swanson, C.D. (1993). Confidentiality and privileged communication. (1993). See American Counseling Association.

Association for Specialists in Group Work. (1989). Ethical Guidelines for group counselors. (1989). Alexandria, VA. See American Counseling Association.

Corey, G., Corey, M.S. and Callanan. (1998). Issues and Ethics in the Helping Professions. Pacific Grove, CA: Brooks/Cole. (Brooks/Cole, 511 Forest Lodge Rd., Pacific Grove, CA 93950) www.thomson.com.

Crawford, R. (1994). Avoiding counselor malpractice. Alexandria, VA. See American Counseling Association.

Forrester-Miller, H. and Davis, T.E. (1996). A practitioner's guide to ethical decision making. Alexandria, VA. See American Counseling Association.

Herlihy, B. and Corey, G. (1996). ACA ethical standards casebook. Fifth ed. Alexandria, VA. See American Counseling Association.

Herlihy, B. and Corey, G. (1992). Dual relationships in counseling. Alexandria, VA. See American Counseling Association.

Huey, W.C. and Remley, T.P. (1988). Ethical and legal issues in school counseling. Alexandria, VA. See American School Counselor Association.

Joint Committee on Testing Practices. (1988). Code of fair testing practices in education. Washington, DC: American Psychological Association. (1200 17th Street, NW, Washington, DC 20036) 202 336 5500

Mitchell, R.W. (1991). Documentation in counseling records. Alexandria, VA. See American Counseling Association.

National Board for Certified Counselors. (1998). National board for certified counselors: code of ethics. Greensboro, NC. (3 Terrace Way, Suite D, Greensboro, NC 27403-3660) 336 547 0607 www.nbcc.org.

National Board for Certified Counselors. (1997). Standards for the ethical practice of webcounseling. Greensboro, NC.

National Peer Helpers Association. (1989). Code of ethics for peer helping professionals. Greenville, NC. PO Box 2684, Greenville, NC 27836. 919 522 3959. nphaorg@aol.com.

Salo, M. and Schumate, S. (1993). Counseling minor clients. Alexandria, VA. See American School Counselor Association.

Stevens-Smith, P. and Hughes, M. (1993). Legal issues in marriage and family counseling. Alexandria, VA. See American School Counselor Association.

Wheeler, N. and Bertram, B. (1994). Legal aspects of counseling: avoiding lawsuits and legal problems. (Videotape). Alexandria, VA. See American School Counselor Association.

Ethical Standards for School Counselors was adopted by the ASCA Delegate Assembly, March 19, 1984. The first revision was approved by the ASCA Delegate Assembly, March 27, 1992. The second revision was approved by the ASCA Governing Board on March 30, 1998 and adopted on June 25, 1998.

APPENDIX B

National Standards for School Counseling Programs

The standards for each content area are intended to provide guidance and direction for states, school systems and individual schools to develop quality and affective school counseling programs. The emphasis is on success for *all students*, no just those students who are motivated, supported, and ready to learn. The school counseling program based upon national standards enables *all students* to achieve success in school and to develop into contributing members of our society.

School success requires that students make successful transitions from elementary school to middle/junior high school to high school. Graduates from high school have acquired the attitudes, skills, and knowledge that are essential to the competitive workplace of the 21st century.

A school counseling program based upon national standards provides the elements for all students to achieve success in school. School counselors continuously assess their students' needs to identify barriers and obstacles that may be hindering success and also advocate for programmatic efforts to eliminate these barriers.

Each standard is followed by a list of student competencies which articulate desired student learning outcomes. Student competencies define specific knowledge, attitudes, and skills that students should obtain or demonstrate as a result of participating in a school counseling program. These listings are not meant to be all inclusive, nor is any individual program expected to include all of the competencies in the school counseling program. The competencies offer a foundation for what a standards-based program should address and deliver. These can be used as a basis to develop measurable indicators of student performance.

The program standards for **academic development** *guide the school counseling program to implement strategies and activities to support and maximize each student's ability to learn.* Academic development includes acquiring skills, attitudes, and knowledge which contribute to effective learning in school and across the life span; employing strategies to achieve success in school; and understanding the relationship of academics to the world of work, and to life at home and in the community. Academic development standards and competencies support the premise that all students meet or exceed the local, state, and national academic standards.

     The program standards for **career** development *guide the school counseling program to provide the foundation for the acquisition of skills, attitudes, and knowledge that enable students to make a successful transition from school to the world of work, and from job to job across the life span.* Career development includes the employment of strategies to achieve future career success and job satisfaction as well as fostering understanding of the relationship between personal qualities, education and training, and the world of work. Career development standards and competencies ensure that students develop career goals as a result of participation in a comprehensive plan of career awareness, exploration, and preparation activities.

     The program standards for **personal/social** development *guide the school counseling program to provide the foundation for personal and social growth as students progress through school and into adulthood.* Personal/social development contributes to academic and career success. Personal/social development includes the acquisition of skills, attitudes, and knowledge which help students understand and respect self and others, acquire effective interpersonal skills, understand safety and survival skills, and develop into contributing members of our society. Personal/social development standards and competencies ensure that students have learned to successfully and safely negotiate their way in the increasingly complex and diverse world of the 21st century.

National Standards for School Counseling Programs

I. Academic Development

Standards in this area guide the school counseling program to implement strategies and activities to support and enable the student to experience academic success, maximize learning through commitment, produce high quality work, and be prepared for a full range of options and opportunities after high school.

     The academic development area includes the acquisition of skills in decision making, problem solving and goal setting, critical thinking, logical reasoning, and interpersonal communication and the application of these skills to academic achievement.

     The school counseling program enables all students to achieve success in school and to develop into contributing members of our society.

     Standard A: Students will acquire the attitudes, knowledge, and skills that contribute to effective learning in school and across the life span.

     Standard B: Students will complete school with the academic preparation essential to choose from a wide range of substantial postsecondary options, including college.

     Standard C: Students will understand the relationship of academics to the world of work, and to life at home and in the community.

Academic Development: Standard A   Students will acquire the attitudes, knowledge, and skills that contribute to effective learning in school and across the life span.

Student Competencies

Improve Academic Self-Concept
     Students will:

- articulate feelings of competence and confidence as learners
- display a positive interest in learning
- take pride in work and achievement
- accept mistakes as essential to the learning process
- identify attitudes and behaviors which lead to successful learning

Acquire Skills for Improving Learning
     Students will:

- apply time management and task management skills
- demonstrate how effort and persistence positively affect learning
- use communications skills to know when and how to ask for help when needed
- apply knowledge and learning styles to positively influence school performance

Achieve School Success

Students will:

- take responsibility for their actions
- demonstrate the ability to work independently, as well as the ability to work cooperatively with other students
- develop a broad range of interests and abilities
- demonstrate dependability, productivity and initiative
- share knowledge

Academic Development: Standard B   Students will complete school with the academic preparation essential to choose from a wide range of substantial postsecondary options, including college.

Student Competencies

Improve Learning

Students will:

- demonstrate the motivation to achieve individual potential
- learn and apply critical-thinking skills
- apply the study skills necessary for academic success at each level
- seek information and support from faculty, staff, family and peers
- organize and apply academic information from a variety of sources
- use knowledge of learning styles to positively influence school performance
- become self-directed and independent learners

Plan to Achieve Goals

Students will:

- establish challenging academic goals in elementary, middle/ junior high and high school
- use assessment results in educational planning
- develop and implement annual plan of study to maximize academic ability and achievement
- apply knowledge of aptitudes and interests to goal setting
- use problem-solving and decision-making skills to assess progress toward educational goals
- understand the relationship between classroom performance and success in school
- identify post-secondary options consistent with interests, achievement, aptitude and abilities

Academic Development: Standard C   Students will understand the relationship of academics to the world of work and to life at home and in the community.

Student Competencies

Relate School to Life Experiences

Students will:

- demonstrate the ability to balance school, studies, extracurricular activities, leisure time and family life
- seek co-curricular and community experiences to enhance the school experience
- understand the relationship between learning and work
- demonstrate an understanding of the value of lifelong learning as essential to seeking, obtaining and maintaining life goals
- understand that school success is the preparation to make the transition from student to community member
- understand how school success and academic achievement enhance future career and avocational opportunities

II. Career Development

Standards in this area guide the school counseling program to implement strategies and activities to support and enable the student to develop a positive attitude toward work, and to develop the necessary skills to make a successful transition from school to the world of work, and from job to job across the life career span. Also, standards in this area help students to understand the relationship between success in school and future success in the world of work. The career development standards reflect the recommendations of the Secretary's Commission on Achieving Necessary Skills (SCANS, 1991) and the content of the *National Career Development Guidelines* (NOICC, 1989).

The school counseling program enables all students to achieve success in school and to develop into contributing members of our society.

Standard A: Students will acquire the skills to investigate the world of work in relation to knowledge of self and to make informed career decisions.

Standard B: Students will employ strategies to achieve future career goals with success and satisfaction.

Standard C: Students will understand the relationship between personal qualities, education, training, and the world of work.

Career Development: Standard A   Students will acquire the skills to investigate the world of work in relation to knowledge of self and to make informed career decisions.

Student Competencies

Develop Career Awareness

Students will:

- develop skills to locate, evaluate and interpret career information
- learn about the variety of traditional and nontraditional occupations
- develop an awareness of personal abilities, skills, interests and motivations
- learn how to interact and work cooperatively in teams
- learn to make decisions
- learn how to set goals
- understand the importance of planning
- pursue and develop competency in areas of interest
- develop hobbies and vocational interests
- balance between work and leisure time

Develop Employment Readiness

Students will:

- acquire employability skills such as working on a team, problem-solving and organizational skills
- apply job readiness skills to seek employment opportunities
- demonstrate knowledge about the changing workplace
- learn about the rights and responsibilities of employers and employees
- learn to respect individual uniqueness in the workplace
- learn how to write a resume
- develop a positive attitude toward work and learning
- understand the importance of responsibility, dependability, punctuality, integrity and effort in the workplace
- utilize time- and task-management skills

Career Development: Standard B   Students will employ strategies to achieve future career goals with success and satisfaction.

Student Competencies

Acquire Career Information

Students will:

- apply decision-making skills to career planning, course selection and career transitions
- identify personal skills, interests and abilities and relate them to current career choices
- demonstrate knowledge of the career-planning process
- know the various ways in which occupations can be classified
- use research and information resources to obtain career information

- learn to use the Internet to access career planning information
- describe traditional and nontraditional career choices and how they relate to career choice
- understand how changing economic and societal needs influence employment trends and future training

Identify Career Goals
Students will:

- demonstrate awareness of the education and training needed to achieve career goals
- assess and modify their educational plan to support career goals
- use employability and job readiness skills in internship, mentoring, shadowing and/or other work experience
- select course work that is related to career interests
- maintain a career-planning portfolio

Career Development: Standard C   Students will understand the relationship between personal qualities, education, training and the world of work.

Student Competencies
Acquire Knowledge to Achieve Career Goals
Students will:

- understand the relationship between educational achievement and career success
- explain how work can help to achieve personal success and satisfaction
- identify personal preferences and interests influencing career choice and success
- understand that the changing workplace requires lifelong learning and acquiring new skills
- describe the effect of work on lifestyles
- understand the importance of equity and access in career choice
- understand that work is an important and satisfying means of personal expression

Apply Skills to Achieve Career Goals
Students will:

- demonstrate how interests, abilities and achievement relate to achieving personal, social, educational and career goals
- learn how to use conflict management skills with peers and adults
- learn to work cooperatively with others as a team member
- apply academic and employment readiness skills in work-based learning situations such as internships, shadowing and/or mentoring experiences

III. Personal/Social Development

Standards in the personal/social area guide the school counseling program to implement strategies and activities to support and maximize each student's personal growth and enhance the educational and career development of the student.

The school counseling program enables all students to achieve success in school and develop into contributing members of society.

Standard A: Students will acquire the knowledge, attitudes and inter-personal skills to help them understand and respect self and others.
Standard B: Students will make decisions, set goals and take necessary action to achieve goals.
Standard C: Students will understand safety and survival skills.

Personal/Social Development: Standard A   Students will acquire the knowledge, attitudes and interpersonal skills to help them understand and respect self and others.

Student Competencies
  Acquire Self-knowledge

- develop positive attitudes toward self as a unique and worthy person
- identify values, attitudes and beliefs
- learn the goal-setting process
- understand change is a part of growth
- identify and express feelings
- distinguish between appropriate and inappropriate behavior
- recognize personal boundaries, rights and privacy needs
- understand the need for self-control and how to practice it
- demonstrate cooperative behavior in groups
- identify personal strengths and assets
- identify and discuss changing personal and social roles
- identify and recognize changing family roles

  Acquire Interpersonal Skills
    Students will:

- recognize that everyone has rights and responsibilities
- respect alternative points of view
- recognize, accept, respect and appreciate individual differences
- recognize, accept and appreciate ethnic and cultural diversity
- recognize and respect differences in various family configurations
- use effective communications skills
- know that communication involves speaking, listening and nonverbal behavior
- learn how to make and keep friends

Personal/Social Development: Standard B   Students will make decisions, set goals and take necessary action to achieve goals.

Student Competencies
  Self-knowledge Application
    Students will:

- use a decision-making and problem-solving model
- understand consequences of decisions and choices
- identify alternative solutions to a problem
- develop effective coping skills for dealing with problems
- demonstrate when, where and how to seek help for solving problems and making decisions
- know how to apply conflict resolution skills
- demonstrate a respect and appreciation for individual and cultural differences
- know when peer pressure is influencing a decision
- identify long- and short-term goals
- identify alternative ways of achieving goals
- use persistence and perseverance in acquiring knowledge and skills
- develop an action plan to set and achieve realistic goals

Personal/Social Development: Standard C   Students will understand safety and survival skills.

Student Competencies
  Safety and Survival Application

- demonstrate knowledge of personal information (i.e., telephone number, home address, emergency contact)
- learn about the relationship between rules, laws, safety, and the protection of individual's rights
- learn the difference between appropriate and inappropriate physical contact
- demonstrate the ability to asset boundaries, rights, and personal privacy

- differentiate between situations requiring peer support and situations requiring adult professional help
- identify resource people in the school and community, and know how to seek their help
- apply effective problem-solving and decision-making skills to make safe and healthy choices
- learn about the emotional and physical dangers of substance use and abuse
- learn how to cope with peer pressure
- learn techniques for managing stress and conflict
- learn coping skills for managing life events

APPENDIX C

Program Goals for Adult Partners in the DAP Model

In a comprehensive school counseling program, counselors have primary responsibility for the growth and development of the student partners of the Domains/Activities/Partners Model. But counselors must also work systematically and holistically to address the needs of all partners in the education of young people. A comprehensive school counseling program, therefore, will also include systemic work with all the adult partners of the DAP model: parents and caregivers, teachers, administrators, other student services professionals (school psychologists, nurses, and social workers), and community colleagues (community mental health professionals, physical health professionals, social service and law enforcement professionals, employers, etc.).

For the work done with our adult partners, goals must be defined that will guide these interactions and provide outcomes that can be measured. This Appendix contains some ideas for goals for adult partners that could become part of the comprehensive school counseling program. These goals are presented here as a beginning for discussions and should be modified based on local needs and priorities as established by the professional school counselor, in consultation with advisory groups. See Chapter 5 for a discussion of advisory committees and the program design process.

A. Goals for All Adult Partners

Goal A	1:	All partners will understand the developmental needs of students from a holistic perspective.
Goal A	2:	All partners will understand the systemic elements of families, schools, and communities that facilitate student development.
Goal A	3:	All partners will understand the systemic elements of families, schools, and communities that impede student development.
Goal A	4:	All partners will understand the academic development process of students and will understand strategies to help students in that process.
Goal A	5:	All partners will understand the career development process of students and will understand strategies to help students in that process.
Goal A	6:	All partners will understand the personal/social development process of students and will understand strategies to help students in that process.
Goal A	7:	All partners will understand their role in the development of students.
Goal A	8:	All partners will demonstrate basic strategies for communicating with secondary school students in developmentally appropriate ways.

Goal A   9: All partners will understand the role of the other partners in the developmental process of students.

Goal A   10: All partners will understand the role of the school counselor and the role of comprehensive school counseling programs in the developmental process of students.

Goal A   11: All partners will feel comfortable approaching the school counselor with questions or concerns about students, families, schools, human development, or other topics.

Goal A   12: All partners will find the school counselor helpful in answering those questions and/or resolving those concerns about students, families, schools, and so on.

Goal A   13: All partners will understand the role of schools in educating young people for the world after secondary school.

Goal A   14: All partners will feel a part of the school community and the larger community and will share responsibility for, responsibility to, and will respond to the needs of those communities.

B. Goals for Parents and Caregivers

Goal B   1: Parents/caregivers will feel welcome in the school environment.

Goal B   2: Parents/caregivers will feel included and invested in the work done with students in the comprehensive school counseling program.

Goal B   3: Parents/caregivers will understand the crucial effects that family can have on the development of young people.

Goal B   4: Parents/caregivers will acquire strategies for creating a healthy family environment for students.

Goal B   5: Parents/caregivers will foster positive interactions between families, schools, and the community on behalf of students.

C. Goals for Colleagues in the Schools

Goal C   1: Colleagues in the schools will understand the philosophy of developmentally appropriate education.

Goal C   2: Colleagues in the schools will feel included and invested in the work of the school counselor in the comprehensive school counseling program.

Goal C   3: Colleagues in the schools will understand the critical effect that schools can have on the development of young people.

Goal C   4: Colleagues in the schools will understand the need for an environment of respect in the school.

Goal C   5: Colleagues in the schools will acquire strategies for promoting an environment of respect in the school.

Goal C   6: Colleagues in the schools will foster positive interactions between families, schools, and the community on behalf of students.

D. Goals for Colleagues in the Community

Goal D   1: Colleagues in the community will feel welcome in the school.

Goal D   2: Colleagues in the community will feel included and invested in the work of the school counselor in the comprehensive school counseling program.

Goal D   3: Colleagues in the community will understand the critical effect that neighborhoods and communities can have on the development of young people.

Goal D   4: Colleagues in the community will understand that civility and respect in the community will have a profound impact on the climate of the school.

Goal D   5: Colleagues in the community will acquire strategies for creating that environment of civility and respect in the community.

Goal D   6: Colleagues in the community will foster positive interactions between families, schools, and the community on behalf of students.

Index